Hands-On ALGEBRA!

Ready-to-Use Games & Activities for Grades 7-12

FRANCES M. THOMPSON

JOSSEY-BASS
A Wiley Imprint
www.josseybass.com

Published by Jossey-Bass
A Wiley Imprint
989 Market Street, San Francisco, CA 94103-1741   www.josseybass.com

Jossey-Bass books and products are available through most bookstores. To contact Jossey-Bass
directly call our Customer Care Department within the U.S. at (800) 956-7739, outside the U.S.
at (317) 572-3986 or fax (317) 572-4002.

Jossey-Bass also publishes its books in a variety of electronic formats. Some content that appears
in print may not be available in electronic books.

Library of Congress Cataloging-in-Publication Data:
Thompson, Frances M. (Frances McBroom)
   Hands-on algebra! : ready-to-use games & activites for grades
7–12 / Frances M. Thompson.
    p.   cm.
   ISBN 0-87628-386-5
   1. Algebra—Study and teaching—Activity programs. 2. Algebra—Study
and teaching (Secondary) I. Title.
   QA159.T48 1998   98-13698
   512.9'071'2—dc21

Printed in the United States of America
PB Printing 10   9   8   7   6   5   4   3   2

This book is dedicated:

. . . . to the junior high and senior high school students and their teachers, who so graciously opened their classrooms and candidly responded to me so that new ideas and techniques might be explored;

. . . . to my undergraduate and graduate students desiring to teach, whose insatiable curiosity and trust motivated me to seek more effective methods of instruction that would increase their own personal success in mathematics;

. . . . to my husband Claude, who made certain we had groceries in the pantry and clean dishes in the cabinets during the writing of the book and who cheered me on through the difficult and long hours of preparing the final manuscript and graphics;

. . . . to my son Brooks, whose own struggles with high school algebra led me to develop many new conceptual models and approaches now included in this book and whose eventual success convinced me that algebra can indeed be for everyone;

. . . . to my beloved parents, Alex and Myrtle McBroom, who supported me in every good thing I ever wanted to do;

. . . . to my editor, Susan Kolwicz, for her understanding and gentle manner; and

. . . . to these times that keep us—as teachers—continuously reaching, teaching, and touching lives for the future.

ABOUT THE AUTHOR

Frances McBroom Thompson has been exploring the many varieties of manipulative materials available for mathematics instruction since 1973. Her investigations have often taken her into the classroom at all grade levels in an effort to provide successful learning experiences for students of all ability levels.

She regularly contributes articles on mathematics teaching to professional education journals and conducts workshops for in-service teachers at the elementary and secondary levels. She has published *Five-Minute Challenges* and *More Five-Minute Challenges,* two activity books in secondary problem solving, and has co-authored *Holt Math 1000* and *Holt Essential Math,* two general mathematics textbooks for high school students. Frances has also developed a training module for algebra teachers under a grant with the Texas Education Agency. Her more recent publication is *Hands-On Math! Ready-to-Use Games and Activities for Grades 4–8,* a teacher's resource book that introduces over 90 mathematical concepts with manipulatives and diagrams.

Frances has taught mathematics full-time at the junior and senior high school levels in Texas and California, and has served as a K–12 mathematics specialist in both Georgia and Texas. She holds a bachelor's degree in mathematics education from Abilene Christian University (Texas) and a master's degree in mathematics from the University of Texas at Austin. Her doctoral degree is in mathematics education from the University of Georgia at Athens. She presently serves as Professor of Mathematics at Texas Woman's University in Denton, Texas, where she offers undergraduate and graduate courses in mathematics and mathematics teaching.

ABOUT THIS BOOK

Algebra is for everyone! This statement has much meaning for society today. With technology changing rapidly, business and industry are requiring more employees to have a better understanding of mathematics than ever before and, in particular, to have a greater knowledge of algebra. In order to fare well in today's job market, most high-school students now need a minimum of one year of high school algebra. Teaching techniques once used for only college-bound students must now be adjusted to better serve students of all ability levels. This book, *Hands-On Algebra! Ready-to-Use Games & Activities for Grades 7–12,* has been designed to help teachers of algebra meet the needs of this greatly increasing population of students. It covers content and contains materials sufficient for a two-semester course in Algebra I.

FOCUS OF CONTENT

Lessons in this book reflect the recommendations of the 1992 Conference, "Algebra for the Twenty-first Century," funded by the National Science Foundation through the National Council of Teachers of Mathematics. Students represent patterns and relationships in a variety of ways: physical models, diagrams, numerical tables, graphs, and algebraic expressions. Graphing is used to explore linear and quadratic functions and their real-world applications, as well as to investigate exponential functions and inverse variations. This graphing is done first by hand, then with graphing calculators or computers. Collected data are analyzed for patterns, then approximated by appropriate curves and algebraic equations. Several methods for solving linear and quadratic equations, and linear inequalities are presented. Problem solving is incorporated throughout the book.

EMPHASIS ON COMMUNICATION AND MODELING

Algebraic notation must be presented in a meaningful way in order for students to understand it. For that reason it must be continually associated with the actions or relationships it represents. This book provides many opportunities for students to describe their procedures and results both orally and in written form. The use of physical and pictorial models enables students to develop mental images and to describe observations easily. In addition, games and calculator/computer activities provide cooperative experiences that encourage the development of a precise mathematical language.

STRUCTURE OF LESSONS

Each objective in *Hands-On Algebra! Ready-to-Use Games & Activities for Grades 7–12* is presented in a sequence of three lessons or activities. Activity 1 involves physical models in the **development** of the concept, and Activity 2 uses pictorial or graphic models to help students **bridge** from the concrete to the abstract level of thinking. Both activities allow students to generate and record a variety of examples from which to seek patterns. Carefully selected examples are provided in all lessons to assist the teacher. From patterns observed in these examples students form hypotheses, then either confirm, or reject and revise them. Through this process they generalize the concept being studied, and express their generalization through verbal and written statements. Activity 3 allows students to further **explore** and **apply** the new generalization. This cooperative activity typically consists of a game, a puzzle, an application program, or a graphing calculator or computer activity. Special extensions of the concept might also occur in Activity 3.

A **learner option** is available to students for most objectives. That is, if a student still needs or prefers to work with manipulatives after Activity 1 has been completed, instructions and exercises have been provided in Activity 2 that will allow that student to continue to build with manipulatives, then draw diagrams to *record* the procedure used, while the teacher and other students in the class only draw diagrams to work the *same* exercises. In order to promote a climate of acceptance in the classroom, *all* students are offered the option and are provided manipulatives on their desks; however, most students will quietly lay aside the manipulatives as soon as they are developmentally ready. Similarly, after Activity 2 is completed, some students may still need to draw diagrams to solve problems, rather than work only with the abstract or algebraic notation. Typically, it will be the same students who needed the manipulatives a little longer during Activity 2. While drawing diagrams, these students will continue to make connections with the abstract notation through the *recording* process. When they finally internalize the procedures, they will begin to work independently with just the notation. Such transitions are extremely learner-dependent and cannot be forced. Activity 2 plays a vital role in enabling students to bridge from manipulative to symbolic work. Finally, even though a set of exercises is provided with each activity of most objectives, some students may need more practice with certain procedures that involve detailed symbolic or algebraic notation. Additional exercises are available in many instructional resource books or publishers' textbooks, and can be easily assigned to those particular students.

Effort has been made to keep the implementation of the lessons manageable and feasible for most classroom situations. An approximate time length is suggested for each lesson; the actual time length will vary from class to class, however, and will ultimately depend on the teacher's overall goals for the lesson and on observed student need. All materials needed for each activity or lesson are listed or described at the beginning of the activity. Suggested manipulatives are accessible to all teachers. In most cases, alternatives to commercial materials have been suggested, and ideas for packaging the manipulatives have also been given.

INSTRUCTIONAL DESIGN

With the increased use of technology in the classroom, it becomes even more vital that students encounter new mathematical ideas initially through hands-on experiences, which encourage them to reflect on the relationships that are present. This book is based on such a philosophy. For example, in Activity 1 students are first asked to solve simple, linear equations with concrete materials. The written algebraic notation is carefully associated with the physical movement of the materials. In Activity 2, students continue similarly with diagrams until they recognize procedures common to all the linear equations they have solved. Finally, from these common procedures students are asked to *generalize* a solution process and apply that process abstractly in Activity 3. Abstract activities are only used after students have discovered new ideas for themselves and are ready to apply them. In particular, graphing calculators or computers are used to generate different sets of functions, but only after students have observed the numerical and graphical changes that occur within and among ordered pairs resulting from their own collected data. Because of the developmental connections that exist among the three activities for each objective, it is extremely important that none of these related activities be omitted. Where time is a factor, Activity 1 should be the favored activity. It is at this concrete level that most students discover the special relationships that are being developed.

LEARNER EXPECTATIONS

For several decades in the United States, mathematics instruction has focused on rote memorization of concepts, skills, and formulas. As a result, far too many students are unable to apply their mathematical knowledge in the real world. Such rote learning is not easily retained and teachers often find themselves reteaching ideas covered in previous units. The author has found that the consistent use of a variety of models helps most students, regardless of ability, to discover mathematical relationships for themselves. Gifted students delve more deeply into new mathematical ideas. Students with dyslexia or with decoding or other processing difficulties find instruction with manipulatives to be quite beneficial. Older students, who might first object to working with manipulatives in algebra, quickly change their attitudes when they begin to experience success in learning. When algebra instruction is correlated with the natural growth process of learning (concrete to pictorial to abstract), most students progress necessarily and attain greater power to think and reason mathematically—a quality needed by all citizens in this world of constantly changing technology and information.

Frances McBroom Thompson

CONTENTS

Section 2
LINEAR FORMS

Section 3
LINEAR APPLICATIONS AND GRAPHING

Section 4
QUADRATIC CONCEPTS

Section 5
SPECIAL APPLICATIONS

Section 1

REAL NUMBERS, THEIR OPERATIONS, AND THEIR PROPERTIES

OBJECTIVE 1: Order the set of integers.

Activity 1: COUNTING OFF

[Developing Action]

Materials: Packet of integer tiles (40 positive and 40 negative units) per pair of students
Unlined paper for building mats (8.5 in. × 11 in.; if white tiles are used, colored paper should be used for mats)
Regular paper
Pencils
Worksheet 1–1–1

Management: Partners (20–30 minutes)

Directions:

1. Give each pair of students a packet of unit tiles and a blank sheet of paper for a building mat. There are several sets of unit tiles available commercially or you may make your own, using the pattern provided in the Appendix. The positive units will be one color while the negative units will be another color. If using the pattern provided, only one color is needed; the plain small squares will be positive units and the small squares with an X drawn inside will be the negative units.

2. Discuss the existence of opposites in everyday life. Ask students to name actions that are opposites. For example, they might mention a door opening and closing, a car moving forward and backward, the sun rising and setting, day and night, hot and cold water, emptying and filling a bottle, etc. The integers are used to quantify such actions or situations. Hot water may be 10 degrees Fahrenheit **above** room temperature (shown as +10); cold water may be 5 degrees Fahrenheit **below** room temperature (shown as –5). A car may go 25 miles **north** (+25) or go 30 miles **south** (–30) from town A. The water level in a large tank may be **raised** 2 feet (+2) or **lowered** 3 feet (–3). *Ask:* "If a door is closed and you open it one time (a +1 action) and then close it one time (a –1 action), what is the final position of the door?" *(closed again; the opening and closing of the door returned the door to its original state; the opening and closing actions neutralized each* *other)* Opposite actions neutralize each other; that is, together they produce no change or have no effect. Hence, when a positive unit and a negative unit occur together in a situation being described, we will refer to them as a 0-pair, i.e., they cancel each other's effect. **Note:** Throughout the activities of this book we will read +1 as "positive one," not "plus one"; and −1 as "negative one," "inverse of one," or "opposite of one," not "minus one." "Plus" and "minus" refer to operations, whereas "positive," "negative," "opposite," and "inverse" refer to certain members of a set of numbers.

3. Ask students to place a positive unit on their building mat, then place **one more unit (+1)** on the mat. *Ask:* "How much do you have now?" *(positive 2 or 2 positive units)* "How does +2 compare to +1? Why?" *(+2 is greater than +1 because +2 is **one more than +1**, i.e., **we increased +1 by a positive unit** to get +2)* An increase is always shown by bringing in positive units. *Ask:* "How can we show +3 on the building mat?" *(place another +1 on the mat with +2)* "How does +3 compare to +2 or to +1?" *(+3 is one more than +2 and two more than +1)* Have students record on their own papers: +2 > +1, +3 > +2, and +3 > +1. Since +1 is one more positive unit than 0, students should also record "+1 > 0" (similarly +2 > 0 and +3 > 0).

4. *Now ask:* "Which is greater: −1 or 0? Remember that a lesser amount can be increased by positive units to make a greater amount." Students should show that 0 (the empty mat) increased by +1 shows +1 on the mat. If −1 is increased by +1, the negative unit and positive unit form a 0-pair on the mat and can be removed to show an empty mat. Thus, 0 > −1 since −1 was the amount that had to be increased to show 0.

5. *Ask:* "Which is greater: −3 or −1? Show this with your tiles on your building mat." If −1 is increased with positive units, the new amount will be 0, +1, +2, etc. If −3 is increased with positive units, 0-pairs will be formed, and the new amount will be −2, −1, 0, +1, etc., depending on the number of 0-pairs removed. Hence, −1 cannot be increased to make −3, but −3 can be increased to make −1; therefore, −1 > −3.

6. Now give students different pairs of integers to try to order with their partners, using their tiles on their building mats. They should record their results on their own papers, using both > and <. For example, since −2 can be increased to make +1, both "−2 < +1" and "+1 > −2" should be recorded. Here are some number pairs to compare: −8 with −3, +2 with +5, 0 with −4, 0 with +3, +7 with −2, +2 with −1, −5 with +4, and +6 with −6. (See Worksheet 1–1–1.)

Activity 2: LINE BUILDING

[Bridging Action]

Materials: Unlined paper (8.5 in. × 11 in.)
Rulers
Regular paper
Pencils

Management: Partners (20–30 minutes)

Directions:

1. Have each pair of students use a regular pencil and ruler to draw a number line down the middle lengthwise on a sheet of unlined paper, marking off equally spaced

Name _____   **Date** _____

WORKSHEET 1–1–1
Counting Off

Use your tiles to compare integers.

1. Circle which integer is greater in the following pairs.

+2 or +1	−3 or +1	+7 or 0	+5 or −6
0 or −1	+2 or −4	+4 or −4	+9 or +3
−3 or −1	0 or −8	−6 or −10	−3 or −5

2. Circle which integer is less in the following pairs.

+3 or +5	+4 or −1	+9 or +12	−14 or +8
−1 or −6	−5 or 0	−10 or +10	0 or +6
−5 or +2	+8 or −8	+8 or +5	−7 or −10

3. Using > and <, write which belongs with the following pairs. The first is completed for you.

−8 __<__ −3	+1 _____ −2	+2 _____ −0
+2 _____ +5	−5 _____ 0	+6 _____ −6
0 _____ −4	+8 _____ −3	−5 _____ +4
+7 _____ −2	−4 _____ +4	+3 _____ −3
0 _____ +3	−3 _____ −8	+10 _____ −1

units and labeling the middle mark as 0. Students should rotate the paper so that the number line extends left-to-right on the desktop in front of them. The number line should cover the full length of the paper and adjacent marks will be about a half-inch apart. All other marks should be unlabeled at this time. There should be 10 marks to the left of 0 and 10 marks to the right of 0. These additional marks will be labeled as part of this activity. Also draw a large number line on the classroom chalkboard.

2. The purpose of this activity is to introduce students to the number line as a representation of the set of integers and to the idea that a countable amount of positive or negative units can be associated with a set of adjacent unit spaces to the right or left of 0. Discuss the idea that traditionally (i.e., we could change it if we wanted to) we place positive integer amounts to the right of 0 on the number line, and **count** unit spaces **to the right** to show **increases**. Since +1 is just one more than 0 and positive, we count one unit space to the right of 0 and label the mark we reach as +1. Since +2 is just one more than +1 and two more than 0, we count two unit spaces to the right of 0 and label the mark reached as +2.

3. Now randomly call out positive integers from +1 to +10 for students to locate on their number lines. Do not call the numbers out in order since students will just label the marks in sequence without thinking about a reason. Have students state which mark should represent the number and why. For example, if +8 is called out, students should state that +8 is eight more than 0 or that 0 can be increased by eight positive units to make +8. Hence, +8 must be at the eighth mark to the right of 0.

4. After all ten marks to the right of 0 are labeled, *ask:* "Where do you think –2 should be on the number line and why?" To help with this, draw two small squares (with a large X inside each square) on the board to represent the two negative units. *Ask:* "How do we increase this amount to make 0? Remember that a unit increase must be made with a positive unit." Hopefully students will suggest that small plain squares for positive units must be drawn to show an increase, and that each 0-pair formed can be marked out since its two opposite units have no effect on the final amount being sought. Two positive units (plain squares) will pair up with the two negative units, leaving a value of 0. Since two positive units were needed, 0 must be two more than –2. This means that 0 must be two unit spaces to the right of –2 on the number line. Have students find the correct location and label the mark to show –2.

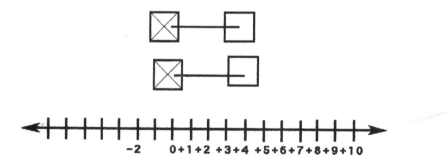

5. Now randomly call out negative integers from –1 to –10 for students to locate on their number lines. Do not call the numbers out in order; this will make students just label the marks in sequence without thinking about a reason. Have students state which mark should represent the number and why. For example, if –5 is called out, students should state that 0 is five more than –5 or that –5 can be increased by five positive units to make 0. Hence, –5 must be at the mark that is five unit spaces to the left of 0 on the line. Have students draw and pair off squares any time they are not sure about the number of unit spaces they need to count off from 0.

Activity 3: BATTLE FOR THE BIGGER!

[Application/Exploration]

Materials: For each team, a deck of integer cards and a packet of integer tiles (from Activity 1)

Management: Teams of 4 students each (20 minutes)

Directions:

   1. Prepare a deck of integer cards for each team. A deck consists of 40 cards, each having an integer (0, positive, or negative) written on it. The cards might be made from small index cards. Have 0 on four of the cards and an equal number of positive and negative integers on the remaining cards. Select 18 integers randomly from –1 to –20 and 18 more from +1 to +20.

   2. Give each team a deck of cards and a packet of integer tiles.

   3. Each team should shuffle its deck of cards, then deal them out equally to all 4 members. Each player should turn his or her set of cards face down on the table. Two members on the team will play against the other two members of the team in the following way: The first member of pair A will play the first member of pair B, then the second member of pair A will play the second member of pair B, followed by the first members playing again. This rotation will continue until one of the four team members runs out of cards or time is called by the teacher.

   4. For a round of play (two members against each other) each of the two players will turn the top card of his or her stack face up on the table. The two players must decide which of the integers showing is the greater. The player with the greater number collects both cards and places them face down at the bottom of his or her own stack. If neither student is sure which number is greater, together they must build the two amounts with the tiles, then show the effect of bringing in positive units to each given amount. The one that can be changed or increased to become the other is the lesser amount. For example, if the two cards show –5 and +3, eight positive unit tiles can be joined to 5 negative units. Five 0-pairs will be formed at first, then the other three positive units will yield +3 in value. Since –5 was increased to make +3, +3 must be the greater number.

   5. As an alternative for comparing the numbers shown on the cards, students might use a copy of a number line that goes from –20 to +20. This method, however, is not encouraged until students are fully aware that integers represent quantities and not just arbitrary marks on some line.

OBJECTIVE 2: Add with integers.

Activity 1: COMBO-MATCH

[Developing Action]

Materials: Packets of integer tiles from Objective 1
Unlined paper for building mats (8.5 in. × 11 in.; if white tiles are used, colored paper should be used for mats)
Regular paper
Pencils
Worksheet 1–2–1

Management: Partners (50 minutes)

Directions:

1. Give each pair of students a packet of unit tiles and a blank sheet of paper for a building mat. The mat should be positioned with its length turned horizontally or left to right to the students. It is assumed that students have already completed the activities of Objective 1 in this section so that they understand the nature of opposites in their daily world.

2. Have students build (+2) + (+3) on their mats by placing 2 positive unit tiles on the left side of the mat and 3 positive unit tiles on the right side. Remind them that addition is just the counting out and combining of two or more groups (**addends**) of objects that are **alike** in some way and the recounting of the total objects (**sum**) in the new group that has been formed. For integer addition, if two unit tiles are both positive (or both negative), they are considered to be alike. Therefore, since all the unit tiles on the mat are positive, they can be combined and the total recounted. There are 5 tiles in all and they are all positive, so the sum is +5.

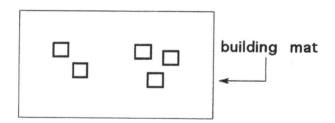

building mat

3. Write the following number sentence on the chalkboard to record the results: (+2) + (+3) = +5.

4. Now have students build (−1) + (−3) on their mats. One negative unit tile should be placed on the left side of the mat and 3 negative unit tiles placed on the right side. Whichever amount is given **first** or written on the left in a horizontal addition exercise (or in an action, whichever amount occurs first) should always be placed on the **left** side of the mat, then the second amount should be placed to the right of that first amount. This consistent positioning will later be used to develop the various properties such as commutativity for integer operations. Again, all the unit tiles on the mat are alike (all negative this time), so they can be recounted to get a total. Since all the tiles are negative and there are four of them, the sum will be −4.

5. Write the following number sentence or equation on the chalkboard to record the results: $(-1) + (-3) = -4$.

6. Now have students build $(-2) + (+5)$ on their mats by placing 2 negative unit tiles on the left side of the mat and placing 5 positive unit tiles on the right side. This time not all the tiles are alike. **Ask:** "Are there any opposites present on your mats? If so, form 0-pairs and remove them from the mat. Why can you remove such pairs from the mat?" *(because 0-pairs are opposites, that is, one is positive and the other is negative, and opposites neutralize or cancel the effect of each other; hence, together as a pair they have no overall effect on the total value, or force, or charge, etc., existing in some situation)* Students should form and remove two positive-negative pairs of unit tiles from their mats. The remaining tiles should then be counted to find the **effective** value or sum of the sets of tiles originally placed on the mat. The value of the 3 positive unit tiles still on the mat will be +3.

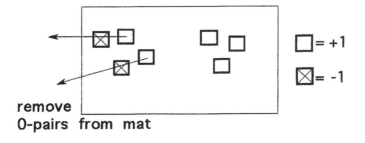

remove
0-pairs from mat

7. Write an equation or number sentence on the board to record the results: $(-2) + (+5) = +3$.

8. Now have students build $(+3) + (-8)$ on their mats. Since opposites exist, 0-pairs should be formed and removed. This will leave 5 negative unit tiles on the mat, so the effective sum is –5. Record this result as $(+3) + (-8) = -5$.

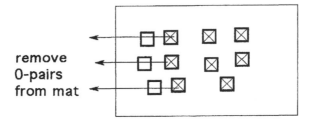

remove
0-pairs
from mat

9. The above four examples represent the four basic types of integer addition and are represented in the practice exercises provided below. These four types must be considered whenever patterns are sought in the addition of integers and will be discussed in more detail in Activity 2.

10. Students should now practice building other addition exercises given below. They should record their results on their own papers, using number sentences or equations. Remind students that if, after all 0-pairs are removed from the mat, no other unit tiles remain on the mat, then the answer or effective sum will be 0. Also, if an addend is 0, no tiles are placed on the mat for that particular addend. (See Worksheet 1–2–1.)

$(+4) + (+2) = ?$	$(-5) + (-7) = ?$	$(+12) + (-2) = ?$	$(+2) + (-2) = ?$
$(-10) + (+6) = ?$	$(+4) + (-4) = ?$	$(+8) + (+8) = ?$	$(-7) + (-10) = ?$
$0 + (-9) = ?$	$(-5) + (+11) = ?$	$(+6) + (-13) = ?$	$(+5) + 0 = ?$
$(-5) + (+5) = ?$	$(+7) + (-7) = ?$	$(-12) + (+8) = ?$	$(+14) + (-5) = ?$

WORKSHEET 1–2–1
Combo-Match

Use your tiles to complete the following sentences with the missing sums.

$(+4) + (+2) =$ _____ $(+12) + (-2) =$ _____

$(-10) + (+6) =$ _____ $(+6) + (-13) =$ _____

$0 + (-9) \quad =$ _____ $(+5) + 0 \quad\quad =$ _____

$(-5) + (+5) \quad =$ _____ $(+14) + (-5) =$ _____

Now write two or three on your own. Briefly explain in writing how you found the sums.

_____

_____

_____

_____

_____

_____

_____

_____

_____

_____

_____

_____

_____

_____

_____

_____

11. After students have built all of the above practice exercises with their tiles and recorded a number sentence for each, ask partners to write two or three sentences on their own paper about the general processes they used to find their sums. Descriptions will vary. Have some students read their paragraphs to the whole class. *Sample comments:* "If any tiles are opposites, match them to make 0-pairs. Count the tiles that are left to get your sum." Do not stress sign patterns at this time. That idea will be developed in Activity 2.

Activity 2: PICTURING SUMS

[Bridging Action]

Materials: Paper
Regular pencils
Red pencils
Colored chalk
Worksheet 1–2–2

Management: Partners (50 minutes)

Directions:

1. Give each pair of students a red pencil. In this activity they will be asked to look for patterns in addition exercises. The four types of addend combinations presented in Activity 1 will also be developed here in diagram format.

2. On the chalkboard show students how to draw a diagram of (+4) + (+6). Draw small, plain squares for the positive units. Four squares should be drawn as a group to the left and six squares should be drawn as a group to the right. Since all the units are positive, draw a path with colored chalk around the entire set of 10 squares on the board. Students should draw the same groups on their own papers, leaving about a finger's width between the two groups of squares. A path should be drawn with red pencil around all 10 squares. Students should avoid drawing extremely small squares that make counting difficult. The completed diagram as shown below should extend across a width equal to half the width of a regular sheet of paper. It might be helpful to have students fold their papers lengthwise so that the fold down the middle of the paper might guide them in making their diagrams large enough.

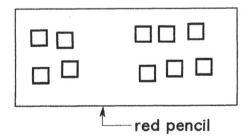
red pencil

3. Students should record a number sentence or equation on their paper below the diagram in order to show their result: (+4) + (+6) = +10. The recording should also be written on the chalkboard.

4. Similarly, have students draw a diagram for $(-5) + (-2)$. Five small squares with a large X in each interior should be drawn to the left and two more such squares drawn to the right. Since all the squares represent negative units, a path should be drawn with red pencil around all 7 units to show a sum of -7. The recording will be $(-5) + (-2) = -7$.

5. Now have students draw a diagram for $(-9) + (+4)$. Nine small squares with a large X in each interior should be drawn to the left and four small, plain squares should be drawn to the right. **Ask:** "When both positive and negative units are to be combined, what should we do first?" *(form all possible 0-pairs)* Show students how to connect opposite units together to represent 0-pairs. This should be done with regular chalk on the board or with regular pencil on paper. After all 0-pairs are formed, five negative units will remain, showing the effective sum of -5. A path should be drawn with red pencil around this set of 5 units. The recording for this result is $(-9) + (+4) = -5$.

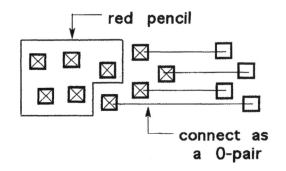

6. Now write $(+10) + (-2)$ on the board for students to draw. Ten plain squares will be on the left and two squares with X's will be on the right. Students should connect opposites to form two 0-pairs, leaving 8 plain squares unconnected. A path should be drawn with red pencil around these 8 remaining squares to show the sum of $+8$. The recording will be $(+10) + (-2) = +8$.

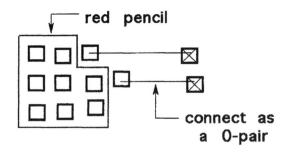

7. Assign the following set of exercises for students to draw in order to find the sums. Each sum should be recorded with a number sentence or equation below its corresponding diagram. Continue to use the red pencil to identify the effective sum each time. Remind students that, if no units remain after all 0-pairs have been formed, then the sum will be 0. Also, if an addend is 0, no squares are drawn for that particular addend. (The starred [*] exercises will also be used later in a pattern search.) (See Worksheet 1–2–2.)

*$(-2) + (-7) = ?$	$(+4) + (+9) = ?$	$(+8) + (-8) = ?$	$(+5) + (-15) = ?$
$(+7) + 0 = ?$	$(-10) + (+8) = ?$	$(+5) + (-2) = ?$	$0 + (-4) = ?$
*$(-3) + (+3) = ?$	*$(-3) + (+14) = ?$	$(+3) + (+2) = ?$	$(-11) + (+5) = ?$
*$(+12) + (+5) = ?$	*$(+6) + (-14) = ?$	*$(+12) + (-12) = ?$	$(+13) + (-6) = ?$

WORKSHEET 1–2–2
Picturing Sums

Draw diagrams of tiles to complete the following sentences with the missing sums.

1. $(-2) + (-7) =$ _____

5. $(+7) + 0 =$ _____

2. $(+4) + (+9) =$ _____

6. $(-10) + (+8) =$ _____

3. $(+8) + (-8) =$ _____

7. $(+3) + (+2) =$ _____

4. $(+5) + (-15) =$ _____

8. $(+13) + (-6) =$ _____

8. After students have drawn diagrams for the above exercises and checked them in class, guide them in a search for patterns among the signs of the integers in the recorded equations. This portion of Activity 2 may actually occur at the beginning of the next class period rather than at the end of the class period when Activity 2 is first introduced. Students must have time to work all the assigned exercises before they are asked to look for any patterns. On the board write the completed equations for the six starred exercises in step 7 above as well as the four equations that were demonstrated at the beginning of Activity 2. Other number sentences may also be included. The idea is to provide at least two samples each of the four types of exercises presented initially in this activity, as well as of the type where the sum is 0. Students need *as a minimum* these ten exercises if they are to search successfully for sign patterns that will help them predict the sign of any sum.

9. Have students look at the ten addition number sentences or equations written on the board, one below the other. With colored chalk, circle the positive or negative sign of each integer, including the sum; do **not** circle the addition or plus sign that indicates the operation.

10. *Ask:* "If we look at the signs on the two addends (the two integral amounts being joined together) and the sign of the sum (unless the sum is 0) in each equation, is there a pattern or relationship among these signs that will help us predict what the sign of the sum will be for any addition exercise like these examples?" Have partners discuss their ideas with each other, then call on several students to share their ideas or conjectures with the class. With each conjecture shared, have the class check all the equations written on the board to see if the conjecture holds true for any equation to which it applies. If not, tell students that the conjecture (or proposed pattern) must be rejected. Here are some possible statements students typically offer:

(a) Some students may suggest that "if both addends are positive, the sum is positive" and "if both addends are negative, the sum is negative." This conjecture is correct for the equations to which it applies. It does not cover equations, however, where the addends have *different* signs.

(b) Other students may offer a conjecture for this latter case: "If the two addends have different signs, then the sum has the same sign as the addend representing the *larger amount* of units." Again, have the class test this idea by checking the appropriate equations. **Note**: Do *not* allow students to say that the sign of the sum is the same as the sign of the *larger number* of the two addends. This implies *value*. −12 represents 12 units and +5 represents 5 units, so *quantity-wise* there are *more* negative units than positive units. The *value* of −12, however, is *less than* the *value* of +5 (see Objective 1 for the ordering of integers).

(c) Another conjecture that students might offer is: "If the two addends have opposite signs but they represent the same number of units (but do not have the same value)—for example, 5 positive units and 5 negative units—then the sum will be 0."

11. The three conjectures above are correct for their applicable equations. Ask students to write a paragraph in their notebooks or journals that will compile the three ideas together for a complete description of the addition process. Have some students read their paragraphs to the whole class. Clarify any unclear statements.

Activity 3: SPIN-AND-ADD

[Application/Exploration]

Materials: Decks of integer cards (described in step 1 below)
Spinner patterns (Worksheet 1–2–3)
Large paper clips
Packets of unit tiles and building mats from Activity 1

Management: Teams of 4 students each (30 minutes)

Directions:

1. Each deck will contain 20 numeral cards, using the integers –9, –8, . . . , –1, 0, +1, . . . , +8, +9 with one numeral per card. Each numeral will be used only once except for 0, which will be used on two cards. The cards may be made with small, blank index cards or cut from lightweight tagboard or cardstock. After a numeral is written on each card, the cards may be laminated for greater durability. Each deck of cards might be prepared with a different color of marker or coded in some way to help keep the different decks separated from each other.

2. Give each team a deck of integer cards, a building mat with a packet of unit tiles, a spinner pattern, and a large paper clip. Students will use the paper clip as a spinner by holding one end of the paper clip at the center of the spinner with the point of a pencil and then hitting the other end to make the paper clip spin.

3. Each team should shuffle its deck of cards, then place them in a stack face down in the center of the table. Team members will take turns spinning the spinner and drawing a card off the top of the stack. The spinner will indicate whether a sum is to be positive, negative, or zero. The integer on the card will be one of the addends for an addition exercise. The player may then name **one to three** different integers to serve as the second addend with the drawn addend so that their sum will have the sign or equal 0 as shown on the spinner. The selected integers, however, may **not** be consecutive; for example, 0, –3, and +2 would be allowed as choices, but 0, –1, and –2 would not be.

4. As an example of a turn, a player might spin the negative sign and draw the +5 card. In order to have a sum that is negative, the player might suggest the integers –4, –7, and –10 for the second addend to be added to +5 (**consecutive** integers –4, –5, and –6 would not be allowed). The player would then need to confirm each choice by showing each addition with the unit tiles on the building mat (–7 or –10 combined with +5 would produce a negative sum as required, but –4 with +5 would produce a positive sum).

5. If the spinner indicates either the positive or the negative sign, a player may earn 1 point for each proposed addend that yields the required type of sum. Therefore, the player in the above example would earn 2 points, 1 point for each correct sum. If the spinner points to 0 and the player suggests the correct integer for the second addend, 4 points may be earned.

6. After all cards have been drawn from the stack, the game is over. The player with the most points is winner.

WORKSHEET 1–2–3
Spinner Pattern for "Spin-and-Add"

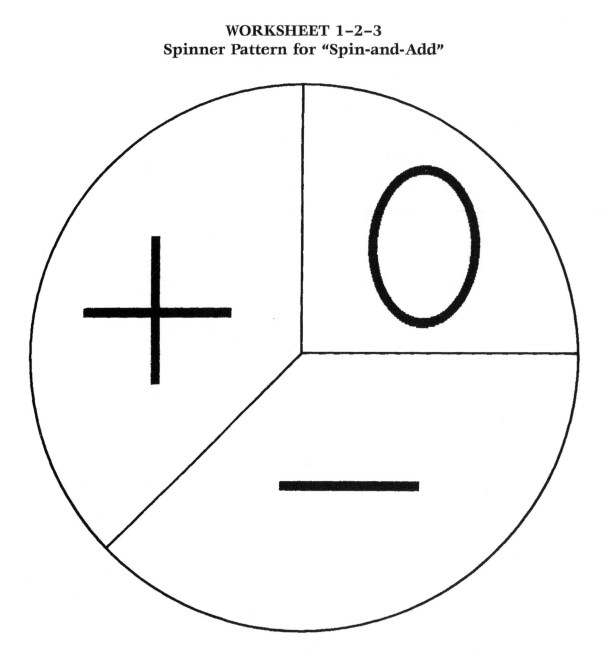

OBJECTIVE 3: Subtract with integers.

Activity 1: TILE TAKE-AWAY

[Developing Action]

Materials: Packets of integer tiles from Objective 1
Unlined paper for building mats (8.5 in. × 11 in.; if white tiles are used,
    colored paper should be used for mats)
Regular paper
Pencils
Worksheet 1–3–1

Management: Partners (50 minutes)

Directions:

1. Give each pair of students a packet of unit tiles and a blank sheet of paper for a building mat. The mat should be positioned with its length turned horizontally or left to right to the students. It is assumed that students have already completed the activities of Objective 1 in this section so that they understand the nature of opposites in their daily world and the neutralizing effect of 0-pairs. The **take-away** model for subtraction will be used in the activities of this objective; it is the model that is most familiar to students. Do not introduce "addition with the inverse" at this time. That procedure will be presented later in Activity 3 as an **alternative** to subtraction, *not* as a **definition** of subtraction.

2. Have students place 6 positive unit tiles on their building mats. Ask them to **take away** or remove 2 positive unit tiles from the tiles already on the mat. (In subtraction, +6, the first term, is called the **minuend** and +2, the second term, is called the **subtrahend.**) Four positive units remain on the mat as the **difference.** This type of exercise is most familiar to students since it corresponds to the whole number subtraction they did in the primary grades.

3. Write the following number sentence or equation on the chalkboard to record the result: $(+6) - (+2) = +4$.

4. Have students place 8 negative unit tiles on the building mat, then remove 3 of the unit tiles from the mat. Counting the remaining tiles, the result will be 5 negative unit tiles or –5. Record this action with the number sentence: $(-8) - (-3) = -5$. Students might also write the number sentences in their own notebooks or journals to show their work with the tiles.

5. The two previous examples required a direct removal of tiles as in whole number subtraction. The next three, however, will involve the application of 0-pairs before any removal of tiles can occur. Have students show +3 with tiles on their mats. *Ask:* "If you want to remove +5 from your mat, can you do it now? If not, what changes might be made to the tiles on the mat to make removal of +5 possible?" *(not enough positive tiles on the mat at first to remove +5; need to build up the amount of positive tiles on the mat in some way)* *Ask:* "What will happen to the amount of tiles and the total value of the tiles on the mat if you place several 0-pairs of unit tiles on the mat with the other +3?" *(extra unit tiles will be on the mat, including both positive and negative tiles; the overall value of the tiles on the mat* *is still +3)* Several 0-pairs (+1 with −1) should now be placed on the mat beside the +3; allow students to decide how many pairs they need. Remind them that their goal is to have enough positive unit tiles on the mat to be able to remove +5. Two 0-pairs are the minimal number needed, but more pairs are acceptable. After the 5 positive unit tiles have been removed from the mat, any remaining 0-pairs should also be removed in order to **simplify** the tiles on the mat and easily reveal the effective value of the tiles that are left. Here, the result will be −2.

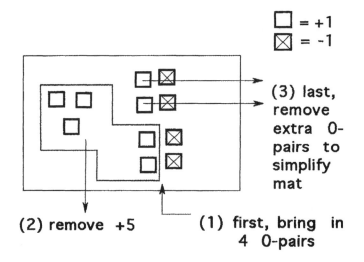

6. In the above illustration, four 0-pairs were used; two pairs were later removed since those tiles were not needed for the subtraction. Hopefully students will realize that only two 0-pairs were actually needed to allow the removal of +5. Now record the action with the equation: (+3) − (+5) = −2.

7. Have students now show (−7) − (+3) with their tiles. Seven negative unit tiles should be placed on the mat initially. *Ask:* "There are only negative units on the mat. What changes must we make in order to be able to remove 3 positive units?" *(bring in 3 or more 0-pairs to the mat; the total tile value on the mat is still −7, but now +3 can be removed)* Students should bring in the necessary 0-pairs (or more) of tiles, then remove 3 positive unit tiles from the mat. (In the illustration below, we chose to bring in three 0-pairs, the minimal number of pairs needed; hence, no simplification was needed.) After the subtraction is completed, they should remove any extra positive-negative pairs that remain on the mat. This will leave 10 negative unit tiles on the mat as the difference or answer. Record the following equation on the board: (−7) − (+3) = −10.

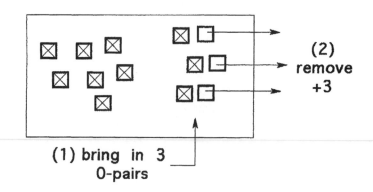

8. Discuss the idea that if no tiles are on the mat, the value shown on the mat is 0. ***Ask:*** "If your mat is empty, how can you subtract or remove –6 from the mat?" *(place 0-pairs of unit tiles on the mat until you can see 6 negative units; the total value in tiles is still 0)* Have students place at least six 0-pairs of unit tiles on their mats, then remove 6 of the negative unit tiles. This will leave +6 on the mat, along with any extra 0-pairs that were used. Students should remove the extra 0-pairs in order to simplify the tiles on the mat. Record the number sentence: 0 – (–6) = +6.

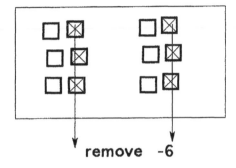

remove -6

9. Now assign additional subtraction exercises for students to work with their tiles. Allow extra time for this activity if needed; students require much practice with the tiles at this stage in order for them to fully understand the addition alternative later. Have students use the **take-away** or removal method with the exercises below, then write a number sentence or equation to record each result. Remind students that when the mat is empty or holds no tiles, whether at the beginning or after the subtraction has occurred, the value represented there is 0. If the amount to be taken away is 0, then no tiles are to be removed from the mat. (See Worksheet 1–3–1.)

(+8) – (+3) = ?	(–5) – (–1) = ?	(+4) – (+4) = ?	(–3) – (+5) = ?
(–2) – (–6) = ?	(+2) – (+7) = ?	(–6) – (+6) = ?	(+2) – (–6) = ?
(–3) – (–3) = ?	(+5) – (+1) = ?	(–7) – (–7) = ?	(–10) – 0 = ?
(+9) – (–2) = ?	0 – (+4) = ?	(+12) – (+4) = ?	(+5) – (–5) = ?
(–10) – (+6) = ?	(+4) – (–7) = ?	0 – (–3) = ?	(–1) – (+8) = ?

10. After all students have completed the above exercises, allow a few minutes for partners to discuss together the work they have done and to comment on anything they have observed about the methods they have used, the recordings made, etc. Then have various students share some of their ideas with the whole class. Do not limit or redirect the discussion at this time to any particular ideas; encourage the students to share anything they might have noticed. Their ideas will be refined later in Activity 3.

Name _____ **Date** _____

WORKSHEET 1-3-1
Tile Take-Away

Use the tiles to complete the following sentences with the missing differences.

$(+8) - (+3)$ = _____

$(+4) - (+4)$ = _____

$(-2) - (-6)$ = _____

$(+5) - (+1)$ = _____

$(+9) - (-2)$ = _____

$0 - (+4)$ = _____

$(-10) - (+6)$ = _____

$(-10) - 0$ = _____

Now write two or three on your own. Briefly explain in writing how you found the differences.

_____

_____

_____

_____

_____

_____

_____

_____

_____

_____

_____

_____

_____

_____

_____

_____

Activity 2: DRAW AND DELETE!

[Bridging Action]

Materials: Paper
Regular pencils
Red pencils
Colored chalk
Worksheet 1–3–2

Management: Partners (50 minutes)

Directions:

1. Give each pair of students a red pencil. In this activity they will continue to work with the different types of minuend-subtrahend combinations presented in Activity 1. These types will be developed here in diagram format.

2. On the chalkboard show students how to draw a diagram for (+7) – (+2). Draw with white chalk small, plain squares for the positive units. Seven squares should be drawn as a group on the board. To show the removal of +2 from this group, mark out two of the squares with white chalk. Draw a path with colored chalk around the remaining 5 squares on the board. Students should draw the same diagram on their own papers. A path should be drawn with red pencil around the unmarked squares. Students should avoid drawing extremely small squares that make counting difficult. The completed diagram as shown below should extend across a width equal to half the width of a regular sheet of paper. It might be helpful to have students fold their papers lengthwise so that the fold down the middle of the paper might guide them in making their diagrams large enough.

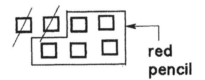

3. Write a number sentence on the chalkboard to record the procedure shown by the diagram: (+7) – (+2) = +5. Students should also write the number sentence or equation below the diagram on their own paper.

4. Now have students draw a diagram for (–12) – (–8) on their papers. Twelve small squares with a large X in each interior should be drawn to represent –12, then 8 of the squares marked out with regular pencil. A path in red pencil should be drawn around the four squares not marked out to show the difference, –4. Students should then record the number sentence: (–12) – (–8) = –4.

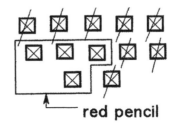

5. The previous two examples involve direct removals from the given amount (the minuend). The next three examples will require the use of 0-pairs of units in order to carry out any removal of units. Have students draw a group of units to show –4. Negative 7 needs to be taken away from this group, but there are not enough negative units in the original group. *Ask:* "What can we do to get more negative units in this group of units without changing the value, –4, of the group?" *(draw extra 0-pairs of positive and negative units)* Have students draw several 0-pairs on their diagrams until they see at least 7 negative units in the whole diagram. In the illustration below, we chose to draw four such pairs. Now 7 negative units should be marked out to show their subtraction or removal from the total group of units in the diagram. Students should also **simplify** their diagrams by marking out any extra 0-pairs that still remain after the subtraction. Finally, only 3 plain squares or positive units have not been marked out. A path should then be drawn in red pencil around this +3, indicating the result or difference. The following equation should now be recorded: $(-4) - (-7) = +3$.

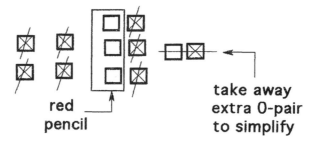

red pencil

take away extra 0-pair to simplify

6. Now ask students to draw a diagram that will represent $(+3) - (-5)$. Positive 3 will be drawn first, but –5 needs to be subtracted or removed and there are no negative units present. *Ask:* "How many 0-pairs of units do we need to draw next to the 3 positive units if we do not want to have any extra pairs at the end?" *(exactly 5 pairs must be drawn in order to provide the 5 negative units we need to subtract)* Students should now draw 5 0-pairs on their diagrams, then mark out –5. This will leave the original +3, along with a new group of +5, making a final difference of +8. A path should now be drawn with red pencil around +8 and the following number sentence recorded: $(+3) - (-5) = +8$.

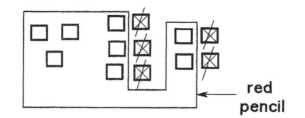

red pencil

7. *Ask:* "How do we begin if we want to draw a diagram for $0 - (+5)$?" (Since 0 is the minuend or original group of units, we start with a blank space on the paper.) *Ask:* "How do we take +5 away from nothing, or 0?" Hopefully students will realize that they can draw 0-pairs of units in the blank space until they see +5 to remove. Five positive units can then be marked out, leaving –5 for the difference. A red path should be drawn around the –5, followed by the recording of the equation: $0 - (+5) = -5$.

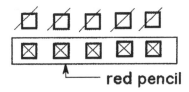

red pencil

8. Now assign more exercises for practice. For each exercise, students should draw a diagram as demonstrated above and write a number sentence or equation that shows the result. Remind students that a 0 at the beginning or at the end is shown by a blank space on their paper. If the amount to be taken away is 0, then no squares are to be marked out on the diagram. (See Worksheet 1–3–2.)

$(-7) - (-5) = ?$	$(+8) - (+1) = ?$	$(-3) - 0 = ?$	$(+3) - (+3) = ?$
$(+10) - (-3) = ?$	$(-1) - (+4) = ?$	$(+3) - (+4) = ?$	$(-2) - (+7) = ?$
$(-2) - (-2) = ?$	$0 - (+8) = ?$	$(+5) - (-5) = ?$	$(-12) - (-5) = ?$
$(+11) - (+6) = ?$	$(+8) - (+14) = ?$	$(-5) - (-10) = ?$	$0 - (-10) = ?$
$(-4) - (+4) = ?$	$(-9) - (-13) = ?$	$(+2) - (-7) = ?$	$(-11) - (+7) = ?$

9. After students have completed and corrected the above exercises, ask partners to work together to write a paragraph of three or four sentences describing the different steps they have learned to use to show subtraction. The paragraphs might be written in students' notebooks or journals. Have several students read their paragraphs to the whole class. Discuss and correct any misunderstandings that occur.

Activity 3: FINDING ALTERNATIVES

[Application/Exploration]

Materials: Paper
Regular pencils
Red pencils
Packets of tiles and building mats from Activity 1
Decks of cards (see step 6 below for the description of a deck)
Worksheet 1–3–3

Management: Teams of 4 students each (50 minutes)

Directions:

1. In this activity students will explore an alternative to subtraction by comparing pairs of "related sentences." Write the following pairs of number sentences or equations, one equation below the other within each pair, on the chalkboard (or see Worksheet 1–3–3 if you prefer):

Pair #1	*Pair #2*	*Pair #3*	*Pair #4*
$(+8) - (-2) = ?$	$(-5) - (+3) = ?$	$(+2) - (-7) = ?$	$(-3) - (+4) = ?$
$(+8) + (+2) = ?$	$(-5) + (-3) = ?$	$(+2) + (+7) = ?$	$(-3) + (-4) = ?$

WORKSHEET 1–3–2
Draw and Delete!

Draw diagrams of tiles to complete the following sentences with the missing differences.

1. $(-7) - (-5)$ = _____

5. $(+11) - (+6)$ = _____

2. $(+8) - (+1)$ = _____

6. $(+8) - (+14)$ = _____

3. $(-3) - 0$ = _____

7. $(-9) - (-13)$ = _____

4. $(+3) - (+3)$ = _____

8. $(+2) - (-7)$ = _____

WORKSHEET 1–3–3
Finding Alternatives

Pair #1	Pair #2	Pair #3	Pair #4
$(+8) - (-2) =$	$(-5) - (+3) =$	$(+2) - (-7) =$	$(-3) - (+4) =$
$(+8) + (+2) =$	$(-5) + (-3) =$	$(+2) + (+7) =$	$(-3) + (-4) =$

Draw a diagram to solve each equation within each pair. Then record the answers to complete the equations.

2. Ask each team to draw a diagram for each equation within a pair, then record the answers to complete the equations. If students prefer, allow them to build the equations on their mats in order to find the answers.

3. After all teams have completed their equations, ask them to look carefully at the equations in each pair and compare their numbers and operations. Have each team write down their observations, then ask various students to share their team's findings. Hopefully the following observations will be made concerning each pair of equations:

   (a) the first numbers are equal in value;

   (b) the two operations, subtraction and addition, are inverses of each other;

   (c) the second numbers are opposites or (additive) inverses of each other; and

   (d) the answers are equal in value, even though the subtraction answer is actually a difference and the addition answer is actually a sum.

4. To check for understanding, **ask:** "If we have the subtraction exercise: $(+3) - (-1) = +4$, what will its **related** number sentence or equation be, based on what we have discovered?" *(the related equation will be $(+3) + (+1) = +4$)* Now **ask:** "Do you think **every** subtraction exercise you worked in Activity 2 has a **related** addition exercise whose sum will be equal in value to the difference you found when you subtracted?" Team members should now try to write a related addition exercise for each subtraction exercise worked earlier in Activity 2, then compare the new sum to the difference already found. The discovery should hold for every subtraction exercise, regardless of the type of exercise used, that is, whether 0-pairs are used or not. For example, $(-6) - (-2) = -4$ and $(-6) + (+2) = -4$ form a related pair, and $(+3) - (+5) = -2$ and $(+3) + (-5) = -2$ form a related pair.

5. The following game will provide students with practice in using related pairs of equations. Emphasis will be on the idea that the answer to a subtraction exercise may now be found by finding the answer to its related addition exercise instead. In other words, students now have an alternative: they may use either subtraction or addition to find their answer, as long as they use related equations as described above in step 3. This discovery provides flexibility to the student. For some numbers, subtraction is easier to use; for example, in $(-9) - (-4)$ where 4 negative units are simply removed from 9 negative units. For other numbers, addition with the related equation might be the easier alternative; for example, in $(+18) - (-2)$ where the alternative that produces the same answer is $(+18) + (+2)$. Students now have a choice.

6. **Game of SUM–DIFF:** Give each team of 4 students a deck of 48 cards, along with the packet of unit tiles and a building mat from Activity 1 that they may already have. The cards may be made with small, blank index cards or cut from light tagboard or cardstock. Each card will contain either an addition exercise or a subtraction exercise. Most exercises have a **related** exercise in the deck as well. Write the following exercises on the cards, one per card. (In the first nine rows below, the first two exercises in each row are related, and the last two exercises in each row are related; in the last three rows, none of the exercises are related.)

$(-2) - (-8)$	$(-2) + (+8)$	$(-7) - (-4)$	$(-7) + (+4)$
$(+8) - (+3)$	$(+8) + (-3)$	$(+5) - (+7)$	$(+5) + (-7)$
$(-3) - (-6)$	$(-3) + (+6)$	$(-11) - (-3)$	$(-11) + (+3)$
$(-2) - (+8)$	$(-2) + (-8)$	$(-8) - (+2)$	$(-8) + (-2)$

$(-5) - (+12)$	$(-5) + (-12)$	$(-10) - (+1)$	$(-10) + (-1)$
$(+12) - (+9)$	$(+12) + (-9)$	$(+3) - (+10)$	$(+3) + (-10)$
$(+12) - (-5)$	$(+12) + (+5)$	$(+3) - (-15)$	$(+3) + (+15)$
$(+18) - (-1)$	$(+18) + (+1)$	$(+7) - (-11)$	$(+7) + (+11)$
$0 - (-7)$	$0 + (+7)$	$0 - (+15)$	$0 + (-15)$
$(-6) - (+9)$	$(-6) - (-9)$	$(-15) + (+10)$	$(-15) + (-10)$
$0 - (-20)$	$0 + (-20)$	$0 + (+3)$	$0 + (-3)$
$(+7) + (-3)$	$(-7) + (+3)$	$(+1) - (-9)$	$(-1) + (+9)$

7. Each team should shuffle its deck of cards, then deal the cards to the team members until each person has 12 cards in hand. Each person must quietly compute the answer to each exercise contained on the cards in her or his hand; this knowledge will be needed in order to select a card for play. Answers may be computed mentally, with a diagram, or with tiles if necessary. Calculators should **not** be used in this particular game since the focus is on learning how the signs relate to each other within an exercise and between exercises. Numbers have been kept small so that computation will be easy to do.

8. The first player places a card face up on the table. Each of the other three players then puts a card down beside the first card. The card with the **greatest value** for its answer wins and the player of that winning card collects the four cards played in that round. If there is a **tie** for the greatest value in a round, the players involved in the tie must each put face down on the table a new card of their own choosing, then turn the cards over at the same time and compare their values. The card of higher value wins and the owner of that card is declared winner of the round and collects the original four cards played for the round as well as the cards played to break the tie. Remind students about the ordering of integers: positive integers are always greater than negative integers in value, 0 is greater than –1, –1 is greater than –2, etc.

9. If a player has a card that contains the **related exercise** of the **initial** card played in a round, and that player chooses to put that particular card down beside the initial card, then this **related** card will win the round. In this case, the higher valued card loses to the related card, regardless of any tie between card **values** in that same round.

10. The player who won the previous round now puts down a new card for the other players to try to beat, either with a higher valued card or with the related card.

11. The rounds continue until one or more players run out of cards. The winner is the player who won the most **cards,** not rounds.

OBJECTIVE 4: Multiply with integers.

Activity 1: ARRAY BUILD-UP

[Developing Action]

Materials: Packets of integer tiles (40 positive and 40 negative units per packet)
Building mats (described in step 1 below)
Paper
Pencils

Management: Partners (50 minutes)

Directions:

1. Give each pair of students a packet of unit tiles and a building mat. The building mat will be a sheet of blank paper (8.5 in. × 11 in.) with a bold stripe drawn midway across the width of the paper. The mat will be rotated so that the longest edge is across the top and bottom of the mat. Use colored paper for the mat if the unit tiles are white.

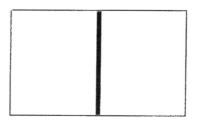

2. Review the meaning of multiplication as the repetition of a set or quantity, a definition common to the elementary school curriculum. To represent 2 sets of 5 objects or 10 objects total, the notation $2 \times 5 = 10$ is used. In integers this becomes $+2 \times +5 = +10$. We interpret the **multiplier** +2 to be the **countable number of sets to build.** Have students build 2 rows of 5 positive units on the left side of their mats and recount to find the total units, +10. A **row** should always be built **horizontally from left to right,** not vertically or up and down, which is called a column. This consistency in building will help later with other interpretations.

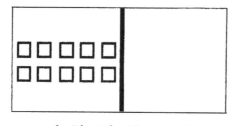

(+2) X (+5) = +10

3. Give students other examples to build on the left side of their mats. For each example, tell them only the ordered factor pair at first. They will build the rows needed, then find the total for themselves. They should then record the result as an integral number sentence on their own papers. Here are some examples to use: $+3 \times +6 = +18$, $+4 \times +2 = +8$, and $+2 \times +4 = +8$. Remember that the first factor is always the multiplier; it tells how many rows or sets to build. Write the completed number sentences on the chalkboard; these will be used later when students search for patterns. Hopefully students will notice that this first group of exercises behaves just like their whole number multiplication.

4. Now ask students to build 3 rows of 4 negative units each and count the total tiles used. Since negative units are being counted, the total will also be in negative units: -12. The number sentence, $+3 \times -4 = -12$, should be recorded on the chalkboard and on students' papers. Have students build several more examples and record them, e.g., $+5 \times -2 = -10$, $+4 \times -8 = -32$, and $+1 \times -9 = -9$.

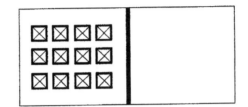

$$(+3) \times (-4) = -12$$

5. The above groups that use a positive multiplier are easy for students to build. A negative multiplier will require some interpretation for them since it will be new to their world of experiences. Remind students that opposite signs are used to describe opposite positions, as well as opposite movement. Discuss and draw on the chalkboard the following situations for 2 rows of 3 band members each, being led by a drum major who always moves in the direction of the parade. (It would be helpful and fun for students to act out each situation in class.)

(a) A single row of 3 band members facing toward the drum major is shown by $+3$; when the 2 rows move in the same direction as the drum major, the direction is shown by a positive multiplier, here $+2$; the final movement of the 6 band members has them all facing in the direction they are moving, or $+6$. The number sentence for this situation is $+2 \times +3 = +6$.

$$(+2) \times (+3) = +6$$

Drum Major

(b) A row of 3 band members with their backs toward the drum major is -3; again, 2 rows moving in the same direction as the drum major is $+2$, regardless of which way the members are facing; the final movement of the 6 band members has them all facing opposite to the direction they are moving, or –6; the number sentence for this is +2 × –3 = –6.

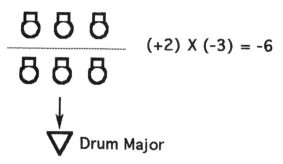

(+2) X (-3) = -6

(c) In each row, 3 band members follow and face toward the drum major at first (+3); when in front of the parade judges, the members continue to face the drum major but the 2 rows suddenly start marching in the opposite direction from the drum major (–2; a negative multiplier indicates that the band has changed its marching direction but each band member does not turn around); the final movement (solid arrow) of the band has them all facing opposite to their new marching direction (–6); the number sentence is –2 × +3 = –6.

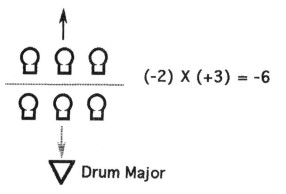

(-2) X (+3) = -6

(d) In each row, 3 band members have their backs toward the drum major (–3); in front of the judges they start marching away from the drum major without turning around (–2); their final movement (solid arrow) has all of them facing the direction they are moving (+6); the number sentence for this situation is –2 × –3 = +6.

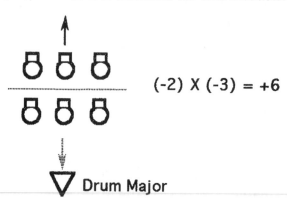

(-2) X (-3) = +6

6. Take time to go over these four situations. Students must be comfortable with the interpretations for position vs. movement before they continue with tiles on the building mats. These two ideas are common in mathematical applications of physics, engineering, etc.

7. Now show how to represent situation (c) on the building mat. For $-3 \times +4$, initially arrange 3 rows of 4 positive units each on the left side of the mat (this corresponds to the initial position of band members facing the drum major). To show the change in direction or movement, on the right side of the mat build the **opposite** of what is seen on the left. Arrange 3 rows of 4 negative units on the right side (this indicates that band members are now moving away from the drum major and in a direction opposite to the way they face). The final sentence, $-3 \times +4 = -12$, should now be written on the chalkboard and on students' papers.

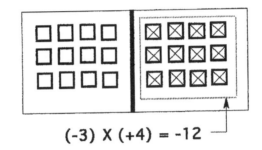

$$(-3) \times (+4) = -12$$

Note: The final equation should only be associated with the arrangement of tiles on the **right** side of the mat. Do not write $+3 \times +4$ on the board at all; it will only confuse students. Also, some will look at the final arrangement on the right and say that it "looks like" $+3 \times -4 = -12$, which it does. The difference that needs to be stressed is that the original group of tiles built on the left side went through a **change** (e.g., band changed its marching direction), as shown by the negative multiplier, whereas $+3 \times -4$ does not indicate a change has occurred.

8. Have students build several tile arrangements on the left side of the mat, then change the tiles by building their opposites on the right side of the mat. Give only the two factors at first, letting students decide what the correct product should be. Each final number sentence should be recorded on the chalkboard and on students' papers. Here are some examples to build: $-2 \times +5 = -10$, $-4 \times +2 = -8$, and $-6 \times +3 = -18$.

9. For situation (d), ask students to build 4 rows of 2 negative units each on the left side of the mat. (This corresponds to band members facing away from the drum major.) To show the change in direction of their movement, i.e., they move away from the drum major, take the opposite of all units on the left by building 4 rows of 2 positive units on the right side of the mat (band members now face the direction in which they are moving). Because of the change that took place both physically and situationally, the arrangement on the right side of the mat can now be represented by the number sentence $-4 \times -2 = +8$.

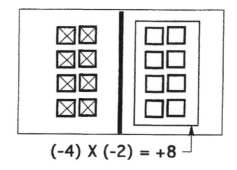

$$(-4) \times (-2) = +8$$

Note: The arrangement on the right side of the mat "looks like" $+4 \times +2 = +8$, but again the positive multiplier does not reflect the **change** that really took place. Number sentences initially should reflect the actions that have occurred in the situation being modeled; equivalent forms should come later.

10. Assign more arrangements of this last type for students to build and record. Here are some examples to use: $-5 \times -3 = +15$, $-1 \times -6 = +6$, and $-3 \times -2 = +6$.

11. During this activity all number sentences built by the students have been recorded on the chalkboard. After everyone seems comfortable with the building process, **ask:** "When you look at these number sentences, what observations can you make about the factors to help you predict when your answer or product will be positive or negative? Discuss your ideas with your partner, then we will share all our ideas." After a few minutes, ask some of the students to share their observations with the whole class. The patterns of signs in multiplication are usually easy for most students to find, but do not press for them if students fail to find them at this time. Accept whatever ideas they suggest as long as the ideas are reasonable and correct for the number sentences shown on the board. Emphasize that you are looking for a pattern or patterns that will hold for all the number sentences, not just a few. (The patterns that will be discovered eventually are that "two factors with like signs have a positive product" and "two factors with unlike signs have a negative product." Students may separate these two categories into smaller ones or word them differently; for example, for the first pattern above students might say instead that "two factors with positive signs have a positive product" and "two factors with negative signs have a positive product.")

Activity 2: VISUALIZING ARRAYS

[Bridging Action]

Materials: Paper
Pencils
Worksheet 1–4–1

Management: Partners (20 minutes)

Directions:

1. Show students how to draw diagrams of arrays (rows of squares) to show different multiplication exercises with integers and to find their products. Quite often if students have been trained to draw pictures for new concepts, they later can replicate such drawings to help them recall the concepts in more abstract form. Use a plain small square for +1 and a small square with a large X inside for −1.

2. Here are examples of drawings for the first two types discussed earlier (the multiplier is positive):

(a) +3 × +5 = ?   (+15)

(b) +4 × −3 = ?   (−12)

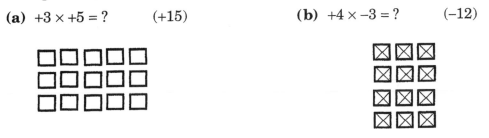

3. For the two types having a negative multiplier, students will need to draw a vertical bar on their papers and show an array on each side of the bar. As an example of type (c), to show −2 × +3, an array for +2 × +3 must first be drawn on the left side of a vertical bar, then the **change** shown by drawing opposites on the right side. The final array on the right will be for −2 × +3 and will have a total of −6. **Note:** After students become comfortable with the meaning of negative multipliers, they tend to mentally picture the initial array on the left side of the vertical bar, leave the left side blank, and draw only the final array on the right side of the vertical bar. This is acceptable as long as they can explain what they are really doing in the exercise.

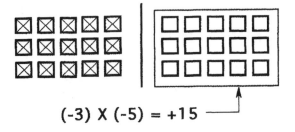

4. Similarly, for type (d) have students draw arrays to show −3 × −5. They will first draw +3 × −5 on the left side of a vertical bar, then show the change indicated by the negative multiplier by drawing the opposite of each unit on the right side. The final array on the right will have a product of +15.

(-3) X (-5) = +15

5. After students have practiced drawing several exercises with the teacher, write a variety of integer multiplication exercises on the chalkboard, omitting the product for each one. Be sure to include 4 or 5 of each type presented above. Have partners work together to draw an array(s), find the product, and record the number sentence for each exercise assigned. (See Worksheet 1–4–1.)

6. When all have finished, ask each pair of students to write a short paragraph about how they might predict the sign of the product for +26 × −38 and for −45 × −67. What

Name _____ **Date** _____

WORKSHEET 1–4–1
Visualizing Arrays

Draw arrays on your own papers to find the products for the following sentences.

$(+3) \times (+5)$ = _____ $(-3) \times (-6)$ = _____

$(-2) \times (+3)$ = _____ $(-4) \times (+3)$ = _____

$(+8) \times (-1)$ = _____ $(+5) \times (-3)$ = _____

$(-5) \times (+5)$ = _____ $(+2) \times (+2)$ = _____

$(+7) \times (-2)$ = _____ $(-7) \times (-5)$ = _____

$(+8) \times (-3)$ = _____ $(+4) \times (+7)$ = _____

$(-5) \times (+3)$ = _____ $(-6) \times (-6)$ = _____

Write a brief paragraph about how you might predict the sign of the product for $(+26) \times (-38)$ and for $(-45) \times (-67)$.

_____

_____

_____

_____

_____

_____

_____

_____

_____

_____

_____

_____

_____

_____

patterns have they seen that might help them with their predictions? Responses might be recorded in student journals, as well as some read to the entire class. (At this point hopefully they have seen the sign patterns described at the end of Activity 1. The first product should be negative because the factors have different signs; the second product should be positive because the factors have like signs.)

7. Mental challenge: Ask students if they can tell what the products will be for +20 × −30 and for −25 × −10, using what they have learned about their arrays and the signs involved. *(−600 and +250)*

Activity 3: TRANSLATION TREKS

[Application/Exploration]

Materials: Blank paper
Pencils
Colored pencils or markers
Worksheet 1–4–2

Management: Teams of 4 students each (30 minutes)

Directions:

1. Prepare a list of number sentences that involve the multiplication of integers, for example, +5 × −8. Be sure to include some number sentences from each of the four types studied earlier in Activities 1 and 2. Assign each team an exercise from this list. Use factors that are between −8 and +8 so that the amount of units involved in the product does not become too large. (See Worksheet 1–4–2.)

2. Ask each team to create a situation (like that of the marching band discussed in Activity 1) that might be represented by their number sentence. Remind them that their situation must include two positions or qualities that are opposites in some way and two movements that are opposites. If a position/quality and a movement are considered to be "in agreement" for some reason, then the product will be positive; if they are not, the product will be negative. Have them draw and color a picture that shows the situation they have chosen.

3. After teams have finished, let them show their artwork and describe the situations they selected. Then the artwork might be displayed in the classroom in some way, if preferred.

4. Here are examples of the kinds of situations needed. Students will have to give careful thought to the different elements needed for their situations. Bold words are used below to identify some of these elements needed.

(a) To satisfy +5 × +4 = +20, 5 boxes of 4 **unbroken** pencils each (+4) are being **saved** in a desk drawer (+5). So 20 good pencils are **being treated correctly** (+20), i.e., being saved. If the pencils were broken, we would use −4; if the 5 boxes were being **thrown away,** we would use −5. If good pencils are being **thrown away by mistake,** we would have −20.

WORKSHEET 1–4–2
Translation Treks

Select one of the number sentences given below. Create a situation (like that of the marching band discussed in Activity 1) that might be represented by your number sentence. Draw a picture that shows your particular situation.

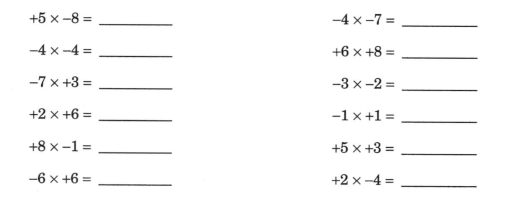

$+5 \times -8 =$ _____ $-4 \times -7 =$ _____

$-4 \times -4 =$ _____ $+6 \times +8 =$ _____

$-7 \times +3 =$ _____ $-3 \times -2 =$ _____

$+2 \times +6 =$ _____ $-1 \times +1 =$ _____

$+8 \times -1 =$ _____ $+5 \times +3 =$ _____

$-6 \times +6 =$ _____ $+2 \times -4 =$ _____

(b) To satisfy $+3 \times -5 = -15$, three groups of 5 motorboats each are positioned with their **front ends pointing upstream** (–5). Front ends **pointed downstream** would be +5. Positive 3 indicates that the groups of boats, no matter which way they are turned, are **moving downstream.** So –15 means that the 3 groups of 5 boats are finally moving downstream, but their front ends are **pointed** upstream, **not in the direction they are moving.**

(c) To satisfy $-2 \times +6 = -12$, there are two groups of 6 race cars each on the race track. Each car is **facing toward the pace car** that is to lead them around the track (+6). Suddenly there is a bad oil slick ahead on the track and it starts burning. The drivers are signaled to back up (but not turn their cars around) and move in an opposite direction away from the oil fire (–2). So –12 is for the total cars **moving backward** on the track, but the 12 cars are **not turned in the direction they are moving.**

(d) To satisfy $-3 \times -2 = +6$, 3 sets of cups can be **filled** (+2) **or emptied** (–2). The 3 sets of cups can be **served** to thirsty customers (+3) **or taken away** from them (–3). Positive 6 indicates that taking away the 3 sets of 2 empty cups each from the thirsty customers is the **agreeable** thing to do since empty cups are of no use to them. To take away 6 filled cups ($-3 \times +2$) would **not** be an **agreeable** action (–6) since the thirsty people need something to drink!

OBJECTIVE 5: Divide with integers.

Activity 1: SEPARATION SAVVY

[Developing Action]

Materials: Packets of integer tiles (40 positive and 40 negative units per packet)
Building mats (described in step 1 below)
Paper
Pencils
Worksheet 1–5–1

Management: Partners (50 minutes)

Directions:

1. Give each pair of students a packet of unit tiles and a building mat. The building mat will be a sheet of blank paper (8.5 in. × 11 in.) with a bold stripe drawn midway across the width of the paper. The mat will be rotated so that the longest edge is across the top and bottom of the mat. Use colored paper for the mat if the unit tiles are white.

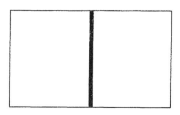

2. Review the meaning of division as the separation of a set of objects into several equal, usually smaller, sets. This is one of the two definitions of division common to the elementary school curriculum. To represent 10 objects separated into 2 equal sets of 5 objects each, the notation $10 \div 2 = 5$ is used. In integers this becomes $(+10) \div (+2) = +5$. We interpret the **divisor** +2 to be the **countable number of sets to build.** Have students place 10 positive units on the left side of their mats and separate them into 2 equal rows, placing one unit at a time per row. A **row** should always be built **horizontally from left to right,** not vertically or up and down, which is called a column. This consistency in building will help later with other interpretations. The row size of +5 is the **quotient** or answer we seek when using this particular definition of division. To emphasize the quotient as the amount of one row, you might have students place a piece of yarn around one row of their choosing or just lay a pencil across one of the rows. It can be any one of the rows built. Do not remove any rows from the left side of the mat, since they show what the original dividend was for the exercise. Record the number sentence, $(+10) \div (+2) = +5$, on the board.

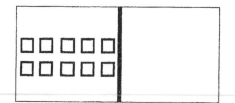

(+10) ÷ (+2) = +5 in each row

3. Give students other examples to build on the left side of their mats. For each example, tell them only the ordered number pair (dividend and divisor), not the answer. They will place the total units on the mat first, build the rows needed, then find the amount per row for themselves. They should then record the result as an integral number sentence on their own papers. Here are some examples to use: (+18) ÷ (+3) = +6, (+8) ÷ (+4) = +2, and (+15) ÷ (+3) = +5. (See Worksheet 1–5–1.) Remember that the first number written is always the **dividend;** it tells how many units total need to be separated. The second number of the pair is the **divisor;** it tells how many rows or sets to build, using the total given. Write the completed number sentences on the chalkboard; these will be used later when students search for patterns. Hopefully students will notice that this first group of exercises behaves just like whole number division where the divisor tells how many sets are to be made and the quotient is the size of each set.

4. Now ask students to place 12 negative units on the left side of their mats and separate them equally into 3 rows. Have them count the number of tiles used in each row to find the row size. Since negative units form the original amount (the dividend), the row size will also be in negative units: –4. The number sentence (–12) ÷ (+3) = –4 should be recorded on the chalkboard and on students' papers. Have students build several more examples and record them, e.g., (–10) ÷ (+5) = –2, (–32) ÷ (+4) = –8, and (–9) ÷ (+1) = –9. (See Worksheet 1–5–1.)

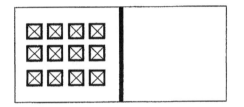

(-12) ÷ (+3) = -4 in each row

5. The above groups of exercises that use a positive divisor are easy for students to build. A negative divisor requires some interpretation for them since it will be new to their world of experiences. Review Activity 1 from the previous lesson on multiplication of integers where the examples of marching bands are discussed. We want to make use of the relationship between division and multiplication so as not to be too tedious, but we also want division to have a meaning all its own. Remind students that opposite signs are used to describe opposite positions, as well as opposite movements.

6. First discuss the two band situations for (+12) ÷ (+3) and (+12) ÷ (–3).

(a) In (+12) ÷ (+3), +12 represents all band members and the positive sign indicates that all members are facing in the direction they are moving. The divisor +3 has a positive sign, which means that the band moves in the same direction as the drum major; it also means that the band is arranged in 3 equal rows. So what does each row look like? How many members are in each row and which way are they facing? [Wow! It's mystery-solving time!] Draw 3 rows of 4 small circles each on the chalkboard; the circles are the hats of the band members, four per row. Show the direction the drum major is moving (broken arrow). Since the **divisor** is **positive,** the **band** (solid arrow) is **moving in the same direction as the drum major. All members must face the same direction the band is moving** (+12), so draw a bill on each hat pointing in the direction of the solid arrow. Thus, the **individual band members** in each row are **facing toward the drum major,** so we use +4 to describe each row. Conclusion: $(+12) \div (+3) = +4$. Record the number sentence on the board.

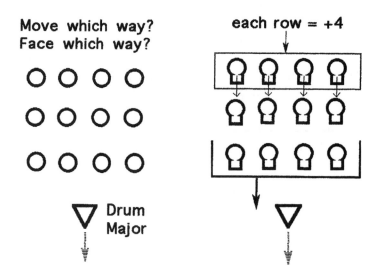

(b) Now what about $(+12) \div (-3)$? Draw 3 new rows of 4 circles each on the board. The divisor -3 tells us that the band moves away from the drum major (broken arrow), so draw a solid arrow to show their opposite direction. The dividend, $+12$, shows that all band members face toward their own direction of movement, so they must all be facing away from the drum major. Then each row size must be -4. Conclusion: $(+12) \div (-3) = -4$. Record this number sentence on the board.

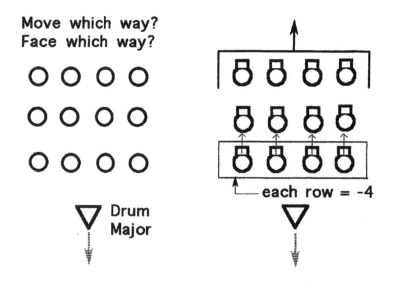

7. Ask: "How do $(+12) \div (+3)$ and $(+12) \div (-3)$ differ?" *(Their divisors have opposite signs.)* "How do the answers or quotients to these two exercises differ?" *(They have opposite signs also.)* So when we have a negative divisor, our answer or quotient will just be the opposite of the answer we would get using the positive form of the divisor. Similar analyses will produce the following drawings for $(-12) \div (+3)$ and $(-12) \div (-3)$. Notice that the divisors and quotients are opposites in these examples as well. Record these two number sentences on the board as well.

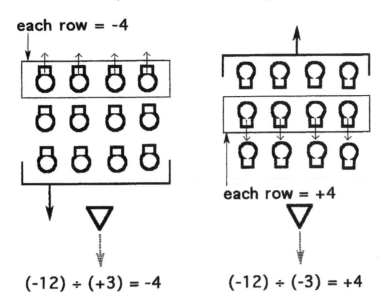

each row = -4

each row = +4

$(-12) \div (+3) = -4$ $(-12) \div (-3) = +4$

8. Now that students have an idea of what happens with the signs, show them how to build division exercises on the mat, using negative divisors. Consider $(+8) \div (-2)$. Have students place 8 positive units on the left side of their mats and separate them into 2 equal rows.

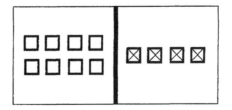

9. This action alone is just $(+8) \div (+2)$. **Ask:** "What changes did we discover when we wanted to use a negative divisor?" *(The answer or quotient changes, too.)* So if the row size for $(+8) \div (+2)$ is +4, to get the row size for $(+8) \div (-2)$, we simply take the opposite of +4. Have students build a single row of units on the right side of the mat, but this time use negative units. The number sentence $(+8) \div (-2) = -4$ should be recorded on the board and on students' papers. **Note:** Just a single row is built on the right side of the mat since for division we really want to know only the row size, not work with the total tile arrangement.

10. Assign more exercises of this type (positive dividend, negative divisor) for students to build and record. Here are some examples to use: $(+15) \div (-5) = -3$, $(+7) \div (-1) = -7$, and $(+6) \div (-3) = -2$. (See Worksheet 1–5–1.)

WORKSHEET 1-5-1
Separation Savvy

Build with tiles to find the quotient of each number sentence below.

$(+15) \div (-5) =$ _____ $(+18) \div (+3) =$ _____

$(+8) \div (+4) \ =$ _____ $(-32) \div (+4) =$ _____

$(+15) \div (+3) =$ _____ $(-10) \div (+5) =$ _____

$(-9) \div (+1) \ =$ _____ $(+6) \div (-3) \ =$ _____

$(-18) \div (-6) =$ _____ $(-20) \div (-4) =$ _____

$(-16) \div (-2) =$ _____ $(+7) \div (-1) \ =$ _____

When you look at the signs on the dividend and divisor and compare them with the sign on the quotient or answer, what do you notice? Is there a way you can predict what the sign will be on your answer just by looking at the signs on the first two numbers in the sentence?

_____

_____

_____

_____

_____

_____

_____

_____

_____

_____

_____

_____

11. Working with a negative dividend and a negative divisor still maintains the "opposites" relationships of the divisors and quotients, as shown in step 7 above. Have students show $(-10) \div (-5)$ by first placing 10 negative units on the left side of the mat and separating them into 5 equal rows. Each row will have –2 in it. Our negative divisor indicates that we need the opposite of this row size for our quotient. Students should build one row of +2 on the right side of their mats. The number sentence $(-10) \div (-5) = +2$ should be recorded on the board and on students' papers for later pattern searches.

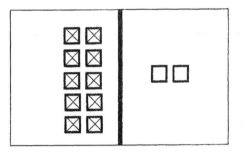

12. Assign more exercises that have a negative dividend and negative divisor for students to build and record. Here are some examples: $(-16) \div (-2) = +8$, $(-18) \div (-6) = +3$, and $(-20) \div (-4) = +5$. (See Worksheet 1–5–1.)

13. When students have finished building all the assigned exercises and the number sentences have been recorded on the board, **ask:** "When you look at the signs on the dividend and divisor and compare them to the sign on the quotient or answer, what do you notice? Is there a way you can predict what the sign will be on your answer just by looking at the signs on the first two numbers in the exercise?" Accept whatever they might suggest at this time as long as it is reasonable and applies to more than one exercise shown on the board. The relationship among the signs in division will be finalized in Activity 2: When the signs of the dividend and divisor are alike, either both negative or both positive, the sign of the quotient will be positive; when the two signs are opposites, the sign of the quotient will be negative.

Activity 2: DIVISION DIAGRAMS

[Bridging Action]

Materials: Paper
Pencils
Worksheet 1–5–2

Management: Partners (30 minutes)

Directions:

1. Show students how to draw diagrams that represent separation into equal sets or rows. The diagrams will be similar to those used for integer multiplication. Use a small plain square for +1 and a small square with an X in its interior for –1. Our goal is to help students visualize the action of division rather than just memorize some number sentences by rote.

2.   Here are examples of drawings for the first two types discussed earlier (the divisor is positive). Encourage students to circle a different row each time to show the answer. Which row is circled is not important; the quotient being sought is the amount in any one row.

   (a) (+15) ÷ (+3) = ?   (+5)   **(b)** (−12) ÷ (+4) = ?   (−3)

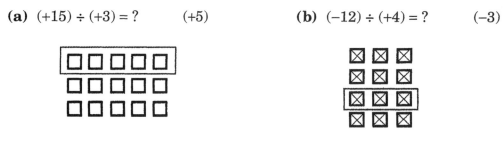

3.   For the two types having a negative divisor, students will need to draw a vertical bar on their paper and show an array on the left side of the bar and a single row on the right side. As an example of a positive dividend, to show (+15) ÷ (−3), an array for (+15) ÷ (+3) must first be drawn on the left side of a vertical bar, then the **change** shown by drawing a row of opposite units on the right side. The final row on the right will be for (+15) ÷ (−3) and will contain 5 negative units, or –5.

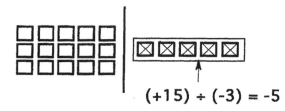

4.   Similarly, for a negative dividend have students draw a diagram to show (−6) ÷ (−2). They will first draw an array for (−6) ÷ (+2) on the left side of a vertical bar, then show the **change** indicated by the negative divisor by drawing the opposite of a single row on the right side. The final row on the right will be for (−6) ÷ (−2), which is +3.

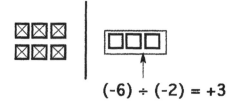

5.   After students have practiced drawing several exercises with the teacher, write a variety of integer division exercises on the chalkboard, omitting the quotient for each one. Be sure to include 4 or 5 of each type presented above. Have partners work together to draw an array, find the quotient, and record the number sentence for each exercise assigned. (See Worksheet 1–5–2.)

6.   When all have finished, ask each pair of students to write a short paragraph about how they might predict the sign of the quotient for (+105) ÷ (−15) and for (−286) ÷ (−22). (Do not encourage computation at this time.) What patterns have they seen that might

WORKSHEET 1–5–2
Division Diagrams

Draw diagrams of tiles on your own papers to find the quotients of the following sentences.

$(+15) \div (+3) =$ $(-12) \div (+4) =$

$(-18) \div (+6) =$ $(+2) \div (-2) \ =$

$(-6) \div (-3) \ =$ $(-15) \div (-5) =$

$(+9) \div (+3) \ =$ $(+4) \div (-2) \ =$

$(+3) \div (-1) \ =$ $(-12) \div (+6) =$

$(-14) \div (-7) =$ $(+16) \div (+4) =$

$(+7) \div (-1) \ =$ $(-8) \div (+2) \ =$

Explain in writing how you might predict the sign of the quotient for $(+105) \div (-15)$ and for $(-286) \div (-22)$. Do not compute at this time.

_____

_____

_____

_____

_____

_____

_____

_____

_____

_____

_____

_____

_____

help them with their predictions? Responses might be recorded in student journals, as well as some read to the entire class. (At this point hopefully they have seen the sign patterns described at the end of Activity 1. The first quotient should be negative because the dividend and the divisor have different signs; the second quotient should be positive because the dividend and the divisor have like signs.)

7. Mental challenge: Ask students if they can tell what the quotients will be for $(+200) \div (-50)$ and for $(-350) \div (-10)$, using what they have learned about their arrays and the signs involved. *(−4 and +35)*

Activity 3: DIVVY UP!

[Application/Exploration]

Materials: One deck of DIVVY UP cards per team (described in step 1 below)

Management: Teams of 4 students each (20 minutes)

Directions:

1. Prepare a deck of 40 cards for each team. Small, unlined index cards might be labeled and decorated uniformly for the playing cards. Label the cards to match by pairs; one card in a pair will have the division exercise and the other will have the quotient for that exercise. For example, one card might contain "$(+10) \div (-2)$" as the exercise, and its matching card would contain "−5" as the quotient. In each deck there should be 5 pairs of each type of integer division studied in Activity 1 and Activity 2. Cards might be laminated to make them last longer. Each complete deck should have its own color of card or decoration so that any sets of mixed cards can be easily separated into their correct decks.

2. Give each team a deck of cards. A team should shuffle its own deck, then equally distribute the cards one at a time to the 4 members, giving each person a playing hand of 10 cards. The players will take turns trying to make matching pairs with the cards in their hands.

3. On a turn, a player may lay down on the table face up at most two possible pairs or "books" he or she can make at that time. The other players must agree that a pair of cards is correctly matched before the pair can be put down on the table. If a player does not have any matched pairs in hand when it is his or her turn, that player must draw a card from the player to the left. If the new card completes a match, the card pair may be played at that time.

4. When one of the players runs out of cards, the game ends. The player with the most matched pairs on the table is the winner.

5. All the cards may then be reshuffled and distributed for a new game if time permits.

OBJECTIVE 6: Develop and apply the distributive property to real numbers.

Activity 1: SPLITTING THINGS APART

[Developing Action]

Materials: Packets of integer tiles (40 positive units and 40 negative units per packet)
Building mats (described below in step 2)
10-inch pieces of cotton yarn or thin bamboo skewers (2 per pair of students)
Paper
Pencils
Worksheet 1–6–1

Management: Partners (30 minutes)

Directions:

1. The distributive property, formally the distributive property of multiplication over addition for real numbers, allows us to organize a quantity in different ways. This activity will provide students with opportunities to separate amounts into different, smaller subsets and to visualize a combination of integers as an array that can be cut either horizontally or vertically, then described with symbols in written form.

2. Give each pair of students a packet of integer tiles, a building mat, and 2 pieces of yarn (or 2 bamboo skewers). The mat should consist of an 8.5 in. × 11 in. sheet of light tagboard with an L-frame drawn on it with a wide marker. The mat might be laminated to make it last longer. An example of the mat is shown in the illustration.

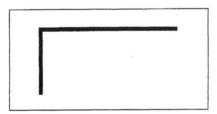

3. Ask students to place 3 positive units, then 5 negative units on their building mats above the L-frame. Have them also place 4 positive units down the left side of the L-frame (see illustration below). The area under the L-frame is for building the product of the left and top quantities placed on the mat. The one or more quantities on top (+3 with –5) indicate the **multiplicand** or the set that is to be copied several times and the quantity on the left (+4) indicates the **multiplier,** which counts the number of copies to be made.

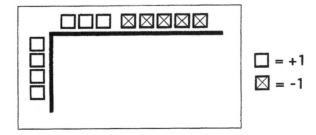

4. Have students build 4 copies of the row of tiles that equals to (+3) + (−5). At first have them build one complete row of tiles before starting the next row. This emphasizes the role of the +4 and the repetition of a complete set of objects in the multiplication process. (Here the "complete set" is a row.) Later they will find their own ways to build with the tiles.

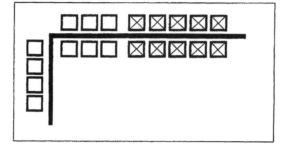

5. Tell students that since they built their 4 copies one complete row at a time, an expression that shows this process is (+4)[(+3) + (−5)]. That is, the +3 and −5 are connected together by the brackets to show they exist in the same row. Record this on the chalkboard. Remind students that when numbers are written beside each other like in (+4)[(+3) + . . .] or (+2)(−6), that is, when only parentheses or brackets are between the numbers, this means multiplication.

6. Now *ask:* "Do you notice how the unit tiles are grouped in the product area below the L-frame?" (*All the positive units are together on the left and all the negative units are together on the right.*) Have students place a piece of yarn (or bamboo skewer) on the building mat between the two groups of tiles. Ask them to describe the two arrays of tiles they now see. (*4 rows of +3 each on the left and 4 rows of −5 each on the right*) So this new way to describe the product can be recorded as **(+4)(+3) + (+4)(−5).** The 3 positive tiles and 5 negative tiles are no longer seen as being connected in one row, so the numbers +3 and −5 are not written together or connected with brackets. Write this new expression on the board below the other expression.

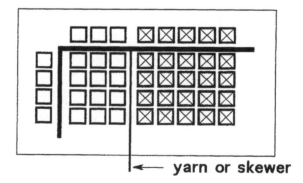

◄── yarn or skewer

7. Now guide students to find other ways to describe the product of tiles. Here are some possibilities. (For each idea, record an expression on the board below the other expressions already given.) If all the positive tiles are viewed together, their value is +12; if the negative tiles are viewed together, their value is −20. So the product can also be expressed as **(+12) + (−20).** If all the tiles are simplified by forming 0-pairs, the product's value is **−8.** (Some students may need to actually move the tiles to form 0-pairs; allow them to do this, but they should restore their tiles to the array format as soon as they have found their numerical answer.) If each row of tiles is simplified to –2 by forming 0-pairs before the 4 copies are made, the product appears as **(+4)(–2)**. Emphasize to students that all these expressions describe the same product of tiles on their building mats, but each expression represents a different way of organizing or viewing the total set of unit tiles. It is extremely important early in the study of algebra that students begin to see the written language of algebra as a way of communicating actions or procedures that have occurred. Such communication will come directly from work with manipulatives and with diagrams throughout this book.

8. Now ask students to show –3 as the multiplier and –2 with +6 as the set to be copied on their mats. Review the lessons for Objective 4 on integer multiplication; remind students that a **negative** multiplier requires **changing** an initial product **to its opposite.** Thus, we need the opposite of whatever 3 complete rows of [(–2) + (+6)] will make as a product. Instead of an array of –6 on the left of the mat, we must build an array for +6. Instead of an array of +18 on the right of the mat, we must build an array for –18. Have students place the yarn or skewer between the two groups of tiles that appear in the mat product. Tell students that since changes did occur in the building process, we need the final expressions to reflect those changes. Hence, the negative multiplier should remain a part of the appropriate recordings. Here are the possible recordings and what the mat should look like when completed:

(–3)[(–2) + (+6)], (–3)(–2) + (–3)(+6), (+6) + (–18), –12, (–3)(+4)

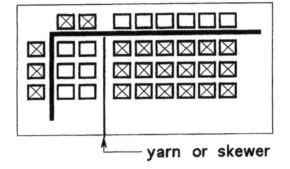

—— **yarn or skewer**

9. Give students other similar sets of tiles to build on their mats. (See Worksheet 1–6–1.) Remind them always to build the multiplier, the first factor or factor-group written in a multiplication exercise, down the left side of the mat. The set to be copied, regardless of how many different amounts are connected together, must be built along the top of the mat above the L-frame. Here are two more examples to try, along with illustrations of their completed products on the mat and the expressions that describe the products in different ways. Student partners might also create exercises of their own to give to other partners to build and record.

(a) 2 rows of –3 with +7

Recordings:

(+2)[(–3) + (+7)]
(+2)(–3) + (+2)(+7)
(–6) + (+14)
+8
(+2)(+4)

(b) the opposite of 5 rows of +1 with –4

Recordings:

(–5)[(+1) + (–4)]
(–5)(+1) + (–5)(–4)
(–5) + (+20)
+15
(–5)(–3)

Name _____ **Date** _____

WORKSHEET 1–6–1
Splitting Things Apart

Build each expression with tiles. Describe each product in four different ways.

$(+3)[(+3) + (-4)] =$ _____ $(-4)[(-5) + (+2)] =$ _____

$[(+2) + (-3)](+5) =$ _____ $[(+5) + (-2)](+2) =$ _____

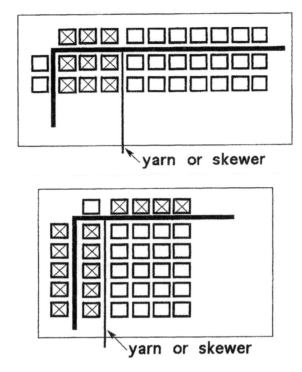

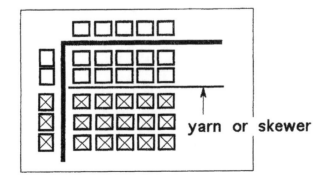

10. Challenge: After students are comfortable with their building and describing, have them show $(+2) + (-3)$ as the multiplier and $+5$ as the set to be copied on their mats. They must build with the $+2$ as part of the multiplier first, then with the -3, like following a recipe step by step. Two rows of $+5$ each should be built, followed by the opposite of 3 rows of $+5$ each. Ask students to place a yarn piece or a skewer between the two groups of tiles formed. The expressions to record, along with the completed mat, are shown below.

$$[(+2) + (-3)](+5), (+2)(+5) + (-3)(+5), (+10) + (-15), -5, (-1)(+5)$$

Note: In the last expression, $(-1)(+5)$, students will simplify the multiplier this time instead of the set or multiplicand $(+5)$. This causes each column (top to bottom) within the product to be simplified to -1, leaving one row of five negative units in the product. The simplified multiplier (-1) is **negative,** however, so this row of negative units is the result of **taking the opposite** of the original $+5$, hence our final expression $(-1)(+5)$.

Activity 2: RENAMING A PRODUCT

[Bridging Action]

Materials: Paper
Pencils
Red pencils
Worksheet 1–6–2

Management: Partners (30 minutes)

Directions:

1. Give each pair of students a red pencil. This will be used to separate the different sets of integer units drawn for the product. Plain, small squares will indicate positive units and small squares with an X in the interior will indicate negative units in each diagram.

2. Have students draw a large L-frame in the upper half of a sheet of paper, then draw a multiplier of +4 to the left of the frame and a multiplicand group of –4 and +2 and –1 above the frame.

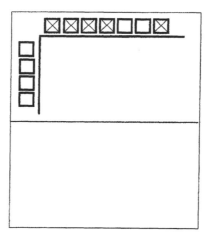

3. *Ask:* "What does the multiplier +4 tell us to do?" *(draw 4 rows with –4 plus +2 plus –1 in each row)* Have students draw the product under the L-frame at this time. Then have them draw red bars with their red pencil to separate the different types of unit squares in the product from each other.

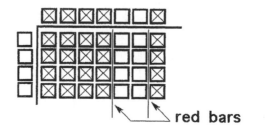
red bars

4. After students finish, ask them how they drew the different sections of small squares to show the product. Some will draw and complete a row at a time, while others will draw all the rows for −4 first, then all the rows for +2 next, and finally all the rows for −1. That they have this option for drawing the product is a direct application of the distributive property they are studying at this time.

5. Now ask students to record on their own paper to the right of their diagram which expression describes drawing their product by drawing one complete row at a time. *(+4)[(−4) + (+2) + (−1)]* **Ask:** "By looking at the red bars that separate your product, can you write another expression that shows how the product might be drawn one section at a time?" *(+4)(−4) + (+4)(+2) + (+4)(−1)* Another expression views the different sections by their total value, here (−16) + (+8) + (−4). If 0-pairs are formed throughout the product, the resulting value would be −12. If each row is simplified to −3 and there are 4 rows, the expression for what remains is (+4)(−3). All these expressions should be recorded on the students' papers. Emphasize that these expressions all describe the same product, but each views the organization of the product's squares in a different way.

6. Draw several different diagrams on the board, showing only the two factors: the multiplier and the multiplicand group. (See Worksheet 1–6–2.) Students should copy the assigned diagrams on their own papers, then draw the correct product for each and separate the different sections of squares with red bars. Beside each completed product, partners should record as many expressions as possible that will describe how that product might be built or viewed. Be sure to include some with negative multipliers. Here is an example (a special situation when we form 0-pairs!) and its possible expressions: (−2)[(+3) + (−5) + (+2)], (−2)(+3) + (−2)(−5) + (−2)(+2), (−6) + (+10) + (−4), 0, (−2)(0).

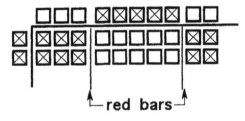

7. When all students are finished, have some read their expressions out loud to the class or write them on the board. Stress correct reading of the expressions. For example, (−2)[(+3) + (−1)] might be read as "negative 2 **of the group,** positive 3 plus negative 1" and (+3)(+2) + (+3)(−7) might be read as "positive 3 **of** positive 2 plus positive 3 **of** negative 7." Discourage readings like "negative 2 **times** positive 3 plus negative 1" because students do not usually understand what "times" really means in terms of actions with objects or diagrams. Remind students that the "distributive property of multiplication over addition" can be remembered as our way of organizing an amount as whole rows or as parts of rows, but the total value remains the same.

WORKSHEET 1–6–2
Renaming a Product

Draw the product for each exercise. Separate the different sections of squares with red bars. Write different expressions for each product.

Product   ## Expressions

Activity 3: FANCY EXPRESSIONS

[Application/Exploration]

Materials: Decks of cards (described in step 1 below)
Paper
Pencils
Calculators

Management: Teams of 4 students each (20 minutes)

Directions:

1. Give each team of 4 students a deck of cards and a calculator. A deck consists of 40 cards, which may be made with small index cards or lightweight tagboard cut to card size. Color-code each deck in some way so that misplaced cards can easily be returned to their correct deck. Laminate the cards so that they will last longer. Each card will have only one expression written on it. Every four cards that contain equivalent expressions will form a "book," which represents an application of the distributive property. One possible set of expressions to use is listed below. The four expressions shown in the same row are equivalent to each other. This particular set has been selected to give students limited practice in applying addition and multiplication sign patterns to other real numbers besides integers. Simple fraction and decimal forms have been used to help students review their basic operations with such numbers and extend the distributive property to mixed types of numbers. The numbers have been kept simple in order for students to recognize the two forms of the distributive property involved and to be able to simplify the expressions, either with the calculator or mentally. If preferred, a deck might be limited to only integers.

Suggested expressions for a deck of cards (one expression per card):

$(+\frac{1}{4})[(-2) + (+0.8)]$	$(+\frac{1}{4})(-2) + (+\frac{1}{4})(+0.8)$	$(-\frac{2}{4}) + (+0.2)$	-0.3
$(+3)[(-0.5) + (-2)]$	$(+3)(-0.5) + (+3)(-2)$	$(-1.5) + (-6)$	-7.5
$(+3)[(+0.5) + (+2)]$	$(+3)(+0.5) + (+3)(+2)$	$(+1.5) + (6)$	7.5
$(-5)[(-2) + (+3)]$	$(-5)(-2) + (-5)(3)$	$(+10) + (-15)$	-5
$5[(-2) + (3)]$	$5(-2) + 5(3)$	$-10 + 15$	5
$(\frac{1}{2})[4 + (\frac{1}{2})]$	$(\frac{1}{2})(4) + (\frac{1}{2})(\frac{1}{2})$	$2 + (\frac{1}{4})$	$+2.25$
$(-2)[(+6) + (-1)]$	$(-2)(+6) + (-2)(-1)$	$(-12) + 2$	-10
$(-2)[(-6) + (+1)]$	$(-2)(-6) + (-2)(+1)$	$12 + (-2)$	$+10$
$(-\frac{1}{2})[(-4) + (-\frac{1}{2})]$	$(-\frac{1}{2})(-4) + (-\frac{1}{2})(-\frac{1}{2})$	$(+2) + (+\frac{1}{4})$	2.25
$-3[0.5 + (-2)]$	$-3(0.5) + (-3)(-2)$	$-1.5 + 6$	$+4.5$

2. Review with the class that a value can be written in different ways. For example, "positive one-half" may be 0.5 or $\frac{1}{2}$ and may or may not show its sign: +0.5 or 0.5, $+\frac{1}{2}$ or $\frac{1}{2}$. Encourage students to change a number to an equivalent form if such a change makes a problem easier to solve. That is, for $(\frac{1}{4})(+0.12)$, we might think of 0.12 divided by 4, which equals +0.03, or use the calculator to find 0.25×0.12. This game is intended to make students think about their notation and what it means without making the expressions too complicated.

3. Each team should shuffle its deck of cards, then equally distribute them one at a time to the 4 team members. Each team player should have 10 cards, and may look at them throughout the game but not give them to another player to hold at any time during the game. A player may only lay one or more cards down on the table when showing them to others in order to help form a "book" of equivalent expressions.

4. The players on a team will take turns laying down the "first card" of a new book, which may be either of the expression forms that show multiplication occurring (i.e., the first or second expression on the left in each row listed in step 1 above). If a player does not have such a card when it is his or her turn to go first, that player may pass.

5. After the "first card" of a new book has been laid on the table, the other three players should look at their hands to see if they have the other cards needed to complete the book. Since this is a cooperative game, the players are allowed to discuss any potential cards they might have and decide together which cards need to be played at that particular time. Remember—no player can touch another player's cards. He or she can only look at or discuss the expressions on the cards. Once the team has decided which 3 cards are equivalent to the first card played, all 4 cards should be stacked together on the table as a book. Then the turn passes to the next person to play a new "first card."

6. The teacher should monitor the teams to be sure that correct forms are being matched together as a book. Variations in notation may need to be discussed with some of the teams if confusion occurs during a game.

7. When all 10 books have been formed, the game is over.

OBJECTIVE 7: Define an order for applying the four operations to the real numbers.

Activity 1: WHAT COMES FIRST?

[Developing Action]

Materials: Packets of integer tiles (40 positive and 40 negative units)
Paper
Pencils
Envelopes containing paper strips with directions (described in step 1 below)
Calculators *(optional)*
Worksheet 1–7–1

Management: Teams of 4 students each (30–45 minutes)

Directions:

1. Give each team of students a packet of unit tiles and an envelope with 16 small paper strips, each strip containing written directions for a single procedure to follow. (See Worksheet 1–7–1.) Here are some suggestions to use (one procedure per strip): add +7, multiply with +3, subtract (take away) +5, divide by +3, add –4, multiply with –2, subtract (take away) –6, divide by –2, add +5, multiply with +2, subtract (take away) +1, divide by +4, add –2, multiply with –3, subtract (take away) –3, divide by –1. Small values have been used to control the total number of tiles needed and also to minimize divisors so that students can easily work with any fractions that might occur. If helpful, fractions might be changed to decimal form. Calculators might then be used as well. The simplified expression"multiply with N" means to use N as the multiplier or number of rows or sets to build; hence, the amount of tiles already on the table serves as the multiplicand or set size. Remind students that a negative multiplier means to take an opposite of what has been built or copied.

2. Each team member should take turns placing a set of unit tiles on the table (select an amount of at most 8 tiles, either all positive or all negative) and randomly drawing 2 slips of paper from the envelope without looking. After the tiles and paper strips have been selected, the team works together to carry out the procedures with the tiles.

3. The team must decide in what order to apply the procedures. For example, if 5 positive tiles are on the table and the two paper strips have "multiply with –2" and "add +7," the students might decide to follow "multiply with –2" first. To do this, they must build 2 rows of +5 each (one row will come from the original +5) to get +10, then take the opposite to get –10 (the +10 tiles should be removed from the table once the –10 are built). To the –10 they must now "add +7" in tiles. When +7 in tiles is joined to the –10 in tiles and 0-pairs formed, the final value will be –3. On a sheet of paper the student who first selected the +5 and two slips of paper should record a number sentence showing what steps were followed. Brackets should be used to indicate which procedure was applied first. For the above example, the number sentence would be $[(-2)(+5)] + (+7) = -3$.

4. The team must now reverse its two directions, build again with tiles, and record the second sentence. For the above example, "add +7" would be applied to the initial +5 to get

Add +7.

Add –2.

Multiply with +3.

Divide by +4.

Subtract (take away) +5.

Multiply with –3.

Divide by +3.

Add –4.

Multiply with –2.

Subtract (take away) –6.

Divide by –2.

Add +5.

Multiply with +2.

Subtract (take away) +1.

Subtract (take away) –3.

Divide by –1.

+12 tiles on the table. The "multiply with –2" is applied to the +12; that is, 2 rows of +12 are built, then replaced with opposites to leave –12 for the final value. The new number sentence is $(-2)[(+5) + (+7)] = -12$. Notice that the numbers in the number sentence are not written in the same left-to-right order as you might "see" them when the paper strips are laid end to end on the table. The number sentence must reflect the order in which the building occurred, and especially which number served as the multiplier. Encourage students to use correct mathematical language.

5. On each turn, a new student will select the tiles and paper strips to use and the team will repeat the above process. After paper strips have been used, they should be placed aside and not returned to the envelope.

6. After teams have finished 6 to 8 turns or rounds of drawing out paper strips and building, ask them to look carefully at the answers they found when they reversed their paper strips or the order of their directions. **Ask:** "When you found different answers after reversing your directions, what operations were involved? When your answers were the same, what operations were used? Were there ever times when the two directions that were drawn used the same operation? If so, how did the two answers compare? Were they the same or different?" Different teams will have different number sentences, so their responses to the above questions will also vary. At this time you mainly want them to observe that changing the order of the directions (hence, the order of the operations in some cases) influences their results.

Activity 2: NO SIGN POSTS!

[Bridging Action]

Materials: Paper
Pencils
Colored pencils (2 different colors)
Worksheet 1-7-2

Management: Teams of 4 students each (30–45 minutes)

Directions:

1. In previous lessons, we focused on the use of parentheses and brackets in notation to indicate what processes were being performed either physically or pictorially. We will expand on that idea to lead to the need for a prior agreement when such markings are not given in the notation.

2. Give each team 2 colored pencils (two different colors) and a copy of Worksheet 1–7–2. Remind students that our four basic operations are "binary," that is, we can only work with two numbers at a time, whether we are adding, subtracting, multiplying, or dividing with them.

3. Discuss how to use Worksheet 1–7–2. For example, in $(+2) \times (+4) + (-5)$, the first exercise, have students draw a bracket **above** the $(+2) \times (+4)$ pair and label it (a), using one of the colored pencils. Then have them draw a bracket **under** the $(+4) + (-5)$ pair and label it (b), using the other colored pencil. Students should now work the exercise by drawing pictures of unit tiles as dictated by the notation. Students should begin with the

WORKSHEET 1–7–2
No Sign Posts!

In each exercise below, draw a bracket **above** the first pair of numbers; label it (a). Draw a bracket **below** the second pair of numbers; label it (b). Follow the teacher's directions to complete the worksheet.

1. (+2) x (+4) + (−5) = ?   (a) _____   (b) _____

2. (−9) + (−6) ÷ (+3) = ?   (a) _____   (b) _____

3. (+5) + (+7) − (−4) = ?   (a) _____   (b) _____

4. (−3) x (+10) ÷ (−2) = ?   (a) _____   (b) _____

5. (+12) ÷ (−3) − (−5) = ?   (a) _____   (b) _____

6. (−7) − (−4) x (+3) = ?   (a) _____   (b) _____

7. (+10) − (−3) − (+4) = ?   (a) _____   (b) _____

8. (+3) + (−5) + (−2) = ?   (a) _____   (b) _____

9. (−4) x (−3) x (+1) = ?   (a) _____   (b) _____

10. (−8) ÷ (+4) ÷ (−2) = ?   (a) _____   (b) _____

pair in bracket (a), that is, show $(+2) \times (+4)$ by drawing two rows of +4 each. The result, +8, then replaces the (a)-pair and students find $(+8) + (-5)$ by drawing tiles for +8 and –5 and forming 0-pairs. The result, +3, should be recorded in the (a) blank beside exercise 1. Repeat the above process, but now begin with the pair in bracket (b), that is, draw tiles to compute $(+4) + (-5)$ and get –1. The –1 then replaces the (b)-pair and students find $(+2) \times (-1)$ by drawing 2 rows of –1 each. The result, –2, should be recorded in the (b) blank beside exercise 1. This latter process might be shown with the illustration below. Student diagrams will vary.

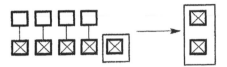

4. Teams should now repeat the above process and work the additional exercises on the worksheet, using the different colored pencils to draw the brackets for each exercise.

5. After all teams have finished the worksheet, ask them to look carefully at the exercises that had two different answers when worked the two different ways. Some had addition with multiplication or with division, or subtraction with multiplication or with division. Some had subtraction used twice or division used twice.

6. *Ask:* "What do you notice about the exercises that had only one answer even though you worked them two different ways?" *Some had only addition or only multiplication, while others had addition with subtraction or multiplication with division.*

7. Ask students to make one final test: rework exercises 3, 4, 8, and 9 by reversing the "directions" given. That is, still use the bracket approach to work each exercise two different ways, but this time work the following: $(+5) - (-4) + (+7) = ?$, $(-3) \div (-2) \times (+10) = ?$, $(+3) + (-2) + (-5) = ?$, and $(-4) \times (+1) \times (-3) = ?$ The first two new exercises now produce two different answers, but the last two exercises each produce only one answer even though worked the two different ways again.

8. Now *ask:* "If we want to be able to agree on a single answer for the same exercise, how can we do this with the least amount of changes in our notation? What can we do so that the notation used on our worksheet is enough to guarantee a single answer every time?" Allow each team a few minutes to try to summarize what they have noticed about the operations and the order in which they occur within an exercise. Have them share their ideas with the class. Hopefully the following observations will be made:

(a) if only addition or only multiplication is used, the order used to compute the numbers does not matter (these cases will be identified as the associative properties of addition and multiplication later in Objective 8);

(b) if addition and subtraction occur together, or if multiplication and division occur together, it does matter which operation is done first (the traditional rule is to work from left to right; that is, compute with the first pair of numbers, then work with the third number; no extra brackets are needed);

(c) if only subtraction or only division is used, the order in which the numbers are computed matters (again, the traditional rule is to work from left to right; that is, compute with the first pair of numbers, then work with the third number; no extra brackets are needed); and

(d) finally, if addition or subtraction is mixed with multiplication or division, the order in which the numbers are paired matters (the traditional rule is to compute the multiplication or division pairs first, then bring in the third number, which involves addition or subtraction).

9. The important focus of this activity is to help students realize that we must have some agreement as to how we approach exercises so that we can obtain the same results. Just the simple rules of (1) doing division or multiplication first, followed by addition and subtraction, then (2) in general working left to right will allow us all to have the same answers—a major concept at a time when global communication requires great accuracy! Activity 3 will give students practice in applying these two rules.

Activity 3: THE RULE OF SIGNS

[Application/Exploration]

Materials: Patterns for spinners A and B (Worksheet 1–7–3)
Large paper clips (for spinner needles)
Sets of cards (Worksheet 1–7–4)
Paper
Pencils
Calculators

Management: Teams of 4 students each (20–30 minutes)

Directions:

1. Give each team a copy of Worksheet 1–7–3 (the two spinners), a large paper clip to serve as a spinner needle, a calculator, and a set of 16 small cards (8 number cards and 8 operation cards). (See Worksheet 1–7–4 and run off several copies.) The cards may be cut from lightweight tagboard, labeled, and laminated. Make the number cards one color and the operation cards another color in order to separate them easily. Use the following numbers, one per card and one card per number, to label the 8 number cards: $-1, -2, -4,$ $-7, +2, +3, +5,$ and $+6$ (these also appear on Spinner A). Then write each operation sign $(+, -, \times,$ and $\div)$ on two cards (one sign per card, 8 operation cards total). The paper clip can serve as a needle by holding one end of it in place with a pencil point at the center of the spinner while hitting the other end to make the paper clip spin around.

2. Players on a team will take turns using the cards to formulate an exercise that has maximum value. This will be done by a player spinning Spinner A three times to select three different number cards and spinning Spinner B twice to select two operation cards (which may be the same operation). If the same number is selected twice by the spinner needle, the player should spin again. All three numbers need to be different. The operation, however, may be repeated.

3. After a player has selected 3 numbers and 2 operations to use, he or she should pull the cards containing those numbers and signs from the team's set of cards and arrange them on the table in a row, using the arrangement of number-sign-number-sign-number; for example, $(+2) + (-4) \div (+6)$. The player must decide which left-to-right order of the

Spinner A

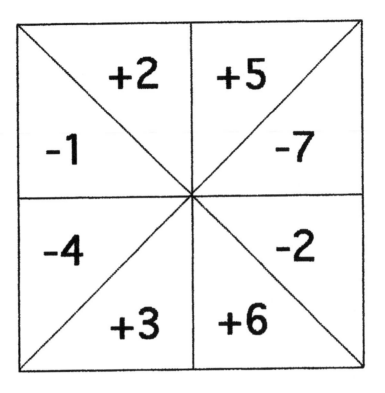

Spinner B

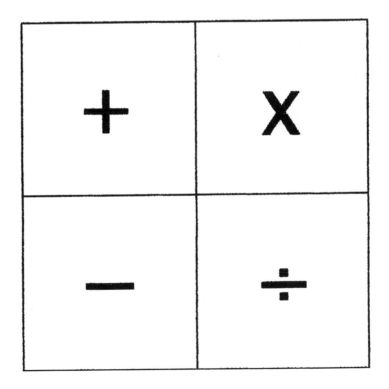

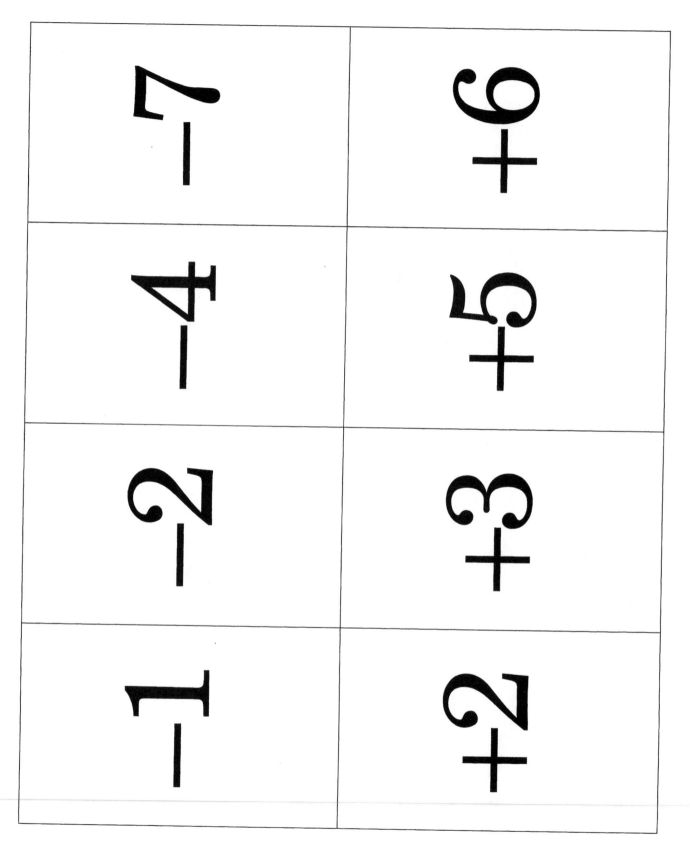

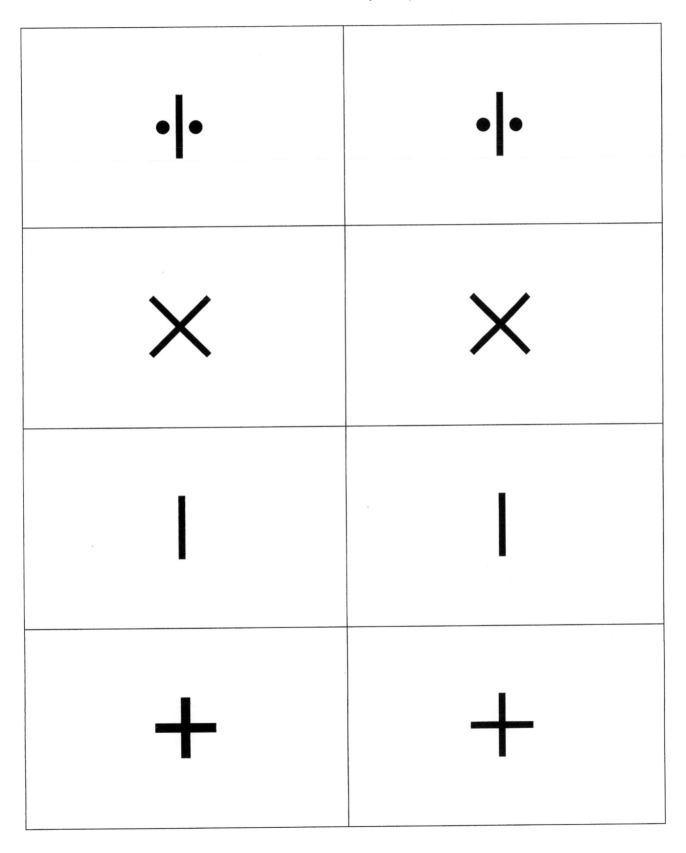

cards will yield the highest value when the "order of operations" discovered in Activity 2 is applied. In the above example, the value will be $(+2) + (-\frac{4}{6})$ or approximately $(+2) + (-0.66)$, which equals $+1.34$. (When preferred, the calculator may be used to change fractions to decimal form. Decimal fractions may be approximated to hundredths with no rounding.) Notice, however, that if the player arranges the cards to show $(+6) + (-4) \div (+2)$ instead, the value becomes $+4$. So the player decides to use this second arrangement and $+4$ is added to the player's accumulating score. Naturally the other players do not want to tell this player about another possible arrangement, $(+2) \div (-4) + (+6)$ or $(-\frac{1}{2}) + (+6)$, which is $+5.5$.

4. Once a player has declared a value for a final card arrangement aloud to the team (several arrangements may be tried before the final choice is announced), the turn passes to another player to spin and draw out cards.

5. Each value claimed for a particular card arrangement should be checked by the other team members (and teacher, if requested) to make certain the "order of operations" is being correctly followed. In addition, the new value acquired from a player's turn must be properly added to that player's previous score; for example, if the previous score was $+5$ and the new value is -1, the new score becomes $(+5) + (-1)$, or $+4$! All team members must monitor the adding on of new values. The calculator may be used for this accumulation to keep the addition from becoming too tedious.

6. Remind students of the order of the real numbers; for example, $+2 > -5$, $0 > -3$, and $-1 > -8$.

7. Play may continue as long as time permits. The player with the accumulated score of greatest worth is winner.

8. Alternative method for scoring: This game can be used as a cooperative activity where players take turns selecting the number cards and sign cards, but once the cards are selected, the team members work together to find the best arrangement that will give them maximum value. Their goal is to make the highest score possible after 8 turns. They can then play another 8 turns to see if they can score higher than they did on the previous game.

OBJECTIVE 8: **Explore other properties of the real numbers: the commutative property of addition and of multiplication, the associative property of addition and of multiplication, and the additive inverse of a sum and of a product.**

Activity 1: NOTATION TALK

[Developing Action]

Materials: Packets of integer tiles (40 positive units and 40 negative units)
15-inch pieces of cotton yarn (one piece per pair of students)
Unlined paper
Regular paper
Pencils

Management: Partners (50 minutes)

Directions:

1. Give each pair of students a packet of unit tiles, a piece of cotton yarn, and two sheets of unlined paper, which will serve as the building mats. A mat should be turned so that the longer edge is at the top of the sheet. In this activity students will explore a variety of properties that govern the way they build with the tiles on the mat. These properties should be freely discussed anytime they occur in building. Notation used to record the number sentences being built will be linked to these physical procedures. Emphasis will be on the appearance of the tile sets on the mat and how two different groups of tiles might compare to each other. Any number sentences, observations, or descriptions students are asked to write should be recorded on their own papers or in their math journals for future reference.

Commutative Property of Addition:

2. Ask students to place 5 negative units on the left half of the mat and 3 positive units on the right half of the mat. They should join the amounts together to form 0-pairs if possible, then count to find the final value, which is –2. Keeping the order of the notation the same as the initial order of the quantities on the mat (left to right), have students record (–5) + (+3) = –2 on their own papers.

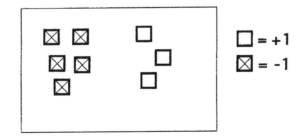

3. Now have the students place 3 positive units on the left half of an empty mat, followed by 5 negative units on the right half of the mat. The two amounts should be joined together and simplified to find the final value, which is also –2. Students should record (+3) + (–5) = –2 below the other number sentence on their papers.

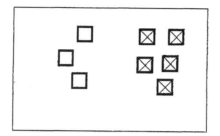

4. Ask students to write a brief description of how the two exercises were alike and how they were different. Have some students share their ideas with the class. Some possible observations: In one exercise, –5 was placed on the mat first and on the left side; in the other, +3 was placed first and on the left; the same two amounts were used in both exercises, just in a different order, and the final value (–2) was the same for both. Tell students to title their paragraph as "The Commutative Property of Addition."

Associative Property of Addition:

5. The addition or joining together of **two** sets of tiles is a **"binary"** action, so addition is easily shown by each hand holding a set of tiles, then the two hands moving together to bring the two sets together. But what happens when we have three sets of tiles and only two hands? Have students place 3 positive units on the left side of the mat, then 6 negative units in the middle of the mat, followed by 2 positive units on the right side of the mat. This left-right order should be carefully maintained. *Ask:* "We do not want to change the order of our three amounts on the mat and we can only join two amounts together each time, so how might we join these three amounts together in order to find their total value?" Hopefully students will observe that initially the middle quantity can be moved over to join the amount on the left side of the mat, or the middle quantity can be moved over to join the amount on the right side of the mat.

6. First guide students to loop their yarn piece loosely around the sets of units on the left and in the middle of the mat. The tiles inside the loop should be joined to form 0-pairs if possible. Once the 0-pairs are removed, the yarn loop should be removed and the other tiles from the loop should be moved over and joined to the tiles on the right. After any new 0-pairs are removed, only –1 remains on the mat. We will use brackets to show which original amounts were in the yarn loop. Have students record the following number sentence to show which actions they used to find their final answer: [(+3) + (–6)] + (+2) = –1.

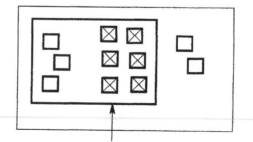

yarn

7. Now have students replace the tiles for +3, –6, and +2 on the mat in their original order, but this time loop the yarn around the middle and right sets of units on the mat. The tiles inside the loop should first be joined and any 0-pairs removed. Then the loop should be removed and its remaining tiles moved over to the set of tiles on the left. After 0-pairs are formed and removed again if possible, the final sum on the mat will be –1. Have students write the following sentence to record the order of their actions: (+3) + [(–6) + (+2)] = –1.

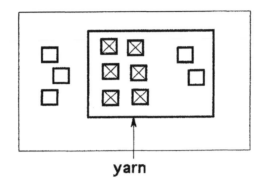

yarn

8. Ask students to write a brief description about the similarities and differences between these last two procedures with +3, –6, and +2 on the building mat. Some of the ideas should then be shared with the class. Hopefully their observations will include the following: The same three amounts were placed on the mat in the same order (left to right) each time; the final answers were the same (–1); the yarn was looped around the left and middle amounts one time, then around the middle and right amounts the other time. Have students title their descriptions as "The Associative Property of Addition."

Additive Inverse of a Sum:

9. Have students place the piece of yarn across the middle of the mat from top to bottom, separating the left and right sides of the mat. Tell them to show –3 with tiles on the left side of the mat. *Ask:* "What tiles need to go on the right side in order for the total tiles on the mat (with the yarn removed) to have the value of 0?" *(3 positive units)* "How are these new units related to the –3?" *(They are opposites of the 3 negative units.)* Since +3 forms the opposite of –3, we can write +3 = –(–3) and read it as **"positive 3 is the opposite or inverse of negative 3."** Students should record the number sentence and its word sentence equivalent on their own papers or in their journals. Another relationship we often ignore is **"negative 3 is the opposite or inverse of positive 3,"** which can be written as –3 = –(+3). Remind students that the symbol (–3) just means **"the opposite or inverse of positive 3"** anyway.

10. Now have students place tiles on the left side of the mat to show +5 with –2 (both +5 and –2 should be seen; do not simplify to +3). *Ask:* "If there are 5 positive units and 2 negative units on the left and we do not want to form 0-pairs, what amounts of tiles might we place on the right so that all the sets on the mat combined would have the total value of 0?" *(–5 and +2 will be needed)* "What is the relationship of this new group of sets, (–5) with (+2), to the first group, (+5) with (–2), shown on the left side of the mat?" *(The group on the right is the opposite of the group on the left since the two groups together equal 0.)* We can then write a number sentence for the new group on the right: [(–5) + (+2)] = –[(+5) + (–2)], which we may read as **"the group of –5 plus +2 is the opposite**

or inverse of the group, +5 plus –2.” We can also think of how +5 and –2 relate to the second group: [(+5) + (–2)] = –[(–5) + (+2)], which may be read as **“the group of +5 plus –2 is the opposite or inverse of the group, –5 plus +2.”** Emphasize the correct use of language; encourage students to be careful with their reading of the different number sentences.

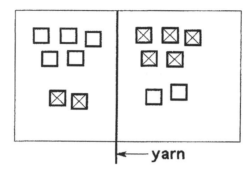

Additive Inverse of a Product:

11.   Again have students place the piece of yarn across the middle of the mat from top to bottom, separating the left and right sides of the mat. Now have students place 3 rows (left to right) of +4 each on the left side of the mat. **Ask:** “Is there another array like this one so that, when all its tiles are joined with these tiles on the left (after the yarn is removed), the total value on the mat will be 0?” A variety of arrays are possible for the right side as long as their own total equals –12. What we would like here is an array shaped like the array already on the left. Typically students should offer 3 rows of –4 each for the right side of the mat. Then each positive unit tile within the array on the left can be paired with an inverse tile in the same location (row and column) within the array on the right. So on the right side of the mat **“the product (+3)(–4) is the opposite or inverse of the product (+3)(+4)”** on the left, which is indicated with the notation, (+3)(–4) = –[(+3)(+4)]. Similarly, on the left side **“the product (+3)(+4) is the opposite or inverse of the product (+3)(–4)”** on the right, which we may show as (+3)(+4) = – [(+3)(–4)]. Have students record these number sentences and word sentences on their own papers or in their journals. **Note:** Some students may recognize that (–3)(+4) will also produce an array that is the opposite of (+3)(+4), so (–3)(+4) = –[(+3)(+4)] as well.

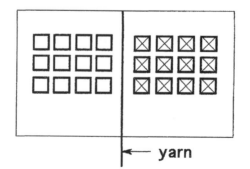

Commutative Property of Multiplication:

12.   Now have students use two sheets of unlined paper for building mats (have longer edge at the top of the mat). On one mat have them build 3 rows of +5 each, which is

(+3)(+5) = +15. On the other mat, build 5 rows of +3 each, which is (+5)(+3) = +15. Remember that a row runs left to right in an array.

13. Ask students to write a brief description about how the two arrays are alike and how they are different. Possible observations: One array looks like the other rotated 90 degrees; both products have the factors +5 and +3; the same total number of positive unit tiles (+15) are in each array, or the arrays have the same value, +15; and the number of rows for one array equals the row size of the other, and vice versa. Students should record their number sentences and their observations in their journals and share them with the class. Use the title "The Commutative Property of Multiplication."

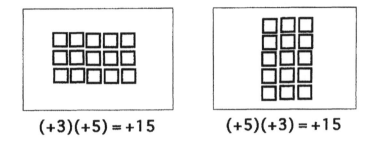

$$(+3)(+5) = +15 \qquad (+5)(+3) = +15$$

14. Challenge: Ask the class, "Will all your observations for the commutative property still hold true if we start with 2 rows of –4 each? According to this property, what must be the first and second factors of the second product if +2 and –4 are the first and second factors of the first product?" Let students discuss the questions with their partners, then ask them to share their ideas. Have them build the first product, (+2)(–4) = –8, on the first mat. For the second product, –4 must be the first factor or multiplier, and +2 must be the second factor or row size. **Ask:** "In integer multiplication, how do we build an array when we have a negative multiplier? What does the negative sign tell us to do?" On the second mat, for (–4)(+2) we must first build 4 rows of +2 each on the left side of the mat. (Use the yarn to temporarily divide the second mat into a left and a right half.) Then build the **opposite** array or product on the right side of the mat. The array on the **right** side represents the product, (–4)(+2) = –8. Both arrays have 8 negative units in them, and one array is a 90-degree rotation of the other. All the criteria in step 13 have been met, so the commutative property of multiplication holds true even for negative multipliers.

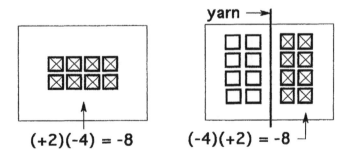

$$(+2)(-4) = -8 \qquad (-4)(+2) = -8$$

Associative Property of Multiplication:

15. The associative property was discovered (but not named) in the previous activities of Objective 7; it occurred when we found that only one answer resulted if only multiplication was used, no matter how the three numbers in the exercise were paired. This property can be shown by building the multiplier and the multiplicand in different ways.

Write (+2)[(+3)(−4)] on the board. Working with the brackets group first, have students build 3 rows of −4 each close together at the top of the building mat. Since +2 is on the left, it is the multiplier for the group just built. Have students place the yarn piece across the mat below the group, then copy that same group on the mat below the yarn piece. There are now 2 groups of (+3)(−4) each, which have a total value of −24. Students should record the number sentence (+2)[(+3)(−4)] = −24 on their own papers.

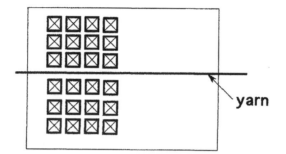

16. Now have students build [(+2)(+3)](−4) on a second mat. Since the last factor (−4) stands alone, it is the multiplicand or row size to be built. The first factor or multiplier involves a group; this means we must arrange the rows being built in a certain way. The (+2)(+3) tells us to build 3 rows, then repeat those 3 rows, that is, form 2 separate sections of 3 rows each. Have students start 3 rows at the top of the mat by placing the first tile of each row (here, −1). There will be a column of 3 negative units, one below the other. The yarn piece should be placed across the mat under this top column, then a copy of that column built below the yarn. Once the row positions have been marked, students should complete each row so that it contains 4 negative units. The total value in tiles will be −24. The number sentence [(+2)(+3)](−4) = −24 should now be recorded on the students' papers.

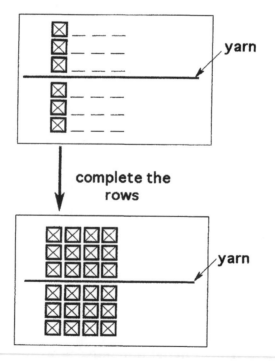

17. Ask students to write a brief description of how the tile arrangements on the two mats differ and how they are alike. Some of the ideas should then be shared with the class. Hopefully their observations will include the following: The same three numbers were used as factors in the same order (left to right) each time; the final answers were the same (–24); when the last two numbers were paired together, 3 rows of –4 were built at the top, then the whole set copied at the bottom; when the first two numbers were paired together, the position of each row was first located—3 positions at the top and 3 positions at the bottom—then each row of –4 was completed. Have students title their descriptions as "The Associative Property of Multiplication."

Activity 2: PICTURING PROPERTIES

[Bridging Action]

Materials: Paper
Pencils
Red pencils
Packets of unit tiles from Activity 1 *(optional)*

Management: Teams of 3–4 students each (30 minutes)

Directions:

1. Give each team a red pencil and a packet of unit tiles (if they prefer).

2. On the chalkboard list the properties that were discussed in Activity 1: commutative property of addition, associative property of addition, additive inverse of a sum, additive inverse of a product, and commutative property of multiplication. Ask each team to draw a diagram of unit tiles for each of the properties. They should review their descriptions of the properties that they recorded earlier during Activity 1. The quantities of tiles they use for their diagrams should be different from those used earlier during the building. Encourage students to build with the tiles first, then draw what they have built if this process will be helpful to them. The red pencil may be used to represent the colored yarn when needed or to indicate special groups. A number sentence should be written under each diagram to show the notation that corresponds to the drawing action.

3. Monitor the drawing carefully to be sure students are representing the properties correctly. Diagrams will vary, but their general appearance should be similar to that of actual tiles on building mats.

4. When all teams are finished, have some members draw their diagrams on the board or on the overhead projector for others to view.

5. Here are some sample diagrams for the listed properties.

(a) Commutative property of addition (different addend order, same value)

$$(-4) + (+5) = +1 \quad \text{and} \quad (+5) + (-4) = +1$$

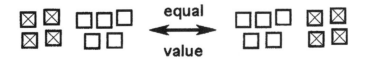

(b) Associative property of addition (different addend grouping, same value)

$$[(+6) + (+3)] + (-5) = +4 \qquad \text{and} \qquad (+6) + [(+3) + (-5)] = +4$$

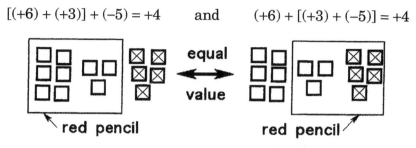

(c) Additive inverse of a sum (sets of opposites add to equal 0)

$$(-7) + (+3) = -[(+7) + (-3)] \qquad \text{and} \qquad (+7) + (-3) = -[(-7) + (+3)]$$

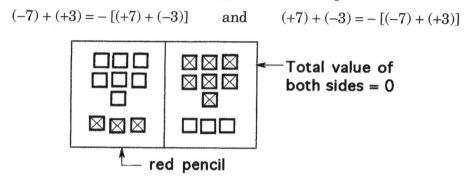

(d) Additive inverse of a product (opposite products add to equal 0)

$$(+3)(+2) = -[(+3)(-2)] \qquad \text{and} \qquad (+3)(-2) = -[(+3)(+2)]$$

Note: Students might recognize that $(-3)(-2)$ also produces an array that is the opposite of $(+3)(-2)$, so $(-3)(-2) = -[(+3)(-2)]$ as well.

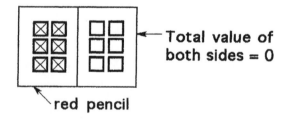

(e) Commutative property of multiplication (different factor order, same value)

$$(-2)(-5) = +10 \qquad \text{and} \qquad (-5)(-2) = +10$$

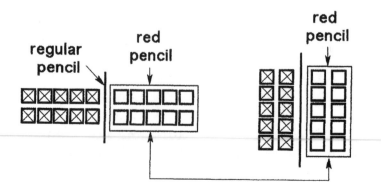

(f) Associative property of multiplication (different use of multiplier, same row size, same value)

$$(+3)[(+2)(+5)] = +30 \qquad \text{and} \qquad [(+3)(+2)](+5) = +30$$

rows drawn first

sets drawn first

Activity 3: NOTATION ROTATION

[Application/Exploration]

Materials: Decks of cards (one deck per team; cards described below in step 9)
Game answer keys
Paper
Pencils

Management: Teams of 4 students each (20 minutes)

Directions:

1. Give each team a deck of cards and an answer key *(optional)*. One team member should be selected as "referee" or "keeper of the answer key." The four members should separate the set of NOTATION cards from the set of VALUE cards, then shuffle each set and place each one face down in the center of the table.

2. The top 12 NOTATION cards should be drawn off the NOTATION stack and placed face up around the two card stacks in positions similar to the 12 numbers on the face of a clock.

3. To play, team members take turns drawing a VALUE card off the top of the VALUE stack and matching it to a NOTATION card of equivalent value or form showing in the circle of cards. Only one VALUE card can be played to each NOTATION card. If the VALUE card cannot be matched to any card in the circle, the player must pass, but keep the VALUE card until it can be matched later on.

4. When a player makes a match, he or she must remove the matched pair from the circle of cards and keep the pair until the end of the game. A position in the circle is now open, so the same player must draw a new card from the top of the NOTATION stack to place in that position. The next player now gets a turn to play.

5. If a player has one or more VALUE cards in his or her hand and it is that player's turn, he or she may make a match with one of the cards being held instead of drawing from the VALUE stack.

6. A player earns a point for each correct match. Also, some VALUE cards show a question mark instead of a numerical value for the expression. If a player can state the correct numerical value for the matched cards at the time when the match is made, he or she earns an extra point. Another point may also be earned if the player can identify the property being represented by the matched pair.

7. Any time a player makes a match or states the numerical value of a VALUE card being played, the other players must approve. Only when there is a question about a match or a value should the "referee" of the team consult the answer key.

8. When all the NOTATION and VALUE cards have been played and matched up, the game is over. The player with the most points from matched pairs or correct numerical values is the winner.

9. Here is a possible set of expressions to use for the NOTATION and VALUE cards. They are listed by matching pairs. Each NOTATION card is numbered, so the list can also be copied and used as an answer key for the different teams. The NOTATION cards should be made from unlined index cards or tagboard of one color and the VALUE cards made similarly but of a different color. The cards might also be laminated to make them last longer. Be sure to include on each NOTATION card that card's position number shown on the list. This reference number will make the answer key easier to use. To help identify misplaced cards, mark all the cards belonging to the same deck with a colored dot, using the same color for all cards in that deck.

"ROTATION NOTATION" MATCHING PAIRS

Code for properties represented by the matching pairs:

Comm(+)—Commutative Property of Addition
Assoc(+)—Associative Property of Addition
Inv Sum—Additive Inverse of Sum
Inv Prod—Additive Inverse of Product
Comm(×)—Commutative Property of Multiplication
Assoc(×)—Associative Property of Multiplication

NOTATION Cards—match to these—VALUE Cards—for these PROPERTIES:

	NOTATION	VALUE	PROPERTIES
1.	$-[(+8) + (-3)]$	$(-8) + (+3)$ or **?** $[-5]$	Inv Sum
2.	$-[(-2) + (-1)]$	$(+2) + (+1)$ or $+3$	Inv Sum
3.	$-[(+5) + (+8)]$	$(-5) + (-8)$ or -13	Inv Sum
4.	$-[(-8) + (+3)]$	$(+8) + (-3)$ or **?** $[+5]$	Inv Sum
5.	$-[(-5)(+4)]$	$(-5)(-4)$ or **?** $[+20]$	Inv Prod
6.	$-[(+7)(+6)]$	$(+7)(-6)$ or -42	Inv Prod
7.	$-[(+10)(-3)]$	$(+10)(+3)$ or **?** $[+30]$	Inv Prod
8.	$-[(+10)(-3)]$	$(-10)(-3)$ or $+30$	Inv Prod
9.	$[(+1) + (-5)] + (-3)$	$(+1) + [(-5) + (-3)]$ or **?** $[-7]$	Assoc(+)
10.	$[(-3) + (-9)] + (+10)$	$(-12) + (+10)$ or -2	Assoc(+)
11.	$(+8) + [(+5) + (-12)]$	$(+8) + (-7)$ or $+1$	Assoc(+)
12.	$(-15) + [(+9) + (+6)]$	$(-6) + (+6)$ or **?** $[0]$	Assoc(+)
13.	$(+8) + (+12)$	$(+12) + (+8)$ or $+20$	Comm(+)
14.	$(-5) + (-9)$	$(-9) + (-5)$ or **?** $[-14]$	Comm(+)
15.	$(+20) + (-13)$	$(-13) + (+20)$ or $+7$	Comm(+)
16.	$(-25) + (+25)$	$(+25) + (-25)$ or **?** $[0]$	Comm(+)
17.	$(-6)(+10)$	$(+10)(-6)$ or **?** $[-60]$	Comm(×)
18.	$(+8)(+5)$	$(+5)(+8)$ or $+40$	Comm(×)
19.	$(-12)(-4)$	$(-4)(-12)$ or **?** $[+48]$	Comm(×)
20.	$(+7)(-11)$	$(-11)(+7)$ or **?** $[-77]$	Comm(×)
21.	$[(+3)(-2)](+5)$	$(+3)[(-2)(+5)]$ or -30	Assoc(×)
22.	$[(-4)(+4)](-2)$	$(-4)[(+4)(-2)]$ or **?** $[+32]$	Assoc(×)
23.	$(-6)[(+3)(+2)]$	$(-18)(+2)$ or -36	Assoc(×)
24.	$(+8)[(-3)(-2)]$	$[(+8)(-3)](-2)$ or **?** $[+48]$	Assoc(×)

OBJECTIVE 9: Find the midpoint of two points graphically and numerically.

Activity 1: FINDING HALFWAY

[Developing Action]

Materials: Packets of integer tiles (40 positive and 40 negative units)
Paper
Pencils
8.5 in. × 14 in. unlined paper for building mats
Thin bamboo skewers (or long, flat toothpicks)
Worksheet 1–9–1

Management: Partners (30 minutes)

Directions:

1. Give each pair of students a packet of unit tiles, two bamboo skewers (or long tooth-picks), a sheet of unlined paper for a building mat (use a contrasting color to the tiles), and Worksheet 1–9–1. On the mat draw a line segment down the middle of the paper lengthwise and another segment perpendicular to the first one at its midpoint. The mat should be turned so that the longer edge of the paper is at the top of the mat. A zero should be written at the intersection of the two segments on the mat.

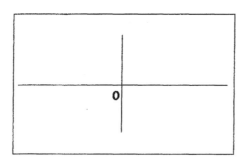

2. Tell students that we want to find where the "halfway" marker is along a road. The zero on the mat represents the 0 marker and is used to locate all other markers. A distance traveled **toward** a destination will be stated as a **positive** distance and measured to the right from the last known marker. A distance traveled **away from** a destination will be stated as a **negative** distance and measured to the left from the last known marker.

3. Suppose a person starts at 0 and travels 8 units to reach a destination. Have students place a skewer across the horizontal segment at 0 to be the beginning marker, then show the distance by placing 8 positive unit tiles along the same horizontal segment, beginning at 0 and extending to the right. At the end of the 8 tiles, place another skewer across the segment as the ending marker. *Ask:* "How do we find the halfway marker of the distance traveled?" The distance traveled will be the number of tiles found between the beginning and ending road markers (the skewers). In this case the person traveled the entire 8 units. The ending marker is at +8 since the person reached the destination after moving 8 units from 0, the beginning marker. When the 8 units of distance traveled are separated into 2 equal groups, the point of separation is to the right of the fourth tile. So the halfway marker for this person will be at +4, or 4 units to the right of 0.

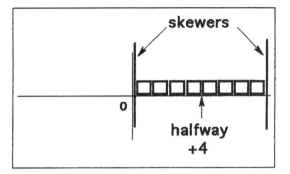

4. Draw a table on the chalkboard to record the marker locations for each example. (See Worksheet 1–9–1.) Make three columns, using the headings from left to right: "Beginning Marker," "Ending Marker," and "Halfway Marker." From the first example above, the entries in the table should be from left to right: 0, +8, and +4.

5. Now suppose a person starts at the +2 road marker (2 positive units from 0) and travels 6 units toward the destination. Have students place 2 positive unit tiles on the horizontal segment, beginning at 0 and extending to the right. At the right end of these tiles is the +2 marker where this new journey begins; a skewer (or toothpick) should be placed across the segment at this point. Then have students place 6 more positive units on the same segment, starting at the skewer where the first 2 tiles ended. Place the second skewer to the right of the new tiles to show the ending marker. *Ask:* "How far did the person move between the two markers toward the destination?" *(6 units or +6)* "Where will the halfway marker be for this person?" *(at the point where the distance traveled splits into two equal sections)* Students should find this separation point; it will be between the fifth and sixth tiles to the right of 0. So the halfway marker is at +5. Complete the table, using in order: +2, +8, and +5.

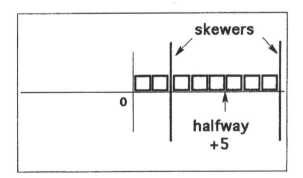

6. Now consider a journey where the person backs up at some point instead of progressing all the time. The person begins at the +11 marker, but goes backward or away from the destination and ends at the +1 road marker. Students should place 11 positive units on the mat to the right of 0 and place a skewer to the right end of these tiles as the beginning marker. Since the person is moving backward, negative unit tiles should be placed beside the positive tiles from the eleventh tile back to and including the second tile. The ending marker or skewer should be placed to the left of the negative tiles, which

Name ____________________ Date ____________________

WORKSHEET 1-9-1
Midpoint Table

Using your set of tiles, find the Halfway Marker for each entry.

Beginning Marker	*Ending Marker*	*Halfway Marker*
0	+8	
+2	+8	
+11	+1	
−3	+5	
−5	+5	
+4	−6	
−2	−8	

Do you see a relationship between the beginning and ending marker numbers and the halfway marker number? Can you use the beginning and ending marker numbers in some way to find the halfway marker number? Explain.

will be between the first and second positive tiles, counting from 0. The distance traveled is –10, that is, 10 away from the destination. The 10 negative units split at a point between the sixth and seventh positive units, so the halfway marker is at +6, or six units to the right of 0. The table entries will be +11, +1, and +6.

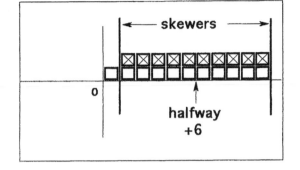

7. Now what if the person has gone backward 3 units past the 0 marker? Then the beginning marker is at –3. The person travels toward the destination, stopping at the +5 marker. Have students place 3 negative units on the segment, starting just left of 0 and extending to the left, then place a skewer to the left of those 3 tiles. Beginning at this skewer, students should place positive units beside the negative tiles and extend them to the right until the fifth unit to the right of 0 has been placed. This is the +5 marker. The second skewer should be placed to the right of this last positive unit. *Ask:* "What was the distance traveled from the –3 marker to the +5 marker?" *(8 positive units or +8)* "When the distance is split into two equal sections, where will the halfway marker be located?" *(at +1 to the right of 0)* Numbers for the table will be –3, +5, and +1.

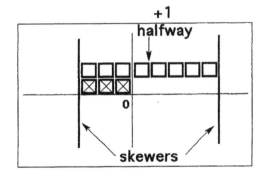

8. Here are three more situations for students to show on their mats and record on their tables, along with illustrations of the tiles on the mat:

(a) beginning marker at –5, ending marker at +5

(dist. traveled = pos.; halfway marker at 0)

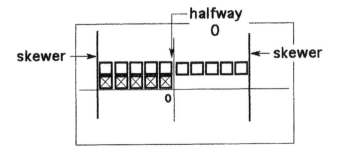

(b) beginning marker at +4, ending marker at –6

(dist. traveled = neg.; halfway marker at –1)

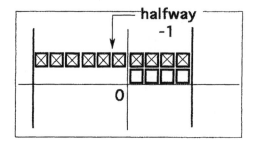

(c) beginning marker at –2, ending marker at –8

(dist. traveled = neg.; halfway marker at –5)

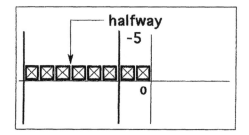

9. After students have finished building the last three situations in step 8, ***ask:*** "Do you see a relationship between the numbers you have for the beginning and ending markers and the numbers you have for the halfway markers? Can we use the beginning and ending marker numbers in some way to find the halfway marker number?" Answers will vary. Do not rush students to see the relationship at this time. They may not be comfortable enough with adding integers yet. The relationship will be finalized in Activity 2. *(Relationship: Add the first two marker numbers and divide by 2 to get the halfway marker number.)*

Activity 2: MARKING MIDPOINTS

[Bridging Action]

Materials: Worksheet 1–9–2
    Regular pencils
    Red and blue pencils (or any two different colors except black)

Management: Partners (30 minutes)

Directions:

1. Give each pair of students a copy of Worksheet 1–9–2 and a red and a blue pencil. Any two colors for the pencils will be acceptable; red and blue are used here for convenience of discussion only.

2. Discuss how to do the first exercise on the worksheet. The number line and its markings represent the road and its distance markers in Activity 1. For the first exercise, consider the beginning marker as +3 and the ending marker as –5. With a red pencil have students draw a bar parallel to the number line from 0 to +3 and circle the point on the number line at +3. With the blue pencil they should then draw a bar parallel to the red bar from +3 back to –5 and circle the point on the number line at –5. The circled points correspond to the markers/skewers used in Activity 1. Have the students count the unit intervals (**not** the points) on the number line to find the length or distance traveled, then find the midpoint or "halfway marker" for this length, which will be –1. With a regular pencil students should draw a vertical bar through the point for –1 and circle the –1. Finally they should complete the table for this exercise by recording +3 in the left column and –5 in the middle column; in the right column, have them write the full number sentence, $2 \times (-1) = -2$, not just –2.

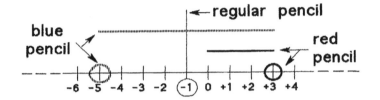

3. Now write on the chalkboard the following ordered pairs of beginning and ending markers for students to use to complete the other exercises on the worksheet. Exercise 1 is included. The midpoint for each pair will be shown in brackets. A finished diagram for Exercise 7 is also provided. If a midpoint is not yet labeled on a particular number line, students should mark and label that number appropriately.

(1) +3 and –5   [–1]
(2) –4 and +8   [+2]
(3) +6 and –6   [0]
(4) +10 and +5 [+7.5]
(5) –3 and –9   [–6]
(6) +4 and +10 [+7]
(7) –5 and +2   [–1.5]
(8) 0 and +6   [+3]

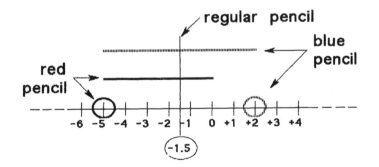

4. After all students have finished their diagrams on the worksheet, write the completed table on the chalkboard. *Ask:* "For each exercise, what seems to be the relationship between the numbers in the left and middle columns and the number in the right

WORKSHEET 1-9-2
Marking Midpoints

Complete the table for each situation. Can you find a way to compute the midpoint of the distance between the given points without drawing a diagram each time? Write your answer on the back of this sheet.

	Markers		2 × Midpt. Marker = ?
	Beg.	End	
1.			
2.			
3.			
4.			
5.			
6.			
7.			
8.			

column?" *(sum of first two numbers equals third number)* "How can we compute the midpoint marker or number of the segment or 'distance travelled' if we know the beginning and ending markers or numbers?" *(add beginning and ending numbers, then divide by 2)* Have students write a statement on their own papers that summarizes this relationship. Ask some to read their statements to the whole class.

Activity 3: MIDPOINT MADNESS!

[Application/Exploration]

Materials: Regular dice
Worksheet 1–9–3
Calculators
Paper
Pencils

Management: Teams of 4 students each (20–30 minutes)

Directions:

1. Give each team of students one regular die, 2 copies of Worksheet 1–9–3, and a calculator. The worksheet contains several number lines with unit intervals marked off but no numbers labeled.

2. Team members will take turns locating beginning and ending markers (or endpoints) for segments on the number line and midpoints of those segments. On a turn, a player will roll the die once to decide what types of integers to use as markers or endpoints. If a 1 or 2 is rolled, both numbers will be positive; for 3 or 4, both will be negative; and for 5 or 6, one number will be negative, the other positive (the player may choose which number will be positive and which will be negative).

3. The player will roll the die another two times to get the numbers to use for endpoints. If a 2 and a 5 are rolled and both are to be positive from the initial roll of the die, then the player will label the necessary markings on a number line to include +2 and +5. Points less than +2 or more than +5 do not need to be labeled. The smaller number of the pair, here +2, may be assigned to the left-most marking on the number line or farther to the right, as the player chooses, as long as enough markings remain to the right to properly locate the larger number of the pair. If both numbers are to be negative, then –2 and –5 will be used; if one is to be positive and one negative, the player must decide whether to use –2 and +5, or +2 and –5.

4. After the player draws and labels the two endpoints or markers on the number line, she or he must find and draw the halfway marker or midpoint of the line segment that is bounded by the two endpoints. A box should be drawn around the number of the midpoint. For example, with endpoints –5 and +2, the midpoint will be at –1.5, so a new marking will need to be made between –1 and –2 on the number line and a box drawn around the number, –1.5.

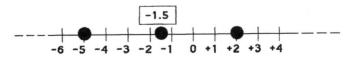

WORKSHEET 1–9–3
Midpoint Madness

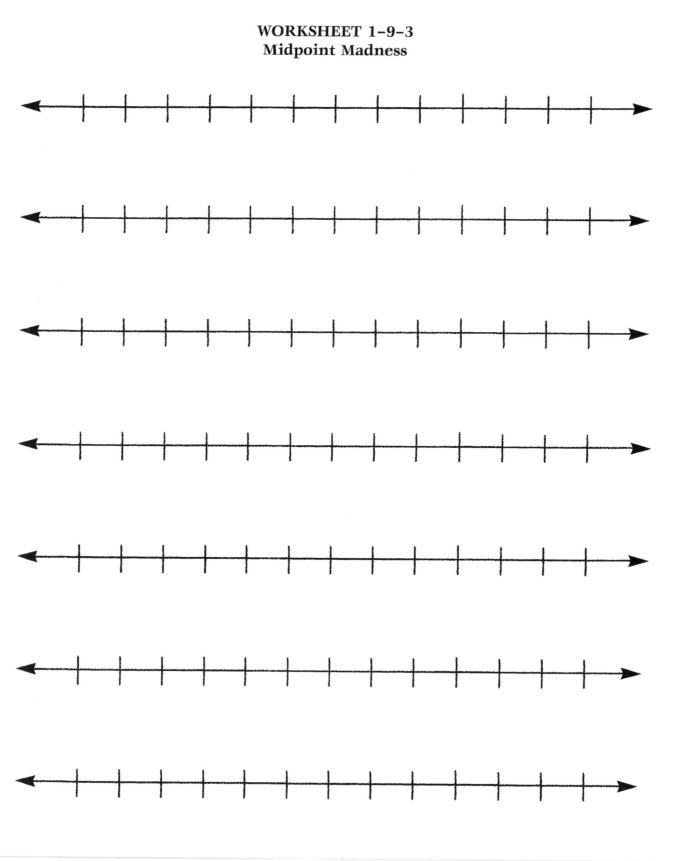

5. In addition to drawing and labeling the three different points on the number line, the player must write a number sentence for computing the midpoint. In the example above with −5 and +2, the player should write $[(−5) + (+2)]/2 = −1.5$. The player must also correctly key this number sentence into the calculator, using the order of operations required by that specific calculator, so that the desired midpoint number is obtained.

6. For each endpoint and midpoint correctly located on the number line, the player earns 1 point. If the number sentence is written correctly for the points involved, another point is earned. If the number sentence has been properly keyed into the calculator so that the calculator answer agrees with the value of the midpoint already shown on the number line, the player earns another point. A maximum of 5 points can be earned by a player on a single turn.

7. All graphing and computing must be approved by other members of the team before any points can be claimed by a player. The teacher needs to monitor the worksheets regularly during the game to be sure that students are correctly identifying and locating points on the number lines and writing correct number sentences.

8. The winner will be the first player on a team to earn 20 or more points.

OBJECTIVE 10: Define and apply the concept of absolute value.

Activity 1: BUILDING DISTANCES

[Developing Action]

Materials: Packets of integer tiles (40 positive and 40 negative units)
Building mats (from Objective 9, Activity 1)
Thin bamboo skewers or long flat toothpicks/coffee stirrers
Paper
Pencils
Worksheet 1–10–1

Management: Partners (30 minutes)

Directions:

1. Absolute value and the previous objective's concept, the midpoint of a segment, are similar in their development in that both involve finding the distance between two points. For the midpoint, we needed to work with half of the distance, but for absolute value we will use the entire distance. The direction of movement is involved at first in the development of both, but eventually will lose its significance. **Absolute value** is defined in applications as **the distance between two points** and sometimes referred to as the "difference" between two points or values. This leads to the notation of |a–b| that we will be using in the activities that follow.

2. Give pairs of students a packet of integer tiles, 2 bamboo skewers (or toothpicks), and a building mat from Activity 1 of Objective 9. The mat should at first be positioned so that a longer edge of the paper is at the top of the mat.

3. Discuss the situation of a car race where the cars are lined up and equally spaced, one behind the other, and the drivers are warming up their engines. A spectator notices that last year's champion, a red car, is the fourth car ahead of a yellow flag at the edge of the track and her favorite, a blue car, is the third car back from the flag. How many cars are lined up between and including the red and the blue race cars? To represent this situation, have students use negative unit tiles for the cars behind or back from the flag and positive unit tiles for the cars ahead of the flag. The 0 on the building mat will represent the flag's position on the track and the horizontal bar will be the track. Students should place 3 negative units beside the horizontal bar of the mat, beginning just to the left of 0 and extending to the left. A skewer should be placed vertically to the left of the last negative tile. Students should also place 4 positive units beside the bar, beginning at 0 and extending to the right. Another skewer should be placed vertically to the right of the last positive tile.

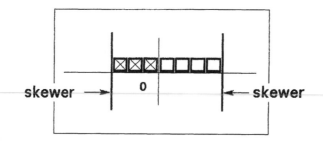

4. *Ask:* "If the tile at the left end is the blue car and the tile at the right end is the red car, how many cars are in this particular lineup?" Students should count the unit tiles, both positive and negative, now on the mat between the two skewers. There should be 7 unit tiles, so there are 7 cars lined up from the blue car to the red car, including the two end cars. Record on the board: "The amount of cars from the –3 car to the +4 car is 7 cars."

5. Now discuss another situation where one telephone line has been laid so that it runs 5 yards above ground and another line has been laid 1 yard below ground. The two lines are parallel to each other and, in general, parallel to the ground. Have students turn their mats 90 degrees so that the long bar is vertical instead of horizontal. Let the 0 mark represent the ground level and a unit tile represent 1 yard of distance. Students should place 5 positive unit tiles on the mat to the left of the long bar, beginning just above the 0 mark and continuing upward. A skewer should be placed horizontally above the last positive tile. This skewer at the upper end of these 5 tiles shows the position of the telephone line running above ground. Then students should place 1 negative unit tile to the left of the long bar but just below the 0 mark. Another skewer placed horizontally at the lower end of this tile shows the position of the telephone line running below ground.

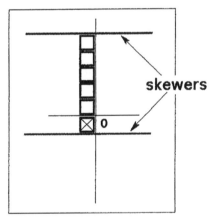

6. *Ask:* "How many yards apart are these two telephone lines?" Students should count the tiles between the two skewers on their mats to get 6 unit tiles, which represents 6 yards of distance between the two lines. Record on the board: "The distance in yards from the +5 yards telephone line to the –1 yard telephone line is 6 yards."

7. While the long bar of the mat is turned vertically, ask students to use their tiles to find the distance between a pipe 6 feet below ground and a pipe 3 feet above the ground. They should place 6 negative unit tiles on the mat to the left of the long bar and below 0 for the 6 feet below ground, and place 3 positive unit tiles to the left of the long bar and above 0 for the 3 feet above the ground. One skewer should be placed horizontally below the last negative tile and another skewer should be placed horizontally above the last positive tile. Since there are 9 tiles total on the mat between the two skewers, there must be 9 feet of distance between the two pipes. Record on the board: "The distance from the –6 feet pipe to the +3 feet pipe is 9 feet."

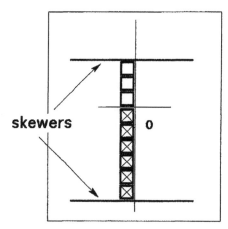

8. Now have students reposition their mats so that a longer edge of the paper is at the top of the mat. Discuss the idea that a piece of ribbon is measured by placing its full length on a meter stick so that one end of the ribbon touches the 2-centimeter mark and the other end touches the 7-centimeter mark. How long is the ribbon? To show this situation, have students place 2 positive unit tiles on the mat beside the horizontal bar and to the right of 0 (0 represents one end of the meter stick). A skewer should be placed vertically to the right of the second tile to show where the left end of the ribbon begins (the 2-cm mark). Now more tiles should be placed to the right of the first two until a total of 7 tiles is on the mat. Another skewer should be placed vertically to the right of the seventh tile to mark where the right end of the ribbon stops (the 7-cm mark). Students can now count the tiles between the two skewers for a total of 5 positive tiles. Record on the board: "The distance from the 2-cm mark to the 7-cm mark is 5 cm, so the ribbon is 5 cm long." (**Note:** If both endpoints from a situation are negative marks, negative tiles will be placed on the mat to the left of 0 and the skewers will be placed accordingly.)

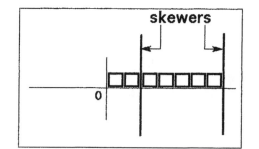

9. Begin a table on the chalkboard to record the endpoints and total distance or amount found for each of the previous situations and to record numbers from future exercises with the tiles. (See Worksheet 1–10–1.) Use the column headings: "First Endpoint," "Second Endpoint," and "Distance/Amount." Students should make a copy of the table on their own papers. It does not matter which endpoint is listed first; the smaller number does not always have to be the first endpoint. Entries from the first four situations above will be as follows: –3, +4, and 7; +5, –1, and 6; –6, +3, and 9; +2, +7, and 5. Notice that we are not writing a + or – sign on the distance amount. This is because we are not concerned about the direction in which we moved while counting the total tiles.

10. Now have students practice with the tiles by telling them where the beginning point and ending point are on the mat and asking for the total distance between the two

Name _____ **Date** _____

WORKSHEET 1-10-1
Building Distances

Using your set of tiles, find the total distance from the first to the second endpoint.

First Endpoint	Second Endpoint	Distance/Amount
−3	+4	
+5	−1	
−6	+3	
+2	+7	
−5	+3	
+6	−4	
0	+7	
+2	+8	
−1	−10	
−5	0	
−2	+5	
+8	−3	
+9	+1	

Looking at the numbers on the table, do you see a relationship between the endpoint numbers and the total distance found? Explain your answer on the back of this sheet.

endpoints. They should continue to record their numbers on their new table. Here are some possible endpoints to use with each total distance to be found by the students given in brackets. (Consider the first number listed as the first endpoint for the table.)

−5 to +3 ; [8]	+2 to +8 ; [6]	−2 to +5 ; [7]
+6 to −4 ; [10]	−1 to −10 ; [9]	+8 to −3 ; [11]
0 to +7 ; [7]	−5 to 0 ; [5]	+9 to +1 ; [8]

11. After all students have finished the exercises and recorded the results on their tables (record all numbers on the table on the chalkboard also), **ask:** "Looking at the numbers on the table, do you see a relationship between the endpoint numbers and the total distance found?" Hopefully students will see that the distance number equals the difference between the two endpoints. How quickly they discover this will depend on how comfortable they are with the subtraction of integers. Do not press for a correct statement of the relationship at this time if students are not ready. More practice will come in Activity 2. Have students write on their own papers some of their observations, however, and share them with the rest of the class. Check their ideas for reasonableness when compared to their actions with the tiles.

Activity 2: ABSOLUTELY PICTURED

[Bridging Action]

Materials: Tables from Activity 1
$\frac{1}{4}$-inch grid paper (8.5 in. by 11 in.)
Colored pencils (not black, gray, or yellow)
Regular pencils
Paper
Transparency pens and a $\frac{1}{4}$-inch transparency grid for overhead projector

Management: Partners (30 minutes)

Directions:

1. Give each pair of students a sheet of $\frac{1}{4}$-inch grid paper and 2 colored pencils (any 2 different bright colors; not black, yellow, or gray). They should also have the table they made in Activity 1. The grid paper should already have a vertical and a horizontal axis drawn with a wide, black marker so that the two axes cross at the center of the paper; the intersection point will be the origin (0,0). The longer axis should be labeled with +H and −H (for horizontal) and the shorter axis should be labeled with +V and −V (for vertical). The grid should be turned so that the longer edge is at the top.

2. For practice have students locate the points at +6 and at −5 on the H axis and draw a segment with one of the colored pencils to connect the two points. They should then count the unit intervals on the axis between the two points; there should be 11 units of distance counted. The numbers should be added to the table already begun in Activity 1. The chosen **beginning** endpoint of the drawing (e.g., +6) might be recorded as the "first endpoint" and the **terminal** endpoint as the "second endpoint" (e.g., −5); the "distance" is 11 units for the above example.

3. Have students locate −3 and −10 on the V axis, then connect the two points with the second colored pencil. If they draw **from** −10 **to** −3, for example, they might have the numbers −10, −3, and 7 entered in their table in that order, with 7 units being the distance.

4. Now tell students to locate the points (−8, +4) and (−8, −5), using the first member of each pair for the H direction and the second member for the V direction. (You may need to review students on how to plot ordered pairs on a grid.) Have them draw from (−8, +4) to (−8, −5). Since the segment that connects these two points runs parallel to the V axis, students should draw the segment with the same color used earlier for the segment on the V axis. (Similarly, if a segment runs parallel to the H axis, the color used earlier for the segment on the H axis should be used.) Also, because the segment only runs in the V direction, only +4 and −5 affect the segment's length and should be entered in the table with the distance, 9. The graphs of the three examples presented thus far are shown in this illustration.

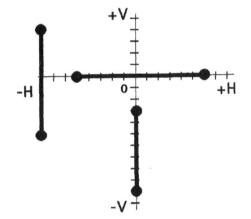

5. Ask students to continue locating pairs of points of their own choosing, but the connecting segments must either be parallel to or on the H axis, or parallel to or on the V axis. In each case, the correct numbers should be entered in the table. The color used for a segment will be determined by the color assigned to its parallel axis, H or V.

6. After students have drawn several segments on their grid paper, allow several to draw their points and segments on a grid transparency on the overhead projector. Record their numbers on a table on the chalkboard. *Ask:* "How can we use the two numbers for the endpoints to find the distance?" Guide them to see that the distance is related to the **difference** between the numbers of the two endpoints, but the distance itself will not have a sign to indicate a direction. (**Note:** Traditionally a number without a sign is considered a positive number, and when direction is not an issue, the + sign is often omitted. If direction is significant in a situation, however, we try to show this by writing the sign with the number, whether + or −. In the case of a distance between two points, the absolute value, direction is not important and we show this by omitting signs.)

7. Once students are comfortable with the **distance between two points as the undirected difference,** introduce them to the notation that describes this relationship, i.e., the absolute value symbol. For example, the distance (without direction) between −5 and +6 on the real line is shown by $|(-5) - (+6)| = 11$ or by $|(+6) - (-5)| = 11$. Sometimes when one of the points is 0, the absolute value group is abbreviated: $|(-3) - 0| = 3$ may be written as $|-3| = 3$. Now have students add this new notation to the distance column of their tables. That is, if a table entry shows +6, −5, and 11, students should change the 11 to "11= $|(+6) - (-5)|$," where the absolute value notation is applied to the two given points +6 and −5. This last number sentence should be read as "11 is the absolute value of positive 6 minus negative 5, or the distance between +6 and −5." Have partners take turns reading some of their own number sentences aloud to each other.

Activity 3: RECTANGLE MANGLE!

[Application/Exploration]

Materials: Decks of absolute value cards (described in step 1 below)
$\frac{1}{4}$-inch grid paper
Colored pencils
Paper
Pencils
Calculators *(optional)*

Management: Teams of 4 students each (30–50 minutes)

Directions:

1. Give each team of students a deck of 48 absolute value cards, a sheet of $\frac{1}{4}$-inch grid paper (like the grids with the two axes from Activity 2), 4 colored pencils (4 different colors, but not black, yellow, or gray), and a calculator (if preferred). The cards will contain absolute value expressions of the form: $|a-b|$, where a and b are integers located on either the horizontal (H) axis or the vertical (V) axis, depending on whether H or V is given on the card with the expression. Tell students that each absolute value expression used will occur four times in the deck; they need to know this in order to develop a playing strategy. Here are some possible expressions to use (copy each expression on 4 different cards):

For Horizontal Axis:	*For Vertical Axis:*
H: $|(-4) - (+2)|$	V: $|(+4) - 0|$
H: $|(-5) - (-10)|$	V: $|(+4) - (+10)|$
H: $|(+5) - (+11)|$	V: $|(-3) - (-8)|$
H: $|(-8) - (-3)|$	V: $|(+2) - (-1)|$
H: $|(+12) - (+9)|$	V: $|(-5) - (+1)|$
H: $|0 - (+5)|$	V: $|(-2) - (+3)|$

2. A team should shuffle the deck of cards, then distribute 6 cards to each member and place the remaining cards in a stack face down on the table. Each member should have a colored pencil different from those of the other three members.

3. Team members will take turns playing their cards. No one is allowed to pass. For a turn, a player will select a card from the 6 in his or her hand and locate the axis and points indicated by the expression on the card. Using the assigned colored pencil, the player may then draw the segment connecting the points directly on the named axis, or may choose to "slide" the segment away from the axis before drawing it. If the original segment is horizontal, it may be slid up or down but not left or right. If the original segment is vertical, it may be slid left or right but not up or down. Obvious dots should be drawn to show the endpoints of each segment, so that original endpoints can be easily identified later during the game.

Here are examples of segments drawn directly on an axis or "slid" to other locations on the grid. (Discuss several examples with students before beginning the game.)

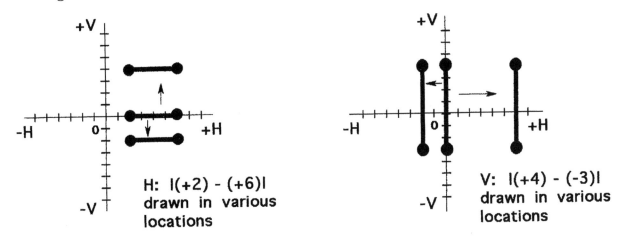

H: |(+2) - (+6)|
drawn in various
locations

V: |(+4) - (-3)|
drawn in various
locations

4. After a card has been played, it should be set aside, and the player draws a new card from the top of the stack on the table in order to keep 6 cards in hand. (Such replacement continues throughout the game until the stack is depleted.) The turn then passes to the next player.

5. The goal is to form rectangles with the drawn segments. A player may "slide" his or her segment on the grid according to the rules in step 3 above until one of its endpoints intersects an endpoint of another segment already drawn on the grid in an effort to make a rectangle. Two segments may form adjacent sides of a rectangle **only** if those two segments connect at their **endpoints.**

Here are acceptable and unacceptable connections of two segments.

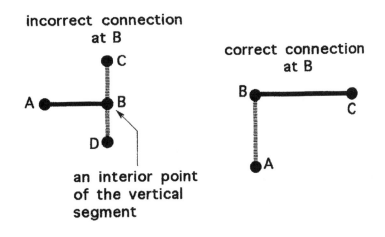

incorrect connection
at B

an interior point
of the vertical
segment

correct connection
at B

6. Since some of the absolute value expressions are for segments that overlap, a major strategy is to decide where to locate a new segment that must be slid off its axis so that it might be eventually connected to other segments to form a rectangle. Students should try to mentally visualize where "vertical" segments and "horizontal" segments described by cards in their hands might be placed. In particular, they should look for any **pairs** of "V" and "H" cards that might produce common endpoints. The ability to visualize "moving" segments improves as experience in graphing increases.

7. Rectangles may overlap each other, but each side of a rectangle must have been drawn as a complete segment for its length to count toward the score. A side cannot be counted if it is merely part of a longer drawn segment or if it is formed by parts of two or more segments. In other words, the sides must be segments specifically drawn for that rectangle. Segments may overlap each other, so drawing segments in different colors and clearly indicating endpoints will help define where complete sides are.

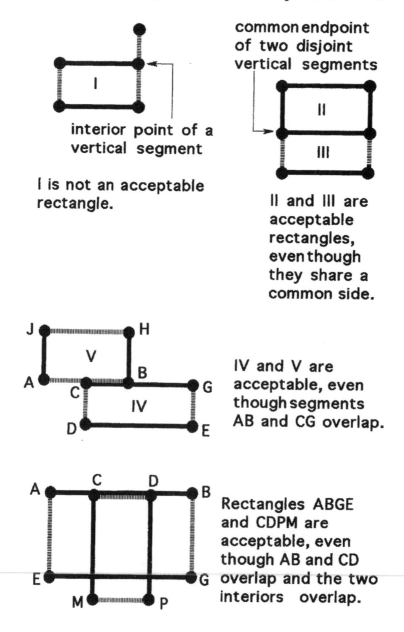

common endpoint of two disjoint vertical segments

interior point of a vertical segment

I is not an acceptable rectangle.

II and III are acceptable rectangles, even though they share a common side.

IV and V are acceptable, even though segments AB and CG overlap.

Rectangles ABGE and CDPM are acceptable, even though AB and CD overlap and the two interiors overlap.

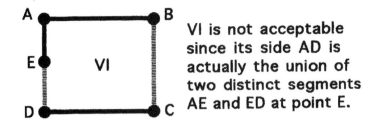

VI is not acceptable since its side AD is actually the union of two distinct segments AE and ED at point E.

8. If a player draws the final segment that completes a rectangle, the player must then add the measures of the four side lengths of the rectangle formed and this sum becomes part of the player's score. That player also writes his or her initials inside the rectangle so that it cannot be claimed later by another player. The player claiming the sum may or may not have drawn any of the other three sides of the rectangle. Any of the sides counted at this moment by this player may also serve as a side or part of a side of another rectangle completed later by another player and thus may be recounted toward another sum.

Here are examples of overlapping rectangles and their sums:

Sum of side lengths for ABCD: 9 + 4 + 9 + 4 = 26 units

Sum of side lengths for GJMP: 7 + 3 + 7 + 3 = 20 units

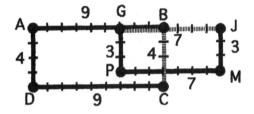

(In the example above, segment AB overlaps segment GJ, but one player may claim the sum for rectangle ABCD while another claims the sum for GJMP.)

9. When all cards in the stack have been drawn, players must use up whatever cards are still in their hands. Once all cards have been played, the game is over. The player with the highest accumulated score from completed rectangles is the winner. The person with the most rectangles completed may not necessarily have the highest score.

10. The teacher may wish to call time after 30 minutes of play. Players will then compare the total points or units they have accumulated in the game thus far.

OBJECTIVE 11: Approximate numerical square roots.

Activity 1: SQUARES AHOY!

[Developing Action]

Materials: Packets of one-inch paper squares or "tiles" (about 75 paper squares in a non-white color per packet)
Inch grid paper for building mats (8.5 in. × 11 in., on white paper)
Scissors
Paper
Regular pencils

Management: Partners (50 minutes)

Directions:

1. Give each pair of students a sheet of inch grid paper and a packet of one-inch paper squares. For convenience, we will use the color red for the paper squares or "tiles."

2. Have students place 4 red tiles in the spaces on the grid paper and arrange them to form a large, square region (no open spaces in the interior of the square). Tell students that the length of each tile edge will be called 1 *unit*. **Ask:** "How long is the edge of this large square?" *(2 units)* Discuss the idea that this edge length is also called the "square root" of the 4-tile square, so *the square root of 4 is +2.* Remind students that this edge measure can be used to find the **area** of the large square: (+2) × (+2) = +4 square units, which is just the number of tiles used to build the large square initially.

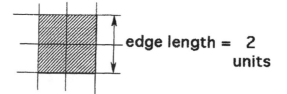

3. **Ask:** "In multiplication of integers we learned that each integer has an opposite or inverse. Does the square root of 4 have an opposite or inverse?" *(yes; since the square root of 4 equals +2, the inverse of the square root of 4 must be –2)* **Ask:** "If, for our 4-tile square, we know that the edge length of +2 units multiplied by itself equals the area of 4 square units, what can we say about –2 with respect to this same area?" *(the product, (–2) × (–2), also equals +4)* Now have students record the following statements on their own papers: "The square root of 4 is +2 and the inverse square root of 4 is –2."

4. Now have students place 20 red tiles on their grid paper and try to arrange them as another large square. A 16-tile square can be made, but the other 4 tiles added on will not form another larger square. **Ask:** "How many more spaces around the 16-tile square need to be filled with tiles in order to make the next larger square?" *(need 9 more tiles placed along two adjacent sides of the 16-tile square in order to form a 25-tile square)* **Ask:** "Is there some way our extra 4 tiles might be cut apart and placed around the 16-tile square in these 9 spaces in order to form at least a little larger square?" *(yes; fold each of the 4 extra tiles in half and cut along the fold; place the half-tiles around the 16-tile square)*

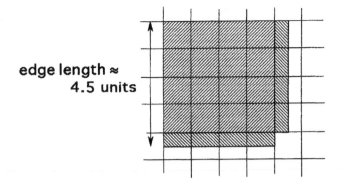

edge length ≈
4.5 units

5. **Ask:** "Even though there is a small corner piece missing from this new square, what might be an estimate of the edge length of this square?" *(the original 4 units plus another half of a unit of length)* Then $4\frac{1}{2}$ becomes an **estimate** for the square root of 20, and $-4\frac{1}{2}$ is the inverse of that square root. Students should record the following: "The square root of 20 is about $4\frac{1}{2}$, and the inverse square root of 20 is about $-4\frac{1}{2}$."

6. Now have students place 11 red tiles on their grid paper and try to arrange them as another large square. A 9-tile square can be made, but the other 2 tiles added on will not form another larger square. **Ask:** "How many more spaces around the 9-tile square need to be filled with tiles in order to make the next larger square?" *(need 7 more tiles placed along two adjacent sides of the 9-tile square in order to form a 16-tile square)* **Ask:** "Is there some way our extra 2 tiles might be cut apart and placed around the 9-tile square in these 7 spaces in order to form at least a little larger square?" *(yes; fold each of the 2 extra tiles in thirds and cut along the two folds of each tile; place the third-tiles around the 9-tile square)*

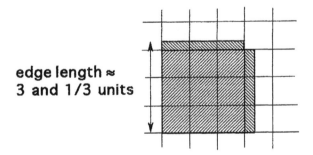

edge length ≈
3 and 1/3 units

7. **Ask:** "Even though there is a small corner piece missing from this new square, what might be an estimate of the edge length of this square?" *(the original 3 units plus another third of a unit of length)* Then $3\frac{1}{3}$ becomes an **estimate** for the square root of 11, and $-3\frac{1}{3}$ is the inverse of that square root. Students should record the following: "The square root of 11 is about $3\frac{1}{3}$, and the inverse square root of 11 is about $-3\frac{1}{3}$."

8. Now assign other amounts of tiles for students to use to build large squares, then find or estimate the edge length or square root of each square built. Students should record statements about their squares similar to the statements in step 3 or 7. Here are some possible amounts to assign. (The fractional parts beside certain numbers indicate the portion of a tile that will be needed in each border space, along with whole tiles in the interior spaces, to approximate a large square; students should find the needed part size through their own exploration.) 9, 16, 25, 36, 6 (halves), 12 (halves), 40 (thirds), 5 (fourths), 18 (fourths), 13 (two-thirds).

Activity 2: ROOTING OUT SQUARE ROOTS

[Bridging Action]

Materials: Centimeter grid paper
Colored markers (fine or medium points; 2 colors)
Worksheet 1–11–1
Paper
Regular pencils
Calculators

Management: Partners (50 minutes)

Directions:

1. Give each pair of students three sheets of centimeter grid paper, two markers in different colors, a copy of Worksheet 1–11–1, and a calculator. In Activity 1, the square root of a number was estimated by cutting apart the extra tiles around a large square made of whole tiles, placing these tile pieces around the whole tiles again to make a larger square, then finding the edge length of this new square. In Activity 2 students will estimate the square root by using the ratio of extra spaces to the total "border" spaces needed to make the next larger square of whole spaces. ("Border" spaces are the whole spaces that would fit along two adjacent edges of a large square in order to form the next larger square.) This ratio will be changed to a decimal fraction and used to estimate the fractional part of the edge length of the large square being represented.

2. Show students how to color 7 square units or spaces on the centimeter grid, starting in the upper left corner of the grid and making the largest square possible. Encourage students to position their squares carefully in order to minimize paper waste. A 2×2 square will be formed and the 3 remaining spaces will lie within a "border" along two adjacent edges of the 2×2 square. The original 7 spaces should be colored in one color (for convenience, we will use red). Then the other border spaces along the two edges should be colored in the second color (for this we will use yellow).

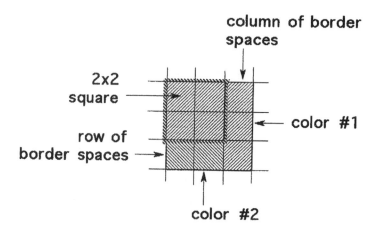

3. Discuss the idea that the extra 3 red spaces only represent 3 of the 5 spaces needed to complete the border and form the larger 3×3 square. If each of these 3 red spaces could be "cut apart" into 5 equal pieces and all 15 such pieces rearranged to fill the 5 border spaces as equally as possible, there would be 3 of these "fifths" in each border space. That is, $\frac{3}{5}$ or 0.6 of each border space would be filled. This imaginary sharing might look like the following:

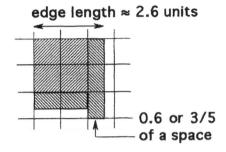

edge length ≈ 2.6 units

0.6 or 3/5
of a space

4. The corner space of the border, however, does not need so much "filling" as the other four spaces do; some of its "filling" could be redistributed to the other four spaces, thereby causing the edge length to increase a little. Hence, the true edge length for a square made with all 7 red spaces will be greater than 2.6 units. Have students find the square root of 7 with their calculators; to the nearest hundredth, it is 2.65. So the method of using the ratio of $\frac{3}{5}$ combined with the edge length of the largest square of whole spaces possible out of 7 spaces (i.e., the edge length of a 2 × 2 square) has produced an estimate for the square root of 7 that is quite close to its computed value. Have students record their results for 7 on their worksheet (entry per column from left to right): 7, $\frac{3}{5}$, 0.60, 2.60, 2.65. Now write the symbol for a square root ($\sqrt{}$) on the chalkboard. This symbol represents the edge length of a square. In the above example, the notation "$\sqrt{7}$" indicates the edge length of a square made with 7 square units or spaces. It is read as "the square root of 7" and has a value of approximately 2.60 or 2.65, depending on the method used.

5. Will this method provide a close estimate every time? Guide students in another example by coloring 10 spaces red on the grid paper and making the largest square possible. A 3 × 3 square can be made, with one extra red space lying in the border. The next larger square would be a 4 × 4 square, so have students color 6 more spaces yellow to complete the border of the 3 × 3 and form the 4 × 4 square.

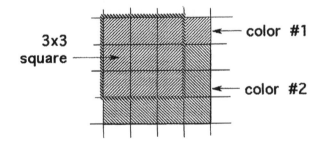

3x3
square

color #1

color #2

6. *Ask:* "What ratio do we need as an estimate of the fractional part of the edge length of a square made with all 10 red spaces if they could be rearranged?" (*the ratio of the 1 extra red space not in the 3 × 3 square compared to the 7 spaces total in the border;* $\frac{1}{7}$ *equals 0.14 to the nearest hundredth*) "Using the edge length of the 3 × 3 square combined with this fractional part, what is our estimate for the square root of 10?" (*3.14 units*) "How does our estimate compare to the value shown by the calculator?" (*very close; calculator value for $\sqrt{10}$ is 3.16*) Students should record the following entries on their worksheet (one per column, left to right): 10, $\frac{1}{7}$, 0.14, 3.14, 3.16.

7. Now assign more numbers for students to draw on their grid paper and apply the above ratio method to estimate the square roots of the numbers. The various columns on

WORKSHEET 1–11–1
Rooting Out Square Roots
(Estimating Square Roots)

Total Spaces Used (N)	Extra Border Spaces (E) ——— Total Border Spaces (T)	E/T as a Decimal (to the nearest 0.01)	Estimate for Edge Length ($\sqrt{N}$)	Calculator Value for $\sqrt{N}$ (to the nearest 0.01)

the worksheet should be completed to show the steps used for each number. Here are some possible numbers to assign, along with their expected entries for the worksheet.

Total Spaces Used (N)	Extra Border Spaces (E) / Total Border Spaces (T)	E/T as Decimal to nearest .01	Estimate for Edge Length (√N)	Calculator Value for √N to nearest .01
7	$\frac{3}{5}$	0.60	2.60	2.65
10	$\frac{1}{7}$	0.14	3.14	3.16
13	$\frac{4}{7}$	0.57	3.57	3.61
18	$\frac{2}{9}$	0.22	4.22	4.24
24	$\frac{8}{9}$	0.89	4.89	4.90
38	$\frac{2}{13}$	0.15	6.15	6.16
50	$\frac{1}{15}$	0.07	7.07	7.07
79	$\frac{15}{17}$	0.88	8.88	8.89
90	$\frac{9}{19}$	0.47	9.47	9.49
118	$\frac{18}{21}$	0.86	10.86	10.86
902*	$\frac{2}{61}$	0.03	30.03	30.03
10,199*	$\frac{199}{201}$	0.99	100.99	100.99

*For an extra challenge: Numbers are too large for grid paper; just use ratio method and calculator.

8. After students have completed their worksheets using the assigned integral values, discuss the accuracy of the ratio method for estimating square roots of positive integers. As shown by the table entries in step 7, the ratio method provides an estimate within a few hundredths of the value obtained from a calculator's programmed method. For very large numbers, the two methods produce equivalent answers if the two obtained values are rounded to the nearest hundredth. Activity 3 will provide students with more practice using the ratio method.

Activity 3: SQUARE ROOT ROLL

[Application/Exploration]

Materials: Dice
Calculators
Worksheet 1–11–2 (score sheet)
Paper
Regular pencils

Management: Teams of 4 students each (30 minutes)

Directions:

1. Give each team one die, a calculator, and 4 copies of Worksheet 1–11–2 (to be used as individual score sheets). This game will give students more practice with the ratio method presented in Activity 2. It will also provide a review of decimal operations and develop a better understanding of the effect of multiplication on decimal fractions.

Students will be using calculators, but are **not** allowed to use the **square root key;** they may, however, use the squaring key. The purpose of the game is to try to find an estimate for a number's square root that is extremely close to the actual root value.

2. To prepare for the game, discuss the procedure to be followed by applying it to the number 54. Assuming that 54 has been obtained by a player rolling the die twice (first roll indicates tens place and second roll indicates ones place for number to be used), have students apply the ratio method to find an estimate for the square root of 54. Since 49 is the largest perfect square that is still less than 54, and 64 is the next larger perfect square, the ratio equals $(54 - 49)/(64 - 49)$, which is $\frac{5}{15}$ or 0.33 when rounded to the nearest 0.01. Then an estimate for the square root of 54 might be 7.33. When a true or exact square root is squared, the new product should equal the original number; however, when an estimate is squared, its product will be just less than or just more than the original number. Generally the estimate found with the ratio method can be improved by increasing the estimate by 0.01 or 0.02. This second estimate is often a better estimate than the first because its square will be closer (either just under or just over) to the original number. So the basic strategy of the game will be to add an extra 0.01 or 0.02 to the root estimate found by the ratio method. Once a player decides by how much to increase the initial estimate, the amount of increase cannot be changed later. For practice, have students increase the 7.33 estimate to 7.34. When 7.34 is squared (or multiplied by itself) on the calculator, the product equals 53.88, rounded to the nearest 0.01. The difference between 54 and 53.88 is 0.12, either positive or negative, depending on which number is keyed into the calculator first. The score for the player will be 0.12 for choosing 7.34 as an estimate of $\sqrt{54}$.

3. Now show students how to record on the score sheet the steps used in the example. Entries for the columns should be as follows, recording from left to right:

Number Rolled (N)	Square Root Estimate ($\sqrt{N}$)	Square of Estimate ($\sqrt{N}$)^2	Difference of Squares	Accumulated Score
54	$\sqrt{54} \approx 7.34$	$(7.34)^2 \approx 53.88$	$54 - 53.88$ $= +0.12$	0.12

4. On her or his second turn, a player will begin adding any new score to the previous total score to get the new accumulated score to be recorded in the last column. For the example above, the score for that turn was 0.12. If that had been the second turn for that player and the score for the first turn had been 0.09, the accumulated score after the second turn would be $0.09 + 0.12$, or 0.21. The score for the third turn would then be added to 0.21.

5. Team members should now take turns finding "best" square roots (i.e., those closest to the true value. On a turn, each player will roll the die to generate the number to be used, then use the calculator to progress through the steps demonstrated previously with 54. That player will record the appropriate numbers on her or his own score sheet. The next player will then repeat the process.

6. After each player has had 4 or 5 turns or time is called, the player with the lowest accumulated score will be the winner, the "greatest with the least," since that person had the closer square root estimates during the game.

Name _____   **Date** _____

WORKSHEET 1–11–2
Square Root Roll
Score Sheet

Number Rolled (N)	Square Root Estimate ($\sqrt{N}$)	Square of Estimate ($\sqrt{N}$)^2	Difference of Squares	Accumulated Score

Section 2

LINEAR FORMS

OBJECTIVE 1: Describe real-world situations with algebraic expressions.

Activity 1: ACTING IT OUT!

[Developing Action]

Materials: Packets of tiles and building mats (described in step 1 below)
Paper
Regular pencils

Management: Partners (50 minutes)

Directions:

1. Give each pair of students a packet of tiles and a building mat. The building mat should be a blank 8.5 in. by 14 in. sheet of white paper. Each packet should contain 8 variable tiles each of two different lengths, and 20 unit tiles. Unit tiles will be used to represent individual objects; variable tiles will be used to show containers or groups of unknown amounts of objects (i.e., they will serve as variables or unknowns). Each size of tile should be in a color different from the other two sizes on the mat. Commercial tiles are available in the different sizes and colors, but a large X must be drawn on one of the largest faces of each tile in order to represent the inverse of that tile when the X faces up. If teacher-made tiles are to be made of tagboard and laminated, the following sizes are recommended: variable tiles, 0.75 in. by 3 in. (color #1) and 0.75 in. by 3.25 in. (color #2); unit tiles, 0.75 in. by 0.75 in. (color #3). Each teacher-made tile should have a large X drawn on one side to show the inverse of that tile. If the tagboard or paper to be used is too thin so that the drawn X will show through to the other side, 8 variable tiles of each size may be made plain and an additional 8 tiles in that size made with the X; prepare unit tiles similarly. A pattern for plain and marked tiles is also available in the Appendix; printed copies of the pattern can be made on colored paper and cut apart into the different tiles.

2. Review the meanings of the four basic operations in terms of *action:*

- Addition is the joining together of two or more sets of objects.

- Subtraction (as used here) is the removal of objects from a given set or the finding of a missing part of a given set.

- Multiplication is the combining of several equal-sized sets of objects.

- Division is the separation of a given amount of objects into equal-sized sets.

3. Have students practice showing various amounts with their variable tiles and unit tiles. Special language will be introduced at this time. If one variable tile represents *some* (unknown) amount, students might show the following amounts by placing the described tiles on their building mats. (Do not simplify at this time.)

5 more than +3—show 3 positive units followed by 5 positive units; "N more than" means to increase the original amount by **bringing in** N **positive** units.

2 less than +4 —show 4 positive units, then remove 2 positive units; "N less than" means to decrease the original amount by **removing** N **positive** units.

3 more than –2—show the original –2 followed by 3 positive units.

4 less than –1 —4 positive units need to be removed from –1; to do this, 0-pairs of units must be brought in and +4 removed, leaving 4 negative units with the original –1; as a result, the **decrease** can also be shown with the original –1 followed by 4 **negative** units.

3 more than some amount—show 1 variable (either size/color; no X showing) followed by 3 positive units.

2 less than some amount—show 1 variable (plain) followed by 2 negative units (X faces up) to show the decrease.

some amount more than +3—show 3 positive units followed by one variable (plain variable represents *some* amount of positive units brought in for the increase).

some amount more than –2—show 2 negative units followed by one variable (plain) to show the increase.

some amount less than +1—show 1 positive unit followed by one inverse variable (use same color as with previous plain variable; show the X side for "less than," the opposite action to "more than"; inverse variable represents *some* amount of negative units brought in for the decrease).

some amount less than –5—show 5 negative units followed by one inverse variable (use same color as above; X side of variable faces up to show *some* negative units brought in to cause a decrease).

Note: The inverse variable will not always be a negative amount; in the above examples, when N must be **removed** to show a **decrease**, it must represent a **positive** amount; an equivalent process is to **add** the **inverse** of N, –N, which in this case must be a **negative** amount.

4. Give students several different story situations that involve one or more of the four operations. Have them demonstrate the actions with their variable tiles and unit tiles. Here are some possible examples:

(a) Addition: *There are 5 goldfish and several guppies in the aquarium. How many fish total are in the aquarium?* Students should place 5 positive unit tiles (as "goldfish") on their building mats, then put a single, plain variable beside them to represent the number of guppies to be joined to the +5. The number of guppies is unknown for the moment. **Note:** When simple objects are being counted, positive unit tiles will be used. When an opposite action is being quantified, negative unit tiles will be used.

(b) **Subtraction (removal):** *Tonya held 6 bags of candies at first. She then gave 2 of the bags to Juan. If all the bags contain the same number of candies, how many candies does Tonya hold now?* Partners should place 6 plain variables of the same color on the building mat, then remove 2 of them. Each variable represents the unknown number of candies in one bag. Emphasize that this is all students can do at this time since they do not know the exact amount of candies per bag yet. *Alternative response:* If you prefer to think in terms of **opposite actions,** then 6 plain variables of the same color might represent the **holding** of 6 bags of candies and 2 inverse variables (X faces up) in the above color might represent the **giving away** of 2 bags of candies. The **combined** actions (addition) of holding followed by giving away would then be shown by placing the set of 6 plain variables **beside** the set of 2 inverse variables. "Opposite" variable tiles would be paired to form 0-pairs, leaving 4 plain variables. This indicates that Tonya is left **holding** 4 bags of candies.

(c) **Subtraction (missing addend):** *Sharesha has some marbles in a bag. She finds 4 more marbles. After combining all the marbles in the bag, how many marbles does she have?* Students should place a plain variable on the building mat to represent the first amount of marbles in the bag, then place 4 positive units beside the variable. Positive units are used because marbles are **put into** the bag. (For an example with negative tiles, use: *Charles has some marbles in an open bag. He drops 5 marbles out of the bag. How many marbles remain in the bag?* A variable (plain) would then be placed on the mat and 5 negative units placed beside the variable. The negative units represent the 5 marbles **dropped out of** the bag.)

(d) **Multiplication:** *There are 5 envelopes in all. All envelopes hold the same number of coupons. How many coupons are there in all?* Students should place 5 variables (plain) of the same color on the mat, each variable representing the (unknown) number of coupons in one envelope. The 5 variables will be the total coupons in all the envelopes.

(e) **Division:** *There are 8 shipping cartons. They all contain the same number of crystal vases. The vases are to be equally distributed to 4 different cities. How many vases will be shipped to each city?* Partners should place 8 variables of the same color on the mat, each variable representing the (unknown) number of vases in one carton. The 8 variables should be separated into 4 equal groups. The 2 variable tiles in each group will represent the number of vases being shipped to one of the cities.

(f) **Addition-multiplication combination (one unknown):** *Kim Lee has 3 boxes of pencils, each box containing the same amount. He has 6 extra pencils in his desk drawer. How many pencils does he have in all?* Three variables (plain) of the same color should be placed on the mat to show the boxes of pencils; each variable represents the (unknown) number of pencils in one box. Then 6 positive units should be placed beside the variables to show the **extra** (known) amount of individual pencils.

(g) **Combinations with division (one unknown):** *There are 6 CD storage cases full of CDs and 9 individual newly-bought CDs that are to be shared equally by 3 friends. How many CDs total will each friend receive?* Six variables (plain) of one color should be placed on the mat, along with 9 positive units. Each variable represents the (unknown) number of CDs in one storage case; a positive unit is for 1 individual **newly-bought** CD. Students should separate the variables into 3 equal groups and also equally distribute the positive units into the same 3 groups. The 2 variables and 3 positive units in one group show the CDs one friend will receive, i.e., an unknown amount of CDs in each of 2 cases plus 3 individual **newly-bought** CDs (+3). (For an example with negative units, use: *There are 6 storage cases containing CDs, but 12 individual CDs are missing from the cases. The same number of CDs is missing from each case. All the remaining CDs are to be shared equally by 3 friends. How many CDs total will each friend receive?* Six variables of one color should be placed on the mat, along with 12 negative units. Each variable represents the (unknown) number of CDs in one storage case; a negative unit is for each individual CD **missing** from a storage case. Students should separate the variables into 3 equal groups and also equally distribute the negative units into the same 3 groups, this latter action occurring because each case is missing the same amount of CDs. The 2 variables and 4 negative units in one group show the CDs one friend will receive, i.e., an unknown amount of CDs in each of 2 cases with a total of 4 individual CDs **missing** from the 2 cases.)

(h) **Addition-multiplication combination (two unknowns):** *Joel has 2 packages of stickers. There are the same number of stickers in each of his packages. Sondra has 3 times as many packages as Joel. All her packages are alike, but they each hold a different amount of stickers than Joel's do. How many stickers do they have together?* Partners should put down 2 variables of one color on the mat, then put down "3 times as many" or 3 sets of 2 variables each, or 6 variables, but in the second color/size. Each variable in the first color represents the number of stickers in one of Joel's packages; each variable in the second color represents the number of stickers in one of Sondra's packages. The group of 2 variables and the group of 6 variables cannot be recounted as a single set of 8 variables to show the total number of stickers because their two colors/sizes represent different amounts of stickers. **Note:** If each of Sondra's packages held the **same** amount of stickers as each of Joel's packages, this situation would involve only **one** unknown. Two variable tiles of one color would be placed on the mat, then 3 sets of 2 variable tiles each, **using the same first color,** would be placed next to the initial 2 variables. Because the variables are all the same color, the 2 variables and 6 variables could be recounted as a single set and the 8 variables together would represent the total number of stickers belonging to Joel and Sondra.

5. If time permits, have teams of 3–4 students create their own story situations, using known and unknown amounts. Actual numbers in the stories should be limited to the quantities of variable tiles and unit tiles available to each team. Ask other students to represent the different amounts in the newly-created stories with their sets of tiles.

Activity 2: VISUALIZING EXPRESSIONS

[Bridging Action]

Materials: Packets of variable tiles and unit tiles from Activity 1
Colored pencils (same colors as variable tile colors)
Worksheet 2–1–1
Regular pencils

Management: Partners (30–50 minutes)

Directions:

1. Give each pair of students a packet of variable tiles and unit tiles, a colored pencil for each color of variable tile they have, and two copies of Worksheet 2–1–1.

2. The worksheet contains the story situations discussed in Activity 1. Partners should now work together and independently of the teacher to build each situation with the variable tiles and unit tiles, then draw a diagram of what they have built. Students should record the diagrams on their own worksheets.

3. Have students draw tall rectangles to represent the variable tiles and color the interiors of these shapes with the color of the variable tile used. A tall rectangle with a large X in the interior will show an inverse variable. Small squares will represent the unit tiles. As used in earlier activities, plain small squares will show positive units, and small squares with a large X in the interior will show negative units.

4. Also have students write a symbolic expression for each diagram. The symbols and their left-to-right order should closely reflect what the students have drawn with shapes on their worksheets. Labels should also be used to identify the objects involved. Here are examples of diagrams and symbolic expressions that might be used for the situations (situations are identified by their numbers on the worksheet).

(1) (+5) + G fish, G = number of guppies

(2) 6C – 2C, or 4C candies, C = number of candies in one bag. Do not overemphasize the 6C-type of notation (i.e., a number beside a letter)—6C just means there are "6 of the C-amount of candies" or C + C + C + C + C + C. In this example, 6 is the multiplier that counts groups, so it is considered positive; in particular, when counting a variable or unknown group, the (+) sign is usually omitted.

(3) M + (+4) total marbles, M = number of marbles in bag at first

(4) M + (−5) marbles left, M = number of marbles in bag at first

(5) 5C coupons, C = number of coupons in one envelope

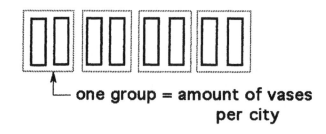

(6) ($\frac{1}{4}$)(8V) = 2V vases per city, V = number of vases in one shipping carton

└─ **one group = amount of vases
per city**

(7) 3P + (+6) pencils, P = number of pencils in one box

(8) ($\frac{1}{3}$)[6D + (+9)] = 2D + (+3) disks per person, D = number of CDs in one storage case

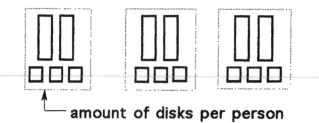

└─ **amount of disks per person**

(9) $(\frac{1}{3})[6D + (-12)] = 2D + (-4)$ disks per person, D = number of CDs in one storage case

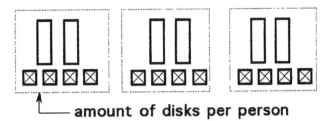

— amount of disks per person

(10) 2J + 6S stickers, J = number of stickers in one of Joel's packages, S = number of stickers in one of Sondra's packages (plain rectangle here indicates one color, shaded rectangle another color)

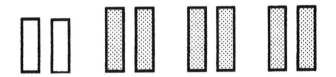

5. Partners can share their work with the rest of the class when all are finished with the worksheet.

Activity 3: MATCH THE MEANINGS!

[Application/Exploration]

Materials: Decks of cards (described in step 1)

Management: Teams of 4 students each (20–30 minutes)

Directions:

1. Give each team of 4 students a deck of 32 cards. Cards can be made with small, colored, unlined index cards, then laminated. Eight cards (set A) should be made of one color and will contain simplified algebraic expressions. The other 24 cards (set B) should be made of a second color and will contain word phrases or algebraic expressions. Each card in set A will match in its meaning to 3 cards in set B. A possible deck is described in step 5. Unknowns in algebraic expressions on the cards will be represented by the words "some amount" in the word phrases. This game provides experience in seeing a positive integer sometimes written without its (+) sign, e.g., 5 instead of +5. Discuss this possibility with the students before they play the game.

2. Each team should shuffle the 8 cards in set A, then turn the stack face down in the center of the table. The 24 cards in set B are then shuffled and distributed equally to the 4 team members. The team will now work together to match cards in their hands to each card in the set A stack.

3. The four members of a team will take turns drawing a card from the top of the stack (set A) and placing it face up on the table near the stack. Then all four members

WORKSHEET 2-1-1
Visualizing Expressions

For each situation below, on another sheet of paper draw a diagram to represent the amounts described and write a symbolic expression based on that diagram. The teacher will give additional instructions.

1. There are 5 goldfish and several guppies in the aquarium. How many fish total are in the aquarium?

2. Tonya held 6 bags of candies at first. She then gave 2 of the bags to Juan. If all the bags contain the same number of candies, how many candies does Tonya hold now?

3. Sharesha has some marbles in a bag. She finds 4 more marbles. After combining all the marbles in the bag, how many marbles does she have?

4. Charles has some marbles in an open bag. He drops 5 marbles out of the bag. How many marbles remain in the bag?

5. There are 5 envelopes in all. All envelopes hold the same number of coupons. How many coupons are there in all?

6. There are 8 shipping cartons. They all contain the same number of crystal vases. The vases are to be equally distributed to 4 different cities. How many vases will be shipped to each city?

7. Kim Lee has 3 boxes of pencils, each box containing the same amount. He has 6 extra pencils in his desk drawer. How many pencils does he have in all?

8. There are 6 CD storage cases full of CDs and 9 individual newly-bought CDs that are to be shared equally by 3 friends. How many CDs total will each friend receive?

9. There are 6 storage cases containing CDs, but 12 individual CDs are missing from the cases. The same number of CDs is missing from each case. All the remaining CDs are to be shared equally by 3 friends. How many CDs total will each friend receive?

10. Joel has 2 packages of stickers. There are the same number of stickers in each of his packages. Sondra has 3 times as many packages as Joel. All her packages are alike, but they each hold a different amount of stickers than Joel's do. How many stickers do they have together?

will look at the cards in their hands to try to find cards that are equivalent to or that describe in words the algebraic expression on the face-up card. When the 3 matching cards are located, they should be placed next to the face-up card. Then another card should be drawn from the stack (set A) and the matching process repeated. Members may discuss their various cards as they search for correct matches, but no one person may hold all the cards from set B during the game.

4. After a team has used all its cards to form matches, give the team an answer key of correct matches so that they may check their work and correct any wrong matches. Discuss any mismatches that occur and correct any errors in the understanding of notation.

5. Here is a possible list of expressions to use for a deck of cards. The list as provided here may also be used as an answer key for the students.

Set A	*Set B*
$2C - 5$	*twice some amount* decreased by 5
	5 less than *2 of some amount*
	$2C + (-5)$
$3M + 1$	*three times some amount* increased by 1
	1 more than *three of some amount*
	1 more than *some amount that has been tripled*
$(+8) - N$	$+8$ decreased by *some amount*
	$(+8) + (-N)$
	some amount less than $+8$
$R - (+3)$	3 less than *some amount*
	some amount decreased by 3
	$R + (-3)$
$B + 5$	5 more than *some amount*
	some amount increased by 5
	$B + (+5)$
$2 + C$	2 increased by *some amount*
	some amount more than 2
	$(+2) + C$
$2A$	*twice some amount*
	some amount doubled
	2 of some amount
$(\frac{1}{3})B - 6$	*a third of some amount* decreased by 6
	6 less than *a third of some amount*
	some amount divided into 3 shares, then each share decreased by 6

OBJECTIVE 2: Evaluate algebraic expressions.

Activity 1: MAKE-AND-REPLACE

[Developing Action]

Materials: Sets of commercial or teacher-made tiles with building mats (described in step 1)
Paper
Pencils
Worksheet 2–2–1

Management: Partners (50 minutes)

Directions:

1.   Give each pair of students a set of tiles and a building mat. The building mat should be a blank 8.5 in. by 14 in. sheet of white paper. Each set should contain three different types (e.g., X, Y, Z) of variable tiles with four tiles of each type, and 30 positive and 30 negative unit tiles. The rectangular tiles for different variables should differ in color and in length, but not in width or thickness. If teacher-made tiles are used, a variable may be represented by a strip of laminated, colored construction paper or lightweight tagboard with a different color used for each type of variable. For example, for one variable a red strip approximately 0.75 inch by 3 inches in size might be used; for the second variable, a blue strip approximately 0.75 inch by 3.25 inches in size; and for the third variable, a yellow strip approximately 0.75 inch by 3.5 inches in size. To correspond to the teacher-made variables, 0.75 in. by 0.75 in. paper squares might be used for the unit tiles; a color different from the variable colors should be used for the units. (The set of tiles used previously in Activity 1 of Objective 1 might be expanded and used for this activity.) To show the inverse of a variable, a large X should be drawn on one side of each variable tile or paper strip. When the X-side is face up, the **inverse or opposite of the variable** is represented. When the plain side is face up, the original **variable** is represented. (Use a similar marking for the unit tiles; the X-side face up would represent –1.) If commercial tiles are being used and each tile is single-colored, a large X can be drawn on one large face of the tile in permanent marking pen in order to represent the inverse or opposite of that tile when the X-side is face up. **Note:** Try to avoid language like "positive variable" or "negative variable." This leads students to incorrectly expect a variable to always be a positive value and the inverse of the variable to be a negative value.

2.   For convenience of discussion, the colors red, blue, and yellow will be used as the colors of the three different variables in our set of tiles. Ask students to place 3 red strips on their building mats, followed on the right by 5 positive unit tiles and 2 blue strips. Tell the students that this set of tiles in order from left to right represents the expression 3R + (+5) + 2B, using R for the red variable tile and B for the blue variable tile. Have them write the expression on their own papers.

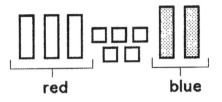

3. Now tell them that each red strip, R, has a value of +4, and each blue strip, B, has a value of +3. Ask the students to trade each strip or variable tile for its stated value in unit tiles, then find the total value of the expression.

4. To do the trading or substitution, students should replace each red strip with 4 positive unit tiles and each blue strip with 3 positive unit tiles. As each new group of unit tiles is placed, it should be kept separated from the other groups of tiles in order to make the final recording process easier. After trading is completed, from left to right on the building mat they should see groups of unit tiles in the following order: (+4) + (+4) + (+4) + (+5) + (+3) + (+3), which yields a total value of +23.

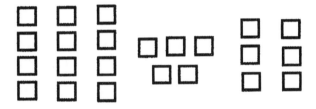

5. *Ask:* "How many groups of +4 do you see on your building mat?" *(3 groups of +4)* "How many groups of +3 do you see?" *(2 groups of +3)* Students should now complete their recording of the expression as follows: **3R + (+5) + 2B = 3(+4) + (+5) + 2(+3) = +23 when R = +4 and B = +3.** At this stage it is helpful to students' understanding to read 3(+4) as "3 of +4" and 2(+3) as "2 of +3."

6. Now write the expression (–B) + (+3) + Y on the board for students to build. The blue strip might be chosen with its X-side face up to represent the inverse of B, and the yellow strip might be chosen for the variable Y (plain side face up).

7. *Ask:* "If B is –2, what is the value of the inverse of B?" *(the opposite of –2, or +2)* Thus, letting Y = –5, have students replace the strip for –B with 2 positive units and the yellow strip for Y with 5 negative units, keeping the original 3 positive units positioned between the two new groups of units.

8. Now have students simplify their three groups of unit tiles by forming 0-pairs; encourage them to do this mentally, but allow them to move the tiles into pairs if necessary. The final effective value will be 0. They should then record their results as follows: **(–B) + (+3) + Y = (+2) + (+3) + (–5) = 0 when B = –2 and Y = –5.**

9. Now write several other algebraic expressions on the chalkboard for students to build. The expressions may involve 1 to 3 different unknowns (variables), and substitution values for those unknowns or variables should be listed. Various letters besides R, B, and Y should now be used for the variables. The substitution values used and the total number of units needed to evaluate an expression will be controlled by the number of units available in the students' sets of tiles.

10. For each expression, partners must decide which color of paper strip or variable tile to use for each unknown, then build that expression on their building mat with the selected variable tiles and unit tiles. After making the required substitutions, students should record the expressions and values on their own papers as shown previously in steps 5 and 8.

11. Here are some possible expressions to use. (See Worksheet 2–2–1.) In the case of subtraction or the presence of the inverse of a variable within an expression, students should be encouraged to view the expression in more than one way. If time permits, students might also create their own expressions for other students to build and evaluate by substitution.

$N + R + (+3) = ?$ when $N = +5$ and $R = +7$.

$P – (+5) = ?$ when $P = +18$. [Build as $P + (–5)$, then use $(+18) + (–5) = +13$; or show P-variable **alone,** then trade it for 18 positive units and remove 5 of those positive units. This latter approach would be recorded as $(+18) – (+5) = +13$.]

$2N + (+7) = ?$ when $N = +8$.

$T + M – (+9) = ?$ when $T = +4$ and $M = +15$. [See two approaches used in $P – (+5)$ expression above.]

$P + 3B = ?$ when $P = –4$ and $B = +5$.

$T + (–W) + N + (–6) = ?$ when $T = +2$, $W = –3$, and $N = –7$.

$4B – B = ?$ when $B = +8$. [This may be considered as 3B after the removal of one B-variable from 4B, or may be worked as $4B + (–B) = ?$]

$3P + (+4) + (–P) = ?$ when $P = +6$. [This may also be considered as $3P + (+4) – P = ?$]

$2T + 3W + 2M = ?$ when $T = +7$, $W = +2$, and $M = –4$.

$4N – 2N + N – (+8) = ?$ when $N = –3$. [Show 4N, remove 2N, then bring in one N, yielding 3N. To remove +8, bring in 8 0-pairs of units with the 3N, then remove +8. This leaves $3N + (–8)$, the alternative approach, with which to begin the substitution process. Students might also use $4N + (–2N) + N$, then bring in the 8 0-pairs, etc.]

Name _____   **Date** _____

WORKSHEET 2–2–1
Make-and-Replace

Here are several algebraic expressions for you to build on mats with variable tiles and unit tiles.

1. $N + R + (+3) = ?$ when $N = +5$ and $R = +7$.

2. $P - (+5) = ?$ when $P = +18$. [Build as $P + (-5)$, then use $(+18) + (-5) = +13$; or show P-variable **alone,** then trade it for 18 positive units and remove 5 of those positive units. This latter approach would be recorded as $(+18) - (+5) = +13$.]

3. $2N + (+7) = ?$ when $N = +8$.

4. $T + M - (+9) = ?$ when $T = +4$ and $M = +15$. [See two approaches used in $P - (+5)$ expression above.]

5. $P + 3B = ?$ when $P = -4$ and $B = +5$.

6. $T + (-W) + N + (-6) = ?$ when $T = +2$, $W = -3$, and $N = -7$.

7. $4B - B = ?$ when $B = +8$. [This may be considered as 3B after the removal of one B-variable from 4B, or may be worked as $4B + (-B) = ?$]

8. $3P + (+4) + (-P) = ?$ when $P = +6$. [This may also be considered as $3P + (+4) - P = ?$]

9. $2T + 3W + 2M = ?$ when $T = +7$, $W = +2$, and $M = -4$.

10. $4N - 2N + N - (+8) = ?$ when $N = -3$. [Show 4N, remove 2N, then bring in one N, yielding 3N. To remove +8, bring in 8 0-pairs of units with the 3N, then remove +8. This leaves $3N + (-8)$, the alternative approach, with which to begin the substitution process. You might also use $4N + (-2N) + N$, then bring in the 8 0-pairs, etc.]

Activity 2: DRAWING TO EVALUATE

[Bridging Action]

Materials: Worksheet 2–2–2
Paper
Pencil
Sets of tiles and building mats from Activity 1 *(optional)*

Management: Partners (30–50 minutes)

Directions:

1. Have students work in pairs. Give each student a copy of Worksheet 2–2–2. The emphasis will be on how to draw diagrams for expressions in order to substitute units for variables found in the expression. Some students may still prefer to work with the tiles; this is acceptable. Have them first build a given expression with tiles, then draw pictures to show the steps they use to evaluate the expression. When ready, such students will begin to draw only, and no longer build with tiles.

2. Show how to draw and label different rectangles with letters in order to represent variables or unknowns in a situation. All rectangles will be drawn with the same approximate length since it is difficult for students to draw different lengths free-hand. As an example, to show the expression 2G + (–4) – A and evaluate it for G = +3 and A = –2, draw the following two stages on the board:

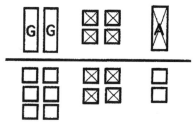

3. To record the work, write the following two statements on the board:

2G + (–4) – A = 2G + (–4) + (–A) = ? and 2(+3) + (–4) + (+2) = +4

Observe that the **removal of the variable A** in the original expression has been replaced with its equivalent process, the **joining of the variable (–A),** a relationship discovered in earlier activities. Encourage students to rewrite the entire equivalent expression rather than just make some sign changes on the original expression. This will help them focus on equivalent processes instead of on what some students perceive as "mysterious sign changes" on numbers. Remind students that 2G means G + G and that 2(+3) means 2 groups of +3. In integer multiplication, this last form might also be written as (+2)(+3). This indicates that the multiplier 2 is considered positive since it counts how many groups are present.

4. Now have students complete their worksheets with their partners. They should first write an expression that depicts the original situation, and simplify it or rewrite it in the

equivalent addition format. After the drawing and substitution are done, a number sentence should be written to show the final value for the original expression.

5. Here are some possible expressions with their diagrams and completed number sentences that students might use for the items on the worksheet. Remind students that amounts of objects they can count and hold will be shown with positive units. Also, rectangles will be labeled with letters to represent different variables instead of being different colors or lengths.

(1) $(+5) + P = ?$ $(+5) + (+7) = +12$ cookies in the basket

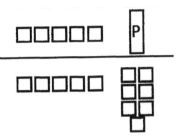

(2) $5B - 2B = 3B = ?$ $3(+10) = +30$ pieces of gum remain

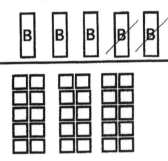

Alternative: $5B - 2B = 5B + (-2B) = 5B + 2(-B) = ?$

$5(+10) + 2(-10) = +30$ pieces

The diagram for this approach would show
5 groups of $+10$ and 2 groups of -10.

(3) $2M + (+4) = ?$ $2(+9) + (+4) = +22$ marbles remain

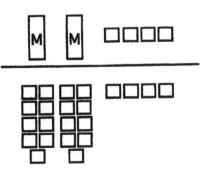

(4) $N - (+5) = N + (-5) = ?$ $(+8) + (-5) = +3$ fish remain in tank

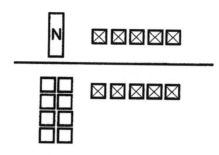

(5) $(\frac{1}{3})[6A + (+9)] = 2A + (+3) = ?$

$2(+5) + (+3) = +13$ pizzas for each employee

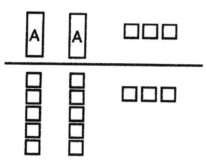

(6) $(\frac{1}{4})[8D - (+16)] = 2D - (+4) = 2D + (-4) = ?$

$2(+10) + (-4) = +16$ disks per student

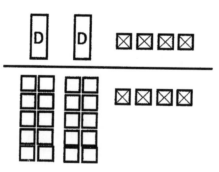

(7) $3Y + 6C = ?$ $3(+5) + 6(+4) = +39$ stickers in all

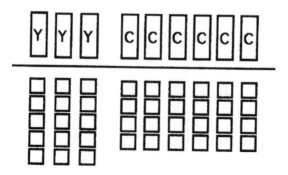

WORKSHEET 2-2-2
Drawing to Evaluate

For each situation below, write an expression and simplify it if possible. Draw a diagram to represent the simplified expression, then draw units to show substitutions for the variables involved. Write number sentences to show the substitutions made. The teacher will give additional instructions.

1. There are 5 chocolate chip cookies and several peanut butter cookies in the basket. How many cookies total are in the basket? [Use P = 7 peanut butter cookies in the basket.]

2. Suzette bought 5 packages of blueberry-flavored gum. She gave 2 of the packages to her brother. If all the packages contain the same number of pieces of gum, how many pieces does Suzette have now? [Use B = 10 pieces per package.]

3. Mario has the same amount of marbles in each of 2 bags. He finds 4 more marbles. After combining all the marbles, how many marbles does he have? [Use M = 9 marbles per bag.]

4. Some flying fish are temporarily placed in a water tank that has no top cover. Five of the fish fly out of the tank and into a nearby bucket of water. How many fish remain in the tank? [Use N = 8 fish in the open tank at first.]

5. On Friday night at Sal's Pizza Parlor, 3 employees teamed together to sell 6 "party packages" of pizza, as well as 9 individual pizzas. What was each employee's fair share of the total pizzas sold? [Use A = 5 pizzas per "party package."]

6. There are 8 boxes containing computer disks, but 16 individual disks are missing from the boxes. The same number of disks is missing from each box. All the remaining disks are to be shared equally by 4 students. How many disks total will each student receive? [Use D = 10 disks per box.]

7. You Hwan has 3 packages of stickers. There are the same number of stickers in each of his packages. Cass has twice as many packages as Hwan. All her packages are alike, but they each hold a different amount of stickers than You Hwan's do. How many stickers do they have together? [Use Y = 5 stickers per package for You Hwan and C = 4 stickers per package for Cass.]

8. Draw to evaluate:

   (a)   A – 2B if A = –4 and B = +3   **(b)**   (–G) + 4M if G = –12 and M = +7

(8a) A – 2B = A + (–2B) = A + 2(–B) = ?   (–4) + 2(–3) = –10

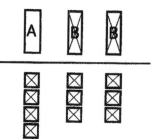

(8b) (–G) + 4M = ?   (+12) + 4(+7) = +40

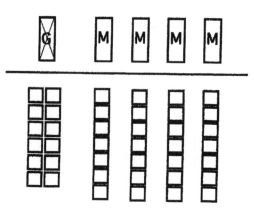

6. After students have completed the worksheet, ask some of them to draw their diagrams and write their number sentences on the board. Discuss any expressions that caused difficulty for anyone. Remind students that algebraic expressions can be simplified or viewed in different ways, particularly when subtraction is involved.

Activity 3: EVALU-MATES!

[Application/Exploration]

Materials: Decks of cards (described in step 1)
Calculators
Paper
Regular pencils

Management: Teams of 4 students each (20–30 minutes)

Directions:

1. Give each team a deck of 16 cards and a calculator. The cards may be made with small, colored index cards and each will contain an algebraic expression similar to those used in Activity 2. A variety of letters will be used for variables. Here is a possible set of expressions to use:

$3B + A = ?$	$(+5) - M + (-2) = ?$	$(\frac{1}{2})N - (-6) = ?$	$(-G) + H = ?$
$(-7) + 5J = ?$	$7X + 2N + K = ?$	$-4B + (-C) + 5 = ?$	$(+8) - M = ?$
$(\frac{1}{5})[10B + (-15)] = ?$	$6W + 5W = ?$	$(-9) - N = ?$	$(+3) + 4A = ?$
$9N - 3N + (+6) = ?$	$2[3M + K] = ?$	$-5[X + (-8)] = ?$	$-3B - (-12) = ?$

2. The team should shuffle its deck of cards, then place the stack face down in the center of the table.

3. Members take turns drawing a card from the top of the stack. The player drawing the card must simplify (if needed) and evaluate the expression on the card. The person to the left of the drawing player will state what values are to be used for the variables appearing on the card.

4. The drawing player will substitute the given values for the variables and compute the total value for the expression. The computation may be done with pencil and paper or with calculator, assuming that the players know how to input data correctly according to the order of operations. The person to the right of the drawing player will check the computation used and the answer found, again either with pencil and paper or with calculator. If there is disagreement, the drawing player and the checker will compare their work to look for any errors. The teacher serves as the final judge in such matters.

5. The person to the left of the drawing player becomes the next player to draw a card from the stack, and the evaluating process continues.

6. Play should continue until all cards are drawn or until time is called.

OBJECTIVE 3: Solve linear equations in one variable by adding-on or removing value.

Activity 1: KEEPING THE BALANCE!

[Developing Action]

Materials: Sets of commercial or teacher-made tiles and building mats (described in step 1)
Coffee stirrers or pieces of colored yarn (approx. 12 in. long)
Paper
Regular pencils
Worksheet 2–3–1

Management: Partners (50 minutes)

Directions:

1. Give each pair of students a building mat, a coffee stirrer or piece of colored yarn, and a set of tiles (minimal set should be equivalent to 1 variable and its inverse variable, 20 positive units, and 20 negative units). The sets of tiles from Objective 1 or Objective 2 might be used for this activity. The mat consists of an 8.5 in. × 14 in. sheet of paper (may be lightweight tagboard and/or laminated). A bold, black bar should be drawn from the midpoint of one longer edge to the midpoint of the other longer edge of the paper. This bar represents the equal sign of an equation. The color of the mat should contrast with the colors of the tiles.

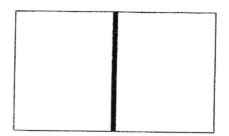

2. Ask each set of partners to show B + (+3) = +5 with tiles on their building mat by placing 1 variable tile to the left of the black bar, then **combining** 3 positive unit tiles with it on the mat. Five positive unit tiles should be placed to the right of the black bar.

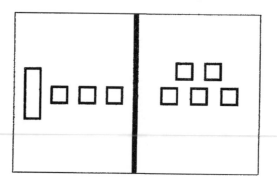

3. Remind students that the mat represents a balance scale where the total value on the left side must equal or "balance" the total value on the right side. Therefore, if the variable tile is on one side of the mat by itself and it balances a group of only positive or negative unit tiles on the other side of the mat, the variable tile must have the same value as the group of unit tiles. *Ask:* "What can we do to change the tiles on the left side and leave the variable tile there alone?" There are two different actions students might suggest: remove the 3 positive unit tiles from the mat's left side, or place 3 new negative unit tiles beside the 3 positive unit tiles (which will form 3 zero-pairs).

4. *Ask:* "If we choose to remove the 3 positive unit tiles from the left, what does this do to the balance of the two sides? How can we keep the balance?" Someone always suggests putting the +3 back on the mat, but since that move just undoes the previous move, remind them that they need the variable tile by itself. Ask students for another idea. They will then suggest removing 3 positive unit tiles from the right side as well.

5. Have the students now remove 3 positive unit tiles from each side of the mat, leaving the single variable tile on the left and 2 positive unit tiles on the right. This shows that the value of the variable must be +2. To confirm this result, tell students to show the original equation on their mats again. They should then replace the variable tile with 2 positive unit tiles. Ask them what they now see. Their response should be that there are 5 positive unit tiles on the left and 5 positive unit tiles on the right, which is a true equality. Thus, +2 must be the correct value for the variable.

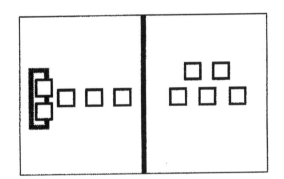

6. Record the steps used to solve the equation by writing the following on the board for students to read (and also write at this time, if preferred):

$$B + (+3) = \quad +5$$
$$\underline{\quad -(+3) \quad -(+3)}$$
$$B \qquad = \quad +2$$

Have someone explain what each row of symbols means in terms of the actions that were taken.

7. For the second approach, have students rebuild the original equation, B + (+3) = +5, on their mats. *Ask:* "If we choose, instead, to place 3 negative unit tiles on the mat's left side to form 0-pairs, what must we do to keep the balance?" Students will then place 3 negative unit tiles on each side of the mat to preserve the balance of the equality. Three 0-pairs will be formed on the left and three 0-pairs will be formed on the right. Tell students to remove from the mat any 0-pairs they have formed. This will leave the single variable tile on the left side and 2 positive unit tiles on the right.

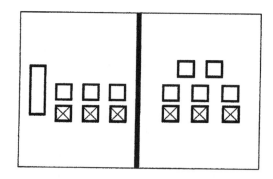

8. Record the new steps used to solve the equation by writing the following steps on the board for students to read and then having someone explain what each row of symbols means:

$$B + (+3) = \quad +5$$
$$\underline{+ (-3) \quad + (-3)}$$
$$B \qquad = \quad +2$$

9. Now write the equation $+3 = W - (+4)$ on the board. Discuss the idea that the notation indicates that +4 is to be **removed** from the value of W; however, the value of W is not known at this time. So enough 0-pairs must be placed on the mat with the variable to allow +4 to be removed. Remember that bringing in 0-pairs to any one side of the mat does not change the total value of whatever else may be there. Hence, bringing in 0-pairs will not affect the value of the variable W or the overall balance of the equation.

10. *Ask:* "How many 0-pairs do we need with W to be able to remove 4 positive units from the total value that W represents?" *(four 0-pairs)* Ask students to build $+3 = W - (+4)$ on their mats. Have students place four 0-pairs (4 positive units and 4 negative units) and also the variable on the right side of the mat. They should then remove 4 positive units from the right side to represent the expression $W - (+4)$. In addition, 3 positive units should be placed on the left side of the mat.

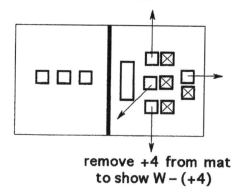

remove +4 from mat
to show W – (+4)

11. Note that the right side now contains $W + (-4)$, a **combination** (addition) equivalent to the **take-away** action shown by the expression $W - (+4)$. ***Ask:*** "What can we do to change the tiles on the right side and leave the variable there alone?" As was the case in step 3 above, students have two choices: (a) place 4 new positive units on the right side of the mat to form 0-pairs with –4, or (b) remove –4 from that side.

12. Method (a): Have students place +4 on the right side, then balance that action by placing another +4 on the left side. Four 0-pairs should now be formed and removed from the right side, leaving the variable there alone. The 4 positive units on the left side combine with the +3 already there to make +7 total. Thus, the value of the variable is +7.

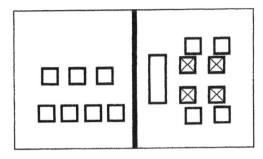

13. Record the steps taken with symbols on the board as follows: [Remember that in building W − (+4) with 0-pairs, we ended up with tiles that showed W + (−4), so we record both forms here.]

$$
\begin{aligned}
+3 &= W - (+4) \\
+3 &= W + (-4) \\
\underline{+ (+4) \qquad + (+4)} \\
+7 &= W
\end{aligned}
$$

Students should confirm their result by placing +3 on the left side of the mat again and the variable with −4 on the right side; +7 should then replace the variable, and any 0-pairs formed on the right side should be removed. This leaves +3 on both sides of the mat, indicating the obviously true equality: +3 = +3. So +7 is the correct value for the variable W. (**Note:** This confirming process is very important for students to experience.)

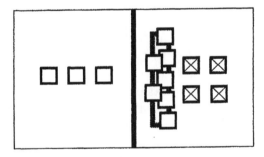

14. Method (b): Now have students show +3 = W + (−4) on their mats again and try the second approach: removing −4 from the right side, then removing −4 from the left to maintain the balance of the equality. The four negative units are easily removed from the mat's right side, leaving the variable alone. To remove that amount from the left side, *at least* four 0-pairs must be combined with the original +3 in order to have enough negative units to remove −4. The total value of the left side becomes +7, indicating the value of the variable on the right.

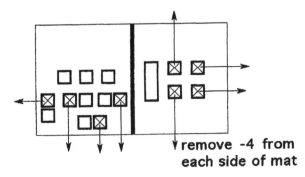

remove -4 from
each side of mat

15. Record these last actions with symbols on the board as follows:

$$+3 = W - (+4)$$
$$+3 = W + (-4)$$
$$\underline{-(-4) \qquad -(-4)}$$
$$+7 = W$$

Have a student read and explain what each row of symbols means.

16. Discuss the idea that, for equations like $(-P) + (+3) = +8$ where the **inverse variable** occurs, they are to solve for the single tile $(-P)$ just as they might solve for P. Read $(-P)$ as "opposite of P" or "inverse of P," and occasionally as "negative P." Once the value of $-P$ is found, P itself must have the opposite value. For example, if $-P = +5$, then $P = -5$; this last statement $(P = -5)$ would simply be written below $-P = +5$ in the symbolic recording. On the mat, the last two steps in solving the equation would be separated by a coffee stirrer or piece of colored yarn and shown as follows.

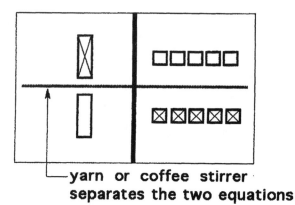

yarn or coffee stirrer separates the two equations

17. Now have students build other equations on their mats to practice solving for the variable. Give them a variety of equations like the examples discussed earlier. (See Worksheet 2–3–1.) Allow them to choose from either of the approaches presented above that are appropriate for a particular equation, but their recording in symbols should reflect the actions used. The value of the variable should also be confirmed each time by rebuilding the original equation and replacing the variable with its suggested value.

18. After all students have built several different equations, have various students share their methods and solutions with the class. Here are several equations to assign to partners for practice. (After students are comfortable with capital letters as variables, you might begin to include some lower case letters.)

1. $B + (-2) = -7$
2. $W - (+5) = +8$
3. $(-3) + (-B) = +2$
4. $-5 = (-5) + W$

5. $+4 = (+3) + B$
6. $-3 = M + (+7)$
7. $-8 = (-P) - (+2)$
8. $0 = (+7) + (-W)$

9. $T - (-1) = -6$
10. $(-B) + (-4) = +1$
11. $(+9) + U = +10$
12. $0 = M - (-6)$

19. **Challenge:** Ask students if they can show the equation $(-3) - W = +4$ with their tiles. Here the **variable** W is to be **subtracted** from -3 on the left side of the equation. To show this, a 0-pair of variables, W and $-W$, must be brought in on the left side of the building mat to combine with -3. Then the variable W can be removed or subtracted from the left side, leaving $-W$ there with -3; this represents the action indicated by $(-3) - W$;

WORKSHEET 2-3-1
Keeping the Balance!

Use your mat and tiles to build these equations to solve for the variables. You may choose from either of the approaches presented during the lesson.

1. $B + (-2) = -7$

2. $W - (+5) = +8$

3. $(-3) + (-B) = +2$

4. $-5 = (-5) + W$

5. $+4 = (+3) + B$

6. $-3 = M + (+7)$

7. $-8 = (-P) - (+2)$

8. $0 = (+7) + (-W)$

9. $T - (-1) = -6$

10. $(-B) + (-4) = +1$

11. $(+9) + U = +10$

12. $0 = M - (-6)$

Challenge: Show the equation $(-3) - W = +4$ with your tiles.

+4 will remain on the right side of the mat. The tiles that finally remain on the left may now be described with the expression $(-3) + (-W)$.

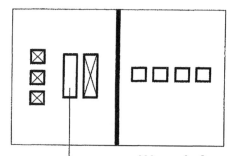

**▼ remove W on left
to show (-3) - W**

Activity 2: PICTURING A SOLUTION

[Bridging Action]

Materials: Paper
Regular pencils
Red pencils
Colored chalk
Commercial or teacher-made tiles for a single variable and units
Building mats from Activity 1 *(optional)*
Worksheet 2–3–2

Management: Partners (50 minutes)

Directions:

1. Have students work with a partner. Give each pair a red pencil. Mats and sets of tiles should be available for all students to use, but emphasis will be on drawing diagrams to represent equations and transforming those diagrams to identify solutions. Students who still prefer to build with tiles should first build, then draw a picture of what they have built, making changes in the picture to show the steps they used with the tiles.

2. To represent the equation $B + (-3) = -5$, draw the following on the board.

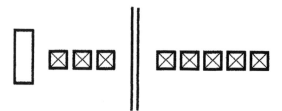

3. Discuss the different ways the equation can be solved for the value of the variable B: (a) **remove** −3 from the left side, and do the same on the right to maintain the equality; or (b) **bring in** +3 on the left and form 0-pairs, and bring in +3 on the right to keep the balance. Show how each method is to be drawn.

4. Method (a): The removal (subtraction) of a tile drawn on the board is shown by marking out the tile with a single mark.

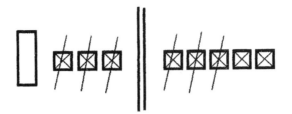

5. The variable remains on the left and –2 remains on the right. Confirm the value of B by redrawing the original diagram, but drawing 2 negative units in red pencil in place of the variable. The diagram now shows the equality –5 = –5. Hence, B = –2 is a true statement.

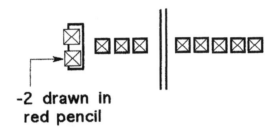

**-2 drawn in
red pencil**

6. Record the drawing steps with symbols on the board, and have a student read and explain each row of symbols.

$$
\begin{array}{rl}
B + (-3) = & -5 \\
- (-3) \quad & - (-3) \\
\hline
B \quad = & -2
\end{array}
$$

7. Method (b): Three positive units are drawn (added) on the left side, then drawn on the right to maintain the balance of the equation. On the left, 0-pairs are formed by connecting opposite units together; only the variable remains unpaired on the left. The pairing is repeated on the right side with –2 remaining unpaired there.

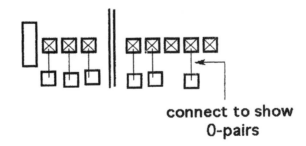

**connect to show
0-pairs**

8. Record the steps in symbols on the board and have a student read and explain the action that each row of symbols means.

$$
\begin{array}{rl}
B + (-3) = & -5 \\
+ (+3) \quad & + (+3) \\
\hline
B \quad = & -2
\end{array}
$$

9. Now write the equation $-1 = (-w) - (+2)$ on the board. The value of $-w$ (often read as "negative w," but the preferred ways in this text will be "inverse of w" or "opposite of w") must first be found, then the opposite value taken for w. Draw the following diagram on the board (a lower-case letter will be used for the variable this time).

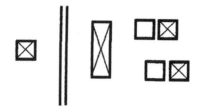

Remind students that, in order to show subtraction from a variable of unknown value, new 0-pairs of units must be drawn beside the variable; note that this does not change the value of the variable. With white chalk (or regular pencil if on paper) mark out +2 on the right side of the diagram above to show the subtraction. This final diagram now represents the action for the original equation, $-1 = (-w) - (+2)$. It would also look like $-1 = (-w) + (-2)$, however, if the marked-out +2 were erased and only the unmarked tiles considered. This shows that the two equations are "equivalent" to each other.

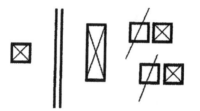

10. Methods (a) and (b) discussed earlier now apply. Show students how the diagram will change for each method and how the recording will be done with symbols. Draw 0-pairs wherever needed; simplify by connecting opposite units to form 0-pairs.

Method (a) [Removal]:

The drawing is done in three stages to help students visually identify the parts that remain.

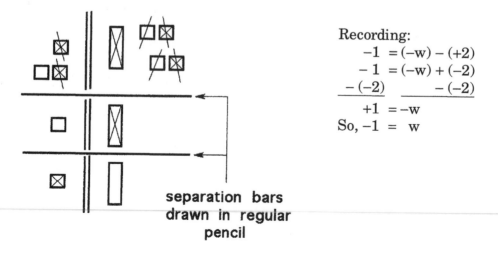

separation bars
drawn in regular
pencil

Recording:
$$-1 = (-w) - (+2)$$
$$-1 = (-w) + (-2)$$
$$\underline{\quad - (-2) \qquad\qquad - (-2)\quad}$$
$$+1 = -w$$
So, $-1 = w$

Method (b) [Add-on]:

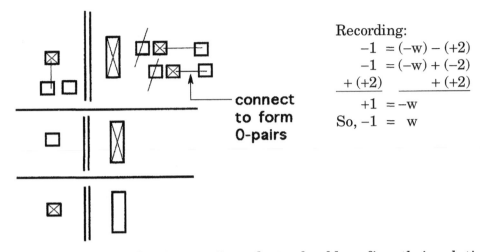

Recording:
$$-1 = (-w) - (+2)$$
$$-1 = (-w) + (-2)$$
$$\underline{+ (+2) \qquad\qquad + (+2)}$$
$$+1 = -w$$
$$\text{So,} -1 = w$$

connect
to form
0-pairs

11. As shown earlier in step 5, students should confirm their solutions to the equations. For example, for method (b) used in step 10, students would redraw their original diagram of the equation $-1 = (-w) - (+2)$, but in red pencil would draw a positive one in place of the inverse variable, $-w$. 0-pairs would then be formed and the equality $-1 = -1$ would remain, confirming that the solution, $w = -1$, is indeed correct.

0-pair connected

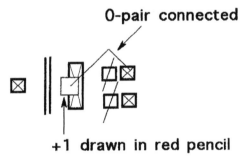

+1 drawn in red pencil

12. Now write other equations on the board for students and their partners to solve. (See Worksheet 2–3–2.) Allow the students to choose from any of the approaches presented above that are appropriate for a particular equation, but their diagrams and symbolic recordings should reflect the actions used. A solution should also be confirmed each time by redrawing the original diagram for the equation, but replacing the variable with its value drawn in red pencil. A numerical equality should result if the solution is correct. Monitor student work carefully, making sure that they can explain what their different pictorial actions and corresponding symbols mean. Some students may still need to build with the tiles. Allow them to build each equation with tiles, but then have them draw a diagram to show what they did with the tiles, as well as make a symbolic recording of their steps. They will stop using the tiles when they are ready to progress to the next level of learning, i.e., the pictorial level.

13. Here are some possible equations to assign:

1. $b + (-5) = -8$	5. $+7 = M + (+2)$	9. $P - (-4) = -3$
2. $(+4) + T = -7$	6. $w - (+1) = +8$	10. $(-6) + (-b) = +2$
3. $-7 = (-W) + (-3)$	7. $+5 = (-B) - (-3)$	11. $m - (-3) = -9$
4. $+10 = (-T) - (+3)$	8. $0 = m - (+4)$	12. $0 = (+7) + p$

WORKSHEET 2–3–2
Picturing a Solution

Here are equations for you to solve with diagrams. Choose from any of the approaches presented during the lesson that are appropriate for a particular equation.

1. $b + (-5) = -8$

2. $(+4) + T = -7$

3. $-7 = (-W) + (-3)$

4. $+10 = (-T) - (+3)$

5. $+7 = M + (+2)$

6. $w - (+1) = +8$

7. $+5 = (-B) - (-3)$

8. $0 = m - (+4)$

9. $P - (-4) = -3$

10. $(-6) + (-b) = +2$

11. $m - (-3) = -9$

12. $0 = (+7) + p$

Challenge: Draw a diagram that might represent the equation $(+3) - (-B) = +5$, where the inverse variable $(-B)$ is being subtracted from $+3$.

14. Challenge: Ask students to draw a diagram that might represent the equation $(+3) - (-B) = +5$, where the **inverse variable** $(-B)$ is being **subtracted** from $+3$. Here is a possible diagram that uses 0-pairs of the variables, B and –B, to show the initial equation.

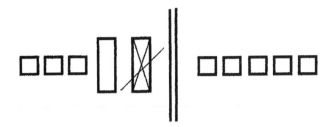

Activity 3: MAKING SOLUTION TRACKS!

[Application/Exploration]

Materials: Dice (2 colors per team)
Worksheet 2–3–3
Pencils
Paper
Tiles and building mats from Activity 1 *(optional)*

Management: Teams of 4 students each (20–30 minutes)

Directions:

1. Give each team of 4 students 2 colored dice (one per color) and two copies of Worksheet 2–3–3. For this activity, some students may still prefer to work with tiles or diagrams; such materials should be available if needed.

2. Each team will play the game as two pairs and at the beginning of the game will decide which die will be die A and which one die B. For each round one pair of students will roll the dice twice, the first time to see which color will represent a negative integer; the die with the lower number on the first roll will be negative. The same pair will then roll the two dice again to get two numbers to complete the number sentence: $N + \underline{(A)} = \underline{(B)}$. Thus, with this procedure, sometimes the number on die A will be positive and sometimes it will be negative; the results will be similar for die B.

3. The pair rolling the dice will then label an unused number line on Worksheet 2–3–3 by locating the point for integer $\underline{(B)}$ on the number line and writing the expression, $N + \underline{(A)}$, above that point. The other pair of students on the team must now solve the equation for N, locate the point for N's value on the number line, and write the letter N above that point. The solving of the equation completes the round. (**Note:** Students should solve the equation by whatever process they prefer: mentally, in symbolic form, with diagrams, or with the tiles. By observing which processes are used by various students, the teacher can quickly assess a student's level of development in solving simple equations.)

4. For example, suppose a team decides at the beginning of the game to call its red die "A" and its white die "B." On one pair's turn they roll the two dice and first get a red 5 and a white 1. Since 1 < 5, the white die will serve as negative and the red die will serve as positive. The pair rolls the dice again, this time getting a red 2 (so A = +2) and a white 6 (so B = –6). The equation becomes N + (+2) = –6, so the two students write N + (+2) above the –6 on a new number line. Now the other pair of students solve the equation by whichever method they choose (either removal or add-on), finding N to be –8. These two students then write N above the –8 on the number line. Hopefully the team will notice that N + (+2) is two units to the right of N or that N is two units to the left of N + (+2); that is, they will become aware of the effect of the +2 on their solution for N.

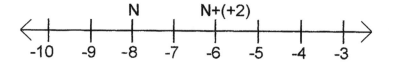

5. The two pairs on a team will rotate the tasks of rolling the dice and solving the equation. Whichever pair solved the equation of the last round rolls the dice for the next round. A new number line is used for each round. After each pair has had the opportunity to solve 4 to 5 equations, the game may be ended if necessary.

WORKSHEET 2-3-3
Making Solution Tracks!

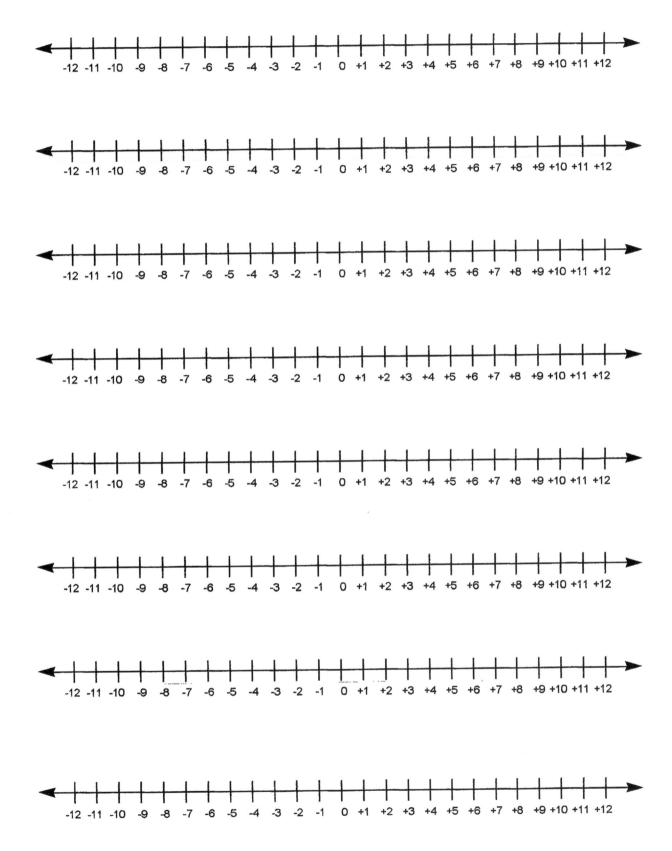

OBJECTIVE 4: Solve linear equations having multiple amounts of one variable by the separation process.

Activity 1: BUILDING FAIR SHARES

[Developing Action]

Materials: Sets of tiles (from Objective 2, Activity 1) and building mats (from Objective 3, Activity 1)
Pieces of colored yarn (approx. 12 in. long) or coffee stirrers
Paper
Regular pencils
Worksheet 2–4–1

Management: Partners (50 minutes)

Directions:

1. Give each pair of students a set of tiles and a building mat (see Activity 1 from Objective 2 and Objective 3 in this section for descriptions of the tiles and mat). Also give each pair a coffee stirrer or piece of colored yarn.

2. Have students place 3 variable tiles of the same size and color on the left half of the building mat and place 6 positive units on the right half of the mat. Discuss the idea that all the variable tiles are the same, so each tile must represent the same amount of units.

3. *Ask:* "If each variable tile represents the same amount of units and the total amount from the variable tiles balances with or equals to the +6 on the right side of the mat, how many positive units must each variable tile equal?" Have students place 6 positive units on the left side of the mat and try to distribute them to the 3 variable tiles until the same number of units (+2) is on top of each variable tile. Some will recognize this sharing situation as that of division and will know immediately that 6 objects shared 3 ways will result in 2 objects per share (or variable tile in this case); they will just place 2 positive units on each variable tile without experimenting.

4. Remind students that in this type of sharing process we want to know how many objects will be in each share. We want to know how many units will equal to just one variable tile. So the answer is +2, or 2 positive units per variable tile. Write the following number sentence on the board: 3P = +6, so P = +2.

5. Now have students randomly place 4 variable tiles that are alike on the right side of the mat and randomly place 12 negative units on the left side. This time ask them to **separate** the 4 variable tiles from each other and line them up along the vertical bar in the middle of the mat. Since the variable tiles have been separated into 4 distinct, equal groups, the 12 negative units on the left must also be separated into 4 distinct, equal groups to maintain the balance of the equality. Students should line up each group of units with a variable tile on the other side of the bar. This procedure will indicate how many units each variable tile must equal. On the board write the sentence: –12 = 4N, so –3 = N. Note that we are recording the sentences in the same left-right order in which they were built on the mat. Discuss the idea that –3 = N can also be written as N = –3.

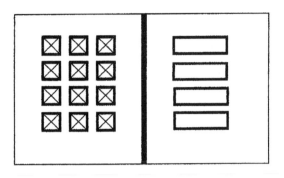

6. Have students confirm their solution of −3 by replacing each variable tile on the mat with 3 negative units. The total number of negative units on the right side of the mat (−12) should equal the total number of negative units on the left side (−12). Therefore, the solution, N = −3, is correct.

7. Now have students place tiles on their mats to show the equation: −5B = +10. Five of the same kind of variable tile should be randomly placed on the left side of the mat with the X-side facing up to show the inverse of the variable B. Ten positive units should be placed randomly on the right side of the mat.

8. Discuss the idea that a group of inverse variable tiles can be separated in the same way that a group of regular variable tiles can be separated. Have students **separate** the five inverse variable tiles from each other and line them up along the vertical bar of the mat. Then the 10 positive units must be separated into 5 equal groups, each group of +2 being lined up with one of the variable tiles.

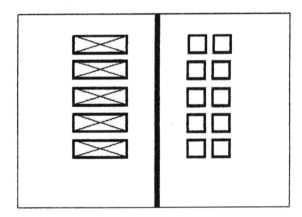

9. Each row of tiles on the mat now represents −B = +2. This shows that B itself will have a value that is the opposite or inverse of +2, which is −2. Generally, when the "solution" to an equation is sought, the value of the original variable, **not** its inverse, is what is needed. (There are situations in real–world applications, however, where the value of the **inverse** variable is the one needed; this will be indicated by conditions of the problem.) To show the final solution, have students place a coffee stirrer or piece of yarn below the last row of tiles on the mat. They should then place below the coffee stirrer or yarn a variable tile (of same type as earlier 5 tiles but now with X-side facing down) on the left and 2 negative units on the right.

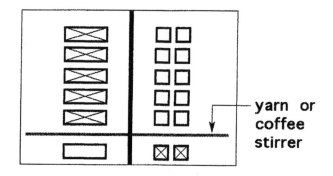

yarn or coffee stirrer

10. On the board write the number sentences: $-5B = +10$, so $B = -2$.

11. Have students confirm that $B = -2$ is indeed the solution for the original equation they built on their mats. If $B = -2$, then $-B = +2$. Each of the 5 inverse variable tiles on the left side of the mat should be replaced with 2 positive units. This shows a total of $+10$ on the left, which matches with the $+10$ on the right side of the mat. Thus, $B = -2$ is the correct solution.

12. Now write several other equations for the students to build on their mats, then solve by applying the **separation** process. (See Worksheet 2–4–1.) Have them record sentences showing each equation and its result on their own papers. Remind them to confirm each solution found. Here are some possible equations to use. (**Note:** If a group of variable tiles equals 0, the variable tiles will be placed on one side of the mat, but the other side of the mat will remain empty. The variable tiles should still be separated; the space on the other side of the mat where the numerical amount would normally be as part of each row will just remain empty of any unit tiles. This shows that each variable tile has a value of 0.)

$2P = +10$	$5M = -15$	$+15 = -3G$	$-7 = 7R$
$-8 = -4N$	$2T = -14$	$0 = 5B$	$-7K = +14$
$+20 = 5K$	$+9 = -3A$	$-6X = -12$	$-4N = -16$

Activity 2: PICTURING SHARES

[Bridging Action]

Materials: Paper
Red pencils
Regular pencils
Colored chalk
Tiles and mat from Activity 1 *(optional)*
Worksheet 2–4–2

Management: Partners (50 minutes)

Directions:

1. Give each pair of students a red pencil. Some students may still need to work with the tiles and building mat; this is acceptable. Encourage them to first build an equation with the tiles, then draw a diagram that shows the steps they used to solve for the

WORKSHEET 2-4-1
Building Fair Shares

Here are equations for you to build on your mats. Then solve them by applying the separation process. Complete each sentence showing each equation and its result.

1. $3P = +6$, so _____.

9. $-5B = +10$, so _____.

2. $-12 = 4N$, so _____.

10. $-7K = +14$, so _____.

3. $-8 = -4N$, so _____.

11. $+9 = -3A$, so _____.

4. $+20 = 5K$, so _____.

12. $+15 = -3G$, so _____.

5. $-7 = 7R$, so _____.

13. $0 = 5B$, so _____.

6. $-2A = 0$, so _____.

14. $-6X = -12$, so _____.

7. $5M = -15$, so _____.

15. $-4N = -16$, so _____.

8. $2T = -14$, so _____.

16. $2P = +10$, so _____.

variable. Students will stop building with tiles when they are cognitively ready to do so, and will move on to the next level, the pictorial level.

2. Write the equation 2N = +8 on the chalkboard. Remind students that multiple copies of the same type of variable must have the same value when they appear in the same equation together. Otherwise, we would never know what each variable represented, and there would be great confusion. Show students how to draw 2 rectangles of equal length for the two variables and 8 small squares for the integral units. The units should be drawn in a random arrangement at first. Parallel, vertical bars will represent the equal sign in the notation.

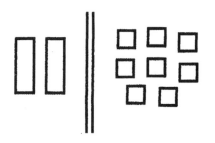

3. Discuss how the variables must be separated into two equal groups on the left. Then to keep the equality of the two sides of the equation, the units on the right side must also be separated into two equal groups. Some students will be able to divide +8 by +2 mentally and simply draw 4 positive units in one row and another 4 positive units in the second row. Others may need to draw one unit per row before drawing a second unit per row, etc., until they have used all 8 positive units. This latter group will be those students who do not immediately recognize the situation as a division situation. **Note:** After students have drawn diagrams for several exercises, they may prefer to omit the first step of showing the units **randomly** arranged and immediately draw the units in equal rows lined up with individual variables; this procedure will be acceptable as long as students can explain why they are forming equal rows on each side of the vertical bars.

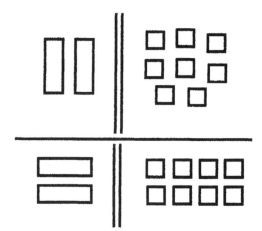

4. Have students draw a path around one row with red pencil to show that one share, or N, will equal +4. (Be sure to vary which row is selected from exercise to exercise to avoid wrong conclusions by students; *which* share is selected is not important.)

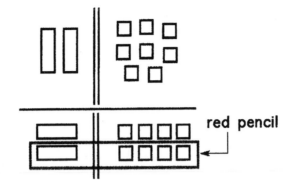

5. Now record additional number sentences on the board to show the steps that were taken:

$$2N = +8$$
$$\tfrac{1}{2}(2N) = \tfrac{1}{2}(+8)$$
$$N = +4$$

6. Use the following language when "reading" the second and third lines of the above recording: "1 of 2 equal shares of 2N is 1 of 2 equal shares of +8, or N equals +4." This is to prepare students for the more general reciprocal or multiplicative inverse approach that will be developed in future lessons. The language "2N divided by 2" should not be used at this time. It is difficult for students to transfer from the division form, $\frac{2N}{2}$, to the multiplication form, $\tfrac{1}{2}(2N)$, when needed later.

7. Students should confirm their answer of N = +4 by drawing in red pencil 4 positive units on top of each variable rectangle in the original diagram. This will show a total value of +8 on the left side, as well as +8 on the right side. Thus, the equality holds and the answer, +4, is correct. Have students write the number sentence 2(+4) = +8 to record the substitution that confirmed their answer. Remind students that this is equivalent to writing +2(+4) = +8, since we usually consider the multiplier 2 to be positive as a counter of groups or sets.

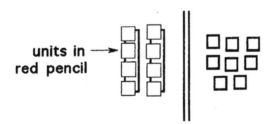

8. Now write the equation −20 = 4B on the board and ask students to draw a diagram to solve for the value of B. Again, draw a random arrangement of units to show −20.

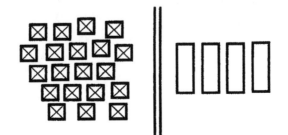

9. *Ask:* "How do we find a single variable, B ?" *(Separate the four variables on the right into four equal groups of one variable each.)* "What does this separation require us to do with the units on the left?" *(Separate them into four equal groups on the left; align each group in a row with one of the variables.)* Students should draw a second diagram below the first one, separating them with a long horizontal bar, and draw a red path around one of the rows to show one share.

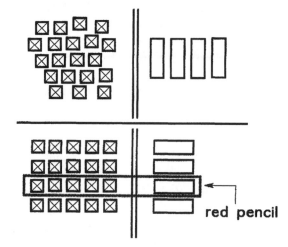

10. Record the steps with symbolic notation:

$$-20 = 4B$$
$$\tfrac{1}{4}(-20) = \tfrac{1}{4}(4B)$$
$$-5 = B$$

11. Encourage students to use the following language to describe the above notation: "1 of 4 equal shares of −20 is 1 of 4 equal shares of 4B, or −5 equals B." Also have them confirm their solution by drawing 5 negative units in red pencil on top of each variable in the original diagram. This will show that −20 equals −20, a true equality. Students should then record the number sentence for their substitution: −20 = 4(−5).

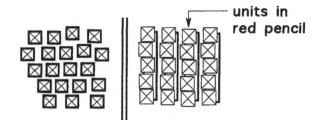

12. Now have students draw diagrams to solve the equation: −3C = +12. Students should view the notation −3C as "3 of the inverse or opposite of variable C." They may also read it as "negative 3C" or "the opposite of 3C."

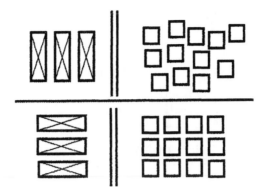

13. Each row now shows an inverse variable with 4 positive units, but we want to find the value of the original variable C, not its inverse. Have students draw a long horizontal bar below the rows of inverse variables and units, then below that bar draw a row that contains "opposites" of the rows drawn earlier. That is, the new row will contain an original variable (the opposite of –C) on the left side of the vertical bars and 4 negative units (the opposite of +4) on the right side. Students should draw a path in red pencil around this last row to show the final amounts they seek, i.e., C = –4.

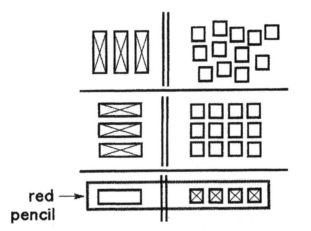

red → pencil

14. Now complete the recording of equations on the board to show the steps that were taken to solve for C:

$$-3C = +12$$
$$\tfrac{1}{3}(-3C) = \tfrac{1}{3}(+12)$$
$$-C = +4$$
$$\text{So, } C = -4$$

15. Use the following language to read or describe these new equations: "1 of 3 equal shares of –3C is 1 of 3 equal shares of +12, or –C = +4. If we want C, the opposite of –C (i.e., the opposite of 'negative C' or of the 'inverse of C'), we need the opposite of +4, or –4. So C = –4."

16. To confirm their solution of –4 for C, students should draw with red pencil four **positive** units on top of each **inverse** variable in the diagram of the original equation. This will show 3 groups of +4 each on the left equaling to +12 on the right, which is a true equality. Have students record their substitution with the number sentence: 3(+4) = +12.

Note: If some students view –3C as "the opposite of 3C," they may record their substitution sentence as –3(–4) = +12, where they use C = –4 instead of –C = +4.

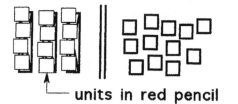

— units in red pencil

17. Now assign other equations for students to solve by drawing diagrams. (See Worksheet 2–4–2.) They should record their solution steps in equation form, then confirm their answers with red pencil and write a substitution equation. All of these drawing and writing stages are important and should not be omitted at this point in the development. Here are some suggested equations for you to assign (lower-case letters will also be used for variables).

$2p = +12$	$3M = -15$	$+15 = -3g$	$0 = 5R$
$-8 = -2N$	$7w = -14$	$+9 = 9A$	$-6k = +18$
$+20 = 5m$	$0 = -3b$	$-6X = +12$	$-4n = -16$

Note: If a group of variables equals 0, draw a "sloppy 0" on the side of the vertical bars where units would usually be drawn. The variables should still be separated, and the space on the other side of the vertical bars, where units should be drawn as part of each row, will contain a "sloppy 0" instead. This shows that each variable has a value of 0. The use of a "sloppy 0" in a space prevents students from later trying to incorrectly draw some units there. Below is a sample diagram for the equation, –2M = 0.

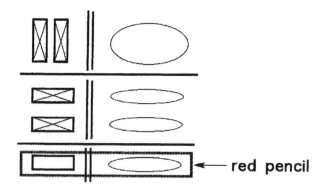

← red pencil

18. After students have solved a variety of equations by drawing diagrams and recording their steps, on the board write the **first two steps** used to solve each of several equations already worked. It is time to search for **patterns** in the **notation.** Here are some examples to use:

(a)	$-20 = 4B$	**(b)**	$2N = +8$	**(c)**	$-3C = +12$
	$\frac{1}{4}(-20) = \frac{1}{4}(4B)$		$\frac{1}{2}(2N) = \frac{1}{2}(+8)$		$\frac{1}{3}(-3C) = \frac{1}{3}(+12)$
(d)	$7w = -14$	**(e)**	$0 = 5R$	**(f)**	$-8 = -2N$
	$\frac{1}{7}(7w) = \frac{1}{7}(-14)$		$\frac{1}{5}(0) = \frac{1}{5}(5R)$		$\frac{1}{2}(-8) = \frac{1}{2}(-2N)$

Name _____ **Date** _____

WORKSHEET 2–4–2
Picturing Shares

Solve these equations by drawing diagrams. Record your solution steps in equation form, then confirm your answers with red pencil and write a substitution equation.

1. $2N = 8$

2. $2p = +12$

3. $-8 = -2N$

4. $+20 = 5m$

5. $0 = 5R$

6. $-20 = 4B$

7. $3M = -15$

8. $7w = -14$

9. $0 = -3b$

10. $-6k = +18$

11. $-3C = 12$

12. $+15 = -3g$

13. $+9 = 9A$

14. $-6X = +12$

15. $-4n = -16$

Challenge: When you are given an equation to solve like these, can you just look at the *notation* involving the variable in the first step, for example, $-3C$, and decide which number to multiply by that variable group in the second step? Explain your answer.

_____

_____

_____

_____

_____

_____

_____

_____

_____

_____

_____

_____

_____

19. *Ask:* "When you are given an equation to solve like these in the first step, can you just look at the *notation* involving the variable, for example, –3C, and decide which number to multiply by that variable group in the second step?" Hopefully, students will recognize that the **denominator** of the unit fraction being multiplied by the variable group (for example, $\frac{1}{3}$ being multiplied by –3C) matches the **digit** that tells how many variables are present (e.g., the 3 in –3C; –3 itself is a number, not a digit). This digit is the **absolute value** of the **coefficient** of the variable C; the coefficient is the numerical factor in the variable group. If students do not see this pattern at first, highlight the numbers involved in colored chalk, e.g., $\frac{1}{3}$ (–3C). Have students look at their recorded steps for the other equations they have already worked to verify whether the pattern holds for them as well. As an extension, *ask:* "What is the special relationship that numbers like $\frac{1}{3}$ and 3, or $\frac{1}{4}$ and 4, have under multiplication?" *(each pair has a product of 1; two numbers whose product is 1 are called* **multiplicative inverses** *or* **reciprocals** *of each other)* The above pattern search will prepare students for another pattern search that will occur in Objective 6.

Note: In the above notation discussion and throughout Activity 1 and Activity 2, a positive fraction (e.g., $\frac{1}{3}$ or $+\frac{1}{3}$, and not $-\frac{1}{3}$) has been used as the multiplier with a negative variable group (e.g., with –3C) because the positive number reflects the type of separation and sharing that has taken place either physically with the tiles or pictorially with the diagram. If we had used a negative fraction instead, a different building or drawing procedure would have been followed. Do not introduce alternative notation at this time; such changes in format will interfere with the consistency of the process being developed in this and following lessons. All symbolic notation must reflect the steps being used with the physical materials and diagrams.

Activity 3: NAME CHANGE!

[Application/Exploration]

Materials: Paper
Regular pencils
Colored markers *(optional)*
Worksheet 2–4–3

Management: Teams of 4 students each (50 minutes)

Directions:

1. Give each team one or two different equations that involve the *separation* or *division* process. Both upper- and lower-case letters will be used for the unknowns in this activity.

2. Students are to create a story problem (preferably a silly one!) to go with each equation. The name of the real object selected to be used in a story should begin with the letter given in the equation as the unknown. If preferred, students might also draw and color illustrations for their story problems.

3. After each team has created one or two story problems, they will exchange only their story problems and illustrations (no equations or unknowns given) with another team, who will have to determine the correct equation and unknown to use for each new problem, then solve the equation and describe the result. Solutions will be shared with the entire class in order to be checked for accuracy. The letter used for each unknown by the solving team might also be compared to the one originally used by the writing team; the letters may differ since the writing team will not have revealed their chosen letter in the story problem. Here are examples of equations and their story problems. (In this activity, equations like aX = b, where *a* and *b* are both negative, will not be used. Refer to Section 1, Objective 4 for more situations involving integers in multiplication.)

(a)   8K = +72

"Eight kangaroos went for a hop together. They spied a big patch of giant kuckaberries. Being quite hungry, they worked together to **gather 72** kuckaberries in all, then shared them equally with each other. That helped some of the taller ones, who found it difficult to reach down to the low bushes. How many delicious kuckaberries did each fortunate kangaroo get to eat?" (K = number of kuckaberries gathered per animal; *K* will be positive to show gathering action)

(b)   5g = –30

"Five elephants decided to go on a diet to lose some extra gazzles they had gained during their last circus tour. After several weeks of drinking only water, they all lost the same amount of weight. Together they **lost 30** gazzles. How many gazzles did each elephant lose?" (g = number of gazzles lost by each elephant; *g* will be negative to show the losing action)

(c)   –6M = +24 (This is the more difficult type of equation to interpret.)

"In Backwardville tuba parades always begin at the courthouse and **march toward the schoolhouse.** One day a hurricane blew through town during a parade, leaving the local band still intact, without the loss of a single tuba or member, but **now marching toward the courthouse.** All band members were still in their original positions. To the amazement of the townspeople, all 24 band members were now **facing** in the direction of their **marching.** If there were six rows of band members marching at the beginning and at the end, how many members were in each row and how was each person moving before the hurricane hit?" (M = number of band members per row; use +24 since all face in the direction they are moving at the end, and use –6 as multiplier to show 6 rows changed the direction of their original march; –4 for M indicates 4 people per row, but each person was marching **backward** at the beginning before the hurricane hit)

4. Here are some possible equations to use for this activity. (See Worksheet 2–4–3.)

14M = +56	+80 = 20j	19w = –57	+99 = 11B
–96 = 8T	40A = +200	+63 = 7e	–25h = +125
+88 = –22X	13k = +91	–144 = 12V	50C = +350

WORKSHEET 2–4–3
Name Change!

Create your own story problems to go with these equations.

1. $14M = +56$

2. $+99 = 11B$

3. $+63 = 7e$

4. $13k = +91$

5. $+80 = 20j$

6. $-96 = 8T$

7. $-25h = +125$

8. $-144 = 12V$

9. $19w = -57$

10. $40A = +200$

11. $+88 = -22X$

12. $50C = +350$

OBJECTIVE 5: Combine processes to solve linear equations of the form: aX + b = c, where *a* is an integer and *b, c* and *X* are real numbers.

Activity 1: BALANCING WITH UNKNOWNS

[Developing Action]

Materials: Sets of tiles (from Objective 1, Activity 1) and building mats (from Objective 3, Activity 1)
Pieces of colored yarn (approx. 12 in. long) or coffee stirrers
Paper
Regular pencils
Worksheet 2–5–1

Management: Partners (50 minutes)

Directions:

1. Give each pair of students a set of tiles and a building mat (see Activity 1 from Objective 1 and Objective 3 of this section for descriptions of the tiles and mat). Ten additional unit tiles will be needed. Also give each pair a coffee stirrer or piece of colored yarn. In this lesson, it is assumed that students have already completed the activities of Objective 3 and Objective 4.

2. Have students place 9 negative unit tiles on the left side of their building mat, and 2 variable tiles of the same size and color (no X-side showing) and 3 negative unit tiles on the right side of their building mat. Discuss the idea that when there is more than one variable tile on the mat and we want to find the value of one variable tile, we must first isolate all the variable tiles together on the same side of the mat. Then we can separate them to find the value of one of the variable tiles.

3. *Ask:* "If we need the variable tiles alone on one side of the mat and, in this example, the 2 variable tiles are on the right side, what must be removed from the right side?" *(the 3 negative unit tiles)* "How can we remove them?" *(by simply taking –3 from the right side of the mat, or by adding on +3 to the right side to form three 0-pairs)* Allow students to choose the approach to use, but remind them that they must keep the two sides of the mat "balanced"; what they do to one side must also be done to the other side.

4. After students have either added +3 to both sides of the mat and removed any 0-pairs formed, or removed –3 from both sides of the mat, 6 negative unit tiles will remain on the left side of the mat and the 2 variable tiles will remain on the right side. The 2 variable tiles should then be separated into two rows lined up against the vertical bar of the mat, and the 6 negative unit tiles should also be separated into two equal rows, each row of unit tiles in line with one of the variable tiles. One complete row on the mat shows that –3 balances with one variable tile. That is, one variable tile has the value of –3.

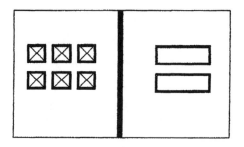

5. Now show students how to record the steps they used. Here are the two methods they might use:

(a) remove and separate:
$$-9 = 2B + (-3)$$
$$\underline{-(-3) \qquad -(-3)}$$
$$-6 = 2B$$
$$\tfrac{1}{2}(-6) = \tfrac{1}{2}(2B)$$
$$-3 = B$$

(b) add-on and separate:
$$-9 = 2B + (-3)$$
$$\underline{+(+3) \qquad +(+3)}$$
$$-6 = 2B$$
$$\tfrac{1}{2}(-6) \quad \tfrac{1}{2}(2B)$$
$$-3 = B$$

6. Have students confirm their solutions by rebuilding the original equation, $-9 = 2B + (-3)$, on their mats. They should then replace each variable tile on the mat with 3 negative unit tiles. The mat now shows -9 on the left side, and 2 groups of -3 and another -3, a total of -9, on the right; this is a true equality. Students should also record the number sentence for their substitution: $-9 = 2(-3) + (-3)$.

7. Now have students build the equation $(+5) + (-3G) = -7$ on their mats. There will be 5 positive unit tiles and 3 inverse variable tiles (of equal length and color) on the left side of the mat, and 7 negative unit tiles on the right side. Allow students to choose which method they use to isolate the inverse variables on one side. For the add-on method, they will just bring in -5 to both sides of the mat and remove the five 0-pairs formed on the left side. For the removal method, they will first need to bring in five 0-pairs on the right side before they can remove $+5$.

8. The 3 inverse variable tiles are now isolated on the left side of the mat and 12 negative unit tiles are on the right side. Students should separate the inverse variable tiles into 3 rows on the left, and should separate the unit tiles into 3 equal rows on the right, each row in line with one of the 3 inverse variable tiles.

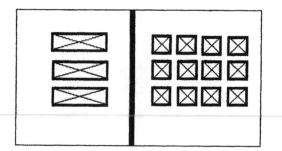

9. Each complete row on the mat shows that –G has a value of –4. Since the value of G is needed instead of the value of –G, have students place a piece of colored yarn or a coffee stirrer below the three rows containing –G, then form a new row of "opposites" below the yarn or coffee stirrer. This shows that G must have the value of +4.

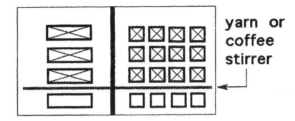

10. Students should record equations that show the steps they used with the tiles to solve for G. Here are the two methods they might use:

(a) remove and separate:

$$(+5) + (-3G) = \quad -7$$
$$- (+5) \qquad\qquad - (+5)$$
$$\overline{\qquad\qquad\qquad}$$
$$-3G = \quad -12$$
$$\tfrac{1}{3}(-3G) = \tfrac{1}{3}(-12)$$
$$-G = -4$$
$$\text{So, } G = +4$$

(b) add-on and separate:

$$(+5) + (-3G) = \quad -7$$
$$+ (-5) \qquad\qquad + (-5)$$
$$\overline{\qquad\qquad\qquad}$$
$$-3G = \quad -12$$
$$\tfrac{1}{3}(-3G) = \tfrac{1}{3}(-12)$$
$$-G = -4$$
$$\text{So, } G = +4$$

11. Again, the solution of G = +4 needs to be confirmed. Students should rebuild the original equation, $(+5) + (-3G) = -7$, on the mat and replace each **inverse** variable tile with –4. Then the left side will show +5 with 3 groups of –4 each, which is a total value of –7, and the right side will show –7. This is a true equality, so G = +4 is the correct solution. Students should record their substitution equation: $(+5) + 3(-4) = -7$. **Note:** Some students may view the 3 inverse variable tiles as "the opposite of 3G" rather than "3 of the opposite of G." In this case, their substitution equation might be written as $(+5) + (-3)(+4) = -7$.

12. Now write several other equations for students to build and solve. (See Worksheet 2–5–1.) For each equation solved, they should also record their steps in symbolic notation, confirm their solution, and write a substitution equation, using the solution found. Here are some possible equations to use. (Remind students that if only variable tiles are on one side of the mat and the other side is empty, i.e., equals 0, then when the variable tiles are separated, each variable tile must equal 0.)

$2P + (-5) = +3$	$3k + (+2) = -7$	$+12 = 5M + (+2)$	$-2n + (+6) = -2$
$-4y + (-1) = +7$	$-5 = (-5) + (-2r)$	$+11 = (-3) + (-7m)$	$+5 = (+2) + 3B$
$(+4) + 5C = +4$	$+14 = -4d + (-2)$	$6p + (-1) = -7$	$+8 = (-2a) + (+4)$

WORKSHEET 2–5–1
Balancing with Unknowns

Here are equations for you to build and solve. For each equation solved, record your steps in symbolic notation, confirm your solution, and write a substitution equation using the solution found.

1. $2P + (-5) = +3$

2. $-2n + (+6) = -2$

3. $+11 = (-3) + (-7m)$

4. $+14 = -4d + (-2)$

5. $3k + (+2) = -7$

6. $-4y + (-1) = +7$

7. $+5 = (+2) + 3B$

8. $6p + (-1) = -7$

9. $+12 = 5M + (+2)$

10. $-5 = (-5) + (-2r)$

11. $(+4) + 5C = +4$

12. $+8 = (-2a) + (+4)$

Activity 2: PICTURING SOLUTIONS

[Bridging Action]

Materials: Paper
Regular pencils
Red pencils
Tiles and mats from Activity 1 *(optional)*
Worksheet 2–5–2

Management: Partners (50 minutes)

Directions:

1. Give each pair of students a red pencil. Some students may still prefer to work with the tiles; this is acceptable. Encourage them to first build an equation with their tiles, then draw diagrams that show the steps they used to solve the equation. Eventually they will lay aside the tiles and begin drawing diagrams to find solutions.

2. Write the equation $3a + (-2) = +4$ on the chalkboard. Show students how to draw a diagram that represents tiles on a mat. All rectangles for variables should be the same size, and small squares should be used for the units. Here is an example of how the diagram should look for this equation.

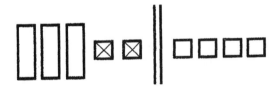

3. *Ask:* "If we want to isolate the 3 variables and we need to remove the −2 on the left, how shall we do this?" Again, two methods are possible, and they involve the same number of changes in the unit tiles. As in Activity 1, allow students to use whichever method they prefer.

4. Here are the two methods shown with diagrams:

(a) add-on [pairings of opposites show 0-pairs]:

(b) remove:

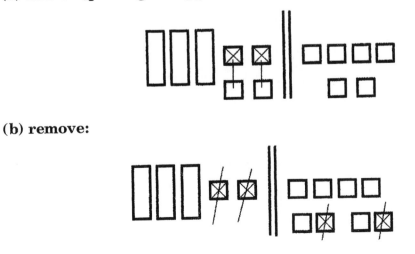

5. Now there are 3 variables on the left and 6 positive units on the right. As shown in Activity 1, the variables need to be separated into 3 rows and similarly the units need to be separated into 3 rows, each row of units lining up with one variable. Have students draw a bar under the first diagram, then draw another diagram that shows the separations into rows. One complete row shows the solution, or the value of the variable in the original equation. Have students draw a red path around one of the rows.

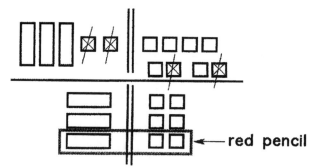

6. All the steps used should now be recorded in symbolic notation. Here are the two ways, depending on the steps used by the students:

(a) add-on and separation:

$$
\begin{aligned}
3a + (-2) &= \quad +4 \\
+ (+2) \quad & + (+2) \\
\hline
3a &= \quad +6 \\
\tfrac{1}{3}(3a) &= \tfrac{1}{3}(+6) \\
a &= \quad +2
\end{aligned}
$$

(b) removal and separation:

$$
\begin{aligned}
3a + (-2) &= \quad +4 \\
- (-2) \quad & - (-2) \\
\hline
3a &= \quad +6 \\
\tfrac{1}{3}(3a) &= \tfrac{1}{3}(+6) \\
a &= \quad +2
\end{aligned}
$$

7. To confirm their solution of a = +2, have students use their red pencils to draw 2 small squares on top of each variable rectangle in the original equation to show +2 replacing each variable. This will reveal 3 groups of +2 and a −2 on the left side, for a total value of +4, and another +4 on the right. This is a true equality, so the solution of +2 is correct. Have students record the substitution equation for the steps they used to check their solution: $3(+2) + (-2) = +4$.

units in red pencil

8. Now write the equation $-15 = (-3) + (-4P)$ on the board for students to draw. Again, allow them to choose their own method; in this case, the removal method might be the easier method for many. The diagrams for both methods are shown below, including the separation step.

(a) removal and separation:

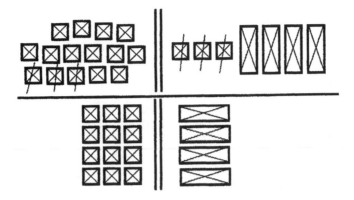

(b) add-on and separation:

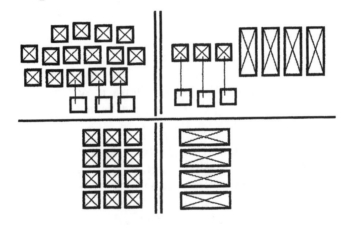

9. One complete row now shows that $-P = -3$, but we need to know the value of P itself. Students should draw another horizontal bar under the last row shown, then draw a row of "opposites," followed by a red path around the "opposites" row. This shows that P equals +3, which is the solution sought.

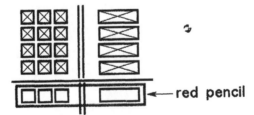

← red pencil

10. Students should record their steps symbolically according to the steps they used. Here are the two possible recordings:

(a) removal and separation:

$$
\begin{aligned}
-15 &= (-3) + (-4P) \\
-(-3) &\quad -(-3) \\
\hline
-12 &= -4P \\
\tfrac{1}{4}(-12) &= \tfrac{1}{4}(-4P) \\
-3 &= -P \\
\text{So, } +3 &= P
\end{aligned}
$$

(b) add-on and separation:

$$
\begin{array}{rcl}
-15 &=& (-3) + (-4P) \\
+(+3) && +\,(+3) \\
\hline
-12 &=& -4P \\
\tfrac{1}{4}(-12) &=& \tfrac{1}{4}(-4P) \\
-3 &=& -P \\
\text{So, } +3 &=& P
\end{array}
$$

11. The solution, P = +3, now needs to be confirmed. Since –P is in the original equation, students should use –P = –3 for the substitution. Here is the confirmed diagram.

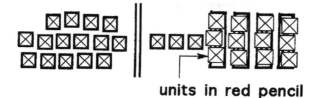

units in red pencil

12. The diagram shows –15 on the left, and a –3 amount along with 4 other groups of –3 on the right (a total value of –15 on the right). This true equality confirms that P = +3 is the correct solution. Students should write the following equation to show their substitution: –15 = (–3) + 4(–3). **Note:** Some students may view –4P as "the opposite of 4P" instead of "4 of the opposite of P"; if so, their substitution equation might be –15 = (–3) + (–4)(+3).

13. Now write several other equations for students to solve by drawing diagrams. (See Worksheet 2–5–2.) All steps drawn must be recorded with symbolic notation. Also, the solution should be confirmed each time and the substitution equation recorded. Here are some possible equations to use. (In these equations, students will receive more experience with the format, aX – b [removing b from aX], which is equivalent to the format, aX + (–b) [adding on the opposite of b to aX]. Discuss these two formats with students. Remind them that the latter format results from bringing in 0-pairs in order to remove b.)

3P + (+3) = –9	(–2) + (–7w) = +5	+6 = (–4) + 2C	(+4) – 3g = –8
+14 = (–2) + (–8k)	+11 = –4M – 9	–9N + (–3) = +15	5X + (+7) = +7
(–5) + 2a = –5	+3 = 6B + (–3)	7y – 9 = +5	–13 = (+5) – 6m

Note: Here is an example of a diagram for an equation where the solution is 0. Students should draw a "sloppy zero" instead of leaving the numerical side of the diagram blank, i.e., a space with no units shown. Otherwise, students will forget why a **blank** space is present and try to draw something there to make it "look right." Here is the diagram for the equation: –2b + (+3) = +3, where –b = 0 and b = 0.

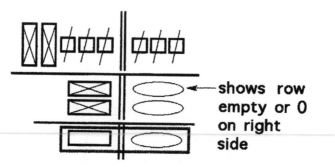

shows row empty or 0 on right side

Name _____ **Date** _____

WORKSHEET 2-5-2
Picturing Solutions

Here are equations for you to solve by drawing diagrams. Record all steps drawn with symbolic notation.

1. $3a + (-2) = +4$

2. $3P + (+3) = -9$

3. $+6 = (-4) + 2C$

4. $+14 = (-2) + (-8k)$

5. $-9N + (-3) = +15$

6. $(-5) + 2a = -5$

7. $7y - 9 = +5$

8. $-15 = (-3) + (-4P)$

9. $(-2) + (-7w) = +5$

10. $(+4) - 3g = -8$

11. $+11 = -4M - 9$

12. $5X + (+7) = +7$

13. $+3 = 6B + (-3)$

14. $-13 = (+5) - 6m$

Activity 3: EQUATION SCRAMBLE

[Application/Exploration]

Materials: Decks of cards (described in step 1)
Calculators
Tiles and mats from Activity 1 *(optional)*

Management: Teams of 4 students each (30 minutes)

Directions:

1. Give each team a deck of 36 cards containing different equations. Each deck will have 12 "books" of cards. A "book" will consist of 3 cards: one card will contain an equation of the form $aX + b = c$; another card will have the equivalent of $aX = c - b$; and a third card will contain $X = (c - b)/a$ or its equivalent. All equations will be simplified. Tell students that, where applicable, the equation in terms of the single inverse variable (e.g., $-X = ?$) will be omitted; only the final solution equation in terms of the single, original variable (e.g., $X = ?$) will be included. The cards may be made from cardstock, tagboard, or unlined, colored index cards, and laminated. Each card should be about 3 in. by 4 in. in size. For ease of reading, equations should be written lengthwise on the cards.

2. Each team should shuffle its deck of cards and distribute the cards equally to the four team members. The first player will start the game by placing a card containing an "initial" equation, i.e., an equation of the form $aX + b = c$ in the center of the table. After that, the players will take turns placing a card in the center of the table in an effort to match to an "initial" equation already played. If a player has no cards that contain other equations in the solution sequence of an "initial" equation already on the table, she or he may play a new "initial" equation to begin a new "book"; if this is not possible, the player must pass.

3. A team will work cooperatively to make the various "books," but no player may give any of her or his cards to another player on the team. Players may only show their cards to the other players as they put cards down on the table to help form a "book." The entire team must approve a card being offered by a player in order for it to remain as part of a "book."

4. Some teams may find it helpful to solve an "initial" equation with the tiles and building mat, or with a calculator. Since the focus of the game is on finding correct solution sequences and not on accuracy of computation, such aids should be allowed. Their use will only strengthen the students' understanding of the solution process. Nevertheless, encourage students to solve mentally whenever possible, instead of using the aids mentioned above or even paper and pencil.

5. When all 3 cards of a "book" have been found, the players must arrange the cards side by side with the "initial" equation on the left, the $aX = c - b$ equation in the middle, and the $X = (c - b)/a$ equation on the right. These 3-card arrangements must be left spread out and face up on the table until all "books" have been found.

6. Then the teacher should check all arrangements for correct cards and correct order, or the team may be given an answer key that lists all the correct arrangements.

Any errors found should be discussed and corrected by the team with the teacher or with an assigned checker.

7. Here is a possible list of equations that might be used for a deck of cards. (Each row reflects a correct left-to-right arrangement for 3 equations in a solution sequence; in some sequences, the left and right sides of an equation may be reversed to increase awareness of the properties of an equality; students will see equation notation in a variety of formats; only one letter will be used as the variable to avoid giving students any hints regarding which cards match.)

$3m + (+5) = -13$	$3m = -18$	$m = -6$
$(-4) + (-5m) = +16$	$-5m = +20$	$m = -4$
$+12 = 2m - 8$	$2m = +20$	$+10 = m$
$-5m + 6.3 = +1.3$	$-5.0 = -5m$	$m = +1$
$4 + 6m = -14$	$-18 = 6m$	$m = -3$
$+11 = -3m - 4$	$+15 = -3m$	$-5 = m$
$+30 = (-12) + 7m$	$+42 = 7m$	$+6 = m$
$9m + 10 = -17$	$-27 = 9m$	$-3 = m$
$(+12) - 10m = +2$	$-10m = -10$	$+1 = m$
$2m - 5.7 = +6.3$	$2m = +12.0$	$m = +6$
$-9 = (-15m) - 9$	$0 = -15m$	$m = 0$
$3m + 1.5 = +7.5$	$3m = +6$	$+2 = m$

OBJECTIVE 6: Solve linear equations involving fractional amounts of a variable.

Activity 1: A WHOLE IN ONE!

[Developing Action]

Materials: Tile sets and building mats from Chapter 2, Objective 5
Paper
Regular pencils
Pieces of colored yarn (approx. 12 in. long) or coffee stirrers
Extra construction paper (use colors that match the variable tiles in the sets)
Scissors

Management: Partners (50–90 minutes)

Directions:

1. Give each pair of students a set of tiles, a building mat, a piece of yarn or coffee stirrer, scissors, and a sheet of construction paper (same color as some of their variable tiles).

2. Have students cut out 6 rectangular strips from their sheet of construction paper. The paper strips should be the same size and color as one of their variable tiles. Show them how to fold the paper strips, mark the creases, and label the parts with fractional names. Two strips should be folded and labeled for halves, two more strips for thirds, and another two strips for fourths. Use the ratio format for the fractional parts, for example, $\frac{1}{2}$, $\frac{1}{3}$, and $\frac{1}{4}$. On one side of each *fractional part* made, have students mark a thin, large X to represent the **inverse** of the fractional part. Be sure that the X does not show through on the other side of the paper. Additional paper strips may be cut out as needed.

3. Ask students to cut the two halves of a variable apart and place one of the halves on the left side of their building mat. Describe this part as "one-half of a variable." Five positive unit tiles should then be placed on the right side of the mat.

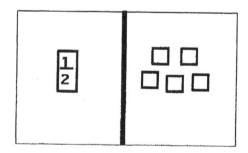

4. Discuss the idea that when we are looking for a *solution* to an equation, we usually are wanting the value of a single, **whole** variable. *Ask:* "**How many in all** of this variable part do we need in order to have a whole variable tile?" (*need two parts, or 2 halves total*) Be careful **not** to ask "**how much more** do we need?"; this question leads to the wrong action for this situation, that is, addition of another part. We are needing multiplication at this point.

5. Have students place another half-variable tile on the left side of their mat. *Ask:* "Since you have **doubled** the number of half-variable tiles on the left, what must you do to the amount of tiles on the right side of the mat to keep the two sides balanced?" (*must **double** the +5; do not say that 5 **more** positive units must be **brought in**—this implies addition; again, we need multiplication here*) Students should now place another group of +5 on the right side and arrange all the tiles as shown.

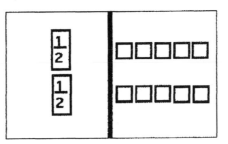

6. *Ask:* "How much of a variable tile do you now have on the left side of your mat?" (*move two halves together to show one whole variable*) "What value does that variable have according to your tiles on the mat?" (*+10*) Show students how to record the steps they have used in the following way. (Read $\frac{1}{2}$B as "one-half of the variable B.")

$$\frac{1}{2}B = +5$$
$$2(\tfrac{1}{2}B) = 2(+5)$$
$$B = +10$$

7. Students need to confirm their solution of B = +10. Have them rebuild the original equation with a half-variable tile on the left side of the mat and +5 on the right. Since B = +10, they should place 10 positive units at the top of the mat on the left side, then separate them into 2 equal groups. Only half of B's value is needed on the left, so $\frac{1}{2}$B should be exchanged for one of the two groups, or +5; the other group of +5 should be removed from the left side of the mat. Now +5 remains on both sides of the mat, showing a true equality. Thus, B = +10 is the correct solution. Have students write equations or number sentences to show the substitution used:

$$\tfrac{1}{2}(+10) = +5$$
$$+5 = +5$$

8. Ask students to cut the four fourths of a variable apart and place one of the fourths with the X-side facing up on the right side of their building mat. Describe this part as "one-fourth of an inverse variable." Three negative unit tiles should then be placed on the left side of the mat.

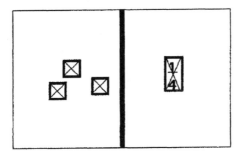

9. *Ask:* "**How many in all** of this variable part do we need in order to have a whole inverse variable tile?" *(need four parts, or 4 negative or inverse fourths total)* Again, be careful **not** to ask "**how much more** do we need?"

10. Have students place other negative fourth-variable tiles on the right side of their mat until they have four parts total. *Ask:* "Since you have **quadrupled** the number of variable parts on the right, what must you do to the amount of tiles on the left side of the mat to keep the two sides balanced?" *(must **quadruple** the −3; do not say that 9 **more** negative units must be **brought in**—this implies addition; again, we need multiplication here)* Students should now place additional groups of −3 on the left side until they have four such groups in all, and arrange all the tiles as shown.

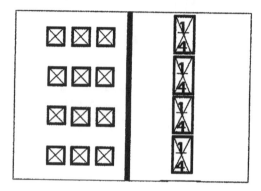

11. *Ask:* "How much of an inverse variable tile do you now have on the right side of your mat?" *(move the four fourths together to show one whole inverse variable)* "What value does that variable have according to your tiles on the left side of the mat?" *(−12)* Generally, a *solution* refers to the value of the original variable, not the inverse variable, so have students place their yarn piece or coffee stirrer below the last row of tiles. Below the yarn or stirrer, a plain variable tile (the **opposite** of the four inverse fourths already on the mat) should be placed vertically on the right side of the mat and 4 rows of +3, or +12 (the **opposite** of −12), should be placed on the left side. This shows +12 to be the solution.

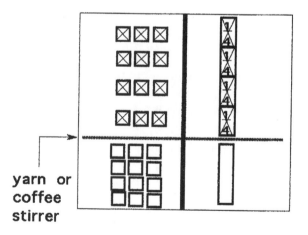

yarn or coffee stirrer

12. Show students how to record the steps they have used with symbolic notation in the following way. (Read $-\frac{1}{4}A$ as "one-fourth of the inverse or opposite of variable A.")

$$-3 = -\tfrac{1}{4}A$$
$$4(-3) = 4(-\tfrac{1}{4}A)$$
$$-12 = -A$$
$$\text{So, } +12 = A$$

13. Students need to confirm their solution of $A = +12$. Have them rebuild the original equation, $-3 = -\frac{1}{4}A$, on the mat. If $A = +12$, but an **inverse** variable part is on the mat, students should place 12 **negative** units at the top of the mat above the variable part on the right side, then separate them into 4 equal groups. Only a fourth of $-A$'s value is needed on the right, so $-\frac{1}{4}A$ should be exchanged for one of the four groups, or -3; the other groups of -3 should be removed from the right side of the mat. Now -3 remains on both sides of the mat, showing a true equality. Thus, $A = +12$ is the correct solution. Have students write equations or number sentences to show the substitution used:

$$-3 = \tfrac{1}{4}(-12)$$
$$-3 = -3$$

Note: Some students may view $-\frac{1}{4}A$ as the "opposite of a fourth of A" instead of "a fourth of $-A$"; hence, they might prefer to write the substitution equation as $-3 = -\frac{1}{4}(+12)$. Either form is acceptable.

14. Now have students cut apart a variable tile folded into thirds and place two of the thirds on the right side of the mat. Four negative unit tiles should be placed on the left side.

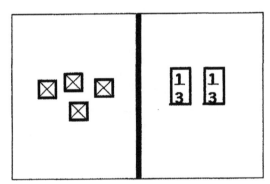

15. *Ask:* "If we only had a single third of a variable tile, how many parts of that size would be needed to make a whole variable tile?" *(three of the parts or thirds make a whole variable tile)* "Then **how much of this set** of variable parts now on the mat do we need in order to have only one third of a variable tile on the mat?" (*half of the set, or one of two equal groups formed from the set of parts;* in this case, a "group" is just one of the thirds) Avoid asking "**how many of these parts** do we need to **remove** or **take-away** from the mat?"; **take-away** is associated with **subtraction,** and multiplication is needed here. Temporarily have students separate the two thirds on the right side from each other, placing one part above the other. This is preparation for later taking **half of** each side of the mat, which is multiplication.

16. Discuss the idea that since two equal groups have been formed on the right, two equal groups should also be formed from the 4 negative units on the left in order to keep the two sides of the mat balanced in their actions. One group of −2 should be lined up with each third of a variable. One complete row of a third of a variable and 2 negative unit tiles may now be removed from the mat. This completes the **"half of"** process.

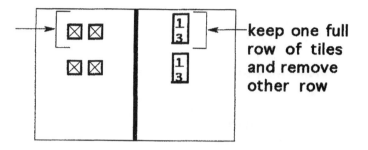

17. Have students record in symbols the steps they have performed so far:

$$-4 = \tfrac{2}{3}N$$
$$\tfrac{1}{2}(-4) = \tfrac{1}{2}(\tfrac{2}{3}N)$$
$$-2 = \tfrac{1}{3}N$$

18. *Ask:* "Since we now have the single part that we said we wanted earlier, **how many in all** of this variable part remaining on the right do we need in order to have a whole variable tile?" *(need three parts, or 3 thirds total)* Again, be careful **not** to ask "**how much more** do we need?"; this question leads to the wrong action for this situation, that is, addition of two more parts. We are still needing multiplication here. Have students place two more thirds of a variable on the right side.

19. *Ask:* "Since we have **tripled** the number of thirds of a variable on the right, what must we do on the left to balance this action?" *(**triple** the number of rows of −2 on the left)* Two more rows of −2 should be placed on the left side of the mat in line with the new fractional variable parts on the right. There should now be three complete rows of tiles on the mat, each row containing 2 negative unit tiles and a third of a variable tile.

Note: The "removal" of a complete row of tiles in step 16 earlier, followed by the present "placing" of a similar row of tiles back on the mat, is necessary in order to establish the procedures needed for this particular objective. Even though the "remove a row, 169 place a row" sequence appears to be a reversal, it really is not. The "removal" involved two rows of tiles, whereas the "placing" involves three rows.

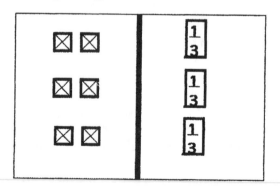

20. The three thirds of a variable tile needed to form a whole variable tile are now present on the right side of the mat. So one whole variable tile must have the value shown on the left, that of –6. Have students record additional equations below the previous ones to show the new steps they have taken:

$$-4 = \tfrac{2}{3}N$$
$$\tfrac{1}{2}(-4) = \tfrac{1}{2}(\tfrac{2}{3}N)$$
$$-2 = \tfrac{1}{3}N$$
$$3(-2) = 3(\tfrac{1}{3}N)$$
$$-6 = N$$

21. The solution, N = –6, now needs to be confirmed. Have students rebuild the original equation on their mats. They should place 6 negative unit tiles at the top of the mat on the right side above the two variable parts. Since two-thirds of the value of the variable N is needed on the right, these six unit tiles should be separated into three equal groups of –2 each, then two of these groups exchanged for the two variable parts on the mat. The two variable parts and the other group of –2 should be removed from the mat. This leaves –4 on the left side of the mat and 2 groups of –2, or a total value of –4, on the right. The mat shows a true equality (–4 = –4), so the solution, N = –6, must be correct.

22. Have students write number sentences to show the substitutions they made:

$$-4 = \tfrac{2}{3}(-6)$$
$$-4 = 2(-2)$$
$$-4 = -4$$

23. Now have students show $-\tfrac{3}{4}P = +6$ with their tiles. A variable tile folded into fourths should be cut apart. A large X should be drawn on one side of each fourth of a variable, yet not show through to the other side. Three of these fourths of a variable should be placed on the left side of the mat with the X-sides facing up (call each part a "fourth of an inverse variable"), and 6 positive unit tiles should be placed on the right side of the mat.

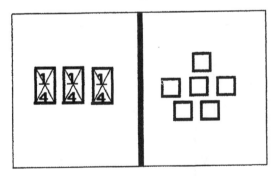

24. A single fractional part of a variable is needed before a whole variable can be found. *Ask:* "**How much of this group** of fractional parts of a variable on the left side do we need in order to isolate a single part here on the left side?" *(one out of the 3 equal parts found in the total group, or **one-third of the group** of fractional parts)* Have students show the separation of the inverse fourths of a variable by placing the three parts directly above each other.

25. **Ask:** "Now that the fractional parts of a variable have been separated into three equal portions (in this case, each portion contains only one part, an inverse fourth of a variable), what must we do to the +6 on the right in order to maintain a balance in the actions on the mat?" *(separate the 6 unit tiles into 3 equal portions of +2 each, or find **one-third of the set** of +6)* Students should now separate +6 into 3 rows of +2 each, lining up each +2 with a variable part on the other side. One complete row of tiles should be kept on the building mat and the other two rows removed; it does not matter which row is kept.

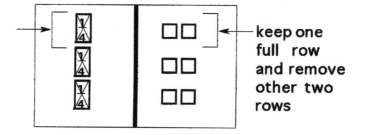

26. Write the following equations on the chalkboard to record the steps used thus far:

$$-\tfrac{3}{4}P = +6$$
$$\tfrac{1}{3}(-\tfrac{3}{4}P) = \tfrac{1}{3}(+6)$$
$$-\tfrac{1}{4}P = +2$$

27. **Ask:** "**How many of** a fourth of an inverse variable $(-\tfrac{1}{4}P)$ are needed in all to equal a whole inverse variable?" *(**four** are needed to make a whole variable here)* Have students place more inverse fourths on the left side of the mat until they have four parts in all. Since the single variable part has been **quadrupled** on the left side, the +2 must also be **quadrupled** on the right side to keep the sides of the mat balanced. The four inverse fourths now represent a whole inverse variable, –P, whose total value is shown by +8 on the right side. (If preferred, students may now replace the 4 inverse fourths on the left with a whole inverse variable tile.)

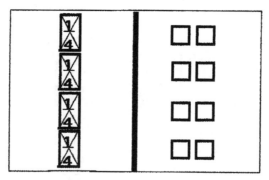

28. Remind students that when a solution is sought, usually the value of the original variable tile, not its inverse, is the value that is needed. Have them place a piece of yarn or coffee stirrer on the mat below the last row of tiles. Below the yarn or coffee stirrer, one regular variable tile (P) should be placed on the left side of the mat to show the opposite of –P, and 4 rows of –2 should be placed on the right side to show the opposite of +8. So, if –P = +8, the solution must be P = –8.

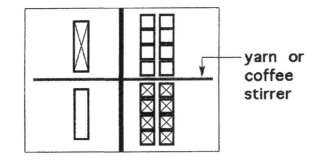

yarn or coffee stirrer

29. Record additional equations below the previous equations to show the final steps used to find the solution:

$$4(-\tfrac{1}{4}P) = 4(+2)$$
$$-P = +8$$
$$\text{So, } P = -8$$

30. The final step is to confirm the solution in the original equation, $-\tfrac{3}{4}P = +6$. Students should rebuild the original equation on their mats. Since $P = -8$, the inverse of P must be $+8$. Eight positive unit tiles should be placed on the left at the top of the mat above the inverse fourths of a variable. Fourths are needed, so the 8 unit tiles should be separated into 4 equal groups of $+2$. Each of the inverse fourths on the mat should be replaced with one of these groups of $+2$; the extra $+2$ should be removed from the mat. Hence, the left side of the mat now shows 3 groups of $+2$ and the right side shows a total of $+6$. The mat contains a true equality, $3(+2) = +6$. Thus, $P = -8$ must be the correct solution.

31. Have students write their substitution equations or number sentences below their other equations:

$$\tfrac{3}{4}(+8) = +6 \ [\tfrac{3}{4} \text{ of } -P \text{ was actually shown on mat}]$$
$$3(+2) = +6$$
$$+6 = +6$$

Note: Some students may view the notation, $-\tfrac{3}{4}P$, as "the opposite of $\tfrac{3}{4}P$," rather than "$\tfrac{3}{4}$ of the opposite of P" as used above. If so, they might prefer to write $-\tfrac{3}{4}(-8) = +6$ for their first substitution equation above.

32. Write several other equations on the board for students to build with their tiles and record their steps with symbolic notation. The solution of each original equation should be confirmed through the substitution process used in the above examples. This confirmation is very important to students' understanding. More variable tiles will need to be cut out of construction paper and folded and labeled according to the number of parts needed to build each equation. Here are some possible equations to assign to the students. (Have them build several equations from Set A before they try to build any from Set B; upper- and lower-case letters will be used for variables.)

Set A	*Set B*
$\tfrac{1}{3}B = +4$	$\tfrac{2}{5}K = +4$
$-2 = \tfrac{1}{5}p$	$-3 = \tfrac{3}{5}B$
$-\tfrac{1}{2}n = +6$	$\tfrac{2}{3}A = +6$
$-4 = -\tfrac{1}{4}C$	$+3 = -\tfrac{3}{4}m$
$\tfrac{1}{4}X = +2$	$-\tfrac{2}{4}w = +6$
$+5 = -\tfrac{1}{3}a$	$-4 = -\tfrac{2}{3}P$

Activity 2: FANCY FRACTIONS

[Bridging Action]

Materials: Paper
Regular pencils
Red pencils
Tiles and mats from Activity 1 *(optional)*
Worksheet 2–6–1

Management: Partners (50 minutes)

Directions:

1. Give each pair of students a red pencil and a packet of tiles with a building mat. Some students may still need to build with tiles in order to solve an equation; this is acceptable, so make the tiles easily available. They will lay the tiles aside when they are comfortable with the steps they are using. Each time they build an equation on the mat, have them make a diagram of their work. Eventually they will omit the tiles and just draw diagrams to solve their equations.

2. Write the equation $-\frac{1}{3}M = +2$ on the chalkboard. To make a diagram of this equation, ask students to draw a short rectangle (but slightly taller than the squares drawn for integral units) on the left side of a pair of parallel line segments (the equal sign). Have them draw a light, but large X in the interior of the rectangle and write the fraction, $\frac{1}{3}$, over the X. This will represent $-\frac{1}{3}M$, read as "one-third of the inverse of the variable M." Avoid the language "negative one-third M" until later. Two small, plain squares should then be drawn on the right side to represent +2.

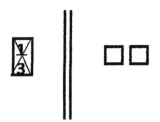

3. Remind students that when we are looking for a *solution* to an equation, we usually want the value of a single, **whole** variable. *Ask:* "**How many in all** of this variable part do we need in order to have a whole variable?" *(need three parts, or 3 thirds total)* Be careful **not** to ask "**how much more** do we need?"; this question leads to the wrong action for this situation, that is, addition of another part instead of multiplication.

4. Have students draw two more thirds of the inverse variable to the left of the vertical bars. *Ask:* "Since you have **tripled** the number of variable parts on the left, what must you do to the amount of units to the right of the vertical bars to keep the two sides balanced?" *(must **triple** the +2; do not say that 4 **more** positive units must be **brought in**—this implies addition; again, we need multiplication here) Students should now draw more groups of +2 on the right in order to have 3 groups total, arranging all the shapes as shown.

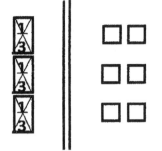

5. **Ask:** "How much of an inverse variable do you now have on the left side of your diagram?" *(draw a larger rectangle around the inverse thirds to show one whole inverse variable)* "What value does this inverse variable have according to your units on the right?" *(+6)* Show students how to record the steps they have used in the following way. (Read $-\frac{1}{3}M$ as "one-third of the inverse variable M.")

$$-\tfrac{1}{3}M = +2$$
$$3(-\tfrac{1}{3}M) = 3(+2)$$
$$-M = +6$$

6. A *solution* typically refers to the original variable, not the inverse of the variable. Have students draw a long bar across their diagram below the rows of shapes, then draw a plain rectangle on the left to represent the variable M, the opposite of –M, and 6 small squares on the right with an X in each interior to show –6, the opposite of +6. The sizes of the rectangles will not be exact, but the plain rectangle should be approximately the length of the three inverse thirds together. Students should now add the equation M = –6 at the bottom of their recording.

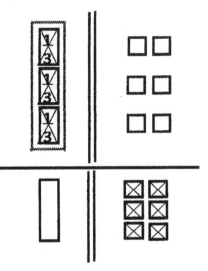

7. Students need to confirm their solution of M = –6. Have them redraw the diagram for the original equation, $-\frac{1}{3}M = +2$. Since the variable part shown in this diagram is an inverse, –M = +6 should be used. Have students draw in red pencil above the diagram 6 small squares for +6; since a third is needed, the 6 small squares should be separated with red pencil into 3 equal groups of 2 squares each. With red pencil students should now draw an arrow through one group of +2 pointed toward the single inverse part and "redraw" 2 red squares on top of the inverse part to indicate the "exchange" of +2 for $-\frac{1}{3}M$

in the diagram. The other two groups of +2 should be marked out with red pencil to show they have not been used. Now +2 is seen on both sides of the vertical bar, showing a true equality. Thus, M = −6 is the correct solution. Have students write equations or number sentences to show the substitution used:

$$\tfrac{1}{3}(+6) = +2$$
$$+2 = +2$$

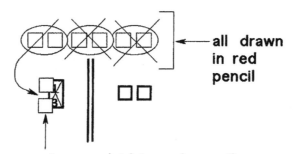

← all drawn in red pencil

units overlaid in red pencil

Note: Some students may view −⅓M as the "opposite or inverse of a third of the variable M," instead of as "a third of the inverse of the variable M." If so, their substitution may be written as −⅓(−6) = +2 instead.

8. Now write the equation, +6 = ⅔A, on the chalkboard. Read ⅔A as "two-fourths, or two out of four equal parts, of the variable A." Students should draw 6 small squares for +6 to the left of the vertical, parallel bars and two taller rectangles marked with ¼'s to the right to show ⅔A.

9. Since only one of the fourths of the variable is needed, have students draw a path around each fourth, creating two equal groups. To keep the diagram balanced, the six unit squares should also be separated into two equal groups with a path drawn around each group of 3 squares. Remind students that to eventually find a whole variable, our strategy is to begin with a single variable part, in this case the fourth. Have students re-draw one group from each side of the diagram in the following way.

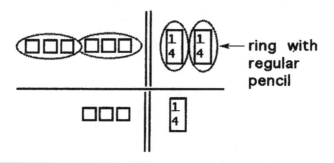

← ring with regular pencil

10. *Ask:* "Now that we have a single fourth of the variable here on the right, **how many fourths** are needed **in all** to make the whole variable?" *(4 parts, or 4 fourths)* Have students draw more fourths on the right, each lined up below the first part shown, until there are four parts in all. *Ask:* "Now that we have **quadrupled** the variable part on the right, what must we do to the units on the left to keep the two sides of the diagram balanced?" (*quadruple* the +3) Extra rows of +3 should now be drawn below the first row of +3 on the left until 4 rows in all are shown.

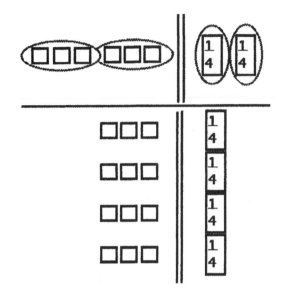

11. Have students draw a larger rectangle around the four fourths on the right to represent the whole variable, A. This final diagram shows that A has the total value of +12. Now write the steps used in symbolic notation on the chalkboard:

$$+6 = \tfrac{2}{4}A$$
$$\tfrac{1}{2}(+6) = \tfrac{1}{2}(\tfrac{2}{4}A)$$
$$+3 = \tfrac{1}{4}A$$
$$4(+3) = 4(\tfrac{1}{4}A)$$
$$+12 = A$$

12. Again, students should confirm their solution, A = +12. Have them redraw the initial diagram used in step 8. Then in red pencil they should draw 12 small squares above their diagram. Since the equation requires fourths of the variable, have them separate the 12 unit squares into four equal groups by drawing a red path around each set of 3 squares. Two fourths are needed, so a red arrow should be drawn through each of two of these groups of squares and pointed toward a fourth. To show the exchange of squares for variable parts, students should then draw 3 red squares overlaid on each variable part. The other two groups of squares should be marked out in red. The new diagram now shows +6 on the left and 2 sets of +3 on the right, which is a true equality. Thus, A = +12 is the correct solution.

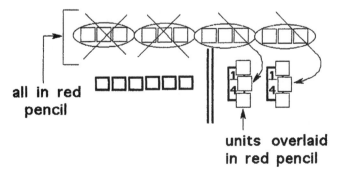

all in red pencil

units overlaid in red pencil

13. The substitution should now be recorded as number sentences:

$+6 = \frac{2}{4}(+12)$

$+6 = 2(+3)$

$+6 = +6$

14. Now write several more equations for students to solve by drawing diagrams. (See Worksheet 2–6–1.) Have them record their steps in symbolic notation, then confirm their solutions and write number sentences for the substitutions used. You might wish to have students rework some of the equations from Activity 1. Here are some additional equations to assign. (Most of these equations can also be built with the tiles if necessary; lower- and upper-case letters will be used for variables.)

Set A	Set B
$\frac{1}{2}P = -6$	$\frac{2}{3}b = +8$
$+2 = \frac{1}{4}c$	$-4 = \frac{2}{4}m$
$-\frac{1}{5}B = +2$	$-\frac{3}{5}A = +6$
$+5 = \frac{1}{3}n$	$-12 = -\frac{3}{4}X$
$-\frac{1}{2}A = -7$	$\frac{4}{5}p = -12$
$-3 = -\frac{1}{6}X$	$+6 = -\frac{2}{6}C$

15. After students have drawn diagrams to solve the equations, write the symbolic notation for only the **first, second,** and **fourth steps** taken from the complete recording of each of several of these equations. It is time for another pattern search similar to that found in Activity 2 of Objective 4. Here are some possible sets of equations to discuss:

(a) $-\frac{3}{4}P = +6$

$\frac{1}{3}(-\frac{3}{4}P) = \frac{1}{3}(+6)$

$4(-\frac{1}{4}P) = 4(+2)$

(b) $-4 = \frac{2}{3}N$

$\frac{1}{2}(-4) = \frac{1}{2}(\frac{2}{3}N)$

$3(-2) = 3(\frac{1}{3}N)$

(c) $\frac{2}{5}K = +4$

$\frac{1}{2}(\frac{2}{5}K) = \frac{1}{2}(+4)$

$5(\frac{1}{5}K) = 5(+2)$

(d) $\frac{4}{5}p = -12$

$\frac{1}{4}(\frac{4}{5}p) = \frac{1}{4}(-12)$

$5(\frac{1}{5}p) = 5(-3)$

16. The pattern discussion will occur in two stages: the combining of steps 2 and 4, and the comparing of the new combined step with step 1. Observations will now be based on the notation itself, rather than the diagrams. First *ask:* "The second step for each original equation involves multiplying the initial variable group (e.g., $-\frac{3}{4}P$) by a unit fraction, and the fourth step involves multiplying the resulting variable group (e.g., $-\frac{1}{4}P$) by a whole number. These two steps work together to produce a single, whole variable at the end. Is there some number by which we could multiply the variable group so that both steps would be carried out at the same time and still produce a single, whole variable at the end? Can we multiply by $\frac{1}{3}$ and by 4 [example (a) above] at the same time? Can we multiply by $\frac{1}{2}$ and by 3 [example (b) above] at the same time?" Give students time to think about this idea and discuss it with a partner. *Hopefully they will realize that the first example is equivalent to multiplying by $\frac{4}{3}$ and the second example is equivalent to multiplying by $\frac{3}{2}$.* Give them some simple exercises to verify this observation. For example, compare $\frac{1}{2}(+8) = +4$, followed by $5(+4) = +20$, to $\frac{5}{2}(+8) = +20$; and compare $\frac{1}{3}(-6) = -2$, followed by $4(-2) = -8$, to $\frac{4}{3}(-6) = -8$. How quickly students see these as equivalent procedures will depend on their level of mastery of fraction multiplication.

WORKSHEET 2-6-1
Fancy Fractions

Solve these equations by drawing diagrams. Record your steps in symbolic notation.

1. $-\frac{1}{3}M = +2$

2. $\frac{1}{2}P = -6$

3. $+2 = \frac{1}{4}c$

4. $-\frac{1}{5}B = +2$

5. $+5 = \frac{1}{3}n$

6. $-\frac{1}{2}A = -7$

7. $-3 = -\frac{1}{6}X$

8. $+6 = \frac{2}{4}A$

9. $\frac{2}{3}b = +8$

10. $-4 = \frac{2}{4}m$

11. $-\frac{3}{5}A = +6$

12. $-12 = -\frac{3}{4}X$

13. $\frac{4}{5}p = -12$

14. $+6 = -\frac{2}{6}C$

17. Once students are comfortable with the combining of steps 2 and 4, replace the two steps in each board example with a single step, which yields the following sets of equations:

(a) $\quad -\frac{3}{4}P = +6$

$\qquad \frac{4}{3}(-\frac{3}{4}P) = \frac{4}{3}(+6)$

(b) $\quad -4 = \frac{2}{3}N$

$\qquad \frac{3}{2}(-4) = \frac{3}{2}(\frac{2}{3}N)$

(c) $\quad \frac{2}{5}K = +4$

$\qquad \frac{5}{2}(\frac{2}{5}K) = \frac{5}{2}(+4)$

(d) $\quad \frac{4}{5}p = -12$

$\qquad \frac{5}{4}(\frac{4}{5}p) = \frac{5}{4}(-12)$

Now you are ready for the second stage of the pattern discussion. We are looking for patterns in the notation. *Ask:* "Look at the new number now being multiplied by the initial variable group (e.g., $\frac{4}{3}$ is being multiplied by the variable group, $-\frac{3}{4}P$) in each of the four sets of equations written on the board. Do you see a relationship between this new number and the original coefficient of the variable (i.e., the number factor with the variable; as an example, $-\frac{3}{4}$ is the coefficient of P)? Given another equation like we have been studying, could you predict what the new number would be just by looking at the variable group?" *Hopefully students will notice that the two numbers involved have a product of +1 or −1.* Their multiplication will lead to a single, whole variable, either the original variable or its inverse. If the absolute value of the coefficient of the variable (e.g., $\frac{3}{4}$ or $+\frac{3}{4}$ from the variable group, $-\frac{3}{4}P$) is considered with the new number ($\frac{4}{3}$ in the above example), their product will be +1, thereby making these two numbers **multiplicative inverses** or **reciprocals** of each other. Have students verify the relationship they have found between the new number and the variable's initial coefficient by checking all their other symbolic recordings made from Activity 1 and Activity 2. Activity 3 will help students apply what they have discovered.

Activity 3: RAGING RECIPROCALS!

[Application/Exploration]

Materials: Decks of cards (described in step 1)
Calculators
Paper
Regular pencils

Management: Teams of 4 students each (30–45 minutes)

Directions:

1. Give each team of students a deck of cards and a calculator. A deck will consist of 20 variable cards and 20 number cards. The variable cards should be one color and the number cards another color. Small, colored index cards or lightweight tagboard or cardstock may be used to make the decks of cards. Any fractions or rational numbers to be written on the cards should have horizontal bars, not slanted bars. For a possible deck, use the following sets of expressions, writing one expression on each card.

Variable Cards: $\frac{1}{3}B$, $\frac{3}{4}A$, $-\frac{1}{5}m$, $-\frac{5}{6}K$, $3c$, $-8d$, $\frac{7}{10}P$, $-\frac{8}{15}R$, $\frac{5}{4}X$, $\frac{1}{9}g$, $-\frac{3}{2}N$, $+\frac{5}{8}a$, $5p$, $+\frac{1}{10}R$, $+\frac{12}{5}V$, $-\frac{1}{18}b$, $-6K$, $-\frac{2}{3}M$, $\frac{5}{3}n$, $-\frac{1}{11}W$

Number Cards: $+2$, -5, $+\frac{3}{4}$, $-\frac{1}{6}$, $+8$, -12, $+25$, -30, $+\frac{5}{4}$, $-\frac{3}{2}$, $+7$, -10, $+\frac{1}{2}$, $-\frac{1}{3}$, $+\frac{1}{10}$, -100, $+\frac{1}{5}$, $-\frac{7}{8}$, $+\frac{3}{5}$, $-\frac{9}{4}$

2. This game is designed to provide review for students in the multiplication of fractions or rational numbers, including the use of whole numbers and improper fractions as factors, while they practice using reciprocals to solve equations. The coefficients of variables will be rational numbers, including some integral forms. Some positive numbers will have the (+) sign, while others will not. Discuss these various possibilities with students and review multiplication of a whole number with a fraction, as well as a fraction with a fraction. Also, have them share different ways for working such problems with their calculators. This game focuses on solving equations by means of reciprocals, not on accuracy in multiplication of rational numbers. Therefore, the calculator is an appropriate tool for the activity.

3. To begin the game, each team should shuffle its set of variable cards and place them face down in a stack in the center of the table. The process should be repeated with the number cards.

4. On each turn, a player will draw the top card off of each stack. The two cards will represent an equation. The player will first record the equation on a sheet of paper; all four players will record on the same paper. Then the player will solve the equation for the stated variable by multiplying the appropriate fraction or whole number by the value of the number card. This may be done with the calculator, mentally, or with paper and pencil. In some cases, the inverse variable will have to be found first. The steps to be recorded on the team paper are minimal, although some students may prefer to write all the details used in Activity 1 and Activity 2. As an example of a turn, suppose a player draws the variable card, $-\frac{8}{15}R$, and the number card, -10. The player records on the team paper the following steps:

$$-\frac{8}{15}R = -10$$
$$-R = \frac{15}{8}(-10) = -18.75 \text{ or } -18.8 \text{ (rounded to nearest tenth)}$$
$$R \approx +18.8$$

5. After a player finishes recording the steps used and the solution found, the previous player should confirm the solution by substitution, using the calculator. In the example shown in step 4, the confirming player might compute $+\frac{8}{15}(-18.8)$ to see that the product, -10.02, was approximately -10. The number sentence would be recorded on the team paper either beside or below the corresponding solution steps: $+\frac{8}{15}(-18.8) = -10.02 \approx -10$.

(*Alternative:* $-\frac{8}{15}(+18.8) = -10.02$ if $-\frac{8}{15}R$ is interpreted as the opposite of $\frac{8}{15}$ of the variable R.)

6. After all the cards have been drawn and 20 equations have been solved and checked by the team, the completed team paper might be turned in to the teacher for credit.

7. If time is limited, the teacher might ask each team to solve and check only 8 to 10 equations.

8. For an alternative activity, each team might solve, but not check, 8 to 10 equations, then exchange team papers with another team, who would then check the first team's solutions.

OBJECTIVE 7: Combine processes to solve linear equations of the form: $(\frac{a}{b})X + c = d$, where *a* and *b* are nonzero integers with a < b, and X, c, and d are real numbers.

Activity 1: SUPER SOLUTIONS!

[Developing Action]

Materials: Tile sets and building mats from Section 2, Objective 5
Paper
Regular pencils
Red pencils
Pieces of colored yarn (approx. 12 in. long) or coffee stirrers
Extra construction paper (use colors that match the variable tiles in the sets)
Scissors
Worksheet 2–7–1

Management: Partners (50 minutes)

Directions:

1. Give each pair of students a set of tiles, a building mat, a piece of yarn or coffee stirrer, a red pencil, scissors, and a sheet of construction paper (same color as some of their variable tiles). This lesson will combine the steps or moves with tiles that were developed in Objective 3 and Objective 6; it is assumed that students have already completed those activities.

2. Use the fractional variable tiles from Objective 6. If these are not available, have students cut out 6 rectangular strips from their sheet of construction paper. The paper strips should be the same size and color as one of their variable tiles. Show them how to fold the paper strips, mark the creases, and label the parts with fractional names. Two strips should be folded and labeled for halves, two more strips for thirds, and another two strips for fourths. Use the ratio format for the fractional parts, for example, $\frac{1}{2}$, $\frac{1}{3}$, and $\frac{1}{4}$. On one side of each *fractional part* made, have students mark a thin, large X to represent the **inverse** of the fractional part. Be sure that the X does not show through on the other side of the paper. Additional paper strips may be cut out as needed.

3. Have students build the equation $+7 = (+2) + \frac{1}{2}C$ on their mats. Seven positive unit tiles should be placed on the left side of the mat, and two positive unit tiles followed by half of a variable tile should be placed on the right side of the mat.

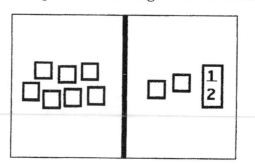

4. Remind students that the goal is to move tiles until only variable tiles are on one side of the mat and only unit tiles are on the other side. Then the variable group can either be separated or multiplied in order to isolate a single, whole variable tile on one side of the mat and show that it balances or equals some amount of unit tiles on the other side.

5. *Ask:* "To have the variable tile by itself, what do we need to do first?" *(must remove +2 from the right side in some way)* At this point students should recognize that +2 can be taken away from the right side of the mat or −2 can be placed on that same side to form two 0-pairs, which can then be taken away. Allow students to use whichever method they prefer, but they must be able to record their chosen steps in symbolic notation later. *Ask:* "Once you decide how to isolate the variable part, what must you do to keep the tiles on the mat balanced in value?" *(if you take away +2 from the tiles on the right side, you must take away +2 from the left; if you join −2 to the tiles on the right, you must place −2 on the left)* Have students carry out their chosen steps with the tiles, then record their steps with symbolic notation. The two possible mat arrangements and their respective notations are shown below:

(a) take-away method:

$$+7 \ = \ (+2) +\tfrac{1}{2}C$$
$$\underline{-(+2) \quad -(+2)}$$
$$+5 \ = \qquad \tfrac{1}{2}C$$

(b) add-on method:

$$+7 \ = \ (+2) +\tfrac{1}{2}C$$
$$\underline{+(-2) \quad +(-2)}$$
$$+5 \ = \qquad \tfrac{1}{2}C$$

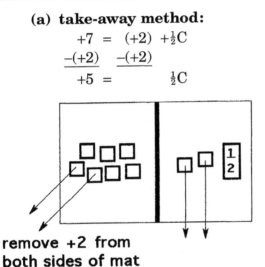

remove +2 from both sides of mat

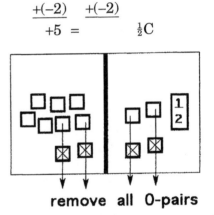

remove all 0-pairs

6. With a half of a variable tile remaining on the right side of the mat, *ask:* "How many halves do we need to form a whole variable tile?" *(two) Ask:* "So if we need two of the amount on the right, what do we need on the left?" *(two of the +5)* Have students double the amount of tiles they have on each side of the mat, then record their steps below the previous notation. The two halves of the variable may be replaced with a whole variable tile, if students prefer.

(a) take-away method:

$$+7 \ = \ (+2) +\tfrac{1}{2}C$$
$$\underline{-(+2) \quad -(+2)}$$
$$+5 \ = \qquad \tfrac{1}{2}C$$
$$2(+5) = \quad 2(\tfrac{1}{2}C)$$
$$+10 \ = \qquad C$$

(b) add-on method:

$$+7 \ = \ (+2) + \tfrac{1}{2}C$$
$$\underline{+(-2) \quad +(-2)}$$
$$+5 \ = \qquad \tfrac{1}{2}C$$
$$2(+5) = \quad 2(\tfrac{1}{2}C)$$
$$+10 \ = \qquad C$$

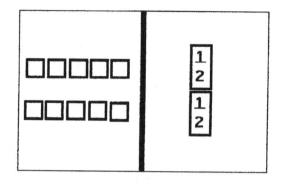

7. Students should always confirm their solutions in some way. In this activity, you should have them rebuild the original equation with tiles, then substitute the variable's discovered value in unit tiles for the variable tile itself to show the true equality. The numerical substitution will be used in Activity 2. For the above example, students should show $+7 = (+2) + \frac{1}{2}C$ on the mat again. Since $C = +10$, 10 positive units should be placed on the right side of the mat just above the variable part. A half of the variable is needed, so the 10 units should be separated into two equal groups of $+5$ each. One group of $+5$ then replaces $\frac{1}{2}C$ on the mat and the other group of $+5$ is removed from the mat. Seven positive unit tiles are now on the left, and 2 positive unit tiles combined with 5 positive unit tiles appear on the right. Since the left and right total values equal or balance each other, $C = +10$ must be the correct solution. Have students make a check mark ($\sqrt{}$) in red pencil beside their solution equation, $C = +10$, to show that they checked its correctness.

8. Now have students build the equation $\frac{2}{3}K - (+3) = -7$ with tiles. A paper variable folded into thirds should be cut apart and two of the thirds placed on the left side of the mat. Since subtraction indicates taking $+3$ off of the mat and there are not 3 positive unit tiles on the left side, three 0-pairs of positive and negative unit tiles should be placed on the left side of the mat, followed by removal of the 3 positive unit tiles. Some students may realize that subtracting $+3$ is equivalent to adding -3; if so, they may simply place -3 on the left side of the mat with the fractional variable tiles instead of working with the 0-pairs first. Finally, seven negative unit tiles should be placed on the right side of the mat.

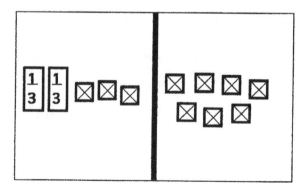

9. *Ask:* "What changes can we make to the mat that will leave the variable tiles by themselves on the left?" *(either take away −3 or bring in +3 on the left)* The students must then repeat whichever action they choose on the right side of the mat and record their steps with symbolic notation.

(a) take-away model:

$$\tfrac{2}{3}K - (+3) = \quad -7$$
$$\tfrac{2}{3}K + (-3) = \quad -7$$
$$\underline{\quad -(-3) \quad -(-3)}$$
$$\tfrac{2}{3}K \qquad = \quad -4$$

(b) add-on model:

$$\tfrac{2}{3}K - (+3) = \quad -7$$
$$\tfrac{2}{3}K + (-3) = \quad -7$$
$$\underline{\quad +(+3) \quad +(+3)}$$
$$\tfrac{2}{3}K \qquad = \quad -4$$

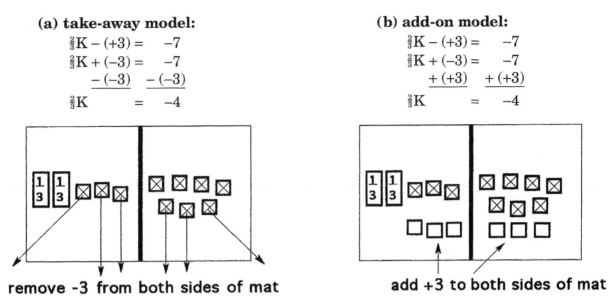

remove -3 from both sides of mat

add +3 to both sides of mat

10. *Ask:* "Two of the thirds of a variable remain on the left by themselves. What do we need to do to find a whole variable tile now?" *(first find a single third of the variable by separating the 2 variable parts or by finding "half" of the present variable group; 3 of this single third will make a whole variable tile)* Remember that you need to use *multiplication* language here, not *addition* language. After students perform these two actions—halving then tripling—on both sides of the mat, have them record their new actions as shown below:

(a) take-away model:

$$\tfrac{2}{3}K - (+3) = \quad -7$$
$$\tfrac{2}{3}K + (-3) = \quad -7$$
$$\underline{\quad -(-3) \quad -(-3)}$$
$$\tfrac{2}{3}K \qquad = \quad -4$$
$$\tfrac{1}{2}(\tfrac{2}{3}K) \quad = \quad \tfrac{1}{2}(-4)$$
$$\tfrac{1}{3}K \qquad = \quad -2$$
$$3(\tfrac{1}{3}K) \quad = \quad 3(-2)$$
$$K \qquad = \quad -6$$

(b) add-on model:

$$\tfrac{2}{3}K - (+3) = \quad -7$$
$$\tfrac{2}{3}K + (-3) = \quad -7$$
$$\underline{\quad +(+3) \quad +(+3)}$$
$$\tfrac{2}{3}K \qquad = \quad -4$$
$$\tfrac{1}{2}(\tfrac{2}{3}K) \quad = \quad \tfrac{1}{2}(-4)$$
$$\tfrac{1}{3}K \qquad = \quad -2$$
$$3(\tfrac{1}{3}K) \quad = \quad 3(-2)$$
$$K \qquad = \quad -6$$

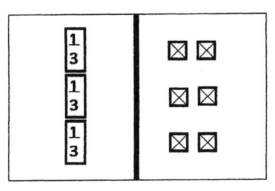

Note: Hopefully after their work with the activities of Objective 6, most students realize by now that the halving-tripling process used above can be combined and shown in the recording as follows:

$$\tfrac{2}{3}K = -4$$
$$\tfrac{3}{2}(\tfrac{2}{3}K) = \tfrac{3}{2}(-4)$$
$$K = -6$$

11. The solution, $K = -6$, should be confirmed by exchanging variable parts for units. Have students rebuild the original equation on their mats and place 6 negative unit tiles on the mat just above the variable tiles. Since thirds are involved, -6 should be separated into 3 equal groups of -2 each. Each variable part on the mat should be replaced with one of the groups of -2. The unused -2 should be removed from the top of the mat. Now 2 groups of -2, along with another group of -3, can be seen on the left side, and -7 appears on the right. Since the two sides have the same total value, $K = -6$ is the correct solution. A red check mark ($\checkmark$) should be written beside the solution equation.

12. Students should now build the equation $(-1) - \tfrac{1}{4}p = -4$ on their mats, using paper fourths of a variable. Each fourth should have an X marked on one side. First have students place -4 on the right side of the mat and -1 on the left side. Discuss the idea that, just as with unit tiles earlier, subtraction of a variable group is equivalent to the addition of the inverse variable group. Hence, after showing a 0-pair of fourths of a variable (one plain fourth and one fourth with an X-side facing up) on the left side of the mat with -1 and then removing $+\tfrac{1}{4}p$, students will have $-\tfrac{1}{4}p$ and -1 still remaining on the left side.

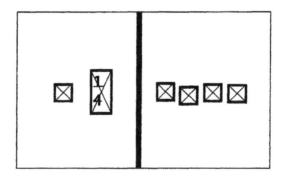

13. Students should now isolate the fourth of an inverse variable by either the take-away or the add-on method. The tiles on each side of the mat should then be quadrupled to yield four variable parts that are equivalent to a whole inverse variable, $-p$. If students prefer, they may replace the four variable parts on the mat with a whole inverse variable tile.

14. Since a solution usually involves a value for the regular variable p, not its inverse, $-p$, a coffee stirrer or piece of yarn should be placed below the last row of tiles on the mat: $-p = -12$. The inverse of $-p$ is p and the inverse of -12 is $+12$; therefore, the regular, whole variable tile should be placed on the mat below the coffee stirrer or yarn and the four fourths of the inverse variable, and 12 positive units should be placed below the negative units and coffee stirrer or yarn on the right. The building and recording are as follows:

(a) add-on method:

$$(-1) - \tfrac{1}{4}p = -4$$
$$(-1) + (-\tfrac{1}{4}p) = -4$$
$$\underline{+\ (+1) \qquad\quad +\ (+1)}$$
$$-\tfrac{1}{4}p = -3$$
$$4(-\tfrac{1}{4}p) = 4(-3)$$
$$-p = -12$$
$$\text{So, } p = +12$$

(b) take-away method:

$$(-1) - \tfrac{1}{4}p = -4$$
$$(-1) + (-\tfrac{1}{4}p) = -4$$
$$\underline{-\ (-1) \qquad\quad -\ (-1)}$$
$$-\tfrac{1}{4}p = -3$$
$$4(-\tfrac{1}{4}p) = 4(-3)$$
$$-p = -12$$
$$\text{So, } p = +12$$

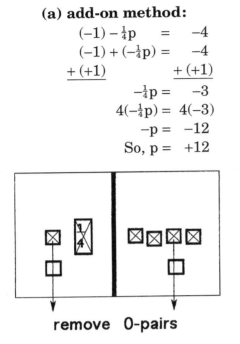

remove 0-pairs

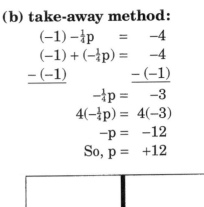

remove -1 from both
sides of mat

Final steps for both methods:

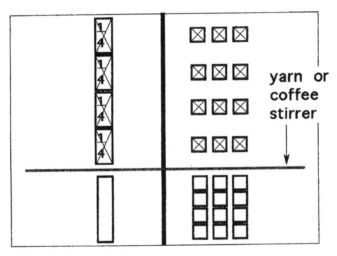

yarn or
coffee
stirrer

15. Finally the solution needs to be confirmed. The original equation should be rebuilt on the mat, including one of the fourths of the inverse variable tile. If p = +12, –p must equal –12; hence, –12 should be placed on the mat above the tiles on the left side. Since a fourth is needed, –12 should be separated into four equal groups of –3 each. One group of –3 should be exchanged with the variable part and the other three groups of –3 removed from the mat. A single, negative unit tile, as well as the group of –3, are now seen on the left side of the mat, and a group of –4 is seen on the right. Both sides of the mat have the same total value, so the solution, p = +12, is correct. A red check mark (√) should be written beside the solution equation.

16. Now write other equations for students to solve with their tiles. (See Worksheet 2–7–1.) They should record the steps they use with symbolic notation and also confirm their solutions by exchanging the appropriate amount of unit tiles for the variable tiles

WORKSHEET 2–7–1
Super Solutions!

Here are equations for you to solve with your tiles. Record the steps you use with symbolic notation. Then confirm your solutions by exchanging the appropriate amount of unit tiles for the variable tiles given in the original equation.

1. $7 = 2 + \frac{1}{2}C$

2. $-1 - \frac{1}{4}p = -4$

3. $\frac{1}{3}B + (+2) = +6$

4. $-5 = \frac{1}{5}p + (-3)$

5. $-\frac{1}{2}n - 5 = +1$

6. $-2 = -\frac{1}{4}C - (-2)$

7. $5 + \frac{1}{4}X = +7$

8. $+3 = (-2) - \frac{1}{3}a$

9. $\frac{2}{3}K - (+3) = -7$

10. $(-6) + \frac{2}{5}K = -2$

11. $-7 = \frac{3}{5}B + (-4)$

12. $\frac{2}{3}A - 4 = +2$

13. $+8 = -\frac{3}{4}m - (-2)$

14. $(-5) + (-\frac{2}{4}w) = +1$

15. $4 = 8 - \frac{2}{3}P$

16. $\frac{3}{2}B + 6 = 0$

given in the original equation. A red check mark (√) should be written beside any solution equation shown to be correct. Here are some possible equations to use:

Set A	***Set B***
$\frac{1}{3}B + (+2) = +6$	$(-6) + \frac{2}{5}K = -2$
$-5 = \frac{1}{5}p + (-3)$	$-7 = \frac{3}{5}B + (-4)$
$-\frac{1}{2}n - 5 = +1$	$\frac{2}{3}A - 4 = +2$
$-2 = -\frac{1}{4}C - (-2)$	$+8 = -\frac{3}{4}m - (-2)$
$5 + \frac{1}{4}X = +7$	$(-5) + (-\frac{2}{4}w) = +1$
$+3 = (-2) - \frac{1}{3}a$	$4 = 8 - \frac{2}{3}P$

Activity 2: SOLUTION DRAW

[Bridging Action]

Materials: Paper
Regular pencils
Calculators
Tiles and mats from Activity 1 *(optional)*
Worksheet 2–7–2

Management: Partners (50 minutes)

Directions:

1. Give each pair of students a calculator and a packet of tiles with a building mat. Some students may still need to build with tiles in order to solve an equation; this is acceptable, so make the tiles easily available. They will lay the tiles aside when they are comfortable with the steps they are using. Each time they build an equation on the mat, have them make a diagram of their work. Eventually they will omit the tiles and just draw diagrams to solve their equations.

2. Write the equation $-\frac{1}{3}M + 5 = +7$ on the chalkboard. To make a diagram of this equation, ask students to draw a short rectangle (but slightly taller than the squares drawn for integral units) on the left side of a pair of parallel line segments (the equal sign). Have them draw a light, but large X (to show the inverse) in the interior of the rectangle and write the fraction, $\frac{1}{3}$, over the X. This will represent $-\frac{1}{3}M$, read as "one-third of the inverse of the variable M." Avoid the language "negative one-third M" until later. Also draw 5 small, plain squares on the left side with the variable rectangle. Seven small, plain squares should then be drawn on the right side to represent +7.

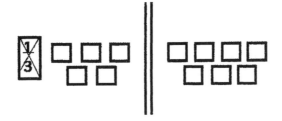

3. To isolate the variable by itself, students have the usual two methods available: remove +5 from both sides of the diagram, or bring in –5 to both sides of the diagram to form 0-pairs of the units. The transformed diagrams will appear as follows:

(a) take-away method: **(b) add-on method:**

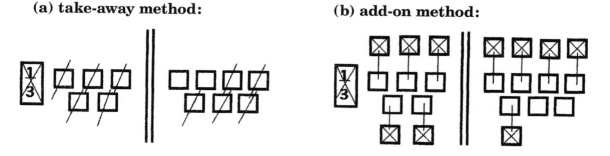

4. A horizontal bar should be drawn below the first diagram that shows the take-away or add-on step, and the remaining shapes for $-\frac{1}{3}$M on the left and +2 on the right should be redrawn below that bar. Students now need to form a whole variable. This is done by drawing more rows of shapes on the second diagram until there are 3 rows in all; each row shows a $-\frac{1}{3}$M on the left of the vertical bars and +2 on the right. Remind students that they now have **3 times as many** $-\frac{1}{3}$**M's** and **3 times as many groups of +2** as they did before they drew the extra amounts on the diagram.

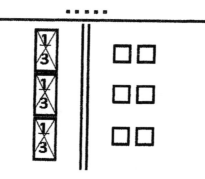

5. Hopefully by this time students will recognize the three inverse thirds of a variable, one drawn above another, as a whole variable and they will not need to draw a new, longer rectangle to show the whole inverse variable. If helpful, have students draw a larger rectangle around the three smaller rectangles to show them grouped together. Since the diagram shows –M = +6, a horizontal bar should be drawn below this diagram and a plain rectangle for M drawn below the bar on the left side and 3 rows of –2 drawn below the bar on the right. That is, inverses have to be taken of –M and +6 in order to solve for the regular variable, M.

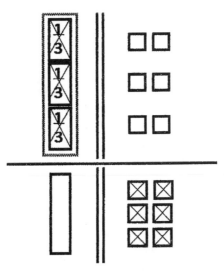

6. Students should record their pictorial steps in symbolic notation. Depending on the method used, their recordings will appear as follows:

(a) take-away/multiplication method:

$$-\tfrac{1}{3}M \; + (+5) = \quad +7$$
$$\underline{\quad -(+5) \quad -(+5)\quad}$$
$$-\tfrac{1}{3}M \qquad = \quad +2$$
$$3(-\tfrac{1}{3}M) \quad = \; 3(+2)$$
$$-M \qquad = \quad +6$$
$$\text{So, M} \qquad = \quad -6$$

(b) add-on/multiplication method:

$$-\tfrac{1}{3}M \; + (+5) = \quad +7$$
$$\underline{\quad +(-5) \quad +(-5)\quad}$$
$$-\tfrac{1}{3}M \qquad = \quad +2$$
$$3(-\tfrac{1}{3}M) \quad = \; 3(+2)$$
$$-M \qquad = \quad +6$$
$$\text{So, M} \qquad = \quad -6$$

7. For this activity, to confirm the solution of $M = -6$, have students write the number sentences that show the substitutions: $-\tfrac{1}{3}M + (+5) = \tfrac{1}{3}(+6) + (+5) = (+2) + (+5) = +7$ [viewing $-\tfrac{1}{3}M$ as "a third of the inverse variable, $-M$," or $\tfrac{1}{3}$ of $+6$]; or $-\tfrac{1}{3}M + (+5) = -\tfrac{1}{3}(-6) + (+5)$ $= (+2) + (+5) = +7$ [viewing $-\tfrac{1}{3}M$ as "the opposite of $\tfrac{1}{3}$ of the variable, M," or $-\tfrac{1}{3}$ of -6]. The $+7$, found after substitution as the value of the left side of the original equation, agrees with the $+7$ given as the right side of the equation. Thus, $M = -6$ must be the correct solution.

8. Now write the equation $-2 = \tfrac{2}{4}A - 8$ on the chalkboard. Read $\tfrac{2}{4}A$ as "two-fourths, or two out of four equal parts, of the variable A." Students should draw 2 small squares (with an X in each interior) for -2 to the left of the vertical, parallel bars. Two rectangles slightly taller than the squares and marked with $\tfrac{1}{4}$'s, along with 8 small squares marked with an X, should be drawn to the right to show $\tfrac{2}{4}A - 8$. Remind students that subtracting $+8$ is equivalent to adding -8. If helpful, some students may prefer to draw $+8$ and -8, or 8 0-pairs of unit squares, on the right with the rectangles, then mark out $+8$ to show the subtraction; -8 will remain on the right with the rectangles, indicating a joining or addition.

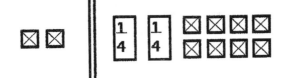

9. The variable group needs to be isolated, so if −8 is considered to be added to the variable group on the right, the add-on method (the bringing in of +8) might be used with the resulting diagram shown here.

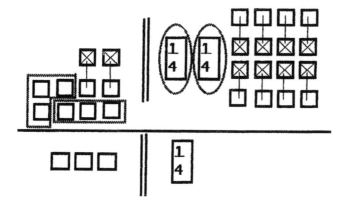

10. Since for the next step only one of the fourths of the variable is needed at first, have students draw a path around each fourth, creating two equal groups. To keep the diagram balanced, the six unit squares still remaining on the left side should also be separated into two equal groups with a path drawn around each group of 3 squares. Remind students that to eventually find a whole variable, our strategy is to begin with a single variable part, in this case the fourth. Have students redraw one group from each side of the diagram in the following way:

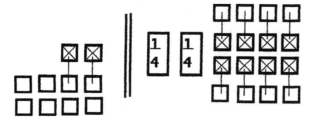

11. *Ask:* "Now that we have a single fourth of the variable here on the right, **how many fourths** are needed **in all** to make the whole variable?" *(4 parts, or 4 fourths)* Have students draw more fourths on the right, each lined up below the first part shown, until there are four parts in all. With four variable groups now drawn on the right, four groups of +3 each are needed on the left side to maintain the balance of the diagram.

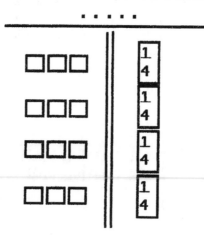

12. If helpful, have students draw a larger rectangle around the four fourths on the right to represent the whole variable, A. This final diagram shows that A has the total value of +12. Discuss the idea that the initial variable group, $\frac{2}{4}$A, was first separated into two groups; that is, half of $\frac{2}{4}$A was found. Then the single fourth of the variable, $\frac{1}{4}$A, was quadrupled. **Ask:** "If the halving process and the quadrupling or '4 times' process are combined together, how do we represent this new single process?" *(multiply $\frac{4}{2}$ by the variable group, $\frac{2}{4}$A)* Students should now write all the steps they used in symbolic notation. Encourage them to record with the combined process discussed above.

$$-2 \;=\; \tfrac{2}{4}A - 8$$
$$-2 \;=\; \tfrac{2}{4}A + (-8)$$
$$\underline{+\,(+8) \qquad\quad +\,(+8)}$$
$$+6 \;=\; \qquad \tfrac{2}{4}A$$
$$\tfrac{4}{2}(+6) = \tfrac{4}{2}(\tfrac{2}{4}A)$$
$$+12 \;=\; \qquad A$$

13. Again, students should confirm their solution, A = +12. Have them write equations to show the substitution used: $\frac{2}{4}A - 8 = \frac{2}{4}(+12) + (-8) = (+6) + (-8) = -2$. Since after substitution the right side of the original equation has the final value of −2 and this agrees with the −2 given on the left side, the solution of A = +12 must be correct.

14. Now write several more equations for students to solve by drawing diagrams. (See Worksheet 2–7–2.) Have them record their steps in symbolic notation, then confirm their solutions by writing number sentences for the substitutions used. You might wish to have students rework some of the equations from Activity 1. Here are some additional equations to assign. (Most of these equations can also be built with the tiles if necessary; lower- and upper-case letters will be used for variables.)

Set A	*Set B*
$(-3) + \frac{1}{2}P = -9$	$\frac{2}{3}b + (+4) = +12$
$-2 = \frac{1}{4}c - 4$	$+3 = (-7) + \frac{2}{4}m$
$-\frac{1}{5}B + (-1) = +1$	$(+5) + (-\frac{3}{5}A) = +11$
$+7 = \frac{1}{3}n - (-2)$	$-18 = (-6) - \frac{3}{4}X$
$-\frac{1}{2}A + 9 = -2$	$\frac{4}{5}p - (-3) = -9$
$+1 = -\frac{1}{6}X + 4$	$-2 = 8 - \frac{2}{6}C$

Activity 3: SOLUTION TAG

[Application/Exploration]

Materials: Paper
Regular pencils
Decks of cards (described in step 1)
Calculators
Tiles and building mats from Activity 1 *(optional)*

Management: Teams of 4 students each (30–45 minutes)

WORKSHEET 2–7–2
Solution Draw

Here are equations to solve by drawing diagrams. Record your steps in symbolic notation. Then confirm your solutions by writing number sentences for the substitutions used.

1. $-\frac{1}{3}M + 5 = +7$

2. $(-3) + \frac{1}{2}P = -9$

3. $-2 = \frac{1}{4}c - 4$

4. $-\frac{1}{5}B + (-1) = +1$

5. $+7 = \frac{1}{3}n - (-2)$

6. $-\frac{1}{2}A + 9 = -2$

7. $+1 = -\frac{1}{6}X + 4$

8. $-2 = \frac{2}{4}A - 8$

9. $\frac{2}{3}b + (+4) = +12$

10. $+3 = (-7) + \frac{2}{4}m$

11. $(+5) + (-\frac{3}{5}A) = +11$

12. $-18 = (-6) - \frac{3}{4}X$

13. $\frac{4}{5}p - (-3) = -9$

14. $-2 = 8 - \frac{2}{6}C$

Directions:

1. Give each team of students a deck of cards, a calculator, and a set of tiles and a building mat (from Activity 1). Each deck contains 48 cards, which will form 12 "books."

Each book consists of a **situation** card, its matching **equation** card, and its **solution** card. An *extra copy* of each solution card will also be included in the deck. The playing cards may be made from blank index cards or from cardstock or lightweight tagboard, then laminated for durability. See step 8 for a suggested deck of cards.

2. Each team should shuffle its deck of cards, then distribute the cards equally to the four team members. Each member will try to complete as many books as possible. To form a book, a situation card must first be placed face up in the center of the table; on a later turn by any player, the matching equation card must be placed beside its situation card; finally, on another turn by any player, the matching solution card must be played. The player who puts down the correct solution card earns the completed book.

3. To begin the game, the first player places a situation card face up in the center of the table. The next player must play the matching equation card, if available; if not, that player must put down a new situation card to begin another book. As the players continue to take turns, they must either play an equation card or solution card on a book begun earlier, or they must put down a new situation card. This process continues until all 12 situation cards have been placed in the center of the table and their equation and solution cards correctly matched to them.

4. In order to decide where to play the solution cards, students must solve the equations shown on the various cards. This may be done in several ways: abstractly with written algebraic symbols only, and with a calculator if needed; with diagrams; or with the tiles. Once a student thinks she or he has found the solution for a situation-equation pair already played, on her or his next turn, the solution card may be placed beside the other two cards. If the other players agree with the solution choice, the book of 3 cards may be removed from the table center and stacked directly in front of the player who completed the book by playing the correct solution card. If another player believes the proposed solution is incorrect, he or she may challenge or **tag** the play and offer another solution card instead. The challenger must show the new solution to be correct by building with tiles or by numerically substituting the value of this new solution for the variable in the equation already matched to the situation. If this second solution is confirmed, the first solution card is discarded or placed aside and the new solution card is placed on the stack of the other two cards, the situation and equation cards; the successful challenger has now earned the book. If the first solution is correct, the completing player earns 1 point for the book; if the second solution is correct, then the challenger earns 3 points for the book instead.

5. Because of the discarding of any solution cards played incorrectly, if there are several such errors during a game, it is possible for a partial book to remain at the end of the game for lack of a solution card in any player's hand. If a team has at least 3 partial books at the end of a game, this will indicate that these particular members need more work on solving procedures used in this game; they need more practice with the tiles or the diagrams and are not yet ready to work independently.

6. A player may not pass during the early part of the game, but may do so near the end of the game if the only cards left in hand are copies of solution cards that have already been correctly played. When all possible books have been made, the teacher might check each team's books for correct matchings or hand out an answer key for the teams to check their own work.

7. The winner on each team is the person earning the most points for completing books, whether by playing the correct solution initially (1 point) or by successfully challenging an incorrect solution (3 points).

8. Here is a suggested set of 12 **situations,** their **equations,** and their **solutions** that might be used for the deck of playing cards. The three categories in each item below represent the three cards that form a "book." For a few situations, the equation reflecting the original action has been simplified on the card. Word names have been used for the numbers in each situation to prevent students from just matching numbers seen in a situation description to numbers seen in an equation without reading carefully. Each variable has been used more than once. Remember to make *two* copies of each **solution** card.

- Two-thirds of a bag of candies remains in a bowl after a party. Eight more candies are put into the bowl. A total of twenty candies are now in the bowl. How many candies were in the bag before it was opened for the party? $\frac{2}{3}C + 8 = 20$; $C = 18$

- Jorge won one-half of a box of rings at the carnival, but on the way home lost three of the rings. Later at home he still had four rings left. How many rings were originally in a full box? $\frac{1}{2}R - 3 = 4$; $R = 14$

- Jaime removed one-third of a cup of jelly beans from a jar that held thirty-five jelly beans at first. She recounted and found that there were still twenty-eight jelly beans in the jar. Approximately how many jelly beans would fill a whole cup? $35 - \frac{1}{3}C = 28$; $C = 21$

- Three-fourths of the Math I class and nine students from the Math II class are planning to go to the museum. Twenty-four students in all will go on the field trip. How many students total attend the Math I class? $\frac{3}{4}M + 9 = 24$; $M = 20$

- Two-thirds of the oil in an oil drum has leaked out. Ten gallons of oil are left in the drum. How many gallons total can the drum hold? $\frac{1}{3}C = 10$; $C = 30$

- Three-fifths of a parking lot is scheduled to be resurfaced with new asphalt. Another two hundred square feet of driveway will also be resurfaced at that time. The contractor has agreed to repave twenty-nine hundred square feet total. What is the size of the parking lot in square feet? $\frac{3}{5}p + 200 = 2900$; $p = 4500$

- A florist has half of a container of roses left for making corsages. She then uses eight of the roses to fill a special order, leaving eighteen roses still in the container. How many roses did the container originally hold? $\frac{1}{2}R - 8 = 18$; $R = 52$

- Three-fourths of the books on a library shelf are arranged in stacks of five books per stack. There are an additional fifteen books on that same shelf that are not in stacks. How many books total are on this shelf? $\frac{1}{4}M = 15$; $M = 60$

- Three-fifths of a box of beads are spilled on the floor where five of the beads roll into a heating vent in the floor and cannot be reached. If thirteen beads are finally picked up, how many beads were in the box before the spill? $\frac{3}{5}p - 5 = 13$; $p = 30$

- One-third of a giant box of crayons are melted to make specialty candles. Eighty-eight crayons are still in the box. How many crayons can such a giant box hold? $\frac{2}{3}C = 88$; $C = 132$

- The school cafeteria is only three-fourths full during lunch time today. Ten students finish eating and go to their next class. Only one hundred ten students are left in the cafeteria. How many students is the cafeteria designed to hold? $\frac{3}{4}M - 10 = 110$; $M = 160$

- A barrel holds fifty gallons of purified water. Sixteen gallons are syphoned from the barrel to fill one-fourth of another smaller barrel. Another five gallons are also added to this second barrel. What is the maximum capacity in gallons of the smaller barrel? $\frac{1}{4}M + 5 = 21$; $M = 64$

OBJECTIVE 8: Solve equations of the form: aX + b = cX + d, where *a, b, c, d* and *X* are real numbers.

Activity 1: SWITCHING TRACKS!

[Developing Action]

Materials: Tile sets and building mats from Section 2, Objective 5
Paper
Regular pencils
Red pencils
Pieces of colored yarn (approx. 12 in. long) or coffee stirrers
Extra construction paper (use colors that match the variable tiles in the sets)
Scissors
Worksheet 2–8–1

Management: Partners (50 minutes)

Directions:

1. Give each pair of students two sets of tiles, a building mat, a piece of yarn or coffee stirrer, a red pencil, scissors, and a sheet of construction paper (same color as some of their variable tiles). This lesson will combine the steps or moves with tiles that were developed in Objectives 3 through 7; it is assumed that students have already completed those activities. Students will be encouraged to vary their sequence of steps in solving an equation when the order of the steps does not matter.

2. Ask students to build the equation N – 2 = 3N + 4 on their mats. Variables now appear on both sides of the mat. Remind students that subtraction has an alternative process; that is, N – 2 or N – (+2), which involves 0-pairs and the removal of +2, can be replaced by N + (–2). This substitution, however, does not imply that "subtraction is equal to addition." The expressions N – 2 and N + (–2) simply produce the same or equivalent results on the building mat.

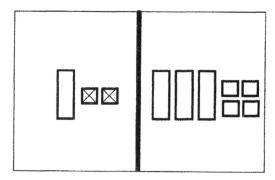

3. Encourage students to use steps that will minimize the number of tiles needed on the mat at any time. Since we still want to isolate the variable tiles on one side of the mat, as a strategy have students look for the side that has more variable tiles, whether positive or negative. In this case, the right side has more; ask students to take away the single variable tile from the left side of the mat. Balancing this action, they should also take away one variable tile from the three variable tiles on the right side. **Ask:** "Why was the take-away method chosen here instead of the add-on method?" *(because the add-on method would have required more tiles on the mat at one time than the take-away method did; extra tiles to be added on would need to be placed on the mat, whereas the take-away method merely removed some tiles that were already on the mat)*

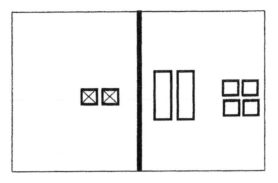

4. ***Ask:*** "Now that the variable tiles are isolated on the right side of the mat, what is the better way to remove the +4 from the right in terms of minimizing the number of extra tiles to be placed on the mat?" *(neither method is better in this case; the same number of extra tiles, 8, must be placed on the mat for both methods; the tiles are just distributed differently on the two sides of the mat)* We can then choose whichever method we want to use; for practice, we will use the add-on method to remove +4. Have students place 4 negative unit tiles on each side of the mat. After the four 0-pairs are removed from the right side, 2 variable tiles remain alone on the right side and –6 remains on the left side.

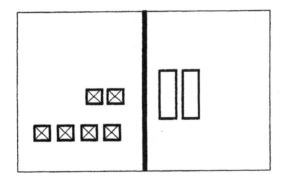

5. Students should now separate the variable tiles into two equal groups of one variable tile per group. The –6 should also be separated into two equal groups with –3 per group. We only need one group on each side, so remove the extra group from both sides. This leaves –3 on the left and the single variable tile on the right. The solution, therefore, is –3 = N or N = –3.

6. The sequence of steps used above should now be recorded in symbols:

$$
\begin{array}{rcl}
N \quad - 2 & = & 3N \quad + 4 \\
N + (-2) & = & 3N \quad + 4 \\
\underline{- N} & & \underline{\quad - N \quad} \\
-2 & = & 2N \quad + 4 \\
\underline{+ (-4)} & & \underline{\quad + (-4)} \\
-6 & = & 2N \\
\tfrac{1}{2}(-6) & = & \tfrac{1}{2}(2N) \\
-3 & = & N
\end{array}
$$

7. Students need to confirm their solution, N = −3. Have them rebuild the original equation on the mat, then replace each variable tile with −3. One group of −3 and another group of −2 will appear on the left; three groups of −3 with a group of +4 will be on the right. Since both sides of the mat have a total value of −5, the solution of −3 must be correct. Have students write a red check mark (√) beside their solution equation to show it is correct.

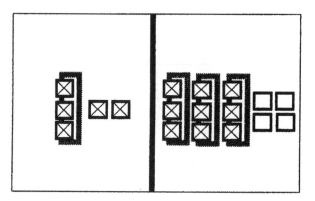

8. Have students build the equation −4b + (−1) = 9 + b on their mats. This time there are more variable tiles on the left side, even though they are actually inverse tiles, so the variable tiles will be isolated on the left side. Remind students that we are concerned only about the quantity of tiles at this point, not their value. In the previous example, the variable tiles were changed first; here, for variety, we will change the unit tiles first and use the add-on method. One positive unit tile should be placed on the left side to form a 0-pair of unit tiles, thus leaving the variable group there alone. This action is balanced by placing another +1 on the right. The mat now shows the equation −4b = +10 + b.

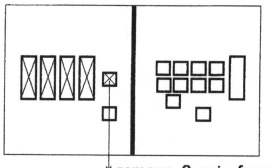

▼ remove 0-pair from mat

9. Now the variable on the right needs to be removed. This can be done by bringing in an inverse variable tile to form a 0-pair of variable tiles, then removing the 0-pair. This action is balanced by bringing in another inverse variable tile on the left, which leaves 5 inverse variable tiles on the left side of the mat and +10 on the right side.

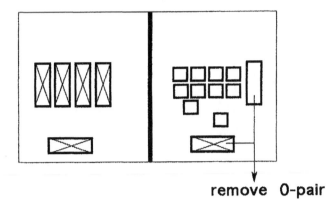

remove 0-pair

10. The equation –5b = +10 now appears on the mat. ***Ask:*** "How do we find the value of *b* from this mat arrangement?" *(separate the 5 inverse variable tiles into 5 equal groups and repeat with the +10; keep one group on each side of the mat and remove all the other groups)* Since the mat shows –b = +2, a yarn piece (or coffee stirrer) should be placed below this complete row of tiles, then the inverse of this row built below the yarn piece. The final row will have a regular variable tile on the left and –2 on the right. The solution is b = –2.

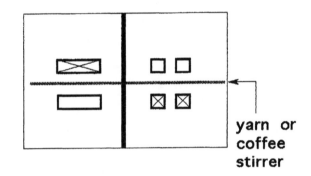

yarn or
coffee
stirrer

11. Students should record their steps for solving this equation as follows:

$$
\begin{array}{rcl}
-4b +(-1) &=& 9 \;+ b \\
\underline{+(+1) \;\;+(+1)} & & \\
-4b &=& +10 \;+ b \\
\underline{+(-b) \qquad\qquad +(-b)} & & \\
-5b &=& +10 \\
\tfrac{1}{5}(-5b) &=& \tfrac{1}{5}(+10) \\
-b &=& +2 \\
\text{So, b} &=& -2
\end{array}
$$

12. Again, have students confirm their solution by rebuilding the original equation on their mats. Both the regular variable tile and its inverse tile appear on the mat this time. The regular variable tile on the right should be replaced by –2, the value of the variable *b;* each of the four inverse variable tiles should be replaced by +2, the value of the inverse variable, *–b.* Four groups of +2 followed by –1 are now on the left side and +9 with –2 are on the right. Since each side has a total value of +7, the solution of b = –2 is correct. A red check mark (√) should be written beside the solution equation to show that it is correct.

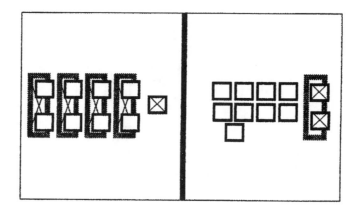

13. This next example will involve mixed numbers. Have students build the equation 3N + 2 = (+11) + 1½N on their mats. They will need to cut out about 3 paper variables and fold and cut each into halves, labeling the plain side of each half with the symbol ½.

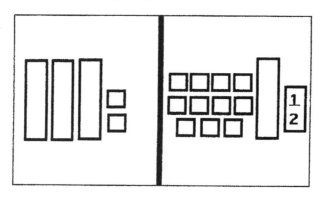

14. There are more whole variable tiles on the left side, so the variable group will be isolated on that side. Using the take-away method, one whole variable tile and a half of a variable tile can be removed from both sides. To complete this subtraction on the left side, a whole variable tile must be exchanged for 2 paper halves. Then one whole variable tile and a half of a variable tile can be removed, leaving one whole variable tile and one of the halves on the left side; +2 will still be on the left and +11 on the right.

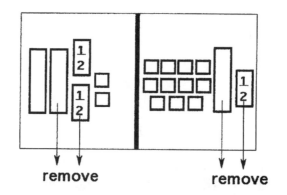

15. *Ask:* "Now that the variable group is isolated on the left, what method is easier to use to remove the +2 from the left, the take-away or the add-on method?" *(in this case, the take-away method because no extra tiles are needed on the mat)* +2 should then be taken away from each side of the mat. This leaves 1 and $\frac{1}{2}$ of a variable tile on the left and +9 on the right.

16. To separate the variable group into smaller, equal groups, all the parts in the variable group need to be the same size. Have students exchange the whole variable tile for 2 paper halves, making a total of 3 halves of a variable on the left side. These can be separated into 3 equal groups, and the +9 on the right can also be separated into 3 equal groups. Then only one group on each side should be kept on the mat, while all the other groups are removed. This will leave the equation $\frac{1}{2}N = +3$ on the mat.

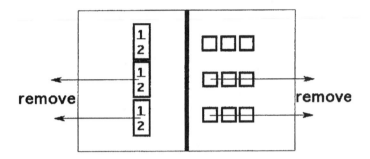

17. *Ask:* "Since a whole variable tile is needed for the solution, what must we do to this half of a variable?" *(double it to make a whole variable tile)* The right side must also be doubled, giving the final equation, N = +6, on the mat.

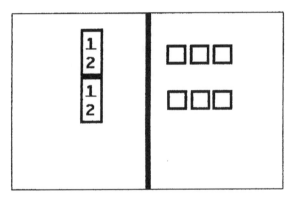

18. The following symbolic steps can be recorded, with the final separation and doubling steps recorded in one equation:

$$3N \;\;+ 2 \;= (+11) + 1\tfrac{1}{2}N$$
$$2\tfrac{2}{2}N \;\;+ 2 \;= (+11) + 1\tfrac{1}{2}N$$
$$-1\tfrac{1}{2}N \qquad\qquad\quad -1\tfrac{1}{2}N$$
$$\overline{1\tfrac{1}{2}N \;\;+ 2 \;= (+11)\qquad\quad}$$
$$\qquad - (+2) \;\; - (+2)$$
$$\overline{1\tfrac{1}{2}N \qquad\;\; = \quad +9}$$
$$\tfrac{3}{2}N \qquad\;\; = \quad +9$$
$$\tfrac{2}{3}(\tfrac{3}{2}N) \quad\;\; = \tfrac{2}{3}(+9)$$
$$N \qquad\quad\;\; = \quad +6$$

19. Finally, the solution of N = +6 must be confirmed. Students will need 40 unit tiles (i.e., use 2 sets of tiles) to complete this particular checking process. The original equation should be rebuilt on the mat. Each whole variable tile should be replaced with +6, and the half of a variable should be replaced with +3. There will be 3 groups of +6 with +2 on the left, and +11 and a group of +6 and a group of +3 on the right. Since both sides have a total value of +20, the solution is correct. A red check mark (√) should be written beside the solution equation to show that it is correct.

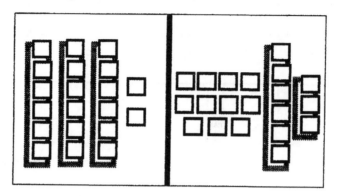

20. Now write other equations for students to build on their mats. (See Worksheet 2–8–1.) They should choose the methods and the sequence of steps they wish to use, show the changes on their mats, and record their steps with symbolic notation. Each solution should be confirmed by substitution into the original equation on the mat, and a red check mark (√) used to show a solution equation is correct. Do not encourage students to take shortcuts with their recording at this time. Other combinations of steps such as with the previous separation-multiplication steps will be allowed later at the pictorial level or in Activity 2. Here are some possible equations to assign to the students. (Remind students that a 0-value on one side of the mat is shown by an empty space.)

$2p + 2 = 5p + 5$ $m - 3 = 4m + 3$ $(-2) + 4X = 2X - (+4)$

$-B + 10 = B + 2$ $1 - 3B = 4 - 2B$ $4C + (-2) = (-7) + (-C)$

$4p - 1 = (-6) + 1\frac{1}{2}p$ $\frac{1}{2}A + 3 = A - 1$ $3m + (-7) = m + (-7)$

$\frac{1}{3}N + (-2) = -\frac{2}{3}N + 7$ $-3R = (-8) + R$ $-5A - 6 = 4A + (-6)$

Activity 2: DRAWING TO SOLVE

[Bridging Action]

Materials: Paper
Regular pencils
Calculators
Whole tiles and mats from Activity 1 *(optional)*
Worksheet 2–8–2

Management: Partners (50 minutes)

Directions:

1. Give each pair of students a calculator and a packet of tiles with a building mat. Even though this activity will emphasize the pictorial level, some students may still need to build with tiles in order to solve an equation; this is acceptable, so make the tiles easily

Name _____   **Date** _____

WORKSHEET 2–8–1
Switching Tracks!

Here are equations for you to build on your mat. Choose the methods and sequence of steps you wish to use, show the changes on your mat, and record your steps with symbolic notation. Confirm each solution by substitution into the original equation on the mat.

1. $N - 2 = 3N + 4$

2. $3N + 2 = 11 + 1\frac{1}{2}N$

3. $m - 3 = 4m + 3$

4. $-B + 10 = B + 2$

5. $4C + (-2) = (-7) + (-C)$

6. $\frac{1}{2}A + 3 = A - 1$

7. $\frac{1}{3}N + (-2) = -\frac{2}{3}N + 7$

8. $-5A - 6 = 4A + (-6)$

9. $-4b + (-1) = 9 + b$

10. $2p + 2 = 5p + 5$

11. $(-2) + 4X = 2X - (+4)$

12. $1 - 3B = 4 - 2B$

13. $4p - 1 = (-6) + 1\frac{1}{2}p$

14. $3m + (-7) = m + (-7)$

15. $-3R = (-8) + R$

16. $N + 1 = 7 + \frac{1}{4}N$

available. They will lay the tiles aside when they are comfortable with the steps they are using. Each time they build an equation on the mat, have them make a diagram of their work. Eventually they will omit the tiles and just draw diagrams to solve their equations.

2. Write the equation $4 - 2M = 1 - 3M$ on the board for students to draw. ***Ask:*** "Looking at your diagrams, which method seems more direct: the take-away method or the add-on method?" *(the take-away method, since there are inverse variables on both sides of the diagram and they can just be marked out)* The add-on method will certainly work, but this lesson focuses on students making decisions about the methods to use. Have students mark out 2 inverse variables from both sides of the diagram. This step begins to isolate a variable form on the right side of the diagram.

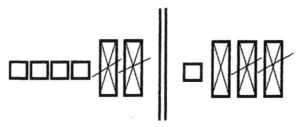

3. Since $+4$ remains on the left, and $+1$ and one inverse variable remain on the right, the take-away method again seems more reasonable. Have students mark out $+1$ on both sides of the diagram. This equal treatment of both sides keeps the equation balanced and finally isolates the inverse variable on the right side of the diagram.

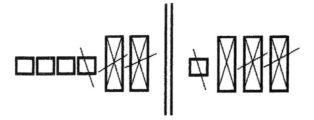

4. We need a value for M as a solution. Students should draw a horizontal bar below the first diagram that now shows $+3 = -M$, then draw a new diagram below that bar to show $-3 = M$ as the inverse of the previous equation, $+3 = -M$.

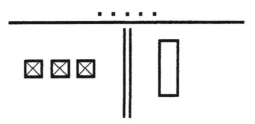

5. The steps used to solve the equation should now be recorded:

$$
\begin{array}{rclcl}
4 & - & 2M & = & 1 \ - 3M \\
4 & + & (-2M) & = & 1 + (-3M) \\
  & - & (-2M) & & \quad - (-2M) \\
\hline
4 & & & = & 1 \ + (-M) \\
-1 & & & & -1 \\
\hline
3 & & & = & -M \\
\text{So, } -3 & & & = & M
\end{array}
$$

6. The solution, M = –3, now needs to be confirmed. Have students write number sentences showing the substitution: 4 + 2(+3) = +10 and 1 + 3(+3) = +10. Since the number sentence for each side of the original equation shows a value of +10, M = –3 is the correct solution. The number sentences used above interpret –2M and –3M as 2 of –M and 3 of –M. If students interpret the expressions as "the opposite of 2M" and "the opposite of 3M," they may use 4 + (–2)(–3) = +10 and 1 + (–3)(–3) = +10.

7. Now write the equation (–2) + 1⅖b = b + 1 on the board for students to solve by drawing a diagram. Because both the variable and the unit will occur in fractional form in this exercise, to avoid confusion with the art work have students label the whole variable rectangle with "b" and each fractional part of the variable with "⅕b." **Ask:** "On what side do you see the larger variable group, regardless of whether they are inverses or regular variable forms?" *(larger amount is on the left of the diagram, so plan to isolate the variable of the equation on the left side this time)* "Which method is easier for removing the –2 on the left side, the take-away or the add-on method?" *(the add-on method since the unit on the right is positive and the units on the left are negative)* Have students draw 2 positive units on the left and on the right side of the diagram, then form 0-pairs. This leaves 1⅖b = b + (+3) still showing on the diagram.

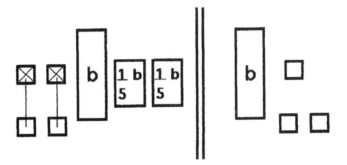

8. Now **ask:** "Since we are trying to isolate the variable on the left side, we need to remove the whole variable on the right. Which method is easier this time, the take-away or the add-on method?" *(the take-away method is easier here because the variables on both sides are of the same form, that is, **not** opposites or inverses of each other)* Have students mark out one whole variable on each side of the diagram. This will leave ⅖b = +3 showing on the diagram.

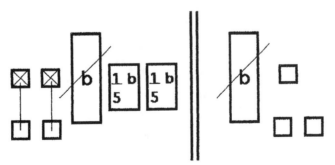

9. Since there are two of the fifths of a variable on the left side, these can be separated into 2 groups. Have students draw a path around each fifth of a variable. Similarly, the +3 on the right must be separated into 2 equal groups. Have students think through the needed action: +1 will be in each group, but the third or remaining +1 must be subdivided into two equal parts or 2 halves. A bar should be drawn vertically or horizontally through the middle of this last unit square to form two half-units. Then a path should be drawn around one whole unit and one of the half-units and a second path drawn around the other whole unit and half-unit. Since the separation into equal groups is division where we are only interested in a single group on each side, have students draw a long, horizontal bar below the first diagram and redraw a rectangle for a fifth of a variable on the left and redraw a group of one whole square and a half-square for $+1\frac{1}{2}$ on the right. The interior of the rectangle on the left should be labeled with "$\frac{1}{5}b$," and the interior of the half-square or half of a unit on the right should be labeled with "$\frac{1}{2}$." It is difficult to draw small, proportional shapes, so the half-unit will probably not be a "true" half of the unit square; that is why the labeling is so important at this time. This new diagram now shows $\frac{1}{5}b = +1\frac{1}{2}$.

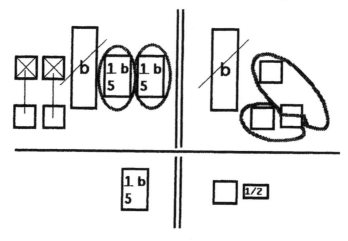

10. *Ask:* "On the new diagram we now see only a fifth of a variable on the left. How many fifths total need to be drawn to make a whole variable *b*?" *(need to draw enough fifths of the variable b to have five total on the diagram)* Have students draw extra $\frac{1}{5}b$'s below the first part on the left in order to show five parts total. Since there are now five equal groups on the left, students should draw more groups of $+1\frac{1}{2}$ below the first group on the right until they have five such groups total. *Ask:* "What is another number name for the total of the five groups of $+1\frac{1}{2}$ each on the right?" *(five whole units and five half-units make seven whole units and a half-unit)* What should now be represented on this last diagram are 5 fifths or 1 whole variable on the left and $+7\frac{1}{2}$ on the right, that is, the equation: $b = +7\frac{1}{2}$.

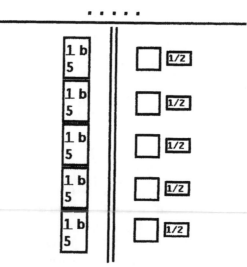

11. Students now need to record their steps in the following way on their own papers. (After completing the recording, have 1 or 2 students explain which drawing action each step represents.)

$$\begin{aligned}
(-2) + 1\tfrac{2}{5}b &= b + 1 \\
+\,(+2) & + (+2) \\
\hline
1\tfrac{2}{5}b &= b + 3 \\
-\,b & -\,b \\
\hline
\tfrac{2}{5}b &= 3 \\
\tfrac{5}{2}(\tfrac{2}{5}b) &= \tfrac{5}{2}(+3) \\
b &= +\,7\tfrac{1}{2}
\end{aligned}$$

Note: In the recording above, the separation process (division by 2) and the multiplication process (drawing 5 rows of a single group) have been combined into one step and shown as multiplication by $\tfrac{5}{2}$. This recording technique was presented in Objective 6 and again in Objective 7. If some students are still not ready for this combined step, have them record the following steps instead:

$$\begin{aligned}
\tfrac{1}{2}(\tfrac{2}{5}b) &= \tfrac{1}{2}\,(+3) \\
\tfrac{1}{5}b &= +1\tfrac{1}{2} \\
5\,(\tfrac{1}{5}b) &= 5\,(+1\tfrac{1}{2}) \\
b &= +\,7\tfrac{1}{2}
\end{aligned}$$

Also at this level some students may be ready to combine other steps in their recording. This should be encouraged as long as they can explain their work clearly. Here is an example of a possible combination:

$$\begin{aligned}
(-2) + 3A &= A + 5 \\
+\,(+2) \;-\, A & -\,A + (+2) \\
\hline
2A &= +7
\end{aligned}$$

12. As usual, students should confirm their solution, $b = +7\tfrac{1}{2}$. At this point, they should write substitution equations for their work. These equations might be written as follows:

(a) left side: $(-2) + 1\tfrac{2}{5}\,(+\,7\tfrac{1}{2}) = (-2) + \tfrac{7}{5}\,(+\tfrac{15}{2}) = (-2) + (+\tfrac{105}{10}) = (-2) + (+10.5) = +8.5$, and

(b) right side: $(+7\tfrac{1}{2}) + 1 = +8\tfrac{1}{2}$.

Since both sides of the equation have the total value of $+8\tfrac{1}{2}$ or $+8.5$, $b = +7\tfrac{1}{2}$ is the correct solution.

13. Now write more equations for students to solve by drawing diagrams. (See Worksheet 2–8–2.) For each equation, they should record the particular steps they chose to use, then confirm their solution by writing substitution equations. Here are some possible equations to assign. If needed by some students, most of these equations can also be solved with the prepared set of tiles, along with some paper variable tiles and paper unit tiles that can be folded.

$4m + (-2) = 3m - 4$	$B + 2 = -B + 10$	$p - 1 = \tfrac{1}{2}p + 3$
$-4A - 5 = 3A + (-5)$	$(+2) + 3K = 8 - K$	$2N + 9 = 10 - 2N$
$(-3) - 5m = 2 - 3m$	$4X - 5 = X - 7$	$7 - 11b = -6b + 7$
$\tfrac{1}{2} + \tfrac{1}{3}A = 1\tfrac{1}{2} - A$	$3B + (-2) = (-11) + 1\tfrac{1}{2}B$	$(-\tfrac{3}{4}) + 2d = \tfrac{1}{2}d + (-3\tfrac{3}{4})$

WORKSHEET 2–8–2
Drawing to Solve

Here are equations for you to solve by drawing diagrams. Record the particular steps you choose to use for each equation. Then confirm your solution by writing substitution equations.

1. $4 - 2M = 1 - 3M$

2. $4m + (-2) = 3m - 4$

3. $p - 1 = \frac{1}{2}p + 3$

4. $(+2) + 3K = 8 - K$

5. $(-3) - 5m = 2 - 3m$

6. $7 - 11b = -6b + 7$

7. $3B + (-2) = (-11) + 1\frac{1}{2}B$

8. $-2 + 1\frac{2}{5}b = b + 1$

9. $B + 2 = -B + 10$

10. $-4A - 5 = 3A + (-5)$

11. $2N + 9 = 10 - 2N$

12. $4X - 5 = X - 7$

13. $\frac{1}{2} + \frac{1}{3}A = 1\frac{1}{2} - A$

14. $(-\frac{3}{4}) + 2d = \frac{1}{2}d + (-3\frac{3}{4})$

Activity 3: DOMINO MATCH

[Application/Exploration]

Materials: Sets of "dominoes" (described in step 1)
Paper
Regular pencils
Calculators
Scissors
Tiles and mats *(optional)*

Management: Teams of 4 students each (30–40 minutes)

Directions:

1. Prepare a set of "dominoes" for each team by drawing a grid on a large piece of colored tagboard where each grid cell is approximately 3 in. × 3 in. There should be 9 such cells or dominoes in the total grid before the dominoes are cut apart. While the grid is still whole, for each interior line segment write an equation of the type being studied on one side of the segment and its solution equation on the other side. Possible equations and their solutions are given after the last step below. See Activities 1 and 2 for additional equations or create other similar equations if you prefer. Also write equations along the border segments of the grid; these should be "distractors" and should not have an equivalent equation or solution equation anywhere else inside the grid. The following list may serve as "distractors"; note that these equations use the same variables as those that will form matches. (For an easier game, do not use "distractor" equations along the border; instead, draw a colorful, decorative trimming along the edges of the grid. This colorful "frame" will aid students in arranging their dominoes later.) For more varied practice, prepare tagboard grids in several different colors; each color will indicate a different set of equations and solutions. Teams can then play with a different color of dominoes each time in order to experience a wider variety of equations. If several sets of dominoes are the same color, code the cards from the same set in some way; for example, mark the same small arrangement of dots on the backs of cards from the same set, or mark the backs with the same letter of the alphabet. Such marking should be done before the grids are laminated. This will help you match any loose cards to their proper sets.

Possible "distractors" to be used with the pairs of equations provided at the end of this activity:

- Type **(e)** distractors [equations to be solved]: $3k - 2 = 3k + 5$; $-7m = 9 + m$; $4A + 3.5 = 2A + 3.5$; $2b + 5 = b - 5$; $6 - 5m = 3 - 5m$; $4k - 100 = 2k + 100$

- Type **(s)** distractors [solution equations]: $A = -2$; $m = 3.8$; $k = -4.1$; $b = 1.3$; $m = \frac{2}{3}$; $b = 0$

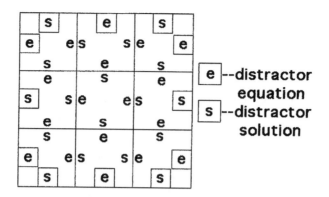

2. The grid can now be laminated, if desired, and the dominoes cut apart along the line segments of the grid, making 9 dominoes. Each set of cards or dominoes may be stored in a closeable plastic bag or brown envelope. If plastic bags are used, punch a small airhole in each bag to make storage of several bags together easier to accomplish (no extra time needed to force out the trapped air!).

3. Give each team a set of dominoes, 2–3 sets of tiles (including some paper for making fractional variable or unit tiles), scissors, and a calculator. The emphasis in this cooperative game is on the processes of adding, removing, multiplying, or separating in solving an equation, not on a student's accuracy with integer or decimal operations; hence, a calculator is appropriate. Remind students that the physical separating, for example, of 18 negative units into 6 equal groups may be described with the **recorded notation** $\frac{1}{6}(-18)$ or $-\frac{18}{6}$, and computed mentally or with paper and pencil to get -3 per group; or it may be computed using the **calculator step** $(-18) \div (+6)$. Similarly, if a decimal number occurs as a coefficient, as in $0.3k = -7.2$, it should be treated in the same format as a whole number coefficient; for example, we will have $\frac{1}{0.3}(0.3k) = \frac{1}{0.3}(-7.2)$ where $(-7.2) \div 0.3$ is used for finding the value of k with the calculator. Also, remind students that subtraction has an equivalent alternative form in addition; for example, $B - 9$ or $B - (+9)$ is equivalent to $B + (-9)$ because of the adding on of 0-pairs. In addition, for this game, correct solution equations will require the regular variable (e.g., A), not the inverse variable (e.g., $-A$).

4. Each team of students should shuffle its set of dominoes and turn the dominoes face down near the center of the table. The first player will draw out a domino from the pile and place it face up in the center of the table. That player will select and write down an equation shown on the drawn domino and solve it, using symbols, diagrams, or tiles, but will not reveal the solution found until a later turn. Other players may secretly solve any equation displayed on the same domino, saving their solutions until later.

5. On each turn after the first domino has been put down, a player may either **make a newly discovered match** of an equation to its solution, using two dominoes **already** face up on the table but not yet matched to each other, or **draw a new domino,** place it face up and try to match it to a previously drawn domino. If no correct match is possible using the newly drawn domino, it should be left face up near the other dominoes already played. A player may rearrange any dominoes already played in order to make another match, assuming all matches made up to that point are correct matches and can still be maintained under the new arrangement. (Since all solutions used in the set given in step 9 are unique, such rearranging will be minimal.) All team members must accept a new matching of an equation with its solution as correct before the two dominoes can be left with their edges touching.

6. Since this is a cooperative game, when a player is trying to solve an equation during a turn, the other team members may **help,** but only by asking **questions** that will guide the player to: (1) think generally about the next step needed, (2) rename a number in some way in order to match it to the form used on a domino, or (3) try other ways to solve the equation (for example, use tiles instead of symbols if more helpful). No solution or specific steps may be offered.

7. The game will be over when a 3-by-3 arrangement has been made with the dominoes and all matches are correct. An answer key may be provided for the team members to check their work. A list of equations and their matching solutions like the ones given below might be provided.

8. To make the game more competitive or to have a scoring method of some kind, each student might record on a sheet of paper any equation and its solution that she or he has been able to match with dominoes. Each correct match earns a point for that player.

9. Here is a possible set of equations and their solutions to write on the touching edges of the dominoes. Each **e–s** pair of equations should be written on an interior line segment of the domino grid [**e**—equation to be solved—on one side of the segment; **s**—solution to that equation—on the other side of the segment] before the grid sections are cut apart. (Seven of these equations can be solved with tiles, using 2 to 3 sets of tiles; most can be solved with diagrams; no solution value is used more than once.)

$e \; ; \; s$	$e \; ; \; s$
$4b - 5 = 7 + b \; ; \; b = 4$	$(+2) + 3A = 8 - A \; ; \; A = 1.5$
$6m - 1 = 5m - 1 \; ; \; m = 0$	$(-3) - 5k = 2 - 3k \; ; \; k = -2\tfrac{1}{2}$
$5b - 8 = b + 5 \; ; \; b = +3.25$	$\tfrac{1}{2} + \tfrac{1}{3}m = 1\tfrac{1}{2} - m \; ; \; m = \tfrac{3}{4}$
$(-35) + 13k = 3k - 46 \; ; \; k = -1.1$	$(-4b) + 1\tfrac{1}{2} = (-7b) + 3 \; ; \; b = \tfrac{1}{2}$
$6A + 9 = 10 - 2A \; ; \; A = \tfrac{1}{8}$	$(-3) + 1.2m = m - 3.08 \; ; \; m = -0.4$
$7 - 11k = -6k + 7 \; ; \; k = 0$	$(-6) + 2.5A = 2A - 10 \; ; \; A = -8$

Section 3

LINEAR APPLICATIONS AND GRAPHING

OBJECTIVE 1: Model linear relationships in real-world situations.

Activity 1: MODELING ACTIONS

[Developing Action]

Materials: Packets of tiles (from Section 2, Objective 1) and building mats (from Section 2, Objective 3)
Worksheet 3–1–1
Paper
Regular pencils
Piece of yarn or coffee stirrer

Management: Partners (50 minutes)

Directions:

1. Give each pair of students a packet of tiles, a building mat, and a piece of yarn or a coffee stirrer. It is assumed that students have mastered the basic skills presented in Section 2 for solving linear equations. Students will now combine those skills and apply them to solve real-world situations. One or two unknowns will be involved, but enough specific information will be available that the values of the unknowns can be found. The focus will be on representing the situation correctly with tiles, then recording the results as an equation in written or symbolic form.

2. Review the meanings of the four basic operations in terms of *action:*

- Addition is the joining together of two or more sets of objects.

- Subtraction (as used here) is the removal of objects from a given set or the finding of a missing part of a given set.

- Multiplication is the combining of several equal-sized sets of objects.

- Division is the separation of a given amount of objects into equal-sized sets.

3. Ask students to place tiles on the building mat to represent the following situation: *There are 3 goldfish and several guppies in the aquarium. If there are 12 goldfish and*

211

guppies in all in the aquarium, how many guppies are in the aquarium? Students should place 3 positive unit tiles (as "goldfish") on the left side of the building mat, then place a single, plain variable tile to the right of the unit tiles but still on the left side of the mat. The variable tile represents the number of guppies to be joined to the 3 goldfish. Since this total on the left must equal 12 fish in all, students should place 12 positive unit tiles on the right side of the mat. **Note:** Whenever a specific amount is given, unit tiles will be used. If the amount is unknown initially, the variable tile will be used. When opposite actions are implied, inverse tiles will be used.

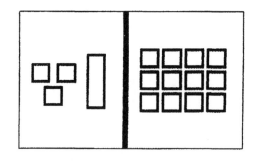

4. Ask students what might be done to isolate the variable tile on one side of the mat by itself. Two methods are possible: remove 3 positive unit tiles from each side of the mat, or add 3 negative unit tiles to each side to form 0-pairs. Allow students to choose which method to use. In either case, the variable tile will remain on the left side of the mat and 9 positive unit tiles will remain on the right side. Select a letter to represent the unknown—for example, G for the number of guppies—and record on the board: **(+3) + G = +12 and G = +9 guppies.**

5. Now have students model the following situation: *Maurice has equal amounts of marbles in 2 bags. One bag has a hole in it, so 4 marbles fall out and are lost. When Maurice empties the remaining marbles into a box and counts them, 6 marbles remain. How many marbles were in each bag initially?* Two plain variable tiles of the same size or color should be placed on the left side of the mat. Four negative unit tiles should be placed on the left side to the right of the variable tiles; these represent the 4 lost marbles. Now place 6 positive unit tiles on the right side of the mat. The tiles on the mat should appear as those in the following illustration.

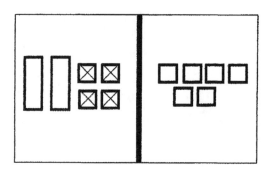

6. Now ask students to find the value of the variable tile by making appropriate moves with their tiles. When they are finished, ask several students to explain the steps they used. Two methods are possible: (a) bring in 4 positive unit tiles on both sides of the mat to isolate the two variable tiles, remove any 0-pairs, then separate the remaining tiles on each side of the mat into two equal rows; or (b) bring in 4 0-pairs on the right side of the mat, then remove 4 negative unit tiles from both sides, leaving 2 variable tiles on the left and 10 positive unit tiles on the right of the mat; a separation of tiles into two equal rows then follows on each side. One complete row of tiles across the mat shows that the variable tile must equal +5. Using the letter M for the number of marbles in one bag, record the following equations or number sentences on the board: **2M + (–4) = +6 and M = +5 marbles per bag.**

7. Now have students model the following situation: *Ito says the distance in blocks from his house to the music store is 3 blocks more than twice the distance from Sonya's house to the same store. Josh argues that Ito's distance is really just 7 blocks further than Sonya's distance to the store. Can Ito and Josh both be right?* Show Ito's amount in tiles on the left side of the mat and show Josh's amount on the right. Use a plain variable tile to represent the distance from Sonya's house to the music store. The tile sets will look like the following illustration on the mat.

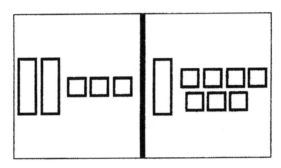

8. ***Discuss:*** "We want to know if the two amounts on the mat are equal or 'balanced.' The mat is only balanced for sure if we see the same value in unit tiles on both sides of the mat. What do we need to know in order to decide if Ito's distance in blocks equals Josh's distance in blocks?" Hopefully students will recognize that, if they know Sonya's distance in blocks, they can then find Ito's and Josh's distances.

9. Have students now apply appropriate steps to move the tiles on the mat and solve for the value of the variable tile (Sonya's distance). Allow them to choose their own approach for isolating the variable tile. Have different students share their approaches with the class. One possible way is to remove 3 positive unit tiles from both sides of the mat and also to remove 1 variable tile from both sides. Then the variable tile must equal +4 if Josh's and Ito's original expressions shown on the mat are to be equal.

10. To test whether the two expressions are equal in value, students should rebuild the original sets of tiles on their mats. Each variable tile should then be replaced with 4 positive unit tiles. Confirming the solution is a very important step for students. The result will be two sets of +4 and another +3 in unit tiles on the left and +4 with another +7 on the right, producing a value of +11 on each side of the mat. So Josh and Ito were both right; they just had two different ways to describe the same distance. Record the original equation and the solution on the board, using the letter S for Sonya's distance in blocks: **2S + (+3) = S + (+7) and S = +4 blocks for the distance from Sonya's house to the music store.**

11. Assign other story problems or situations for students to build and solve with their tiles. (See Worksheet 3–1–1.) Equations should be written that describe: (a) the original

Name _____ **Date** _____

WORKSHEET 3–1–1
Building Models of Real-World Situations

For each situation, build a model with tiles to represent the situation. Choose a letter for each variable used. Write an equation that describes the initial appearance of the tiles on the mat (or shows the steps taken in some cases) and any other equations that are required by the situation or by your teacher.

1. There are 4 envelopes in all. All envelopes hold the same number of coupons. There are 20 coupons in all. How many coupons are in each envelope?

2. There are 8 shipping cartons. They all contain the same number of electric generators. The generators are to be equally distributed to 4 different city hospitals. Each hospital will receive 4 generators. How many generators total are to be shipped to the hospitals?

3. Heidi has 3 boxes of pencils, each box containing the same amount. She has 6 extra pencils in her desk drawer. Her total number of pencils is 5 more than José has in his storage closet. If Heidi has 4 pencils in each of her boxes, can you find how many pencils José has?

4. Use tiles to show the mean or average of the two values represented by $C + 7$ and $3C - 1$. If the mean is +13, what are the original two values?

5. On Tuesday the reported temperature in Celsius was 13 degrees higher than on Monday. On Wednesday the temperature was 10 degrees less than twice the Monday temperature, yet it was the same as the temperature on Tuesday. What was the temperature on Tuesday?

tiles on the mat in some way, (2) the solution, or value of the variable tile, and (3) any other equations or results the problem may require. Allow plenty of class time for students to share their results and to explain their methods to each other. Such verbalizing of their ideas and processes is extremely important in the learning of mathematics.

12. Here are some possible equations for the items on Worksheet 3–1–1. The formats used for the equations may vary, but try to give the original tile arrangements before simplifying them. Letters chosen for variables will also vary. Emphasis should be on writing equations that reflect the actions in the situations as closely as possible.

(1) $4E = +20$, $E = +5$ coupons per envelope

(2) $(\frac{1}{4})(8C) = +4$, $C = +2$ generators per carton, $8C = +16$ generators total; $2C = +4$ may also be given, but it does not show the initial condition of 8 cartons

(3) $3H + 6 = J + 5$, $H = +4$ pencils per box (given for Heidi), $J = +13$ pencils for José

(4) $(\frac{1}{2})[(C + 7) + (3C - 1)] = +13$, $C = +5$, values are $+12$ and $+14$; $2C + 3 = +13$ may also be given, but it does not show the initial forms for the values

(5) $M + 13 = 2M - 10$, $M = +23$ degrees Celsius on Monday, $M + 13 = +36$ degrees Celsius on Tuesday

Activity 2: VISUALIZING SITUATIONS

[Bridging Action]

Materials: Building mats and packets of variable tiles and unit tiles from Activity 1
Worksheet 3–1–2
Regular pencils
Red pencils *(optional)*

Management: Partners (30–50 minutes)

Directions:

1. Give each pair of students a packet of tiles, a building mat, and 2 copies of Worksheet 3–1–2. Students should build with the tiles to represent situations described in items 1–4 of the worksheet. After they have solved a problem with the tiles, they should draw a diagram that shows the steps they followed with the tiles. If students do not need the tiles, allow them to represent the situations initially with diagrams, but still mark the diagrams to show the steps needed to solve the problem. Allow time to discuss the various diagrams students draw for this activity. Using diagrams to analyze a problem and to determine the equations needed to solve the problem is a major strategy in mathematics and is a skill that must be taught; most students do not naturally know how to draw diagrams and need to be shown how to make some of the simpler forms. Also, the diagram for a particular problem will not be unique, but must have meaning for the artist and must lead easily to an equation.

2. To prepare students for the worksheet, have them build with tiles, then draw a diagram for the following situation (item 1 of worksheet): *Suzette held 5 small bags of candies at first, along with 4 single candies. She then gave 2 of the bags to Juan. When*

WORKSHEET 3–1–2
Visualizing Situations

For items 1–4, draw a diagram of variables and units to represent each situation described. Build with tiles first if helpful. Write an equation that reflects the original diagram, then make changes to the diagram to solve the problem. Record the solution as an equation also. Record any other information required by the problem.

1. Suzette held 5 small bags of candies at first, along with 4 single candies. She then gave 2 of the bags to Juan. When Suzette counted all the candies she had left, she had 22 candies. If all the bags contain the same number of candies, how many candies were in each bag?

2. Each winner in a contest is to receive a storage case full of CDs, as well as 4 single CDs. There are 3 winners. A total of 21 CDs will be given to the winners. How many CDs are in each storage case?

3. John has 3 more baseball trading cards than Georg, but Carol has 7 fewer cards than twice Georg's number. John and Carol are surprised to learn that they have the same number of cards. How many cards does John have?

4. Four angles in a design each measure $(n - 2)$ degrees. Their total measure equals 32 degrees. How many degrees does each angle measure?

WORKSHEET 3–1–2 *(cont.)*
Visualizing Situations

For each of items 5–8, draw a simple diagram (unless already shown) of some kind, one not based on tiles this time but that will still represent the situation. Then write an equation that reflects the diagram. You do not need to solve for values of the variables.

5. Beatrice walked at a steady speed on level ground for 3 hours and covered 12 miles of trail. Draw a diagram that relates her walking speed, R, and the other details, then write an equation for the situation.

6. Using the given diagram of 4 squares of side length y lined up beside 2 larger squares of side length w, write an equation that relates the lengths k, w and y in some way. The length k is indicated on the diagram.

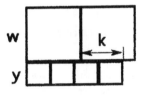

7. Three books cost X dollars each and five books cost N dollars each. The total cost of the books is \$55. Draw a diagram to represent the books bought and their cost. Using the diagram, write an equation.

8. A retail store ordered at wholesale prices two \$8 shirts for every \$13 shirt ordered. The cost of the total order was \$870. Draw a diagram to represent the shirts ordered and their cost. Using the diagram, write an equation. **Challenge:** How would you find the total number of shirts ordered?

Suzette counted all the candies she had left, she had 22 candies. If all the bags contain the same number of candies, how many candies were in each bag? For the diagrams, use vertical rectangles for variables and small squares for unit tiles. Draw a large X inside a shape to represent its inverse form. Be sure to show all the initial conditions when possible. (**Note:** To indicate *different* variables in a diagram, write the letter used for each variable inside its rectangle; otherwise, all rectangles will be drawn the same size. On the mat, the variable tiles will be different colors and lengths.) The above situation might have the following diagram (similarly for the mat).

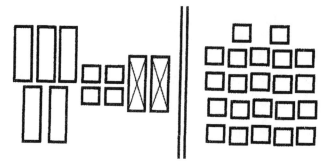

3. Students should write an equation to the right of their diagram to describe their work in symbols. Allow the class to choose the letter for each variable or unknown when the entire class is working together on the same problem. In the above problem, we might use B for the number of candies in one bag. The initial model with either the tiles or the diagram might have the following equation: $5B + 4 - 2B = +22$, or possibly $5B + (+4) + (-2B) = +22$.

4. Two 0-pairs of variables can be formed on the left side and 4 positive units can be removed from both sides of the mat or diagram. The remaining 3 variables must then be separated into 3 rows on the left; the 18 positive units must also be separated into 3 equal rows of +6 each on the right. The mat work or the diagram now indicates that each variable has the value of +6. Since students have worked with diagrams of tiles in depth in Section 2, they may draw a path around one complete row to show the solution, using either a regular or a red pencil. So B = +6 candies in each bag.

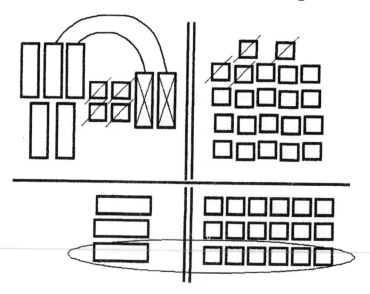

5. In items 5–8 emphasis will be on making the diagrams and writing equations for them, not on solving the problems. In fact, some of the problems do not provide enough information for a solution to be found. Discuss item 7 with the class and different ways they might make a diagram. One simple method is to draw a small rectangle or square for each book and write the cost of the book inside the shape. Draw a row of 3 rectangles with $X written inside each shape, then extend the row to the right by drawing 5 rectangles with $N written inside each one. All 8 rectangles may be the same size since each has its own label to identify it. Draw a double-headed arrow below the row of rectangles that extends the full length of the row. At the midpoint of the arrow, write "$55 total cost." No other labeling is necessary.

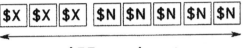

$55 total cost

6. Discuss the idea that in such a diagram, when several shapes are in a row together, addition is implied. Also, if a particular shape is repeated several times, this implies multiplication. The arrow, whose length matches the row length of the combined shapes, indicates that the value shown on the arrow ($55) equals the value of the combined shapes. So an equation for this diagram might be: $3(\$X) + 5(\$N) = \$55$.

7. Partners should now work together to make diagrams and write equations for the other items on the worksheet. When all are finished, have different students draw their particular diagrams on the board and explain what each part means to them. Remind students that their diagrams for the same problem may vary greatly, but that is acceptable. The only requirement is for all the conditions of the problem to be represented in the diagram in some way.

8. Here are some possible diagrams and equations for the other items on Worksheet 3–1–2. Refer to Section 2 on how each diagram of tiles needs to be changed to show the solution.

Item 2: $3(S + 4) = +21$ where S = number of CDs in storage case (S = 3)

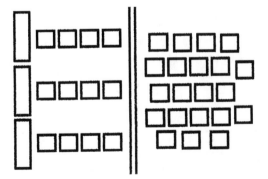

Item 3: $G + 3 = 2G - 7$ where G = Georg's number of baseball cards (G = 10)

Item 4: $4(n - 2) = +32$ where n is some real number not identified (n = 10)

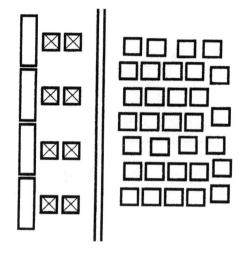

Item 5: $3R = +12$ where R is the walking speed or miles walked each hour

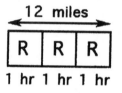

Item 6: $4y = w + k$, or $y + y + y + y = w + k$ where y = side length of smaller square, w = side length of larger square, and k= some length along length w

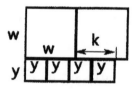

Item 8: $N(\$8 + \$8 + \$13) = \$870$ where N = number of groups purchased with 2 \$8 shirts and 1 \$13 shirt per group; total number of shirts bought can be found from $N(3)$ when the value of N is found because there are 3 shirts in each group purchased

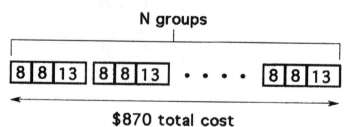

Activity 3: LINEAR RELATIONSHIPS

[Application/Exploration]

Materials: Centimeter grid paper
Colored pencils (4 different colors per team)
Calculators
Paper
Regular pencils
Worksheet 3–1–3

Management: Teams of 3–4 students each (2 parts, 30 min. each)

Directions:

1. This activity contains two parts: Part A involves finding a table of values for each of four different linear relationships and plotting the four sets of ordered pairs on the same grid to see what patterns appear; Part B presents a multi-step problem with a linear relationship for students to explore and solve. You may assign either or both parts to your students, depending on the available time.

Part A

2. Give each team of students a sheet of centimeter grid paper, 4 colored pencils (4 different colors), and a calculator. Write the following four formulas on the board for the teams to copy on their own papers:

Wm = 72H – 260 where Wm = ideal weight for male in pounds, H = adult male's height in feet

Wf = 60H – 200 where Wf = ideal weight for female in pounds, H = adult female's height in feet

V = 50K where V = volume of a box in cu. cm, K = width of bottom of box in centimeters

C = \$35 + T(\$40) where C = cost of a repair, T = time needed in hours to make repair

Discuss the idea that each formula contains two different variables and is supposed to show us how values for the two variables relate to each other.

3. So that all four formulas can be represented on the same grid, have students number the lower horizontal axis of their grid from 1 to 7 and write "Units for Values of H, K, or T" below the axis. Space the marks evenly across the axis. Also have them number the left vertical axis of their grid (the longer side of the paper) in intervals of 20: 20, 40, 60, 80, etc., evenly spaced along the axis. On the left beside the vertical axis, students should write "For Values of Wf, Wm, V, or C." This labeling of the two axes will allow all four sets of ordered pairs to be plotted on the same grid.

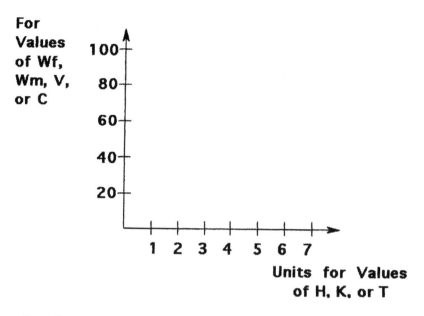

For Values of Wf, Wm, V, or C

Units for Values of H, K, or T

4. Each team should now use their calculators to prepare a table of values for each of the four formulas. The tables will be for the pair types: (T, C), (K, V), (H, Wf), and (H, Wm). Use the values 1 through 7 for the first member of each type of pair to calculate the second member. **Note:** For Wm and Wf, H = 1, 2, 3, or 4 will produce a negative or an unreasonable weight for an adult. That is because the formulas were originally developed for adults; hence, there is an expected minimum for H. Discuss this idea with the students. Have them simply delete the ordered pairs that have negative second members from their tables and not plot them.

5. The seven ordered pairs for each formula should be plotted on the grid, using a different color for each formula's points. That is, there will be four sets of points on the grid and each set will be in its own color. Do not connect the points with line segments at this time. Students should also prepare a color key somewhere on the grid to indicate which color has been used for each formula.

6. After each team has plotted their four sets of points, have students write some sentences about what they notice about the sets of points. Ask several to share their ideas with the class. Hopefully they will notice that each set of points (whether the four points for Wm or Wf, or the seven points for V or C) appears to form a straight path on the grid. Some paths will be steeper than others. The C-set looks like it will cross the vertical axis; the V-set is pointed toward the origin; and the Wm-set and the Wf-set both look like they will cross the horizontal axis. Tell students that when the points for a formula's ordered pairs make a straight path on a grid, the formula describes a **linear** relationship between its two variables. The word "linear" is based on the word "line." We will be learning more about these special relationships in future lessons.

Part B

7. Give each team a copy of Worksheet 3–1–3. Discuss the problem of enlarging the animal pen and the condition of wanting the least amount of additional fencing possible. Review how the area of a rectangular region may be found. Remind students that the new section of the pen will have an area of 4 square meters. Also, diagrams should be drawn and labeled before any effort is made to write equations. Remember that the focus

Name _____ **Date** _____

WORKSHEET 3-1-3
How Much Additional Fencing?

A rectangular animal pen is 5 meters by 20 meters. It needs to be enlarged by an additional 4 square meters. The area will be increased by moving only one side of the pen outward and attaching additional fencing to close any gaps formed when the one side is moved. Which two sides of the pen will need to be extended and by how much per side when the other side is moved if the owner wants to use the least amount of additional fencing possible? (Draw several diagrams of the original pen and label the side measures. On each diagram, show a different way of extending the pen. Write equations that relate the total area of the new pen to the areas of the old pen and the new section. Solve to find the amount of extension needed in each case. Decide which new pen design better satisfies the owner's conditions.)

of this objective is to learn to draw diagrams, which then determine what equations are needed.

8. Each team should now draw several diagrams to represent different ways to extend the pen. The length by which an original side must be extended is the variable or unknown value in the problem; a letter must be selected by team members to label that part of the pen diagram. Once all the different lengths are identified, equations can be written to equate areas of the different sections formed.

9. Students will discover that there are two ways to enlarge the pen: (a) by extending the two sides that measure 5 meters each, or (b) by extending the two sides that measure 20 meters each. If the 5-meter sides are extended by K meters each, a possible equation to relate the areas will be: $20(5 + K) = 20(5) + 4$ sq. meters. If the 20-meter sides are extended by N meters each, a possible equation will be: $5(20 + N) = 5(20) + 4$ sq. meters. Diagrams that might be drawn for each case are shown below:

Case (a):   *Case (b):*

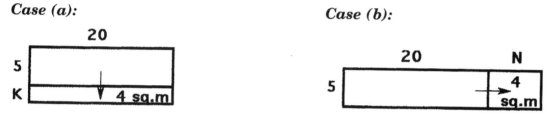

10. When the equations described in step 9 above are solved, we have $N = \frac{4}{5}$ of a meter and $K = \frac{4}{20}$ or $\frac{1}{5}$ of a meter. So if the 5-meter sides of the pen are extended, $2(\frac{1}{5})$ or $\frac{2}{5}$ of a meter of additional fencing will be needed. If the 20-meter sides are extended, $2(\frac{4}{5})$ or $\frac{8}{5}$ meters of additional fencing will be needed. **Conclusion:** The owner will prefer to extend the two shorter sides of the pen. Allow time for different teams to present their findings and to show the diagrams and labels they used to obtain their equations. Such discussions effectively increase mathematical understanding in students.

OBJECTIVE 2: Investigate linear relationships in geometry.

Activity 1: FOLD-R-TEAR

[Developing Action]

Materials: Worksheets 3–2–1 and 3–2–2
Scissors
Unlined paper
Calculators
Colored pencils (2 different colors)
Regular pencils and paper
Rulers

Management: Partners (3 parts, 30 minutes per part)

Directions:

1. There are 3 parts to this activity. They may be done at different class times or in any order.

Part A: Side Relationships in Triangles

2. Give each pair of students a copy of Worksheet 3–2–1, a pair of scissors, and a calculator. Worksheet 3–2–1 contains two large triangles for students to cut out. For each triangle, one side has a length indicated and the perimeter is given. Students must fold the other two sides against each other to find their relationship. The triangles will not be drawn to scale, so students cannot just measure to find the lengths of the two unmarked sides of each triangle. They must set up an equation that reflects the relationships they have found in each triangle in order to find the unknown lengths. Review how to find the perimeter of a triangle.

3. When the two unmarked sides of triangle #1 are folded together, their lengths match. Students should label these two sides with the same letter as the variable. An equation can now be written for the perimeter, using the information from the three sides. A possible equation to use might be: $N + N + 15 = 39$ units of perimeter, where N is the length of each unmarked side. Students should then solve the equation symbolically to find $N = 12$ units of length for each unmarked side. Emphasis should be on writing the equation and showing the changes made or steps taken to find the missing side length, even though some students may be able to solve the equation mentally. Translating from a situation to an equation should be stressed in this activity.

4. Students should repeat the above folding process with triangle #2. When the two unmarked sides are folded together, one side will be approximately twice as long as the other. This can be confirmed by marking the shorter side off on the edge of another sheet of paper, then transferring this marked length to the longer side to see how many times it will fit. A possible equation for the perimeter might be: $G + 2G + 21 = 48$ units of perimeter where G is the length of the shorter, unmarked side. The original equation needs to reflect the combining of the three distinct side lengths; hence, do not simplify to $3G + 21 = 48$ as the first equation to be recorded. The variables should be combined in a

The triangles below are *not* drawn to scale. Only the general length relationship between the unmarked sides may be used with the given measures to form equations. Cut out each triangle and follow the teacher's directions to find the missing side lengths.

Triangle #1:

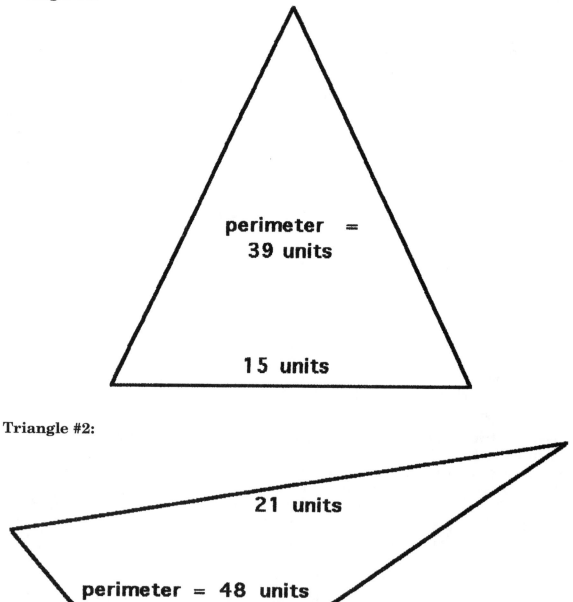

perimeter = 39 units

15 units

Triangle #2:

21 units

perimeter = 48 units

later step. The solution to the equation will be G = 9 units of length for the shorter un-marked side. The length of the longer unmarked side will be 2G = 2(9) or 18 units. As a final check, we have 9 + 18 + 21 = 48 units for the perimeter.

Part B: Total Angle Measure of a Triangle

5. Give each pair of students a copy of Worksheet 3–2–2, a ruler, scissors, a calculator, and 2 differently colored pencils (1 per color). For convenience, we will use the colors red and blue. Have students color the interior of each corner of triangle #1 in red (the whole inside of the triangle does not need to be colored) and the interior of each corner of triangle #2 in blue. The coloring will help students keep the pieces of the two triangles separated later. The three corners of each triangle should now be torn off so that the label of each angle is included in the torn corner piece.

6. Now have students draw a line segment vertically down the middle of a sheet of paper and draw a dot at the midpoint of the segment. Review what a straight angle looks like and that its angle measure is 180 degrees. The red corner pieces from triangle #1 should now be placed next to the line segment so that the vertex point of each corner piece touches the dot on the segment. The straight edges (from sides of triangle) of each corner piece should be either touching the line segment or touching the edge of another corner piece; the pieces should not overlap each other. If the pieces are placed carefully, they will appear as follows:

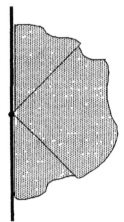

7. Discuss how the three pieces together represent the total rotation or measure of the three angles of triangle #1. Since the line segment represents a straight angle with its vertex at the dot and the 180-degree rotation around the dot matches the total rotation for the three angles from triangle #1, we can state that the combined angle measures from triangle #1 equal 180 degrees.

8. With this new information, students should be able to write an equation that relates the angle measures to 180 degrees. One possible equation might be: (m+3) + (m+5) + 40 = 180 degrees total. Students should solve their equation symbolically to find m = 66 degrees. Then the two unknown angle measures will be m + 3 = 69 degrees and m + 5 = 71 degrees. The final angle measures should be tested to see if their total still equals 180: 69 + 71 + 40 = 180 degrees.

9. Now have students repeat steps 6–8, using the three blue corner pieces from triangle #2. Again, the three pieces will fit into the straight angle's interior (that is, the

WORKSHEET 3-2-2
Total Angle Measure of a Triangle

The two triangles below are *not* drawn to scale. Cut out each triangle and color the interior of each of its corners with the same color. Use one color for triangle #1 and a different color for triangle #2. Tear off the three corners of each triangle, making sure the number or algebraic expression for each angle measure is showing on the torn-off corner. Follow the teacher's directions to find the missing angle measures of each triangle.

Triangle #1:

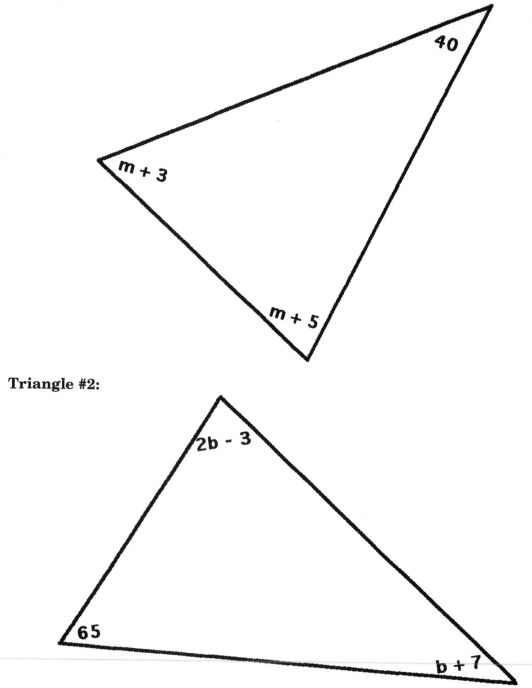

40

m + 3

m + 5

Triangle #2:

2b - 3

65

b + 7

measured rotation across the 3 pieces matches the measured rotation of the straight angle). A new equation can be written to relate these angle measures: $65 + (2b - 3) + (b + 7) = 180$ degrees. Solving the equation, we find $b = 37$ degrees. The two unknown angle measures will be $2b - 3 = 71$ degrees and $b + 7 = 44$ degrees. For a final test of the measures: $65 + 71 + 44 = 180$ degrees. Ask some students to explain what steps they used to solve their equations.

Part C: Transversals of Parallel Line Segments

10. Give each pair of students 3 plain, unlined sheets of paper and a colored pencil. Number the sheets near a corner as #1, #2, and #3. Show students how to fold their sheets as follows (short edge folds toward long edge of paper):

Sheet #1   **Sheet #2**   **Sheet #3**

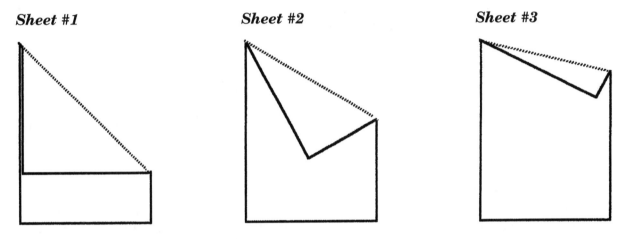

11. After each sheet is creased firmly along the fold, it should be unfolded and the crease redrawn with a colored pencil. The fold line now forms several angles with the left and right edges of the paper. Label the interior of each distinct angle in the order shown.

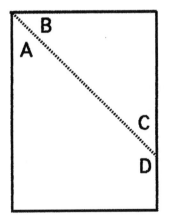

12. Have students trace each angle A onto another sheet of paper, then slide the tracing over each of the other three angles on the same sheet of paper to see if it matches or fits any of them. If there is a match, the letter A should be written and circled in colored pencil beside the letter of the other angle. Here are the matches students should find for A:

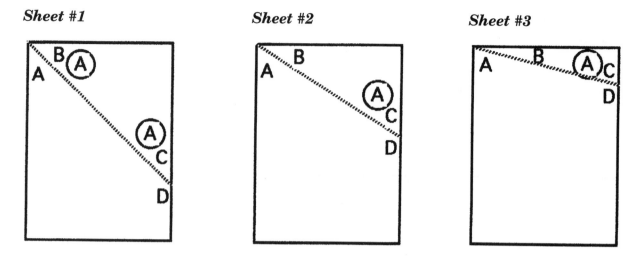

Sheet #1   **Sheet #2**   **Sheet #3**

13. Ask students why angle A matches angle B on sheet #1, but not on sheets #2 and #3. Hopefully they will notice that sheet #1 was folded so that the top edge of the paper touched the left edge of the paper, thereby forming two angles of equal measure (A and B). The other two sheets of paper were not folded that way. On all three sheets, however, angle A matches angle C in measure. Observe that the left and right sides or edges of each sheet of paper are parallel to each other, as are the short sides to each other. The fold line connects from one long side over to the other long side on all three sheets; this connecting line (actually a segment here) between two parallel edges is called a *transversal*. Notice that the acute angles A and C are on opposite sides of the transversal and both lie between the two long, parallel edges of each sheet of paper. Therefore, A and C are called *alternate interior angles* with respect to the transversal and the two parallel edges that it connects. Any two angles related in this way will always be equal in measure. An equation that reflects this special "transversal-parallel" relationship might be written as follows: $m\angle A = m\angle C$, where $m\angle A$ and $m\angle C$ denote the measures of angle A and angle C, respectively.

14. Encourage students to look for other angle relationships on their papers. Two other possibilities are: (1) angles A and B are *complementary* angles because the *two* angles together match or fit into a right angle (the corner of the paper makes a 90-degree angle); and (2) angles C and D are *supplementary* angles because the *two* angles together match or fit into a straight angle (the straight, right edge of the paper makes a 180-degree angle, its vertex being the point where the fold line intersects the right edge of the paper). Two equations that reflect these angle relationships are: (1) $m\angle A + m\angle B = 90$ degrees, where $m\angle A$ and $m\angle B$ denote the degree measures of complementary angles A and B, respectively; and (2) $m\angle C + m\angle D = 180$ degrees, where $m\angle C$ and $m\angle D$ denote the degree measures of supplementary angles C and D, respectively.

Activity 2: GEOMETRIC DIAGRAMS

[Bridging Action]

Materials: Paper
Regular pencils
Colored pencils (at least 3 different colors)
Calculators
Worksheets 3–2–3, 3–2–4, and 3–2–5

Management: Partners (3 parts, 30–50 minutes per part)

Directions:

1. The three major concepts introduced in Parts A–C of Activity 1 will be developed further here in Activity 2. Carefully connect the work done in each part in Activity 1 with the work done in its corresponding section here. Consistently follow the recording format presented in Section 2 for solving equations. Do not suggest "shortcuts" to students; even though such a technique might seem clear to you as the teacher, the change in approach and format at this time could be detrimental to students' understanding. Students eventually will discover their own abbreviated ways to record their steps; self-discovery is the best way to learn a "shortcut."

Part A: Side Relationships in Triangles

2. Give each pair of students 2 copies of Worksheet 3–2–3, a calculator, and 2 colored pencils (any color; do not have to be same color). On Worksheet 3–2–3 there are several triangles with labeled sides and given perimeter. Some perimeters will be specific values; others, algebraic expressions. On their own paper, students should write an equation for each triangle that reflects the sides-perimeter relationship, then solve the equation symbolically to find the missing measures of the triangle.

3. As an example, discuss item #5 on the worksheet. Since perimeter involves combining the lengths of the three sides, to help the tactile or visual learner, have students use a colored pencil to draw a path around the outside of the triangle, encircling each side measure encountered along the way.

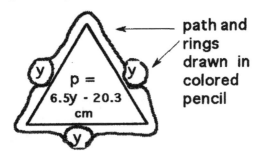

4. Students should now write the following equation on their own papers: $y + y + y = (6.5y - 20.3)$ cm. The three separate side lengths should be reflected in the equation at first. The given perimeter indicates the unit of measure for the side lengths of the

WORKSHEET 3–2–3
Diagrams for Side Relationships

For each triangle below, use the labels for the side lengths to write an equation for the given perimeter. Solve the equation to find the missing lengths or perimeter. Under each triangle, write its name(s) according to its sides. Possible names: (a) equilateral—all 3 sides are equal; (b) isosceles—2 or 3 sides are equal; or (c) scalene—0 or no sides are equal. (Triangles are *not* drawn to scale.)

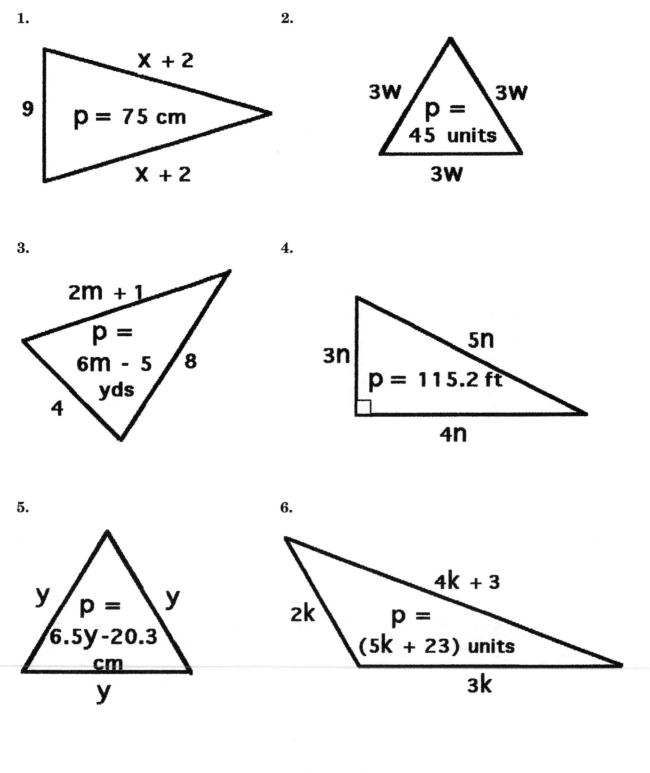

1.

$X + 2$
9
$p = 75$ cm
$X + 2$

2.

3W $\quad$ 3W
$p =$ 45 units
3W

3.

$2m + 1$
$p =$
$6m - 5$ $\quad$ 8
yds
4

4.

3n $\quad$ 5n
$p = 115.2$ ft
4n

5.

y $\quad$ y
$p =$ 6.5y -20.3 cm
y

6.

$4k + 3$
2k
$p =$ (5k + 23) units
3k

triangle as well as for the perimeter. Students should record all the steps needed to solve the equation. Here is one possible way to show the solution steps:

$$
\begin{aligned}
y + y + y &= (6.5y - 20.3) \text{ cm} \\
3y &= 6.5y + (-20.3) \\
\underline{-(3y) \quad -(3y)} & \\
0 &= 3.5y + (-20.3) \\
\underline{+ (+20.3) \qquad + (+20.3)} & \\
+20.3 &= 3.5y \\
(\tfrac{1}{3.5})(+20.3) &= (\tfrac{1}{3.5})(3.5y) \\
+5.8 &= y
\end{aligned}
$$

So each side length is 5.8 cm, and the perimeter is $(6.5)(5.8) - 20.3 = 17.4$ cm.

Note: The reciprocal-factor approach has been used here to find 1y, instead of the divisor approach where 3.5 would be written directly under 20.3. The factor notation makes it easier for students to work with fractional or decimal coefficients and to recognize reciprocals more quickly. Many students only seem comfortable with divisor notation when the divisor is a whole number. In addition, if needed, allow students to solve the equation by drawing diagrams. For values like –20.3, they can simply write 20.3 in a small square instead of drawing whole or partial individual units. A large X should be lightly drawn over the number to indicate the negative or inverse form. If some amount is to be added to or subtracted from –20.3, the square with the –20.3 can just be marked out and a new square drawn nearby with the new amount recorded inside it. Individual units can still be drawn for amounts less than 10, and vertical rectangles can still be drawn for variables.

5. After the values of the unknown side lengths have been found, students should write those values (each 5.8 cm) with colored pencil on the appropriate sides of the triangle on the worksheet. Be sure to make the final test: $5.8 + 5.8 + 5.8 = 17.4$ cm as the perimeter. Also, below the triangle, they should write all names that apply to the triangle with respect to its sides. In this example, the triangle has *three* equal side lengths, so it is an *equilateral* triangle, as well as an *isosceles* triangle. Record both names. Encourage students to pronounce the words correctly and to spell them correctly. (**Note:** An isosceles triangle may have *2 or 3* equal sides.)

6. Now have students complete the other exercises on the worksheet. When all are finished, have different students write their equations on the board and explain the steps they used. Discuss the types of triangles they found.

Part B: Total Angle Measure of a Triangle

7. Give each pair of students 2 copies of Worksheet 3–2–4, a calculator, and 2 colored pencils (any color; do not have to be same color). On Worksheet 3–2–4, there are several triangles with indicated angle measures. Using the fact that the sum of the three angle measures equals 180 degrees, students will write and solve equations to find the missing angle measures.

8. As an example, discuss item #3 from Worksheet 3–2–4 with students. Review their experience from Activity 1 where they discovered that the rotational measure of the three cut-off corners of a triangle matched the measure of a straight angle. Again, to help the tactile or visual learner, have students write 180 in the center of the triangle

WORKSHEET 3–2–4
Total Angle Measure Using Diagrams

For each triangle below, use the labels for the angle measures to write an equation for the total angle measure of the triangle. Solve the equation to find the missing angle measures. Under each triangle, write its name according to its angles. Possible names: (a) acute—3 acute angles; (b) right—2 acute angles and 1 right angle; or (c) obtuse—2 acute angles and 1 obtuse angle. (Triangles are *not* drawn to scale.)

1.

2.

3.

4.

5.

6.

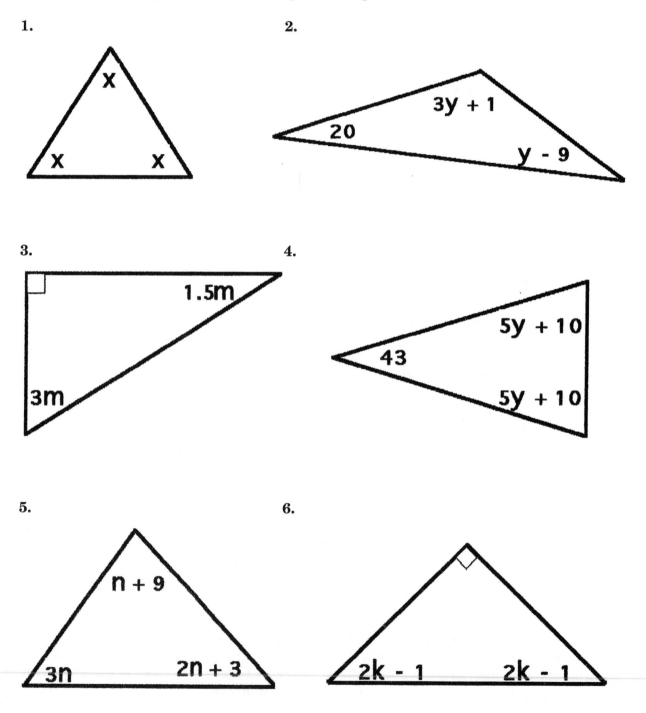

and 90 beside the box symbol, then draw a ring around the value or expression given for each angle measure and draw an arrow from that expression toward the 180.

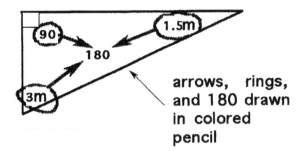

arrows, rings, and 180 drawn in colored pencil

9. On their own papers, students should now write an equation that relates the three angle measures to 180, recording *degrees,* the units used, with the 180 at the end of the equation. All three angles should be represented separately in the initial equation: 90 + 3m + 1.5m = 180 degrees. Students should record all the steps needed to solve the equation. Here is a possible way to record the solution steps:

$$
\begin{aligned}
90 + 3m + 1.5m &= 180 \\
90 \qquad + 4.5m &= 180 \\
-90 \qquad\qquad &\;\; -90 \\
\hline
4.5m &= 90 \\
(\tfrac{1}{4.5})(4.5m) &= (\tfrac{1}{4.5})(90) \\
m &= 20
\end{aligned}
$$

So the two unknown angles are (1.5)(20) = 30 degrees and 3(20) = 60 degrees.

Note: Regarding the matter of factor vs. divisor, refer to the "Note" in step 4. Also, if needed, allow students to solve the equation by drawing diagrams. For large values like 180, they can simply write 180 in a small square instead of drawing 180 individual units. Then if some amount is to be added to or subtracted from 180, the square with the 180 can just be marked out and a new square drawn nearby with the new amount recorded inside it. Individual units can still be drawn for amounts less than 10, and vertical rectangles can still be drawn for variables.

10. After the new value of m has been used to find the unknown angle measures, students should write those values (30 degrees and 60 degrees) with colored pencil near the appropriate vertices of the triangle on the worksheet. Be sure to make the final test: 90 + 30 + 60 = 180 degrees. Also, below the triangle, they should write all names that apply to the triangle with respect to its angles. In this example, the triangle has two acute angles and one right angle, so it is a *right* triangle. Encourage students to pronounce the terms correctly and to spell them correctly.

11. Now have students complete the other exercises on the worksheet. When all are finished, have different students write their equations on the board and explain the steps they used. Also, discuss the different types of triangles they found.

Part C: Transversals of Parallel Line Segments

12. Give each pair of students 2 copies of Worksheet 3–2–5, a calculator, and 3 colored pencils (3 different colors). On Worksheet 3–2–5, students will color with the same color the interiors of any two angles whose measures are *equal.* Angles with different measures will have different colors. A single arc in a third color will be drawn across any two angles that are *supplementary.* Equations will be written and solved in order to find any

WORKSHEET 3–2–5
Transversals Across Parallel Line Segments

For each set of line segments below, any two segments that appear oriented the same way will be considered parallel to each other. (Equal numbers of small arrows pointing in the same direction will also show that lines are parallel.) A value or algebraic expression written in the interior of an angle represents the degree measure for that angle. Write equations that relate various angles to each other. Several equations are possible for each exercise. Use logical reasoning to find the measures of angles marked with "?" or "??."

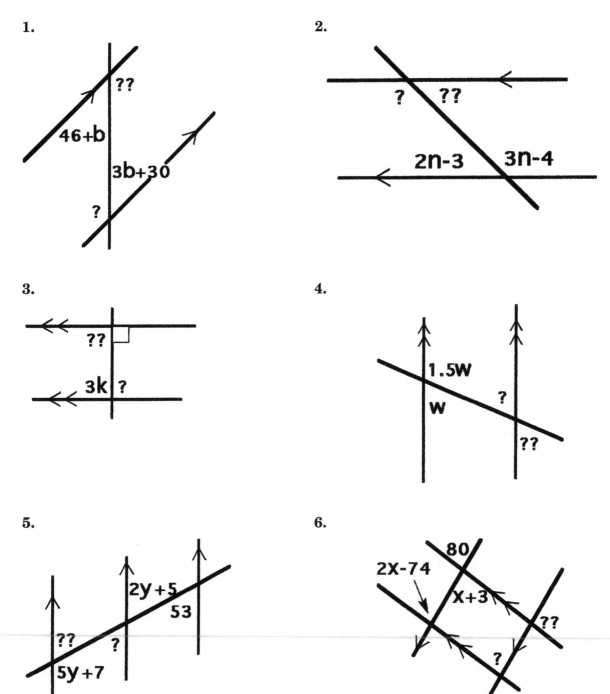

1.

2.

3.

4.

5.

6.

missing angle measures described with algebraic expressions. *Logical reasoning* will also be used to find additional angle measures marked with "?" or "??."

13. Discuss item #2 on Worksheet 3–2–5 with students. The interiors of the two angles labeled with expressions lie on a line segment and share a common side. In Activity 1, we learned by folding and tracing that these two angles are supplementary and have a total measure of 180 degrees. Have students draw an arc in color #1 (their choice) across the interiors of these two angles. (See the illustration in step 15.)

14. On their own papers, they should now write the equation that relates the measures of these two angles to each other: $(2n - 3) + (3n - 4) = 180$ degrees. All steps needed to solve this equation should also be recorded. Here is one possible way to record the solution steps:

$$(2n - 3) + (3n - 4) = \ 180$$
$$5n + (-7) = +180$$
$$\underline{+ (+7) \quad + (+7)}$$
$$5n = +187$$
$$(\tfrac{1}{5})(5n) = (\tfrac{1}{5})(+187)$$
$$n = 37.4$$

Using the new value, $n = 37.4$, the missing angle measures (71.8 degrees and 108.2 degrees) can be found and written in colored pencil within the corresponding angle interiors of the triangle on the worksheet.

15. Ask students how they can find the angle measures marked with "?" and "??." Ask if they see any relationships between one of these angle measures and the angle measures already found. If needed, students may compare the various angle measures by tracing one angle on another sheet of paper, then moving the tracing around to try to match it to any of the other angles formed by the line segments. Hopefully they will recognize that ? and $(3n - 4)$ are measures of alternate interior angles; that is, the angles lie between the two parallel line segments but are on opposite sides of the transversal segment. $(2n - 3)$ and ?? also are measures of alternate interior angles. Since each such pair is equivalent, students should color the interiors of the first pair with color #2 and the interiors of the second pair with color #3. Another arc in color #1 might also be drawn across the interiors of the angles having ? and ?? measure if students recognize the two angles as supplementary angles.

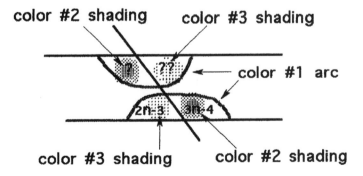

16. Equations may now be written for these new relationships: $? = 3n - 4$ and $?? = 2n - 3$. Since the values of n, $3n - 4$, and $2n - 3$ are already known, students may simply write the following on their papers: $? = 108.2$ degrees and $?? = 71.8$ degrees, then record the values in their proper places on the set of line segments.

17. Now have students complete the other exercises on the worksheet. When all are finished, have different students write their equations on the board and explain the steps they used. What equations are actually solved in detail will depend on which relationships are used first. Always have students explain which angle relationships they are using to work a particular exercise. In each exercise, other angles are present that have not been labeled. Students may certainly find the measures of these angles as well, if interest and time permit.

Answer Key to WORKSHEET 3–2–3

1. $(X + 2) + (X + 2) + 9 = 75$ cm, $X = 31$;
   $X + 2 = 33$ cm;
   isosceles triangle

2. $3W + 3W + 3W = 45$ units, $W = 5$;
   $3W = 15$ units;
   equilateral and isosceles triangle

3. $(2m + 1) + 8 + 4 = (6m - 5)$ yds, $m = 4.5$;
   $2m + 1 = 10$ yds, $p = 6m - 5 = 22$ yds;
   scalene triangle

4. $3n + 4n + 5n = 115.2$ ft, $n = 9.6$;
   $3n = 28.8$ ft, $4n = 38.4$ ft, $5n = 48$ ft;
   scalene triangle

5. $y + y + y = (6.5y - 20.3)$ cm, $y = 5.8$;
   $y = 5.8$ cm, $p = 6.5y - 20.3 = 17.4$ cm;
   equilateral and isosceles triangle

6. $2k + (4k + 3) + 3k = (5k + 23)$ units, $k = 5$;
   $2k = 10$ units, $3k = 15$ units, $4k + 3 = 23$ units, $p = 5k + 23 = 48$ units;
   scalene triangle

Answer Key to WORKSHEET 3–2–4

1. $X + X + X = 180$ degrees, $X = 60$;
   $X = 60$ degrees;
   acute triangle

2. $20 + (3y + 1) + (y - 9) = 180$ degrees, $y = 42$;
   $3y + 1 = 127$ degrees, $y - 9 = 33$ degrees;
   obtuse triangle

3. $90 + 1.5m + 3m = 180$ degrees, $m = 20$;
   $1.5m = 30$ degrees, $3m = 60$ degrees;
   right triangle

4. $43 + (5y + 10) + (5y + 10) = 180$ degrees, $y = 11.7$;
   $5y + 10 = 68.5$ degrees;
   acute triangle

5. $3n + (n + 9) + (2n + 3) = 180$ degrees, $n = 28$;
   $3n = 84$ degrees, $n + 9 = 37$ degrees, $2n + 3 = 59$ degrees;
   acute triangle

6. $90 + (2k - 1) + (2k - 1) = 180$ degrees, $k = 23$;
   $2k - 1 = 45$ degrees;
   right triangle

Answer Key to WORKSHEET 3-2-5

Several possible equations and the angle measures for each exercise are provided in this answer key; no color coding is included.

Equations

1. $46 + b = 3b + 30$, $b = 8$
   $?? + (46 + b) = 180$ degrees
   $? + (3b + 30) = 180$ degrees

2. $(2n - 3) + (3n - 4) = 180$ degrees, $n = 37.4$
   $? = 3n - 4$
   $?? = 2n - 3$

3. $3k = 90$ degrees
   $3k + ? = 180$ degrees
   $?? + 90 = 180$ degrees

4. $1.5w + w = 180$ degrees
   $? = w$
   $? = ??$

5. $2y + 5 = 53$ degrees
   $?? + (5y + 7) = 180$ degrees
   $? = (2y + 5)$ degrees
   $? = ??$

6. $X + 3 = 80$ degrees
   $X + 3 = 2X - 74$
   $? = (2X - 74)$ degrees
   $?? + 80 = 180$ degrees

Solutions

1. $46 + b = 54$ degrees
   $3b + 30 = 54$ degrees
   $?? = 126$ degrees
   $? = 126$ degrees

2. $2n - 3 = 71.8$ degrees
   $3n - 4 = 108.2$ degrees
   $? = 108.2$ degrees
   $?? = 71.8$ degrees

3. $k = 30$ degrees
   $? = 90$ degrees
   $?? = 90$ degrees

4. $w = 72$ degrees
   $? = 72$ degrees
   $?? = 72$ degrees

5. $y = 24$ degrees
   $??$ or $?$ or $(2y + 5) = 53$ degrees
   $5y + 7 = 127$ degrees

6. $X = 77$ degrees
   $(2X - 74)$ or $? = 80$ degrees
   $?? = 100$ degrees

Activity 3: GEO-VEXATION

[Application/Exploration]

Materials: Worksheet 3–2–6
   Colored pencils (at least 2 different colors)
   Regular pencils and paper
   Calculators

Management: Teams of 4 students each (30–50 minutes)

Directions:

   1. This activity assumes that all *three* parts (A, B, and C) of Activity 1 and Activity 2 have been completed. Give each team one copy of Worksheet 3–2–6 (enlarged if possible),

WORKSHEET 3-2-6
Geo-Vexation

Follow the teacher's instructions to play this game. Angles and line segments are not drawn to scale. Any line segments with small arrows oriented in the same direction are parallel to each other. Any numbers or expressions in brackets, [—], represent segment lengths.

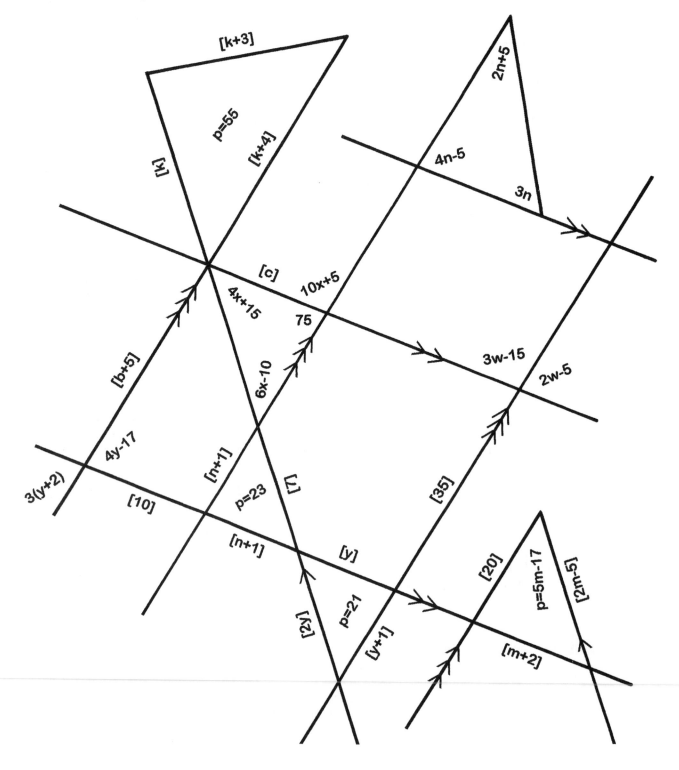

2 colored pencils (1 per color), and 1 or 2 calculators. Each team will form two pairs of partners; one pair of partners will compete against the other pair on the same team. Each pair will have its own colored pencil and its own calculator, if possible. On the worksheet, which serves as a gameboard, the angles and line segments are not drawn to scale; students should not assume that two angles or two segments are of equal measure just because they "look like they are equal." All values or expressions for segment lengths are shown in brackets, [—], on the worksheet; values or expressions for angle measures are not. A marked length applies only to the shortest segment on which it is written; a label for an angle measure applies only to the smallest angle in whose interior it lies. The value or expression for the perimeter of a triangle will be identified as "p" in the interior of the triangle.

2. On each team, the two pairs of students will take turns applying the relationships studied in Activities 1 and 2, but only one relationship may be applied on a turn. This chosen relationship must be stated at the beginning of the turn by the playing pair. A relationship may occur in the following ways on the worksheet: (1) a triangle solved for 2 or 3 of its side lengths; (2) a triangle solved for 2 or 3 of its angle measures; (3) a pair of supplementary angles solved for one or both of the angle measures; (4) a pair of alternate, interior angles solved for one or both angle measures; (5) a pair of vertical angles solved for one or both angle measures; or (6) a pair of corresponding angles on parallel line segments solved for one or both angle measures. A few others are possible, but have not been studied yet; accept them if students recognize them and can explain them.

3. As stated previously, more than one relationship may not be used during a single turn. For example, supplementary angles A and B at the intersection of two line segments may be found, but angle C that is supplementary to angle B at the same intersection may not be labeled with a value during the same turn (even though the players may easily know its value!) since it does not relate to A *and* B in the *same way*. If the next pair to play has paid attention, they can quickly state the value of angle C without any computational effort. They will be using the relationship of B supplemental to C. The turn then goes back to the previous pair of partners. It will be possible in several places on the worksheet to find a single angle measure merely by knowing that angle's relationship to other nearby angles that lie within a set of parallel or intersecting line segments. Only two acute angles on the worksheet cannot be labeled with values; you might offer bonus points to the partners on each team who locate them first. These two angles will be marked on the answer key!

4. Partners should record and circle their newly found values on the worksheet in the appropriate places, using their own color of pencil. The next turn then goes to the other pair of partners, who repeat the process.

5. During the game, a pair may "pass" or not play on a turn if they temporarily cannot find another angle or side to evaluate, but they may only pass two times during a game. If a third pass is necessary, the game will end.

6. When one pair of partners is unable to play for the third time or when both pairs of partners are unable to evaluate any more angles or marked segments on the worksheet, each pair will simply count all the numbers written on the worksheet in their particular color. The pair with the most numbers recorded will be the winning pair.

Answer Key to WORKSHEET 3–2–6, Geo-Vexation

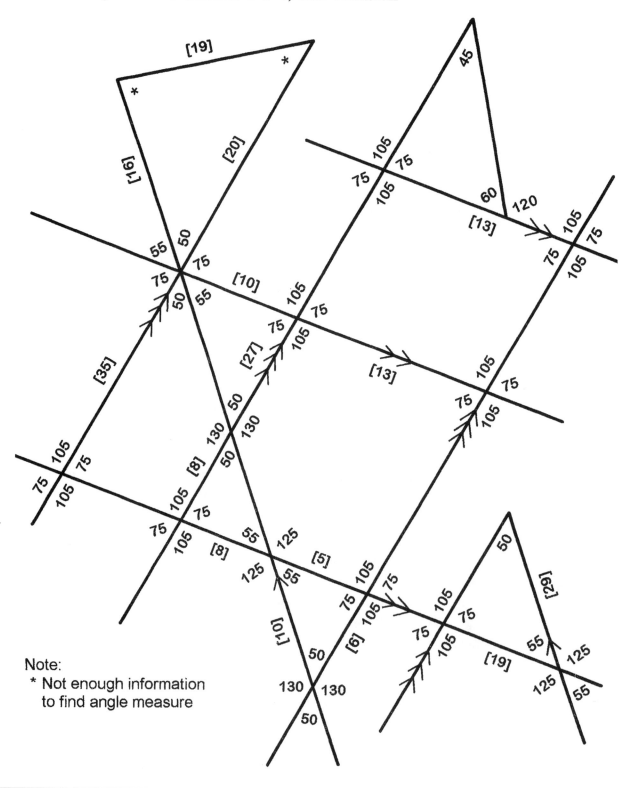

Note:

* Not enough information
to find angle measure

OBJECTIVE 3: Explore ratio and proportion in rates, probability, percent, and other topics.

Activity 1: BUILDING WITH RATIOS

[Developing Action]

Materials: Sets of variable and unit tiles (see Section 2, Objective 1 for details, if needed)

Counters such as small blocks, cubes, or 1-inch paper squares (2 colors; 20 per color)

Ratio building mats (described in step 1)

Paper

Regular pencils

Worksheet 3–3–1

Management: Partners (50 minutes)

Directions:

1. Give each pair of students a set of variable and unit tiles, 20 counters in each of two colors, and a ratio building mat. The building mat may be made by drawing sections on an 8.5″ × 14″ sheet of unlined paper and labeling them in the following way:

2.5 in.	6.5 in.	5 in.	
Basic Ratio:			2 in.
Secondary Ratio:			6.5 in.

In the discussion, the two *blank* columns of the mat will be called the "left" and "right" columns. **Proportions** make up a **major** strategy in mathematical problem solving. Do not rush the development of this concept. Allow maximum time for both Activity 1 and Activity 2 in order to ensure full understanding by all students.

2. Different basic or simplified ratios can be shown on the mat by placing one color of counter in the upper section of the left column and another color of counter in the upper section of the right column. We will limit the amounts used in the basic ratio to the counting or natural numbers. The two numbers used in a basic ratio will usually be relatively prime; that is, they will not have a common divisor greater than one.

3. As an example, have students show the basic ratio of 4 dollars earned for every hour of work done. This type of ratio that involves a *single unit* of one element in the comparison (here, time) is called a **rate.** Students should place 4 counters of one color (e.g., blue) in the upper left section of the mat and 1 counter of the other color (e.g., red) in the upper right section of the mat. For discussion purposes, we will continue to refer to red and blue as our two colors for the counters and will choose to place blue counters in the left column and red counters in the right column each time.

4. Discuss how this basic relationship of 4 dollars to 1 hour must be maintained, no matter how many dollars or hours are involved. To show this, have students place 2 rows of 4 blue counters each in the lower left section of the building mat and 2 rows of 1 red counter each in the lower right section of the mat. Each row across the mat represents 4 dollars being earned in or compared to 1 hour. The secondary ratio is always built by repeating the basic ratio several times. The building mat should now appear as follows:

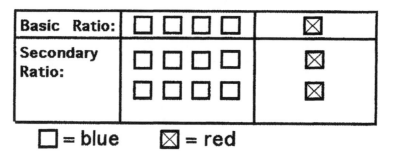

5. Ask students to find the new secondary ratio for *dollars to hours* by counting the counters in the two lower sections of the mat. Students should have 8 blue counters and 2 red counters. The new ratio is therefore *8 dollars to 2 hours,* reading from left to right on the mat. The basic ratio and the secondary ratio are placed on the mat in the same order; that is, if we decide to show dollars in the left column and hours in the right column of the upper level of the mat, then we must keep that order in the lower level also. Have students record the following on their own papers: *4 dollars compares to 1 hour like 8 dollars compares to 2 hours.* Here an alternative recording might be: *4 dollars earned in 1 hour is like 8 dollars earned in 2 hours.*

6. Assign several other basic ratios for students to show on the upper level of their building mats and then extend to secondary ratios by making two to five rows or copies of the basic ratio on the lower level of the mat. (See Worksheet 3–3–1.) Have them write a sentence like the example in step 5 to describe each result. Use 1 to 5 for each number in the basic ratio. The total number of counters used in each column (upper and lower sections combined) is limited to 20, the number of counters available in each color. Here are some examples of basic ratios to use: 3 girls to 4 boys; 1 quarter to 5 nickels; 2 pencils to 5 cents; 3 cups to 2 teaspoons; 4 chairs to 1 table; 3 deliveries to 5 miles; 5 pizzas to 4 teenagers.

7. Another version of the initial procedure presented in steps 4 and 5 consists of giving students a *secondary ratio* and *one part of a basic ratio.* The missing part of the basic ratio must then be found. Students would still record their sentences in the same way. As an example, consider this problem from **probability:** "The chance that a striped ball will drop out of the spinning basket whenever one ball is released is 1 out of 4. If 12 balls have been released, how many might we expect to be striped?" There are at least two ways we can define "basic ratio" in probability problems. In this activity we will define it to be the number of striped balls (i.e., 1 striped ball) mentioned in the probability of lowest terms compared to the number of striped balls expected in some larger sampling of released balls. For the secondary ratio, the lower sections will show the total released balls given in the probability of lowest terms compared to the total number of released balls in the larger sampling. (A similar interpretation is applied to **percent** in Activity 2.) To represent what is known initially, students should place 1 blue counter (for 1 striped ball) in the upper left section of the mat, and *randomly* place 4 blue counters (for 4 balls total from probability of lowest terms) in the lower left section. Twelve red

WORKSHEET 3–3–1
Building with Ratios

Use tiles or colored counters to build the following ratios on your ratio mat according to your teacher's instructions. Write a sentence to record each result.

1. 4 dollars to 1 hour

2. 1 striped ball out of 4 balls total

3. 8 cats to 12 dogs

4. 12 students to 3 boxes of doughnuts

5. 15 guppies to 10 goldfish

6. 6 wieners to 15 buns

7. 4 cars to 12 people

8. 2B to 1B

9. 1G to +3

10. −2C to +4

11. 2A to −1

12. −K to −5

counters should be *randomly* placed (not in rows yet) in the lower right section of the mat. The upper right section, which should hold the number of expected striped balls in the larger sampling of 12 balls, is empty at first.

   8. Since the secondary ratio must contain rows that match the row in the basic ratio, students must discover how many rows of 1 blue counter each can be made with the 4 blue counters in the lower left section of the mat; 4 such rows can be made. Now, since the lower left section has 4 rows, the 12 red counters in the lower right section must be arranged into 4 equal rows; this forces 3 red counters to be in each row. Each row of counters in the lower right section must match the one row of red counters in the upper right section. Hence, students should now place one row of 3 red counters in the upper right section of the mat. This new amount indicates that in the larger sampling of 12 balls total, we should expect 3 of the released balls to be striped. Because of the way we defined our sections earlier, students should now record: *1 striped ball compares to 3 striped balls like 4 total balls compare to 12 total balls.* An alternative way to say this in probability language is the following: *1 striped ball out of 4 balls total is equivalent to 3 striped balls out of 12 balls total.*

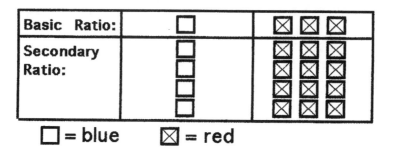

   9. After students have had practice initially with generating a secondary ratio from a given basic ratio, reverse the procedure. Give them a *secondary ratio* and have them try to find the basic ratio. This corresponds to the traditional practice of "reducing or simplifying a ratio to lowest terms." See step 2 for the requirements for a basic ratio.

   10. As an example, ask students to show *8 cats to 12 dogs* as the secondary ratio on the lower level of their building mat. Since *cats* are mentioned first in the expression, 8 blue counters should be placed in the lower left column. Twelve red counters should then be placed in the lower right column to represent *dogs*.

   11. Students must now try to form rows of counters so that the same number of rows is seen in both lower sections and the number of blue (or red) counters found in one row is also found in each of the other rows in the same column. Students might form two rows first, showing 4 blue and 6 red counters in each row. Since the blue counters and red counters in one row can still be regrouped into two groups of 2 blue and two groups of 3 red, that is, 4 and 6 can both be divided by 2, students must separate their blue and red counters into more rows. Hence, the final arrangement for the secondary ratio becomes four rows of 2 blue counters and 3 red counters each.

   12. This last combination of 2 blue counters and 3 red counters per row is the basic ratio being sought and should be *copied* by placing 2 new blue counters in the upper left section and 3 new red counters in the upper right section of the mat. Students should now write the following: *8 cats compare to 12 dogs like 2 cats compare to 3 dogs.*

   13. Have students simplify several other secondary ratios to basic ratios and write sentences for their results like the sentence given in step 12. Here are some possible secondary ratios to try: 12 students to 3 boxes of doughnuts; 15 guppies to 10 goldfish; 6 wieners to 15 buns; 4 cars to 12 people.

14. Now that students are comfortable with building countable amounts on their mats, introduce them to problems that will involve the variable tiles. Using the unit tiles is similar to using the red and blue counters, so we can easily include them later with the variable tiles for more ratio practice. Give students the basic ratio of 2B to 1B (or B) and ask what is needed in a secondary ratio to compare to 4B. Students should place 2 of the variable tiles horizontally in one row in the upper left section of the mat and place 1 variable tile horizontally in the upper right section. Since they are looking for the amount "to compare to 4B," 4 variable tiles should be placed *randomly at first* in the lower right section of the mat.

15. Variable tiles must follow the same arranging procedure that has been used with the colored counters (or unit tiles). That is, the row of tiles in the basic ratio must be copied in the secondary ratio. Since there is just one variable tile in the upper right section, the 4 variable tiles in the lower right section of the mat must be arranged in rows, using 1 variable tile per row. Therefore, there will be 4 rows of 1 variable tile each in the lower right section. This requires the lower left section to have 4 rows also, so students should now build 4 rows of 2 variable tiles each in the lower left section of the mat. Students should record the following: *2B compares to 1B like 8B compares to 4B.* The final arrangement of tiles on the mat will be as follows:

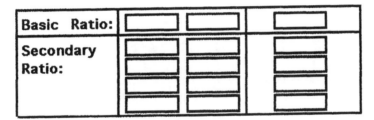

16. For additional practice, use basic ratios involving variable and also unit tiles. Have students practice building the secondary ratio by copying the basic ratio row from one to four times. They should record their results each time. Along with the given basic ratio, you may sometimes want to give them one amount of the secondary ratio and have them find the other amount (see steps 14–15). Some basic ratios to use: 1G to +3; –2C to +4; 2A to –1; and –K to –5.

Activity 2: DRAWING PROPORTIONS

[Bridging Action]

Materials: Worksheet 3–3–2
                Regular pencils

Management: Partners (50 minutes)

Directions:

1. Give each pair of students 4–6 copies of Worksheet 3–3–2, which contains blank ratio frames for students to complete. Use the small boxes above the frames for numbering the

Name _____   Date _____

WORKSHEET 3–3–2
Drawing Proportions

Complete the frames below to find equivalent ratios. Write number sentences about what you find. Use the small boxes above the frames to number your exercises.

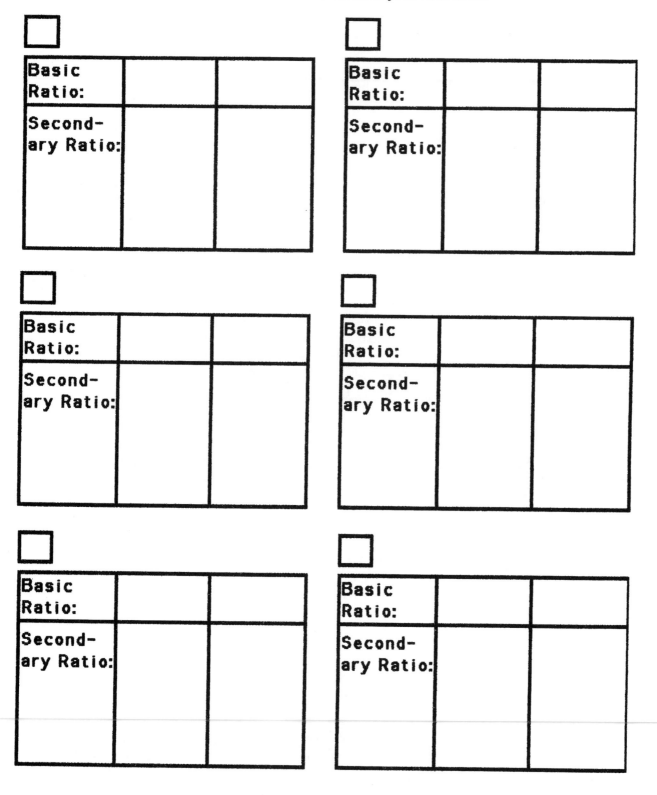

WORKSHEET 3–3–2 *(cont.)*
Drawing Proportions

Draw these exercises on ratio frames, following your teacher's instructions.

1. 3 circles to 4 triangles

2. 2 circles to 1 triangle

3. 9W to –12

4. 25% of $40

5. 1 circle to 3 triangles (use 3 circles)

6. 3 circles to 2 triangles (use 4 triangles)

7. 2M to +5 (use 6M)

8. –A to –2 (use –8)

9. 16 circles to 4 triangles

10. 15 circles to 6 squares

11. 6P to –4

12. –3N to +9

13. 50% of 16 crates

14. 7 boxes are 20% of _____

15. 5 is _____% of 20

16. 2 blue balls out of every 6 balls (use 15 balls total)

frames in order as needed. When given the basic ratio, students will draw that ratio on a frame of the worksheet, then draw the number of rows indicated by the teacher in order to find the corresponding secondary ratio. For other exercises, students will be given the secondary ratio to draw, then must apply a *trial-and-error* strategy to find the corresponding basic ratio. Number sentences will be recorded under each frame that compare the two ratios shown there.

2. For this activity we will use simple shapes like triangles, squares, or circles to represent ratio quantities, or we will draw models of the variable tiles and unit tiles. For the first exercise, have students draw the basic ratio, *3 circles to 4 triangles*, on the first frame of the worksheet. One row of 3 circles should be drawn in the upper left section of the frame and one row of 4 triangles (equilaterals will be just fine) in the upper right section. Ask students to make two copies or draw two rows of the basic ratio in the lower sections of the frame to form a secondary ratio. The secondary ratio will be *6 circles to 8 triangles*. The frame should appear as follows:

3. Below the completed frame, students should record the final proportion they have drawn in the following way: *3 to 4 = (2 × 3) to (2 × 4) = 6 to 8*. Discuss the idea that the notations (2 × 3) and (2 × 4) simply refer to the two rows of 3 circles and the two rows of 4 triangles that were drawn in the secondary ratio. The last ratio, 6 to 8, represents the total circles and total triangles drawn for the secondary ratio.

4. Now have students draw the basic ratio, *2 circles to 1 triangle,* and tell them to use *5 triangles* in the secondary ratio. Since there is only 1 triangle in the basic ratio, the required 5 triangles will need to be drawn as 5 rows of 1 triangle each. This means that we will need 5 rows of circles in the secondary ratio, with 2 circles per row. So the secondary ratio becomes *10 circles to 5 triangles*. The following number sentence should be written below the completed frame: *2 to 1 = (5 × 2) to (5 × 1) = 10 to 5*.

5. Work with variables and individual units should follow the same procedures as used previously with countable quantities. Because of the size of the ratio frame on the worksheet, we will represent the variable tile by drawing a vertical rectangle, and the unit tile by drawing small circles. A large X in the interior of each shape will indicate the inverse form. For this exercise, give students the secondary ratio, 9W to –12, and ask them to find the basic ratio, that is, the row with the least amount of variables and units in it that can still be repeated to make 9W and –12. To accomplish this, students need to draw the greatest number of rows possible, using 9 variables and 12 negative units. Students may have to find the number of rows needed by first drawing the shapes on scratch paper. All rows must have the same combination of rectangles (variables) and circles (units). Here, three rows will be the most rows possible. There will be 3 rectangles and 4 circles (with X in the interior) drawn in each row; hence, 3 rectangles and 4 "inverse" circles need to be drawn in the basic ratio sections of the frame. The following illustration shows the completed frame.

Basic Ratio:	‖ ‖ ‖	⊗ ⊗ ⊗ ⊗
Secondary Ratio:	‖ ‖ ‖	⊗ ⊗ ⊗ ⊗
		⊗ ⊗ ⊗ ⊗
		⊗ ⊗ ⊗ ⊗
		⊗ ⊗ ⊗ ⊗

6. Students should now record the following number sentence: *9W to –12 = (3 × 3W) to (3 × –4) = 3W to –4.* An alternative form with *variables* might be preferred: *9W to –12 = 3(3W) to 3(–4) = 3W to –4.*

7. Another type of proportion is **percent.** Using the definition that 25% means "25 parts out of 100 parts total" and a modified pictorial model for larger numbers, have students draw on a frame to represent the problem: "What amount in dollars is 25% of $40?" To show 25% on the frame, students should first draw a small square in the upper left section of the frame and write the number 25 inside the square. Since there are four 25's in 100, four squares (with one square per row to match the one square in the basic ratio above) should be drawn in the lower left section of the frame. (If we had chosen to show 25 with a row of five squares, a 5 written in each square, then we would have to show 100 with four rows of five squares, a 5 inside each square.) As we did earlier with the probability problem (see Activity 1, steps 7 and 8), we are defining the basic ratio to be the *number of parts wanted* out of 100 parts total compared to the *number of dollars wanted* out of some total number of dollars being considered. In other words, the basic ratio represents the *portions* of two sets being compared and the secondary ratio represents the *totals* of the two sets being compared. This interpretation is being used to provide continuity between recording formats.

8. Because of the four rows of 25 used to show 100 in the lower left section of the frame, the $40 (the total in dollars) must also be shown in four rows. This requires us to use $10 per row. On the frame in the lower right section, students should draw four rows of one small square each, with $10 written inside each square. The final frame will appear as follows:

Basic Ratio:	25			$10
Secondary Ratio:	25			$10
	25			$10
	25			$10
	25			$10

9. The upper right section shows one square of $10, the solution to the percent problem. Students should record the proportion number sentence: *100 to $40 = (4 × 25) to (4 × 10) = 25 to $10* (use of $ here is optional). An alternative recording in percent language would be: *25% of $40 is $10.* (**Note:** In the recent proportion number sentence, we cannot write "100% to $40" instead of "100 to $40," because **100** and % in this case are synonymous.)

10.   Provide additional practice problems for students to draw on the frames and record as number sentences. The teacher should indicate the number of rows (up to 5 rows) for students to draw to form the secondary ratio when only the basic ratio is given.

   (a)   Some basic ratios to use (a possible quantity of the secondary ratio is given in parentheses): 1 circle to 3 triangles (3 circles); 3 circles to 2 triangles (4 triangles); 2M to +5 (6M); –A to –2 (–8) [draw vertical rectangles for variables]

   (b)   Some secondary ratios to simplify to the basic ratio: 16 circles to 4 triangles; 15 circles to 6 squares; 6P to –4; –3N to +9

   (c)   Some applications to solve as proportions [if necessary, write larger amounts in small squares drawn on frame]: 50% of 16 crates = ?; 7 boxes are 20% of how many boxes total?; 5 is what percent of 20?; probability for selecting blue is 2 blue balls out of every 6 balls, so we expect how many blue out of 15 balls total?

11. Change in recording format: After students seem comfortable with the drawing and recording of various types of proportions, we want to move them to a new way of recording the four quantities of a proportion (i.e., a basic ratio with one of its secondary ratios). On their own papers, have them draw several 2 by 2 grids that look similar to the frames used to show ratios pictorially, but the ratio labels are omitted. Here is an example of what we shall call a "ratio table":

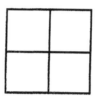

12.   On the "ratio table," the top row will still be used for the basic ratio and the bottom row will be for the secondary ratio. Using their previous recordings or drawings from Activity 1 or Activity 2 exercises, have students transfer the numbers for the amounts either built or drawn in the four different sections of the mat or frame to their *corresponding* sections in the new ratio table. Labeling the rows and columns will also be helpful. For example, in the percent problem described in steps 7–9 above, the ratio table should be completed as follows [do not write the % symbol in the boxes with 25 and 100; the presence of 100 eliminates the need for the %]:

	percent	dollars
part	25	$10
total	100	$40

The numbers from the probability problem in Activity 1, steps 7 and 8, might be recorded in a ratio table as follows:

	sm sample	lg sample
striped	1	3
total	4	12

13. On the classroom board, draw several of the ratio tables prepared by the students. For each ratio table, ask students to look for special relationships among the four numbers shown. Discuss any ideas they may have. Encourage them to find a relationship or a general statement that holds true for all the ratio tables, regardless of the specific numbers used. After several ideas have been shared, if not already mentioned, present the idea of **multiples**—the major thread in **proportions.** For example, in the percent ratio table in step 12 above, the *fourth* multiple of 25 is 100 and the *fourth* multiple of $10 is $40. In the probability ratio table, the *fourth* multiple of 1 is 4 and the *fourth* multiple of 3 is 12; also, the *third* multiple of 1 is 3 and the *third* multiple of 4 is 12. Show these special relationships directly on the ratio tables in the following ways. (For consistency, draw arrows to point from the smaller number to the larger one each time; also, as an example to clarify the "multiple" notation, the "4X" on the arrow from 25 to 100 should be correctly read as "4 of 25 equals 100.")

14. Ask students to draw and label similar arrows on all their other ratio tables, at least wherever the multiples are *obvious*. Original quantities were selected carefully, so every ratio table from Activities 1 and 2 should have at least one *obvious* pair of arrows, pointing in the same direction either vertically or horizontally, and each arrow in the pair should have the same "multiple" label. Notice that, in the probability ratio table mentioned previously, both vertical and horizontal arrows were present. This property is true for *all* proportions. Have students investigate the percent ratio table shown earlier to see if they can find some number (not a nice integer this time!) that will multiply by 10 to equal 25 and that will also multiply by 40 to equal 100. A few calculators would be helpful at this time. The number that finally works is 2.5. Horizontal arrows pointing from $10 to 25 and from $40 to 100 should now be added to the percent ratio table; each arrow should be labeled with "2.5X." Now **ask:** "Can you create a special factor from 10 and 25 that, when multiplied by 10, will equal 25? Some fractional numbers might be helpful here." Hopefully students will realize that the fractional form, $\frac{25}{10}$, multiplied by 10 will equal 25, i.e., $(\frac{25}{10}) \times 10 = 25$. This technique for identifying the factor is very important. No matter what form the two numbers in the ratio table may take (e.g., decimals or fractions), setting them up initially as a special factor in the manner given above will allow students to later simplify the new factor into a more usable form. For example, if we start with the form, $\frac{25}{10}$, we can then carry out the suggested division on the calculator to find 2.5. If we start with $\frac{3}{0.75}$, then the division will yield the "nice" number 4; if we have $3/(\frac{3}{4})$ instead, then we can change it to $3 \times (\frac{4}{3})$ to get 4. It is important for students to set up the factor *first* according to the special *pattern* they have found, then change it to some other form of their choosing. Otherwise, they become confused by the different numerical forms like decimals and fractions that are not comfortable to them and lose sight of the overall process they need to follow.

15. The purpose of the ratio table and arrows is to provide students with a reliable, yet *visual* way of setting up a proportion correctly and then of identifying the operation and numbers needed to find any missing part. The use of the four sections of the table and the labeling of the columns and rows helps students put the numbers in their proper order within the proportion (a task that is otherwise difficult for many students), and the arrows help them set up the correct equations needed. In addition, a large portion of real-world problems that students encounter in algebra can be solved with the ratio table technique. This will be demonstrated in Activity 3. In other words, students now have a single procedure that can be applied to a variety of situations, for example, to percent, probability, or rate situations. **Proportion** becomes the "big idea" through which we present the many different "little ideas."

Answer Key to WORKSHEET 3–3–2

Abbreviated proportions are given here. Students will be asked to write their results in various formats after drawing their basic and secondary ratios on ratio frames. Specific answers for certain situations are given in parentheses.

1. 3 to 4 = 6 to 8
2. 2 to 1 = 10 to 5
3. 9W to –12 = 3W to –4
4. 100 to $40 = 25 to $10
5. 1 to 3 = 3 to 9
6. 3 to 2 = 6 to 4
7. 2M to +5 = 6M to +15
8. –A to –2 = –4A to –8

9. 16 to 4 = 4 to 1
10. 15 to 6 = 5 to 2
11. 6P to –4 = 3P to –2
12. –3N to +9 = –N to +3
13. 100 to 16 = 50 to 8 (8 crates)
14. 20 to 7 = 100 to 35 (35 boxes total)
15. 100 to 20 = 25 to 5 (25%)
16. 6 to 15 = 2 to 5 (5 blue balls)

Activity 3: MIXING IT UP!

[Application/Exploration]

Materials: Worksheet 3–3–3
Calculators
Paper
Regular pencils

Management: Teams of 3–4 students each (50 minutes)

Directions:

1. Give each student a copy of Worksheet 3–3–3 and each team a calculator. On each team, students will take turns explaining how to set up a ratio table for a problem on the worksheet and how to write an equation for finding the missing part of the table. Other students on the team may help if the explaining student has difficulties with the selected problem. The problems on the worksheet do not have to be worked in the order in which they are given. Students may choose the problem they want to work when it is their turn. There are enough problems that you may wish to have the teams solve only certain problems in class, then assign some of the other problems as independent homework. Several problems require an additional step besides the ratio table or require possibly two ratio tables. Encourage students to read carefully.

WORKSHEET 3-3-3
Mixing It Up!

Work with a team to solve the problems below. Follow the teacher's directions for showing all your work on ratio tables. Calculators will be helpful. Read carefully! Be sure to answer the *questions* that are actually *asked!* Sometimes you will need to do more than just complete a ratio table. Some answers will be *algebraic expressions* instead of numerical values.

1. If a freight train travels a distance of 212 miles in 4 hours, what is its average speed in miles per hour (miles in one hour)?

2. Amanda wants to buy ice cream cones for herself and 4 friends. The cones cost about $6 in all. Approximately what will one cone cost?

3. When Dr. Emerson filled her car tank with gas, she found that she had driven 315 miles on 15 gallons of fuel. How many miles per gallon did her car get?

4. The ratio of a rectangular floor's width to length is 2 to 3. The length of the floor is 12 meters. Find the perimeter of the floor in meters.

5. Jana works 13 hours a week and earns $75.40. How much money does Jana earn per hour?

6. The weight of a sack of grain and another third of this weight equals 24 pounds in all. What is the weight of just one sack of grain in pounds?

7. Classified ads in a newspaper cost $1.50 for every 25 words. How many words must be deleted from the text of an 86-word ad to make the ad cost $4.50?

8. Jonathan earns a commission of $1 for every $4 he sells. If his total sales are $300, what will his commission be?

9. If 5 = 2b + 3, what number will equal 12b + 18?

10. The Fragaras buy a box of laundry detergent that contains 40 cups. If one box is enough to do 32 loads of laundry, how much detergent is used per load?

11. A flat, circular area of 4π sq. in. on a map is surveyed. The *map scale* for *distance* is 1 inch = 60 miles. Find the area in square miles of the land that was surveyed. (Remember: π is just a special number! Can you still use it in your ratio table?)

12. 54% of the registered voters in a district actually voted in a recent election. If the district has 350 registered voters, how many of them voted?

13. Ona spins a game spinner 100 times. The needle lands on yellow 20 times; red, 40 times; green, 20 times; and blue, 20 times. If the spinner is divided into 5 equal sections, how many sections would you expect to be colored red?

14. 3% of (A + G) is 12. What does G equal if A = 135?

15. Jim travels an average speed of M miles per hour. How many hours are needed at this same speed to go 400 miles?

16. An automatic camera is set so that the shutter opens every 31 seconds. To the nearest whole minute, about how many minutes will it take the camera's shutter to open 29 times?

17. The edge around a metal frame has a perimeter of 42 inches. The frame is shaped like an equilateral triangle. What is the length of each side of the metal frame?

18. The radius of circle A forms a ratio of 1 to 3 with the radius of circle B. What ratio does A's circumference form with B's circumference? If all the radius and circumference numbers are put in a ratio table in proper order, will they follow the arrow patterns of a proportion? What does this tell you about the change to expect in a circumference when the radius changes?

19. Joni biked 36 miles in 2 days, and her friend Marcus biked 24 miles in that same amount of time. For every 3 miles that Joni traveled, how many miles did Marcus travel?

20. A miller keeps 10% of the flour she grinds for customers as a service fee. If she gives a customer (W + 2) tons, how much flour was ground in all for that order?

21. A distance of 700 miles on the ground is represented by 3.5 inches on a certain map. What distance on the ground is represented by 1 inch on the map (i.e., what is the map scale)?

22. Yu Hwan wants to draw a Galactic Space Ring out of a bowl of rings at the school carnival. He knows only 18 Galactic Space Rings are in the bowl of 45 rings total. What is the percent probability that Yu Hwan will draw this special ring?

23. A store promotion offers to customers a refund of 5% of the amount they spend. If a person spends $80, what will be the amount of the refund?

24. If a car has traveled 150 miles in 3 hours and continues at the same rate, how far will it travel in the next 2 hours?

25. Abra-Dab-Rah granola bars are packed 6 per box and each bar supplies 2 grams of protein. How many such boxes would supply 36 grams of protein?

26. Alexa has asked one of her friends to feed her 3 dogs while she is away on vacation. Each dog eats $1\frac{1}{2}$ bags of dog food per week. How many bags of food should Alexa leave for her dogs to eat if she will be gone for 4 weeks?

2. Before the teams begin to work, discuss the procedure they will use by applying it to two problems. Consider the problem of enlarging a photograph: "The original photograph is 3 inches by 5 inches. If the **enlargement** (a proportional relationship) is to have a width of 12 inches, what will the new length be?" This is an application of **similar shapes.** Have students draw a ratio table. Since the top row is always for the basic ratio (the smaller numbers), the 3 and 5 will be written there. Allow the students to decide whether the width or the length is to go in the first column, then label the columns accordingly. This will also determine where the 12 is to go. Assuming the width is to go in the first column, the number 3 should be written in the upper left section and the number 5 written in the upper right section. The number 12 will be in the lower left section. To help with the equation writing later, the variable N should be written in the empty section (here, the lower right section).

3. A vertical arrow should now be drawn from the smaller number, 3, to the larger number, 12. Our arrow pattern discovered in Activity 2 requires that a partner arrow be drawn vertically from the number, 5, to the section containing the variable, N. The factor for the first arrow must be 4, so 4 must also be the factor needed for the second arrow. Here is the completed table:

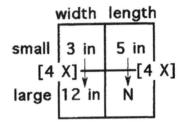

4. An equation can now be written that reflects the arrow relationship involving the variable N. Always start with the number in the basic ratio, and set the product equal to the number in the secondary ratio, regardless of where the variable may be. The *strategy* is to have a technique that is independent of the number that is missing in the proportion. For this current problem, the equation will be: $4 \times 5 = N$ inches. Thus, N equals 20 inches, which will be the length of the enlarged photograph. **Note:** The arrow factor (here, 4) is always written first in the product, since it is in the role of the **multiplier** for multiplication.

5. Discuss one more problem with the class, one where the missing part is in the basic ratio. Consider the following: "Early on Monday morning a butcher delivers 300 pounds of meat to a restaurant. That day the restaurant uses 54 pounds of the meat to make special entrees and hamburgers. What percent of the 300 pounds of meat will be available to the chef on Tuesday?" Remind students that for percent, the basic ratio will be the portion of 100 needed (i.e., the percent) compared to the portion of 300 pounds needed. We will choose to write the percent numbers in the left column and the pounds numbers in the right column. Write 54 in the upper right section, 300 in the lower right section, and 100 in the lower left section. The variable N should be written in the empty section (here, the upper left section).

6. Looking for obvious multiples first, either vertically or horizontally, we find that 3 of 100 will equal 300. So horizontal arrows can be drawn and labeled as shown below.

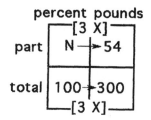

7. The basic ratio can now be used to write an equation to solve for N. Keeping the correct order for the factor-multiplier, the equation becomes $3 \times N = 54$, which may be written as $3N = 54$ because of the presence of the variable N. If some students still need to build with tiles on a mat or draw shapes on a frame to solve equations, allow them to do so in an accepting manner, but carefully guide them in recording their steps in symbols. Hopefully most students will be able to solve the equation abstractly. Encourage them to consistently apply the techniques they learned in Section 2. The recorded steps for the current equation should be as follows:

$$3N = 54$$
$$(\tfrac{1}{3})(3N) = (\tfrac{1}{3})(54)$$
$$N = 18$$

The number 18 *over the 100* in the ratio table indicates that 54 pounds will be 18 *percent* of the 300 pounds. As mentioned in previous lessons, writing the second step above (where the reciprocal, $\tfrac{1}{3}$, is used as a factor with 54 instead of writing 54 over 3 for division) is the preferred format because of the flexibility it provides for the problem solver. But the question in the problem has not been answered. We need to find out what percent of the meat will be available on Tuesday. Since 18% was used on Monday, we need to find 100% − 18%, which is 82%. So the final answer will be: "82 percent of the 300 pounds of meat will be available to the chef on Tuesday."

8. In the "meat" problem above, students most likely will use the relationship between 100 and 300 to draw their arrows; however, if the numerical relationship is not so obvious, students must have a way to form a factor to use. Discuss this idea with them (see step 14 of Activity 2). For practice, suppose we needed to draw a vertical arrow to relate 54 to 300 instead; their relationship is not obvious. The factor would be formed from 54 and 300, and be written in a ratio form: $(\tfrac{300}{54})$. In other words, we would have the number sentence: $(\tfrac{300}{54}) \times 54 = 300$. The equation for N would then be the following: $(\tfrac{300}{54})N = 100$. To solve, we would write the next two steps: $(\tfrac{54}{300})(\tfrac{300}{54})N = (\tfrac{54}{300})(100)$ and $N = (\tfrac{54}{300})(100) = 18$, the same answer we found earlier. The benefit of this approach is that, regardless of the types of numbers involved, students can choose the order of operations they wish to follow on their calculators to calculate the value of N.

9. Students should now work with their teams to solve the assigned problems on Worksheet 3–3–3. When all have finished, have various team members write their ratio tables and equations on the board and explain their solution steps to the class. Each presenter must also make a final statement that expresses the solution in terms of its situation; for example, in step 7 above, the statement would be "82 percent of the 300 pounds of meat will be available to the chef on Tuesday."

10. Worksheet 3–3–3 contains a variety of problems, some requiring just a simple ratio table with whole numbers, others with an additional step beyond the table or with unfamiliar numbers. Ordering the problems from simpler to more difficult has been intentionally avoided. Most of these problems have often been worked with other methods; the focus in this activity is on the ratio table, which unites all these seemingly different types of problems into one major category. **All** students must be given the opportunity to work **all** of the problems so that they can see just how versatile the technique really is. Class discussion on how to *set up* each problem into some kind of ratio table (for example, what labels go on the columns and on the rows) is **vital**.

Answer Key to WORKSHEET 3–3–3

Here are suggested ratio tables to use and solutions for the exercises on the worksheet. Several initial equation set-ups are possible for each ratio table. The *vertical arrow pattern* has been used to set up each equation unless the horizontal arrow pattern is specifically indicated.

1.

	miles	hrs
rate	N	1
total	212	4

$4N = 212$

$N = 53$ miles per hour

2.

	am't	cost
single	1	N
total	5	$6

$5N = 6$

$N = \$1.20$ per cone

3.

	miles	gal
rate	N	1
total	315	15

$15N = 315$

$N = 21$ miles per gallon

4.

	width	length
basic	2	3
actual	N	12

$4(2) = N$

$N = 8$ meters width; perimeter = $2(8) + 2(12)$ or
$2(8 + 12) = 40$ meters

5.

	$$	hrs
rate	N	1
total	$75.40	13

$13N = \$75.40$

$N = \$5.80$ per hour

6.

	# sacks	lbs
rate	1	N
total	$1\frac{1}{3}$	24

$(\frac{4}{3})N = 24$

$N = 18$ lbs per sack

7.

	# words	cost
rate	25	$1.50
total	N	$4.50

$3(25) = N$

$N = 75$ words for ad; $86 - 75 = 11$ words to delete

8.

	comm.	sales
rate	$1	$4
total	N	$300

horizontal arrow pattern used

$4N = \$300$

$N = \$75$ commission earned

9.

	sum	value
basic	2b + 3	5
total	12b + 18	N

6(5) = N

N = 30, value of 12b + 18

10.

	loads	cups
rate	1	N
total	32	40

32N = 40

N = 1.25 cups per load of laundry

11.

	map	land
area scale	(1)(1)	(60)(60)
area total	4π	N

4π(60)(60) = N

N = 14,400 π sq. miles of land area

12.

	%	voters
part	54	N
total	100	350

horizontal arrow pattern used

$(\frac{350}{100})(54) = N$

N = 189 people voted

13.

	sections	spins
red part	N	40
total	5	100

horizontal arrow pattern used

20N = 40

N = 2 red sections on spinner

14.

	%	am't
part	3	12
total	100	A + G

horizontal arrow pattern used

4(100) = A + G

A + G = 400 = 135 + G; G = 265

15.

	miles	hrs
rate	M	1
total	400	N

$(\frac{400}{M})(1) = N$

$N = (\frac{400}{M})$ hours to go 400 miles

16.

	# openings	time (sec)
rate	1	31
total	29	N

(29)(31) = N

N = 899 seconds ≈ 15 minutes

17.

	general	specific
side	A	N
perim.	3A	42

3N = 42

N = 14 inches

18.

	A	B
radius	1R	3R
circum.	2πR	6πR

circum(A) to circum(B) = 2πR to 6πR = 1 to 3

Ratio table vertical and horizontal arrow patterns hold. Circumference changes in same way radius changes.

19.

	Marcus	Joni
part	N	3
total	24	36

$12N = 24$

$N = 2$ miles for Marcus

20.

	%	tons
cust. part	90	W + 2
total	100	N

$(\frac{100}{90})(W + 2) = N$

$N = (1.1W + 2.2)$ tons total

21.

	map	land
scale	1	N
total	3.5	700

$3.5N = 700$

$N = 200$ miles

22.

	%	am't
part	N	18
total	100	45

$(\frac{45}{18})N = 100$

$N = (\frac{18}{45})(100) = 40$ (40% probability)

23.

	%	$$
part	5	N
total	100	$80

$20N = \$80$

$N = \$4$ refund

24.

	miles	hrs
dist. #1	150	3
dist. #2	N	2

horizontal arrow pattern used

$50(2) = N$

$N = 100$ miles

25.

	bars	grams
basic	1	2
total	N	36

$18(1) = N$

$N = 18$ bars have 36 grams

	bars	boxes
basic	6	1
total	18	M

horizontal arrow pattern used

$6M = 18$

$M = 3$ boxes have 36 grams

26.

	bags	weeks
basic	1.5	1
total	N	4

horizontal arrow pattern used

$(1.5)(4) = N$

$N = 6$ bags for 1 dog for 4 weeks

	dogs	bags
basic	1	6
total	3	M

$3(6) = M$

$M = 18$ bags total for 3 dogs for 4 weeks

OBJECTIVE 4: Investigate linear or arithmetic sequences, using figurate numbers; find an expression for the N-th term.

Activity 1: BUILDING BY PATTERNS

[Developing Action]

Materials: One-inch square tiles (or one-inch paper squares)
Paper
Regular pencils
One reclosable plastic bag for tiles per pair of students

Management: Partners (50 minutes)

Directions:

1. Give each pair of students a reclosable plastic bag of about 100 square tiles.

2. Have students build "windmills" with their tiles, building them in order of size with the smallest one first. Show them the following shapes already drawn on a transparency; do not draw the shapes in front of the students. They must decide *how* to build each new windmill for themselves.

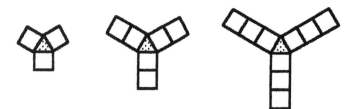

3. Have them make a 2-column table on their own paper to record their work. Use the headings: *Which Shape* (e.g., write "1" for first shape built) and *Total Tiles in Shape*. The left column for *Which Shape* should show 1, 2, 3, . . . and the right column should show the totals 3, 6, 9, ...

4. Ask several students to tell how the first and second shapes are alike and how they are different. (Possible responses: Both shapes have 3 blades; #2 has 1 more tile in each windmill blade than #1 has, or #2 has 2 tiles in each blade instead of 1 tile.) Ask how the second windmill was changed to make the third one. (Responses should be similar to those for #1 and #2.)

5. Ask students to build the fourth windmill (it should have 3 blades with 4 tiles per blade) to the right of the first three.

6. Have some students describe in their own words what each windmill looks like. Encourage the following type of details: *The first shape has 1 tile per blade for 3 blades; #2 has 2 tiles/blade for 3 blades; #3 has 3 tiles/blade for 3 blades; etc.* A second approach might say the following: *#1 has 1 ring of 3 tiles; #2 has the first ring of 3 tiles plus 1 more ring of 3 tiles, or 2 rings of 3 tiles; #3 has 1 more ring of 3 tiles than #2, or 3 rings of 3 tiles; etc.*

7. Ask the students to predict how the tenth windmill might look and how many tiles total will be needed, based on their descriptions given in step 6. (Examples: Method (a)*#10 has 10 tiles/blade for 3 blades;* Method (b) *#10 has 10 rings of 3 tiles each*) Have them complete their table through the tenth shape with its total tiles, 30 tiles. Some students may need to build the other windmills (#5–#9) to confirm their predictions of the total tiles needed for the tenth shape. Discuss how the numbers in the *Total* column change (increase by 3 each time for either method).

8. Now ask them to try to describe how to find the total tiles needed for making the N-th windmill. The algebraic expression should follow the language pattern used in step 6: Method (a) *The N-th shape will use N tiles per blade for 3 blades, or 3 × N or 3N tiles total;* Method (b) *The N-th shape will use N rings of 3 tiles each, or N(3) tiles total.* Have students write the letter N above the *Which Shape* column of their table and their particular expression [3N for method (a), or N(3) for method (b)] above the *Total* column. **Note:** Do not rewrite N(3) as 3N at this stage; physically, they have different meanings and students must be allowed to see the difference. N(3) is N rings of 3 tiles each, whereas 3N is 3 sets of N tiles each.

9. Show 3 new shapes on a transparency for students to build with their tiles, again building them in order of size with the smallest one first.

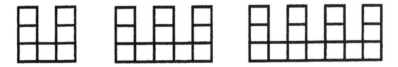

10. Have students make a 4-column table on their own paper to record their work. Use the headings: *Which Shape, Towers in Shape, Single Stories, Total Tiles.* The first three rows of the table would be for the first three shapes shown, and would have the following numbers (left to right by row): 1, 2, 1, 7; 2, 3, 2, 11; and 3, 4, 3, 15.

11. Ask students to build the fourth shape (it should have 5 towers of 3 tiles each with 1 single story between each pair of towers) to the right of the first three. The numbers 4, 5, 4, 19 should be recorded in the table.

12. Have some students describe in their own words what each shape looks like. Encourage the following type of details: *The first shape has 2 towers of 3 tiles each and 1 single story between the towers; #2 has 3 towers of 3 tiles each and 2 single stories; #3 has 4 towers of 3 tiles each and 3 single stories; #4 has 5 towers of 3 tiles each and 4 single stories.*

13. Ask if anyone has a different way of describing the shapes; encourage them to explain what they see. Another possible way is as follows: *#1 has 1 tower of 3 tiles and a set of 4 tiles (1 single plus 1 tower of 3) added on the right; #2 has 1 tower on the left followed by 2 of the sets of 4; #3 has 1 tower on the left followed by 3 of the sets of 4; #4 has 1 tower on the left followed by 4 of the sets of 4.*

14. Based on how they have previously described the shapes, ask different students to predict what the tenth shape might look like and how many tiles will be needed. Some students may need to build shapes #5–#9 first before they can decide about shape #10. They should continue to record their numbers in the table. Following the description method used in step 12, the tenth shape should *have 11 towers of 3 tiles each and 10 single stories.* The description method used in step 13 would lead to *1 tower of 3 tiles on the left followed by 10 of the sets of 4.*

15. Ask students to describe how the N-th shape will look, according to their chosen description method. Here are possible statements for the two approaches above: Method (a) *The N-th shape will have (N + 1) towers of 3 tiles each and N single stories;* Method (b) *The N-th shape will have 1 tower of 3 at the left followed by N of the sets of 4 tiles.* For total tiles in the N-th shape, method (a) yields the expression: $(N + 1)(3) + N$ tiles, and method (b) yields the expression: $3 + N(4)$ tiles. **Note:** The expression used must closely represent the method and language used by the students to build the shapes. Do *not* simplify the expressions at this time, even though they are mathematically equivalent. Also, keep the multiplier of a situation in its correct position as the first factor of the product; for example, if the counter of sets (multiplier) is N, as in $N(4)$ above, do not rewrite the product as $4N$. Students should now write N above the *Which Shape* column of their table and the expression for their particular method [e.g., $(N + 1)(3) + N$, or $3 + N(4)$] above the *Total* column.

16. If time permits, lead the class through the building of other sequences of shapes, following the same procedure and questioning used in steps 2–15. Be sure that the sequences are arithmetic, that is, each shape's total tiles must equal the previous shape's total files increased by a constant amount. For each sequence, have students record their numbers in a 2-column table; use *Which Shape* for the first heading and *Total Tiles* for the second heading. Encourage alternative descriptions of the sequence. Here are two possible sequences to use, along with descriptions of:

- the type of language needed to describe the shapes;
- the N-th shape's description and the expression for its total tiles;
- the test of the N-th expression for total tiles for shape #1.

Example 1:

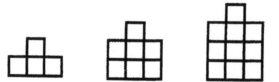

(a) Language (additive approach): Shape #1 has 1 row of 3 tiles with a single tile centered in second row; shape #2 has 2 rows of 3 tiles each with 1 tile centered in third row; shape #3 has 3 rows of 3 tiles each with 1 tile centered in fourth row; etc.

(b) N-th shape: N-th shape has N rows of 3 tiles each and 1 tile centered in (N+1)-st row; total tiles = $N(3) + 1$ tiles.

(c) Test for shape #1: $(1)(3) + 1 = 4$ tiles. $\checkmark$

Possible alternative description:

(a) Language (subtractive approach): Shape #1 has 2 rows of 3 tiles each, with 2 tiles removed from top row; shape #2 has 3 rows of 3 tiles each, with 2 tiles removed from top row; shape #3 has 4 rows of 3 with 2 tiles removed from top; etc.

(b) N-th shape: N-th shape has $(N + 1)$ rows of 3 with 2 tiles removed from top row; total tiles = $(N + 1)(3) - 2$ tiles.

(c) Test for shape #1: $(1 + 1)(3) - 2 = 4$ tiles. $\checkmark$

Example 2:

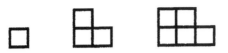

(a) Language (additive approach): Shape #1 has 1 tile; shape #2 has 1 stack of 2 tiles each and 1 tile extra on right in bottom row; shape #3 has 2 stacks of 2 tiles each and 1 tile extra at lower right; etc.

(b) N-th shape: N-th shape has (N – 1) stacks of 2 tiles each and 1 tile extra at lower right; total tiles = (N – 1)(2) + 1 tiles.

(c) Test for shape #1: (1 – 1)(2) + 1 = 1 tile. $\checkmark$

Possible alternative description:

(a) Language (subtractive approach): Shape #1 has 1 tile; shape #2 has 2 rows of 2 tiles each with 1 tile removed from upper right; shape #3 has 2 rows of 3 tiles each with 1 tile removed from upper right; etc.

(b) N-th shape: N-th shape has 2 rows of N tiles each with 1 tile removed from upper right; total tiles = 2N – 1 tiles.

(c) Test for shape #1: (2)(1) – 1 = 1 tile. $\checkmark$

Activity 2: PATTERN DRAW

[Bridging Action]

Materials: Paper
Regular pencils

Management: Partners (30–50 minutes)

Directions:

1. Follow the procedure used in steps 2–15 of Activity 1, except that students will be drawing the shapes rather than building them with tiles.

2. For each sequence discussed, show them the first three shapes of the sequence already drawn on a transparency. Do not allow them to see the shapes being drawn. Deciding how to draw the shapes helps students see the differences in the sequence terms.

3. Show the class the first three shapes of the first sequence. Have students work with a partner, but draw the sequence of shapes on their own papers.

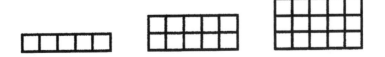

4. Discuss likenesses and differences: *Shape #2 has 1 more row of 5 than #1 has,* etc. Have students describe each shape: *#1 has 1 row of 5 squares; #2 has 2 rows of 5; #3 has 3 rows of 5.*

5. Ask students to draw the fourth shape according to the changes they have seen. (*#4 should have 4 rows of 5 squares.*) Then have them predict how the tenth shape will look (*#10 should have 10 rows of 5 squares each.*)

6. All should now complete a table on their own papers for the sequence, using column headings (left to right) *Which Shape* and *Total Squares*. The left column will have 1, 2, 3, . . . and the right column will have 5, 10, 15, ... Students should record information for the first ten shapes of the sequence. Discuss how the numbers in the *Total* column change (increase by 5 each time).

7. Ask students to describe the N-th shape in the sequence. Following the language used for the earlier shapes, the N-th shape should have N rows of 5 squares each, or $N \times 5$ or N(5) squares total. Use $N \times 5$ or N(5) instead of 5N here because N is the counter of the rows and hence should be written in the multiplier position. Testing for shape #1, we have (1)(5) = 5 squares total.

8. Here is a second sequence to show to the students:

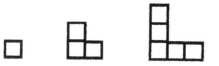

9. Ask students to draw the fourth shape and describe what they see. One possible description might be the following: *Shape #1 is 1 square; shape #2 is a stack of 2 squares with 1 square on the right; #3 is a stack of 3 squares with 2 single squares on the right; #4 is a stack of 4 squares with 3 single squares on the right.*

10. Students should record, for each shape drawn, the shape number and its total squares in another 2-column table like the one described in step 6. Discuss how the totals are increasing by the same amount each time.

11. Have them predict what the tenth shape will look like; if necessary, they should draw shapes #5–#9 to confirm their predictions. Following the descriptions in step 9, shape #10 will have 1 stack of 10 squares with 9 single squares extending to the right from the stack.

12. The N-th shape or term should now be described: The N-th shape will have 1 stack of N squares with (N − 1) single squares in a row extending to the right from the stack. The total squares in the N-th shape will equal N + (N − 1) squares. Testing for shape #1, we have 1 + (1 − 1) = 1 square as the total.

13. This second sequence might also be described in another way: *Shape #1 has 1 square; shape #2 has 1 square in the lower left corner with 1 more square above it and 1 more square on the right; shape #3 has 1 square in the lower left corner with 2 more squares above it and 2 more squares extended on the right;* etc.

14. Then the N-th shape will be described as 1 square at the lower left corner with (N − 1) squares above it and (N − 1) squares extended to the right. Total squares will equal [1 + (N − 1) + (N − 1)] or 1 + 2(N − 1) squares. Testing for shape #1, we have 1 + 2(1 − 1) = 1 square total.

15. Continue to show sequences to the class, following the procedure and questioning of steps 2–14 of this activity. Two-column tables should still be completed for the different shapes drawn and observations made about how the numbers change for each new shape. The algebraic expression recorded for the N-th shape in a sequence must represent closely the language used to describe the different shapes drawn previously in the sequence. Two possible sequences are given below, including alternative descriptions for each.

Example 1:

Method (a):

(1) Language: Shape #1 has a stack of 2 squares and 1 single square on the right; #2 has a stack of 3 squares, then a stack of 2 squares; #3 has a stack of 4 squares, then a stack of 3 squares; etc.

(2) N-th shape: The N-th shape has a stack of $(N + 1)$ squares, then a stack of N squares; total squares $= (N + 1) + N$ squares.

(3) Test for shape #1: $(1 + 1) + 1 = 3$ squares total. $\checkmark$

Method (b):

(1) Language: Shape #1 has 1 row of 2 squares and a single square on top; #2 has 2 rows of 2 squares each with 1 square on top; #3 has 3 rows of 2 squares each with 1 square on top; etc.

(2) N-th shape: The N-th shape has N rows of 2 squares each with 1 square on top; total squares $= N(2) + 1$ squares.

(3) Test for shape #1: $(1)(2) + 1 = 3$ squares total. $\checkmark$

[Note: A *subtractive* method sees the N-th shape as $(N + 1)$ rows of 2 squares each with 1 square *removed* from the upper right corner.]

Example 2:

Method (a): [additive method]

(1) Language: Shape #1 has 1 row of 3 squares; #2 has 1 row of 3 squares on top and 1 row of 5 squares on bottom; #3 has 1 row of 3 squares on top and 2 rows of 5 squares on bottom; #4 has 1 row of 3 on top and 3 rows of 5 on bottom; etc.

(2) N-th shape: The N-th shape has 1 row of 3 on top and $(N - 1)$ rows of 5 on bottom; total squares $= 3 + (N - 1)(5)$ squares.

(3) Test for shape #1: $3 + (1 - 1)(5) = 3$ squares total. $\checkmark$

Method (b): [subtractive method]

(1)   Language: Shape #1 has 1 row of 3 squares; #2 has 2 rows of 5 squares each with 2 squares removed from the top row; #3 has 3 rows of 5 squares each with 2 squares removed from the top row; etc.

(2)   N-th shape: The N-th shape has N rows of 5 squares each with 2 squares removed from the top row; total squares = N(5) – 2 squares.

(3)   Test for shape #1: (1)(5) – 2 = 3 squares total. $\checkmark$

Activity 3: A GRAPHING PERSPECTIVE

[Application/Exploration]

Materials: Bags of square tiles from Activity 1
Worksheet 3–4–1
Calculators
Paper
Colored pencils
Regular pencils

Management: Teams of 4 students each (30 minutes)

Directions:

1.   Give each team of students a bag of square tiles, a copy of Worksheet 3–4–1, a calculator, and a colored pencil (not brown, black, or yellow). In this activity students will reverse the process used in Activities 1 and 2; that is, they will be given an **unsimplified** algebraic expression for the N-th term of a sequence and they will either build or draw what they think the first 4 shapes or terms will be. They will complete a table for each sequence, then plot the ordered pairs from the table onto the adjacent grid to form a scatterplot.

2.   Write the following expression on the board to represent the N-th term of a sequence: N(4) + 2 tiles or squares total. Each team should now build the first 4 shapes described by this expression. In N(4), the N is the counter of groups and the 4 tells how many tiles or squares must be in each group. Three possible ways are shown below. (Others are possible, too.)

Row design:

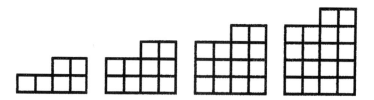

WORKSHEET 3–4–1
A Graphing Perspective

Follow the teacher's directions to complete the two tables below and plot their ordered pairs on the grids. Compare the two scatterplots you make. What do you notice?

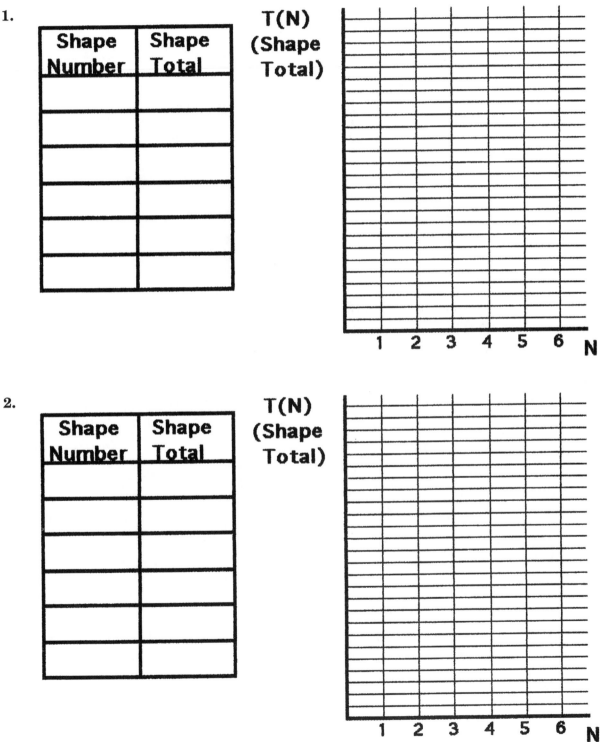

1.

Shape Number	Shape Total

T(N) (Shape Total)

1 2 3 4 5 6   N

2.

Shape Number	Shape Total

T(N) (Shape Total)

1 2 3 4 5 6   N

Tower design:

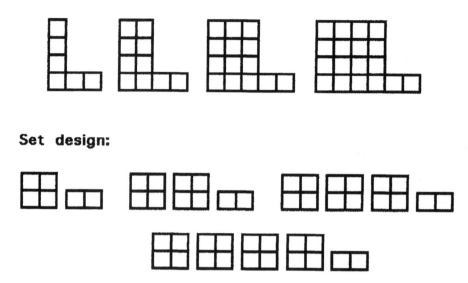

Set design:

3. A table on Worksheet 3–4–1 should be completed that shows the shape number and its total tiles or squares. Students should write N above the first column of the table and N(4) + 2 above the second column. Also have students use the algebraic expression for the N-th shape to *compute* the total tiles or squares for N = 5 and N = 6. These values should be recorded in the table as well. The ordered pairs should be plotted on the grid next to the table. The pairs will be: (1,6), (2,10), (3,14), (4,18), (5,22), (6,26). The six points of the scatterplot should be connected with a colored pencil.

4. Now write another expression on the board: (1)(N + 1) + (N − 1) tiles or squares total. In (1)(N + 1), the first factor (1) is the multiplier and tells that 1 group is involved of size (N + 1). The (N − 1) added on indicates that an (N − 1) amount of tiles or squares is joined to the (1)(N + 1) arrangement in some way. Students should build the first 4 shapes of the sequence. A variety of shape designs will be possible, such as the following:

Tower design:

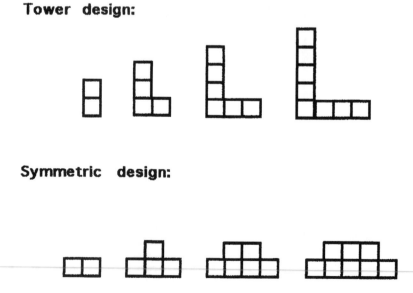

Symmetric design:

5. After the four shapes are built or drawn, each team should complete a table on Worksheet 3–4–1 that shows each shape number and its total tiles or squares. Students should write N above the first column of the table and (1) (N+1) + (N −1) above the second column. Also have students use the algebraic expression for the N-th shape here to *compute* the total tiles or squares for N = 5 and N = 6. These values should be recorded in the table as well. The ordered pairs should be plotted on the grid next to the table. The pairs will be: (1,2), (2,4), (3,6), (4,8), (5,10), (6,12). The six points of the scatterplot should be connected with a colored pencil.

6. Ask students to look at the scatterplots they have made and decide how they are alike and how they are different. Hopefully they will notice that each set of six points connects to form a straight path. This will be true for all **arithmetic** or **linear sequences,** i.e., the sequences where the totals increase by a constant amount. Also, one path appears steeper than the other. (This activity provides an introduction to **linear functions,** which will be studied later in this section.)

OBJECTIVE 5: Transform linear expressions in X and Y (e.g., cX + dY = e) to show X in terms of Y or Y in terms of X.

Activity 1: BUILD AND TRANSFORM

[Developing Action]

Materials: Packets of tiles (see Section 2, Objective 1, Activity 1 for details)
Building mats (see Section 2, Objective 3, Activity 1 for details)
Coffee stirrers or pieces of colored yarn (approx. 12 inches long)
Paper
Regular pencils
Worksheet 3–5–1

Management: Partners (50 minutes)

Directions:

1. Give each pair of students a packet of tiles and a building mat. The packet of tiles should contain a minimum of 12 variable tiles each of two different lengths, and 20 unit tiles. If necessary, prepare more variable tiles to add to packets used in previous lessons. One side of each tile should be marked with a large X to show the inverse form of the tile. Each size of tile, whether variable or unit, should be in a color different from the other two sizes of tile or the mat. In Section 2 lessons focused on linear expressions in several variables and linear equations in one variable. For this present objective, students will extend the solution techniques learned for one variable to the two-variable case. In Activity 1 they will practice isolating each variable type that occurs in a two-variable equation by building with tiles on a mat. For convenience, we will refer to the short variable tile as the variable A and to the long variable tile as the variable B during this lesson. We will limit the exercises to only integral coefficients and constants. (See Worksheet 3–5–1.)

2. Ask students to place tiles on the building mat to show the equation: +5 − B = A + 2B. One short variable tile and two long variable tiles should be placed on the right side of the mat (to the right of the bold, vertical bar), and 5 positive unit tiles and one long inverse variable tile placed on the left side (to the left of the bar). Students are to solve the equation for one of the variables, using the methods studied in Section 2. Do not take "shortcuts" of any kind at this stage. Review the methods and language used in Section 2, if necessary.

3. Have students now isolate the variable A by bringing in 2 of the inverse tiles of variable B on both sides of the mat. Two 0-pairs can be formed with the B and −B variable tiles on the right side of the mat; these two pairs can then be removed from the mat. The mat and tiles appear as follows while the 0-pairs are being formed:

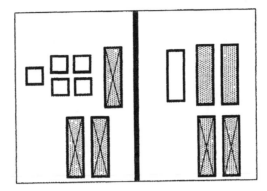

4. Once the 0-pairs of variable tiles have been removed, the variable tile A will remain on the right side of the mat, and 5 positive unit tiles and 3 of the inverse variable tiles (−B) will be on the left side. Have students record this final equation and statement on their own papers:

A is *in terms of B* when A = (+5) + (−3B) or A = 5 − 3B.

Notice that we have rewritten the equation with the variable A on the left side; the symmetric nature of an equation allows us to do this. This writing technique helps emphasize the variable A more in the above statement.

5. In Section 2 students learned to evaluate algebraic expressions. Connect to that experience by having them evaluate the variable tile A when given a value for the variable tile B. Ask them to replace each variable tile B on the mat with 4 positive unit tiles, then simplify the final amount of unit tiles. Since only three of the inverse variable tiles (−B) are on the left side of the mat now with 5 positive unit tiles, each inverse variable tile must be replaced with 4 negative unit tiles. After 0-pairs are formed and removed from the mat, the variable tile A will remain on the right side of the mat and 7 negative unit tiles will be on the left side. Have students record this additional statement below the one given in step 4: **A = −7 when B = +4.**

6. Have students now show the equation 4A − 2B = +6 with tiles on the mat. Four of the variable tile A and 2 of the inverse variable tile (−B) should be placed on the left side of the mat, and 6 positive unit tiles should be on the right side.

7. We want to isolate the variable tile B, so students should bring in 4 of the inverse variable tile (−A) to each side of the mat (as shown below). Four 0-pairs formed by the variable tiles A and −A can now be removed from the left side of the mat. This will leave 2 of the inverse variable tile (−B) on the left, and 6 positive unit tiles and 4 of the inverse variable tile (−A) on the right.

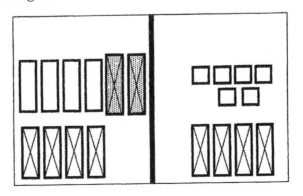

WORSHEET 3–5–1
Build and Transform

Build each equation with tiles to solve for the indicated variable. Record the new equation found and the result of the required substitution.

1. $+5 - B = A + 2B$ [A; +4]

2. $4A - 2B = +6$ [B; –5]

3. $B + A = -10$ [B; –3]

4. $2B = A + 1$ [A; +6]

5. $-3A + 15 = 3B$ [B; +1]

6. $2A - B = 3B + 8$ [A; +5]

Name —————————————————— **Date** ——————————

7. $5B - 3A = -3A$ [B; –8]

8. $6B - 3 = 3(2A + 1)$ [A; +7]

9. $-4C - G = 7G$ [C; –3]

10. $2(X - 3) = 2W$ [X; –10]

11. $-M + P + 3 = +2$ [M; 0]

12. $2R + 5 = -K + 2R$ [K; +4]

8. The two inverse tiles on the left must be separated into two equal rows of one tile each. The 6 unit tiles and 4 inverse tiles on the right must also be separated into two equal rows; there will be 3 positive unit tiles and 2 inverse tiles in each row on the right side of the mat. Since we are only interested in one complete row across the mat, the second row of tiles should be removed from the mat.

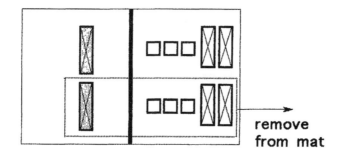

9. We want to solve for the variable B itself, but the mat presently shows the inverse variable ($-$B) on the left. Students should now place a coffee stirrer or piece of yarn across the mat below the remaining row of tiles. A new row of opposites should be built below the stirrer or yarn piece; this row will contain the variable tile B on the left side of the mat and 3 negative unit tiles and 2 of the variable tile A on the right side.

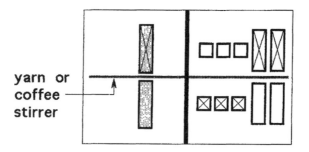

10. The equation has been solved for the variable tile B. Have students record the following statement and equation on their own papers:

B is *in terms of* A when B = ($-$3) + 2A.

11. Ask students to find the value of the variable tile B when A = $-$5. Each variable tile A presently on the right side of the mat should be replaced with 5 negative unit tiles, then all the unit tiles simplified. Hence, we have the variable tile B on the left side of the mat and 13 negative unit tiles on the right side. Have students record the following statement under the other one about B: **B = $-$13 when A = $-$5.**

12. Assign several other equations for students to build on their mats, then solve for one variable in terms of the other variable. After all are finished, have some of the students explain their steps to the entire class. The emphasis here is on the use of the expression "in terms of." Encourage students to state their results in the format recorded on their papers. Remind them that "A in terms of B" simply means that A equals some expression in units and variables where the variable used is B.

13. Here are some more equations for students to solve by building with tiles on their mats. They should solve for the variable indicated in the brackets beside the equation; the integer value listed on the right in the brackets is the value to be substituted for the other variable in the equation. For example, [B; –1] means to solve for B in terms of A, then find the value of B when A = –1. For each equation worked, the original equation itself and two statements in the same formats used in steps 4–5 or steps 10–11 should be recorded. Remind students that the variable for which they are to solve may sometimes be on the right side, not just on the left.

For exercises 1–6, use the short variable tile as A and the long variable tile as B:

1. B + A = –10 [B; –3]

2. 2B = A + 1 [A; +6]

3. –3A + 15 = 3B [B; +1]

4. 2A – B = 3B + 8 [A; +5]

5. 5B – 3A = –3A [B; –8]

6. 6B – 3 = 3(2A + 1) [A; +7]

For exercises 7–10, students should decide which variable tile to use for each letter in the equation. It will be helpful if they write down their choices each time before they start to solve, so that they will make proper substitutions at the end and will refer to the variables correctly in their concluding statements.

7. –4C – G = 7G [C; –3]

8. 2(X – 3) = 2W [X; –10]

9. –M + P + 3 = +2 [M; 0]

10. 2R + 5 = –K + 2R [K; +4]

Activity 2: ISOLATION DRAW

[Bridging Action]

Materials: Calculators
Paper
Regular pencils
Red pencils
Colored chalk

Management: Partners (50 minutes)

Directions:

1. Give each pair of students a red pencil and a calculator for their use as needed. In this activity fractional coefficients and fractional constants will be included. Review the method and language used in Objectives 6–8 of Section 2. Vertical rectangles will be drawn to represent variables; their interiors will be labeled with their variable names, including fractional names. Small squares will be drawn for units. Any rectangles drawn for whole or fractional variable amounts should be drawn at least a little taller than the unit squares used. Similarly, rectangles for whole variables should be drawn taller than a rectangle for a fractional variable. Exactness of size, however, is difficult to achieve, so will not be a major concern here; that is why the labeling is used for the variable shapes. The interior of a rectangle or square will be marked with a large X to show its inverse form.

2. Write the equation $6M - 3R = +9$ on the board and draw it in the following way for students to copy on their own papers. [Note: The ‖ represents the equal sign.]

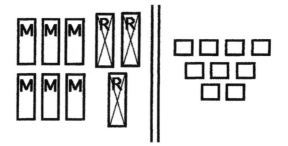

3. Ask students to isolate the variable R. They are to solve for R in terms of M by making changes to their diagrams. Six rectangles with X's for –6M need to be added to both sides of the frame, then 0-pairs marked as follows:

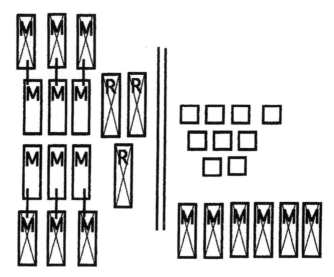

4. There are 3 of the inverse variable, –R, remaining on the left, and we need only one. Students should draw a path around each –R to form 3 equal groups. Then 3 equal groups need to be formed on the right side as well. Each group will contain +3 and –2M. A horizontal bar should be drawn below the diagram with the groups. In the separation process we only want one complete group, so below the bar a single –R should be drawn on the left, and one group of +3 and –2M should be drawn on the right.

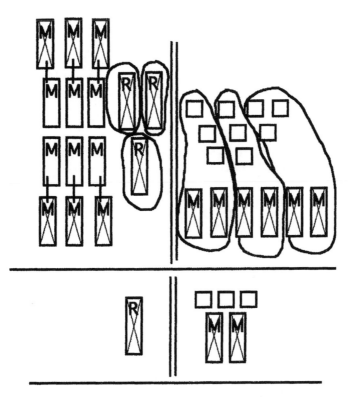

5. Since we are solving for the variable R, students should draw another horizontal bar below the −R grouping in order to show opposites. A single R should finally be drawn on the left of the diagram and 3 small squares with X's inside and 2 rectangles for the variable M should be drawn on the right.

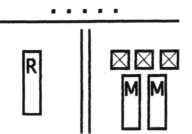

6. Have students record the steps they used to solve for R, then write a statement about their results:

$$6M - 3R = +9$$
$$\underline{+ (-6M) \qquad\qquad\qquad + (-6M)}$$
$$-3R = (+9) + \quad (-6M)$$
$$\tfrac{1}{3}(-3R) = \tfrac{1}{3}[(+9) + (-6M)] \quad [\text{separate}]$$
$$-R = \tfrac{1}{3}(+9) + \tfrac{1}{3}(-6M) \quad [\text{distribute}]$$
$$-R = \quad (+3) + \quad (-2M) \quad [\text{simplify}]$$
$$R = \quad (-3) + \quad (+2M) \quad [\text{opposites}]$$
$$\text{or } R = \quad -3 + \quad\quad 2M$$

So R *in terms of M* equals −3 + 2M.

7. Now that the variable R has been expressed in a format that uses the variable M, ask students to find R when M = –5. Have them draw in red pencil 5 small squares, each containing a large X, on each rectangle for M in the final step of the diagram. In other words, –5 will replace each M in the expression for R. The value for R becomes –13. Students should now write beneath the statement in step 6 the additional sentence: **R = (–3) + 2(–5) = –13 for M = –5.**

8. As another example, write the equation $-\frac{2}{3}B - 1 = 2A$ on the board for students to copy on their own papers. Ask them to solve for B in terms of A, using a diagram of the equation. The initial diagram should appear as shown:

9. After +1 is added to both sides of the diagram and a 0-pair formed on the left, the $-\frac{2}{3}B$ will need to be separated into two equal groups and similarly for 2A and +1 on the right. This requires the small square for +1 to be subdivided into two halves (we will use a square with $\frac{1}{2}$ written inside it to show $+\frac{1}{2}$). Only one group from each side of the diagram is then redrawn. These steps are shown here.

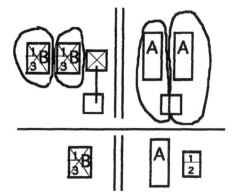

10. Since a whole variable is needed, three of the $-\frac{1}{3}B$ are needed on the left to form –B; this requires three groups on the right as well. Opposites can be drawn to find the final expression for B itself.

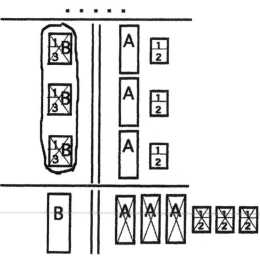

11. Now have students record the steps they have used on their diagrams. Since fractional coefficients were studied in Section 2, encourage students to combine steps and show the reciprocal used [see method (a) below]. If this is still difficult for some, allow them to record the separate steps instead [see method (b) below].

Method (a):

$$-\tfrac{2}{3}B - 1 = 2A$$
$$-\tfrac{2}{3}B + (-1) = 2A$$
$$\underline{\quad + (+1) \qquad + (+1)\quad}$$
$$-\tfrac{2}{3}B = 2A + 1$$
$$\tfrac{3}{2}(-\tfrac{2}{3}B) = \tfrac{3}{2}(2A + 1)$$
$$-B = \tfrac{3}{2}(2A) + \tfrac{3}{2}(1)$$
$$-B = 3A + \tfrac{3}{2}$$
$$B = -3A + (-\tfrac{3}{2}) \qquad [\text{or } B = -3A - 1\tfrac{1}{2}]$$

So B *in terms of* A equals $-3A - \tfrac{3}{2}$.

Method (b):

$$-\tfrac{2}{3}B - 1 = 2A$$
$$-\tfrac{2}{3}B + (-1) = 2A$$
$$\underline{\quad + (+1) \qquad + (+1)\quad}$$
$$-\tfrac{2}{3}B = 2A + 1$$
$$\tfrac{1}{2}(-\tfrac{2}{3}B) = \tfrac{1}{2}(2A + 1)$$
$$-\tfrac{1}{3}B = A + \tfrac{1}{2}$$
$$3(-\tfrac{1}{3}B) = 3(A + \tfrac{1}{2})$$
$$-B = 3A + \tfrac{3}{2}$$
$$B = -3A - \tfrac{3}{2} \qquad [\text{or } -3A - 1\tfrac{1}{2}]$$

So B *in terms of* A equals $-3A - \tfrac{3}{2}$.

12. Working with fractional coefficients is tedious; consequently, students have difficulty with them. Encourage them to carefully record the separation-multiplication steps that are used to form a whole variable (here, −B, then B). If they are consistent with the process, then the use of the reciprocal or multiplicative inverse will have meaning for them. Allow plenty of time for students to discuss and transform their diagrams, then record their steps; do not rush this activity.

13. For another opportunity to show substitution in the new expression for B, ask students to find a value for B by replacing A with the value 0. On the last level of the diagram, students should draw in red pencil a large zero on each rectangle for the variable −A, since when A = 0, −A also is 0. They can then write the new statement: **B = 3(0) − $\tfrac{3}{2}$ = −$\tfrac{3}{2}$.** (If they prefer, they may write **B = −3(0) − $\tfrac{3}{2}$ = −$\tfrac{3}{2}$,** using the "inverse of 3A" instead of "3 of −A" for the expression, −3A.) Remember that our major purpose is always to connect the written notation to the actions performed either on the building mat or with the diagram.

14. Assign more problems to give students practice with diagrams. A few will involve fractional coefficients, while others will have only constants that are fractions. As an extension, two equations have been included that have three variables instead of two. Emphasize to students that the process is the same, no matter how many variables are present. A new rectangle labeled with the new variable merely has to be drawn. Have students follow the same procedure presented in the previous examples, including the statement and substitution. As in Activity 1, brackets with a letter and a value (or values) will indicate which variable to solve for and what value to substitute for the other variable(s) in the final equation.

1. $(-5) + 3C = P + 8$ [P; −4]
2. $2C + M = -C + 5$ [M; −2]
3. $K = (-7) + 3A$ [A; +2]
4. $\frac{1}{2}A + 2B = -1$ [A; +$\frac{3}{2}$]
5. $A - 3B = +9$ [B; +2]
6. $\frac{3}{4}N + 6 = 3K$ [N; −1]
7. $X + W - 4N + 5 = 0$ [W; X = +1, N = +2]
8. $A + \frac{1}{3}R = \frac{1}{2}M - \frac{3}{4} + 2A$ [R; M = +$\frac{1}{2}$, A = +1]

Activity 3: GRAPHING CAPERS

[Application/Exploration]

Materials: Worksheet 3–5–2
Calculators (alternative: graphing calculators)
Colored pencils
Paper
Regular pencils

Management: Teams of 4 students each (30–40 minutes)

Directions:

1. Give each team of students a copy of multi-page Worksheet 3–5–2, a colored pencil (preferably not black, brown, or yellow), and a calculator. For each equation given on the worksheet, students should solve the equation for the stated variable (#2) **in terms of** the other variable (#1). Using selected values for variable #1 and the expression found for variable #2, students may then use a 4-operations calculator to compute values for variable #2 and record them appropriately in the table on the worksheet. Also, for each exercise, the expression found for variable #2 should be written as the heading of the right column of the table. Points should be plotted on the grid for the ordered pairs listed in the table of values, and line segments drawn in colored pencil to connect the points. The scale for the horizontal axis will be given on each grid, but students must select their own equal intervals to use for the vertical axis in each case.

2. As an alternative, if graphing calculators are available, students may plot their expression for the stated variable (#2) by renaming both their variables. Use the variable **Y** instead of the stated variable (#2) and use the variable **X** instead of variable #1. This exchange now gives us Y **in terms of** X. The procedure used will be a reversal of the one described in step 1 for the 4-operations calculator. Here the graph will be found first from Y = (expression in X). Using the TRACE key, a cursor will be moved along the resulting curve (a **linear** curve, but we will discuss this at the end of the activity) and, at selected points, the X and Y values at that point will be recorded in the table. (In step 1, we found the table values first, then plotted the points.) You will need to help students select an appropriate viewing window to use for each problem. Using values from 0 to +4, however, will be quite adequate for each *domain*. Students must decide which 5 pairs to record along the way, hopefully at equal intervals. Typically when a curve is being traced, the X and Y values will not be "nice" integral values; students will have to accept decimal values. In turn, these decimal values will have to be approximated in order to locate their corresponding points on the worksheet grid. The values shown in the left column of each table on the worksheet will need to be changed to the X values indicated in the viewing window for the chosen points on the curve.

Name _____ **Date** _____

WORKSHEET 3-5-2
Graphing Capers

Read about each equation below, then—on your own paper—solve for one variable in terms of the other as requested in the problem. Find different values for the new expression by substituting values 0–4 for the **independent** variable in the expression. Complete the table of values and plot points on the grid for the ordered pairs found. Connect adjacent points with line segments drawn in colored pencil. Answer any questions asked about an equation. Follow additional directions given by your teacher.

1. The cost in dollars, C, for the repair of a home appliance depends on the number of hours (H) needed to make the repair. The equation, $C - \$30\,H = \$25$, relates the cost to the time needed in hours for the repair. Solve for C *in terms of H*. Find C in dollars when H = 0, 1, 2, 3, or 4 hours. What cost might be expected if the repair person takes only 10 minutes to look at the appliance and tell you what's wrong with it, then leaves? What value of H is used to determine this cost?

2. The adjusted weight of a barrel while empty is considered to be 0 pounds. After each hour of water running continuously into the barrel, the barrel's weight is measured in pounds. The equation $80\,T = 2\,W$ relates the number of hours (T) the water has been flowing into the barrel to the weight of the barrel in pounds (W) at the end of that time period. Solve for W *in terms of T*. Find W in pounds when T = 0, 1, 2, 3, or 4 hours. Does the expression for W give the expected weight of the barrel when T = 0 hours? Explain.

3. The equation $D = 50\,T$ relates the distance (D) in miles traveled to the time (T) in hours traveled by a car averaging 50 mph. Find D in miles for T = 0, 1, 2, 3, or 4 hours. Make a scatterplot to represent the ordered pairs (T, D). When the car has not yet moved, what are the values of T and D? Does the equation correctly relate these two values?

4. Repeat Exercise 3, using $D = 60\,T$ for the equation. Here, the car is averaging 60 mph. After both scatterplots have been drawn and adjacent points connected with colored line segments, select a distance (your choice) from the vertical axis and on each graph mark a point on the curve that has that same vertical value. This point will not be in the same location for both graphs. For each graph, extend a path from this point down perpendicularly to the horizontal axis to find the time in hours when the selected distance was traveled by the car. How long did the 50-mph car take to travel your selected distance? How long did the 60-mph car take to travel this same distance? What does this information tell you about the effect of different speeds on travel time?

WORKSHEET 3–5–2 *(cont.)*
Graphing Capers

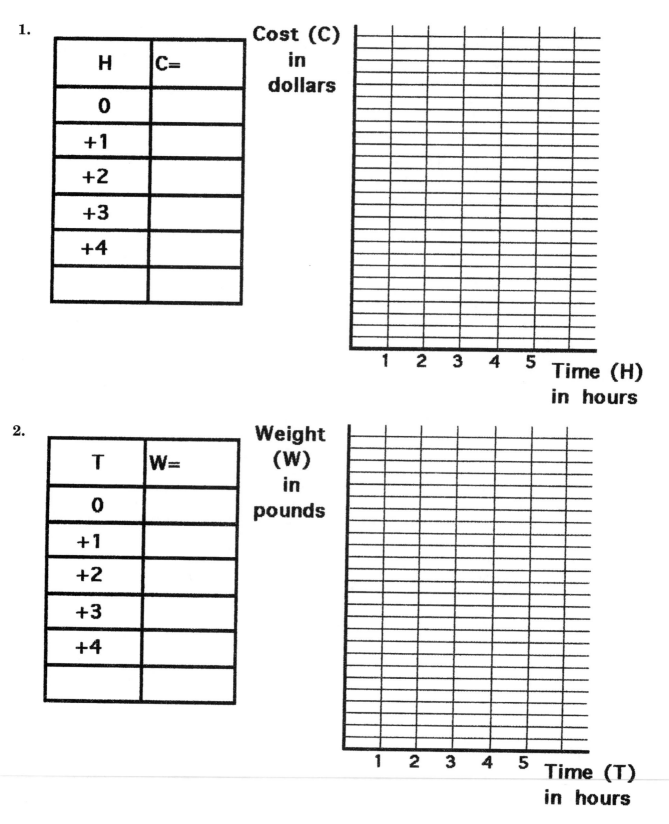

1.

H	C=
0	
+1	
+2	
+3	
+4	

Cost (C) in dollars

Time (H) in hours
1 2 3 4 5

2.

T	W=
0	
+1	
+2	
+3	
+4	

Weight (W) in pounds

Time (T) in hours
1 2 3 4 5

Name _____   Date _____

WORKSHEET 3–5–2 *(cont.)*
Graphing Capers

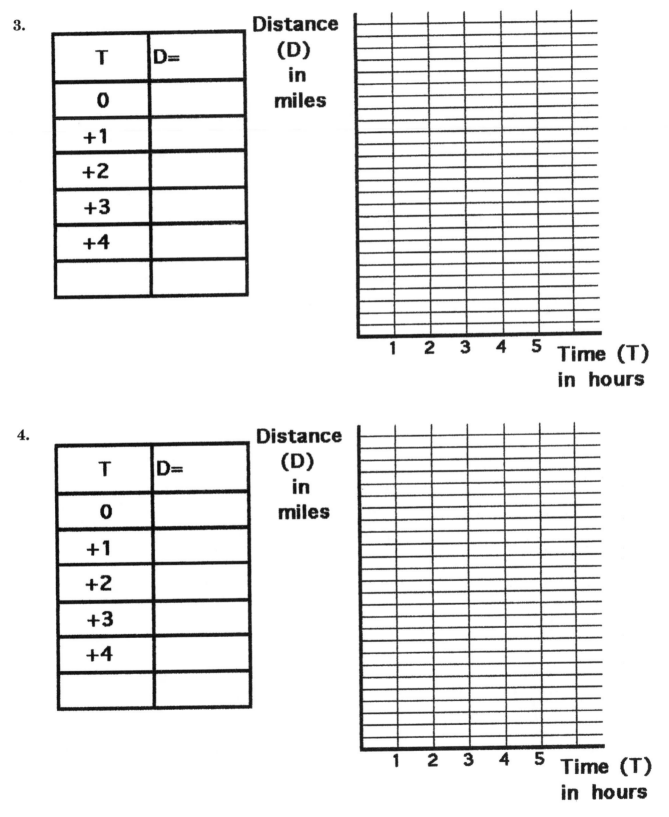

3.

T	D=
0	
+1	
+2	
+3	
+4	

Distance (D) in miles

Time (T) in hours

4.

T	D=
0	
+1	
+2	
+3	
+4	

Distance (D) in miles

Time (T) in hours

3. After all four graphs are completed, ask students to make observations about the paths formed by the different sets of points. All paths should be relatively straight, but will vary in their steepness. Because each value substituted for variable #1 (or X) in the expression produces a single value for the stated variable (#2 or Y) and the path of the points is straight, the set of ordered pairs or data obtained for each problem is called a **linear function.**

4. Another investigation for teams to do involves the last two equations: $D = 50T$ and $D = 60T$. Ask students to find some distance (vertical value) that is the same on both graphs; choices will vary. By tracing over each of the two curves shown on a graphing calculator, they will find points on the two curves or paths (one point per curve) that share the same (or somewhat close) Y-value. Otherwise, in place of the graphing calculator, students will just locate such points on their graphs drawn on the worksheet. Once the common value of variable #2 (in this case, D) or Y is selected, the corresponding value of variable #1 (or T) or X must be identified on each graph, either visually estimated on the graph of the worksheet or by tracing along the curve shown in the viewing window. These last two values for T or X will differ and represent the two different times needed for the two cars to travel the same distance. The purpose of this graphical investigation is to help students become more familiar with the reading and plotting of ordered pairs and to provide experience in comparing simple curves in order to find new information. The following is an example of marking off points on the two distance curves.

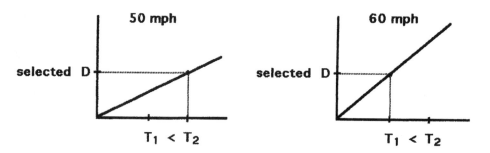

5. Possible answers to discussion questions on Worksheet 3–5–2:

(1) Since the repair person did not stay a full hour or do any repairs, we use $H = 0$ in either the equation or the expression to get $C = \$25$, which is the service fee charged for just the call.

(2) When $T = 0$, this is before water begins to run into the barrel. The equation gives W as 0 lbs. when $T = 0$, which is the adjusted weight given for the barrel when it is still empty. So the equation correctly relates W and T at the beginning of the situation, not just after the water begins to run into the barrel.

(3) When the car has not yet moved, T will be 0 hrs. and D will be 0 mi. For $T = 0$ and $D = 0$ in the equation, we still get a true number sentence: $0 = 0$. So the equation correctly relates T and D at the beginning of the travel, as well as during the travel.

(4) See response for Exercise 3 above. When comparing the 50-mph car to the 60-mph car, the 60-mph car will take less time than the 50-mph car to travel the selected distance (assuming $D > 0$ miles). Conclusion: The faster car requires less time to make the same trip, assuming the faster speed is still a safe speed!

Example of time comparison: To travel 60 miles, the 60-mph car will take $\frac{60}{60}$ or 1 hour; the 50-mph car will take $\frac{60}{50}$ or 1.2 hours.

OBJECTIVE 6: **Compare the vertical change (change in Y or dependent variable) to the horizontal change (change in X or independent variable) between two points on a given line or linear graph.**

Activity 1: OVER AND UP

[Developing Action]

Materials: Large grid sheets and small colored markers (described in step 1)
Thin bamboo skewers or straight wire pieces (10–12 inches long)
One-inch paper squares (marked with either A, B, C, or D; may be laminated)
Paper
Regular pencils
Calculators
Worksheet 3–6–1

Management: Teams of 3–4 students (50 minutes)

Directions:

1. Give each team a large grid sheet, 5 small colored markers (1 marker per color), 4 one-inch paper squares (one labeled with A, one with B, one with C, one with D), a calculator, and 1 bamboo skewer or wire piece. The wire should be only thick enough to keep it from bending too easily. The small markers might be commercially available colored centimeter cubes, colored flat buttons (approximately 0.5-inch diameter), or square or hexagonal metal nuts (approximately 0.5-inch diameter; spray-painted in 5 colors, 1 color per nut) from a hardware store. Other materials are possible; the markers just need to be in 5 different colors and about 0.5 inch in diameter. The grid may be drawn off on heavy bulletin board paper to form approximately a 14 in. × 16 in. grid (unit length of 1 inch), or a grid may be drawn on two sheets of 8.5 in. × 14 in. paper, which can then be taped together at their longer edges to make the larger grid that is needed. Laminating the final grids will make them more durable. Packaging the 5 small markers in a snack-size, closable, plastic bag will also make distribution of materials easier and quicker. This activity will introduce students to the idea of a **ratio** or **rate** in real-world situations corresponding to the **slope** of a line (vertical rise to horizontal run) in a graphical setting. Connections will also be made to the ratio table used in this section in Objective 3 on ratio and proportion.

Real-Life Example:

2. Describe the following situation to students: *A salesperson receives a commission of $1 for every $4 in total sales. What is the commission from an $8 sale? from a $12 sale? from a $14 sale?* For each of the given sales, have students make a ratio table, recording *Total Sales* amounts in the left column and *Commission* amounts in the right column. (See Worksheet 3–6–1.) The top row will be used for the basic ratio and the bottom row will be for the secondary ratio. Both pairs of arrows should also be drawn and labeled on each table as review, even though only one pair is needed to find the missing commission

Name _____ **Date** _____

WORKSHEET 3-6-1
Over and Up

Follow your teacher's instructions to complete the ratio tables below.

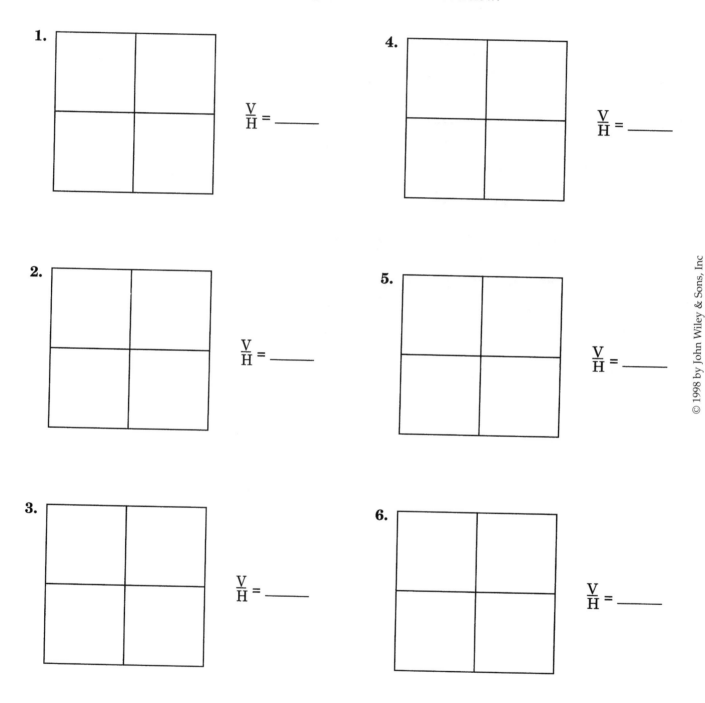

1.

$\dfrac{V}{H} =$ _____

4.

$\dfrac{V}{H} =$ _____

2.

$\dfrac{V}{H} =$ _____

5.

$\dfrac{V}{H} =$ _____

3.

$\dfrac{V}{H} =$ _____

6.

$\dfrac{V}{H} =$ _____

in dollars. (Refer to Section 3, Objective 3 for details on ratio tables.) Discuss the idea that the Total Sales amount is the **independent** value that we use to compute the Commission amount, the **dependent** value. That is, when the Total Sales amount changes, it causes the Commission amount to change as well. Here are the three completed ratio tables:

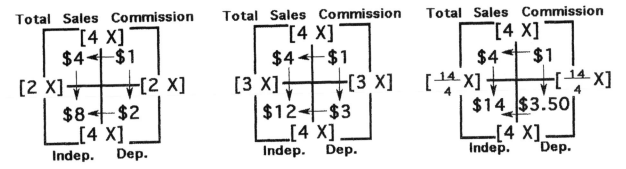

3. For this example, on the large grid we will consider the unit length on each axis scale to represent the value of $1. Each grid should be positioned so that the longer edge is the *horizontal* axis. The lower left corner of the grid will be the origin. Discuss with students that this axis is traditionally used for the **independent** value in a relationship, so it will be used to show Total Sales. The vertical axis is traditionally used for the **dependent** value, so it will be used to show the Commission.

4. For ease of communication, we will use red, blue, orange, yellow, and green for the colors of the small markers. Have students locate on the grid the point that represents the ordered pair for the basic ratio ($4 sales, $1 commission); place the blue marker there and also the paper square marked A, which names the point. They should also place the green marker and the B marker at the point for ($8 sales, $2 commission) from the first ratio table. Finally have them place the red marker at the point for ($8, $1), which is the point of intersection of the horizontal grid line passing through point A and the vertical grid line passing through point B.

5. Ask students to count the horizontal (H) unit lengths between point A and the red marker, which should be 4 units. Then have them count the vertical (V) unit lengths between the red marker and point B, which should be 1 unit. These two lengths should be written as a ratio beside the first ratio table that contains the ordered pairs or coordinates for points A and B. Since on our graph, 1 unit of length represents $1, the following format should be used: $\frac{V}{H} = \frac{1\ \mathbf{DOLLAR}}{4\ \mathbf{DOLLARS}}$. This tells us that from A to B, a $4 increase in sales led to a $1 increase in commission.

6. The third ordered pair ($12 sales, $3 commission) (from the secondary ratio in the second ratio table) should now be located with the orange marker and the C marker. The red marker should be moved over to the new intersection point ($12, $1), and the steps or units counted from point A over to the red marker, then counted from the red marker up to point C. The ratio of these new distances should be recorded beside the ratio table containing $12 in sales: $\frac{V}{H} = \frac{2\ \mathbf{DOLLARS}}{8\ \mathbf{DOLLARS}}$. This ratio tells us that from A to C, an $8 increase in sales produced a $2 increase in commission.

7. Repeat the process to show ($14 sales, $3.50 commission) with the yellow marker and the D marker. The red marker should be moved to ($14, $1). The new ratio will be: $\frac{V}{H} = \frac{\$2.50}{\$10}$. Last, the ratio is recorded beside the ratio table containing $14 in sales.

11. Students should now count the unit lengths between the blue marker and the red marker. There should be 6 unit line segments counted for this horizontal distance. **_Ask:_** "To find the vertical distance, we must count the unit lengths between the red marker and the green marker. How can this be done? How many such units will there be?" *(since the red marker is directly on top of the green marker, there must be 0 unit lengths between the two markers)* The ratio of the two distances will be: $\frac{V}{H} = \frac{0}{6} = 0$. (No labels should be used here for final 0 since it is the *counter* of H-sets matching to the V-set; compare only distances here since no value has been assigned to each unit length.) So the line that contains points A and B is a **horizontal line** and has a distance ratio or **slope of 0.**

12. Now have students place the orange marker and C marker at the point for (7, 2) on the grid, and place the yellow marker and D marker at the point for (7, 6). **_Ask:_** "If the red marker must move horizontally from point C until it is in line with point D, where should the red marker be placed?" Allow students time to explore the situation and share their ideas. The red marker can only be placed on top of the orange marker if it is to be in line with C and D simultaneously.

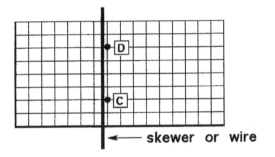

← **skewer or wire**

13. **_Ask:_** "You need to count the horizontal unit lengths between the orange marker and the red marker. How can you do this?" Since the red marker is on top of the orange marker, there must be 0 unit lengths between the two markers horizontally. **_Ask:_** "To find the vertical distance, we must count the unit lengths between the red marker and the yellow marker. How many such units will there be?" Students should count the unit lengths along the vertical grid line between the red marker and the yellow marker; there will be 4 unit lengths. The ratio of the two distances will be: $\frac{V}{H} = \frac{4}{0}$. **_Ask:_** "What do we know about the answer when we divide by 0? Reversing the problem to think of it in another way, we need a number that will multiply by 0 to equal 4. Can you think of such a number?" Students may suggest several different answers like 0 or even 4. Test each suggestion to see if it works in the multiplication sentence; for example, test **0** as the answer: **0 × 0 = 4**, which is not true, so 0 cannot be the answer. Testing **4** as the answer: **4 × 0 = 4**, which also is not true. Since no answer can be found, the ratio of $\frac{4}{0}$ will not have a numerical value. Hence, we cannot find a *slope value* to assign to this particular line. The line that contains points C and D is a **vertical line** for which **the slope does not exist.** We may also say that the slope is "not defined" for a vertical line, or that the slope is "undefined." **Note:** A line having a "slope of 0" is *not* the same as a line having "no slope at all."

Activity 2: DRAWING DISTANCES

[Bridging Action]

Materials: Colored pencils (at least 4 different colors)
Centimeter grid paper
Calculators
Regular pencils
Paper
Worksheet 3–6–2

Management: Partners (50 minutes)

Directions:

1. Give each pair of students 4 colored pencils (4 different colors; 1 pencil per color), 2 sheets of centimeter grid paper, and a calculator. The procedure for this activity will be similar to the one followed in Activity 1, except students will draw the distances in color on the grid each time. Also negative slope will be explored and a special recording notation introduced. On the grid, the shortest segment marked on each axis will now represent multiple units instead of a single unit of length.

2. Describe the following situation to the students: *University campus architects and planners have designed parking lots on the campus so that 2 parking spaces will be available for every 3 cars registered by students. How many parking spaces are expected to be available for 12 cars? for 36 cars? for 58 cars?* Have students draw three ratio tables on their own papers, using 3 cars to 2 parking spaces as the basic ratio each time. (See Worksheet 3–6–2.) For each table, they should draw and label one pair of arrows that can be used to find the missing number of parking spaces for that table. We will assume that the *expected* number of cars on campus (i.e., expected number of students registering) controls the number of parking spaces that have been provided. Thus, the number of cars will be our **independent** value and the number of parking spaces will be our **dependent** value. Three possible completed ratio tables are shown below:

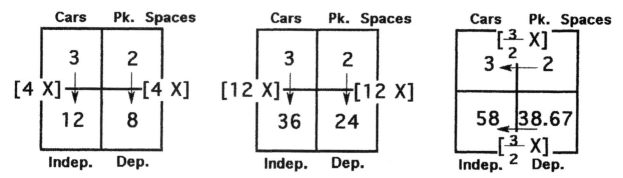

3. Discuss the meaning of 38.67 parking spaces found in the third ratio table. It is frustrating enough for 3 cars to have to fight for 2 parking spaces, but there's no way anyone can use 0.67 of a parking space! So in reality this fraction of a space is useless; only the 38 spaces will be of use to the drivers of the cars. This is a situation where we do not round up a number. Thus, the more meaningful ratio might be 58 cars to 38 parking spaces. Students should still try to approximate the rounded 38.7 on their grids when they plot points later in order to preserve a linear appearance in their graph.

Name _____   **Date** _____

WORKSHEET 3-6-2
Drawing Distances

Follow your teacher's instructions to complete the ratio tables below.

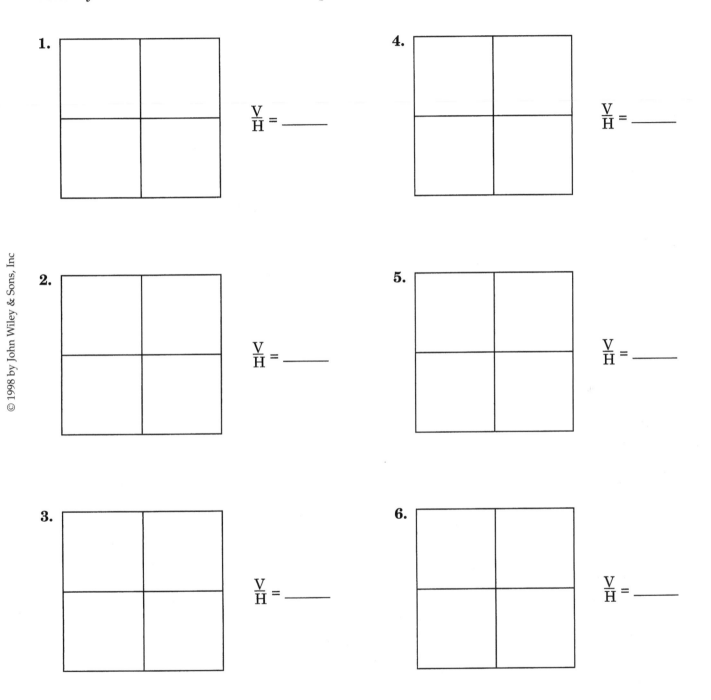

1. $\dfrac{V}{H} =$ _____

2. $\dfrac{V}{H} =$ _____

3. $\dfrac{V}{H} =$ _____

4. $\dfrac{V}{H} =$ _____

5. $\dfrac{V}{H} =$ _____

6. $\dfrac{V}{H} =$ _____

4. Guide students to decide on the scale sizes they will need for their particular grid. One possibility, which we will use in our discussion here, is to have each segment length on the long side of the grid represent 3 cars and each segment length on the short side represent 4 parking spaces. After students have labeled the two axes of their grids (long side for cars, short side for parking spaces), have them locate and label points for A (3, 2), B (12, 8), C (36, 24), and D (58, 38.7). The four points should be connected in regular pencil with broken line segments.

5. To compare points A and B, students should begin by identifying a rectangle on the grid that has A and B at opposite corners and that has its sides aligned with the vertical and horizontal line segments of the grid. The rectangle should be drawn lightly in regular pencil. This process will help students identify and label P, the other point needed for the comparison of distances (the role of the red marker in Activity 1). Two adjacent sides of the rectangle should then be selected and outlined in colored pencil, each side in a different color (there are two such pairs of adjacent sides; students may choose to work with either pair). In our example, we will use red and blue for the two colors. The lower right corner of the rectangle will be chosen for point P.

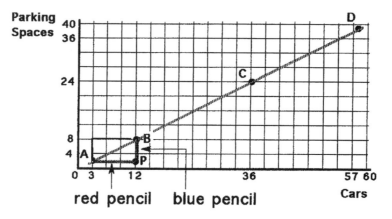

6. Ask students to begin at point A and count the horizontal grid segments equal to the distance from A to point P. In our example, each grid segment has a value of 3 cars, so the 3 segments counted will represent a value of 3×3 cars, or 9 cars. Students should then count the vertical grid segments equal to the distance from P to point B. Each vertical segment has a value of 4 parking spaces, so the 1 and $\frac{1}{2}$ segments will represent the value of 1.5×4 parking spaces, or 6 parking spaces. The distances (in segments) found are now replaced by a new *value* ratio, which should be recorded beside the ratio table containing the entry, 12 cars: $\frac{V}{H} = \frac{6\ \text{SPACES}}{9\ \text{CARS}}$. The following sentence should also be recorded beside the ratio table: **This ratio tells us that from A to B, an increase of 9 cars led to an increase of 6 parking spaces.** Alternative statement: **From A to B, there is an increase of 6 parking spaces because of (for) an increase of 9 cars.**

7. Now have students compare some of the other pairs of points they have plotted: A and C, A and D, B and C, B and D, and C and D. (For this section, they should always start with the point in a pair that is farthest to the left on the grid. In the next section, we will discuss the effects of direction on counting the grid segments.) The value ratios found from these pairs for "increase in spaces compared to increase in cars" ($\frac{V}{H}$) will be $\frac{22}{33}$, $\frac{36.67}{55}$, $\frac{16}{64}$, $\frac{30.67}{46}$, and $\frac{14.67}{22}$, respectively. Each of these ratios, if simplified to a decimal number, will round to 0.67. Again, observe that the **basic ratio,** 3 cars to 2 parking spaces (we choose to write the values in this order to correspond to their order in a *table of values*), could be reworded as a **rate**: "2 parking spaces per 3 cars" (using number of cars as the **independent** value) and written in the form: $\frac{V}{H} = \frac{2}{3}$, which simplifies to 0.67 as well.

Sample of a rectangle to use to compare points B and C (move from B to P, then from P to C):

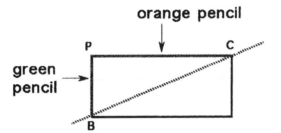

8. Finally ***ask:*** "When you look at the four points plotted on your grid, what do you notice about their appearance? As you move from A to D, what is the direction of your path?" Students should notice that all four points are lined up together; point D may be off-line a little since its vertical coordinate was an approximation. Hence, the collection of four ordered pairs is called a **linear function.** As you move from A to D, the path seems to go uphill to the right. Thus, the line that passes through the four points is described as having a **positive slope.** In conclusion, it does not matter which two points are compared; for all pairs, the ratio of the vertical change in value compared to the horizontal change in value will be the same.

Geometric Examples:

9. Our purpose in Activity 2 is to have students view the change in a dependent element caused by a change in an independent element in a variety of ways: tables of values, graphs/scatterplots, ratios, rate statements, etc. In this section we will look at some general cases graphically. Have students copy the following graph on their own grid paper, assigning each grid segment a value of one.

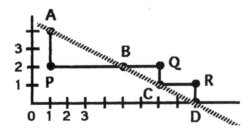

10. Ask students to draw segment AP in one color and segment PB in a different color. Similarly, they should color BQ and QC, then CR and RD. For clarity, any two segments that have a common point should be drawn in different colors.

11. *Ask:* "If you go from having $5 in your pocket to having $12 in your pocket, how do you calculate this increase?" *(usually $12 − $5 = $7 increase)* "If you start at the 3-mile marker on a highway and drive to the 10-mile marker, how do you mentally compute how many miles you have driven?" *(usually 10 − 3 = 7 miles increase)* Discuss the idea that in each case we typically subtract the **starting** number from the **ending** number. We will apply this idea to our grid to find the vertical or horizontal distance between two given points. The markings on the appropriate axis will identify our starting and ending numbers.

12. To compare vertical and horizontal changes occurring as we move from A to B, have students mark arrowheads on segments AP and PB as shown.

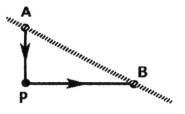

13. Consider the distance from point A to point P. Since the segment is vertical, we must use the vertical scale or axis to find our two numbers. Ask students to locate the marking directly left of A (starting number = 4) and the marking directly left of P (ending number = 2). On their own paper they should write and compute $(2 - 4) = -2$, then record the -2 on segment AP on their grid. Next consider the distance from P to B. Finding the horizontal marking directly below P (starting number = 1) and the marking directly below B (ending number = 5), students should write and compute $(5 - 1) = 4$ on their own paper, then record 4 on segment PB on their grid. This method provides the two distances needed to form the ratio, $\frac{V}{H}$. On the segment AB, have students record: $\frac{V}{H} = -\frac{2}{4}$.

14. Now have students repeat the procedure used in step 13, but have them begin at point B and move to P, then to A. From B to P, the distance becomes $(1 - 5) = -4$; from P to A, the distance becomes $(4 - 2) = 2$. ***Ask:*** "Using these new values, what will the ratio, $\frac{V}{H}$, be?" $(\frac{V}{H} = \frac{2}{(-4)})$ "How does this ratio compare to the first ratio you found?" $(-\frac{2}{4}$ *is equivalent to* $\frac{2}{(-4)}$; that is, both simplify to -0.5, or if both are recorded in a *ratio table,* they will be related by a factor of -1) "To find $\frac{V}{H}$ does it matter whether you move from A to P to B or go from B to P to A?" (*no*; ratios are equivalent; use either form)

15. Have students repeat the procedure used in steps 12–14 to compare the vertical and horizontal changes between B and C, and between C and D. In other words, the ratio $\frac{V}{H}$ should be found in two ways, that is, by moving in opposite directions. As an extra challenge, ask several students to compare the changes between A and C, or between B and D.

16. After students have completed their different computations and labeled the various segments connecting the four points with the appropriate $\frac{V}{H}$ ratios, ask for observations about the various ratios found for this line and the physical appearance of the line. Possible comments: All the ratios are equivalent or can be simplified to the same negative value, -0.5 or $-\frac{1}{2}$; the path through the four points appears to go downhill to the right. Since a specific value can be found by simplifying the ratios and the four points line up together, the four ordered pairs are considered a **linear function.** The line sloping downhill to the right is described as having a **negative slope,** which is also indicated by the **negative value of the $\frac{V}{H}$ ratios** computed.

17. For additional practice, if needed, draw other grids on the board with 3 or 4 collinear points located on each. Have them spaced across different quadrants so that students can practice with negative numbers as starting or ending numbers. Some sets of points should have positive slopes, while others might have negative slopes, a zero slope, or no slope.

Activity 3: RATIO SMASH!

[Application/Exploration]

Materials: Card Decks A and B (Worksheets 3–6–3 and 3–6–4)
Calculators
Paper
Regular pencils
Large grids
Bamboo skewers or pieces of wire
Small markers from Activity 1

Management: Teams of 4 students (20–30 minutes)

Directions:

1. There are two versions of this game; the two card decks represent the two different versions. **For Version A:** Give each team one set of Card Deck A, a large grid with a bag of 5 markers, a bamboo skewer or piece of straight wire, and a calculator. **For Version B:** Give each team one set of Card Deck B, a large grid with a bag of 5 markers, a bamboo skewer or piece of straight wire, and a calculator. Card Deck A will consist of 20 cards, each having a list of ordered pairs randomly arranged and appropriate for the large grid's dimensions. Card Deck B will consist of 20 cards, each having a ratio for vertical distance to horizontal distance ($\frac{V}{H}$) that can be used to describe a line passing through Quadrant I (shown on the large grid). Some ratios will be simplified, and some will list an ordered pair that indicates a point that the line must touch or contain. Each version will be described separately in steps below, and possible ratios or ordered pairs for the different card decks will also be provided.

2. *Game Version A:* Each team will shuffle Card Deck A and place the stack of cards face down on the table. They will take turns drawing a card off the top of the stack and determining if the set of ordered pairs on the card makes a **linear function.** A player chooses one of two ways to test the set of pairs: (a) place a marker on the grid for each point named by an ordered pair and place the skewer or wire next to the markers to see if all the points line up; or (b) reorder the pairs according to the increasing order of the horizontal values, and either mentally or with the calculator compute the ratio of vertical-horizontal differences ($\frac{V}{H}$) for each adjacent pair to see if all the ratios exist and are equivalent.

3. If method (a) [easier] is used and all the markers on the grid line up against the skewer and are **not** vertically arranged, the player should state that the ordered pairs make a **linear function.** If correct, the player earns **1 point.** If method (b) [harder] is used and all the ratios are equivalent and equal some *real value,* the player should state the simplified value of the ratios and that the pairs make a **linear function.** If correct, the player earns **5 points.** After all cards have been drawn, the game is over. The player with the most points wins.

4. Worksheet 3–6–3 gives 20 possible sets of pairs to use for the cards. An answer key is also provided. These sets of pairs may be recopied onto 2 in. × 3 in. pieces of cardstock by hand, or a photocopy may be made of this list, then each list of pairs cut out and glued onto a 2 in. × 3 in. piece of cardstock and laminated. To keep different decks separated,

WORKSHEET 3-6-3
Ordered Pairs for Card Deck A

1. (1, 2) (2, 4) (3, 6) (4, 8) (5, 10)	**2.** (5, 7) (8, 1) (11, 7) (16, 1)	**3.** (4, 0) (5, 4) (6, 8) (7, 12)	**4.** (1, 12) (2, 9) (3, 6) (4, 3)
5. (6, 3) (0, 0) (10, 5) (15, 7.5)	**6.** (3, 1) (6, 10) (4, 1) (6, 3) (6, 7)	**7.** (6, 3) (4, 3) (3, 5) (7, 5) (5, 1)	**8.** (3, 8) (12, 8) (14, 8) (7, 8)
9. (1, 4) (2, 4) (4, 4) (5, 4) (3, 4)	**10.** (4, 0) (12, 8) (15, 11) (7, 3)	**11.** (8, 0) (8, 13) (8, 2) (8, 10)	**12.** (2, 2) (8, 11) (4, 5) (10, 14) (6, 8)
13. (3, 14) (9, 2) (10, 0) (4, 12)	**14.** (3, 10) (5, 7) (7, 2) (9, 8)	**15.** (2, 0) (4, 5) (4, 9) (5, 1)	**16.** (5, 3) (5, 7) (5, 11) (5, 12)
17. (3, 14) (9, 6) (12, 2) (6, 10)	**18.** (2, 6) (6, 10) (8, 8) (4, 8) (10, 6)	**19.** (5, 12) (6, 11) (10, 7) (14, 3)	**20.** (1, 1) (2, 4) (3, 7) (4, 10) (5, 13)

WORKSHEET 3-6-4
Ratios and Ordered Pairs for Card Deck B

1. $0; (4, 1)$	**2.** $0; (9, 5)$	**3.** $-\frac{4}{3}; (9, 6)$	**4.** $+2$
5. $+4; (5, 4)$	**6.** no slope exists (∞); $(0, 0)$	**7.** $\frac{-3}{+4}$	**8.** $\frac{-1}{+2}$
9. $\frac{+2}{+3}$	**10.** $+3$	**11.** $+\frac{3}{2}; (6, 8)$	**12.** -1, or $\frac{-1}{+1}$
13. $+1$, or $\frac{+1}{+1}$	**14.** -2, or $\frac{-2}{+1}$	**15.** 0	**16.** no slope exists (∞); $(3, 8)$
17. $-3; (2, 9)$	**18.** $-2; (10, 0)$	**19.** $+\frac{1}{2}$	**20.** $\frac{-1}{+4}$

use a color code or dot code of some kind and mark all cards in the same deck with the same code or symbol before laminating them.

Answer Key for Card Deck A:

Sets that are **linear functions** followed by their $\frac{V}{H}$ ratios:

> 1 (+2); 3 (+4); 4 (−3); 5 (+$\frac{1}{2}$); 8 (0); 9 (0); 10 (+1); 12 (+$\frac{3}{2}$); 13 (−2); 17 (−$\frac{4}{3}$); 19 (−1); 20 (+3)

Sets that are **not** linear functions: 2; 6; 7; 11; 14; 15; 16; 18

5. *Game Version B:* Each team shuffles Card Deck B and places the stack of cards face down on the table. Players take turns drawing a card off the top of the deck. The card will show a ratio in $\frac{V}{H}$ form (e.g., $\frac{-2}{+1}$) or its simplified value (e.g., −2). Remind students that if only a simplified value for the ratio is given, it should be rewritten in a numerator-denominator format (e.g., −4 might be rewritten as $\frac{-4}{+1}$ or even $\frac{-8}{+2}$). Keeping the denominator positive is merely a convenience; the numerator (−4) may now be used for the vertical difference and the denominator (+1) may be used for the horizontal difference in the $\frac{V}{H}$ ratio. The player must place 3 markers on the large grid to indicate points whose ratios of vertical to horizontal differences for adjacent points will be equivalent to the ratio shown on the card. The player must give the ordered pair for each point selected on the grid and explain why the three points satisfy the given ratio. On some cards an ordered pair will also be given; this pair should also be shown with a marker on the grid. The skewer or wire should be placed on the grid so that it touches the 3 new points and the extra point, if given, to show that the 3 (or 4) points do line up. If all the points line up and are not in a vertical arrangement, the player should state that the set of ordered pairs represented by the markers is a **linear function.** If an extra ordered pair is not given on the card, the player is free to pick any three points on the grid whose $\frac{V}{H}$ ratios are equivalent to the given ratio and that lie in the same line, i.e., are **collinear.**

6. If the player is successful in locating and justifying the selection of the 3 (or 4) collinear points and naming their ordered pairs, the player will earn 2 points. When all cards have been drawn from the stack, the game will be over. The player with the most points will be the winner.

7. Worksheet 3–6–4 gives 20 possible ratios (with or without an ordered pair) to use for the cards in Deck B. Each individual ratio, or ratio with an ordered pair, should be written on a 2 in. × 3 in. piece of cardstock. Each card within the same deck should be coded in some way, then laminated. An answer key given below shows line orientations for required slopes and where selected points might be located. Specific grid positions are shown if a specific point is given.

Answer Key for Card Deck B:

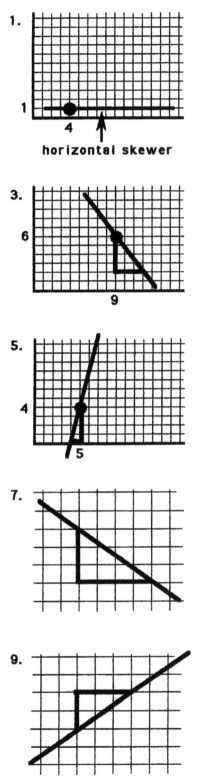

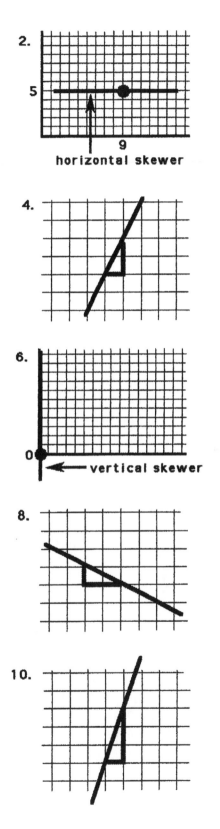

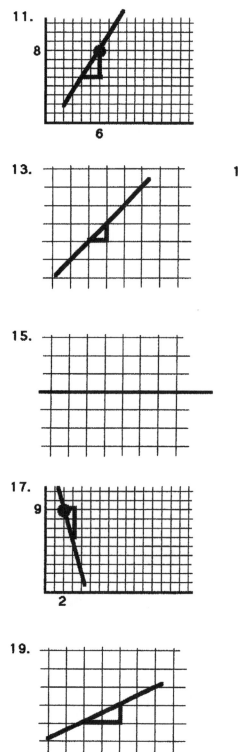
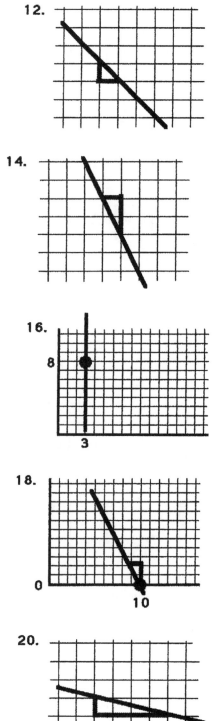

OBJECTIVE 7: Explore minimal numerical conditions needed to determine the specific graph and algebraic form of a linear function.

Activity 1: "I HAVE A LINE THAT . . . "

[Developing Action]

Materials: Small colored markers, thin bamboo skewers or wire pieces (approximately 12 inches long), and large grids from Activity 1, Objective 6
One-inch paper squares (see details in step 1)
Calculators
Paper
Regular pencils

Management: Partners (50 minutes)

Directions:

1. Give each pair of students a large grid, a bag of 5 colored markers, a skewer, and a calculator. Instead of a skewer, a piece of stiff wire or two connected drinking straws (slit end of one straw inserted in end of other straw and overlapping ends taped together) might be used, but either must be straight and not easily bent. Each pair also needs 3 one-inch paper squares, one marked as P(X,Y), one as X, and one as Y; these should be laminated to make them more durable. In this activity students will try to discover the minimal information needed to locate a line in a coordinate plane.

2. *Ask:* "**I have a line that** passes through the point representing the ordered pair (8,3). Put a colored marker at that point on your grid. Can you place your skewer on the grid to show my line?" Skewers will be placed on grids so that they touch the marker for (8,3), but they will have various orientations. Ask a student to name another point that touches her or his skewer, for example, (3,5). *Ask:* "Does anyone else have the same point touching your skewer?" *(some may; others will not)* "If your skewers do not touch the same point, are they in the same position on the grid?" *(no; to be in the same position implies that the skewers touch exactly the same set of points on the grid)* Offer a second point (4,8) to help students locate the mystery line. Students should place a marker at (4,8), then position their skewers to touch both of the points named. Have them look at the skewer positions on nearby grids. All skewers should be in the same approximate position. Have students record on their own paper: **Two points on the grid located the same line for all students.**

3. Have students place their skewer on the grid so that it shows a vertical-horizontal difference ratio ($\frac{V}{H}$) of $+\frac{1}{3}$. No colored markers are used at first. Several positions on the grid are possible as long as the ratio is maintained. (This same idea was used earlier in Game Version B of Activity 3, Objective 6.) Ask a student to name a point that the skewer touches, for example, (6,3). Ask other students if their skewers also touch the same point. (Some literal thinkers will say "no, because the skewer is too short." Tell them to imagine that the skewer can be stretched. Some students, however, cannot visualize this way. If so, give them another skewer to place end-to-end with their first skewer, still maintaining the original orientation but extending toward the point in question to see if the extended skewers will touch the point.) Some skewers will touch this stated point; others will not.

4. *Ask:* "What else do I need to tell you besides the vertical-horizontal differences ratio to help all of you find the line I want?" *(another point will suffice)* Tell students to place a colored marker at the point for (6,5), then slide their skewers over on the grid to touch the marker, keeping the same ratio of $+\frac{1}{3}$. Have them look at nearby grids; all skewers should be in the same position on their grids. *Ask:* "Does it matter which point I give? Is there a point on the vertical axis that I could tell you to use that would belong to this same line you have just shown?" *(the given point can vary; (0,3) is also on the line, but on the vertical axis of the grid)* "Will this same line have a point on the horizontal axis of our grid?" *(not on this grid, because we are working only with the first quadrant; if we extend our horizontal axis to the left for negative values, our line will eventually cross it)* Have students record on their own papers: **If we all use the same $\frac{V}{H}$ ratio for a line and any one point that is on the line, all our lines will be the same; the one point may or may not be on an axis. A point on an axis is an intercept point.**

5. For another example using **two given points,** have students place colored markers on their grids to show the points for (3,2) and (9,6). The skewer should be positioned on the grid to touch these two markers. *Ask:* "What if you are told that the point (6,3) is on the same line? Is this true or false?" *(students can see on the grid that (6,3) is below the skewer)* "How can we decide what value of N is needed in order for (6,N) to be on the line?" Remind students that for a line, the $\frac{V}{H}$ ratios for all pairs of points on that same line will be equivalent (review Objective 6, if needed). First have them find the ratio for the two given points (3,2) and (9,6). For variety, follow the paths shown in the illustration in step 6. Moving from (3,2) horizontally to the right to the point just above 9 on the horizontal axis will give the difference (9 − 3), where 3 is the starting number and 9 is the ending number. Then moving vertically upward from this "turning point" to the point (9,6), which is even with the number 6 on the vertical axis, students will find the difference (6 − 2), where 2 is the starting number and 6 is the ending number. The $\frac{V}{H}$ ratio is then $\frac{(6-2)}{(9-3)}$, or $\frac{4}{6}$. Thus, for (6,N) to be on the same line, it must form a ratio with another point on the line, say, (3,2), that is equivalent to the ratio, $\frac{4}{6}$. A possible equation would be $\frac{(N-2)}{(6-3)} = \frac{4}{6}$, which simplifies to $\frac{1}{3}N - \frac{2}{3} = \frac{4}{6}$. Solving this equation, N will have to equal 4.

6. Now have students place a third colored marker next to the skewer to represent some unknown point on the line. For convenience, place the marker somewhere on the skewer between the other two colored markers. The new point does not have to be at an intersection of a vertical and a horizontal grid line. Use the 3 paper squares labeled **P(X,Y), X,** and **Y** on the grid to help identify the new point. Place the square P(X,Y) beside this new colored marker. The paper square X should be at or on the horizontal axis directly below the paper square for P(X,Y), and the Y-square should be at or on the vertical axis directly left of P(X,Y). Here is a sample grid to show a possible arrangement. (Arrow paths indicate suggested directions to be used when finding vertical and horizontal differences for the change ratios of two different pairs of points.)

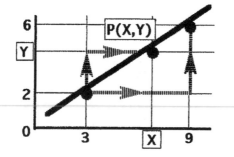

7. Have students now find a new ratio, using (3,2) and P(X,Y) as the pair of points. Moving from the point for (3,2) vertically upward to a point even with the Y-square on the vertical axis will give the difference (Y – 2), where 2 is the starting number and Y is the ending number. Then moving from this new "turning point" in a horizontal direction to P(X,Y), which is directly above the X-square on the horizontal axis, will give the difference (X – 3), since 3 is the starting number and X is the ending number. The new ratio for these two points becomes $\frac{(Y-2)}{(X-3)}$. Since the points (3,2), (9,6) and P(X,Y) are on the same line, they should pairwise have equivalent ratios. Students should record the following equation to show the two equivalent ratios. (Do not simplify at this time.) $\frac{(Y-2)}{(X-3)} = +\frac{4}{6}$.

8. For more practice with **a given ratio and a given point,** ask students to show the line that passes through the point (7,0) and has a difference ratio, $\frac{V}{H}$, of $\frac{-3}{+2}$. A colored marker should be placed on the grid at (7,0) and the skewer positioned next to the marker according to the given ratio. Discuss the idea that (7,0) is where the line intercepts the horizontal axis, so it is called the horizontal intercept (traditionally, the **X-intercept**). *Ask:* "Is the point (5,3) on this same line? Test it by finding the difference or change ratio for this point and (7,0)." Students should find either $\frac{(0-3)}{(7-5)}$ or $\frac{(3-0)}{(5-7)}$, both of which are equivalent to the given ratio, $\frac{-3}{+2}$. Thus, (5,3) is on the line also. A colored marker should be placed on the grid beside the skewer to show this point as well.

9. *Ask:* "Can you apply the given ratio and count backward to find the vertical intercept (or **Y-intercept**) for this line?" Reversing the directions shown in the ratio and counting left 2 units from either (7,0) or (5,3), then up 3 units on the grid to find another point on the line, then repeating this process several times, students will eventually reach the vertical axis. The intercept will be (0,10.5). Place another colored marker beside the skewer at this point. Students might verify that this point is actually on the line by finding the ratio of change between (0,10.5) and (7,0), the **given** point.

10. Finally have students place a fourth colored marker next to the skewer to show some unknown point on the line. For convenience, place the marker somewhere along the skewer on the other side of (5,3) from (7,0). The new point does not have to be at an intersection of a vertical and a horizontal grid line. Use the 3 paper squares labeled **P(X,Y), X,** and **Y** on the grid to help identify the new point as we did earlier. An illustration of the placement of the markers and paper squares is shown below, along with arrows for possible paths to follow to compute differences or changes.

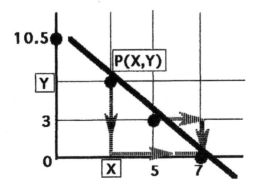

11. For variety, from P(X,Y), which is directly to the right of the Y-square on the vertical axis, we want to move downward to the X-square on the horizontal axis; this point is level with (7,0). The vertical change or difference is described as $(0 - Y)$, Y being the starting number and 0 being the ending number. From this "turning point," move horizontally to the right to the point (7,0). The horizontal difference will be $(7 - X)$, where X is the starting number and 7 is the ending number. The change or differences ratio becomes $\frac{(0-Y)}{(7-X)}$ for the two points P(X,Y) and (7,0). Since this ratio must be equivalent to the **given** ratio, have students record the following equation: $\frac{(0-Y)}{(7-X)} = \frac{-3}{+2}$. Again, do not simplify at this time. In Activity 2 students will be guided through the thought processes needed to clear the variable from the denominator. Then they will be able to simplify the proportions recorded in this activity and solve for Y in terms of X.

Activity 2: LINE FIND

[Bridging Action]

Materials: 5-mm grid paper
Calculators
Rulers or straight edges
Colored pencils (any bright color except yellow)
Paper
Regular pencils
Worksheet 3–7–1

Management: Partners (50 minutes)

Directions:

1. Give each pair of students 4 sheets of 5-mm grid paper, 2 colored pencils (2 different colors), a ruler or straight edge, and a calculator. Partners will work together to find their lines, and will take turns drawing them on their grid paper. In this activity all four quadrants of the coordinate plane will be used. Students will draw their own axes on the grid paper as needed, drawing one pair of axes in the upper half of the paper and another pair in the lower half. The horizontal axis should include [−16,+16] and the vertical axis should include [−10,+10]. Once the necessary points are located in the quadrants, the straight edge or ruler will be used to draw the line in regular pencil.

2. For the first example, have students mark the two points, (−2,9) and (4.5,3), on a set of axes drawn on their grid paper (use 1 grid segment for 1 unit of value). Using the ruler or straight edge and a regular pencil, they should draw the line located by the two points. Ask students to draw arrows to show the path to follow to compute the change or differences ratio for the two given points. Draw the horizontal arrow in one color and the vertical arrow in the second color. If the path goes down from (−2,9), then turns and moves right to (4.5,3), the resulting ratio of differences will be $\frac{(3-9)}{(4.5-(-2))}$, or $\frac{-6}{+6.5}$. Do not simplify this ratio at this time. It will serve as the **basic ratio** in our ratio table.

3. Have students select a new point on their line and label it as P(X,Y); also label the two axes appropriately with X and Y. Sufficient distance along the line should be left between this new point and either of the two given points. A new path should now be drawn in the two colors to show the horizontal and vertical changes between P(X,Y) and one of the **given** points, say, (4.5,3). If we follow the path indicated in the illustration, we will have the following ratio: $\frac{(3-Y)}{(4.5-X)}$. This will serve as the **secondary ratio** in our ratio table.

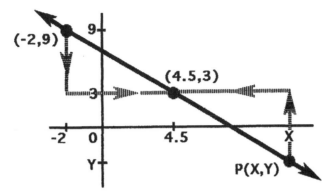

4. Remind students that the ratio table has been used in previous lessons to record equivalent ratios and to look for patterns among the four sections of the table. Now have students record their two ratios in a ratio table as shown, writing vertical differences in the left column and horizontal differences in the right column.

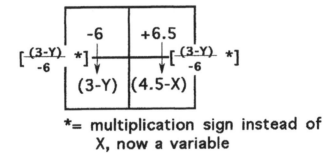

5. Draw vertical arrows pointing down to show the relationship between the value and the expression in each column. As we learned in previous ratio lessons, when the relationship between two amounts is not obvious, the factor or multiplier needed can be expressed as a fractional form of the two amounts. In this example, the factor for the left column will be $\frac{(3-Y)}{(-6)}$ so that $[\frac{(3-Y)}{(-6)}] * (-6) = (3 - Y)$. [Use * for the multiplication sign since × serves as a variable in this problem.] Since this same factor must also relate the two amounts in the right column, we obtain the equation: $[\frac{(3-Y)}{(-6)}] * (+6.5) = (4.5 - X)$. (Notice that this approach eliminates the need to explain variables in the denominator, an algebraic form not yet presented in this text.)

6. Have students write the equation found in step 5 on their own papers. Ask them to simplify the left side, then solve the equation for Y in terms of X. Also ask them to transform the equation for Y into an equation that shows X and Y on one side of the equation and a constant or numerical value on the other side. At this point you may need to remind students that $\frac{(3-Y)}{(-6)}$ is just another way to write $(\frac{1}{-6})(3 - Y)$, the format used earlier to show the separation step in solving an equation of the type: aX = c. Since our original numbers involve tenths, we will round any calculated values to the nearest tenth. We will also try to adhere to the notation style used in the lessons on solving linear equations in Section 2, even though this may put a decimal number in the denominator for a few steps. Such consistency in notation is very helpful to students. Here are possible steps students might want to record:

$$\tfrac{1}{-6}(3 - Y)(+6.5) = 4.5 - X$$
$$\tfrac{1}{-6}(+6.5)(3 - Y) = 4.5 - X \text{ [associative property]}$$
$$\tfrac{+6.5}{-6}(3 - Y) = 4.5 - X$$
$$-1.1(3 - Y) = 4.5 - X$$
$$(-3.3) - (-1.1Y) = 4.5 - X \text{ [distributive property]}$$
$$+ (+3.3) \qquad\qquad + (+3.3)$$
$$+1.1Y = 7.8 - X$$
$$\tfrac{1}{+1.1}(+1.1Y) = \tfrac{1}{+1.1}(7.8 - X)$$
$$Y = \tfrac{1}{+1.1}(7.8) - \tfrac{1}{+1.1}X \text{ [distributive property]}$$
$$\mathbf{Y = 7.1 - 0.9X} \text{ [Y in terms of X]}$$

By adding +0.9X to both sides, we obtain the other equation format we wanted, which is: **0.9X + Y = 7.1.**

7. Ask students to observe the coefficient on the X term in the first equation for Y in terms of X: **Y = 7.1 − 0.9X.** Have them simplify the original ratio they found and round it to the nearest tenth: $\frac{-6}{+6.5}$ **= −0.923, rounded to −0.9.** To the nearest tenth, the differences ratio and the coefficient on X in the equation for Y are equal.

8. For a second example, give students **a single point (0,−4)** and the ratio of change, $\frac{V}{H} =$ **+2.** Students should draw a new set of axes on the lower half of their grid paper and mark the point (0,−4). Rewriting the ratio value in a numerator-denominator format, $\frac{+2}{+1}$, students can move right 1 unit from (0,−4), then up 2 units to find another point that will be on the line meeting the given conditions. This "right 1, up 2" process can continue to find other points as well. One such point is (5,6). Once two or more points are located, the line should be drawn that touches those points.

9. A new point Q(X,Y) should be marked on the line where there is obvious distance between this point and any other point already located on the line. For convenience, we will place it in the first quadrant. The points on the axes for X and Y should also be marked appropriately. The example below also shows the arrows for a possible path to use to find the change or differences ratio for the two points (0,−4) and Q(X,Y). Students should draw these arrows (or others of their choosing) in two different colored pencils.

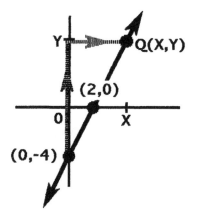

10. Moving from (0,–4) upward to the Y marker on the vertical axis yields the vertical difference or change, (Y – (–4)), where –4 is the starting number and Y is the ending number. Turning at Y and moving right to Q(X,Y), which is directly above the X marker on the horizontal axis, the horizontal change becomes (X – 0), where 0 is the starting number and X is the ending number. The ratio of change for (0,–4) and Q(X,Y) is now $\frac{(Y-(-4))}{(X-0)}$ or $\frac{(Y+4)}{X}$. Since all differences ratios for pairs of points on the same line are equivalent, the two ratios should be recorded in a ratio table, using $\frac{+2}{+1}$ as the **basic ratio.** The arrows and the factor-multiplier should be shown on the ratio table to show the relationship between the basic ratio and the secondary ratio.

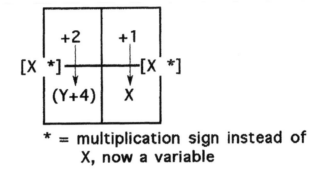

* = multiplication sign instead of
X, now a variable

11. Since +1 appears in the ratio table, finding a factor for its column is easiest; the factor will simply be X. To keep the pattern, the left column must use the same factor or multiplier. Hence, we have the equation: **X * (+2) = (Y + 4).** Students should simplify this equation to get 2X = Y + 4. By removing +4 from both sides of the equation, we have **2X – 4 = Y,** an equation for **Y in terms of X.** By removing Y from both sides of 2X = Y + 4, we find **2X – Y = +4,** an equation with the X term and Y term on one side of the equation and the numerical constant on the other side. In the equation for Y in terms of X, ask students what they notice about the coefficient on the X term. It is **+2,** the same value as the **given** change ratio for the line.

(a)   X (+2) = Y + 4
        2X = Y + 4
     – (+4) – (+4)
    2X – 4 = Y

(b)   2X = Y + 4
        – Y – Y
   2X – Y =   4

12. Assign other sets of points or differences ratios that students may use to locate and draw lines on their grid paper. (See Worksheet 3–7–1.) They should follow the procedures presented in the above examples. For each exercise, using a ratio table, they should develop an equation or proportion that relates two ratios from the same line. This equation should be simplified into (a) an equation for Y in terms of X, and (b) an equation that has X and Y on one side of the equation and only a (numerical) constant on the other side. Later, when discussing the results of each exercise, have students compare the simplified value of the differences ratio to the coefficient on the X in the equation found for Y in terms of X. Also discuss which lines identified will represent sets of points that are linear **functions.** (In the exercises suggested in step 13, only #3 will not represent a *function;* that is, at least two points in the line have the same horizontal value, but different vertical values. It does, however, still represent a *linear* relation or set of ordered pairs.)

Name _____ **Date** _____

WORKSHEET 3–7–1
Line Find

Locate and draw a line on grid paper for each set of points or differences ratios ($\frac{V}{H}$) provided below. Write an initial equation based on a ratio table, then (a) solve the equation for Y in terms of X, and (b) rewrite the equation in the form: $aX + bY = c$.

1. (0,0) and (8,6)

2. (–3,0) and (0,–2)

3. (–2,3) and (–2,–4)

4. $\frac{V}{H} = +0.5$ with (0,0)

5. $\frac{V}{H} = 0$ with (3,–5)

6. $\frac{V}{H} = \frac{-2}{+3}$ with (–1,7.5)

13. Here are some possible sets of values to assign:

1. $(0,0)$ and $(8,6)$

2. $(-3,0)$ and $(0,-2)$

3. $(-2,3)$ and $(-2,-4)$

4. $\frac{V}{H} = +0.5$ with $(0,0)$

5. $\frac{V}{H} = 0$ with $(3,-5)$

6. $\frac{V}{H} = \frac{-2}{+3}$ with $(-1,7.5)$

Answer Key for WORKSHEET 3–7–1

For each exercise listed in step 13 of Activity 2, a ratio table and its initial factor-generated equation, an equation for Y in terms of X, and an equation in the form $aX + bY = c$ are provided below. Other equivalent ratio tables and equations are possible.

1.

+6	+8
Y	X

$(\frac{X}{+8})(+6) = Y$

$(\frac{3}{4})X = Y$; $(\frac{3}{4})X - Y = 0$

2.

−2	+3
Y	X + 3

$(\frac{+3}{-2})Y = X + 3$

$Y = (-\frac{2}{3})X - 2$; $Y + (\frac{2}{3})X = -2$

3.

+7	0
Y − 3	X + 2

$[\frac{(Y-3)}{+7}](0) = X + 2$

$X = -2$ [or $(0)Y = X + 2$; $(0)Y + X = -2$]

4.

+0.5	+1
Y	X

$X(+0.5) = Y$

$0.5X = Y$; $0.5X - Y = 0$

5.

0	+1
Y + 5	X − 3

$(X - 3)(0) = Y + 5$

$-5 = Y$ [or $(0)X - 5 = Y$; $(0)X - Y = +5$]

6.

−2	+3
Y − 7.5	X + 1

$(\frac{+3}{-2})(Y - 7.5) = X + 1$

$Y = -0.7X + 6.8$; $Y + 0.7X = +6.8$

Notes on Certain Exercises:

3. The line will be vertical. Use $\frac{V}{H} = \frac{(3-(-4))}{((-2)-(-2))} = \frac{7}{0}$ and $\frac{V}{H} = \frac{(Y-3)}{X-(-2)} = \frac{(Y-3)}{(X+2)}$ for the ratio table (this latter ratio came from moving *toward* (X,Y); the ratio from moving *away from* (X,Y) could also be used). Avoid 0 as a factor-multiplier since it tends to eliminate *both* X and Y from the initial equation; from the ratio table shown below, we find $[\frac{(Y-3)}{7}] * 0 = X + 2$, leading to $-2 = \mathbf{X}$. There will be no equation for Y in terms of X unless we want to write $0(Y) = X + 2$. (**Note:** 0 as a factor-multiplier from 7 to 0, however, will work in this case, since $0 * (Y - 3) = X + 2$ still preserves X in the initial equation.)

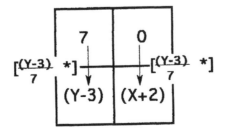

5. The line will be horizontal. Use $\frac{V}{H} = \frac{0}{+1}$ and, if moving toward (X,Y), $\frac{V}{H} = \frac{(Y-(-5))}{X-3} = \frac{(Y+5)}{(X-3)}$ for the ratio table. It is easy to use (X − 3) as the factor-multiplier from +1 to (X − 3). For the left column we then find (X − 3) * 0 = Y + 5, which leads to **−5 = Y.** Note that 0 could be used as a factor from +1 to 0, yielding 0 * (X − 3) = Y + 5 and the same final equation for Y. Y will not be in terms of X, unless we want to write Y = 0(X) − 5.

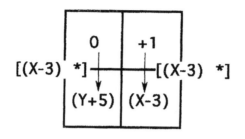

6. The ratio from (−1,7.5) to (X,Y) is $\frac{V}{H} = \frac{(Y-7.5)}{(X-(-1))} = \frac{(Y-7.5)}{(X+1)}$. Using $\frac{+3}{-2}$ as the factor from −2 to +3 in the ratio table, we find from the lower row the relationship: $(\frac{+3}{-2})$ * (Y − 7.5) = X + 1. This initial equation can easily be solved for Y in terms of X. Changing $\frac{+3}{-2}$ to the decimal, −1.5, and rounding calculations to the nearest tenth, the final equation might be written as follows: Y = −0.7X + 6.8.

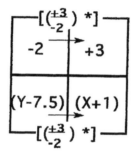

Activity 3: LINE BATTLE

[Application/Exploration]

Materials: Worksheet 3–7–2 (2 spinner patterns)
Large paper clips (for spinner needles)
5-mm grid paper
Calculators
Rulers or straight edges
Paper
Regular pencils

Management: Teams of 4 students each (20–30 minutes)

Directions:

1. Give each team 4 sheets of 5-mm grid paper, a calculator, a ruler or straight edge, a large paper clip, and a copy of Worksheet 3–7–2. The large paper clip will be the needle for the two spinners. A pencil point through one end of the paper clip will hold the paper

Spinner A:

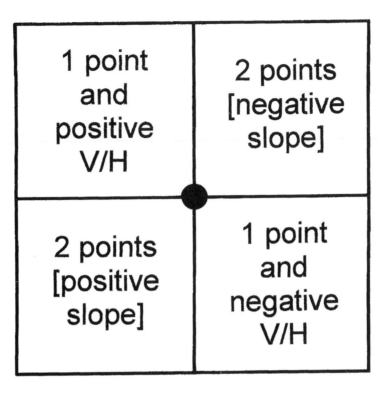

Spinner B:

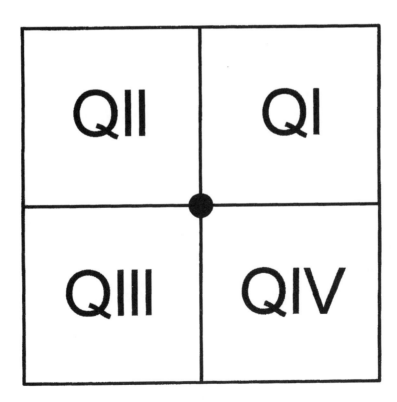

clip in place at the center point of the spinner. Then the other end of the paper clip can be spun around the pencil. Each grid paper should be folded in half so that a set of axes can be drawn in the upper half of the grid and a second set drawn in the lower half. Use 1 grid segment as 1 unit of value. Each pair of students on a team will have their own grid paper to draw on and will compete against the other pair of students on the same team.

2. On each team, Pair A will take turns with Pair B, one pair drawing a line and the other pair trying to copy the line. For example, if it is Pair A's turn to draw, they will spin Spinner A to decide what type of information to give to the other pair, then spin Spinner B to decide where to draw their original line. The quadrant selected with spinner B must contain a portion of the line to be drawn and copied; that is, at least one of the points named by Pair A for Pair B to use must be located in the selected quadrant. This procedure helps randomize the given information, so that a variety of lines will be drawn by the players.

3. Depending on what has been spun on the spinners, the *drawing* pair will draw a line on their own grid paper, blocking their work from the view of the other pair (a piece of cardboard might be helpful in screening their work from the other pair of students). They will then tell the other pair: (1) what the $\frac{V}{H}$ ratio is for the line and name one point on the line in the selected quadrant; or (2) name two points on the line, having at least one of the points in the selected quadrant. Without actually seeing the drawn line, the other pair will try to *copy* the original line on their own grid paper, using the given information.

4. When the *copying* pair is finished, they must state: (1) the ordered pair of another point on the line if they were given the $\frac{V}{H}$ ratio and one point; or (2) what the differences ratio, $\frac{V}{H}$, is if they were given 2 points. They will also compare their new line with the original line of the *drawing* pair. This might be done by overlaying one set of axes with its line on the other set and holding the papers up to the light. If the two lines and axes match **and** the stated information is correct (or equivalent in the case of ratios), the *copying* pair earns 2 points; if the two lines do **not** match **or** the stated information is incorrect, the *drawing* pair earns the 2 points. The pair with the most points after 3 completed rounds (or when time is called) wins. A *round* is completed when each pair has had a turn at both drawing a line and copying a line.

OBJECTIVE 8: Explore the role of the constant b in Y = aX + b, where *a*, *b*, X, and Y are real numbers.

Activity 1: LINE ROLL

[Developing Action]

Materials: Large one-inch grids, small colored markers, and 12-inch bamboo skewers
(or wire pieces or drinking straws) from Activity 1, Objective 6
Calculators
Regular pencils
Paper
Worksheet 3–8–1

Management: Teams of 3–4 students each (30–50 minutes)

Directions:

1. Give each team a large grid, a skewer (or wire piece or taped drinking straws), a bag of 6 colored markers, a calculator, and Worksheet 3–8–1. Additional markers may need to be added to the original set used in Objective 6. Each of the 6 markers should have a unique color. In this activity we will focus on the behavior of the vertical axis intercept (the **Y-intercept**) as the position of a line changes on a grid.

Line	Point 1	Point 2	Point 3	V/H
#1				
#2				
#3				

2. Ask each team to record in its table on the row for "line #1" the three ordered pairs in the given columns: (0,5) as "point #1," (4,5) as "point #2," and (8,5) as "point #3." A colored marker, say blue, should be placed on the grid at the first point, (0,5), and another marker, say orange, should be placed at the third point, (8,5). A skewer should be placed on the grid beside and touching the two markers; it should be on the side of the markers opposite from the horizontal axis (to allow skewer to roll upward on grid without rolling over the markers).

3. On each team, one student, rotating the grid so that its horizontal axis is nearest her or him, should place both hands flat on the skewer, one hand near each end of the skewer, and slowly roll the skewer away from the markers, being careful not to turn the skewer while rolling it. The skewer should be rolled until it touches the point (0,9) on the same vertical grid line but above the first point (0,5), and similarly touches the point (8,9) above the third point (8,5). **Ask:** "What point directly above (4,5) does the skewer touch in its new position?" *(the skewer should be near or touching (4,9))* A red marker should now be placed at (0,9) and a green marker at (8,9). The ordered pairs for these three new points should be recorded in the table in the row for line #2 and in the given

WORKSHEET 3–8–1
Line Roll

Follow your teacher's instructions to complete each table below.

1.

Line	Point 1	Point 2	Point 3	$\frac{V}{H}$
#1				
#2				
#3				

2.

Line	Point 1	Point 2	Point 3	$\frac{V}{H}$
#1				
#2				
#3				

3.

Line	Point 1	Point 2	Point 3	$\frac{V}{H}$
#1				
#2				
#3				

order: (0,9), (4,9), and (8,9). The value of the change ratio, $\frac{V}{H}$, should also be computed and recorded in the table for the first two lines; both skewer positions will have a ratio value of 0. ***Ask:*** "What do you notice about the red and the green marker positions when compared with the blue and the orange markers?" *(the blue-orange pair lines up parallel to the red-green pair, and similarly the blue-red pair lines up parallel to the orange-green pair; the red marker is 4 grid units above the blue marker, and the green marker is 4 units above the orange marker)* "Looking at the ordered pairs, what do you notice about the numbers in the two sets of pairs?" Hopefully students will notice that the **abscissa** or first coordinate remains the same in corresponding ordered pairs on the two lines, and that the **ordinate** or second coordinate has increased by 4 in all three ordered pairs on the second line when compared with the pairs on the first line. Observe that the vertical intercept point changes the same way that other points on the same line change.

4. Repeat the process in step 3, but have students roll the skewer, without turning its path, from the original position back or down to the points (0,2) and (8,2). Place the skewer on the side of the original blue and orange markers that is nearer the horizontal axis before rolling it to the new points. Ask what point the skewer touches that is directly below the point (4,5); it should be (4,2). A brown marker should be placed at the point (0,2) and a yellow marker placed at (8,2). The $\frac{V}{H}$ ratio for this third skewer position will also be 0. The brown marker will be 3 grid units below the blue marker, and the yellow marker will be 3 units below the orange marker. The parallel relationships between marker pairs of the first line and this third line still hold as well. Again, observe that the point that is the vertical intercept undergoes the same changes that the other two points on the line do. Remind students that when the $\frac{V}{H}$ ratio is 0 (or when the **slope** equals 0), the **position** of the skewer will be level or **horizontal** with respect to the grid.

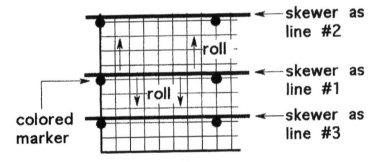

5. Now have students place the skewer on the grid so that it touches the points (6,0) and (6,8); it will be in vertical position. ***Ask:*** "Does this skewer touch points that represent ordered pairs for a **linear function**?" *(no, because one **independent** or horizontal value has several **dependent** or vertical values)* "What do you know about the differences ratio, $\frac{V}{H}$, for this skewer or the line it represents?" *(the $\frac{V}{H}$ ratio or **slope** equals no real value and is said to be **undefined** (shown as ∞); the **position** of the skewer is **vertical**)* "What is the vertical intercept when the skewer is in this position?" *(in this position it has no intersection point with the vertical axis)* Have students roll the skewer over to the vertical axis of the grid, carefully rolling with two hands to prevent the skewer from turning to the side as it rolls. ***Ask:*** "What point serves as the vertical intercept for the skewer in this new position?" *(no **single** point is the intercept now; all points on this new line are intercepts on the vertical axis; hence, the vertical intercept is not unique in this case)* No colored markers need to be placed on the grid in this example unless some students need to see the markers to help them visualize the various points on the lines as they are discussed. Also, no numbers should be recorded in a table at this time.

6. For another example, have students place the blue marker on the grid at the point for (0,6) and the orange marker at (10,3.5), then place the skewer touching the markers on their side away from the horizontal axis. Ask students to name another grid intersection point that the skewer touches, say, (4,5). These three ordered pairs should be recorded in a new table in the row for line #1; the $\frac{V}{H}$ ratio should also be computed and recorded in the table ($\frac{V}{H} = \frac{-1}{4}$). **Note:** The skewer may "touch" points on the grid in a variety of ways; for example, it may literally lie on top of and physically or tangentially touch a point, or it may just be near a point so that the point can be seen when viewed from directly above the skewer. In this activity and previous activities where colored markers are used to locate points, the skewer will lie next to the markers; other points not indicated by markers will then appear slightly to the side of the skewer. Whatever approach is used, the same "viewing angle" must be used for all points represented by the skewer. In our activities with the skewer, only whole units or half-units of distance will be needed to facilitate the naming of points represented by the skewer on the grid.

7. Students should roll (with both hands) the skewer on the grid until it touches a point on the vertical axis that is 5 units above the blue marker or (0,6). Ask them to identify the three new points touched by the skewer that are on the vertical grid lines directly above the three points used for the first line. They should find the points: (0,11)—use red marker; (4,10); and (10,8.5)—use green marker. **Ask:** "What is the change ratio between (0,11) and (4,10)?" ($\frac{-1}{4}$) "How can you check your point for the green marker since it is not directly on an intersection point of the grid?" *(it should have a $\frac{V}{H}$ ratio of $\frac{-1}{4}$ with (0,11) also)* The three new ordered pairs and the $\frac{V}{H}$ ratio should now be recorded on the table for line #2. Students should observe that all three new pairs reflect a 5-unit increase in the second number of each pair, but maintain the same first number when compared to the pairs of line #1. So when the vertical intercept changed from (0,6) to (0,11), all points on the first line changed the same way. Hence, the new line is parallel to the first line.

8. Repeat the procedure used in step 7, but the skewer should be rolled from the line #1 position toward the horizontal axis until it touches the point for (10,1). **Ask:** "What changes occurred when the skewer moved from (10,3.5) to (10,1)? How did this change affect the other points we used on line #1: (4,5) and (0,6)?" *(a 2.5 vertical decrease occurred for the three points on line #1; new points for line #3 are (0,3.5)—use brown marker, (4,2.5), and (10,1)—use yellow marker)* Students might confirm their visual estimates for the ordered pairs by computing the $\frac{V}{H}$ ratio for each two points of the three points in line #3; the ratio will equal $\frac{-1}{4}$ each time. Again, the intercept of the vertical axis changes like other points on the same line, and such a change produces parallel lines.

9. For additional practice, students might work with the points (0,0) and (5,2). The points (2.5,1) and (10,4) are possible third points to use in the table. The skewer should be rolled upward on the grid until another grid intersection point directly above either (0,0) or (5,2) is found. The differences ratio, $\frac{V}{H}$, will be $\frac{+2}{+5}$. As before, changes in the ordered pairs should be discussed, along with the idea of equivalent $\frac{V}{H}$ ratios. Observe that vertical change in points of a line leads to another line that is parallel to the first line and that the vertical intercept goes through the same vertical change as other points on the same line.

Activity 2: *PARALLEL DRAW*

[Bridging Action]

Materials: 5-mm grid paper
Rulers
Colored pencils (at least 2 different bright colors)
Calculators
Paper
Regular pencils
Worksheet 3–8–2

Management: Partners (30 minutes)

Directions:

1. Give each pair of students a calculator, 2 sheets of 5-mm grid paper, a ruler (inch or centimeter), and 2 colored pencils (any 2 different bright colors; not black, brown, or yellow). Have students draw a set of coordinate axes in the upper half of a grid paper and another set in the lower half of the paper. All four quadrants will be used in this activity. Use 1 grid segment for 0.5 unit, or 2 segments for 1 unit of value to mark off and label the axes.

2. Have students use their ruler and regular pencil on a set of axes to draw a line that passes through the two points (0,–3) and (4,0). Arrows should be drawn at the ends of the line to show that it might be extended if necessary. *Ask:* "Remembering what we learned in Activity 1, if we want to draw a new line that is parallel to this one and we want it to pass through the point (4,5), what will be the new intercept on the vertical axis?" *(the point (4,0) was changed vertically by 5 units, so (0,–3) must also be changed vertically by 5 units, giving the new point (0,2))* Students should draw the new line in regular pencil through the points (0,2) and (4,5).

3. Have students find the differences ratio $\frac{V}{H}$ for each line, using the two points now marked on each line. Both lines will have a ratio of $\frac{+3}{+4}$.

4. Students should now mark a point P(X,Y) on the first line between the two points (0,–3) and (4,0) already located, and also appropriately mark an X and a Y on their corresponding axes. Following the procedure developed in Objective 7 to find an equation for a line that expresses Y in terms of X, students should draw an arrow path from one of the given points, say, (4,0), to the point P(X,Y). An arrow should be drawn in color #1 from (4,0) down to the horizontal grid line that is even with Y on the vertical axis. The vertical change or difference is (Y – 0). From this new point, an arrow is drawn in color #2 over to P(X,Y), which is directly below X on the horizontal axis. The horizontal change is (X – 4). Thus, the change ratio, $\frac{V}{H}$, is $\frac{(Y-0)}{(X-4)}$ or $\frac{Y}{(X-4)}$ between (4,0) and P(X,Y).

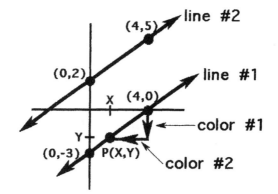

5. Since $(0,-3)$, $(4,0)$, and $P(X,Y)$ are on the same line, the differences ratios between any two of these points will be equivalent. Thus, we have $\frac{Y}{(X-4)} = \frac{+3}{+4}$. Writing these four expressions in a ratio table, from $+3$ to $+4$ we obtain the factor or multiplier $\frac{+4}{+3}$ and can write the equation: $\left(\frac{+4}{+3}\right) * Y = X - 4$. Notice that if we go from $+4$ to $+3$, the factor becomes $\frac{+3}{+4}$ and we get the equation: $Y = \frac{+3}{+4}(X - 4)$, which only needs simplifying on the right side. Students may use either approach.

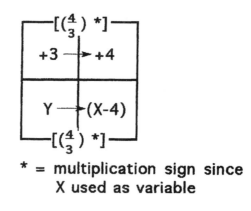

* = multiplication sign since
X used as variable

6. For practice, we will use the first equation found in step 5 above. Students should now apply the methods learned in Section 2 to solve this equation for Y in terms of X. Here are possible steps to record (avoid shortcuts; keep $\frac{+3}{+4}$ in obvious ratio format):

$$\frac{+4}{+3}Y = X - 4$$
$$\frac{+3}{+4}\left(\frac{+4}{+3}Y\right) = \frac{+3}{+4}(X - 4)$$
$$Y = \frac{+3}{+4}X - \left(\frac{+3}{+4}\right)(4)$$
$$\mathbf{Y = \frac{+3}{+4}X - 3}$$

7. Ask students to compare what they know about the first line's $\frac{V}{H}$ value, $\frac{+3}{+4}$, and its vertical intercept, which is -3, to the numbers that serve as coefficients (numbers with the variables) or constants in the new equation for Y found in step 6. They should notice that the $\frac{V}{H}$ ratio and the coefficient on X are equivalent, and that the vertical intercept and the constant following the X-term in the equation are the same if we use the form, $\frac{+3}{+4}X + (-3)$. **Note:** If students want to use decimals in the solution process, then all fractional forms need to be changed to decimals: $\frac{V}{H} = +0.75$; ratio table factor = $+1.33$ (use two decimal places since 0.75 is to two decimal places); initial equation $+1.33\,Y = X - 4$. The final equation becomes $Y = +0.75\,X - 3$. The values to be compared must be in the same form if students are to recognize their equality easily.

Name _____ **Date** _____

WORKSHEET 3–8–2
Parallel Draw

Follow your teacher's instructions for each pair of lines described below.

1. first line through (–2,1) and (3,–2); second line through (3,2)

2. first line through (–3,–2) and (4,–2); second line through (0,–5)

3. first line through (0,0) and (5,4); second line through (0,6)

4. first line through (5,1) and (–5,–1); second line through (5,–3)

8. A similar procedure should be applied to the second line that passes through the points (0,2) and (4,5), which produce a differences ratio of $\frac{+3}{+4}$ also. If we locate a point Q(X′,Y′) on the second line between the two indicated points and mark X′ and Y′ on the appropriate axes, an arrow path drawn from, say, (0,2) to Q(X′,Y′) yields $\frac{V}{H} = \frac{(Y'-2)}{(X'-0)} = \frac{(Y'-2)}{X'}$. Using the ratio table and going from +4 to +3 to find a factor, we can get the equation: $\left(\frac{+3}{+4}\right)$ * X′ = Y′ − 2. By simply adding +2 to both sides, we will have Y′ in terms of X′: **Y′ = $\frac{+3}{+4}$X′ + 2.** Again have students compare the numbers in the equation with the differences ratio, $\frac{+3}{+4}$, and the vertical intercept at (0,2).

9. Write the two equations on the board: Y = $\frac{+3}{+4}$X − 3 and Y′ = $\frac{+3}{+4}$X′ + 2. Ask students to compare how the two *equations* differ with how the two *parallel lines* differ. For example, the coefficients on the variables match; that is, Y and Y′ have +1 and X and X′ have $\frac{+3}{+4}$. The constants −3 and +2 differ by 5 units, just as the two parallel lines are 5 units apart on the vertical axis. Other corresponding points on the two lines also differ vertically by 5 units.

10. Assign other pairs of points for students to use to locate and draw lines. (See Worksheet 3–8–2.) For each line, they will draw a second line parallel to the first line and passing through a given point. Using $\frac{V}{H}$ ratios and given points, students should find an equation for each line in a pair of parallel lines and solve each equation for Y in terms of X. After partners have found the equations for each pair of lines, have them confirm the presence of the $\frac{V}{H}$ ratio and the vertical intercept (Y-intercept) in each line's equation. Reinforce the idea that the Y-intercept and the $\frac{V}{H}$ ratio can help students locate a line on the grid quickly and also write an equation for Y in terms of X that describes the points on the line. Have students summarize their findings by writing the following in their own notebooks: **Any point (X,Y) on a line can be found by using the equation Y = (differences ratio $\frac{V}{H}$ for line) X + (Y-intercept of line). Another way to state this idea is Y = (slope value of line) X + (Y-intercept of line). A symbolic way to write this is Y = mX + b.**

11. Here are some suggested sets of points to assign. (If students easily understand the numerical relationships they have discovered and recorded in words in step 10, after they have worked the first two exercises below, encourage them to apply their discoveries directly to the given points to find their equations rather than go through the entire solution process to find the equations; however, they must always be able to explain their reasoning for each equation they write.)

(a) first line through (−2,1) and (3,−2); second line through (3,2)

(b) first line through (−3,−2) and (4,−2); second line through (0,−5)

(c) first line through (0,0) and (5,4); second line through (0,6)

(d) first line through (5,1) and (−5,−1); second line through (5,−3)

Answer Key to WORKSHEET 3–8–2

1. Vertical change from line 1 is +4;
   points for line 2: (3,2) and (−2,+5)

   line 1:

−3	+5
Y − 1	X + 2

   $\left[\frac{(X+2)}{+5}\right](-3) = Y - 1$; Y = −0.6X − 0.2

line 2:

−3	+5
Y′ − 5	X′ + 2

$[\frac{(X'+2)}{+5}](-3) = Y' - 5$; $Y' = -0.6X' + 3.8$

2. Vertical change from line 1 is −3, using (0,−2) to (0,−5);
   points for line 2: (0,−5) and (4,−5)

line 1:

0	+7
Y + 2	X + 3

$[\frac{(X+3)}{+7}](0) = Y + 2$; $Y = -2$

line 2:

0	+4
Y′ + 5	X′

$(\frac{X'}{+4})(0) = Y' + 5$; $Y' = -5$

3. Vertical change from line 1 is +6;
   points for line 2: (0,6) and (5,10)

line 1:

+4	+5
Y	X

$(\frac{+5}{+4})Y = X$; $Y = +0.8X$

line 2:

+4	+5
Y′ − 6	X′

$(\frac{+5}{+4})(Y' - 6) = X'$; $Y' = +0.8X' + 6$

4. Vertical change from line 1 is − 4;
   points for line 2: (5,−3) and (−5,−5)

line 1:

+2	+10
Y + 1	X + 5

$+5(Y + 1) = X + 5$; $Y = +0.2X$

line 2:

+2	+10
Y′ + 5	X′ +5

$+ 5(Y' + 5) = X' + 5$; $Y' = +0.2X' - 4$

Activity 3: DUELING LINES

[Application/Exploration]

Materials: Graphing calculators
Regular pencils
Paper

Management: Teams of 4 students each (20–30 minutes)

Directions:

1. Give each team of students a graphing calculator. Two of the team members, Pair A, will duel the other two, Pair B, in trying to match lines. The two pairs will take turns graphing a line on the graphing calculator for the other pair to identify and regraph. Use the viewing window: X ε [–10,10] and Y ε [–10,10], scale = 1.

2. As an example, on their turn, Pair A will graph an equation of the form: Y = mX + b, without revealing the actual equation to Pair B. (For an easier version of the game, restrict the values for m and b to integers; otherwise, restrict their values to real numbers expressed to the nearest tenth.) If the graph of the chosen line is not in the viewing window, Pair A must adjust the b or Y-intercept value in their initial equation until the line does appear in the viewing window; the graph of this new equation then becomes the target for Pair B. Pair B then looks at the line in the viewing window. Using only the markings on the axes, Pair B will determine by *visual estimation* a differences ratio or slope value (i.e., $\frac{V}{H}$ or m) and a Y-intercept for the displayed line. Pair B will write an equation for a new line in the Y = mX + b format and must show their equation to Pair A. Pair B will then graph their new line over the line of Pair A. They are allowed only one opportunity to graph an equation on the calculator; no adjustments are allowed once the PLOT or Y= screen has been accessed. **Note:** When the PLOT screen is accessed, the equation used by Pair A will be visible to Pair B.

3. Scoring: (a) If the graphs of the two lines either coincide or are parallel so that the vertical distance between any two corresponding points on the two graphs is less than 1 unit, according to the vertical axis of the viewing window, then Pair B earns 5 points.

Method(a)

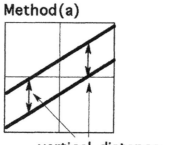

vertical distance <1

(b) If the two lines intersect each other and both cross the viewing window from the left side to the right, then the greatest vertical distance between corresponding points of the two lines (use points located at the left or right edge of the viewing window) must be less than 1 unit; similarly, if the two lines cross the viewing window from the upper edge to the lower edge, then the greatest horizontal distance between corresponding points located at the upper or lower edge of the viewing window must be less than 1 unit. If either of the above conditions, vertical or horizontal, is met, Pair B earns 2 points.

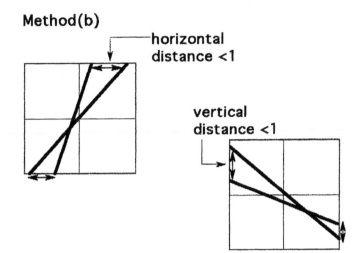

Method(b)

horizontal distance <1

vertical distance <1

(c) If neither the conditions of (a) nor the conditions of (b) are met, Pair B earns 0 points. Sample graphs show the scoring methods (a) and (b) described above.

4. The turn then passes to Pair B, who will clear the screen and graph a new line for Pair A to try to match. Play continues until time is called. The winning pair is the pair with the greater total in points.

5. *Alternative method of play:* Instead of *visually* estimating a line's Y-intercept or its $\frac{V}{H}$ ratio, each pair might use the TRACE key and move the cursor along the initial line to be matched; the X- and Y-coordinates for various points on the line may then be read at the bottom of the viewing window and used to determine the desired equation. The new equation will probably have decimal numbers for the values of m and b. This equation will then be graphed and its line compared with the first line for a score. TRACE and cursor movement may also be used to find X- or Y-values for either line near the edge of the screen; these values are then used to compute distances needed for scoring.

OBJECTIVE 9: Fit linear curves to given sets of points on a grid and fit algebraic forms to those linear curves in real-world situations.

Activity 1: POINT LINE-UP

[Developing Action]

Materials: Large inch grids, small colored markers, and 12-inch bamboo skewers from Activity 1, Objective 8
Rulers
Calculators
Paper
Regular pencils
Worksheet 3–9–1

Management: Partners (30 minutes)

Directions:

1. Give each pair of students a large inch grid, 6 colored markers, a skewer (or wire piece or 2 taped drinking straws), a calculator, and Worksheet 3–9–1. Read the following story aloud to the class: *Mahesh needs to improve his dart throwing. He throws 6 darts at his dart board, then measures how far each dart hits from the bull's-eye. Here are the measurements: Throw #1, 6 inches away; #2, 3 inches; #3, 4 inches; #4, 3 inches; #5, 4 inches; #6, 2 inches. Can you find an equation that can be used to estimate his distances for the 6 throws?*

2. Use the longer horizontal axis of the large grid to represent the number of the throw made, and use the shorter vertical axis to represent the distance of the hit in inches from the bull's-eye. Have students place colored markers at the points on the grid that represent the results of Mahesh's 6 different dart throws. Markers should be placed on the grid at (1,6), (2,3), (3,4), (4,3), (5,4), and (6,2).

3. Ask students to carefully place their skewer on the grid so that it touches the most markers possible. Allow time for students to try several different positions. Then ***ask:*** "Which points did you decide to use?" Several positions are possible that only touch two markers. Three markers, however, can be touched if the points (1,6), (3,4), and (4,3) are used; this is the most points possible for this situation. ***Ask:*** "Where are the other markers not touched by the skewer?" *(2 are on one side of the skewer, and 1 is on the other side)* The skewer positioned at the three points represents the **best-fit line** for *estimating* the distances from the bull's-eye since it touches the maximum number of markers possible in this situation.

4. Have students find an equation of the form $Y = mX + b$ that will describe their skewer's position on the grid. Encourage students to apply what they learned in Objective 8 about the roles of m and b regarding an equation for a line. If students still do not understand these roles, have them find their equation by applying the change ratios and ratio table approach directly to two of the three selected points and to a general point $P(X,Y)$ located somewhere on the skewer. Hopefully students will be able to use two of

Name _____ **Date** _____

WORKSHEET 3-9-1
Point Line-Up

Place markers on your grid to represent each situation described below. Write an equation of the form Y = mX + b for each line located.

1. Mahesh needs to improve his dart throwing. He throws 6 darts at his dart board, then measures how far each dart hits from the bull's-eye. Here are the measurements: Throw #1, 6 inches away; #2, 3 inches; #3, 4 inches; #4, 3 inches; #5, 4 inches; #6, 2 inches. Can you find an equation that can be used to estimate his distances for the 6 throws?

2. Jill takes a 10-point quiz after she completes each lesson of a special study unit in her Biology class. For the first six quizzes she has made the following scores, which are arranged in the order they were taken: 7, 9, 6, 9, 8, and 10 points. Can you find an equation that can be used to estimate her score for each quiz taken?

their 3 points to compute the ratio $\frac{V}{H}$ and estimate a point on the vertical axis where the skewer would touch if it were extended to that axis. The best-fit line should intersect the vertical axis at (0,7), so students should use +7 as their value for b in the equation. If we choose the points (1,6) and (4,3), for example, to compute $\frac{V}{H}$, we will get the ratio, $\frac{(3-6)}{(4-1)}$ or $\frac{-3}{+3}$, which simplifies to –1. Hence, –1 may be used as the value of m, which is the **slope** of the line.

5. Students should write the following equation on their own papers: **Y = –1X + 7.** Do not simplify –1X to –X at this time; the value of m needs to remain visible to students. *Ask:* "If we look at just the first, third, and fourth throws, and ignore the other three throws, what seems to be happening as Mahesh throws more darts?" *(he seems to be getting closer to the bull's-eye; perhaps he is "improving with practice"???)* "If Mahesh could throw all 6 darts similar to his first, third, and fourth throws, what does our equation predict the distance from the bull's-eye would be on the second, fifth, and sixth throws?" Students should substitute the values 2, 5, and 6 for X (number of throw made) in the equation and compute to find the corresponding values of Y (distance in inches of dart from bull's-eye). They should find 5 inches for the second throw, 2 inches for the fifth throw, and 1 inch for the sixth throw.

6. If time permits, share another story with the students and repeat the above process for finding the best-fit line for the data of the situation and an equation that describes all points on the line. Here is another possible story: *Jill takes a 10-point quiz after she completes each lesson of a special study unit in her Biology class. For the first six quizzes she has made the following scores, which are arranged in the order they were taken: 7, 9, 6, 9, 8, and 10 points. Can you find an equation that can be used to estimate her score for each quiz taken?*

7. Use the horizontal axis for the number of each quiz taken and the vertical axis for the score or number of points made on each quiz. Students should place markers on their grid to show points for the following ordered pairs: (1,7), (2,9), (3,6), (4,9), (5,8), and (6,10). They should then place the skewer on the grid so that it touches the most points possible. Allow time for students to explore different positions for the skewer. In this situation, the skewer will touch at most 2 points, and several different pairs of points are possible.

8. Ask students to position the skewer so that the four points it does **not** touch are at least **as close as possible** to the skewer. Again, allow time for exploration. We will assume that the best-fit line in this case should pass through (1,7) and (6,10). (**Note:** Various pairs of students may choose a different pair of points; have them present reasons for their choices and find an equation based on their own choices. Activity 2 will present a method for minimizing the distances of points from the chosen line.) Extending the skewer to the vertical axis yields +6.5 as an approximate value for the Y-intercept or b in the equation. Using the two chosen points, we find that the ratio $\frac{V}{H}$ equals $\frac{(10-7)}{(6-1)}$ or $\frac{+3}{+5}$. Then the new equation for our best-fit line becomes Y = $\frac{+3}{+5}$ X + 6.5. Since 6.5 is a decimal number, we might rewrite the equation as **Y = 0.6X + 6.5.** This equation may now be used to estimate Jill's scores for the second, third, fourth, and fifth quizzes. If Jill could steadily improve from one quiz to the next like she improved overall between quiz #1 and quiz #6, we would estimate her scores on quizzes 2–5 respectively to be as follows: 7.7, 8.3, 8.9, and 9.5.

Activity 2: FINDING A CLOSER FIT

[Bridging Action]

Materials: Centimeter grid paper
Centimeter rulers
Index cards (3 in. × 5 in.)
Calculators
Colored pencils (any bright color)
Regular pencils
Paper

Management: Partners (30 minutes)

Directions:

1. Give each pair of students 1 sheet of centimeter grid paper, a centimeter ruler, an index card, a colored pencil (any bright color; not brown, black, or yellow), and a calculator. Have them fold the grid paper in half so that the upper half of the grid may be used for one exercise and the lower half for another. We will use the same two situations presented in Activity 1. For each situation, the original ordered pairs will be graphed on the centimeter grid paper, using the same labels for the axes as before. The original line selected as best-fit will be drawn on the grid. Then, instead of the visual and maximizing-points-touched approach used in Activity 1, students will apply a *numerical* approach to test the **closeness** of the line's fit to the data.

2. On the upper half of the sheet of grid paper first have students plot the ordered pairs for the dart throws: (1,6), (2,3), (3,4), (4,3), (5,4), and (6,2). The labeling of the axes should be the same as that used in Activity 1. The line through (1,6) and (4,3) should also be drawn on the grid paper. Using an index card to draw line segments that are perpendicular to the newly drawn line, students should now draw with the colored pencil a segment from each point not on the line to a point on the line so that the segment is perpendicular to the line.

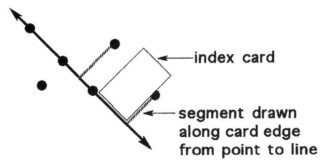

3. The centimeter ruler should now be used to measure the length in centimeters (to the nearest tenth) of each line segment drawn from a point to the line. Each length found should be recorded on the segment it represents. The total of the lengths should be computed and recorded on the graph as the **closeness measure** for this particular line. Discuss the idea that another line might have been chosen that would produce a smaller closeness measure. If so, then that new line would become the **best-fit line** for this data or set of points.

4. On the lower half of the grid paper have students plot the points for the quiz scores from the second story in Activity 1: (1,7), (2,9), (3,6), (4,9), (5,8), and (6,10). Label the axes as in Activity 1. For these points students were only able to find two points that would determine a best-fit line. Earlier there was question as to which pair of points would provide the line of best fit. Ask students to test their particular choice of line, or assign different pairs of points to various students for testing so that several different lines will be tested. Some partners may have time to try more than one line. If so, a second color should be used for the segments drawn to this second line on the same grid paper. The segment lengths to a particular line and their total measure should be recorded on the graph in the same color used to draw the line segments. When all have finished their measurements, have different students share their results. The line that produces the **least** total measure or closeness measure will be declared the best-fit line for the given quiz score data. So which line will it be? Can we improve on our "visual" choice of line made in Activity 1?

Activity 3: FITNESS CHALLENGE

[Application/Exploration]

Materials: 12-inch bamboo skewers and small colored markers from Activity 1,
Objective 8
Calculators
Index cards (3 in. × 5 in.)
Inch grid paper
Centimeter rulers
Colored pencils (at least 2 different colors)
Regular pencils
Paper

Management: Teams of 4 students each (20–30 minutes)

Directions:

1. Give each team 6 sheets of one-inch grid paper, a skewer (or wire piece or taped drinking straws), a bag of 6 colored markers, a centimeter ruler, a calculator, an index card, and 2 colored pencils (2 different colors). One pair of students within a team (Pair A) will compete against the other pair (Pair B) on the same team. Pairs will take turns tossing the markers onto the one-inch grid paper, then selecting a **best-fit line** and computing its **closeness measure.** A new sheet of grid paper will be used for each toss. Students should label one corner as 0 for the origin, then label a longer edge of the grid as the horizontal axis and a shorter edge as the vertical axis so that the grid paper represents the first quadrant of a coordinate plane. When the markers are tossed onto the grid paper, the point on the grid where each marker lands will be marked, then the marker removed.

2. As an example of play, suppose Pair A has the turn to toss the markers. They toss the 6 markers onto the grid, mark their landing points, then remove the markers. Pair B then positions the skewer in order to find a line of best-fit, that is, a line that minimizes the total distance of the 6 points from that line. When they are satisfied with their choice of position, Pair B traces along the skewer to mark the line of their choice (or they may mark two points identified by the skewer and use the ruler with the two points to draw the line). The chosen line may or may not pass through any of the original 6 points marked on the grid. Using a colored pencil (color #1) and the index card, Pair B will draw the necessary line segments from the *off-line* points to the line, measure the segments to the nearest tenth of a centimeter, and find the total of the segment lengths. They will then record with their colored pencil the total on the graph as the **closeness measure** for their proposed line.

3. Pair A may **challenge** Pair B's proposed line. If they choose to challenge, Pair A will place the skewer back on the grid to find a new position that they believe will be closer to all the given points. They will draw their new line, then use the index card and their colored pencil (color #2) to draw the necessary line segments. Pair A will measure their segments and find their total length. This new total will be recorded in color #2 on the graph as the closeness measure for Pair A's proposed line.

4. If Pair B has the smaller closeness measure, they earn **5** points. If the challenging pair, here Pair A, has the smaller closeness measure, they earn **10** points. The line with the smaller closeness measure should be marked with a star or an asterisk, and the words "best-fit" written on the line. The turn to toss now goes to Pair B, and Pair A gets first choice for locating a line. A new grid sheet will be needed for each new toss.

5. Play continues until time is called or until 3 complete A–B rotations have occurred. The pair with the higher number of points will be the winners or **best-fit champions.**

6. Extension: On each turn, after the best-fit line has been identified, have Pair A and Pair B work together to find an **equation** for the best-fit line, using 2 points **on** that line. These two points may be among the six original "tossed" points, or, if the selected line does not pass through any of the original six points, two new points will be identified directly from their grid positions on the line. If a point does not fall on the intersection of two grid lines, its vertical and horizontal locations should be estimated to the nearest fourth of an inch (inch = grid unit length). Half-units and fourth-units can then be converted to decimal form in order to use the calculator to find the vertical and horizontal differences for the $\frac{V}{H}$ ratio or slope value m. For their equation, have students use the form: $Y = mX + b$. The values used for m and b should be rounded to the nearest tenth. The simplified equation should then be recorded on the grid paper near the best-fit line that it describes. The completed graphs and equations may later be turned in to the teacher for a *team* grade on Activity 3.

OBJECTIVE 10: **Given the expression for the general or N-th term of a linear sequence and its numerical value for some N, find the value of N.**

Activity 1: BUILDING LARGER TERMS

[Developing Action]

Materials: Packet of tiles and building mats from Section 2, Objective 3
Pieces of colored yarn (approximately 12 inches long) or coffee stirrers
Regular pencils
Paper
Worksheet 3–10–1

Management: Partners (50 minutes)

Directions:

1. Give each pair of students a building mat, a packet of tiles, and a piece of colored yarn or a coffee stirrer. The packet of tiles should contain a minimum of 5 plain variable tiles and 5 inverse variable tiles of the same size or length and same color, and 30 positive unit tiles and 30 negative unit tiles. In this activity students will represent the N-th term of a linear sequence with tiles and equate that set of tiles to the value of a particular term expressed in unit tiles. While solving linear equations with tiles, students will make connections to the figurate number sequences developed in Objective 4 of this section. It is assumed that students have completed the three activities of Objective 4 as preparation for this lesson. They will also be using the skills developed in Objective 1 of this section.

2. Write the following on the board: *The total unit tiles or value for the N-th term of a linear sequence will equal 3N + 5.* **Ask:** "Looking at the algebraic expression, 3N + 5, as a building pattern for the N-th term, can you use the positive unit tiles to build the first term? the second term? What does the 3N tell you to build? the +5?" Using 3N as 3 rows of N unit tiles per row, students should build a *first* term and a *second* term as shown in the illustration below. Have them count the total tiles used to build each term, then record the following number sentences on their own papers: **T(1) = +8 and T(2) = +11 when T(N) = 3N + 5.** Read T(1) as "total unit tiles in the first term, or T of 1," and similarly for T(2).

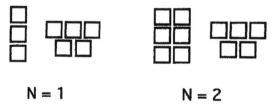

N = 1   N = 2

3. **Ask:** "If one of the terms in this sequence uses 20 positive unit tiles in its design, how can we decide which term it is and what the term will look like?" Some students may offer their opinions at this point. Listen to their ideas, then ask them to show the relationship with their tiles on the building mat. Using a variable tile for N, three plain variable tiles (arranged as 3 rows of an unknown) and 5 positive unit tiles should be placed on the left side of the mat to show 3N + 5, and 20 positive unit tiles should be placed on the right side of the mat to show +20. Ask students to solve the equation for the value of the variable tile. The steps are shown below.

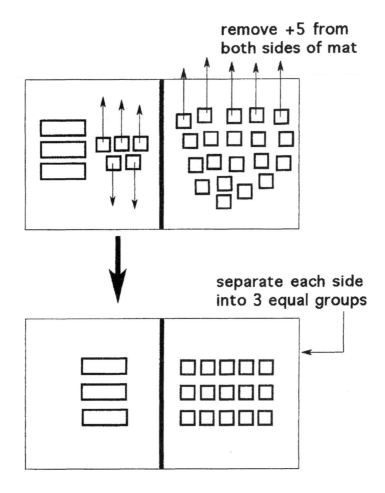

4. One complete row of tiles on the mat shows the solution; the variable N must equal +5. This indicates that the term having a value of **+20** must be the **fifth** term in the sequence. Ask students to build the fifth term with their positive unit tiles, following their earlier pattern for the first and second terms. There should be 3 rows of 5 positive unit tiles each, followed by an extra 5 positive unit tiles (not in a row). Have students count the total tiles used to confirm that the fifth term indeed requires 20 of the positive unit tiles. Students should finally record: **T(5) = +20.** Again, read T(5) as "total unit tiles in the fifth term, or T of 5."

5. Now write the following on the board: *The total unit tiles or value for the N-th term of a linear sequence will equal −2N − 1.* Discuss the idea that this algebraic expression may be considered as some amount with +1 removed, or as some amount with −1 added to it.

6. Ask students to build the *third* term of this new sequence with their unit tiles. Remind them that −2N may be read as "2 of the inverse of N." After building, students should count the total tiles used and record the following number sentences or equations on their own papers: **T(3) = –7 when T(N) = –2N – 1.** Two different ways are possible to build the third term, as shown here.

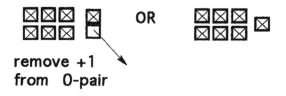

OR

remove +1
from 0-pair

7. *Ask:* "How can we find the term of this sequence that requires 17 negative unit tiles to build it? Can you build an equation on the building mat to help you decide which term it will be?" For variation, have students place 17 negative unit tiles on the *left* side of the mat, and place 2 rows of 1 inverse variable tile each, along with one negative unit tile, on the right side of the mat. The right side will represent the algebraic expression, –2N – 1, for the total unit tiles in the N-th term. Mat steps needed to solve for the variable N are shown below.

**(1) add +1 to both sides;
     remove 0-pairs**

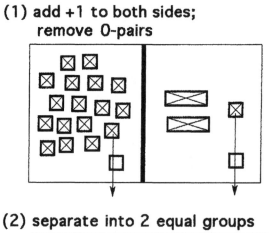

(2) separate into 2 equal groups

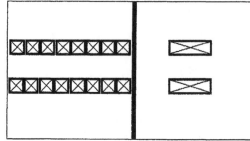

(3) take opposites

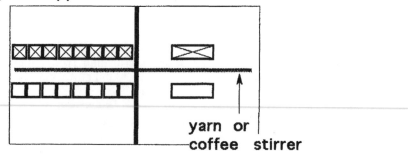

yarn or
coffee stirrer

8. The solution, N = +8, indicates that the **eighth** term should have a total tile value of **–17**. Have students build the eighth term according to the pattern they used for the third term earlier. Since –2N means "2 of the inverse of N," they should build 2 rows of 8 negative unit tiles each (N itself is 8 positive unit tiles) with an extra negative unit tile added on (or a 0-pair of unit tiles added on, followed by removal of the positive unit tile). Upon counting the total unit tiles to confirm that the eighth term indeed has a value of –17, students should record on their own papers: **T(8) = –17**.

9. Assign other sequences for which students will find specific terms when given their total value in unit tiles. (See Worksheet 3–10–1.) After solving each equation for N by building with the tiles, students should build the indicated term in unit tiles according to the pattern represented by the algebraic expression. This will confirm that the term does have the required value. This confirming process will also reinforce students' understanding of the algebraic expressions as *models of situations*. Here are some possible expressions to assign, as well as a term value for which to find N:

1. T(N) = N + 4; +14
2. T(N) = –4N; –24
3. T(N) = 5 – N; –3
4. T(N) = (+2) – 3N; –19

5. T(N) = N – 6; +3
6. T(N) = +5N; +20
7. T(N) = 2N + 3; 15
8. T(N) = 3N – 4; 11

Activity 2: PICTURING SPECIAL TERMS

[Bridging Action]

Materials: Paper
Regular pencils
Calculators *(optional)*
Tiles and building mats from Activity 1 *(optional)*
Worksheet 3–10–2

Management: Partners (30–50 minutes)

Directions:

1. Provide selected pairs of students with a calculator, or with a packet of tiles and a building mat, if they need help with their computation or if they still prefer to work with the tiles. Be accepting of their learning needs. Encourage them to explain the steps they are using as they work through the various exercises and also to draw diagrams of their actions with the tiles. Hopefully, by this time most students are proficient with solving linear equations. Then the diagramming technique used in this activity will give them simply another strategy to apply to *situations* involving sequences.

2. Write the following equation on the board: **T(N) = –3N + 1.** Ask students to calculate T(1) and T(2) and record their work on their own papers as number sentences: **T(1) = –3(1) + 1 = –2 and T(2) = –3(2) + 1 = –5.** *Ask:* "What type of arrangement of tiles is suggested by the algebraic expression, –3N + 1?" *(3 rows of the inverse of some value for N, which are combined with a single positive unit)* "Can you draw a diagram that **equates** this *description* of any term in the sequence with the term *value* of –20?"

Name ______________________________ Date ____________________

WORKSHEET 3-10-1
Building Larger Terms

Build with tiles to find the specific term of each sequence that has the given value.

1. $T(N) = N + 4; +14$

2. $T(N) = -4N; -24$

3. $T(N) = 5 - N; -3$

4. $T(N) = (+2) - 3N; -19$

5. $T(N) = N - 6; +3$

6. $T(N) = +5N; +20$

7. $T(N) = 2N + 3; 15$

8. $T(N) = 3N - 4; 11$

3. Students should draw a series of diagrams to solve the equation for N, the number of the term needed. A possible series to use is as follows:

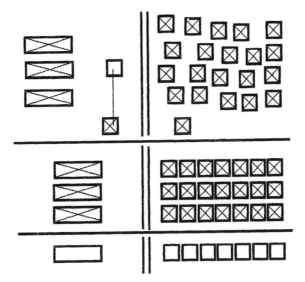

4. After students have completed their diagrams and found N = +7, have them record their steps in symbolic notation as follows:

$$-3N + 1 = -20$$
$$\underline{+ (-1) \quad + (-1)}$$
$$-3N \qquad = -21$$
$$\tfrac{1}{3}(-3N) = \tfrac{1}{3}(-21)$$
$$-N = -7$$
$$N = +7$$

5. Since N = +7 means the **seventh** term in the sequence, students should test the seventh term in the expression that describes the arrangement of that term to confirm that it has a value of **–20.** They should record these substitution steps on their own papers: **T(7) = –3(7) + 1 = –20.** Hence, the seventh term of the sequence has a value of –20.

6. Now assign other sequences for students to solve for a particular term. (See Worksheet 3–10–2.) The procedure used in steps 2–5 should be followed. T(1) and T(2) should be calculated first, then a diagram drawn to represent the particular term whose *value* has been given. Once the term's position in the sequence has been identified, symbolic steps should be recorded and a test made to confirm that term's value with respect to the general expression given for all the terms in the sequence. Later, when checking students' work in class, occasionally ask students to describe the unit tile arrangement for T(1) or T(2) or the new term found for a given expression (with respect to number and size of row and any extra units included).

7. Here are suggested general expressions for the N-th term, along with the values of the terms being sought, that might be assigned to students:

1. T(N) = N – 5; +11
2. T(N) = –2N; –18
3. T(N) = 2N – 1; +17
4. T(N) = 8 – N; –4
5. T(N) = –6 – N; –16
6. T(N) = 5 + 2N; +21
7. T(N) = –N + 4; –9
8. T(N) = 3N + 4; +28

WORKSHEET 3–10–2
Picturing Special Terms

For each general expression, compute T(1) and T(2). Draw a diagram of tiles and use it to solve for N when T(N) equals the term *value* given with the expression.

1. $T(N) = N - 5; +11$

2. $T(N) = -2N; -18$

3. $T(N) = 2N - 1; +17$

4. $T(N) = 8 - N; -4$

5. $T(N) = -6 - N; -16$

6. $T(N) = 5 + 2N; +21$

7. $T(N) = -N + 4; -9$

8. $T(N) = 3N + 4; +28$

Answer Key to WORKSHEET 3–10–2

1. T(1) = –4, T(2) = –3, T(16) = +11

2. T(1) = –2, T(2) = –4, T(9) = –18

3. T(1) = +1, T(2) = +3, T(9) = +17

4. T(1) = +7, T(2) = +6, T(12) = –4

5. T(1) = –7, T(2) = –8, T(10) = –16

6. T(1) = +7, T(2) = +9, T(8) = +21

7. T(1) = +3, T(2) = +2, T(13) = –9

8. T(1) = +7, T(2) = +10, T(8) = +28

Activity 3: BACKTRACKING POINTS

[Application/Exploration]

Materials: Centimeter grid paper
Red pencils
Regular pencils
Rulers or straight edges
Calculators *(optional)*

Management: Partners (30 minutes)

Directions:

1. Give each pair of students 4–5 sheets of centimeter grid paper, a ruler or straight edge, and a red pencil. Provide calculators to those students who might need such assistance. Remind students that a **linear sequence** is just a special type of **linear function** where the first member of each ordered pair is a positive integer or natural number (1,2,3, . . .). The second member is a value that has been formed according to a specific pattern, which is described with an algebraic expression. It is the set of **values,** listed according to the order of the first members of the pairs, that students typically see and consider to be the sequence itself.

2. Write the equation **T(N) = 4N – 3** on the board. Ask students to compute **T(1)** and **T(2)** on their own papers as follows: T(1) = 4(1) – 3 = 1 and T(2) = 4(2) – 3 = 5. Using (N, T(N)) as the form for the ordered pairs, students should record the ordered pairs found: (1,1) and (2,5), in a 2-column table with headings N and T(N); the pairs should then be plotted on a sheet of the centimeter grid paper. The longer edge should be the (left) vertical axis, labeled as "Term Value T(N)"; the shorter edge should be the (lower) horizontal axis, labeled as "Term Number N" or "Term Position N." Each grid segment should equal 1 unit for the scales. Once the two points are marked on the grid, students should draw a line segment through the points in red pencil. The graph of points will have a linear path since we are working with a linear sequence or function.

3. *Ask:* "If we are looking for the term in this sequence that has the value 21, how might we find the point on our line that belongs to that term?" Various ideas will be shared, but guide students to focus on the ordered pairs. The point being sought has the ordered pair (N, 21); the vertical distance, 21, should be located and "boxed" on the vertical axis, then that position "tracked" over to the red line segment by drawing in regular pencil a horizontal path that will intersect with the line segment. This point of intersection should be marked and circled on the line segment. *Ask:* "What mark on the

horizontal axis lies directly below this new point on the line?" Another path or "track" should be drawn vertically from the new point on the line down to the horizontal axis; the axis mark will be at +6. A box should be drawn around +6. **Note:** Every number found on the horizontal axis by this "backtracking" method will be an *integer,* since this axis represents the term *positions* (counting numbers) in the sequence.

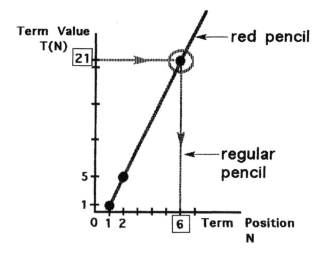

4. The +6 indicates the position of the term whose value is 21. Have students test this solution by substituting +6 in the general expression for a term's value in the sequence: $T(6) = 4(6) - 3 = 21$. So the **sixth** term does indeed have the value **21.** Students should now record their new ordered pair (6,21) in their 2-column table.

5. For more practice with this *same* sequence, give students the term value of 13 to "track." The corresponding N will equal 4. For *new* sequences, assign the general expressions (with given term values) listed below, each expression to be plotted on a separate sheet of grid paper. When larger numbers are given for term values, select scales for the vertical axis accordingly. For each expression, students should compute $T(1)$ and $T(2)$; prepare a table of ordered pairs; plot points and connect them with a red line segment; "backtrack" from the given term value to the term position; and last, test the N found. Ask several students to explain their work when all are finished.

1. $T(N) = 25 - 2N$; +5

2. $T(N) = -3 + 3N$; +21

3. $T(N) = 3N + 8$; +53

4. $T(N) = -5N + 64$; +29

OBJECTIVE 11: Locate points in disjoint regions formed by one or two given boundary points on a number line (one-dimensional space).

Activity 1: TESTING THE MARK

[Developing Action]

Materials: Building mats (described in step 1)
One-inch paper squares (labeled with X, Y, Z, or W)
Regular pencils
Paper

Management: Partners (30 minutes)

Directions:

1. This activity prepares students for solving inequalities (Objective 12) by introducing them to *intervals* and how a variable may sometimes represent *infinitely many* values, rather than *one* or *two* values. Students are also exposed to the idea of **shifts** on an axis that will occur later in the study of conics and other special relations and their graphs. To begin, give each pair of students a building mat and 4 one-inch paper squares, each labeled with a different letter: X, Y, Z, or W (one letter per square). The squares might be laminated for durability. The building mat should be drawn on an 8.5 in. by 14 in. sheet of paper and may be laminated for durability as well. In order to help students remain aware of how single-variable situations (one-dimensional space) fit within the framework of two-variable situations (two-dimensional space), the mat will show *two coordinate axes,* even though only the horizontal axis will actually be used. That is, the vertical distance will remain at 0 in the case of single-variable situations. Hopefully this will make the later transition from single-variable inequalities to two-variable inequalities easier for the students. The mat should be drawn and labeled as follows. (Do not label any marks on the axes except those indicated; adjacent marks should be 1 inch apart.)

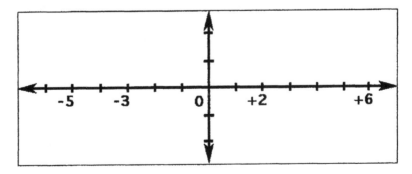

2. *Ask:* "Where might the paper square labeled with the variable X be placed on the horizontal axis of your building mat to mark a number that is less than +2?" Partners should place their X marker on any mark to the left of the mark for +2. (Some students may realize that *unmarked* points on the axis may also be used.) Have different students tell the numbers they selected. If an *unlabeled* mark is used, students should determine the number that the mark represents. Possible integral mat choices for the X marker will range from –6 to +1. **Ask:** "Can we also place the X marker at $+\frac{1}{2}$ and still have it less than +2? at $-3\frac{1}{2}$ and still be less than +2?" *(yes; each point on the axis represents a real number, so there will be other numbers, besides the integers already found, whose points are to the left of +2)* Discuss the idea that X may have many possible values when it is described as **a number less than +2.** Have students write on their own papers the expression that represents all the different numbers they chose for the X marker on the horizontal axis: **X < +2.** This expression should be read *from left to right* as **"X is any real number less than +2."**

3.   Continue with the other letters or variables. Students should place the requested marker on the axis in various positions that will satisfy the stated inequality. Ask students to look at all the different positions found by other nearby students; this awareness of multiple positions is extremely important in the study of **inequalities.** Students tend to think of a variable as always in an *equality* setting where it typically represents just a few numbers, not infinitely many numbers as in an *inequality*. Have students record each inequality in symbols and take turns reading aloud the statements they have written. Here are some possible questions to ask and the recording to use for each:

"Where can we place

- the variable Y to show a number **greater than** –3?" *(Y > –3)*

- the variable Z to show a number that is **between** 0 **and** –5 (endpoints excluded)?" *(–5 < Z < 0 or 0 > Z > –5)* [example: –5 < Z < 0 is read as "–5 is less than Z, which is less than 0"]

- the variable W to show a number that is **more than** 0 **and less than** +6?" *(0 < W < +6, read as "0 is less than W, which is less than +6"; or +6 > W > 0, read as "+6 is greater than W, which is greater than 0")*

- the variable X to show a number that is **more than** 0 *and* **less than** –3?" *(not possible; the X marker cannot be to the right of 0 at the same time that it is to the left of –3)*

- the variable Y to show a number that is **more than** 0 or **less than** –3?" *(in this case the Y marker may be placed anywhere to the right of 0 or anywhere to the left of –3; students should try placing the marker in each of the two intervals [but not simultaneously]; the logical **or** does not require both conditions to be satisfied at the same time; record as **two** statements: Y < –3 or Y > 0)*

4.   Now ask students to place their four variable markers on the horizontal axis of the building mat in the following positions: X between 0 and +1; W between –1 and 0; Y between +4 and +5; and Z between –3 and –2. Remind students that if a variable marker is placed between two numbers, say –1 and 0, the value of the variable could be just greater than –1 or the value could be just less than 0; the variable will not necessarily equal the middle-most number, here $-\frac{1}{2}$. We want students to think of the variable as ranging across the unit interval in which it lies on the axis.

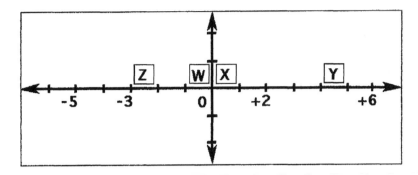

5. With the variable markers now in position, write the following inequalities on the board and ask students to decide whether each is true or false:

Is X < W? *[False]*   **Is (X + Z) < 0?** *[True]*   **Is (Y – X) > 0?** *[True]*

Is 3W > X? *[False]*   **Is (Z)(Z) < W?** *[False]*   **Is (X)(X) < X?** *[True]*

In each case, students should consider the minimum and the maximum values possible for the variables in their assigned positions. For example, to test whether (Z)(Z) < W or not, consider that if Z is close to –3, then (Z)(Z) is close to +9; if Z is close to –2, then (Z)(Z) is close to +4. Since (Z)(Z) lies between +4 and +9, and W lies between –1 and 0, clearly (Z)(Z) cannot be less than W; hence, the inequality is false. (**Note:** We have used a *product* form for Z here, rather than a *power* form, since we have not yet presented powers of variables in this text.) To test (Y – X) > 0, students need to minimize and maximize the difference: the maximal difference will be close to (5 – 0) or +5, and the minimal difference will be close to (4 – 1) or +3. Thus, (Y – X) ranges between +3 and +5. Hence, the difference will always be greater than 0, so the inequality is true. Notice that for (X)(X) < X, it will not be enough to look at the endpoints of the interval for X; fractional values within the interval, for example, ¼, will need to be tested as well.

6. Allow time for partners to discuss their ideas with each other. Then have various students share their conclusions and their reasoning with the class.

Activity 2: IDENTIFYING INTERVALS

[Bridging Action]

Materials: Worksheet 3–11–1
Colored pencils (any bright color)
Regular pencils

Management: Partners (30 minutes)

Directions:

1. Give each pair of students 4 copies of Worksheet 3–11–1 and 2 colored pencils (colors may or may not be the same). Partners will work together, but each individual student will complete one or two worksheets. In Activity 1, students found solutions to an inequality by considering individual points that satisfied the given condition. Although most points identified were for integers, students were encouraged to test other real numbers as well. In Activity 2, emphasis will be on solutions that include nonintegral numbers; this will be done by coloring entire intervals on the horizontal axis rather than by just locating individual points. Worksheet 3–11–1 contains several sets of coordinate axes for this purpose.

2. Write the statement **X < –2** on the board. Ask a student to read the statement (example: "X is any real number less than –2"). Ask students to find the mark or point for –2 on the first set of axes on Worksheet 3–11–1. Since only one variable is involved, have students work only with the horizontal axis to find –2. **Ask:** "Can X equal –2 according to the inequality statement?" *(no; X can only be numbers **less than** –2)* Since X will not be –2, have students draw a circle around the mark for –2; do not shade the interior of the circle. **Ask:** "Where on the axis will we find numbers that are less than –2? Can you name some of these numbers?" *(any point to the left of –2 will represent a number less than –2; examples might be –3, –4.5, –10½, etc.)* Encourage students to name and give the general location on the axis of a variety of numbers that will be less than –2, that is, numbers that are decimals, mixed numbers, etc. (real numbers, not limited to integers). At least two such numbers should be marked on the axis. After several numbers have been suggested and located, have students color the entire portion of the horizontal axis that is to the left of the circled –2. To show that other numbers not visible on the axis will also be included, the left arrowhead should also be colored. Discuss the idea that –2 acts as a **boundary point** in that it appears to separate the horizontal axis into two portions or intervals, not counting –2 itself; the portion to the left of –2 contains **all** the solution points found by the students, and the portion to the right of –2 does **not** contain any solution points. In this particular example, the boundary point itself is not a solution point either. Within the colored portion of the axis a random solution point should be marked and labeled as X to show the variable involved in the inequality. Finally students should write the statement **X < –2** below the axis portion that has been colored.

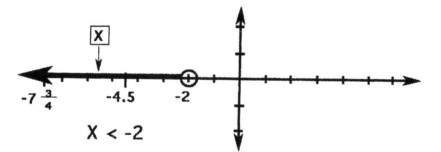

3. Now write the statement, **+3 ≥ W > –4** on the board. We will follow a procedure similar to that used in step 2 and graph our results on a second set of axes on the worksheet. Ask a student to read the statement (example: "3 is greater than W or equal to W, and W is greater than –4"). **Ask:** "Where are the boundary points for this inequality?" *(+3 and –4)* "Can W be a number that equals +3?" *(yes)* "Can W be a number that equals –4?" *(no; W can only be numbers greater than –4)* Have students draw a circle around the point for +3 and color the interior of the circle to show that +3 can be a solution point. A circle should also be drawn around the point for –4, but the interior not colored since –4 is not a number that satisfies the inequality.

4. Ask: "Can you describe the different intervals that the boundary points, +3 and –4, have created on the axis?" *(possible description: interval to left of –4 contains all numbers less than –4; interval between –4 and +3 contains all numbers greater than –4, but less than +3; interval to right of +3 contains all numbers greater than +3)* "In what interval or intervals are the numbers that will satisfy this inequality?" *(only in middle portion since*

WORKSHEET 3-11-1
Identifying Intervals

Follow the teacher's directions for this worksheet. On each set of axes below, count each segment of length as one unit of value.

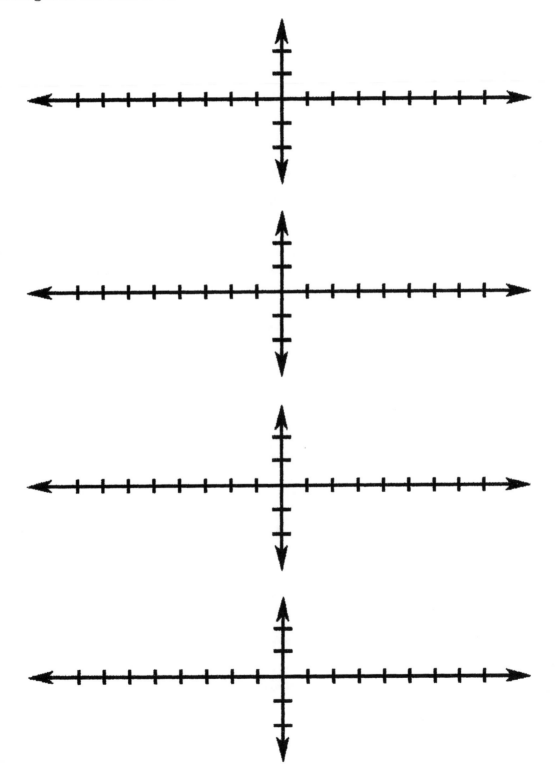

choices for W must be less than +3, but greater than –4; +3 will also be a solution, but being a boundary point, it is not counted in this *interval* discussion) Have students color this middle portion and locate and label two real numbers (not both integers) in this interval that will satisfy the conditions of the inequality. A random point in this interval should be marked for the variable W being used to find the solution points. Finally, the inequality should be written below the colored interval on the axis.

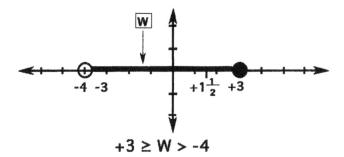

$$+3 \geq W > -4$$

5. Repeat the above procedure, giving students different inequalities for which to locate solution points and hence to color solution intervals on the horizontal number line. If ≤ or ≥ is used, students should circle the boundary point given and then color the interior of the circle to indicate that the boundary point or endpoint is included as a solution point for the inequality. In each case, discuss the boundary point(s) and identify the portions or intervals on the axis that are created by the boundary point(s). Students should find and label on the axis at least two real numbers (not both integers) that will satisfy the condition of the inequality, then color the portion(s) that contain all real solution points. A random solution point should be marked for the variable involved. The statement for the inequality should finally be recorded below the colored interval on the axis.

6. Here are some suggested inequalities to assign:

(a) W ≤ +4   (d) 0 < X < +3

(b) X > –1   (e) –1 ≥ W ≥ –5

(c) Z < +2   (f) Z < –4 or Z ≥ +5

Activity 3: SHIFTING BOUNDARIES

[Application/Exploration]

Materials: Colored paper strips (described in step 1 below)
Large building mats from Activity 1
Regular pencils
Paper
Worksheets 3–11–2 and 3–11–3
Scissors

Management: Teams of 4 students each (30 minutes)

Directions:

1. Give each team a building mat from Activity 1 and two sets of colored paper strips (preferably laminated). (See Worksheet 3–11–2.) The two sets of paper strips should

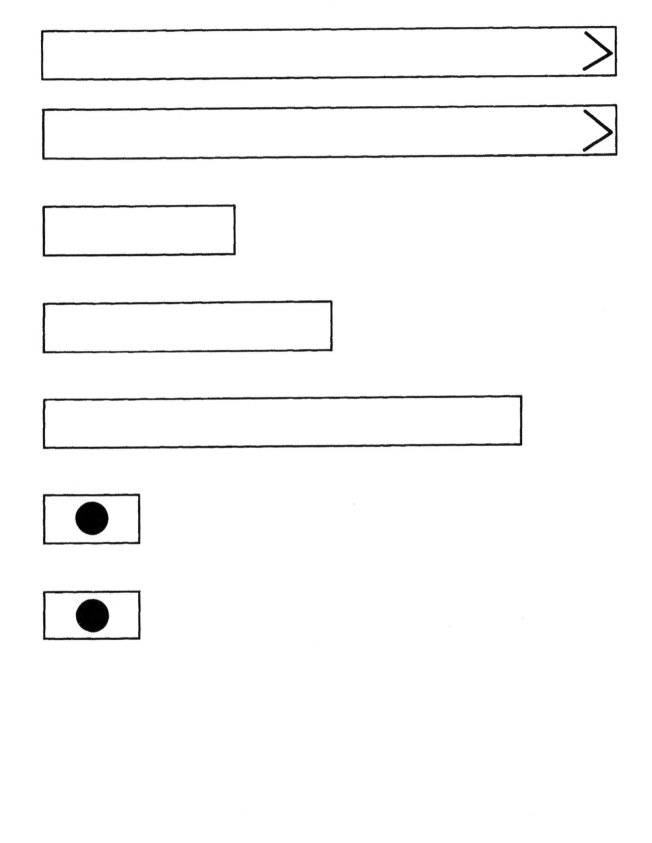

contain strips that are 0.5 inch wide; one set will be one color, the other set a different color. Each set will contain the following strips: two 6-inch strips with a large arrowhead drawn at one end of each strip; one 2-inch strip, one 3-inch strip, and one 5-inch strip, with all three of these left plain; and two 1-inch strips, each with a large dot centered on the strip.

2. Members of each team will work in pairs, Pair A and Pair B. The two pairs will take turns stating the problem. The pair stating the problem will set up some interval on the mat, write the inequality for the interval, and tell how the interval should be changed. The other pair will show the required change on the mat and write an inequality for the new interval. The pair who made the *change* will then state the next problem. The paper strips will be used to show the intervals on the building mat, and the small strips with the large dots will be used to mark a boundary or endpoint that is included in an interval. In order to cover the exact length of a given interval, the plain strips may need to overlap at their ends.

3. For example, suppose it is Pair A's turn to state the problem. They write $X \geq -4$ on a sheet of paper, place a colored arrowhead strip, say blue, on the horizontal axis of the mat so that the plain end of the strip is touching -4 and the arrowhead end is pointing to the right. Since X can be equal to -4, Pair A will also place a small strip with a large dot on top of the longer blue strip, but directly in line with the axis mark for -4.

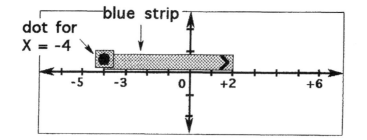

4. Pair A then tells Pair B that "every number in our interval is greater than or equal to -4 and is represented by X," and that they want Pair B to show "another interval where each number is **5 greater than** some number in this first interval." Pair A will then name and record a *nonintegral* number in the *interior* of their interval, say -1.5, that Pair B must match in their new interval. (See end of step 4 for the recording format.) This latter step is to help students realize that there are *other* numbers in an interval besides the boundary points listed or marked on the axis. Realizing that the boundary point must also reflect this increase, Pair B now places their colored arrowhead strip, say red, on the mat so that the plain end is aligned with $+1$ on the horizontal axis and the arrowhead end is pointing to the right. This long red strip may be placed *above* or *below* the horizontal axis, but should be next to, not on top of, the long blue strip already there. A new paper strip with a large dot will be positioned on the plain end of the longer red strip to show that the new interval of numbers will include $+1$. Pair B then states that "if the values of X in the first interval are changed by $+5$, our new values must be greater than or equal to $+1$ and will be represented by $X + 5$. The number in our new interval that matches -1.5 in the first interval is $+3.5$." Pair B then writes $X + 5 \geq +1$ **where** $+3.5 \geq +1$ on the paper below the original inequality and selected number, which were recorded earlier as follows: $X \geq -4$ **where** $-1.5 \geq -4$. The turn now goes to Pair B.

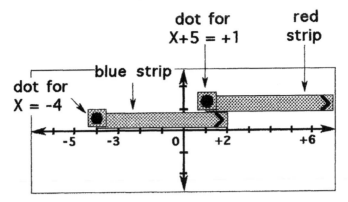

5. As another example, Pair B on their turn might decide to show the interval **−2 < W ≤ +3** on the mat. (Students should vary the letters used for the variable; possible choices might be X, W, V, or Z. Y will not be used here because it often identifies the vertical intercept; similarly, X will not be used for the vertical axis in later lessons because it often identifies the horizontal intercept.) Since this interval has two boundary points, they will use one or more of the plain red strips placed end-to-end (or partially overlapped if necessary to show correct length needed) to extend from −2 to +3 on the horizontal axis. A small strip with a large dot will be placed on top of the red strip at +3 to show that +3 is included in the interval. Pair B now states that "every number in our interval is greater than −2, but less than or equal to +3, and W represents any number in our interval." Pair B asks Pair A to "show a new interval where each number is **2.5 less than** some number in our interval." They then name and record a *nonintegral* number in the *interior* of this interval, say +0.2, for Pair A to match.

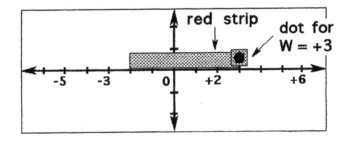

6. Pair A, realizing that the **two boundary points** must change in the same way all other numbers in the interval must change, places one or more plain blue strips from −4.5 to +0.5. A small blue strip with a large dot is placed on top of the longer blue strip to mark +0.5 as a member of the new interval. Pair A identifies −2.3 as their number that is 2.5 less than Pair B's number, +0.2. Pair A also states that "if W represents the numbers that are greater than −2, but less than or equal to +3, then our new numbers that are 2.5 less than these first numbers will be greater than −4.5, but less than or equal to +0.5, and W − 2.5 represents each number in our new interval." Pair A then writes **−4.5 < W − 2.5 ≤ +0.5 where −4.5 < −2.3 ≤ +0.5** on the paper below the inequality and number: **−2 < W ≤ +3 where −2 < +0.2 ≤ +3.** The turn now goes to Pair A.

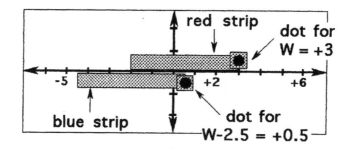

7. The two examples described above are given to show the different ways partners might build their initial intervals. Disjoint intervals might also be used, such as **Z < –3 or Z > +2.** In such cases, both intervals would go through the same amount of **shift,** and a specific number would be identified in each of the two intervals. Students should be encouraged to vary the types of intervals they use. (See Worksheet 3–11–3.) Have the teams turn in the papers containing their recorded inequalities so that you can see the types they actually used. Monitor the teams carefully as they work to make certain that they show and verbalize the locations of their intervals, name a specific nonintegral number in the interior of the first interval and its match in the second interval of each turn, and correctly record their inequalities and specific numbers to show the changes or shifts made on the intervals.

8. As an alternative procedure for Activity 3, each pair of students might select an inequality from the list on Worksheet 3–11–3 and make the change that is requested. The pair must name one nonintegral value in the original interval(s) and match it via the change to a value in the new interval(s). Hence, each pair will be carrying out the steps attributed to both Pair A and Pair B in the original procedure given for Activity 3.

WORKSHEET 3-11-3
Shifting Boundaries

Directions: When it is your turn (with your partner), select an inequality from the list below and show it with paper strips on the building mat. Choose a number that is *not* an integer from within the interval. Show the required change in your inequality with new paper strips on the mat, and tell what your "matching number" will be in the new interval. Describe and record your inequalities and matched numbers according to your teacher's instructions.

1. $X > +2$; change by +3

2. $V \leq 0$; change by −2

3. $−2 \leq W < +4$; change by −1

4. $−1 \geq X > −6$; change by +5

5. $V > +1$ or $V < −3$; change by −3

6. $W \leq −4$ or $W > +2$; change by +2

7. $X \leq −1$; change by +5

8. $V > +3$; change by −4

OBJECTIVE 12: Solve linear inequalities in one variable and graph the solutions.

Activity 1: AN UNEVEN BALANCE

[Developing Action]

Materials: Sets of tiles from Objective 10
Inequality building mats and paper "equals" markers (described in step 1)
Axes building mats and paper strips from Objective 11
Regular pencils
Paper
Colored pencils
Worksheet 3–12–1

Management: Partners (50 minutes)

Directions:

1. Give each pair of students a colored pencil (any color), a set of variable and unit tiles (from Objective 10), an axes building mat and 2 sets of paper strips (one set per color from Objective 11; extra sets may need to be made for this activity), and an inequality building mat with a paper "equals" marker. It is assumed that students have completed all activities for Objective 11 and now understand that an **interval** on an axis represents infinitely many different real numbers and that the interval will have one or two **boundary points** that help identify the other numbers in the interval itself. The paper "equals" marker may be a 2 in. by 3 in. plain index card with an equals sign (=) drawn on it. The inequality building mat should be drawn on a sheet of 8.5 in. by 14 in. paper and laminated for durability. The dotted line segment on the given sample is a guideline for drawing the bold V on the paper and should not appear on the final mat.

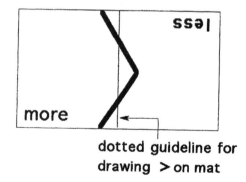

dotted guideline for
drawing $>$ on mat

2. Write the inequality $A - 4 \geq +1$ on the board. Remind students of the following: "When we graphed intervals in our last lesson, we learned that when the variable X represents the numbers in a certain interval, which has one or two boundary points on the horizontal axis, then the variable expression (X + 3) will represent numbers in another interval where each new boundary point is 3 more than each corresponding boundary point of the first interval. Also, each number in the new interval matches to and is 3 more than some number in the first interval. So if we said that X represented numbers less than 0, then we knew that (X + 3) represented numbers that were less than +3."

3. Now **ask:** "What do you know about the interval and boundary point for this new inequality, A − 4 ≥ +1? What does (A − 4) mean with respect to the interval? What does +1 tell us?" **Discuss:** The +1 indicates a boundary point that can be shown on the horizontal axis, and the expression (A − 4) represents every real number that is greater than +1 or that equals to +1. Have students place their paper arrowhead strip (color #1) on the horizontal axis with the plain end at +1 and the arrowhead end pointing to the right on the axis. Also a small strip with a large dot (color #1) should be placed at the +1 position to indicate that +1 is also in the interval. **Ask:** "So what do we now know about A and the numbers it represents?" Since (A − 4) represents numbers that are **4 less than** the numbers A represents, we should reverse this process and describe a number for A as being **4 more than** a number for (A − 4). So, since (A − 4) is for numbers greater than or equal to +1, A itself must be for numbers greater than or equal to +5. Have students place a paper arrowhead strip (color #2) beside their first paper strip (color #1), but place the plain end at +5 and have the arrowhead end pointing to the right. A small strip with a large dot (color #2) should be placed at +5 to show that +5 is also a value for the variable A.

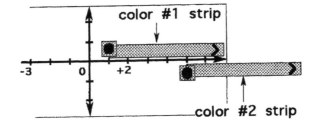

4. Now have students show the same inequality, **A − 4 ≥ +1,** with *tiles* on their *inequality building mat.* The mat should be rotated to show the word "more" in the lower left corner when partners, sitting beside each other, view the mat. The bold separation bar should appear as a "more than" sign to the students working on the mat; the tiles having the greater *value* (not the greater *amount of tiles*) will be on the left side of the bold bar. One plain variable tile and 4 negative unit tiles should be placed on the left side of the mat, and 1 positive unit tile should be placed on the right side. Since (A − 4) may also equal +1, the paper "equals" marker should be placed at the top edge of the mat. Students should now isolate the variable tile on the left by adding on 4 positive unit tiles to both sides of the mat. The 0-pairs should be removed, leaving the variable tile A on the left side of the mat and 5 positive unit tiles on the right. The following illustration shows the mat while 0-pairs are being formed.

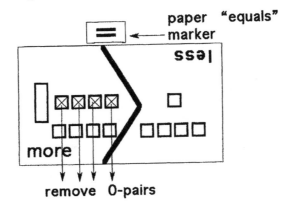

5. *Ask:* "How does your work with the tiles compare to your graph of the two intervals on the axes building mat?" Hopefully students will realize that the original inequality, A − 4 ≥ +1, shown with tiles, corresponds to the first interval shown with the color #1 paper strips, and that the final inequality, A ≥ +5, shown with tiles, corresponds to the second interval shown with the color #2 paper strips. Students need to see this close connection between the work done with tiles and the graphing work done on the axes. Remind students that if one interval includes its boundary point(s), then the new interval will also include its own boundary point(s). In other words, we know that if (A − 4) can equal +1 (boundary point) in the present example, then A alone can equal +5 (boundary point). Hence, when we first set up an inequality with tiles, if we place the "equals" marker at the top of the inequality building mat to show that the boundary point is to be included, then the marker will apply to the solution inequality as well. Finally, write the following on the board: **If (A − 4) > +1 or (A − 4) = +1, then A > +5 or A = +5.** We will record the > and = statements separately in Activity 1 to help students become more aware of what the combined sign implies.

6. For another example, write the inequality **6 − 3c < c − 2** on the board. Discuss the idea that boundary points are not obvious at first, so the graphs of the intervals cannot be shown immediately on the axes building mat. Instead, ask students to show the inequality with tiles on their inequality building mat. The mat should be rotated to show the word "less" in the lower left corner when partners view the mat together. The bold separation bar should appear as a "less than" sign to the students working on the mat; the tiles having the lesser *value* (not the lesser *amount of tiles*) will be placed on the left side of the bold bar. Since only the "less than" relation is involved this time, the paper "equals" marker will not be needed. Students should place 6 positive unit tiles and 3 inverse variable tiles (all 3 of same color and size) on the left side of the mat and place 1 plain variable tile (same color and size of inverse variable tile used) and 2 negative unit tiles on the right side.

7. Ask students to add-on or remove variable tiles until no *inverse* variable tiles remain on the mat and all plain variable tiles left are together on one side of the mat. (**Note:** This approach of *removing* all *inverse* variable tiles allows us to avoid changing directly to **opposites** [our method used with linear **equations** in Section 2], which with inequalities would require a sign change. Such sign changes are very confusing to most students.) At first, when all inverse variable tiles are removed, some unit tiles may be found on the same side of the mat as the plain variable tiles, but *only* unit tiles will be on the other side of the mat. Students may do this transformation in various ways, but one possible way is to add 3 plain variable tiles to each side of the mat. 0-pairs may then be removed from the left side. This leaves 6 positive unit tiles on the left side of the mat, and leaves 4 plain variable tiles and 2 negative unit tiles on the right. Write **6 < 4c − 2** on the board below the original inequality given in step 6.

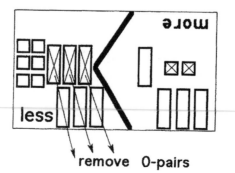

remove 0-pairs

8. At this point students may just solve for the variable c, but first have them investigate what is happening to the **intervals** on the axes building mat with each step taken with the tiles. ***Ask:*** "In the inequality, 6 < 4c − 2, where are the numbers represented by (4c − 2)?" *(all real numbers greater than +6)* Students should place a paper arrowhead strip (color #1) above the horizontal axis of the axes mat with the plain end aligned with +6 and the arrowhead end pointing to the right. ***Ask:*** "Where is the interval represented by 4c then?" *(every real number that is 2 more than some number in the interval for (4c − 2); using boundary points to aid us, the interval for 4c will contain all real numbers that are greater than 2 more than +6, that is, greater than +8)* Students should place just below the horizontal axis an arrowhead strip (color #2) with its plain end aligned with +8 and the arrowhead end pointing to the right. Now ***ask:*** "If the interval for 4c is greater than +8, where is the interval represented by c itself?" *(a new challenge for the students; until now, they have only worked with shifting to lesser values or to greater values, that is, with subtracting or adding; do not rush this development)* Discuss the idea that the numbers in the interval associated with 4c must be **4 times the value** of the matched numbers in the interval associated with c; hence, if we reverse this, we say that each number in the interval for c must be **a fourth** of the value of each matched number in the interval for 4c. Looking at boundary points for help, since 4c represents numbers greater than +8, we know that c must represent numbers greater than a fourth of +8, which is +2. Have students place a third paper arrowhead strip (use color #1 again since only two colors are available; if repeating color #1 confuses some students, provide a third color) on the axes mat with the plain end below and aligned with +2 on the horizontal axis and the arrowhead end pointing to the right. The third strip placed on the mat shows the *solution interval* for the original inequality. That is, the variable c represents all real numbers that are greater than +2. See the following illustration for the positions of the three strips.

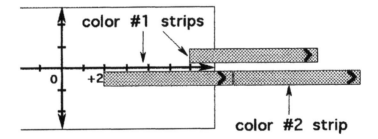

9. Now return to the inequality building mat to finish solving for c. Actually you will be solving for the **boundary point** of the interval of numbers represented by the variable c. Students should add 2 positive unit tiles to both sides of the mat and remove 0-pairs from the right side. Eight positive unit tiles are now on the left side and 4 plain variable tiles are on the right side. The variable tiles must now be separated into 4 rows of 1 variable tile each; the 8 unit tiles on the left must also be separated into 4 rows, each row having 2 positive unit tiles. Since a solution only requires 1 variable tile, one complete row of 2 positive unit tiles on the left and 1 variable tile on the right should be left on the mat. Observe that the tiles remaining on the mat now show the inequality, **+2 < c,** which corresponds to the third paper strip placed on the axes mat to show the interval of numbers represented by c, that is, all real numbers greater than +2. The final inequality should now be written in a statement on the board with the original inequality in the following way:

If 6 − 3c < c − 2, then +2 < c.

8. *Ask:* "Based on data in the three ratio tables, we have compared points A and B, points A and C, and points A and D on the grid. What do you notice about the 4 points on the grid?" (*the 4 points lie in a line together;* the skewer or wire should be placed on the grid across or touching the 4 colored markers for points A, B, C, and D) "Look at the three numerical ratios for $\frac{V}{H}$ that you found. What do you notice about them? If you change each to a decimal number, what happens?" (*each ratio simplifies to the value 0.25, so the three ratios are equivalent, which we already knew from our ratio table work;* this is simply another way to view the same problem)

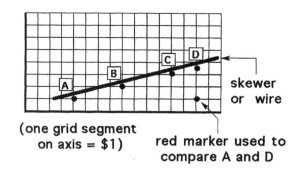

(one grid segment
on axis = $1)

red marker used to
compare A and D

9. Have students investigate the ratio, $\frac{V}{H}$, that results if they move the red marker again to similarly compare points B and C; points B and D; and points C and D. They should find the ratios: $\frac{\$1}{\$4}$, $\frac{\$1.50}{\$6}$, and $\frac{\$0.50}{\$2}$, respectively. Discuss the idea that no matter which two points are compared to find $\frac{V}{H}$, the resulting value will be the same. Also, if the numbers in the **basic ratio** from the original situation, $4 in sales to $1 commission, are stated as a **rate,** "$1 per $4 sales," this may also be written as $\frac{\$1}{\$4}$, which is equivalent to the $\frac{V}{H}$ ratios found earlier. One final observation: As the total sales (independent value) increase, the commission (dependent value) also increases. Thus, the points for the ordered pairs appear to move uphill to the right, and the line containing the points is described as having a **positive slope.**

Geometric Examples:

10. To further pursue the ratio of vertical distance-value to horizontal distance-value, we will look at some special lines on the grid. Ask students to place the A marker and blue marker at the point on the grid for (5, 3) and the B marker and green marker at the point for (11, 3). Place the skewer or wire on the grid so that it touches the blue and green markers. *Ask:* "In order to compare points A and B and find their ratio, $\frac{V}{H}$, the red marker should be placed on the horizontal grid line that contains point A and on the vertical grid line that contains point B. Where should the red marker be placed?" Have students slide the red marker horizontally from point A toward point B. The movement will stop when the red marker reaches and is placed on top of the green marker. In this position, the red marker is also vertically in line with point B. At any other location on the grid, the red marker would not be in line with both A and B at the same time.

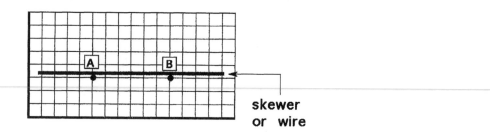

skewer
or wire

Name _____ **Date** _____

WORKSHEET 3–12–1
An Uneven Balance

Build with tiles to solve each inequality given below and complete the sentence with your solution. Show each solution interval with paper strips on the axes mat, then make a sketch of your final graph with a colored pencil on the axes below the sentence.

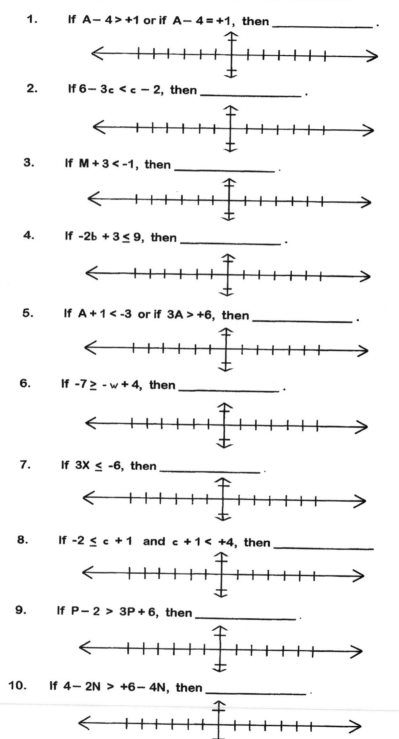

1. If $A - 4 > +1$ or if $A - 4 = +1$, then _____ .

2. If $6 - 3c < c - 2$, then _____ .

3. If $M + 3 < -1$, then _____ .

4. If $-2b + 3 \leq 9$, then _____ .

5. If $A + 1 < -3$ or if $3A > +6$, then _____ .

6. If $-7 \geq -w + 4$, then _____ .

7. If $3X \leq -6$, then _____ .

8. If $-2 \leq c + 1$ and $c + 1 < +4$, then _____

9. If $P - 2 > 3P + 6$, then _____ .

10. If $4 - 2N > +6 - 4N$, then _____ .

10. Assign other inequalities for students to solve by building with tiles on the inequality building mat. (See Worksheet 3–12–1.) At this time, only *final* intervals or *solution* intervals need to be shown with plain or arrowhead paper strips on the axes building mat. For each exercise, the original inequality and the solution inequality should be recorded together as a sentence on each student's own paper, along with a free-hand, but properly labeled *drawing* of the final interval(s) shown on the axes mat. The interval "strip" itself in the drawing should be drawn with a colored pencil. For *compound* inequalities, have students first solve each *separate* inequality with the tiles. Both solution intervals for the same compound inequality should then be shown simultaneously with the strips on the axes mat. In the case of **and** or **between** situations, students must decide what *final* interval on the mat will represent numbers belonging to *both* of the separate solution intervals. Here are suggested exercises that might be assigned:

$M + 3 < -1$	$-7 \geq -w + 4$	$P - 2 > 3P + 6$
$-2b + 3 \leq 9$	$3X \leq -6$	$4 - 2N > +6 - 4N$
$A + 1 < -3$ OR $3A > +6$	$-2 \leq c + 1 < +4$	$+7 \geq G + 1$ AND $-5 \leq G - 4$

Answer Key for WORKSHEET 3–12–1

Solution statements are shown below without their graphs.

1. $A > +5$ or $A = +5$	**6.** $w > +11$ or $w = +11$
2. $+2 < c$	**7.** $X < -2$ or $X = -2$
3. $M < -4$	**8.** $-3 < c$ or $-3 = c$, and $c < +3$
4. $-3 < b$ or $-3 = b$	**9.** $-4 > P$
5. $A < -4$ or $A > +2$	**10.** $N > +1$

Activity 2: PICTURING INEQUALITIES

[Bridging Action]

Materials: Worksheet 3–12–2
Colored pencils
Calculators
Regular pencils
Paper

Management: Partners (50 minutes)

Directions:

1. Give each pair of students a copy of Worksheet 3–12–2, a colored pencil (any bright color; not yellow, black, or brown), and a calculator. In this activity they will draw diagrams on their own papers to solve inequalities, then graph their solution intervals on the axes shown on the worksheet.

2. Write the following inequality on the board: **−m + 2 < −3 − 2m.** Instead of drawing vertical, parallel line segments as used previously with linear equations to separate two

Name _____ **Date** _____

WORKSHEET 3–12–2
Picturing Inequalities

Follow the teacher's directions for graphing solution intervals of inequalities on the axes given below.

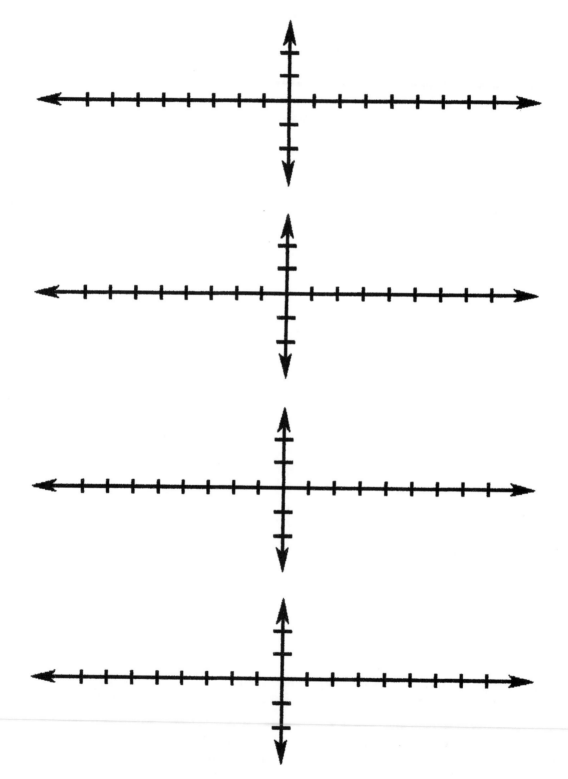

equal expressions, we will now draw a double-V to separate two unequal expressions. As before with equations, all rectangles will serve as variables and small squares will serve as units. A large X drawn in the interior of a shape will indicate its inverse form. Have students draw the following diagram on their own paper.

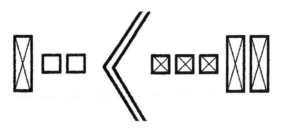

3. Remind students that with inequalities we want to add or remove the variables so that the plain variable is isolated rather than the inverse variable. Since we are **not** dealing with an **equality,** we are not able as the last step to just take *opposites of both sides* in order to find the value of the plain variable that we seek. The add-remove approach to isolating only the *plain* variable avoids the often confusing step of reversing the inequality sign when the inverse variable has been isolated first. Discuss the possible ways that the variable m might be isolated. One way would be to remove or mark out an inverse variable from each side. This leaves one inverse variable on the right side with none on the left side. To remove the inverse variable that remains, a plain variable might be drawn or added to both sides; the 0-pair of variables formed on the right would then have no effect and a plain variable would remain on the left side. Another way would be to add 2 plain variables to both sides; this move would produce two 0-pairs of variables on the right and one 0-pair of variables on the left. One plain variable would then remain on the left side. We will show the diagram for this latter method in the diagram below. Students finally need to isolate this variable by drawing 2 small squares (with X in interior) for 2 negative units on both sides of the inequality; two 0-pairs of units should then be formed on the left.

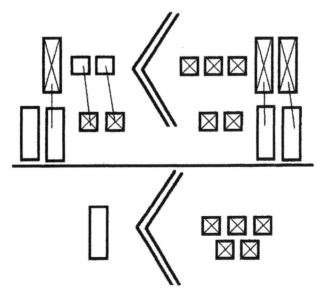

4. Have students record their drawing steps with symbols on their own paper. Recording steps should match the method used in the diagram; the steps recorded below will match the method shown in step 3. Below their final solution step, students should also write the *statements* shown below:

$$-m + 2 \ < \ (-3) - \quad 2m$$
$$-m + 2 \ < \ (-3) + (-2m)$$
$$\underline{+(+2m) +(-2) \quad +(-2) + (+2m)}$$
$$m \qquad < \quad -5$$

Solution: The variable m represents all real numbers less than –5. The point for –5 is the boundary point for the solution interval.

5. On a set of axes on Worksheet 3–12–2, students should now record their solution graphically by marking the boundary point, –5, then coloring an arrow on the horizontal axis pointing left from –5. The horizontal axis should be labeled with the variable letter, m. To emphasize that –5 is **not** one of the numbers in the solution interval, a plain circle (no shaded interior) should be drawn around the axis point at –5.

6. Now write another example on the board: $\frac{2}{3}B - 1 \geq +3$. Students should draw a diagram for this inequality as shown, labeling a short rectangle for each third of the variable (the rectangles should be a little taller than the squares drawn for units). Since the left side may equal +3 in value, as well as be greater than +3, an "equals" sign will be drawn with the "greater than" bar in the diagram.

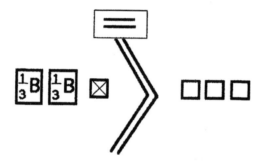

7. Since the fractional parts of the variable are only on the left side and are not inverse forms, we may easily isolate the variable on the left side. A small square should be drawn on both sides of the inequality bar and a 0-pair of units connected on the left side. Following procedures taught in Section 2, have students draw a ring around each third of the variable to form two equal groups; also draw a ring around each two positive units on the right in order to form two equal groups. This separation process indicates that one group on the left (a third of B) is greater than or equal to one group on the right (+2). The **third of B** must be drawn **3 times** on the left to form the whole variable B that is needed. Similarly, the group of +2 must be drawn 3 times on the right in order to keep the actions equivalent. The diagram now reveals the variable B to be greater than or equal to +6.

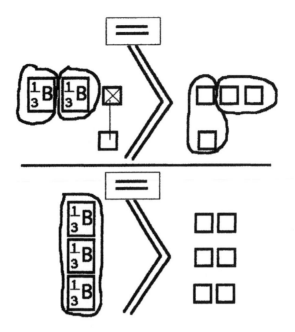

8. Students should now record their steps with symbols and state their conclusion:

$$\tfrac{2}{3}B - 1 \geq +3$$
$$\tfrac{2}{3}B + (-1) \geq +3$$
$$\underline{\phantom{\tfrac{2}{3}B}+(+1) \quad +(+1)}$$
$$\tfrac{2}{3}B \qquad \geq +4$$
$$\tfrac{3}{2}(\tfrac{2}{3}B) \quad \geq \tfrac{3}{2}(+4)$$
$$B \qquad \geq +6$$

Conclusion: The variable B represents all real numbers greater than or equal to +6. The point for +6 is the boundary point for the solution interval.

Note: In the above algebraic notation, the separation of variable parts and the completion of a whole variable have been recorded as one step: multiplication by the reciprocal, $\tfrac{3}{2}$, rather than multiplication first by $\tfrac{1}{2}$ [separation], then by 3 [completion of the whole]. Some students may need to see the two steps recorded separately for a while. Refer to Section 2, Objective 6 for details on this procedure.

9. On another set of axes on Worksheet 3–12–2, students should now record their solution graphically by marking the boundary point, +6, then coloring an arrow on the horizontal axis pointing right from +6. The horizontal axis should be labeled with the variable letter, B. To emphasize that +6 is **also** one of the numbers in the solution interval, a circle should be drawn around the axis point at +6 and its interior shaded.

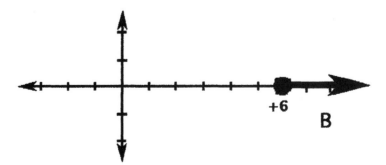

10. Additional exercises need to be assigned for students to practice solving inequalities by drawing diagrams, then recording the symbolic steps used. They should also represent their solution intervals as graphs, using extra copies of Worksheet 3–12–2 if necessary. Original inequalities should be written beside their solution graphs on the worksheet. Suggested exercises will be given below. For a *compound* inequality, such as –3 < 4 – X < +5, have students rewrite it as two *separate* inequalities, e.g., –3 < 4 – X **and** 4 – X < +5, then solve each independently of the other. To graph the two solutions together on the same axes (since they both belong to the original inequality), students must determine what interval(s) of real numbers will satisfy **both** solution inequalities. A single interval may be possible. For example, in the compound inequality given above, the solutions are –1 < X **and** X < +7. Students need numbers that are greater than –1, yet less than +7. Using –1 and +7 as the **boundary points,** students should graph the single solution interval from –1 to +7, excluding the boundary points themselves in this case.

P – 5 > 7 – 3P	–1 – m ≤ 6 + 2m	$\frac{1}{4}$A + 5 < +4
–9 ≥ 2.5d – 1	0.6w + 1.6 < –2.3	–5 ≥ X + $\frac{1}{2}$ OR X > $\frac{1}{2}$X – 1
2 > N + 3 ≥ –4	c + 4 < –2c < –5	0.5B ≥ 0 OR B – 2 < –3

Activity 3: BOUNDARY CHASE

[Application/Exploration]

Materials: Decks of cards (described in step 1)
Calculators
Regular pencils
Paper
Worksheet 3–12–3

Management: Teams of 4 students (30–50 minutes)

Directions:

1. Give each team of students a deck of cards (see Worksheet 3–12–3) and a calculator. Each deck of cards will contain 48 cards, 6 of which will be distractors (3 graphs and 3 solution inequalities). The other 42 cards in the deck will make 14 books of 3 cards per book. Each book consists of an original linear inequality in one variable on one card, the solution inequality on another card, and the graph of the solution on the third card. Cards can be made of small index cards or light tagboard and laminated. Each complete deck should be coded in some way for easy sorting when decks become mixed together. Discuss the meanings of compound inequalities: (a) OR implies that numbers may belong to *either* interval to be considered solutions; and (b) AND implies that numbers must belong to *both* intervals in order to be solutions. Inequalities requiring AND are often presented in a *betweenness* format, such as –3 < X + 1 < +7.

2. To start the game, the deck should be shuffled, then 5 cards dealt to each player. The remaining cards should be placed in a stack face down in the center of the table. At that time, each player may place face up on the table any complete book of 3 cards that may have been dealt in the first hand.

3. After removing any books from their initial cards, the four players will take turns either drawing an unknown card from the hand of the player to their right or drawing a

WORKSHEET 3-12-3
Inequalities/Graphs for Cards by Book

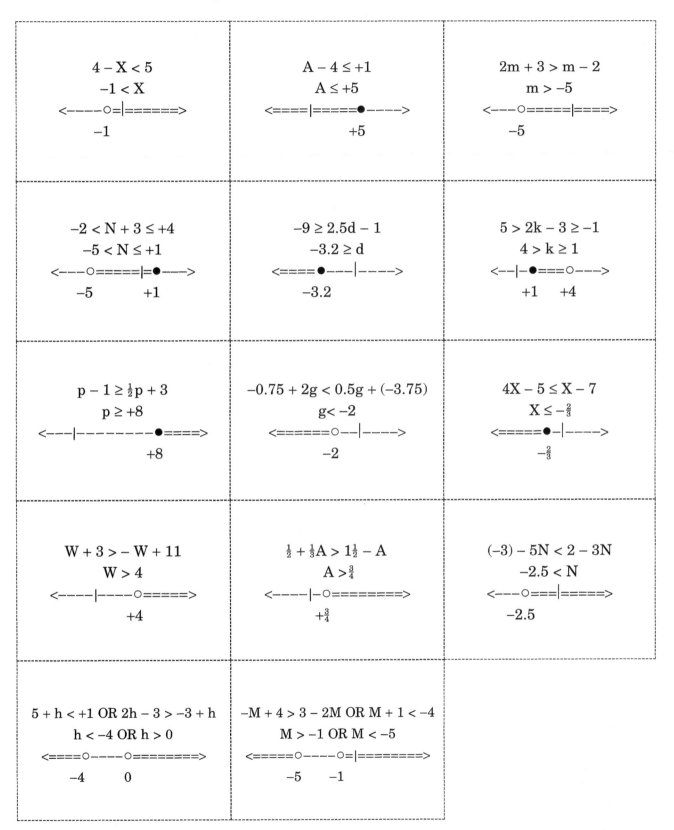

$4 - X < 5$
$-1 < X$
<———○=|======>
-1

$A - 4 \leq +1$
$A \leq +5$
<====|=====●———>
$+5$

$2m + 3 > m - 2$
$m > -5$
<———○=====|====>
-5

$-2 < N + 3 \leq +4$
$-5 < N \leq +1$
<———○=====|=●———>
-5 $+1$

$-9 \geq 2.5d - 1$
$-3.2 \geq d$
<====●———|————>
-3.2

$5 > 2k - 3 \geq -1$
$4 > k \geq 1$
<——|—●===○———>
$+1$ $+4$

$p - 1 \geq \frac{1}{2}p + 3$
$p \geq +8$
<———|————————●====>
$+8$

$-0.75 + 2g < 0.5g + (-3.75)$
$g < -2$
<=====○——|————>
-2

$4X - 5 \leq X - 7$
$X \leq -\frac{2}{3}$
<=====●—|————>
$-\frac{2}{3}$

$W + 3 > -W + 11$
$W > 4$
<————|————○=====>
$+4$

$\frac{1}{2} + \frac{1}{3}A > 1\frac{1}{2} - A$
$A > \frac{3}{4}$
<————|—○========>
$+\frac{3}{4}$

$(-3) - 5N < 2 - 3N$
$-2.5 < N$
<———○===|=====>
-2.5

$5 + h < +1$ OR $2h - 3 > -3 + h$
$h < -4$ OR $h > 0$
<====○————○=======>
-4 0

$-M + 4 > 3 - 2M$ OR $M + 1 < -4$
$M > -1$ OR $M < -5$
<=====○————○=|========>
-5 -1

WORKSHEET 3–12–3 *(cont.)*
For Six Distractor Cards

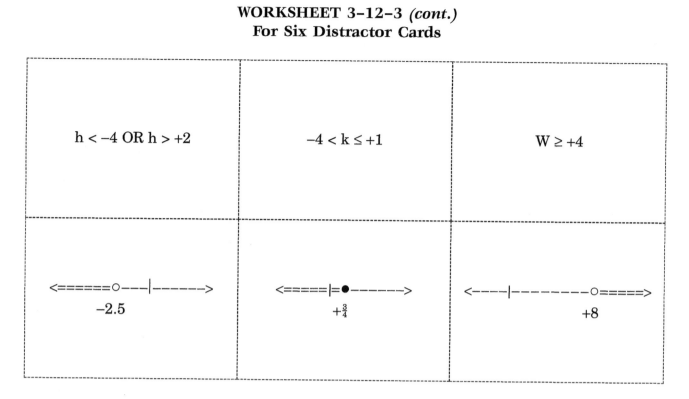

card from the top of the face-down stack in the center of the table. After drawing a new card, a player may lay down the book that the new card has completed, if such occurs, but only one book may be laid down on each turn.

4. Play continues until all cards, except the six distractors, have been drawn and matched in books. The player with the most books will be the winner.

5. Worksheet 3–12–3 gives a possible list of inequalities and graphs for the deck of cards. Each two statements and 1 graph that make a **book** are grouped together. The six distractors are labeled as such and also grouped together. At the end of the game a copy of this list of "books" might be given to each team as an **answer key** by which to check the correctness of any card matches made during the game.

Section 4

QUADRATIC CONCEPTS

OBJECTIVE 1: Develop the concept of exponents (positive, negative, and zero).

Activity 1: POWER SHAPES

[Developing Action]

Materials: Inch grid paper (on white paper)
Colored paper (8.5 in. × 11 in., unlined, bright colors)
Rolls of transparent tape
Scissors
Colored markers (fine point, dark colors)

Management: Teams of 3–4 students each (50 minutes)

Directions:

1. Give each team of students 4 sheets of inch grid paper, 3 sheets of colored paper, a roll of tape, 1 to 2 pairs of scissors, and a colored marker. The three sheets of colored paper should be taped together with their short edges touching to form a longer sheet of paper (approximately 8.5 in. × 33 in.). A baseline should be drawn lengthwise on this new "long" sheet of colored paper and midway between the two long edges of the paper. This baseline will guide students in mounting cut-out paper shapes on the colored paper later during the activity.

2. Ask students to draw, then cut, a 1×2 rectangle from the inch grid paper; that is, using the shortest grid segment as an inch of length, the rectangle will be 1 inch wide and 2 inches long. Its area is 2 sq. inches, which should be recorded in the interior of the shape. This shape should then be taped on the colored paper at the baseline 8 inches from the margin as shown in step 5.

3. A second shape should be drawn by first drawing another 1×2 rectangle on the grid paper, then mentally "sliding" that shape across its longer side to double its size and form a new 2×2 rectangle. The new 2×2 shape should be labeled with its area of 4 sq. inches, then cut out and mounted to the right of the first shape. (A half inch of space should be allowed between each two adjacent shapes.)

4. A third shape should be drawn by drawing another 2×2 shape, then "sliding" it across its "longer" side to double its size and form a new 2×4 shape; this shape should also be labeled (8 sq. in) and cut out. Continuing this process, another 2×4 shape should

367

be drawn, then slid across its longer side to double and form a 4 × 4 shape. Repeat with the 4 × 4 shape to make a 4 × 8 shape. All five cut-out shapes should be arranged and taped on the colored paper in the order and orientation shown in step 5. Each shape should be carefully placed on the baseline. Notice that the *height* of each nonsquare rectangle, when mounted, is always the shorter side or edge; the longer edge lies on the baseline. Hence, a "2 × 4 shape" implies a shape of height 2 and length 4. This differentiation is important to our pattern development for exponents. Have students also record under each shape its product of factors of 2 as indicated in order to reflect the doubling that has occurred while extending the sequence of shapes. Remind students that the first factor on the left in a product is always the *multiplier*, which tells how many or how much of a set to make. The single factor or factor group on the right indicates the set *(multiplicand)*.

5. After each team has properly mounted its shapes, have teams record the **product of 2's** for each shape as a **power of 2** above the shape on the colored paper. For example, above the 4 × 8 shape write **2^5** and above the 1 × 2 shape write **2^1**.

33 inches

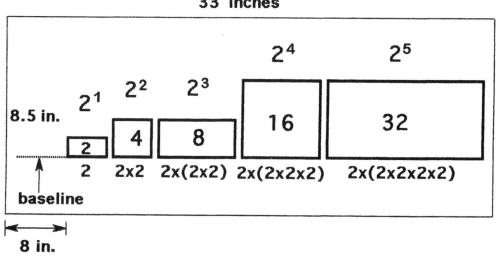

6. Ask students what they notice about the sequence of shapes. Typically, they will notice that the shapes alternate between **nonsquare** rectangles and **square** rectangles. (Do not use "rectangle" versus "square," which would be incorrect; all five shapes are rectangles.) Have them observe how each shape is changed to make the next shape to the right. Encourage the following language to describe the building pattern reflected in the sequence of shapes: "The 1 × 2 *doubles upward* to make the 2 × 2; the 2 × 2 *doubles to its right* to make the 2 × 4; the 2 × 4 *doubles upward* to make the 4 × 4; and the 4 × 4 *doubles to its right* to make the 4 × 8." Ask students to predict how the next shape in the sequence should be formed and what its size, product, and power of 2 will be (the 4 × 8 will double upward to make a new shape that is 8 inches tall and 8 inches wide; the product will be $2 \times (2 \times 2 \times 2 \times 2 \times 2)$ and the power will be 2^6).

7. *Ask:* "What if we begin with the largest shape at the end of the sequence and work backward to describe each new shape to the left? How can we change each shape to form the next shape to the left?" Encourage students to reverse the language used earlier in step 6: "The 4 × 8 is *halved to its left* to make the 4 × 4; the 4 × 4 is *halved downward* to make the 2 × 4; the 2 × 4 is *halved to its left* to make the 2 × 2; and the 2 × 2 is *halved downward* to make the 1 × 2." *Halved to its left (or downward)* indicates that the shape is cut into two equal parts (at least mentally) and only the left half (or lower half) is kept as the new shape.

8. *Ask:* "If we continue this reversal of our building pattern, what will the next shape to the left of the 1×2 shape look like? What will we do mentally to the 1×2 shape to find this new shape?" Since the 1×2 shape is nonsquare, it must be *halved to its left,* thus forming a 1×1 shape. Have students cut out a 1×1 rectangle and tape it onto their colored paper to the left of their 1×2 rectangle. The area of 1 sq. inch should be recorded on the paper square. Since we are focusing on 2's as factors to show a pattern—either in the numerator or in the denominator—and we are halving each shape now to get the next shape to the left, have students write the product $\frac{1}{2} \times 2$ below the new shape. Do not discuss the exponent format at this time.

9. Continuing this process, students should cut out and mount three more shapes. All shapes should be placed carefully on the baseline and in the correct orientation as shown below. The areas in order found will be $\frac{1}{2}$ sq. in., $\frac{1}{4}$ sq. in., and $\frac{1}{8}$ sq. in. The paper shapes may be too small to record these areas; if so, just discuss what the amounts are. Below each shape write the product, using **only** factors of 2 or $\frac{1}{2}$, that shows how the shape was formed from the previous shape on the right: (in order found) $\frac{1}{2}$, $\frac{1}{2} \times \frac{1}{2}$, and $\frac{1}{2} \times (\frac{1}{2} \times \frac{1}{2})$.

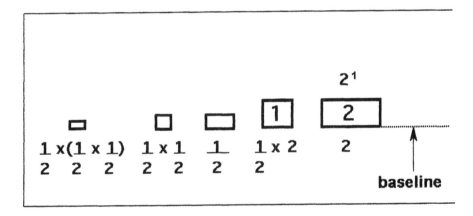

10. Now ask students to look at the powers of 2 on the original five shapes, beginning at the right. The exponents 5, 4, 3, 2, and 1 are decreasing to the left. *Ask:* "If this number pattern continues across our new shapes, what should we expect the other exponents to be?" *(the next four exponents should be 0, –1, –2, and –3)* Have students write the appropriate power of 2 above each of the four new shapes. At this stage, these powers come strictly from the decreasing integer pattern seen in the first five powers recorded, not from the products found.

11. After the new powers have been recorded on the colored sheet, **ask:** "How did you decide what exponent to use for each of the original five shapes?" *(counted the factors of 2 in the product each time)* "If we then look at the four new shapes, how does each new exponent we expect compare to the 2's seen in its shape's product?" Hopefully for each new negative exponent, students will notice that the **negative** integer shows how many 2's are used in the product **in denominator positions.** For the zero exponent, students should notice that there is **one 2 in a numerator position** and **one 2 in a denominator position.** Since the positions of these 2's counter or "neutralize" each other, their overall exponential effect for the product is represented by **0.** At this time do not emphasize the idea that any real number to the 0 power is equivalent to 1.

12. Have students prepare a 3-column table for the different amounts or labels assigned to each shape in the sequence. Use the headings: *Product, Power, and Shape Area.* Record the amounts in decreasing order. The final table will appear as follows:

Product	Power	Shape Area
$2 \times (2 \times 2 \times 2 \times 2)$	2^5	32
$2 \times (2 \times 2 \times 2)$	2^4	16
$2 \times (2 \times 2)$	2^3	8
2×2	2^2	4
2	2^1	2
$\frac{1}{2} \times 2$	2^0	1
$\frac{1}{2}$	2^{-1}	$\frac{1}{2}$
$\frac{1}{2} \times \frac{1}{2}$	2^{-2}	$\frac{1}{4}$
$\frac{1}{2} \times (\frac{1}{2} \times \frac{1}{2})$	2^{-3}	$\frac{1}{8}$

Activity 2: TEST 'N CHECK

[Bridging Action]

Materials: Half-inch grid paper (on white paper)
Colored markers (bright colors, fine points)
Calculators
Regular paper
Regular pencils

Management: Partners (50 minutes)

Directions:

1. Give each pair of students 2 to 3 sheets of half-inch grid paper, a colored marker, and a calculator. This activity is an extension of Activity 1 to other bases, but involves the same patterns found in the sequence of shapes and in the exponents for that activity.

2. Have students prepare a 3-column table like the one used in Activity 1. Headings should be *Product, Power,* and *Value* (*Shape Area* was used earlier instead of *Value*). In decreasing order, the powers of 3 should now be written in the *Power* column: 3^4, 3^3, . . . , 3^{-2}, and 3^{-3}. Since we are working with 3 as the base, we will be tripling or taking a third of a shape.

3. Ask students to make a sequence of shapes by first drawing along the longer side of the grid sheet (longer side turned horizontally to student), then drawing elsewhere on the grid when more space is needed. These shapes will not be cut out this time, so the product and value of each shape will be recorded on the table as soon as the shape is drawn on the grid paper. At first a 1×3 shape should be drawn with the colored marker (the 3-unit edge should be along the longer edge of the grid paper); for the table entries, the product 3 and the value 3 should be recorded in their columns in the same row as the power 3^1.

4. Remind students of the method of "sliding upward across the longer side" or "sliding to the right" that was used with the base 2 earlier. We will use the same approach with the **base 3,** but we must **triple** instead of double to make the next shape. Thus, on the grid paper to the right of the 1×3 drawing, another 1×3 rectangle should be lightly outlined, then mentally "slid upward" to triple itself and form a 3×3 shape; the new 3×3 shape should be drawn with the colored marker. The product 3×3 and the value 9 should be recorded in the table on the row with the power 3^2.

5. Another 3×3 shape should now be lightly outlined to the right of the first 3×3 shape on the grid paper, then mentally tripled by "sliding to the right" to form a new shape, a 3×9 rectangle. This new shape should be drawn with the colored marker and its product $3 \times (3 \times 3)$ and value 27 recorded in the table in line with the power 3^3.

6. Students should continue the tripling process by "sliding" a 3×9 shape "upward" to draw a 9×9 rectangle. This new shape will probably need to be drawn on the grid paper above the original 1×3 shape. The product will be $3 \times (3 \times 3 \times 3)$ and the value will be 81 for the power 3^4. This is as high as we will go unless your students want to try drawing a shape for the product $3 \times (3 \times 3 \times 3 \times 3)$, which will be a 9×27 rectangle!

7. Now we want to reverse our tripling-sliding procedure, beginning with the largest shape drawn, the 9×9 rectangle in this case. Remind students that they now want a **third** of this rectangle to make the next smaller shape, the 3×9 shape. This is done by mentally cutting across the 9×9 shape, then **sliding** these thirds **downward** to fit into the lower 3×9 shape; that is, we will keep only the lower third of the 9×9 shape. Continuing, the 3×9 shape is mentally cut into thirds and the middle and right thirds are **slid left** to fit into the left third, which is a 3×3 shape. The horizontal thirds of the 3×3 shape will slide downward to fit into the lower 1×3 rectangle. Here is a sketch to show the process.

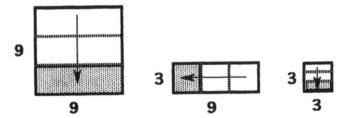

8. Now guide students to discover additional shapes with this reversal process. Have them look at the 1×3 shape on their grid paper, then lightly with a pencil subdivide it into thirds (3 1×1 parts) and mentally slide the middle and right thirds to the left to yield a 1×1 shape. A new 1×1 shape should now be drawn elsewhere on the grid paper (or on another sheet of grid paper if necessary) with a colored marker. The product for this new shape will be $\frac{1}{3} \times 3$ and the value will be 1; the corresponding power in the table will be 3^0. Since the products now involve fractions, have students record both the common fraction and its equivalent decimal fraction for each new value in the table. Use calculators to convert the common fractions to decimal fractions, rounding to the nearest thousandth in each case. The last four shapes drawn will be 1×1, $\frac{1}{3} \times 1$, $\frac{1}{3} \times \frac{1}{3}$, and $\frac{1}{3} \times (\frac{1}{3} \times \frac{1}{3})$. The following illustration shows the forming of these last four shapes, as well as their products and values for the table.

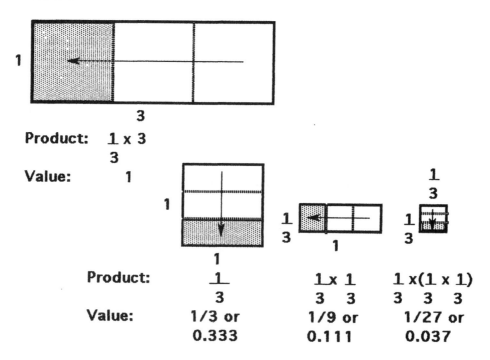

9. After the table is complete, review the idea that factors of 3 in the **numerator** are in an **opposite position** to factors of 3 in the **denominator**. Thus, it is natural to use **opposite signs** on the exponents to represent these opposite positions. Discuss the product $\frac{1}{3} \times 3$, recorded to show the process used for making the 1×1 shape; as found with the base 2 in Activity 1, a factor of 3 in the numerator matches to a factor of 3 in the denominator. Since these two positions are opposites of each other, the exponent used must be 0 to show that the numerator and denominator factors balance or neutralize each other. We will use this same comparison in Objective 2 when we develop some of the *properties* of exponents.

10. At this time we want to guide students to *generalize* about the powers of *any real number*. This is readiness for later work with *variables*. Using the letter N for any real number, help students apply the "sliding" process to N with freehand diagrams. Since we do not know the value of N, we cannot double, triple, or find any other *specific* multiple of a given shape; however, we do know that *even* exponents identify square rectangles and *odd* exponents identify nonsquare rectangles. So when a square should be slid to the right to make a larger nonsquare rectangle, we will simply draw a rectangle whose width equals the side length of the square, but whose length is *obviously* greater (at least visually; no measuring is actually done) than the side length of the square. If a nonsquare rectangle must be slid upward to make a square, then the new square will have a side length equal to the length of the nonsquare rectangle being used. Similarly, if a nonsquare rectangle must be subdivided into an N-amount of equal parts that are slid to the left to fit on the leftmost part, which becomes the next smaller shape, this new shape will be drawn as a square whose side length equals the width of the nonsquare rectangle being used. If a square rectangle must be subdivided and the parts are slid down to the bottom part, this bottom part is drawn as a nonsquare rectangle whose length equals the side length of the square being used and whose width is *obviously* less than the side length of the square. The illustrations below show how the general diagrams are made for some real number N. The products and powers are also shown, but no values can be shown since we do not know what N equals. Allow students time to practice making their own diagrams and labeling them. Their first shape should always be a nonsquare rectangle representing the $1 \times N$ shape. The new sequence of shapes should be drawn in the same order followed for base 2 and for base 3. Carefully connect the sliding process and patterns being used for N to those same processes and patterns used for base 2 and base 3.

(drawn freehand)

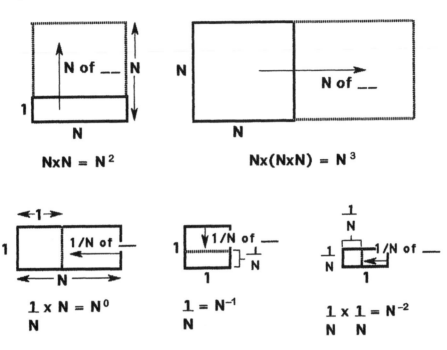

Activity 3: EXPONENT OPPONENTS

[Application/Exploration]

Materials: Worksheet 4–1–1 (spinner pattern)
Dice
Regular paper
Regular pencils
Calculators with exponent/power key
Large paper clips (for spinner needles)

Management: Teams of 4 students (30 minutes)

Directions:

1. Give each team 2 dice, a large paper clip (spinner needle), a calculator, and one copy of Worksheet 4–1–1 (spinner for exponent). Each team should draw a 3-column table on a blank sheet of paper, using the headings: *Power, Computed Value,* and *Calculator Value.* One pair of students on each team will compete against the other pair on the same team. On a turn, one pair will use the spinner and do the computation while the other pair confirms the decimal answer with the calculator; the pairs will exchange roles on the next

Spinner for Exponents

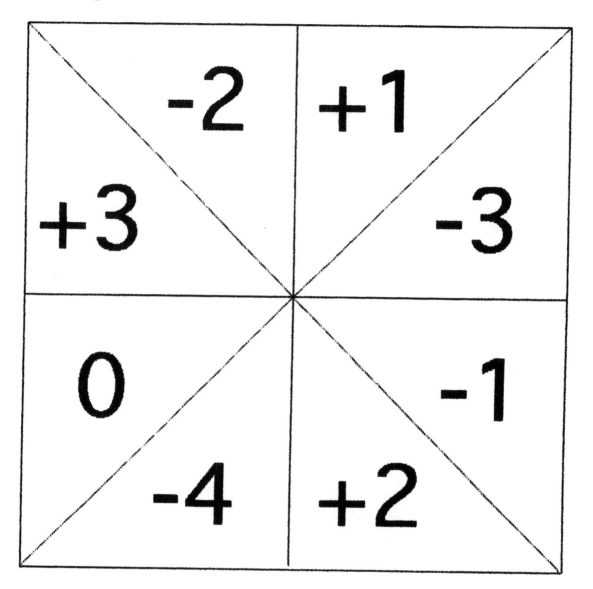

turn. Both pairs will use the calculator for their respective roles. Be sure that students know how to use the exponent or power key (**y^x**) correctly for their particular calculator model.

2. As an example of play, on a turn, Pair A rolls the 2 dice and takes their **sum,** which is **8;** 8 becomes the new base. Pair A then spins the paper clip on the spinner (a pencil point holds the paper clip at the center point of the spinner) and gets the exponent **–2.** Pair A records **8^{-2}** in the first row of the *Power* column of the table. While Pair B watches, Pair A writes the following in the *Computed Value* column: $\frac{1}{8} \times \frac{1}{8} = \frac{1}{64} = 0.016$ (rounded to nearest thousandth). (Alternative recording students might use: $\frac{1}{8} \times \frac{1}{8} = 0.125 \times 0.125 = 0.016$ rounded.) Pair A may only use the **X** and ÷ keys on the calculator, not the exponent or power key (**y^x**), to find their computed value. Finally, Pair B uses the exponent/power key on the calculator to directly find the decimal value of 8^{-2}, which rounds to 0.016 also. Pair B records their 0.016 in the *Calculator Value* column of the table. Since Pair A's value has been confirmed by Pair B's value, Pair A earns 1 point. To show this, Pair A might write their initials in the right margin of row one of the table. If Pair A's value is not confirmed, an X might be recorded in the right margin instead. The turn now passes to Pair B to roll the dice and spin the spinner.

3. Play may continue until time is called. If the teacher prefers, at the end teams might turn in their completed tables for further assessment by the teacher.

OBJECTIVE 2: **Develop the properties of exponents: $(cb)^n = c^n b^n$ and $(c^n)^m = c^{nm}$, where b and c are real numbers and n and m are integers.**

Activity 1: BUILD-R-FOLD

[Developing Action]

Materials: Positive unit tiles
Unlined paper (8.5 in. × 11 in., white)
Colored markers or pencils
Worksheet 4–2–1 (record sheet for Activity 1 and Activity 2)
Regular pencils and paper

Management: Partners (50 minutes)

Directions:

1. The first property stated in the objective above will be developed in Activity 1 and Activity 2. The second property, along with extensions of the definition of an exponent and extensions of the first property, will be developed in Activity 3. Give each pair of students 40 positive unit tiles, 2 sheets of unlined paper, 4 colored markers or pencils (4 different colors), and 2 copies of Worksheet 4–2–1 (one per student). In this activity students will build arrays of unit tiles to model the effects of positive exponents and will fold paper to model the effects of negative exponents. It is assumed that they have completed Objective 1 and have developed definitions for positive, negative, and zero exponents. Students will record number sentences or equations on their own papers to show their steps, but will record the results of their steps on Worksheet 4–2–1.

2. Remind students that the integral exponent indicates how many times the base number occurs as a factor, whether in the numerator (positive exponents) or in the denominator (negative exponents). The zero exponent indicates that the base number appears as a factor the same number of times in the numerator as in the denominator; that is, the two groups of factors neutralize each other, producing a final value or area of 1 square unit. In this activity we will model positive exponents first, beginning with the simple case of 1. The exponent 0 will also be modeled initially so that at the end of the activity we will have covered all types of integral exponents and thus be able to look for a generalization.

3. Write the expressions (a) $(2 \times 5)^1 = ?$ and (b) $2^1 \times 5^1 = ?$ on the chalkboard (the expressions are already listed on Worksheet 4–2–1 for later use).

Expression (a): The exponent in expression (a) shows one factor of the *group* (2×5) in the numerator position, so have students use their positive unit tiles to build 2 rows of 5 unit tiles each, which is a rectangular array with an area of 10 unit tiles total. Students should then copy on their own notebook paper: (a) $(2 \times 5)^1 = (2 \times 5) = 10$ unit tiles. Parentheses are used with the second form of (2×5) to preserve the sense of the original group indicated by the exponent.

Name _____   **Date** _____

WORKSHEET 4–2–1
Build-R-Fold

Exponent Form to Build/Draw	*Area of Shape Built/Drawn*
$(2 \times 5)^1$	
$2^1 \times 5^1$	
$(3 \times 4)^0$	
$3^0 \times 4^0$	
$(3 \times 2)^2$	
$3^2 \times 2^2$	
$(2 \times 3)^{-2}$	
$2^{-2} \times 3^{-2}$	
$(3 \times 5)^2$	
$3^2 \times 5^2$	
$(5 \times 2)^{-1}$	
$5^{-1} \times 2^{-1}$	
$(3 \times 4)^{-2}$	
$3^{-2} \times 4^{-2}$	

After you've completed Activity 2: When two areas are equal, what do you notice about the exponents and factors or bases on the matching expressions in the left column? Describe the pattern you notice.

Expression (b): In expression (b), the exponents imply one factor of 2 and one factor of 5 in a product, both in the numerator position. So again an array of unit tiles may be built to show the product 2×5 and its area of 10 unit tiles. Students will then record on their own papers: (b) $2^1 \times 5^1 = 2 \times 5 = 10$ unit tiles.

4. Now write the expressions (a) $(3 \times 4)^0 = ?$ and (b) $3^0 \times 4^0 = ?$ on the chalkboard. Following the development used previously in Objective 1 to show a 0 exponent, rewrite each expression to show the base group (or individual base number) as one factor in the numerator position and one factor in the denominator position. Students should write the following on their own papers: (a) $(3 \times 4)^0 = \frac{1}{(3 \times 4)} \times (3 \times 4)$ and (b) $3^0 \times 4^0 = (\frac{1}{3} \times 3) \times (\frac{1}{4} \times 4)$.

Expression (a): Simplifying expression (a) by applying the multiplication facts within each group, we have $\frac{1}{12} \times 12$. To model this (assuming that students are **not** comfortable with fraction multiplication), have students place 12 unit tiles in a group. To take $\frac{1}{12}$ of that group means to separate the group into 12 individual parts, then keep one of the parts. In this case, each part contains only one unit tile. Hence, expression (a) yields an area of 1 unit tile. Students should extend the equation begun for expression (a) on their own papers with the following: $\frac{1}{12} \times 12 = 1$ unit tile.

Expression (b): Now guide students in analyzing expression (b). Notice that the first *group*, $(\frac{1}{3} \times 3)$, serves as the multiplier and the second *group*, $(\frac{1}{4} \times 4)$, serves as the multiplicand or set to use. Hence, the set should first be shown as 4 positive unit tiles. Students should then separate the 4 unit tiles into four equal parts and remove three of the parts, leaving one part or 1 unit tile as the new set. The multiplier group indicates that we will first build 3 copies of our set (now 1 unit tile), but finally we will keep only one of the 3 copies. Students should bring in extra unit tiles to make a new set of 3 unit tiles total. This new set is then separated into three equal parts and two of these parts removed, leaving one part or 1 unit tile again. Have students now record 1 unit tile as the answer to the equation they started on their own papers for expression (b). (**Note:** This is a simple procedure, but students need to work through it in preparation for later expressions that use only fractions as factors.) Review the steps that were actually followed in defining expression (b): starting with the factor 4 on the right as the set, the factor $\frac{1}{4}$ was applied as multiplier to the 4 to make a new set of 1; the factor 3 was then used as multiplier of the set of 1, making a new set of 3; finally, $\frac{1}{3}$ served as multiplier to the set of 3, leaving the final set of 1 unit tile. In summary, for expressions in the form of (b), we may simply begin with the last factor as the original set, then apply each remaining factor in order from right to left as a multiplier of the most recent set found. This is an example of the associative property of multiplication in action. We will apply this procedure to future expressions involving fractions.

5. The previous sets of expressions represent the simpler cases and have introduced students to some general procedures for interpreting factors in products. Now write the expressions (a) $(3 \times 2)^2 = ?$ and (b) $3^2 \times 2^2 = ?$ on the chalkboard.

Expression (a): In expression (a), the exponent 2 implies that the factor group (3×2) is used twice; students should write on their own papers the following: $(3 \times 2)^2 = (3 \times 2) \times (3 \times 2) = 6 \times 6 = 36$ unit tiles. By simplifying the expression numerically, we have assumed an understanding of the meaning of multiplication of whole numbers. Students would only need to build 6 rows of 6 unit tiles each to model their product, 6×6. To reinforce the final procedure used in step 4, however, have students build according to the meaning of the groups in $(3 \times 2) \times (3 \times 2)$ in order to confirm their answer of 36 unit tiles. In other words, starting with the factor 2 at the far right of the product as the original set, students should build 3 rows of 2 unit tiles each (6 tiles total) to show the new set. Applying the group factor (3×2) on the left of the product, they should now show 2 copies of the 6 tiles; last, these 2 copies should be shown 3 times. A possible arrangement to show this procedure is given in the illustration below. Notice that the total is 36 unit tiles.

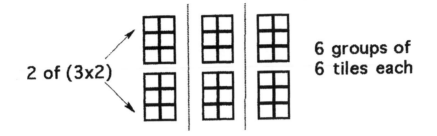

**6 groups of
6 tiles each**

2 of (3x2)

Expression (b): Have students write the following simplification on their own papers: $3^2 \times 2^2 = (3 \times 3) \times (2 \times 2) = 9 \times 4 = 36$ unit tiles. Applying the procedure from step 4 in order to model their numerical result, have students start with 2 unit tiles (from the last factor of 2 in the expression) as their initial set. For (2×2), they should build 2 rows of 2 unit tiles each. The right-most factor of 3 in the multiplier group 3×3 tells us to build 3 copies of the 2×2 group of tiles; the left factor of 3 then requires those 3 copies to be shown 3 times. The total tiles will be 36. Here is a possible arrangement to represent expression (b):

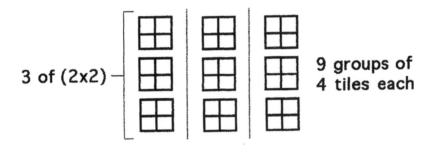

3 of (2x2)

**9 groups of
4 tiles each**

6. Now write the following expressions on the chalkboard: (a) $(2 \times 3)^{-2} = ?$ and (b) $2^{-2} \times 3^{-2} = ?$ These expressions involve fractions as factors, so will be modeled through paper-folding. Students will need the two sheets of unlined paper and four colored markers or pencils at this time.

Expression (a): Have students define the expression by writing the following on their own papers: $(2 \times 3)^{-2} = \frac{1}{(2 \times 3)} \times \frac{1}{(2 \times 3)} = \frac{1}{6} \times \frac{1}{6}$ (applying multiplication facts directly since within a factor group). Based on the procedure developed for negative integral exponents in Objective 1 earlier, each factor group is the denominator of a distinct fraction; hence, we have two fractions as factors. Considering one sheet of paper as the whole, ask students to fold the paper accordion-style along its length into 6 equal parts (see example below), then *leave the paper folded* and outline the section showing on top with one color of pencil or marker. This outlined section represents 1 of 6 parts, or $\frac{1}{6}$ of the whole paper, and serves as the initial set in the product, $\frac{1}{6} \times \frac{1}{6}$ (i.e., the right-most factor $\frac{1}{6}$ indicates the set). The left factor or multiplier, $\frac{1}{6}$, requires this new set, the colored section, to be folded accordion-style along its length into 6 equal parts where the interior of 1 of these 6 parts is completely shaded in a second color. Even though the folded paper is thick, this second folding is still possible; the creases will not be very sharp, but will be visible. After students have completed this second round of folding, **ask:** "How can we describe this final section that we have colored with respect to the whole sheet of paper?" At this point students need to unfold the paper to see the creases formed by their two stages of folding. The small section colored last will be one of 36 equal parts covering the whole sheet of paper. Thus, students should recognize that this section is "$\frac{1}{36}$ of the whole paper" and record this on their own papers as the answer to expression (a).

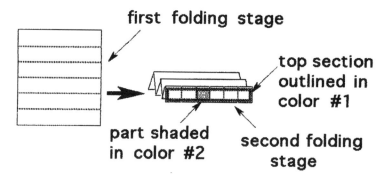

Expression (b): Students should now write the following to define expression (b): $2^{-2} \times 3^{-2} = (\frac{1}{2} \times \frac{1}{2}) \times (\frac{1}{3} \times \frac{1}{3})$. Since we are only assuming mastery of the multiplication facts for whole numbers in this activity, we must model this product that involves only fractions. As we did in step 4, begin with the right-most factor, $\frac{1}{3}$, as the initial set. Have students fold another sheet of unlined paper (accordion-style along its length) into 3 equal parts. Leaving the paper folded, they should outline the top section with a colored pencil or marker (color #1) to show this first set. The other factors should then be applied from right to left as multiplier of each new set formed. To begin, the top section in color #1 should be folded along its length into 3 equal parts, then 1 of these 3 parts outlined in color #2. Leaving the new part exposed as a top section, students should apply the right factor of $\frac{1}{2}$ by folding this new top section along its length into 2 equal parts, then outlining 1 of the 2 parts in color #3. Continuing to leave the paper in its most recent folded form, the left factor of $\frac{1}{2}$ is finally applied to the color #3 section; 2 equal parts are formed and 1 of the 2 parts is shaded in color #4. Have students unfold their sheet of paper and **ask:** "How can we describe your final set, the completely shaded section, with respect to the whole sheet of paper?" Students should count all the small sections now visible in the paper to get a total of 36 sections; the shaded section represents $\frac{1}{36}$ of the whole paper. Have them record on their own papers "$\frac{1}{36}$ of the whole paper" as the answer for expression (b). Also have them notice that if fraction multiplication had been applied at the beginning, the numerical steps would have yielded the same result: $\frac{1}{4} \times \frac{1}{9} = \frac{1}{36}$. Many students have learned fraction multiplication by rote; therefore, they need the above folding experiences to confirm their memorized rules. **Note:** For the above expressions, all folding was done accordion-style along the length of the section being subdivided. This was to ease the difficulty of folding several layers of paper. Certainly, the folds could have been made in other ways as long as equal parts were produced.

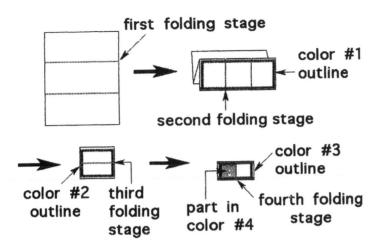

7. To complete Activity 1, have students record their corresponding answers (the areas found in unit tiles or as portions of a whole sheet of paper) to the expressions in the table of Worksheet 4–2–1. Do not make any observations about possible equivalent forms at this time. That will be done at the end of Activity 2. Accept, but do not discuss, whatever responses students might offer at this time.

Answer Key to WORKSHEET 4–2–1

$(2 \times 5)^1 = 10$ unit tiles

$2^1 \times 5^1 = 10$ unit tiles

$(3 \times 4)^0 = 1$ unit tile

$3^0 \times 4^0 = 1$ unit tile

$(3 \times 2)^2 = 36$ unit tiles

$3^2 \times 2^2 = 36$ unit tiles

$(2 \times 3)^{-2} = \frac{1}{36}$ of whole paper

$2^{-2} \times 3^{-2} = \frac{1}{36}$ of whole paper

$(3 \times 5)^2 = 225$ square units

$3^2 \times 5^2 = 225$ square units

$(5 \times 2)^{-1} = \frac{1}{10}$ of small whole rectangle

$5^{-1} \times 2^{-1} = \frac{1}{10}$ of small whole rectangle

$(3 \times 4)^{-2} = \frac{1}{144}$ of large whole rectangle

$3^{-2} \times 4^{-2} = \frac{1}{144}$ of large whole rectangle

Activity 2: *GRIDDING FOR EXPONENTS*

[Bridging Action]

Materials: Millimeter grid paper
Colored pencils or markers (fine points)
Worksheet 4–2–1 from Activity 1
Answer Key for Worksheet 4–2–1
Regular pencils

Management: Partners (50 minutes)

Directions:

1. Give each pair of students 3 sheets of millimeter grid paper and 4 colored pencils (4 different colors). They should already have Worksheet 4–2–1 from Activity 1. We will continue to assume that students are comfortable with models of multiplication facts (whole numbers), but are not familiar with models of products of fractions.

2. Write the following on the board: $(3 \times 5)^2 = (3 \times 5)(3 \times 5) = 15 \times 15 = 225$. Have students draw in the upper left section of a sheet of millimeter grid paper a rectangle that is 15 mm by 15 mm in size. The shortest line segment on the grid (1 mm) will represent 1 *unit* of length. **Ask:** "What is the area of the rectangle in square units?" (*225 sq. units;* some students may not realize that the computed product written on the board is also the area of the drawn rectangle and may start to count the individual square units in the interior of the rectangle; this may indicate that their understanding of area is not fully developed) Students should record the expression $(3 \times 5)^2$ in the left column of Worksheet 4–2–1 and record the area **225 square units** on the same row in the second column.

3. Now write on the board: $3^2 \times 5^2 = (3 \times 3)(5 \times 5) = 9 \times 25 = 225$. In the upper right section of the first sheet of grid paper, have students draw another rectangle that is 9 mm by 25 mm in size. **Ask:** "What is the area in square units for this rectangle?" (*225 sq. units*) Students should now record the expression $3^2 \times 5^2$ in the left column of the worksheet and record the area **225 square units** on the same row in the second column.

4. Negative exponents will now be explored. In the lower section of the first sheet of grid paper have students draw two rectangles that are 20 mm by 20 mm in size. Write the following on the board: $(5 \times 2)^{-1} = \frac{1}{5 \times 2} = \frac{1}{10}$ **of the small, whole rectangle.** (Here we have only simplified the product 5×2 as 10; fraction multiplication has not been used.) Remind students that the negative exponent simply means to place the *base* (5×2) in an opposite location, that is, in the denominator instead of the numerator. Discuss the idea that $\frac{1}{10}$ of a whole means to find 1 of 10 equal parts of whatever serves as the whole or unit. Using the first small rectangle as the **whole** or **unit,** students should use the grid markings to help them subdivide the rectangle's interior into 10 equal parts (there are several ways to do this), then shade one of the parts with a colored pencil. **Ask:** "How much of the small, whole rectangle is represented by the shaded part?" (*$\frac{1}{10}$ of the small, whole rectangle*) Have students record the expression $(5 \times 2)^{-1}$ in the first column of Worksheet 4–2–1 and record $\frac{1}{10}$ **of small, whole rectangle** on the same row in the second column.

5. On the board, write the expression:

$$5^{-1} \times 2^{-1} = \tfrac{1}{5} \times \tfrac{1}{2} \text{ of the small, whole rectangle}$$

Now we must give meaning to the product of the two fractions. Using the approach from Activity 1, the product should be read as "one-fifth of one-half of the whole rectangle." Thus, we start with the second factor, $\frac{1}{2}$. Ask students to find $\frac{1}{2}$ of the second small rectangle (the whole) they have drawn on the first grid sheet. They should subdivide the rectangle into 2 equal parts, then only *outline* one of the parts with a colored pencil (color #1). We now need $\frac{1}{5}$ of this *outlined* section. (**Note:** You need only $\frac{1}{5}$ of the section at this stage, not $\frac{1}{5}$ of the whole rectangle.) Students should use the grid markings to subdivide this section into 5 equal parts, then shade the interior of one of these parts with color #2 (we shade instead of outline, since the left factor in the original product is finally being applied). **Ask:** "How can we decide how much of the small, whole rectangle is represented by this shaded section?" Hopefully students will realize that they need to extend their subdivision markings to cover the entire interior of the rectangle. Ten parts total are then formed and only one is shaded; hence, the shaded section is $\frac{1}{10}$ of the whole rectangle.

Students should record the expression $5^{-1} \times 2^{-1}$ in the left column of their worksheet and $\frac{1}{10}$ **of small, whole rectangle** in the right column.

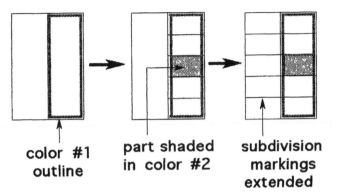

color #1   part shaded   subdivision
outline   in color #2   markings
                                       extended

6. For more examples with negative exponents, have students draw a rectangle that is 144 mm by 144 mm in size on each of the other two sheets of millimeter grid paper. This rectangle will represent the **whole** or **unit** for the next two expressions. Write the following on the board:

$$(3 \times 4)^{-2} = \frac{1}{3 \times 4} \times \frac{1}{3 \times 4} = \frac{1}{12} \times \frac{1}{12} \text{ of the large, whole rectangle}$$

Again, the product 3×4 has just been simplified; no fraction multiplication has been performed yet. Read the last product as "one-twelfth of one-twelfth of the large, whole rectangle." Have students subdivide the large rectangle drawn on the second sheet of grid paper into 12 equal parts and outline one of the parts with a colored pencil (color #1). We then need $\frac{1}{12}$ of this *outlined* section (not $\frac{1}{12}$ of the whole rectangle again). Students should subdivide this outlined section into 12 equal parts and shade (the left fraction factor is being applied here) the interior of 1 of these parts in color #2. These last 12 subdivision markings must finally be extended across the whole rectangle, forming 144 total parts for the rectangle. Only 1 of the 144 equal parts is shaded. Thus, the expression $(3 \times 4)^{-2}$ should be recorded in the left column of the worksheet and $\frac{1}{144}$ **of large, whole rectangle** should be recorded in the right column.

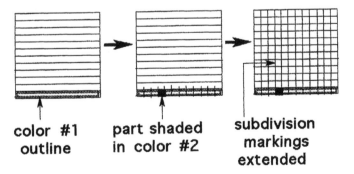

color #1   part shaded   subdivision
outline   in color #2   markings
                                       extended

7. Now write the following on the board:

$$3^{-2} \times 4^{-2} = (\tfrac{1}{3} \times \tfrac{1}{3})(\tfrac{1}{4} \times \tfrac{1}{4}) \text{ of the large, whole rectangle}$$

Students should use the large rectangle on the third grid sheet as their **whole** or **unit.** There are four factors in the product this time. As we did in Activity 1, we will begin by applying the right-most factor to the whole rectangle in order to find our new set. Then we will apply the next factor to the left to this new set found, producing another new set. This process will continue until we apply the left-most factor in the original product. Beginning with the right-most factor $\frac{1}{4}$, students should subdivide the whole rectangle into 4 equal parts and *outline* one of them with color #1. Then $\frac{1}{4}$ of this outlined section (color #1) is needed, so this section is subdivided into 4 equal parts and one part outlined with color #2. Continuing, $\frac{1}{3}$ of the color #2 section is needed, so that section is subdivided into 3 equal parts and one of the new parts is outlined with color #3. Last, the left-most factor $\frac{1}{3}$ is applied to find and *shade* in color #4 one of 3 equal parts of the color #3 section. As done earlier, ***ask:*** "How much of the large, whole rectangle does our shaded part represent?" Students must extend all their subdivision markings, as well as add more, to cover the whole rectangle, thus forming 144 equal parts total for the rectangle. Therefore, 1 of 144 parts is shaded. The illustration below shows one of several ways the rectangle might be subdivided according to the order of the fractions in the product. Students should now record the expression $3^{-2} \times 4^{-2}$ in the left column of their worksheet and write $\frac{1}{144}$ **of the large, whole rectangle** in the right column.

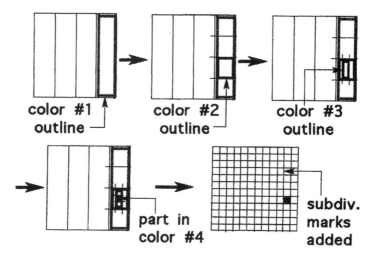

color #1 outline   color #2 outline   color #3 outline

part in color #4   subdiv. marks added

8. At this stage, students should have 14 rows completed on Worksheet 4–2–1, 8 rows from Activity 1 and 6 rows from Activity 2. (See Activity 1 for an answer key for Worksheet 4–2–1.) Ask students to look at the amounts of area recorded in the right column and see what they notice. Hopefully they will observe that the amounts occur in pairs. ***Ask:*** "When two areas are equal, what do you notice about the exponents and factors or bases on the matching expressions in the left column? Do you see a pattern for the exponents?" The pattern that has been developed is symbolically shown as $(cb)^n = c^n b^n$. Encourage students to describe the pattern in their own words, first orally, then in written form. If there is space at the bottom of Worksheet 4–2–1, they might write their description there. This pattern, along with extensions of it, will occur again in Activity 3. One possible description might be the following: "When a product of two integers is raised to a power, it equals the product of each of those integers separately raised to that same power."

Activity 3: FACTOR TRACKS

[Application/Exploration]

Materials: Sets of Factor Cards and sets A and B of Exponent Cards (see step 1 for card details)
Worksheet 4–2–2 (Record Sheet)
Scientific calculators
Regular paper
Regular pencils

Management: Teams of 4 students each (50 minutes)

Directions:

1. Allow plenty of time at the end of the game for students to discuss the exponential patterns discovered during the game. Give each team one set of factor cards and one set each of sets A and B of exponent cards, a calculator (must have exponent key), and one copy of Worksheet 4–2–2. Cards may be made with 2-inch by 3-inch index cards or card stock; after cards are labeled, they should be laminated. A different color should be used for each *type* of card (factor, exponent A, or exponent B). A set of factor cards consists of 12 cards with *2* on each card and 12 cards with *3* on each card. Exponent sets A and B each contain 14 cards, each card having an exponential expression; each expression in Set A matches to an equivalent expression in Set B. Several cards in Set B will contain the same expression, which is equivalent to several different expressions in Set A. Here are the 14 expressions to use for each set, including any repeated expressions and listed as matching pairs:

Set A matches Set B		*Set A matches Set B*	
$(2^3)^2$	2^6	$(2 \times 3)^5$	$2^5 \times 3^5$
$(4^3)^2$	2^{12}	$(3^2)^2$	3^4
$(2^4)^2$	2^8	$(9^2)^3$	3^{12}
$2^3 \times 2^5$	2^8	$3^2 \times 3^4$	3^6
$(3^2)^4$	3^8	$(2^4 \times 3^2)^3$	$2^{12} \times 3^6$
$2^4 \times 2^3$	2^7	4^3	2^6
9^4	3^8	$3^5 \times 3^7$	3^{12}

2. Each team will lay the 14 cards from Set A face up in two equal rows in the center of the table; using the 14 cards from Set B, two more equal rows will be made, placing these cards face up and adjacent to the Set A cards. That is, there will be four rows of 7 cards each, all cards facing up. The factor cards should be placed face up in stacks near the exponent cards, with the **2**'s in one stack and the **3**'s in another stack.

3. On each team, students will work together in pairs. The two pairs will take turns trying to match a card in Set A with a card in Set B. On a turn, a pair will select a card from Set A, placing it in front of them. The two partners will then arrange on the table as a product the appropriate amount of factor cards to show what the card's exponential expression represents. They will rearrange the factor cards, if necessary, then try to find a card in Set B that contains a simpler, but equivalent, exponential form for their

WORKSHEET 4–2–2
Factor Tracks

In the proper columns below, record the expressions from each match you make. When finished, follow other directions your teacher will then give.

Set A Expression ⟷	Set B Expression
1.	
2.	
3.	
4.	
5.	
6.	
7.	
8.	
9.	
10.	
11.	
12.	
13.	
14.	

product. If a matching card is found and the other pair of students agrees that the match is correct, the playing pair will then remove the two cards from the rows of cards on the table and record their two matched expressions in the two columns on Worksheet 4–2–2. If the other pair challenges the match, they should use the calculator to compute the numerical values of the two matched products or powers. If the values are not the same, then the match is incorrect and the two cards must be returned to their original positions among the other cards. The turn then passes to the other pair of students to select the next card from Set A.

4. Here are two examples of how students should use the cards.

(a) 4^3 from Set A is selected; since only factors of 2 or 3 are available, each 4 must be shown as two 2's; to show the third power of 4, the factor cards should first be laid down as a "string" of three *pairs* of 2's; each 2 shown in brackets here represents a factor card; spacing shows the grouping by *pairs:* [*2*][*2*]   [*2*][*2*] [*2*][*2*]. To simplify the factor cards, since only 2 is involved as the base, all six factor cards should be moved closer together so that no grouping is implied: [*2*][*2*][*2*][*2*][*2*][*2*]. This new arrangement (our "factor tracks") now shows 6 factors of 2; the card in Set B that matches this product is 2^6. 4^3 and 2^6 are then recorded on Worksheet 4–2–2 in their proper columns, but on the same row.

(b) $(2^4 \times 3^2)^3$ is selected from Set A; the exponent 3 indicates that 3 *groups* of factors are needed; each factor group should first be shown with the following string of factor cards: [*2*][*2*][*2*][*2*][*3*][*3*]. This grouping of cards should be shown three times on the table, with spacing between each two adjacent groupings. To simplify the cards, all the factors of 2 should then be moved together and all the factors of 3 should be moved together. When the factor cards are all lined up beside each other as a "string" of cards (our "factor tracks" again), they show a product of 12 factors of 2, followed by 6 factors of 3. No new factors of 6 can be formed from a 2 and a 3 since no factor card is available for 6. The card from Set B that matches this product is $2^{12} \times 3^6$. The expressions $(2^4 \times 3^2)^3$ and $2^{12} \times 3^6$ are then recorded in their proper columns on the same row on Worksheet 4–2–2.

5. After each turn, the factor cards should be returned to their original stack for use by the next playing pair. Both pairs will record their matches on the same copy of Worksheet 4–2–2. Play continues until all cards have been matched. The pair completing more matches will be the winner. *Alternative:* For a less competitive game, one pair of students may help the other pair if they are having difficulty making a match. The helping pair may not identify the correct card in Set B, but may help the playing pair set up the correct arrangement of factor cards. The playing pair must then match the correct card in Set B to the product of factor cards shown. Again, the final match should be confirmed with the calculator.

6. When each team has completed the game, ask all students to look at the matches they have recorded on Worksheet 4–2–2. **Ask:** "On your record sheet, when you look at the exponential expressions from Set A and Set B that are equivalent, do you see a pattern among the exponents? For example, do you see the pattern you discovered earlier in Activity 1 and Activity 2? Do you see other patterns as well?" Several patterns have been used, but only with positive integers at this point. Hopefully, students will notice one or more of the following patterns with respect to the expressions they have used, but they should verbally describe the patterns in their own words. (Vary the letters used as **bases**

or **exponents** in expressions; use the letter x, however, only to show multiplication with *numerical* bases.)

For positive integers a, b, c, n, m, and k,

(a) $(cb)^n = c^n b^n$

(b) $(c^n b^m)^k = c^{nk} b^{mk}$

(c) $(c^n)^m = c^{nm}$

(d) $a^n a^m = a^{n+m}$

(e) $4^n = 2^{2n}$

(f) $9^m = 3^{2m}$

(g) $(4^n)^m = 2^{2nm}$

(h) $(9^n)^m = 3^{2nm}$

Patterns (e) through (h) are shown with specific values 4 and 9, because only these two values were factored to lesser bases; hence, no generalization with regard to bases is expected at this time. Some students, however, may suggest the possibility of extending to other values besides 4 and 9. Have students write on their own papers a few sentences that will describe the patterns they have found. Encourage them to use words, rather than equations or formulas, to describe what they have seen. For example, for pattern (d), they might write: "A base raised to power #1 multiplied by the same base raised to power #2 will equal the same base raised to the sum of power #1 and power #2." Review with students that the *expression* 2^3 is called a *power of 2* and is usually read as *2 to the third power* or as *2 cubed*.

7. Lesson Extension: The game "Factor Tracks" uses only positive integers. Now have the teams of students use the exponent key on their calculators to test the discovered patterns with decimals as bases and with negative integers as exponents. Allow students to create their own expressions to test. They should record each exponential expression and its numerical value found on the calculator, and should record equivalent expressions and their calculated values on the same line of their papers. For example, if a team decides to test pattern (c) above, using $(2.5^3)^{-4}$ and 2.5^{-12}, on their paper they will record the following: $(2.5^3)^{-4} = 0.000016777$ and $2.5^{-12} = 0.000016777$. Remind students to use parentheses when keying in a negative exponent on their calculators, or they will not get the correct value for their power. Have them test each pattern that has been found and discussed.

OBJECTIVE 3: Combine like terms, using linear and quadratic terms in one variable.

Activity 1: SORTING TILES

[Developing Action]

Materials: Packets of variable and unit tiles (described in step 1 below)
Legal-sized plain paper or light tagboard (for building mats)
Regular paper
Regular pencils

Management: Partners (50 minutes)

Directions:

1. Give each pair of students a packet of tiles and a sheet of plain paper or tagboard (approx. 8.5 in. × 14 in.) for a building mat. If preferred, laminate the mats to make them more durable. Mats define a specific space on which to represent a problem being solved. If teacher-made tiles are used, each packet should contain the following in different colors of laminated tagboard: 8 square (quadratic) variable tiles, each 3 in. by 3 in. (color #1); 12 rectangular (linear) variable tiles, 0.75 in. by 3 in. (color #1); and 20 unit tiles, 0.75 in. by 0.75 in. (color #2). Each tile should have a large X drawn on one side to show the inverse of that tile. Use tagboard that is thick enough so that the X will not show through to the other side. (**Note:** A similar packet of tiles was used in Sections 2 and 3; however, additional tiles will be needed for Section 4. These extra tiles may be made and added to the earlier packets.) Commercial tiles are also available in different sizes and colors, but a large X must be drawn on one of the largest faces of each tile in order to represent the inverse of that tile when the X faces up. A pattern for plain and marked tiles is also available in the Appendix; printed copies of the pattern can be made on colored paper and cut apart into the different tiles.

2. The large square tile is being introduced for the first time in this activity. Therefore, we need to develop its special meaning with respect to the other tiles: the long rectangular tile (the linear variable) and the small square tile (the integral unit). Have students place a rectangular variable tile (call it variable A) horizontally on the mat, then have them place two more variable tiles below and parallel to the first tile on the mat. **Ask:** "How can we describe the arrangement indicated by these tiles on the mat?" *(3 rows of A)* "What product is this?" *(3A)* **Ask:** "How can we show A rows of A on the mat if we do not know what the value of A is?" Show students how to build several rows of one variable tile each, using one variable tile A as the multiplier or "ruler" that indicates when to stop putting tiles in the product on the mat (see illustration below). When the product is finished, the multiplier tile should be removed from the mat. Depending on the dimensions used for the tiles, whether commercial or teacher-made, the width across several rectangular tiles placed with their longer sides touching may or may not match the length of the longer side of the same type of tile. Such a match is not important and should be deemphasized since the variable tile A is not considered to have a specific length or value in unit tiles. Therefore, even though 4 of the variable tile A may appear to match to one variable tile length as shown on the mat below, do not allow students to say that A rows of A equal 4A.

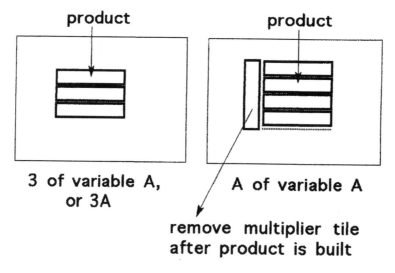

product

product

3 of variable A, or 3A

A of variable A

remove multiplier tile after product is built

3. Ask: "Is there another single block that will cover the same surface area on the mat that this product covers?" (*yes, the large square tile in color #1*; its side length equals the length of the variable tile A) Again, discuss the idea that the large square tile in color #1 may or may not fit perfectly on top of the "A rows of A" tile arrangement; it will be close enough. Since both the square and rectangular tiles in color #1 are representing variables without known values, we want to maintain their variable nature as much as possible. Physical models like the tiles naturally have specific dimensions that affect or limit areas being built with the tiles, but for our purpose, we will assume that **only the unit tiles may be used to represent exact amounts.** We will now assign the large square tile the name of **A-squared** or A^2. Hence, **A rows of A equal A^2.** From now on, whenever A rows of A are needed, the large square tile will be used to show that amount on the mat.

4. Have students place 3 large square tiles, 2 long rectangular tiles, and 5 negative unit tiles on the building mat. Any such group of tiles is called a **polynomial,** that is, a combination of variable tiles and/or unit tiles. Using A for the linear variable name, ask students to describe the tiles on the mat. A possible response might be **3 of A-squared, 2 of A, and −5.** Have students record this set of tiles on their own papers as $3A^2 + 2A + (−5)$ or as $3A^2 + 2A − 5$. Leaving this set of tiles on the mat, have students place additional tiles: **the inverse of A-squared, 3 of A, and +2,** on the mat below the other tiles. The X-side of the large square tile should be showing to represent the inverse tile. The new set of tiles should be recorded with the first set on students' papers as follows: $(3A^2 + 2A − 5) + (−A^2 + 3A + 2)$. **Ask:** "Can any 0-pairs be made and removed from the mat?" (*one 0-pair of the large square tiles and two 0-pairs of the small unit tiles should be formed and removed from the building mat*) "Can you now describe the total in tiles on the mat?" Since tiles for two of A-squared, 5 of A, and −3 remain on the mat, students should complete the recording of the exercise on their papers: $(3A^2 + 2A − 5) + (−A^2 + 3A + 2) = 2A^2 + 5A − 3$.

5. Now write the following on the board: $(4A^2 − 3A + 4) − (A^2 + 2A − 2) = ?$ **Ask:** "What does the subtraction symbol between the two polynomial groups require us to do?" (*remove each term in the second group from the first group*) Have students place tiles on their mats to show the first group. There should be 4 of the large square tile, 3 of the long rectangular tile with the X-side showing for the inverse variable, and 4 positive unit tiles on the building mat. *Ask:* "Can we remove 1 large square tile from the original 4? If so, what tiles will be left?" *(yes; 3 large square tiles, or $3A^2$, will remain)* "Can 2A be removed from −3A? If so, how?" *(since only inverse variable tiles are present, 0-pairs of A and −A will need to be added to the mat until 2 of the variable A are seen; then 2A can be removed, leaving 5 of −A on the mat)* Similarly, −2 will be removed from +4 by first adding two 0-pairs of +1 and −1 to the mat; −2 can then be removed from the mat, leaving +6. Have students complete the original exercise by writing an expression for the tiles left on the mat: $(4A^2 - 3A + 4) - (A^2 + 2A - 2) = 3A^2 - 5A + 6$. *Ask:* "From our work in earlier sections, what was another process we discovered that we could use instead of subtraction? That is, the method gave us the **same answer** as subtraction would, so was considered **equivalent** to subtraction?" Hopefully students will remember that when they use 0-pairs of a tile and remove one form of the tile (e.g., positive), then the other form (e.g., negative) remains to be added to the other tiles on the mat. Show students that when they needed to remove 2A from the mat earlier, two 0-pairs of A and −A were placed on the mat. After 2A was removed to show subtraction, the two inverse variable tiles, −2A, still remained on the mat to be combined with the other tiles for the final answer. Hence, a **removal** of a tile from the mat is equivalent to **adding the inverse** or opposite of that tile to the mat. To confirm this, have students place the original group of tiles $(4A^2 - 3A + 4)$ on the mat again; the opposites needed: $-A^2$, $-2A$, and $+2$, should then be placed on the mat and combined with the original tiles (remove any 0-pairs formed), leaving $3A^2$, $-5A$, and $+6$ on the mat as the answer. Finally, have students write another equation on their papers below the subtraction equation, this time showing the alternative method that uses addition: $(4A^2 - 3A + 4) + (-A^2 - 2A + 2) = 3A^2 - 5A + 6$. Encourage students to use whichever of these two methods seems comfortable to them.

6. Tiles may be thought of as having simply a *numerical* value, without any concern for the size of the tile, or they may be considered for their *geometric* qualities. Discuss the dimensions of the three types of tiles with the students. (**Note:** Inverse tiles will be excluded in this discussion, since area involves only positive measures.) The unit tile may be considered to have an edge length of 1 unit; in other words, it determines the unit of measure for all the other tiles. Thus, the linear variable tile A will have a width that also equals 1 unit; since it represents an unknown, we may claim that its *length* equals A units. Finally, the large square or quadratic tile will have an edge length equal to the length of the variable tile A. Using these measures, we may describe the amount of **area** each type of tile covers on the mat. The unit tile covers 1×1 or 1 square unit of area; the linear variable tile covers $1 \times A$ or A square units, and the quadratic variable tile covers $A \times A$ or A^2 square units of area. Notice that the *area amounts* are the same as the labels used earlier for the tiles' *numerical values,* but the roles differ. Ask students to build the following arrangement of tiles on their mats with the tiles touching each other; tell them that the tiles represent a room floor plan.

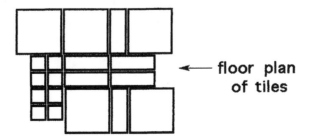

←— floor plan
of tiles

7. Ask them to find the total area of the room's floor, measuring in the square units discussed earlier. Recording the area contributed by each tile or a group of adjacent tiles, one possible partially simplified equation might be: $2A^2 + A + A^2 + 8 + 4A + A^2 + A + A^2$ $= (3A^2 + 8 + 6A + 2A^2)$ **square units of area.** *Ask:* "Could you arrange the tiles in the floor plan differently to make your totaling of the different tile areas easier to do?" *(yes)* Have students rearrange their tiles so that *like* tiles are adjacent to each other, then write a new expression for the total area. Remind students that even though 4 unit tiles might seem to fit along the edge of a variable tile A, we cannot use 4 units as the length of A since A is representing an unknown amount in our model. Here is one possible arrangement that directly yields the area expression: $(5A^2 + 6A + 8)$ **square units of area.** (**Note:** The purpose of this particular exercise is to show the advantages of using the commutative and associative properties of addition whenever possible.)

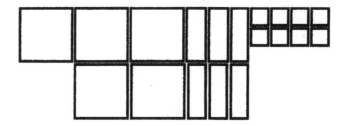

8. For additional practice in adding or subtracting polynomials, have partners work together, taking turns setting up tiles for a new exercise. On the first round, addition will be used. Partner #1 will place two separate groups of tiles on the building mat (at least two different tile sizes must be used in each group; at least one inverse tile must be included in the total set of tiles placed on the mat). Partner #2 must record the polynomial expression for each tile group on paper in an equation, combine and simplify the tiles, and then record the final polynomial answer to complete the equation. For example, if partner #1 places 2 of A-squared, 3 of −A, and +1 together on the mat, followed by 4 of A with −5, partner #2 will record the expressions: $(2A^2 - 3A + 1) + (4A - 5),$ combine the tiles and remove any 0-pairs, then finish the recording as: $(2A^2 - 3A + 1) + (4A - 5) =$ $2A^2 + A - 4.$ Then the turn goes to partner #2 to set up another addition exercise for partner #1 to work. A second round begins when it is partner #1's turn again. For this round, subtraction will be used. Partner #1 places a new group of tiles on the mat, using the conditions given earlier (to provide variety in the exercises), then states what group of tiles needs to be removed. Partner #2 must record the polynomial expression for the first group and also record what polynomial is to be subtracted. After carrying out the removals (or adding opposites, whichever method is preferred) on the mat and simplifying the remaining tiles, partner #2 will finish the recording by writing the polynomial answer found. The turn then passes to partner #2 to set up the next subtraction exercise. On the third round, addition is used again. The partner and operation rotations continue until time is called.

Activity 2: *PICTURING POLYNOMIALS*

[Bridging Action]

Materials: Worksheet 4–3–1
Regular paper
Regular pencils

Management: Partners (50 minutes)

Directions:

1. Have students work together, but they should draw the diagrams separately on their own papers. Large squares will be drawn for the quadratic variable, a long rectangle whose length equals an edge length of the large square will be drawn for the linear variable, and a small square will represent the integral unit. A large X should be drawn in the interior of a shape to show the inverse of that shape. Since each exercise will involve only one variable, letters will not need to be written on the drawn shapes to identify different variables. Different letters, however, will be used in the exercises in order to give students experience with a variety of variable names.

2. Write the following expression on the board: $(-3b^2 + 2 + b) + (b^2 - 4b + 1) = ?$ Students should draw the necessary shapes on their papers to represent each polynomial. The shapes for the first polynomial may be drawn in a row from left to right following the order of the given terms. The shapes for the second polynomial should be drawn as a second row below the first row, but students may rearrange the shapes and draw them below other like shapes in the first row. 0-pairs should be connected; remaining shapes will then be counted and recorded as the answer. A sample drawing is shown below. The final equation will be as follows: $(-3b^2 + 2 + b) + (b^2 - 4b + 1) = -2b^2 - 3b + 3$. At this point begin to encourage students to record the terms of a polynomial with their exponents in decreasing order.

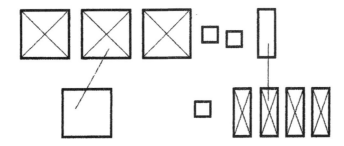

3. Now write the following subtraction exercise on the board: $(m^2 + 5m - 3) - (2m^2 + 3m + 4) = ?$ Since students have had extensive work with subtractive diagrams in Sections 1 and 2, the methods used here should only be viewed as an extension to include the new quadratic variable (the large square). Allow students to choose whether they use the "removal" approach or the "adding of opposites" approach. The shapes remaining or not marked out in the finished diagram will be the answer. Depending on the approach used, the completed equation recorded on students' papers will be: (a) removal: $(m^2 + 5m - 3) - (2m^2 + 3m + 4) = (m^2 - 2m^2) + (5m - 3m) + (-3 - 4) = -m^2 + 2m - 7$; or (b) adding of opposites: $(m^2 + 5m - 3) - (2m^2 + 3m + 4) = m^2 + (-2m^2) + 5m + (-3m) - 3 + (-4) = -m^2 + 2m - 7$. At this stage all combining steps are being shown; eventually, students

should find their own techniques for documenting the steps they take mentally. Here are diagrams for the two approaches.

(a) removal:

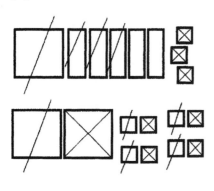

(b) adding of opposites:

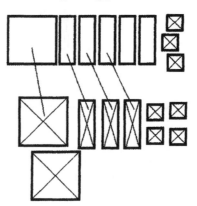

4. Assign additional exercises for students to solve by drawing diagrams and recording their results as symbolic equations. Distribute Worksheet 4–3–1 to students. For subtraction exercises, allow students to use whichever of the two methods they prefer. One method will usually be quicker than the other, depending on the terms used in the exercise. A few exercises will require students to evaluate their answers, using a given value of the variable involved. When checking students' work, always allow time for students to explain their steps; do not just check for answers. Students need to practice expressing their ideas mathematically. Such verbal sharing is also very beneficial to *auditory learners*. Here are some possible exercises to assign: (symbolic answers shown in brackets)

3. $(N^2 + 5N + 8) + (2N^2 - 3N + 4) = ?$
   $[3N^2 + 2N + 12]$

4. $(7A - 1) + (-3A^2 + 2A) = ?$
   $[-3a^2 + 9A - 1]$

5. $(5p^2 + 3) - (2p^2 + 1) = ?$ $[3p^2 + 2]$

6. $3w - (-w^2 - 5) = ?$ $[w^2 + 3w + 5]$

7. $-4M^2 + (-5 + 3M - M^2) = ?$
   $[-5M^2 + 3M - 5]$

8. $(4B - 2 + B^2) + (-6 - 2B) = ?$
   $[B^2 + 2B - 8]$

9. $(6d^2 - d + 3) - (d^2 + d - 3) = ?$
   $[5d^2 - 2d + 6]$

10. $3v^2 - v + 6 - (6 - v + 3v^2) = ?$ $[0]$

12. $(2T^2 + 3T) + (5T - 2T^2 + 3) = ?$
    (Evaluate result for T = –5.)
    $[8T + 3; -37]$

11. $3X - 2X^2 - 5 + X - 8 + 3X^2 = ?$
    (Evaluate result for X = +2.)
    $[X^2 + 4X - 13; -1]$

13. $(7a - 2a^2 + 3) - (-2a^2 + 3 + 7a) = ?$
    $[0]$

14. $(5y^2 - 4) - (5y^2 - 4 - y) = ?$ $[y]$

15. $-k^2 + 3k - (-2) - (+4k) + (-k^2) = ?$
    (Evaluate result for k = 0.)
    $[-2k^2 - k + 2; 2]$

16. $(-m + 2m^2 - 1 + 3m^2) + 5 - 4.5m = ?$
    [draw *half* a rectangle for 0.5m]
    $[5m^2 - 5.5m + 4]$

WORKSHEET 4–3–1
Picturing Polynomials

Draw a diagram on your own paper to solve each exercise below. Record your answer with symbols on this worksheet. Evaluate an answer if a value is given for the variable.

1. $(-3b^2 + 2 + b) + (b^2 - 4b + 1) =$ _____

2. $(m^2 + 5m - 3) - (2m^2 + 3m + 4) =$ _____

3. $(N^2 + 5N + 8) + (2N^2 - 3N + 4) =$ _____

4. $(7A - 1) + (-3A^2 + 2A) =$ _____

5. $(5p^2 + 3) - (2p^2 + 1) =$ _____

6. $3w - (-w^2 - 5) =$ _____

7. $-4M^2 + (-5 + 3M - M^2) =$ _____

8. $(4B - 2 + B^2) + (-6 - 2B) =$ _____

9. $(6d^2 - d + 3) - (d^2 + d - 3) =$ _____

10. $3v^2 - v + 6 - (6 - v + 3v^2) =$ _____

11. $3X - 2X^2 - 5 + X - 8 + 3X^2 =$ _____
    [evaluate for X = +2]

12. $(2T^2 + 3T) + (5T - 2T^2 + 3) =$ _____
    [evaluate for T = −5]

13. $(7a - 2a^2 + 3) - (-2a^2 + 3 + 7a) =$ _____

14. $(5y^2 - 4) - (5y^2 - 4 - y) =$ _____

15. $-k^2 + 3k - (-2) - (+4k) + (-k^2) =$ _____
    [evaluate for k = 0]

16. $(-m + 2m^2 - 1 + 3m^2) + 5 - 4.5m =$ _____

Activity 3: POLYNOMIAL MODELING

[Application/Exploration]

Materials: Worksheet 4–3–2
Regular paper
Regular pencils
Packets of tiles from Activity 1 *(optional)*

Management: Teams of 4 students each (50 minutes)

Directions:

1. The technique of drawing diagrams to analyze and solve nonroutine problems is an important strategy that is often neglected in mathematics instruction. In this activity, and later in Objective 4, students will be guided through the construction and labeling of diagrams in order to gain experience with this particular strategy. If necessary, review Objective 1 of Section 2 for simpler drawing techniques. Emphasis should be more on how to create and interpret illustrations or diagrams than on what the solutions might be.

2. Write the following problem on the board: "Four students collected N dollars each for participating in a Walkathon, a special fund-raising event for a local charity. Three other students also walked; each of these raised twice as much money as anyone in the first group of four students. Three more people collected $60 altogether. Find the average (mean) dollar amount collected per person by these three groups combined, and express that amount in terms of N." Ask each team to draw and label a simple diagram that represents the situation. Diagrams will vary from team to team. An unsimplified algebraic equation should be written to represent the different components in the diagram and the steps needed to solve the problem. Finally, the result of the equation should be simplified as needed and labeled appropriately as the solution to the problem. For the given problem, first review the processes involved in finding an average or mean: combine the different dollar amounts collected by the groups (addition), then separate the total amount into equal shares, one share per person involved in the original groups (division); the dollar amount of one share will be the **average** or **mean.** Students should try to draw a diagram to show these two steps before they write any equations. The diagram will dictate the equations needed if done properly. A possible drawing is shown below. An equation for combining the different dollar amounts might be: 4N + 3(2N) + $60 = Total dollars collected by the people in the three groups. There are 4 + 3 + 3 = 10 people, who collected the total dollars. So the average or equal share will be $(\frac{1}{10})$(4N + 3(2N) + $60), which simplifies to (N + 6) dollars per person.

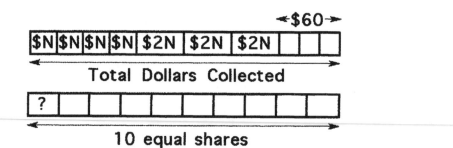

3. Discuss another example with the class. On the board write the following: "A professional tiler has 3 basic tile shapes for making different flooring designs. The large square tile has an area of P^2 square inches; the small square tile has an area of 1 square inch; and the long rectangular tile that is 1 inch wide has an area of P square inches. If the tiler uses one large square tile, four of the long rectangular tiles, and four of the small square tiles to make a design that is a larger square tile than the other two basic square shapes, what will be an expression in P for the side length of the new square and what will be an expression in P for its area in square inches? No broken or cut basic tiles may be used in the design." Have students draw each basic shape needed for the new design, then record the shape's dimensions and area directly on the shape itself. **Ask:** "If the long rectangular tile is 1 inch wide and has an area of P square inches, how does this tile compare to the large square tile?" (*its length must equal the side length of the large square tile, which is P inches;* the rectangular tile is 1 in. by P in. and the large square tile is P in. by P in.) Have students explore several different arrangements of the given tiles. If needed, allow students to **build** physical arrangements with the **tiles** used in Activity 1. Moving different tiles around is helpful to students who have difficulty *mentally* visualizing with shapes. The original shapes and two possible designs are shown below. An expression for the side length of the new square will be **(P + 2) inches** and an expression for the area will be **(P + 2)² square inches.** Do not require students to multiply to find a simpler expression for the area at this time; variable multiplication will be studied in depth in Objective 4. At this stage we only want to use the idea that the area of a square *may* be found by multiplying the side length by itself; hence, we record a **squared** expression to show the area of the new square design in the same sense that we record P^2 as the area for the original P by P square tile.

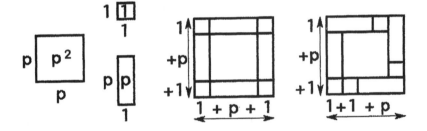

4. Now give each team member a copy of Worksheet 4–3–2. Each team should try to illustrate the problems on Worksheet 4–3–2 in some way. Two problems involve only linear forms and constants, while the other two involve quadratic forms as well. After all teams have completed or at least attempted each problem, ask various students to show their illustrations to the entire class. In particular, select students who have illustrated the same problem but in different ways to share their work; it is important for students to realize that drawings of situations are not unique. Monitor the drawings, however, to insure that all conditions of a problem have been met. Discussions of the worksheet problems are provided here.

WORKSHEET 4–3–2
Polynomial Modeling

Draw diagrams to represent each problem below. Write any expressions or equations required by the problems. Be ready to share your work with the entire class.

1. If $AC = 5n - 3$ and $AB = 2n - 6$ on the line segment shown below, find the length BC in terms of n.

2. Each long, rectangular tile in the given design has an area of B square units and is 1 unit wide. Write an expression for the area of the inner square of the design and an expression for the area of the outer square of the design, giving both expressions in terms of B. Can you write an equation in B that uses the rectangular tiles in some way to compare the areas of the two squares?

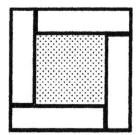

WORKSHEET 4–3–2 *(cont.)*
Polynomial Modeling

3. At a carpet sale, there is a stack of carpet remnants available. Such pieces can be used to cover a small floor space like a storage closet or a playhouse. José finds a large square piece of blue carpet with area X^2 square feet and 5 blue carpet strips that are X feet long and 1 foot wide. This is enough blue carpet for his child's playhouse floor. He also finds some gold carpet remnants in large squares and 1-foot wide strips, but the longer edge length of each gold piece is Y feet, which equals only half the length of each blue piece. Express in terms of X the total area in square feet of the blue carpet needed for the playhouse, then express in terms of Y a total area of gold carpet that is equivalent to the amount of blue carpet needed.

4. Consider the set of numbers {8, 5, 7, 5, 10}. If each number in the set is decreased by the amount d, the arithmetic mean of the new set of numbers will be 4. Find the value of d.

Discussion of WORKSHEET 4–3–2

(1) A possible drawing for this problem:

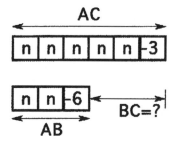

The drawing shows that BC is a *difference* between a whole and a part of the whole, so a possible equation might be $(5n - 3) - (2n - 6) = 3n + 3$. So BC = $3n + 3$, in terms of n. Some students may still need to use diagrams of tiles to solve the equation; this is allowable.

(2) Students should label the original illustration with dimensions, those given and those inferred. Since a rectangular tile has an area of B square units and is 1 unit wide, the tile must have a length of B units ($1 \times B = B$).

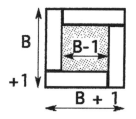

The area of the inner square will be $(B - 1)^2$ square units since its side length is $(B - 1)$ units. The area of the outer square will be $(B + 1)^2$ square units since its side length is $(B + 1)$ units. The area of the 4 rectangular tiles combined with the inner square's area will equal the area of the outer square. Here is a possible equation: $(B - 1)^2 + 4B = (B + 1)^2$ square units. Do not perform the multiplication to simplify the equation; variable multiplication will be discussed in Objective 4. Only the basic idea of length multiplied by width is applied here to set up the expressions for the different areas.

(3) Students should draw each blue carpet piece and label its dimensions as follows:

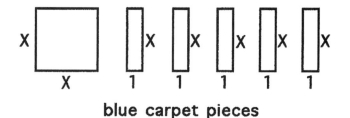

blue carpet pieces

The expression for the total area in terms of X for the blue carpet pieces will be $(X^2 + 5X)$ square feet. The gold carpet pieces might be drawn as overlays on the larger blue pieces as follows:

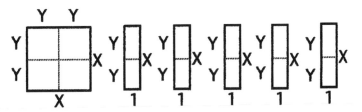

gold carpet pieces

Looking at the adjusted drawings, we see that there are 4 of the gold squares that fit inside the blue square and 2 gold strips that fit inside a blue strip. So the total area in terms of Y for the gold carpet will be $4Y^2 + 5(2Y) = (4Y^2 + 10Y)$ square feet.

(4) Review the steps involved in finding the **mean** of a set of 5 numbers: combine 5 numbers together for a total, then redistribute into 5 new equal amounts, where the new amount is the mean or equal share. Here is a possible diagram to show this combining and redistribution.

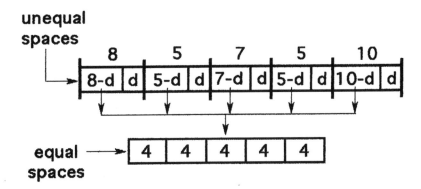

Equations to represent the steps in the problem might be the following: $(8–d) + (5–d) + (7–d) + (5–d) + (10–d) = (35 – 5d)$ for the total, and the redistribution as $(\frac{1}{5})(35 – 5d) = (\frac{1}{5})(35) + (\frac{1}{5})(–5d) = 7 – d$, which is the mean. We must have $7 – d = 4$, so $7 – 4 = d$, or $3 = d$.

OBJECTIVE 4: Find products of second degree, using polynomial factors in one or two variables.

Activity 1: BUILDING PRODUCTS

[Developing Action]

Materials: Building mats and packets of variable and unit tiles (described in step 1 below)
Worksheet 4–4–1
Regular paper
Regular pencils

Management: Partners (50 minutes)

Directions:

1. Give each pair of students a packet of tiles, a building mat, and Worksheet 4–4–1. The building mat should be a blank 8.5 in. by 14 in. sheet of white paper (or light tagboard if preferred) containing a bold L-frame drawn with a wide, black marker (see illustration below). A one-inch margin should be allowed between each segment of the L-frame and the paper's edge. Laminate the mats to make them more durable. If teacher-made tiles are used, each packet should contain the following in different colors of laminated tagboard: 8 square (quadratic) variable tiles each 3 in. by 3 in. (color #1); 4 square (quadratic) variable tiles each 3.25 in. by 3.25 in. (color #2); 12 rectangular (linear) variable tiles, 0.75 in. by 3 in. (color #1); 8 rectangular (linear) variable tiles, 0.75 in. by 3.25 in. (color #2); 20 unit tiles, 0.75 in. by 0.75 in. (color #3); and 4 rectangular variable tiles, 3 in. by 3.25 in. (color #4). Each tile should have a large X drawn on one side to show the inverse of that tile. Use tagboard that is thick enough so that the X will not show through to the other side. (**Note:** A similar packet of tiles was used in Objective 3 of this section and also in Sections 2 and 3; however, additional tiles will be needed for this present objective. These extra tiles may be made and added to the earlier packets.) Commercial tiles are also available in different sizes and colors, but a large X must be drawn on one of the largest faces of each tile in order to represent the inverse of that tile when the X faces up. A pattern for plain and marked tiles is also available in the Appendix; printed copies of the pattern can be made on colored paper and cut apart into the different tiles.

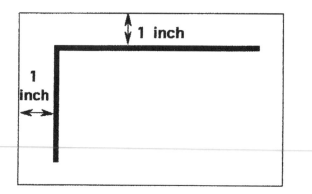

2. Section 2 introduced multiple amounts of variables, that is, expressions like 3B or −2m. In the lesson on arithmetic sequences in Section 3, students generalized from sequences of quantities like **1 of 3 tiles, 2 of 3 tiles, 3 of 3 tiles, . . .** to get **N of 3 tiles,** written as **N(3)** rather than 3N, which would mean 3 of N tiles. In Activity 1 we will develop the meaning of N(3) further; that is, the variable N in the multiplier role (the counter of sets) will be explored with numbers or other variables (besides itself) as the multiplicand or set size. Other expressions equivalent to N(3) will also be investigated. Our model for multiplication will combine the idea of "repetition of sets" with that of "area," in particular, the surface area covered by the variable or unit tiles when arranged in an **array.** Remember that a *row* in an array is in a horizontal or *left-to-right* position. (See Section 1 for more details on arrays in integer multiplication.)

3. To introduce students to the building mat, have them place 2 positive unit tiles vertically to the left of the L-frame and place 3 positive unit tiles horizontally above the L-frame as shown below. The +2 is in the **multiplier** (or counter of sets) position on the mat and the +3 is in the **multiplicand** (or set size) position.

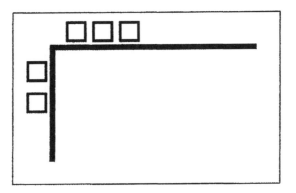

4. Since the tiles on the mat represent the arrangement 2 rows of +3 each, have students place 3 positive unit tiles on the mat in a first row directly under the original +3, then repeat in a second row as shown. The space under the L-frame is for the **product,** which is +6 in this case. We may think of this product as 6 countable, individual unit tiles, or we may think of it as covering an area equal to 6 square units. Students may place tiles so that they touch in order to form a continuous surface area, or they may leave the tiles apart as shown in the illustration below.

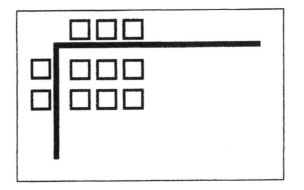

5. Similarly, have students place a rectangular variable tile (color #1) above the L-frame on the mat and place 3 positive unit tiles to the left of the L-frame. Discuss the idea that the variable tile represents some quantity, but we do not know what that quantity is. Calling the variable tile A, we can only repeat the variable tile as our set three times, resulting in the product, 3A.

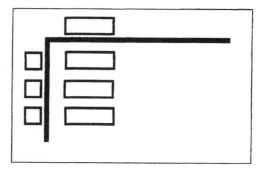

6. Now have students build each of the following arrangements one at a time on their mats (one should be removed before the next is built): 2 rows of +1, 5 rows of +1, and 8 rows of +1. Their respective products placed vertically under the L-frame below the original +1 will be +2, +5, and +8. **Ask:** "How does the number of rows compare to the product found each time?" *(both are represented by the same number name)* Have students place the rectangular variable tile A (color #1) in the multiplier position and +1 in the multiplicand position on the mat. Discuss the idea that since we do not know what value the variable tile A represents, we do not know what specific number of rows to build on the mat. Thus, what is shown on the mat can only be described as "A rows of +1." Using the relationship found earlier when "counting" single unit tiles, we can say that "A rows of +1 equal the product A." Therefore, students should also place a linear or rectangular variable tile A in the product space on the mat. Again, the product A may be viewed as simply a tile representing some total value in counting units, or it may be viewed as a tile covering an area of A square units on the mat.

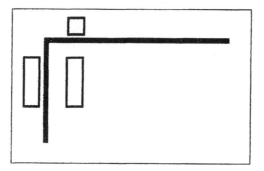

7. Now ask some students to show "4 rows of variable A" with tiles on their mats and ask others to show "A rows of +4." The products should also be shown. **Ask:** "What do you notice about the tiles for the two products?" *(both products contain 4 of the variable tile A; one set is oriented vertically and the other is oriented horizontally)* "How does the surface area covered on the mat by one product compare to the surface area covered by the other product?" *(both products cover the same amount of surface area; some students may need to slide each set of 4 variable tiles together, then place one set on top of the other to verify that the two sets cover the same space on the mat)* Hence, the products 4A and A(+4) are equal in value, and we can replace one expression with the other whenever necessary or convenient.

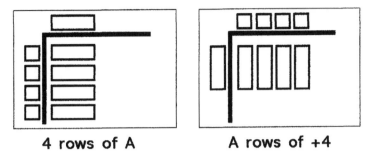

4 rows of A   A rows of +4

8. Have students place a rectangular variable tile A on the mat in the multiplier position and another variable tile A in the multiplicand position. (**Note:** It is helpful for students to hear and use correct terminology for multiplication as often as possible.) ***Ask:*** "How can we describe the arrangement indicated by these two tiles on the mat?" *(A rows of A)* "What will the product look like?" Review the work done in Activity 1 of Objective 3; remind students that **A rows of A** will be represented by the large square tile in color #1, which is called **A-squared.** This large square tile should be placed on the mat in the product position. Again, discuss the idea that the square variable tile in color #1 may or may not fit perfectly on top of the actual "A rows of A" tile arrangement; it will be close enough. Since both the square and rectangular tiles in color #1 (same idea applies for color #2 tiles) are representing variables without known values, we want to maintain their variable nature as much as possible. Remind students that **only the unit tiles may be used to represent exact amounts.**

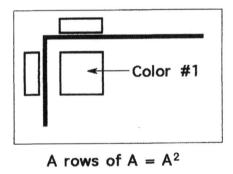

A rows of A = A^2

9. A development similar to that for the variable tile A can be followed for the longer rectangular variable tile in color #2; we will call this tile B. Have students show **B rows of B** on their mats, then replace the product with the square variable tile in color #2 (call it **B-squared** or **B^2**).

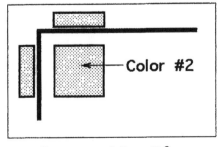

B rows of B = B^2

10. Inverse tiles may also be used as factors when multiplying with tiles. As an example, have students place 5 negative unit tiles to the left of the L-frame and 2 of variable tile A above the L-frame on the mat. These two factors (multiplier and multiplicand) should be read as "the opposite of 5 rows of two A-variable tiles each" or "the opposite of 5 rows of 2A." From their work in Section 1, students should know that for each row of 2A needed, they will actually build a row of inverse tiles (i.e., each A-tile in the product is flipped over to show the X side). The final product will consist of 10 of the inverse of variable tile A, or 10 of –A.

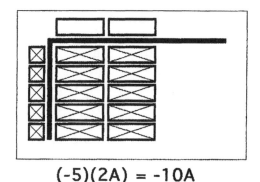

$$(-5)(2A) = -10A$$

11. Working similarly with an *inverse variable* tile as *multiplier,* ask students to show (–A)(2B) on their mats. The first factor –A requires opposites to be taken for the final product. We need "the *opposite of* A rows of 2B each." First, however, students should notice that A rows of B can be replaced by the rectangular variable tile in color #4; in this case, the new tile represents the product AB. (Notice that one edge of this tile has the length of the variable tile A and that the adjacent edge has the length of the variable tile B.) Hence, for every A rows of B, the opposite becomes the inverse of the variable tile AB, which we write as –AB. Observe that the *opposite of* B rows of A would produce the same variable tile, but it would be rotated 90 degrees on the mat and would be written as –BA. Thus, the two products are equivalent; similarly, AB and BA are equivalent to each other. The final product, –2AB, for the original problem being discussed here is shown below:

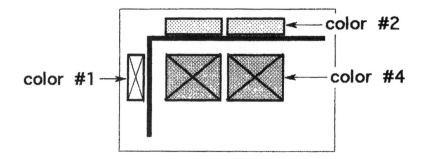

12. Students have now built the basic products they will need for more complex products. The distributive property will allow them to build products for various polynomial factors. To demonstrate this, have students place 1 variable tile A and 2 negative unit tiles to the left of the L-frame and place 1 inverse variable tile, –A, followed by 1 variable tile B and 3 positive unit tiles, above the L-frame. This represents the exercise: **(A – 2)(–A + B + 3) = ?** Ask students to build the product for these factor groups. Remind them that each group of tiles is called a **polynomial,** that is, a combination of variable tiles and/or unit tiles. Working with one tile at a time in the multiplier, students should build in the product space the row that corresponds to that tile. The row built for the variable tile A will show $-A^2$ with AB and 3A; the row for each -1 will have A with $-B$ and -3. To record the final product on their own paper, students should combine any tiles that are the same type. Hence, the final equation recorded will be: **$(A - 2)(-A + B + 3) = -A^2 + AB + 5A - 2B - 6.$**

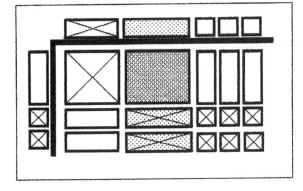

13. Write several different exercises on the board for students to build on their mats, then record on their own papers in equation format. (See Worksheet 4–4–1.) Some possible exercises are provided below. We will continue to use the letters A and B for the rectangular variable tiles in our set. Other letters will be used in Activity 2. Typically the final expression for a product will be obtained by recording the tiles in the upper rows on the mat first, followed by recording the tiles in the lower rows. Different groups of the same type of tile can just be counted together to get one total for that type of tile; sometimes 0-pairs may occur in such combinations. The order of the terms in the final answer, however, is not unique. Encourage students to share any patterns they think they see, but do not emphasize any particular pattern at this time. Specifically, avoid such "shortcut" methods as "foil"; the tile arrangements on the mat and the product grids will create visual and geometric images that incorporate the same pairing of terms that "shortcuts" produce, but the images formed will have greater meaning and be retained more easily.

Additional exercises with answers for Worksheet 4–4–1:

10. $3(2A + 1) = ?$ [6A + 3]

11. $-2(B - 4) = ?$ [-2B + 8]

12. $A(A + B - 2) = ?$ $[A^2 + AB - 2A]$

13. $-B(3B + 1) = ?$ $[-3B^2 - B]$

14. $(-2A + B - 3)(A + 4) = ?$
    $[-2A^2 - 8A + BA + 4B - 3A - 12]$

15. $(B - 1)(A + 2) = ?$ [BA + 2B - A - 2]

17. $(B - A + 3)(-A + 2B + 1) = ?$
    $[-3AB + A^2 + 2B^2 + 7B - 4A + 3]$

16. $(A + 2)(A - 2) = ?$
    $[A^2 - 2A + 2A - 4, \text{ or } A^2 - 4]$

19. $(B - 4)(B + 4) = ?$ $[B^2 - 16]$

18. $(A + 3)(A + 2) = ?$ $[A^2 + 5A + 6]$

21. $(2A + 3)(2A - 3) = ?$ $[4A^2 - 9]$

20. $(-B + 1)(B - 1) = ?$ $[-B^2 + 2B - 1]$

WORKSHEET 4–4–1
Building Products

Build with your tiles to solve the given exercises. Record the symbolic answer or product on the worksheet.

1. 2 rows of +3 = _____

2. 3 rows of A = _____

3. 4 rows of A = _____

4. A rows of +4 = _____

5. A rows of A = _____

6. B rows of B = _____

7. opposite of 5 rows of 2A = _____

8. opposite of A rows of 2B = _____

9. $(A - 2)(-A + B + 3) =$ _____

10. $3(2A + 1) =$ _____

11. $-2(B - 4) =$ _____

12. $A(A + B - 2) =$ _____

13. $-B(3B + 1) =$ _____

14. $(-2A + B - 3)(A + 4) =$ _____

15. $(B - 1)(A + 2) =$ _____

16. $(A + 2)(A - 2) =$ _____

17. $(B - A + 3)(-A + 2B + 1) =$ _____

18. $(A + 3)(A + 2) =$ _____

19. $(B - 4)(B + 4) =$ _____

20. $(-B + 1)(B - 1) =$ _____

21. $(2A + 3)(2A - 3) =$ _____

Activity 2: PRODUCT DRAW

[Bridging Action]

Materials: Worksheet 4–4–2
Paper
Regular pencils

Management: Partners (50 minutes)

Directions:

1. In this activity students will be encouraged to look for specific patterns in products and to apply product diagrams to solve a few nonroutine problems. Since specific multiplication patterns are merely an extension of the multiplication process and are generally intended for efficiency or speed in computation, students do not need to master such patterns; rather, they need to fully understand how to apply the distributive property to the terms within each factor group in order to obtain the product. Nevertheless, pattern awareness is fundamental to effective mathematical thinking, so students should be encouraged to search for patterns in various products, whether or not they master their usage. In this activity, we will include several exercises that result in the difference of two squares, and some that involve the squaring of a binomial. Regarding the application or nonroutine problems, even though the problems may be difficult for some students, all students still need to experience the strategies and analytical thinking involved in solving such problems.

2. Have students draw L-frames on their own paper. Each frame should be drawn so that the vertical segment is about 1 inch to the right of the left margin (i.e., 2 inches from the left edge of the paper) and about 2.5 inches long (i.e., about a third of the length of the paper). The horizontal or top segment of the L-frame should be about 4 inches long. Early efforts to draw L-frames should be closely monitored to make sure that students are allowing enough space to easily draw the different shapes that will form their factors and products. Extremely small or crowded shapes increase the possibility of error. As in earlier lessons, long rectangles will be drawn as models for variable tiles. Since it is difficult to free-hand draw rectangles of consistent length, we will label each long rectangle with the letter of the variable it represents. If only one type of variable is involved in an exercise, such labeling will not be necessary. Large squares with edge length equal to the length of the corresponding variable rectangle will represent that variable squared. Small squares will continue to be used for the units. A large X inside a shape will indicate the inverse of that shape. Adjacent shapes may be drawn touching each other or with space between them.

3. Have students draw shapes on an L-frame to represent the multiplier, **(A + 3),** and the multiplicand, **(A − B − 2).** The top row of the product that is produced with the variable A in the multiplier might be drawn first, followed by the last three rows that are produced by +3. This is recommended practice until students become quite comfortable with applying the distributive property; later, they might decide to draw the shapes in the left column of the product first, then the next column to the right, etc. Have different students explain what the various shapes mean in their products. For example, the top row will contain "A-amount of A, or A-squared," "A-amount of the inverse of B, or −AB," and

"A-amount of –2, or –2A." The next row will contain "1 of A," "1 of the inverse of B," and "1 of –2." Notice that we sometimes describe the units in the multiplicand together as a group; for example, we used "A-amount of –2" rather than "A-amount of –1," followed by another "A-amount of –1." The last two rows will be repeats of the second row. As an alternative, since the last three rows involve units (constants) as multipliers, these 3 positive units might be combined together as +3, but 3 distinct rows of shapes must still be drawn to align with each individual unit. The combined description would then be "3 of A," "3 of the inverse of B," and "3 of –2." At the beginning, however, it is helpful to students to focus on and draw one row of shapes at a time. Have students record each partial product (i.e., each region under the L-frame where adjacent shapes are alike) with algebraic symbols on a *product grid,* as shown below. Observe that two 0-pairs can be formed from 2A and –2A, since they are being joined or added together in producing the product; if helpful, have students mark out 2 of A and 2 of –A on their diagrams or drawings. Students should then write the final equation **(A + 3)(A – B – 2) = A² –AB + A – 3B – 6** on their papers, either below or to the right of their diagram and product grid for the exercise. The right member of the equation is the simplified result after the 0-pairs have been removed. Here is an illustration of how the final drawing and product grid should look.

Diagram: Product Grid:

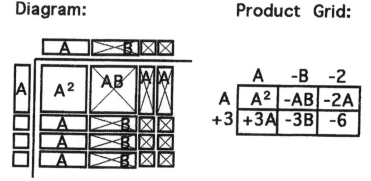

4. Now have students draw a diagram for **(m – 2)(m + 2)**. We are using different letters to denote variables in this activity. Also, since only one type of variable (here, **m**) is used, we do not need to label the shapes in the drawing. The first row of the product diagram will contain "m-amount of m," or m-squared, and "m-amount of +2," or +2m; the next two rows together will show the "opposite of 2m," or –2m, and the "opposite of 2 rows of +2," or –4. The shapes in the four disjoint regions of the product should be recorded in the product grid to the right of the diagram. ***Ask:*** "What do you notice about the two regions containing the linear variable m? Where are these two regions? What is their sum when combined?" (*one partial product of shapes is the opposite or inverse of the other: –2m is the opposite of +2m, and +2m is the opposite of –2m; the regions are diagonal to each other under the L-frame; the sum will equal 0 since the four shapes involved form two 0-pairs*) Students should observe that the symbols in the product grid show this same information. Finally, have students write an equation for the simplified result: **(m – 2)(m + 2) = m² – 4.**

Diagram: **Product Grid:**

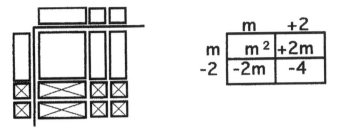

5. Write the exercise $(-2g + 3)^2 = ?$ on the board for students to draw and solve. Discuss the idea that the exponent 2 indicates that two factor groups of $(-2g + 3)$ are needed. Students should write the expanded form $(-2g + 3)(-2g + 3)$ immediately after the given power on their own papers. For the first two rows of the diagram, the partial product for $(-2g)(-2g)$ should be described as the "opposite or inverse of 2g of $-2g$," which equals "4 of g-squared" or $4g^2$. Have students similarly describe the other partial products they find and record them on the product grid. Remind them that the multiplier is mentioned first; for example, if the last three rows are grouped together as like shapes, the left partial product should be described as "3 of $-2g$," not as "2 of $-3g$" or as the "opposite of 2g of $+3$." The final diagram and grid are shown below. Ask students what they notice in the product about the arrangement of shapes in the upper left region, in the upper right and lower left regions, and in the lower right region. Hopefully they will notice that the large squares are themselves in a 2×2 square-shaped arrangement; the long rectangles are rotated arrangements of each other (lower left has 3×2 arrangement, and upper right has 2×3 arrangement); and the positive units form a 3×3 square-shaped arrangement. This type of discussion emphasizes the visual and geometric elements in algebra, which are essential to many students when learning new concepts. Guide students to compare the partial product arrangements in the diagram to the notation recorded in the product grid. The upper left term involves two numerical squares, 4 and g^2, or 2g squared; the upper right and lower left terms are equal; and the lower right term, $+9$, is a perfect square. Finally, have students write below their diagram or their grid the following equation: $(-2g + 3)^2 = (-2g + 3)(-2g + 3) = 4g^2 - 12g + 9.$

Diagram: **Product Grid:**

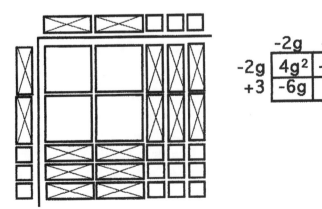

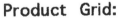

6. *Application:* Write the following problem on the board: **"(p + 2) apple pies are cut into (p + 3) equal slices per pie. Express the total number of slices of pie in**

Name _____ **Date** _____

WORKSHEET 4–4–2
Product Draw

On your own paper draw a diagram to solve each exercise provided and record its result with symbols in a *product grid*. On the worksheet complete each equation by writing its answer in symbols.

1. $(A + 3)(A - B - 2) =$ _____

2. $(m - 2)(m + 2) =$ _____

3. $(-2g + 3)^2 =$_____

4. $(p + 2)$ apple pies are cut into $(p + 3)$ equal slices per pie. Express the total number of slices of pie in terms of p.

5. $B(2B - 3) =$ _____

6. $(y - 1)(y + 1) =$ _____

7. $(3k + 1)(m + k + 2) =$ _____

8. $(P + 5)(P - 5) =$ _____

9. $(2N - R)(4 - 3R) =$ _____

10. $(A + 2)(2A - 5 + C) =$ _____

11. $(J - M)(J - M) =$ _____

12. $-3M(M + 2 - P) =$ _____

13. $(b + 4)(b - 4) =$ _____

14. $(y + 2b)(y + 2b) =$ _____

15. $(3r - 1)^2 =$ _____

16. $(2g - 3p)(-2g - 3p) =$ _____

17. $(-3m + 4d)^2 =$ _____

18. $(2R + 3N)(2R - 3N) =$ _____

19. Find the volume of a right rectangular prism in terms of d if the base of the prism is d units wide and $(d + 2)$ units long. The prism is 7 levels high, and each level is 1 unit high. Illustrate the steps you use to find the solution.

Compare the different factor groups in exercises 1–19 to the different regions in their diagrams. Are there any patterns to help you predict the final products?

terms of p." Ask students to draw a simple illustration of how many pies they have. Illustrating the situation or relationships described in a problem is an extremely important strategy in effective problem solving. From such pictures students are usually able to determine the operations and other steps needed to carry out a solution. Whenever specific amounts are not known, dots or dashes must be used in illustrations to represent unknown amounts. Here is a possible way to show the pies and their number of slices.

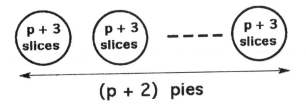

7. Since (p + 2) tells how many pies, or sets of (p + 3) slices, are needed, (p + 2) is the multiplier and (p + 3) is the multiplicand. Have students draw a diagram to find the product, which will be the total number of slices of pie obtained from all the pies. Remind students that the multiplier should be written as the first or left factor of a product. From the diagram and product grid, they should then express their result by writing the equation: **(p + 2)(p + 3) = (p² + 5p + 6) slices of pie in terms of the variable p.**

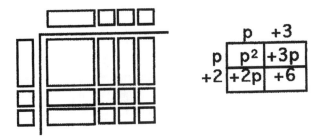

8. Assign additional exercises (see Worksheet 4–4–2) for students to solve by drawing diagrams and recording symbols in product grids. The left factor should always be drawn along the vertical bar of the L-frame; later, after much experience with products, students may begin to apply the commutative property of multiplication. Some possible exercises are listed below, along with another application or nonroutine problem. If two or more different variables occur in the same exercise, each variable rectangle must be labeled with the letter of the variable it represents; if only one variable is involved, no labeling is needed. Students should also write a simplified equation for each exercise worked. A discussion of the application will be provided below the set of exercises.

Additional exercises shown on Worksheet 4–4–2. (Symbolic answers are in brackets.)

5. B(2B − 3) = ?   [2B² − 3B]

6. (y − 1)(y + 1) = ?   [y² − 1]

7. (3k + 1)(m + k + 2) = ?
        [3km + 3k² + 7k + m + 2]

8. (P + 5)(P − 5) = ?   [P² − 25]

9. (2N − R)(4 − 3R) = ?
        [8N − 6NR − 4R + 3R²]

10. (A + 2)(2A − 5 + C) = ?
        [2A² − A + AC − 10 + 2C]

11. (J − M)(J − M) = ?   [J² − 2JM + M²]

12. −3M(M + 2 − P) = ?
        [−3M² − 6M + 3MP]

13. (b + 4)(b − 4) = ?   [b² − 16]

14. (y + 2b)(y + 2b) = ?   [y² + 4by + 4b²]

15. $(3r - 1)^2 = ?$ $[9r^2 - 6r + 1]$

16. $(2g - 3p)(-2g - 3p) = ?$ $[-4g^2 + 9p^2]$

17. $(-3m + 4d)^2 = ?$
     $[9m^2 - 24md + 16d^2]$

18. $(2R + 3N)(2R - 3N) = ?$ $[4R^2 - 9N^2]$

19. Find the volume of a right rectangular prism in terms of d if the base of the prism is d units wide and (d + 2) units long. The prism is 7 levels high, and each level is 1 unit high. Illustrate the steps you use to find the solution.
     $[(7d^2 + 14d)$ cubic units$]$

Discussion of application problem:

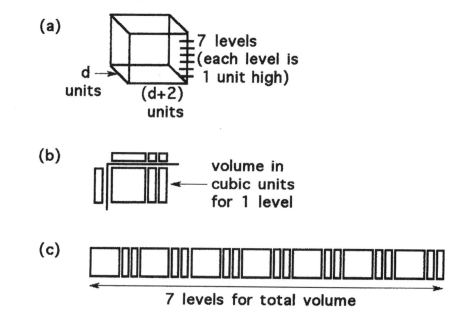

(a) Students might draw an outline of a prism and label the appropriate edges with the given dimensions; this helps clarify the definition of a prism.

(b) The *volume of one level* of the prism may be found by multiplying the two expressions given as dimensions of the base. The diagram shows that the volume of a single level of the prism is $(d^2 + 2d)$ cubic units.

(c) Since there are 7 levels in the prism, 7 of the polynomials, $(d^2 + 2d)$, need to be combined (added) together. Since this skill was covered in Objective 3, many students may be able to compute this sum (or product) mentally. The emphasis here, however, is on the strategy of drawing to find a solution; students should still try to illustrate the sum in some way. The result will be $(7d^2 + 14d)$ cubic units of volume for the entire prism.

Students should write algebraic equations for the steps they used. For the examples above, we would write the following: **$d(d + 2) = d^2 + 2d$ and $7(d^2 + 2d) = 7d^2 + 14d$. So the prism's volume in terms of d is $(7d^2 + 14d)$ cubic units.** [**Note:** Some students may prefer to combine both steps into one equation: $7d(d + 2) = 7(d^2 + 2d) = 7d^2 + 14d$; this is acceptable.]

9. After students have completed their diagrams and product grids, *ask:* "When you compare the different regions in your diagrams to the terms in the factor groups of the original exercises, do you see any patterns that might help you predict how the simplified, written equation will look for the final product?" Encourage students to look for regions of shapes under the same L-frame that: (1) are equal to each other [exercises 7, 10, 11, 13]; (2) are opposites of each other [exercises 2, 4, 9, 14]; or (3) are square arrangements [exercises 2, 4, 7, 9–14]. Exercise 12 may be used to clarify what sign agreement is needed on the first and second terms of particular binomials when predicting a trinomial (product) from the square of a binomial, or when predicting a product that results in the difference of two squares. If students recognize the pattern: $(a + b)(a - b) = a^2 - b^2$ (product as difference of two squares), ask them to predict the simplified, symbolic product for $(2k + 3m)(2k - 3m)$ *without* drawing a diagram. Confirm their prediction by then *drawing* a diagram. If students recognize the pattern: $(c + d)^2 = c^2 + 2cd + d^2$ (product as trinomial from squaring a binomial), ask them to predict the simplified, symbolic product for $(-3m + 5)^2$ without drawing a diagram. Again, confirm their prediction with a diagram. As stated at the beginning of this activity, if students do not easily recognize these two patterns, do not press for memorization. It is sufficient for them to be comfortable with the distribution concept of forming one row of partial products at a time, then simplifying to find the final product.

Activity 3: DRAWING STRATEGIES

[Application/Exploration]

Materials: Worksheet 4–4–3
Regular paper
Regular pencils

Management: Teams of 4 students each (50 minutes)

Directions:

1. Give each student a copy of Worksheet 4–4–3. It contains several nonroutine problems that involve the multiplication of variables in some way. Team members should work together to modify the given illustrations, and to identify the geometric and measurement concepts that need to be applied in order to find solutions. After all teams have completed or at least attempted the problems, ask different students to explain their drawings and their procedures to the entire class. If team illustrations differ for the same problem, discuss these variations with the class in terms of the problem's conditions.

2. Possible modified illustrations, along with computation steps, for the worksheet problems are provided here.

(1) Since a product grid is actually shown for this first problem, students merely need to fill in the spaces with the appropriate partial products. An equation for the total area might be written as follows:

$(b + 3)(b + 2 + b) = b^2 + 2b + b^2 + 3b + 6 + 3b = (2b^2 + 8b + 6)$ for total area in terms of b.

	b	+2	+b
b	b^2	+2b	b^2
+3	+3b	+6	+3b

WORKSHEET 4–4–3
Drawing Strategies

Use drawing techniques to solve the given problems. Be ready to discuss your ideas with the entire class.

1. Find the total area of the following figure in terms of b, using the given dimensions.

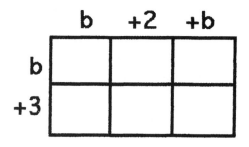

2. Square ABCD has a side length of m. E and F are midpoints of side AD and side BC respectively. What is the area of the shaded regions in terms of m?

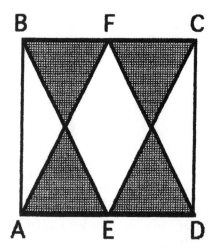

3. In the large square with ten connected regions, the areas of the disjoint regions have been indicated. Using the implied dimensions of these regions, what are some possible expressions for combined segments whose total length will equal the length y?

x^2	xy		
xy	b^2	ba	
	ba	n^2	nt
		nt	t^2

4. Figure ABCD is a square with a side length of 2m feet. E is the midpoint of segment BC and G is the midpoint of the segment CD. Express the area of the shaded region in terms of m.

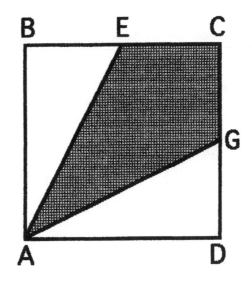

5. Figure ABCD is a square with a side length of k units. The square is contained within two overlapping circles with centers at B and D. In terms of k, what is the perimeter of the solid curved shape formed by the two circles?

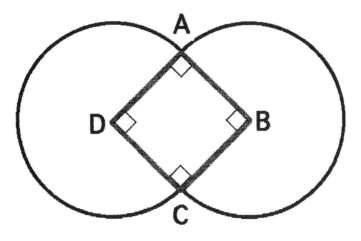

(2) Broken segments may be drawn on the original figure and certain sections numbered to show that shaded sections #1, 2, and 3 in the lower half of the figure might be rotated mentally into the "empty" sections with corresponding numbers in the upper half of the figure. If helpful, students might trace the lower shaded sections onto another sheet of paper, then rotate or cut out the tracings to place them over their matched sections in the upper half of the figure and confirm that the empty sections indeed are filled. The new shaded portion is now a rectangular region that is m units long and $\frac{1}{2}$m units wide. A product grid that shows only the pertinent measures might be helpful to some students at this stage. An example of an equation would be the following:

$(\frac{1}{2}m)(m) = \frac{1}{2}m^2$ square units of shaded area.

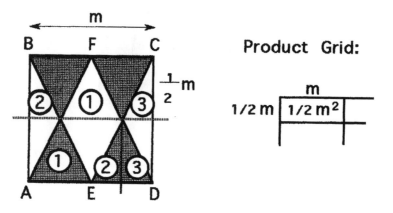

(3) To work this problem, students must use "backward thinking"; that is, they must think which measures or factors would produce the partial product shown as the area of each space in the figure. For example, the lower left space or region has an area of xy and it connects to a square region above that must have a side length of x units. This indicates that the lower left region must have a horizontal side length of x units and a vertical side length of y units. Similarly, since the square region of area b-squared must have side lengths of b units, the lower region of area ba must have a vertical side length of a. Students should continue this process in order to label the different segments on the figure with their measures. The vertical measures that compare to the vertical y-measure are circled on the figure. (Horizontal measures could be compared in a similar way.) So possible expressions equivalent in length to y are (b + a) and (b + n + t).

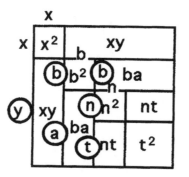

(4) The numbered, unshaded triangles in the figure are congruent since both are right triangles with one leg of length 2m feet and the other leg of length m feet (from E and G being midpoints of sides of the original square). If these two numbered regions are

removed from the figure, only the shaded region will remain. The area of each triangle equals $(\frac{1}{2})(2m)m$, or m^2 square feet, and the total area of the figure equals $(2m)(2m)$, or $4m^2$ square feet. Thus, the area of the shaded region may be computed as $4m^2 - m^2 - m^2 = 2m^2$ square feet, which is in terms of m.

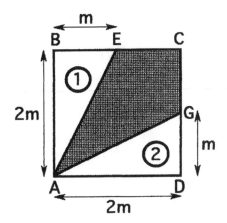

(5) To help students see how much arc length of each circle is being used to make the solid curved figure, a separate circle might be drawn to show the effect of the 90-degree central angle. Three-fourths of each circle forms the original figure; hence, $\frac{3}{4}$ of each circle's *circumference* will be added to find the perimeter of the solid curved figure. Using 3.14 to approximate the value of pi, each circle's circumference equals 3.14(2k), where 2k is the diameter, and $\frac{3}{4}$ of that circumference equals 0.75(3.14)(2k). Since two of this last product will be needed, the total perimeter of the solid curved figure is approximated with 2(0.75)(3.14)(2k), which equals 9.42 k units in terms of k.

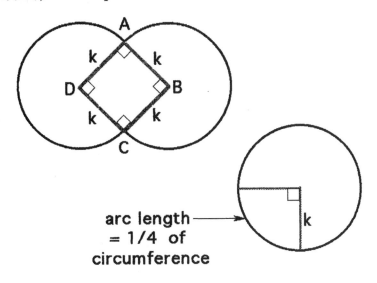

OBJECTIVE 5: Graph points (X, P(X)) where *X* is a measure of length for the polynomial region having "area": P(X) = aX² + bX + c, where *X*, *a*, *b*, and *c* are real numbers.

Activity 1: BUILDING FLOOR COVERS

[Developing Action]

Materials: Packets of tiles from Objective 3
Building mats from Objective 4
Calculators
Regular pencils
Regular paper
Worksheet 4–5–1

Management: Partners (50 minutes)

Directions:

1. Give each pair of students a building mat, a packet of tiles, and a calculator. In this activity students will build a "floor cover" or rectangular array of tiles as the product of two binomials in the same variable N. Each linear tile will have a width of 1 unit (based on the edge length of each unit or integer tile); the variable letter N will represent the length of the linear tile in units, as well as the tile's area in square units ($1 \times N = N$). Since each tile has a numerical area, we will assume that such areas have an *inverse* as well; that is, if a tile has an area of +25, then the inverse of the tile's area will be –25. Students will assign a length to N and, through their recording, *mentally* replace each variable tile (linear or quadratic) in the product or polynomial region with appropriate numerical values and compute the total area P(N) for the region. Each ordered pair (N, P(N)) found will be recorded in a table of values.

2. As an example, have students place tiles on the building mat to show (2N – 2)(3N + 2). Remind students that the first factor group is the multiplier (or "counter" of sets) and should therefore be built to the left of the L-frame on the mat; the second factor group is the multiplicand (or set to be copied) and should be built above the L-frame. Students should build the product on the mat according to the concepts developed in Objective 4; for example, an **N-amount of N** (or **N²**) will be shown with the large square tile, **N of +1** (or **N**) will be shown with the long, rectangular tile, and (–1)(3N), which is the **opposite of 1 set of 3N** (or **–3N**), will be shown with a row of 3 of the inverse variable tile, –N. The completed product is as follows:

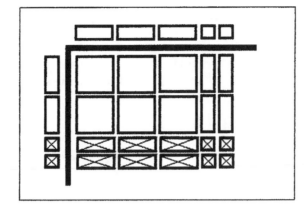

3. Have students write on their own papers a polynomial expression in N for the total area P(N) for their product of tiles: **P(N) = 6N² + 4N + (−6N) + (−4)** [recording the upper level of partial products first, followed by the lower level of tiles]. Working with one section of *like* tiles at a time, have students use +2 as the length of the linear variable tile and find the area of each tile in the product. Thus, for the 1 by N linear tile, the area will be 2 square units and the inverse of that area will be −2 square units; for the N by N quadratic tile, the area will be 4 square units; and the inverse of that area will be −4 square units. Students should now record the area (or inverse of the area) of each tile in the product by recording the following: **P(+2) = 6(+4) + 4(+2) + 6(−2) + (−4) = 24 + 8 − 12 − 4 = 16 square units of area when N = +2.**

4. Now have students repeat the above substitution process, using the value of N as +5, +10, then +50. The four ordered pairs (2, 16), (5, 136), (10, 576), and (50, 14896) should then be recorded in a 2-column table of values where the left column heading is **N** and the right column heading is **P(N)**. *Ask:* "As the value of N increases, in what way is the area P(N) changing? Is the area change a slow change or a fast change?" (*P(N) is also increasing and seems to make a fast change compared to the change in N;* as N changes by tens, the value of P(N) changes by the hundreds).

5. Now assign several other products for students to build and evaluate, using at least four different length values for N. (See Worksheet 4–5–1.) At least one value of N should be between +50 and +100; one or two values may be between 0 and +10. For Activity 1, we will consider only positive values for N; negative values will be introduced in Activity 2, as well as other variable names. Follow the procedures discussed in steps 3 and 4 above. Here are some possible products to assign.

(1) P(N) = (N + 4)(2N + 3)   (4) P(N) = (−N + 2)(N − 5)

(2) P(N) = (3N − 1)(N − 2)   (5) P(N) = (2N + 3)(−2N − 1)

(3) P(N) = (−4N + 3)(−N + 2)   (6) P(N) = (3N − 2)(2N − 1)

WORKSHEET 4–5–1
Building Floor Covers

For each product, build a "floor cover" with tiles. Find the area P(N) of the "floor cover" for four different length values of N between +1 and +100. At least one value of N must be between +50 and +100.

Example: $P(N) = (2N - 2)(3N + 2)$

Substitution Equations for Area P(N) with length N:	N	P(N)
P(+2) =	+2	
P(+5) =	+5	
P(+10) =	+10	
P(+50) =	+50	

Evaluate the following areas or products:

1. $P(N) = (N + 4)(2N + 3)$

2. $P(N) = (3N - 1)(N - 2)$

3. $P(N) = (-4N + 3)(-N + 2)$

4. $P(N) = (-N + 2)(N - 5)$

5. $P(N) = (2N + 3)(-2N - 1)$

6. $P(N) = (3N - 2)(2N - 1)$

Activity 2: DRAW 'N GRAPH

[Bridging Action]

Materials: 5-millimeter grid paper
Calculators
Regular paper
Regular pencils
Colored pencils (any color)
Worksheet 4–5–2

Management: Partners (50 minutes)

Directions:

1. Give each pair of students 3 sheets of 5-millimeter grid paper, a colored pencil (any color), and a calculator. Ask students to fold each grid sheet in half to form a top half and a bottom half of the sheet. Each half-sheet will be used to graph one exercise. For each graph, an interval of –5 to +5 will be used for the horizontal axis and an interval of –10 to +10 used for the vertical axis. In this activity, students will draw diagrams or use product grids (see Objective 4 for details) to find product regions as **simplified polynomials.** An equation will be written for each value selected for the variable; from that equation, the total area of the region will be found. Each ordered pair (length, area) found will then be graphed, and the approximate path formed by the points will be drawn on the graph. Changes in the "area" caused by changes in the length (or in the inverse of the length's value) will be discussed. (**Note:** In this activity we will continue to view the polynomial product as a *geometric region* having area, even though we will now begin to use negative values for the linear variable. The geometric approach is helpful to students who are visual learners. For our purpose here, we may view the use of negative values as an *extension* of the computations with real measures to the *inverses* of those measures.)

2. Write the product P(X) = (X + 2)(X – 2) on the board and ask students to find the polynomial form of the product by drawing a diagram on a sheet of plain paper. The diagram should represent the tiles and the L-frame used in Activity 1, and is shown below. The drawing technique is the same one used in Activity 2 of Objective 4 earlier. [**Note:** Later in this activity, as an alternative technique to drawing shapes, students will be allowed to record the product in a *product grid* (see Objective 4). An example is given below for the present exercise.] Using the diagram students should write the product as a simplified polynomial: **P(X) = (X + 2)(X – 2) = X² – 4.**

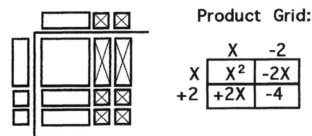

Product Grid:

	X	-2
X	X²	-2X
+2	+2X	-4

3. Ask students to find the total area of the product region for at least *five* different values or lengths of X, the linear variable. Instruct students to use zero, as well as negative and positive integers for X, whichever values will give them a "complete picture" of how the area P(X) of the product region changes as the value of X changes within the given intervals of the set of axes. For this example, X might be –3, –1, 0, +2, and +3. For each value chosen, the substitution should be recorded. For example, for X = –3, each plain linear variable shape (long rectangle) will have an "area" of $(1) \times (-3) = -3$ and each *inverse* linear variable shape (long rectangle with X inside) will have an area that is the *opposite* of –3, or +3. The quadratic variable shape (large square) will have an "area" of $(-3) \times (-3) = +9$. If helpful, for a given variable length students might write the different area values lightly on the appropriate shapes in the diagram to help them understand the more abstract substitution process. Students should now record the following on their own papers: **P(–3) = (–3)² – 4 = 9 – 4 = 5.** Each ordered pair (X, P(X)) found should be recorded in a 2-column table with **X** and **P(X)** as the column headings. Finally, each ordered pair should be located on a set of axes on a grid sheet. Have students label the horizontal axis as **Length X** and the vertical axis as **Area P(X);** similar labels will be used for other exercises, but the variable letter will change. After students have located their first five points, *ask:* "If these five points lie in a path formed by many other points that belong to this same polynomial, do you think you can accurately predict what the path will look like? Do you need more points to help you with this prediction? What other values of X might you try?" This is the first experience with parabolic curves for most students. Often they do not realize that the curve *gradually* turns and will be *symmetrical;* when connecting adjacent points on the grid, students will draw line segments rather than nonlinear curves. For this first example, to have a more complete "picture" of the path, ask students to also find the total area for X = –2 and X = +1 (if they have not already done so). A **curving** path should be drawn in colored pencil through all the points that have been plotted on the set of axes. The final graph should have the given appearance:

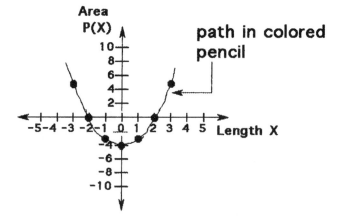

4. Now assign other products for additional practice. (See Worksheet 4–5–2.) Students should represent some products in a *diagram* and others in a *product grid*. For each product, an equation should be written, which shows the simplified polynomial found. Each variable substitution should be recorded in polynomial format as shown in step 3 before giving the final total value. A 2-column table should be prepared for all ordered pairs computed. After all ordered pairs for a given product are plotted on their own set of axes, the points should be connected with a curved path drawn in colored pencil. Do not allow students to draw straight segments between adjacent points.

WORKSHEET 4–5–2
Draw 'N Graph

Procedure:

1. Draw a diagram or product grid for each product.

2. Write an equation to record the results.

3. Evaluate the final polynomial for 5 different values of the variable (use 0 and some positive and negative values).

4. Make a table for the 5 ordered pairs found.

5. Plot the ordered pairs on graph paper.

Products to use:

Draw a diagram for exercises 1 through 3.

1. $P(m) = (-m + 1)(-m + 2)$

2. $P(N) = (N + 3)(2N + 1)$

3. $P(k) = (k - 1)(k + 1)$

Draw a product grid for exercises 4 through 6.

4. $P(R) = (R - 1)(-R - 2)$

5. $P(a) = (-a - 2)(a + 2)$

6. $P(w) = (0.5w + 1)^2$

5. Here are some possible products to assign. Have students draw diagrams with shapes for exercises (1) through (3), then use only product grids for exercises (4) through (6).

(1) $P(m) = (-m + 1)(-m + 2)$

(4) $P(R) = (R - 1)(-R - 2)$

(2) $P(N) = (N + 3)(2N + 1)$

(5) $P(a) = (-a - 2)(a + 2)$

(3) $P(k) = (k - 1)(k + 1)$

(6) $P(w) = (0.5w + 1)^2$

6. When all students have completed their graphs, discuss the appearance of the resulting curves: some open downward, some upward; all are symmetrical about a vertical line; some are narrower or do not spread open as much as others do; parts of a curve may be above or below the horizontal axis; etc. This type of curve is called a **parabola** or a **parabolic curve.** On various graphs, select a value on the horizontal or "length" axis, say –2, and *ask:* "As we move horizontally to the right from –2, how does the 'total area' or numerical value of the vertical height of the path change?" As an example of a response to a particular graph, students might observe that the path increases in its height until we reach +1 on the horizontal axis; beyond +1, the height of the path begins to decrease. Responses will vary, depending on where we start on the horizontal or independent axis. If we start far enough to the right, the vertical height may only decrease or increase. Always move in an increasing direction (or to the right) on the horizontal axis; this helps students develop a more consistent idea of vertical change with respect to horizontal change. Be sure to discuss the idea that some points of a path might be below the horizontal axis and thus have negative values for their vertical height or "total area." Remind students that when they move in an **increasing** direction **horizontally** (i.e., to the right) along a curve or path, if their vertical height changes from –8 to a vertical height of –1 or of +3, then the vertical height has **increased** with respect to the horizontal axis.

Activity 3: FACTOR LINES VS. PRODUCT CURVES

[Application/Exploration]

Materials: Worksheet 4–5–3
            Graphing calculators
            Colored pencils (at least 3 different dark, bright colors)
            Rulers or straight edges
            Regular pencils
            Regular paper

Management: Teams of 4 students each (50 minutes)

Directions:

1. Give each team of students 4 copies of Worksheet 4–5–3, a graphing calculator, a ruler or straight edge, and 3 different colored pencils (1 per color). In this activity, each team will graph the polynomial form (or the binomial factors, if preferred) of a given product on the graphing calculator, using a viewing window of $X\varepsilon[-5, +5]$ and $Y\varepsilon[-10, +10]$ with a scale of +1. (It is assumed that students have already used the graphing calculator to study linear functions in Section 3; therefore, only a minimum of instruction or review should be needed for this activity.) Students will then graph each binomial factor (or linear function) separately over the graph of the polynomial (actually the polynomial **function**). Team members will copy the parabolic curve in regular pencil and the two lines in color #1 pencil onto the same small grid on their own worksheets. The points on the horizontal axis where the lines cross the curve will be circled with the color #2 pencil and the point where the two lines intersect each other will be circled with the color #3 pencil. After the worksheet is completed, students will look for patterns among the graphs and their corresponding algebraic products. This activity is an application of linear graphs studied previously in Section 3 (particularly Objective 9). Even though students will be graphing the linear functions on their calculators, this would be a good time to review what the vertical intercept, as well as the slope or ratio of vertical and horizontal differences, tells us about locating a line on a graph.

2. As an example, write **P(w) = (w + 3)(−2w + 1)** on the board. Remind students that for this activity any letter used as the variable in a product will need to be keyed in as X since graphing calculators typically are set up to use that letter for the independent variable in graphing. Instead of P(w), graphing calculators are set up to use the letter Y for the dependent variable. In real applications, however, other letters may be more appropriate choices; hence, we want students to make conscious changes here. Ask students what the simplified polynomial will be for the given product. Encourage them to use the *Product Grid* (see Objective 4) to find the answer, if necessary. The result will be **P(w) = −2w² − 5w + 3.** Have students graph P(w) on their calculators, using Y for P(w). This may be done by inputting either the polynomial form or the binomial factor form. On the same graphing screen have students also graph each binomial factor as a linear function; that is, they should graph **F(w) = w + 3** and **G(w) = −2w + 1.** (The three different functions may actually be keyed in as Y$_1$, Y$_2$, and Y$_3$ on the calculator.)

3. Students should now copy their three graphs onto one of the grids on Worksheet 4–5–3, matching carefully to corresponding grid markings. The curve should be drawn in regular pencil and the two lines drawn with the color #1 pencil. Students should then use the color #2 pencil to circle the points where the lines cross the curve on the horizontal axis, and use the color #3 pencil to circle the point where the two lines intersect each other. A complete equation for the product should be recorded below the grid. An illustration of the completed drawing is shown here.

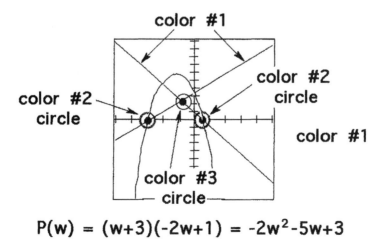

$$P(w) = (w+3)(-2w+1) = -2w^2-5w+3$$

WORKSHEET 4–5–3
Factor Lines vs. Product Curves

Using the graphing calculator, for each product of factors assigned, graph each binomial factor and their product on the same view screen. Copy the three graphs onto a grid on the worksheet. Record an equation for the product below the grid.

1.

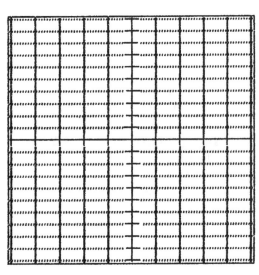

2.

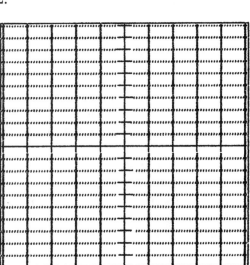

3.

4.

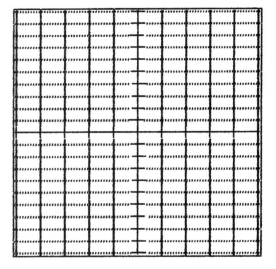

WORKSHEET 4–5–3 *(cont.)*
Factor Lines vs. Product Curves

5.

6.

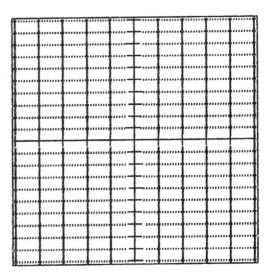

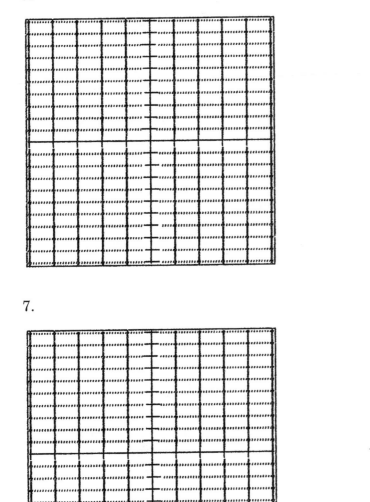

7.

8.

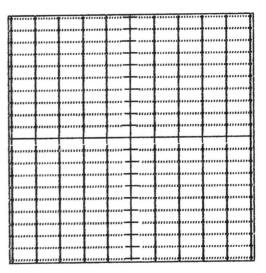

4. Now have students graph other products and their separate binomial factors. They should copy the graphs onto grids and circle the proper intersection points as shown in step 3 above. Here are some possible products to assign:

(1) P(m) = (m − 3)(m + 3)   (5) P(a) = (−a + 2)(a + 2)

(2) P(B) = (2B + 3)²   (6) P(p) = (−p + 3)(−p − 3)

(3) P(k) = (−3k − 2)(−3k + 2)   (7) P(d) = (−d + 1)²

(4) P(X) = (−X + 1)(X − 1)   (8) P(N) = (−3N − 2)(3N + 2)

5. After the teams have completed their graphing, ask them to look at the positions of the lines and the curve in each graph and compare what they see to the types of linear factors used in the product. Remind them of the special patterns found in products of binomial factors in Objective 4: the difference of squares, and the square of a binomial. Several patterns are possible; students should test any conjectures they form by graphing other products that have the same characteristics observed in an assigned product. In general, all product curves are symmetrical, and all lines involved will intersect their product curve at the horizontal axis. Here are other patterns students might find: (a) exercises 1, 3, and 6 yield differences of squares; the curve opens upward and the two lines are parallel; there are two different points on the horizontal axis where the curve intersects one of the lines; if an inverse variable occurs in both binomial factors, the lines have a negative slope; (b) exercises 2 and 7 involve the squaring of a binomial; the curve opens upward and there is only one line, which intersects the curve at only one point on the horizontal axis; the line has a negative slope if an inverse variable is used in the binomial; (c) exercises 4 and 8 have factors that are additive inverses; the curve opens downward and the two lines intersect the curve at the same and only one point on the horizontal axis; the slopes of the two lines are additive inverses, so one line is the reflection across the horizontal axis of the other line; and (d) exercise 5 involves variables that are additive inverses, but the two constants are not inverses; the curve opens downward and the two lines intersect each other but not on the curve; the two lines intersect the curve at different points on the horizontal axis. (Since exercise 5 does not have another related product in the assigned set, other similar exercises need to be tested by students to see if the identified characteristics occur consistently.)

Answer Key for WORKSHEET 4–5–3

1. P(m) = (m − 3)(m + 3) = m² − 9   **2.** P(B) = (2B + 3)² = 4B² + 12B + 9

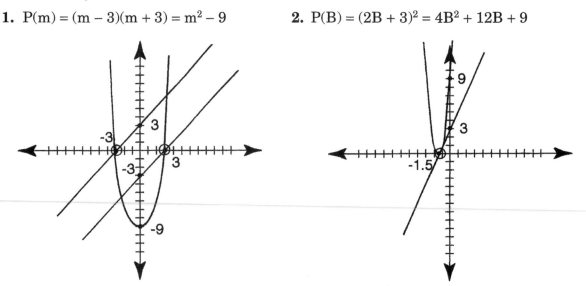

3. $P(k) = (-3k - 2)(-3k + 2) = 9k^2 - 4$

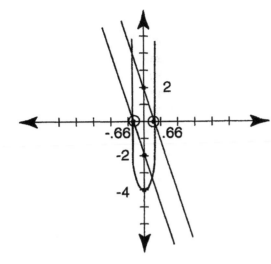

4. $P(X) = (-X + 1)(X - 1) = -X^2 + 2X - 1$

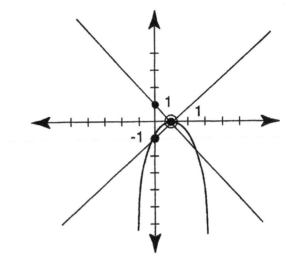

5. $P(a) = (-a + 2)(a + 2) = -a^2 + 4$

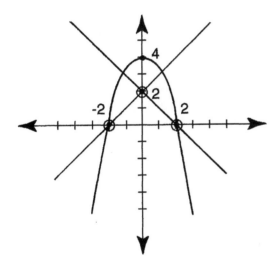

6. $P(p) = (-p + 3)(-p - 3) = p^2 - 9$

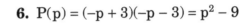
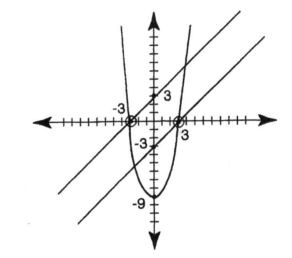

7. $P(d) = (-d + 1)^2 = d^2 - 2d + 1$

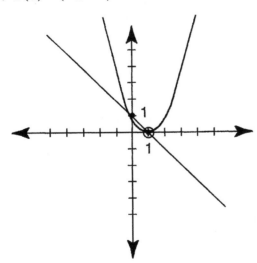

8. $P(N) = (-3N - 2)(3N + 2) = -9N^2 - 12N - 4$

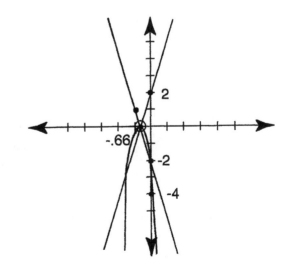

OBJECTIVE 6: Factor polynomials of second degree in one variable.

Activity 1: BACKWARD MOVES!

[Developing Action]

Materials: Packets of tiles from Objective 3
Building mats from Objective 4
Regular paper
Regular pencils
Worksheet 4–6–1

Management: Partners (50 minutes)

Directions:

1. Give each pair of students a packet of tiles (8 large square tiles, 12 long rectangular tiles, and 20 small square tiles) and a building mat. As a review, have students build the product $(B + 2)(2B - 3)$ on the building mat (refer to Objective 4, if necessary). Remind students that the first factor, $(B + 2)$, is the multiplier and is always placed to the left of the L-frame. Notice that the tiles in the product under the L-frame form a rectangular shape. Discuss the four different subregions that these tiles have formed under the L-frame and how each subregion contains only one type of tile: the upper level contains 2 large square tiles (B^2) on the left and 3 inverse rectangular tiles ($-B$) on the right, and the lower level contains 4 rectangular tiles (B) on the left and 6 inverse small square tiles (-1) on the right. These disjoint subregions only exist because of the way we originally arranged the two binomial factors around the L-frame on the mat; like tiles were grouped together within each factor group, and the linear variable tiles were placed in the upper position of the multiplier and in the left position of the multiplicand or set. This ordering does not need to be followed; theoretically, the tiles for each factor can be arranged more randomly. The result, however, is a random mix of tiles within the final product with no obvious patterns being formed by the tiles. To invoke and benefit from students' visual memories, we will always use the ordered approach when building products. Consequently, when multiplying two binomials of the form $(aX + b)$, we will expect to find the quadratic variable or large square tiles in the upper left section of the product and the unit or small square tiles in the lower right; the linear variable or long rectangular tiles will be in both the upper right section and the lower left. This consistent tile arrangement will greatly aid us in the factoring of polynomials of second degree in one variable.

2. Have students clear their mats, then place 1 quadratic variable tile, 5 linear variable tiles, and 6 unit tiles in the product region under the L-frame. *Ask:* "If these tiles represent a product of two binomials, they can be arranged to form a rectangular design. Applying what we have learned about the order or pattern of the four different subregions of tiles in our products, can you arrange these tiles under the L-frame so that we can tell what the two binomial factors should be?" Once students arrange the tiles according to the pattern described in step 1, they should be able to identify which tiles must be in each factor group's position on the mat by *thinking backward;* in other words, which two tiles would be needed as factors to yield each individual tile shown in the final product?

Two possible tile arrangements on the mat are shown below. Have students rearrange their tiles on their mats to show both ways. The arrangement used determines which factor serves as the multiplier or first factor to be recorded in the final equation. Using B as the variable letter in Activity 1, students should record on their own papers both equations found: $B^2 + 5B + 6 = (B + 2)(B + 3)$ or $B^2 + 5B + 6 = (B + 3)(B + 2)$. They should also draw a *product grid* to represent each arrangement. (**Note:** Some students may notice that inverse forms are also possible as factors; for example, $(-B - 2)(-B - 3)$. Acknowledge such ideas as correct, but we will not *record* them in this activity.)

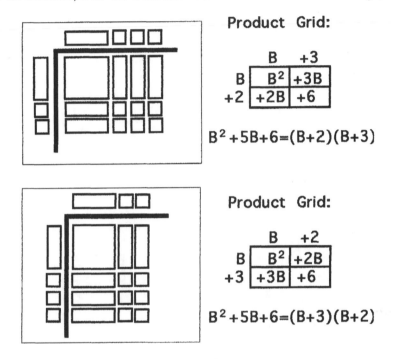

Product Grid:

	B	+3
B	B^2	+3B
+2	+2B	+6

$B^2 + 5B + 6 = (B+2)(B+3)$

Product Grid:

	B	+2
B	B^2	+2B
+3	+3B	+6

$B^2 + 5B + 6 = (B+3)(B+2)$

3. Now have students clear their mats, then place 1 quadratic variable tile and 4 inverse unit tiles on the mat under the L-frame. **Ask:** "Remembering which type of tile is in each subregion, where should these new tiles be placed?" (*the quadratic variable tile will be in the upper left or within the corner of the L-frame and the inverse unit tiles will be in the lower right in some **random grouping** at first*) "Since a tile product for two polynomials always has a rectangular shape with several subregions, where are the linear variable tiles that should be in the upper right and lower left sections of our product region in order to complete the rectangular shape? Remember that each subregion must contain only one type of tile." Allow students time to think about this situation. Eventually, but not immediately, remind them of the important concept of **0-pairs.** Hopefully, they will realize that the only way they can fill the empty subregions is to bring in 0-pairs of the linear variable tile; this method will not change the overall value of their original product tiles. Have students bring in the 0-pairs to the mat one pair at a time, placing the plain variable tile (B) in one of the empty subregions and the inverse variable tile (–B) in the other empty subregion; at this time, it does not matter which tile goes to which subregion. As new 0-pairs are added, all inverse variable tiles must be grouped together and all plain variable tiles grouped together. Students must now begin to "play" with their 4 inverse unit tiles to see how they will fit with the new linear variable tiles being added to the mat. The strategy of **trial-and-error** is needed here; allow students time to struggle with the tiles. If necessary, remind them that for an inverse tile to be in the product, one of the factors producing that tile must also be an inverse tile of some kind. Finally, when they discover an arrangement that works, have them draw the product grid and write the equation for that particular arrangement. Then the students should rebuild their tiles to show the other possible arrangement, and draw its product grid and write its equation. Have students observe the relationship between the partial product in each product grid space and the algebraic expressions that serve as labels for the row and column that determine that grid space. For example, in the first product grid in step 1 above, $-3B$ is in the row of B and the column of -3, showing that $-3B$ factors into $B(-3)$. Below are the two distinct ways, along with their product grids and equations:

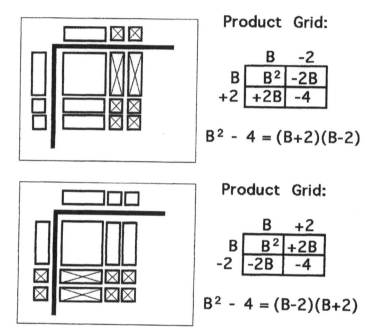

Product Grid:

	B	-2
B	B^2	-2B
+2	+2B	-4

$$B^2 - 4 = (B+2)(B-2)$$

Product Grid:

	B	+2
B	B^2	+2B
-2	-2B	-4

$$B^2 - 4 = (B-2)(B+2)$$

4. Now that students have factored polynomials where both factors are *binomials* (this will be the basic pattern for our factoring), they need experience with a *monomial* factor. Ask students to place 2 inverse quadratic variable tiles and 5 linear variable tiles on the mat under the L-frame and arrange the tiles in a rectangular shape. They will probably try to separate the linear variable tiles into two groups, putting some in the upper right region and some in the lower left region. This will form a lower right space that is **empty,** since no unit tiles were given originally. Hence, students must move all the linear variable tiles together, either to the upper right space on the mat or to the lower left space. These two positions determine the two ways to build the product: the monomial might be the *multiplier* so that only the upper level (left and right sections) of the mat is used for tiles, or it might be the *multiplicand* so that only the left column (upper and lower sections) is used. Since inverse tiles are used, students also have a choice as to where to place the inverse factors. Here are the possible ways to describe what is built: (a) upper level only—$B(-2B + 5)$ or $-B(2B - 5)$; or (b) left column only—$(-2B + 5)B$ or $(2B - 5)(-B)$. Be sure that the multiplier is written in the correct position. Students should still draw a 2 by 2 grid for the product grid, even though only one row or one column is really needed, because the 2 by 2 grid represents the basic pattern and creates the visual image for all products. Here is a factoring arrangement that uses the upper level of the mat's product region, along with its corresponding product grid and equation.

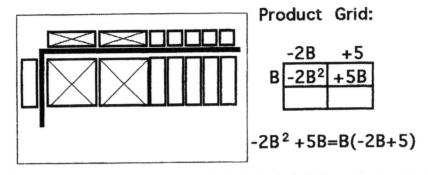

Product Grid:

	-2B	+5
B	$-2B^2$	$+5B$

$-2B^2 + 5B = B(-2B + 5)$

5. Sometimes in division, polynomials for both the dividend (product) and divisor (factor) will be known. The basic pattern of the product region, combined with the given divisor (one of the desired factors), will lead to the other missing factor, which will be the quotient. Write the following on the board: $(X^2 + 5X + 6) \div (X + 2) = ?$ or $\frac{(X^2 + 5X + 6)}{(X + 2)} = ?$ Have students place one quadratic variable tile, 5 linear variable tiles, and 6 positive unit tiles on the mat under the L-frame, and place one linear variable tile and 2 positive unit tiles to the left of the L-frame. This last group of tiles has been placed in the multiplier position for discussion purposes, but the group could also be placed above the frame in the multiplicand position if students prefer. Recalling the basic pattern of subregions within the product (or dividend), students should place the quadratic variable tile in the dividend-product in the same row as the linear variable tile in the divisor-multiplier. Since linear variable tiles occupy the lower left region of the product, two such tiles should be positioned so that each lies in the same row as one of the unit tiles in the divisor-multiplier. The other 3 linear variable tiles must then be placed in the upper right region, and the 6 positive unit tiles must be arranged as 2 rows of 3 tiles each in the lower right region of the product. This final arrangement indicates that the missing factor (quotient) that goes above the L-frame must be $(X + 3)$. Have students complete a product grid and write the following equations on their own papers to show their results: $(X^2 + 5X + 6) \div (X + 2) = (X + 3)$ or $\frac{(X^2 + 5X + 6)}{(X + 2)} = (X + 3)$.

6. Assign more sets of tiles as products for students to build on their mats and find the factors. (See Worksheet 4–6–1.) For each product, continue to have students build the tiles in the two distinct arrangements, then draw the appropriate product grids and record the appropriate equations. This will reinforce their understanding of the *commutative property of multiplication*. For some products, however, only **one** distinct arrangement will be possible—those products that are **perfect squares**. In such cases, students should only draw one product grid and one equation. (**Note:** Since B^2 can always be factored as either $(B)(B)$ or the inverses $(-B)(-B)$, we will not require the inverse form at this time. It will be helpful for future studies, however, if you occasionally ask students to describe the inverse factors for a given exercise.) Here are some possible products to assign:

(1) $2B^2 + 7B + 3 = ?$

(2) $2B^2 + 5B + 2 = ?$

(3) $B^2 + B - 2 = ?$

(4) $B^2 - 9 = ?$

(5) $-B^2 + 2B = ?$

(6) $-B^2 + 4B - 3 = ?$

(7) $2B^2 + 8B = ?$

(8) $(-B^2 - 3B - 2) \div (B + 2) = ?$

(9) $4B^2 - 4 = ?$

(10) $(B^2 - 6B + 9) \div (B - 3) = ?$

WORKSHEET 4-6-1
Backward Moves!

Build with tiles in two ways, if possible, to find factor pairs for the given products. On your own paper draw a product grid for each factoring that is built. Record an equation for each product grid below the grid. For two exercises, only one factor needs to be found.

1. $2B^2 + 7B + 3 = ?$

2. $2B^2 + 5B + 2 = ?$

3. $B^2 + B - 2 = ?$

4. $B^2 - 9 = ?$

5. $-B^2 + 2B = ?$

6. $-B^2 + 4B - 3 = ?$

7. $2B^2 + 8B = ?$

8. $(-B^2 - 3B - 2) \div (B + 2) = ?$

9. $4B^2 - 4 = ?$

10. $(B^2 - 6B + 9) \div (B - 3) = ?$

Answer Key for WORKSHEET 4–6–1

Only the different factor pairs are shown below in symbolic form. Product grids themselves have not been included.

1. $(B + 3)(2B + 1)$ and $(2B + 1)(B + 3)$

2. $(2B + 1)(B + 2)$ and $(B + 2)(2B + 1)$

3. $(B + 2)(B - 1)$ and $(B - 1)(B + 2)$

4. $(B + 3)(B - 3)$ and $(B - 3)(B + 3)$

5. $B(-B + 2)$ and $(-B + 2)B$; or $-B(B - 2)$ and $(B - 2)(-B)$

6. $(-B + 1)(B - 3)$ and $(B - 3)(-B + 1)$; or $(B - 1)(-B + 3)$ and $(-B + 3)(B - 1)$

7. $(B + 4)(2B)$ and $(2B)(B + 4)$; or $B(2B + 8)$ and $(2B + 8)B$

8. $(-B - 1)$

9. $(2B + 2)(2B - 2)$ and $(2B - 2)(2B + 2)$

10. $(B - 3)$

Activity 2: FACTOR DRAW

[Bridging Action]

Materials: Regular paper
Regular pencils
Worksheet 4–6–2

Management: Partners (50 minutes)

Directions:

1. Students will draw their own L-frames on their own papers. For each exercise, the L-frame should be drawn midway across the width of the paper with a third of the paper's width to the left and a third of the width to the right. Each leg of the L-frame should be about 2.5 inches long. The variables and units in the polynomial to be factored should be drawn on the left side of the L-frame and the product grid and equation will be recorded on the right side of the frame in the right third of the paper's width. These measurements allow for three exercises per sheet of paper (upper, middle, and lower sections) and prevent diagrams from being overcrowded and being difficult to read.

2. Have students show the polynomial $N^2 + 3N + 2$ by drawing (free-hand) a large square, 3 long rectangles, and 2 small squares near the left edge of the paper. The length of each rectangle should be equal approximately to the side length of the large square. An L-frame should then be drawn to the right of the shapes about midway across the width of the paper, and a 2 by 2 product grid should be drawn farther to the right near the right edge of the paper. *Ask:* "Because of what you know about the basic pattern of the product region, what spaces in the product grid can you complete before you even begin to draw any shapes under the L-frame?" *(the upper left with N^2 and the lower right with +2)* Students should write these two expressions in the grid at this time, then draw a copy of the large square (quadratic variable) inside the corner of the L-frame and mark out the original large square at the left to show it has been used. ***Ask:*** "Since we know the 2 positive units (small squares) must go in the lower right section either horizontally or vertically adjacent to each other, what does this tell us about the 3 linear variables (long rectangles)?" *(some must go in the upper right section and some in the lower left section)* Encourage students to lightly sketch the 2 small squares and 3 rectangles in different positions under the L-frame until proper rows and columns are formed. Once the product region is complete, students should mark out the original shapes shown at the left and should draw the shapes that form the factors in their proper places on the L-frame. The two remaining spaces in the product grid should now be completed, as well as the correct expressions for row/column labels that indicate the factors. An equation should be written below the product grid that shows the particular factors used in the drawing. Some students will have $(N + 2)$ as the multiplier; others will have $(N + 1)$ in that position. Whenever product grids are completed, have students check each factor pair to confirm their match with the expression in the grid space; for example, $(N)(N) = N^2$, $(N)(+1) = +N$, $(+2)(N) = +2N$, and $(+2)(+1) = +2$ in the grid shown below. (**Note:** In product grid work, it helps students to show *all* signs on the expressions, whether positive or negative. It controls for error when the two linear terms must be combined.) Here is one way for the factoring to be illustrated and recorded.

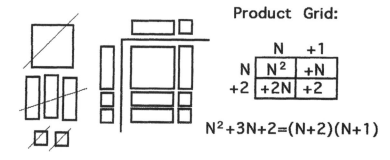

Product Grid:

	N	+1
N	N^2	+N
+2	+2N	+2

$$N^2 + 3N + 2 = (N+2)(N+1)$$

3. Now have students draw a new L-frame below the previous frame and draw 4 quadratic variables and 9 inverse units to the left of the L-frame near the left edge of the paper. Also have them draw a blank product grid near the right edge of the paper. ***Ask:*** "Remembering which type of variable or unit is in each subregion, where under the L-frame should these new shapes be drawn?" *(the quadratic variables will go in the upper left or within the corner of the L-frame and the inverse units will go in the lower right)* Students should record the quadratic expression **4d²** in the upper left space of the grid and **–9** in the lower right space. "Since a product for two polynomials always has a rectangular shape with several subregions, where are the linear variables that should go in the upper right and lower left sections of our product region in order to complete the rectangular shape? None are shown in our original set of shapes at the left edge of your paper. Remember that each subregion must contain only one type of variable or unit." Allow students time to think about this situation. Eventually, but not immediately, remind them of the important concept of 0-pairs. Hopefully, they will realize that the only way they can fill the empty subregions is to draw 0-pairs of the linear variable; they must not change the overall value of their original product tiles. Discuss the idea that these two subregions must have the same *number* of shapes, but one group will be the inverse of the other. Under that condition and because of the way the linear variables are positioned (lower left variables are horizontal lengthwise, and upper right variables are vertical lengthwise), the inverse units must be drawn in a *square* configuration. Similarly, the quadratic variables must be drawn in a *square* configuration. Students should now draw the four quadratic variables (d^2) near the corner of the L-frame as 2 rows of 2 large squares each. The original four large squares at the left side of the paper should now be marked out. Have students begin to draw 0-pairs of the linear variable, one pair at a time, lightly sketching the plain variables (d) in one of the empty subregions and the inverse variables (–d) in the other empty subregion; it does not matter which subregion is chosen for each linear variable form (d or –d), but each rectangle must be aligned with the edge of a large square already drawn under the L-frame. As a row and a column of linear variables begin to come together at a point, an inverse unit should be drawn where the row and column appear to "meet." The drawing continues until 3 rows of 3 inverse units each have been drawn, forming the lower right section of the product as expected. The original 9 inverse units drawn near the left edge of the paper should now be marked out. Students should begin to identify and draw appropriate shapes in the factor positions as their corresponding product shapes are drawn under the L-frame. The strategies of **trial-and-error** and **logical reasoning** are needed here; students must go back and forth from shapes within factors to the shape within the product that they produce, continually confirming that the matches are correct. Finally, when students have drawn an arrangement that works (that is, all factor pairs correctly match to their specific shapes in the product region), have them complete the last two spaces in the product grid (**–6d** and **+6d**) and write the equation for their particular arrangement. Have students also test the factor pairs recorded on their *grids* to see if they correctly match the expression in their corresponding grid space. Below are two possible factorings (not counting the inverse forms) with their product grids and equations:

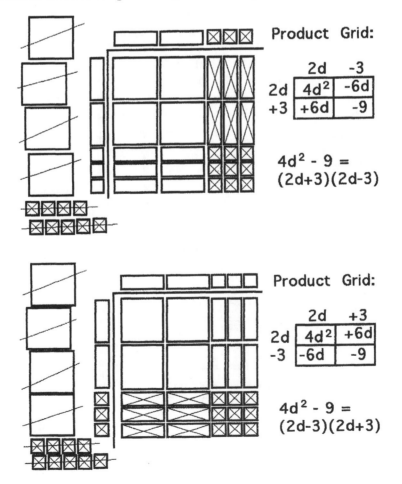

Product Grid:

	2d	-3
2d	4d²	-6d
+3	+6d	-9

$$4d^2 - 9 = (2d+3)(2d-3)$$

Product Grid:

	2d	+3
2d	4d²	+6d
-3	-6d	-9

$$4d^2 - 9 = (2d-3)(2d+3)$$

4. Now give students an exercise where both the product (dividend) and a factor (divisor) will be known. Remind students that the basic pattern of the product region, combined with the given divisor (one of the desired factors), will lead to the other missing factor, which will be the quotient. Write the following on the board: $(-2X^2 + 3X + 2) \div (-X + 2) =$ **? or** $\frac{(-2X^2 + 3X + 2)}{(-X + 2)} = ?$ Have students center an L-frame on their own papers and draw 2 inverse quadratic variables, 3 linear variables, and 2 positive units to the left of the L-frame near the left edge of their paper, then draw one inverse linear variable and 2 positive units to the left of the L-frame as the divisor-multiplier. This last group of shapes has been drawn in the multiplier-divisor position for discussion purposes, but the group could also be drawn above the frame in the multiplicand position if students prefer. Recalling the basic pattern of subregions within the product (or dividend), students should draw the 2 inverse quadratic variables in the dividend-product in the same row as the inverse linear variable in the divisor-multiplier. The two large squares in the group at the left should now be marked out. Because of the inverses in the dividend and the divisor, a plain variable must be drawn in the multiplicand or quotient position above each inverse quadratic variable. The expressions $-2X^2$ and $+2$ in the product spaces, $-X$ and $+2$ in the left factor, and $2X$ in the upper factor should be recorded in the product grid at this time. Continuing, since linear variables occupy the lower left region of the product in our pattern, long rectangles must be drawn below the two quadratic variables in the product. Since these rectangles must also line up with the 2 units in the divisor-multiplier, 2 rows of 2 plain rectangles each are needed in the product; however, there are only 3 such rectangles available in the group shown at the left of the L-frame. An extra rectangle or linear variable needs to be added to the original group of shapes in the dividend, but this can only be done if it comes in as part of a 0-pair. Students should now draw another linear variable and its inverse shape near the original group of shapes. Thus, the two rows of 2 linear variables each may now be drawn in the lower left region and an inverse linear variable must be drawn in the upper right region of the product. All linear variables drawn in the group of shapes at the left should be marked out, and the expressions $+4X$ and $-X$ should be recorded in their appropriate spaces in the product grid. **Ask:** "Since we know that the 2 positive units go in the lower right region so that they line up with the 2 units in the divisor-multiplier, what do we finally know about the missing factor or quotient?" *(a positive unit must be in the quotient with the 2 linear variables)* Have students complete the diagram for the product and record $+1$ over the right column of the product grid. Finally, have students write the following equations on their own papers to show their results: $(-2X^2 + 3X + 2) \div (-X + 2) = (2X + 1)$. **(Note:** In this exercise, one factor was already given; therefore, inverses of the two factors, $(-X + 2)$ and $(2X + 1)$, will not represent another solution.)

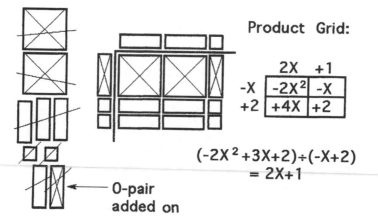

Product Grid:

	2X	+1
-X	$-2X^2$	-X
+2	+4X	+2

$(-2X^2 + 3X + 2) \div (-X + 2)$
$= 2X + 1$

O-pair
added on

WORKSHEET 4-6-2
Factor Draw

On your own paper draw diagrams to find the different factor pairs for each product given below. Draw a product grid for each factoring found. Record an equation for each product grid. For two exercises, only one factor needs to be found.

1. $2A^2 + 5A + 3 = ?$

2. $w^2 - w - 2 = ?$

3. $3m^2 + 5m + 2 = ?$

4. $4B^2 - 1 = ?$

5. $(X^2 + 4X + 4) \div (X + 2) = ?$

6. $-2k^2 + 6k = ?$

7. $-2y^2 - 5y - 2 = ?$

8. $9H^2 + 6H + 1 = ?$

9. $(N^2 - 16) \div (N - 4) = ?$

10. $6p^2 - 4p = ?$

5. Now assign other polynomials for partners to factor by drawing shapes under an L-frame. (See Worksheet 4–6–2.) Before they begin to draw shapes, however, they should try to write as many expressions in the *product grid* (both factor terms and partial products) as they can determine through their reasoning about the patterns found in the product region. They will then test these expressions as they continue to draw shapes to complete their product. (**Note:** The goal is eventually to be able to use *only* the product grid, along with trial-and-error and with logical reasoning, to find the factors of a given second-degree polynomial in one variable. This process is equivalent to other methods used in past curricula, but it provides students with a much more *visual* way of accounting for all needed partial products.) When factoring each polynomial, students should follow the drawing and labeling procedure used in steps 2 through 4 above. When all are finished, have various students explain their work to the whole class; this will continue to support the idea that more than one arrangement or equation is usually possible when factoring a polynomial. Here are some possible polynomials to assign:

(1) $2A^2 + 5A + 3 = ?$

(2) $w^2 - w - 2 = ?$

(3) $3m^2 + 5m + 2 = ?$

(4) $4B^2 - 1 = ?$

(5) $(X^2 + 4X + 4) \div (X + 2) = ?$

(6) $-2k^2 + 6k = ?$

(7) $-2y^2 - 5y - 2 = ?$

(8) $9H^2 + 6H + 1 = ?$

(9) $(N^2 - 16) \div (N - 4) = ?$

(10) $6p^2 - 4p = ?$

Answer Key for WORKSHEET 4–6–2

Only factors in symbolic form are provided; product grids and factoring diagrams are not included.

1. $(2A + 3)(A + 1)$ and $(A + 1)(2A + 3)$

2. $(w + 1)(w - 2)$ and $(w - 2)(w + 1)$

3. $(3m + 2)(m + 1)$ and $(m + 1)(3m + 2)$

4. $(2B + 1)(2B - 1)$ and $(2B - 1)(2B + 1)$

5. $(X + 2)$

6. $k(-2k + 6)$ and $(-2k + 6)$; or $(k - 3)(-2k)$ and $(-2k)(k - 3)$

7. $(-y - 2)(2y + 1)$ and $(2y + 1)(-y - 2)$; or $(y + 2)(-2y - 1)$ and $(-2y - 1)(y + 2)$

8. $(3H + 1)(3H + 1)$

9. $(N + 4)$

10. $(2p)(3p - 2)$ and $(3p - 2)(2p)$

Activity 3: FACTOR CHALLENGES

[Application/Exploration]

Materials: Worksheet 4–6–3
Regular paper
Regular pencils
Tile packets and building mats from Activity 1 *(optional)*

Management: Teams of 3–4 students each (50 minutes)

Directions:

1. Give each team of students one copy of Worksheet 4–6–3 (only one copy per team causes students to work together as a team rather than as individuals). The worksheet contains four different types of problems, each requiring the factoring of polynomials in some way. Encourage students to draw a **product grid** when factoring a polynomial. It will help them account for all the partial products involved. Allow students to use the tiles and building mats if they are not quite ready to work abstractly with the algebraic notation. The first problem on the worksheet requires students to transform and label parts of a diagram in order to find a solution. The other problems are designed to make students aware of processes being used and to give them experience with alternative solutions. Additional problems like those on Worksheet 4–6–3 may be found in the following resource books:

- Thompson, Frances M. (1988). *Five-Minute Challenges for Secondary School* (Activity Resources Co. Inc., P.O. Box 4875, Hayward, CA 94540). ["What Doesn't Belong?" and "What's Missing?"]

- Thompson, Frances M. (1992). *More Five-Minute Challenges for Secondary School* (Activity Resources Co. Inc., P.O. Box 4875, Hayward, CA 94540). ["Squiggles"]

2. After teams have completed Worksheet 4–6–3, have different students share their strategies and answers with the class. For each problem in the "What Doesn't Belong?" category, several responses will be possible; ask for the different choices and the reason for each choice. For the "Squiggles," have students draw their solutions on the board; different networks are created when the polynomial labels for the points are reassigned to new points. The strategy of **trial-and-error** is certainly involved here, and **logical reasoning** must be applied because polynomials cannot always be randomly assigned to a network of points.

Discussion of Problems on WORKSHEET 4–6–3

1. If the segment PR is drawn, a square AQRP will be formed, whose area is twice the area of the triangle, or $2(2N^2) = 4N^2$. Four quadratic variable tiles in a square arrangement must have 2N for the length of each side. So AP = AQ = 2N, which should be labeled on the diagram. Since P is a midpoint, the length PS also equals 2N. Each side length of the large square ABCS must then equal 2N + 2N, or 4N, and the perimeter will be 4(4N) or 16N.

2. The empty space should have $-10N(N + 2)$, the factored form of the given binomial.

3. The empty space should have $(X - 2)^2$, the factored form for the perfect square.

WORKSHEET 4–6–3
Factor Challenges

Solve the following problems with your teammates. Be ready to explain your solutions to the entire class.

1. In the given diagram, shape PQRS is a parallelogram and shape ABCS is a square. Points P and Q are the midpoints of their respective sides of the square. The area of the shaded region is $2N^2$. Modify the diagram as needed and label all known measures, then find the perimeter of shape ABCS.

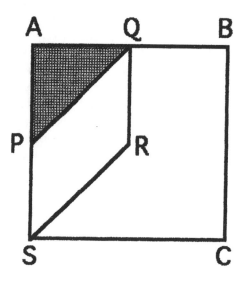

What's Missing?

In each problem, two algebraic expressions are being changed to new formats, using the same procedure. The arrows point to the new expressions. One of the spaces is empty. Can you decide what belongs there? Give a reason.

2.   3.

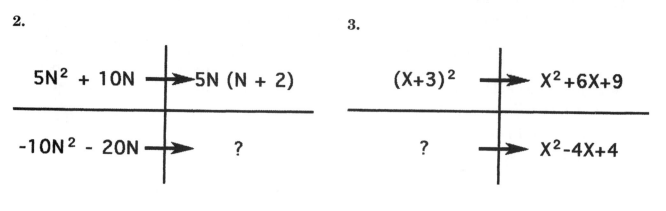

WORKSHEET 4–6–3 *(cont.)*
Factor Challenges

What Doesn't Belong?

Three of the four expressions in the boxes have something in common. The other one differs from them in some way. Which one does not belong? Give a reason. (Several responses may be possible, but for different reasons.)

4.   **5.**

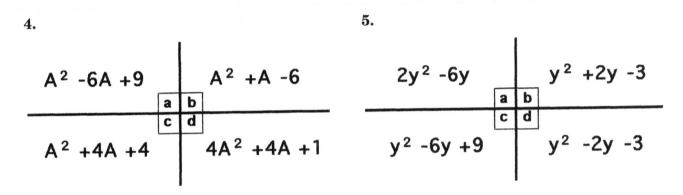

Squiggles

A rule is given with each squiggle to tell how terms or expressions at adjacent points on the network should relate to each other. Assign each expression in the given set to its own unique point on the squiggle. One point has already been labeled. Solutions for labeling points will vary.

6.   **7.**

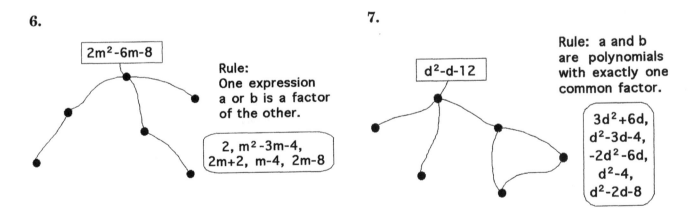

4. Several choices are possible that do not belong for the stated reasons: (a) has an inverse variable or has a negative coefficient on the linear term; (b) is not a perfect square, or it has a negative constant; (c) has the same amount of linear variables as units; or (d) has more than one of the quadratic variable.

5. Several choices are possible that do not belong for the stated reasons: (a) has a monomial factor; (b) does not have a (y–3) factor; or (c) is a perfect square.

6. and **7.** Each polynomial in the set will be written beside a point in the squiggle, so that adjacent or connected polynomials share a common factor. Assignments of polynomial to point can be done in a variety of ways.

One possible solution for (6):

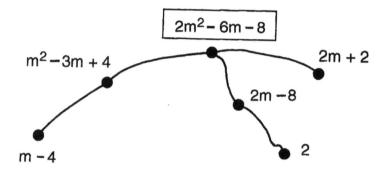

One possible solution for (7):

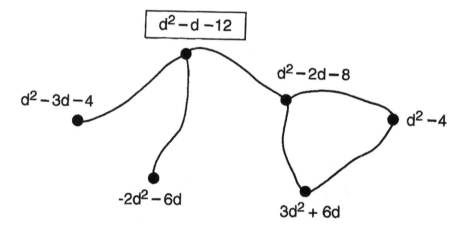

OBJECTIVE 7: Investigate quadratic sequences of figurate numbers to generate quadratic functions; find an expression for the N-th term.

Activity 1: BUILDING BY PATTERNS

[Developing Action]

Materials: One-inch square tiles (or one-inch paper squares) in reclosable plastic bags
Paper
Regular pencils

Management: Partners (50 minutes)

Directions:

1. Give each pair of students a reclosable plastic bag of about 100 square tiles.

2. Have students build rectangular regions with their tiles, building them in order of size with the smallest one first. Show them the following shapes already drawn on a transparency; do not draw the shapes in front of the students. Students must decide *how* to build each new rectangular region for themselves.

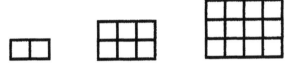

3. Have them make a 2-column table to record their work. Use the headings: *Which Shape* (e.g., write "1" for first shape built) and *Total Tiles in Shape*. The left column for *Which Shape* should show 1, 2, 3, . . . and the right column should show the totals 2, 6, 12, ... The amount of tiles in each shape represents a **rectangular number.**

4. Ask several students to tell how the first and second shapes are alike and how they are different. (*Possible responses:* Both shapes are rectangular where each has equal rows of tiles; #2 has 1 more row and 1 more tile per row than #1 has, or #2 has 2 rows instead of 1 row and 3 tiles per row instead of 2 tiles.) Ask how the second shape differs from the third one. (Responses should be similar to those for #1 and #2. Some students may see shape #2 as *adding 1 more* tile to the row of #1, then *adding 1 more* row of 3 tiles; then to get shape #3, 1 more tile may be added to each row in #2 and then another row of 4 tiles added on. This approach is an *additive* approach and will result in a *finite series,* $2 + 4 + 6 + \ldots + 2(N-1) + 2N$, for the N-th term, which we do not want at this stage since we are focusing on quadratic sequences, that is, sequences whose N-th term is a second-degree polynomial. To avoid the additive approach, encourage students to view each new term or shape as a complete arrangement or array of tiles rather than a shape formed by joining new sections to previous sections.)

5. Ask students to build the fourth shape (it should have 4 rows with 5 tiles per row) to the right of the first three.

6. Have some students describe in their own words what each shape looks like. Encourage the following type of details: *The first shape has 1 row of 2 tiles; #2 has 2 rows of 3 tiles each; #3 has 3 rows of 4 tiles each; etc.*

7. Ask the students to predict how the tenth shape might look and how many tiles total will be needed, based on their descriptions given in step 6. (Example: *#10 has 10 rows of 11 tiles each.*) Have them complete their table through the tenth shape with its total tiles, 110 tiles. Some students may need to build the other shapes (#5 through #9) to confirm their predictions of the total tiles needed for the tenth shape. They will not have enough tiles to keep all shapes built concurrently; they will need to dismantle earlier shapes in order to build each new, larger shape that follows shape #5. Discuss how the numbers in the *Total* column change (increase by a different amount each time) as the shape number increases by 1.

8. Now ask them to try to describe how to find the total tiles needed for making the N-th rectangular shape. The algebraic expression should follow the language pattern used in step 6: *The N-th shape will use N rows of (N + 1) tiles per row, or N × (N + 1) or N(N + 1) tiles total.* Have students write the letter N above the *Which Shape* column of their table and their expression N(N + 1) above the *Total* column. **Note:** Do not rewrite N(N + 1) as $N^2 + N$ at this stage; physically, they may have different meanings and students must be allowed to see the difference. N(N + 1) is N rows of (N + 1) tiles each, whereas $N^2 + N$ implies some amount N has been *added* to a squared amount.

9. Show 3 new shapes on a transparency for students to build with their tiles, again building them in order of size with the smallest one first. Each shape will be a "staircase" of tiles.

10. Have students make a 2-column table to record their work. Use the headings: *Which Shape* and *Total Tiles*. As before, the first three rows of the table will be for the first three shapes shown, and will have the following numbers (left to right by row): 1,1; 2,3; and 3,6. The amount of tiles in each staircase represents a **triangular number.**

11. Ask students to build the fourth staircase to the right of the first three. The bottom row will have 4 tiles, the next step will have 3 tiles, then 2 tiles, and 1 tile. The number pair 4,10 should be recorded in the table.

12. Have some students describe in their own words what each shape looks like. Their first response will probably be similar to the following: *The first staircase has 1 step of size 1; staircase #2 has 1 step of size 2 and 1 step of size 1; staircase #3 has 1 step of size 3, 1 step of size 2, and 1 step of size 1; etc.* This is an *additive* approach. We need the students to view the staircases in a *multiplicative* way if we are to avoid having a finite series: N + (N - 1) + . . . + 3 + 2 + 1, for the N-th term later.

13. Ask students to look at the staircases differently and think of each staircase as part of something larger, yet familiar to them. *Ask:* "If we just look at the second and third staircases, can we use the complete staircase in some way to form a rectangular shape? That is, we want to use a whole staircase, not parts of steps, to make the new shape." Hopefully students will notice that two of the same staircase can be rotated and joined together to make a rectangular shape. This can be done in two different ways as shown below. A description of the tile arrangement is written below each "doubled" staircase. Each original staircase will need only "half" of the tiles used in the doubled staircase.

(a)   (b)

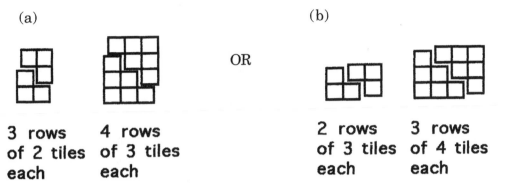

OR

3 rows
of 2 tiles
each

4 rows
of 3 tiles
each

2 rows
of 3 tiles
each

3 rows
of 4 tiles
each

14. Ask students to apply both doubling methods to the first and fourth staircases to see if it will work with them as well. When doubled, the first staircase under method (a) becomes 2 rows of 1 tile each, and under method (b) becomes 1 row of 2 tiles. The fourth staircase doubled under method (a) becomes 5 rows of 4 tiles each, and under method (b) becomes 4 rows of 5 tiles each. So staircase #1 will need half of 2×1 tiles or half of 1×2 tiles; staircase #4 will need half of 5×4 tiles or half of 4×5 tiles.

15. Based on how the previous staircases have been described, ask different students to predict what staircase #10 might look like and how many tiles will be needed. Some students may need to build staircases #5 through #9 first before they can decide about staircase #10. They may have to dismantle the smaller staircases in order to have enough tiles to build each of the larger ones. They should continue to record their numbers in the table. Following the description methods used in steps 12 through 14, staircase #10 should have *1 step of 10 tiles, 1 step of 9 tiles, . . . , 1 step of 2 tiles, and 1 step of 1 tile.* Under method (a), its total tiles will be half of 11×10 tiles; under method (b), its total tiles will be half of 10×11 tiles.

16. Ask students to describe how the N-th staircase will look, according to their chosen description method. Here are possible statements for the two approaches above. Method (a): *The N-th staircase will have half of (N + 1) rows of N tiles, or ($\frac{1}{2}$)(N + 1)N tiles;* Method (b): *The N-th staircase will have half of N rows of (N + 1) tiles, or ($\frac{1}{2}$)N(N + 1) tiles.* **Note:** The expression used must closely represent the method and language used by the students to build the shapes. Do *not* simplify the expressions to ($\frac{1}{2}$)(N^2 + N) at this time, even though they are mathematically equivalent. Also, keep the multiplier of a situation in its correct position as the first factor of the product; for example, if the counter of sets (multiplier) is N, as in N rows of (N + 1) tiles above, the product should be written as N(N + 1), not as (N + 1)N. Students should now write N above the *Which Shape* column of their table and the expression for their particular method (either ($\frac{1}{2}$)(N + 1)N or ($\frac{1}{2}$)N(N + 1)) above the *Total* column.

17. If time permits, lead the class through the building of other sequences of shapes, following the same procedure and questioning used in steps 2 through 16. Be sure that the sequences are quadratic, that is, each shape's total tiles involves the squaring of the shape's position number in some way. For each sequence, have students record their numbers in a 2-column table; use *Which Shape* for the first heading and *Total Tiles* for the second heading. Encourage alternative descriptions of the sequence. Here are two possible sequences to use, along with descriptions of:

- the type of language needed to describe the shapes;

- the N-th shape's description and the expression for its total tiles; and

- the test of the N-th expression for total tiles for shape #1.

Example 1:

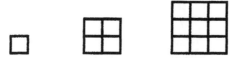

1. *Language:* Shape #1 has 1 row of 1 tile; shape #2 has 2 rows of 2 tiles each; shape #3 has 3 rows of 3 tiles each; etc. Remember that, for consistency of interpretation, **rows** of tiles are always defined as left-to-right or horizontally connected tiles.

2. *N-th shape:* N-th shape has N rows of N tiles each; total tiles = N(N) or N^2 tiles. The power form is used here as another name for the monomial; this is not considered *simplification* (at least as defined in this objective) since the multiplication does not produce any other terms of a final polynomial. The tile totals form the sequence of **squared** numbers.

3. *Test for shape #1:* (1)(1) = 1 tile. $\checkmark$

Example 2:

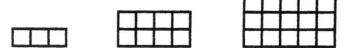

1. *Language:* Shape #1 has 1 row of 3 tiles; shape #2 has 2 rows of 4 tiles each; shape #3 has 3 rows of 5 tiles each; etc.

2. *N-th shape:* N-th shape has N rows of (N + 2) tiles each; total tiles = N(N + 2) tiles. This is another sequence of **rectangular** numbers.

3. *Test for shape #1:* (1)(3) = 3 tiles. $\checkmark$

Activity 2: PATTERN DRAW

[Bridging Action]

Materials: Paper
Regular pencils

Management: Partners (30–50 minutes)

Directions:

1. Follow the procedure used in steps 2 through 16 of Activity 1, except that students will be drawing the shapes rather than building them with tiles.

2. For each sequence discussed, show them the first three shapes of the sequence already drawn on a transparency. Do not allow them to see the shapes being drawn. Deciding how to draw the shapes helps students see the differences in the sequence terms.

3. Show the class the first three shapes of the first sequence. Have students work with a partner, but draw the sequence of shapes on their own paper.

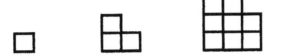

4. Discuss likenesses and differences: *Shape #2 has 1 stack of 2 squares more than #1 has; shape #3 is taller and wider than #2; etc.* Have students describe each shape: *#1 has 1 square; #2 has 1 stack of 2 squares and 1 square; #3 has 2 stacks of 3 squares each and 1 stack of 2 squares.*

5. Ask students to draw the fourth shape according to the changes they have seen. (#4 should have 3 stacks of 4 squares each and 1 stack of 3 squares.) Then have them predict how the tenth shape will look. (#10 should have 9 stacks of 10 squares each and 1 stack of 9 squares.)

6. All should now complete a table for the sequence, using column headings (left to right) *Which Shape* and *Total Squares*. The left column will have 1, 2, 3, 4, . . . and the right column will have 1, 3, 8, 15, ... Students should record information for the first ten shapes of the sequence. Discuss how the numbers in the *Total* column change (increase by a varying amount as the first column increases by 1 each time).

7. Ask students to describe the N-th shape in the sequence. Following the language used for the earlier shapes, the N-th shape should have (N–1) stacks of N squares each and 1 stack of (N – 1) squares, or (N – 1)N + (N – 1) squares total. Testing for shape #1, we have (0)(1) + 0 = 0 squares total, which is not correct, even though the rule or formula does work for all the other shapes. In such cases, we say that for N = 1, shape #1 will have 1 square, but for all other N, shape #N will have (N – 1)N + (N – 1) squares total. Often in sequences the first (and sometimes even the second) term must be given specifically, along with a general rule or formula for all other terms of the sequence.

8. The above method was *additive* in that each shape was seen as a combination of two different groups of squares. The shapes may also be viewed in a *subtractive* sense; that is, a shape may be viewed as part of a larger set of squares from which some squares have been removed. In the present sequence, we may view each shape as a squared arrangement where 1 square has been removed from the upper right corner. In other words, shape #2 has 2 rows of 2 squares each less 1 square, shape #3 has 3 rows of 3 squares each less 1 square, etc. Shape #N will have N rows of N squares each less 1 square, or $(N^2 - 1)$ total squares. Testing shape #1, we have 1 row of 1 square decreased by 1 square, or 0 squares, which is again incorrect. So once again we must state what shape #1 is, then apply the rule to find the total squares in all other shapes in the sequence.

9. Here is a second sequence to show to the students.

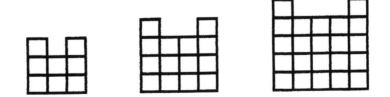

10. Ask students to draw the fourth shape and describe what they see. One possible description might be the following: *Shape #1 is 2 rows of 3 squares each and 2 extra squares on top; shape #2 has 3 rows of 4 squares each and 2 extra squares; shape #3 has 4 rows of 5 squares each and 2 extra squares; etc.*

11. Students should record, for each shape drawn, the shape number and its total squares in another 2-column table like the one described in step 6. Discuss how the totals are increasing by different even amounts each time.

12. Have them predict what the tenth shape will look like; if necessary, they should draw shapes #5 through #9 to confirm their predictions. Following the last descriptions used in step 10, shape #10 will have 11 rows of 12 squares each and 2 extra squares.

13. The N-th shape or term should now be described: The N-th shape will have $(N + 1)$ rows of $(N + 2)$ squares each and 2 extra squares. The total squares in the N-th shape will equal $[(N + 1)(N + 2) + 2]$ squares. Testing for shape #1, we have $(2)(3) + 2$ or 8 squares as the total, which is correct.

14. This second sequence might also be described in another way: *Shape #1 has 3 rows of 3 squares each with 1 square removed; shape #2 has 4 rows of 4 squares each with 2 squares removed; shape #3 has 5 rows of 5 squares each with 3 squares removed; etc.*

15. Then the N-th shape will be described as $(N + 2)$ rows of $(N + 2)$ squares each with N squares removed. Total squares will equal $[(N + 2)(N + 2) - N]$ squares. Testing for shape #1, we have $(3)(3) - 1$ or 8 squares total, which is correct.

16. Continue to show sequences to the class, following the procedure and questioning of steps 2 through 15 of this activity. Two-column tables should still be completed for the different shapes drawn and observations made about how the numbers change for each new shape. The algebraic expression recorded for the N-th shape in a sequence must represent closely the language used to describe the different shapes drawn previously in the sequence. Two possible sequences are given below.

Example 1:

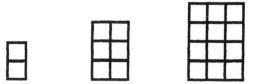

1. *Language:* Shape #1 has 2 rows of 1 square each; shape #2 has 3 rows of 2 squares each; shape #3 has 4 rows of 3 squares each; etc.

2. *N-th shape:* The N-th shape has $(N + 1)$ rows of N squares each; total squares = $(N + 1)N$ squares.

3. *Test for shape #1:* $2(1) = 2$ squares total. $\checkmark$

Example 2:
The shapes for the sequence are the "frames" consisting of unshaded squares.

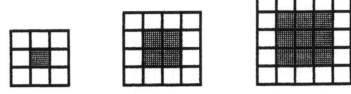

1. *Language:* Shape #1 has 3 rows of 3 squares each less 1 middle square shaded; #2 has 4 rows of 4 squares less the middle 4 squares (2 rows of 2) shaded; #3 has 5 rows of 5 squares less the middle 9 squares (3 rows of 3) shaded; #4 has 6 rows of 6 squares less the middle 16 squares (4 rows of 4) shaded; etc.

2. *N-th shape:* The N-th shape or "frame" has (N + 2) rows of (N + 2) squares each less the middle N rows of N squares shaded; total unshaded squares = [(N + 2)(N + 2) – N(N)] squares.

3. *Test for shape #1:* (3)(3) – (1)(1) = 9 – 1 = 8 squares total. √

Note: The above method was *subtractive* since squares were removed via the shading. An *additive* method might be used that groups the top and bottom rows together, then groups the remaining side squares together. The N-th shape might be described as 2 rows of (N + 2) squares each and 2 columns of N squares each; total unshaded squares = [2(N + 2) + 2N] squares. To test shape #1, we have 2(3) + 2(1) = 8 squares. √

Activity 3: A GRAPHING PERSPECTIVE

[Application/Exploration]

Materials: Bags of square tiles from Activity 1
Worksheet 4–7–1
Calculators
Paper
Colored pencils
Regular pencils

Management: Teams of 4 students each (30 minutes)

Directions:

1. Give each team of students a bag of square tiles, a copy of Worksheet 4–7–1, a calculator, and a colored pencil (not brown, black, or yellow). In this activity students will reverse the process used in Activities 1 and 2; that is, they will be given an **unsimplified** algebraic expression for the N-th term of a sequence and they will either build or draw what they think the first 4 shapes or terms will be. They will complete a table for each sequence, then plot the ordered pairs from the table onto the adjacent grid to form a scatterplot.

2. Write the following expression on the board to represent the N-th term of a sequence: N(N + 3) + 2 tiles or squares total. Each team should now build the first 4 shapes described by this expression. In N(N + 3), the N is the counter of groups and the (N + 3) tells how many tiles or squares must be in each group. One possible way is shown below; others are possible, too.

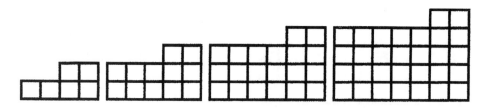

3. A table on Worksheet 4–7–1 should be completed that shows the shape number and its total tiles or squares. Also have students use the algebraic expression for the N-th shape to *compute* the total tiles or squares for N = 5 and N = 6. These values should be recorded in the table as well. The ordered pairs should be plotted on the grid next to the table. The pairs will be (1,6), (2,12), (3,20), (4,30), (5,42), (6,56). The six points of the scatterplot should be connected with a colored pencil.

4. Now write another expression on the board: N(2N – 1) tiles or squares total. The first factor N is the multiplier and tells that N groups are involved of size (2N – 1). Students should build the first 4 shapes of the sequence. Here is one possible way to show the shapes:

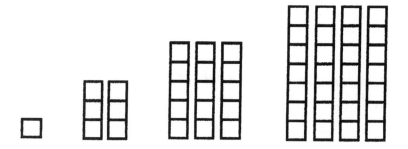

5. After the four shapes are built or drawn, each team should complete a table on Worksheet 4–7–1 that shows each shape number and its total tiles or squares. Also have students use the algebraic expression for the N-th shape here to *compute* the total tiles or squares for N = 5 and N = 6. These values should be recorded in the table as well. The ordered pairs should be plotted on the grid next to the table. The pairs will be (1,1), (2,6), (3,15), (4,28), (5,45), (6,66). The six points of the scatterplot should be connected with a colored pencil.

6. Ask students to look at the scatterplots they have made and decide how they are alike and how they are different. Hopefully they will notice that each set of six points connects to form a path that curves upward to the right. This will be true for certain **quadratic** or **second-degree sequences,** i.e., the sequences where the totals are increasing by a different but increasing amount as N increases by 1 each time. Also, compared to the first path, the second path appears to start lower at the left, but end steeper and higher at the right. (This activity continues our preparation for **quadratic functions,** which will be studied in the next objective.)

Name _____ **Date** _____

WORKSHEET 4–7–1
A Graphing Perspective

Follow the teacher's directions to complete the two tables below and plot their ordered pairs on the nearby grids. Compare the two scatterplots you make. What do you notice?

1. $T(N) = N(N + 3) + 2$

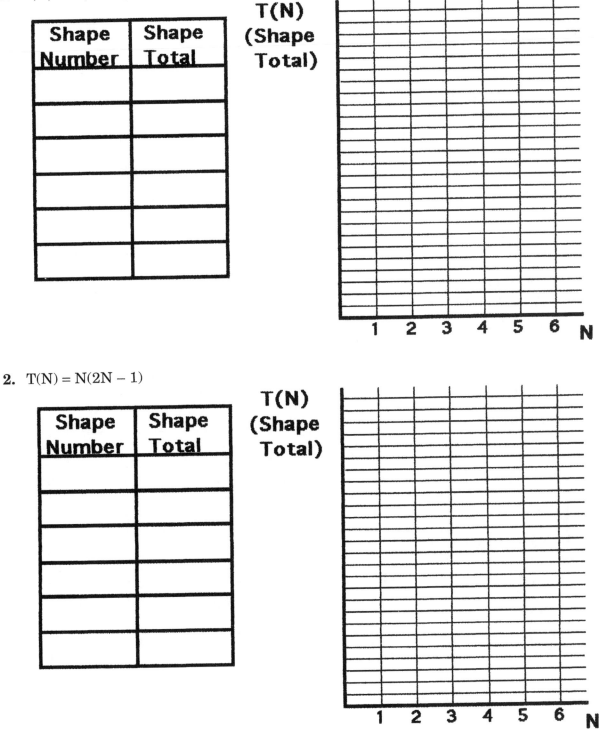

Shape Number	Shape Total

T(N) (Shape Total)

1 2 3 4 5 6 N

2. $T(N) = N(2N - 1)$

Shape Number	Shape Total

T(N) (Shape Total)

1 2 3 4 5 6 N

OBJECTIVE 8: Explore quadratic functions and the effects on their graphs when coefficients and constants are varied.

Activity 1: SLIDING CURVES

[Developing Action]

Materials: Large grid paper and small colored counters or markers (described in step 1)
12-inch lengths of plastic- or rubber-coated electric wiring ($\frac{1}{8}$-inch width, flat, bendable and maintains shape; three different colors if possible)
Calculators
Regular pencils
Regular paper
Worksheet 4–8–1

Management: Teams of 4 students each (50 minutes)

Directions:

1. Give each team a large grid, two pieces of electric wiring (2 different colors, 1 wire per color), a bag of 8 colored counters or markers (2 markers per color, 4 different colors), and a calculator. The small markers might be commercially-available colored centimeter cubes, colored flat buttons (approximately 0.5-inch diameter), or square or hexagonal metal nuts (approximately 0.5-inch diameter; spray-painted in 4 colors, 2 nuts per color) from a hardware store. Other materials are possible; the markers just need to be in 4 different colors and about 0.5-inch in diameter. A similar set of markers used in Activity 1 of Objective 6, Section 3 might be used for this activitiy, but additional markers may need to be added to that original set. The grid may be drawn off on heavy bulletin board paper to form approximately a 12-in. × 24-in. grid (unit length of 1 inch), or several smaller grids might be taped together to make the larger grid that is needed. Using an inch grid segment as a unit of length on an axis, draw a horizontal axis to show the interval [−5,+5] and a vertical axis to show the interval [−12,+12]. Laminating the final grids will make them more durable. Packaging the 8 small markers in a snack-size, closable, plastic bag will also make distribution of materials easier and quicker. In this activity we will focus on the symmetry of the curve and the behavior of the vertical axis intercept (generally called the **Y-intercept**) as a curve slides vertically up or down on the grid. Have each team draw a table with three columns on their own paper. (See Worksheet 4–8–1.) The column headings should be from left to right "Curve #1," "Curve #2," and "Curve #3." Curve #1 will be used for the **basic** or **parent** curve for each family of curves discussed in this activity. Seven ordered pairs will be recorded in each column.

2. Ask each team to record in their table on the first line under the heading of the "Curve #1" column the polynomial function, $P(N) = N^2$. This will serve as the basic function to which to compare the other two. Have students compute the value of $P(N)$ for $N = −3, −2, −1, 0, +1, +2,$ and $+3$, then record the corresponding ordered pairs in the "Curve #1" column in the order listed here for N. For each point located on the large grid, a small

Name ____________________ Date ____________

WORKSHEET 4–8–1
Sliding Curves

For each table, find ordered pairs for and build each of three curves on the large grid. Make a quick sketch and label the three curves on the axes to the right of the table.

1.

Curve #1	***Curve #2***	***Curve #3***
$P(N) = N^2$	$P(N) = N^2 + 2$	$P(N) = N^2 - 2$
(−3,)		
(−2,)		
(−1,)		
(0,)		
(+1,)		
(+2,)		
(+3,)		

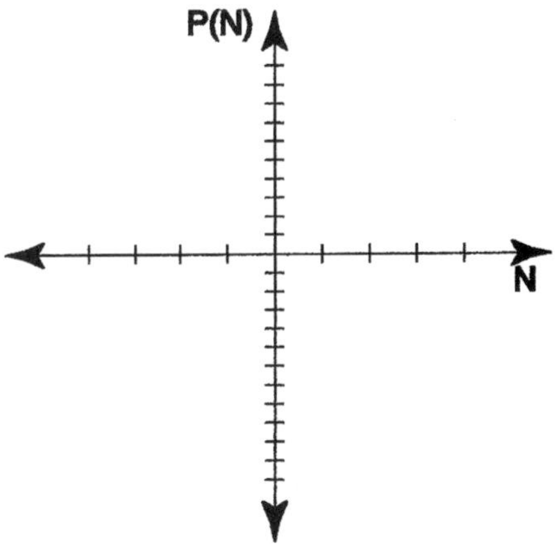

How are the curves alike? different?

2.

Curve #1	***Curve #2***	***Curve #3***
$P(N) = -N^2$	$P(N) = -N^2 + 3$	$P(N) = -N^2 - 1$
(−3,)		
(−2,)		
(−1,)		
(0,)		
(+1,)		
(+2,)		
(+3,)		

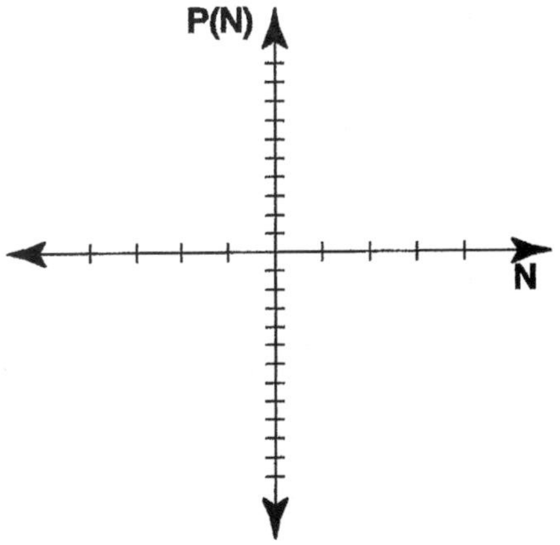

How are the curves alike? different?

3.

Curve #1	Curve #2	Curve #3
$P(N) = (N-1)^2$	$P(N) = (N-1)^2 + 2$	$P(N) = (N-1)^2 - 2$
(−2,)		
(−1,)		
(0,)		
(+1,)		
(+2,)		
(+3,)		
(+4,)		

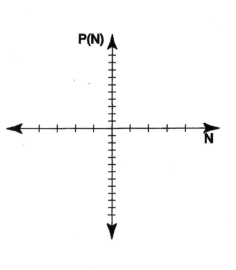

How are the curves alike? different?

4.

Curve #1	Curve #2	Curve #3
$P(N) = 2N^2$	$P(N) = 2N^2 + 3$	$P(N) = 2N^2 - 1$
(−3,)		
(−2,)		
(−1,)		
(0,)		
(+1,)		
(+2,)		
(+3,)		

How are the curves alike? different?

marker or counter should be placed at that point. The markers should be placed according to their colors as follows: color #1 for N = 0 (used to indicate the **vertex** of the curve), color #2 for N = −1 or +1, color #3 for N = −2 or +2, and color #4 for N = −3 or +3. The same color of marker will be used for two points that are images of each other with respect to the line of symmetry for the curve, or more specifically, for the two points with the same **ordinate** value; this will provide a visual cue to help students become aware of the **symmetry** of any quadratic curve. Because of future steps in this activity, it will be helpful to place a small piece of rolled masking tape or poster putty on the bottom of each marker to hold it more securely on the grid. The masking tape should not tear the grid paper if it is pressed down lightly. If the grid has been laminated, rather than the moveable markers, washable colored marking pens might be used to draw large dots directly on the grid to mark points.

3. Once the seven points have been located on the grid, students should take one 12-inch piece of electric wiring (wire color #1) and fold it at its midpoint to make a U-shaped curve. Holding the midpoint or "point of bend" of the wiring with one finger at point (0,0) on the grid, a student should gradually bend the wiring to shape it to touch each of the other six markers on the grid. Discuss the different characteristics of the curve being represented by the bent wiring: there is a **least ordinate** (or a **greatest ordinate** in later examples) in the ordered pairs, which indicates the **turning point** or **vertex** of the curve; the curve opens upward; touches the vertical axis at (0,0); is symmetrical with respect to the vertical axis (i.e., the vertical axis serves as the line of symmetry for the curve); each colored marker (except for the vertex marker) has a matching marker horizontally across the vertical axis (line of symmetry) from itself; the distances of matching markers from the vertical axis (line of symmetry) are equal; etc.

4. Teams should repeat steps 2 and 3, using $P(N) = N^2 + 2$ as "Curve #2" and then $P(N) = N^2 - 2$ as "Curve #3" on the 3-column table. Wire color #2 should be used for curve #2 and wire color #3 should be used for curve #3. For each new curve, the colored markers used for the **parent** or **basic curve** or curve #1 should be carefully lifted from the grid (if masking tape is used), then moved to their new positions on the grid. Once the new curve's wiring is in place on the markers, the basic curve's wiring should be returned to its original position on the grid for comparison purposes. As each curve is built on the grid, students should draw a free-hand sketch of that curve on their own paper; all 3 curves should be drawn on the same set of axes and labeled with their P(N) description. Have students compare and contrast curve #1 to curve #2, and again to curve #3. Here are several ideas to discuss with students: (a) curve #2 crosses the vertical axis 2 units higher (curve #3 is 2 units lower) than the basic curve; this change in the vertex corresponds to the constant +2 (or −2) added to the N^2 in the general polynomial expression P(N); (b) the vertical distance or **ordinate** value of each original marker (curve #1) on the grid has changed by +2 (or −2); (c) the line of symmetry is the same for all three curves; and (d) the horizontal distances of image points from the line of symmetry remain equal, and these distances for the same N values are equal on all three curves (that is, the two color #2 markers used for N = −1 or +1 on curve #1 and again on curve #2 will be the same distance from the line of symmetry (vertical axis), and similarly for the other marker colors).

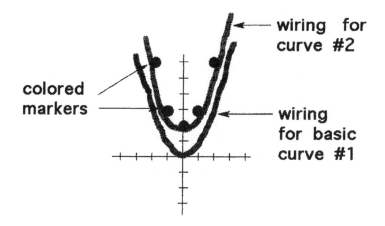

colored markers

wiring for curve #2

wiring for basic curve #1

5. Now repeat steps 2 through 4, using $P(N) = -N^2$ as the basic curve #1, and $P(N) = -N^2 + 3$ and $P(N) = -N^2 - 1$ as the other two curves. These three curves will all open downward; otherwise, their characteristics should be similar to those of the previous set of curves. Also, for each N used for the curve, the ordinate or vertical distance in $P(N) = -N^2$ will be the **inverse** of the ordinate in $P(N) = N^2$ for the same N. Additional sets of curves to use, depending on available time, are the following: (a) $P(N) = (N - 1)^2$ as basic curve, with $P(N) = (N - 1)^2 + 2$ and $P(N) = (N - 1)^2 - 2$; and (b) $P(N) = 2N^2$ as basic curve, with $P(N) = 2N^2 + 3$ and $P(N) = 2N^2 - 1$. When a curve in set (a) is formed, markers of the same color will still be assigned to points having the same **ordinate** value as before, but these image points will no longer have N values that are inverses of each other. Because of this, students should use $N = -2, -1, 0, +1, +2, +3$, and $+4$ to find their ordered pairs for this set of curves. A special characteristic for set (a) is that all points on each of the three curves will be 1 unit farther to the right than their corresponding points and curve in the $P(N) = N^2$ *family* or set of curves; the line of symmetry becomes $N = +1$ instead of $N = 0$. A special characteristic for set (b) is the U-shape of each curve is more closed or does not spread open so widely as the corresponding curve in the $P(N) = N^2$ family of curves.

6. After students have built the various sets or families of curves, have them select one of the curve families they have built on the grid and write a paragraph about that particular group of curves. In the paragraph they should discuss the different characteristics of their curves that they have discovered. Remind students that since each curve built in this lesson represents a set of ordered pairs where each N value (the **independent** variable) yields **only one** vertical distance (the **dependent** variable)—even though other N values may have that same vertical distance—the set of ordered pairs may be called a **function.** When the ordered pairs produce a **parabolic curve** like those in this lesson, then we have a **second-degree polynomial function** or a **quadratic function.** A quadratic function will be generated by a general expression that contains at least one quadratic variable, that is, the linear variable squared. **Note:** In this activity, we have used each of the following: N^2, $-N^2$, $(N - 1)^2$, and $2N^2$, as the expression for the **basic curve** of some family of curves. This was to make observations of likenesses and differences easier for the students. In a more general sense, however, the expression N^2 describes the basic or parent curve for **all** of the curves built during the activity.

Activity 2: PARABOLA DRAW

[Bridging Action]

Materials: Worksheet 4–8–2
5-millimeter grid paper
Colored pencils (at least 3 different bright colors)
Graphing calculators
Paper
Regular pencils

Management: Partners (50 minutes)

Directions:

1. Give each pair of students a copy of Worksheet 4–8–2, a graphing calculator, 4 sheets of 5-millimeter grid paper, and 3 colored pencils (any 3 different bright colors; not black, brown or yellow). Have students draw a set of coordinate axes on each sheet of grid paper, placing the origin at the center of the paper. All four quadrants will be used in this activity. Use 1 vertical grid segment for 4 units, and 1 horizontal segment for 1 unit of value to mark off and label the axes on the grid. Discuss the idea that the functions listed on the worksheet use the variable N and P(N), but the graphing calculators may use the variable X and Y (or possibly F(X) instead of Y). Students need to have experience with a variety of variable names. Initially set the window on the graphing calculators for $X\varepsilon[-7, +7]$, scale of 1, and $Y\varepsilon[-20, +20]$, scale of 2. (**Note:** Vertical scales used on the grid and the viewing screen differ by design need; however, this variance will cause students to apply scales rather than just match spaces when transferring graphs.) Students may choose to adjust the window later. In this activity students will be graphing quadratic functions on the graphing calculator, tracing to read six appropriate ordered pairs directly from each graph, and copying the graph onto their own grid paper. Four different families or sets of curves will be investigated.

2. Ask students to graph each set of functions shown on Worksheet 4–8–2. Students need to graph all three functions in each set on the same grid or viewing screen for comparison purposes. They should graph the functions in a set one at a time and in the order listed, so that they can observe differences between the new graph and any previous graphs already on the screen. They also need to trace each new graph to find at least 5 points on the curve (the **vertex** and 2 points on each side of the vertex, or at least appropriate choices of N to show a "complete picture" of the curve) and use those points to copy the curve onto a sheet of grid paper. Just as with the viewing screen, all 3 curves should be copied onto the same grid paper or set of axes. Use a different color of pencil to draw each curve on the grid and label the curve with its polynomial expression for P(N).

3. On the grid paper below the 3 graphs, students should describe the differences and likenesses they observe among the three curves. When all have finished graphing and writing about the different sets of functions, have various students share their ideas with the entire class. For each set of functions, after students have stated how changing a certain coefficient or parameter has produced certain changes in the graphs, encourage them to test their conjecture by trying new coefficients and predicting how the new curves will look. [*Possible observations:* adding (or subtracting) a linear term to the

WORKSHEET 4–8–2
Parabola Draw

With a partner, graph the following sets of polynomial quadratic functions on a graphing calculator. Graph all functions in the same set on the same viewing screen, then copy the three graphs of the set onto grid paper, using the same vertical and horizontal axes. Each graph within a set should be drawn in a different color. Write about the likenesses and differences you see among the three functions and their graphs in each set.

1. **(a)** $P(N) = N^2$

   (b) $P(N) = N^2 + 6N$

   (c) $P(N) = N^2 - 6N$

2. **(a)** $P(N) = 5N^2 - 6$

   (b) $P(N) = N^2 - 6$

   (c) $P(N) = 0.5N^2 - 6$

3. **(a)** $P(N) = -3N^2 - 4$

   (b) $P(N) = -N^2 - 4$

   (c) $P(N) = -0.3N^2 - 4$

4. **(a)** $P(N) = N^2 + 5.4N - 1$

   (b) $P(N) = 0.4(N^2 + 5.4N - 1)$

   (c) $P(N) = -1.0(N^2 + 5.4N - 1)$

quadratic term causes the **basic** curve, $P(N) = N^2$, to lower and shift left (or right); a positive (or negative) coefficient on the quadratic term causes the curve to open upward (or downward); absolutely increasing (or decreasing) the coefficient on the quadratic term causes the curve to become more narrow (or wider).] Additional coefficient changes might also be explored that have not been included on Worksheet 4–8–2. For example, students might explore the presence of an unchanging linear term with a changing constant, using the following: $N^2 + 6N$, $N^2 + 6N + 5$, and $N^2 + 6N - 5$. The constant indicates where the curve will intersect the vertical axis. Another possibility would be to change the linear coefficient while keeping it either positive or negative, but not change the quadratic coefficient or the constant.

Answer Key to WORKSHEET 4–8–2

Some possible likenesses and differences are provided for each set of curves.

  1. All 3 curves pass through (0,0) and open upward; vertex of (a) is at (0,0); vertex of (b) is at (–3,–9) and vertex of (c) is at (+3,–9).

  2. Curve (a) opens up the least and curve (c) opens up the most; all 3 curves open upward with vertices at (0,–6).

  3. All 3 curves open downward with vertices at (0,–4); curve (c) opens widest and curve (a) opens least.

  4. Curve (c) is reflection of curve (a) across horizontal axis; all three vertices occur at $N \approx -2.680$; curves (b) and (a) open upward, but vertex of curve (b) is higher than vertex of curve (a); curve (b) opens wider than other two curves do.

Activity 3: CURVE TRANSFORMERS

[Application/Exploration]

Materials: Graphing calculators
Regular pencils
Paper
Worksheet 4–8–3

Management: Teams of 4 students each (20–30 minutes)

Directions:

  1. Give each team of students a graphing calculator. Two of the team members, Pair A, will compete with the other two, Pair B, in trying to transform the parabolic curve of the **basic quadratic function,** $P(N) = N^2$. The two pairs will take turns stating a change for the other pair to make in the basic curve, using a graphing calculator. Review the words: **domain** (values for the independent variable) and **range** (values for the dependent variable) of a function. Students must also state the domain and the range of each new curve they create. Use the viewing window: $X\varepsilon[-7,+7]$, scale of 1, and $Y\varepsilon[-20,+20]$, scale of 2. (See Worksheet 4–8–3.)

  2. As an example of play, on their turn, Pair A will first *clear* the graphing screen of any previous curves, then graph $P(N) = N^2$. Pair B will state how the basic curve now showing on the graphing screen should be changed. Pair A will graph a new quadratic function whose graph will reflect the requested change, and will describe the **domain** and **range** of the new function. As an example, the domain for the new curve might simply be given as "N, the independent variable, may equal any real number," and the range might be given as "P(N), the dependent variable, will equal any real number that is equal to or less than −6." If Pair B agrees that the requested change has been made and that the stated domain and range are correct, Pair A earns a point. It is possible that other changes, besides the requested one, may also occur in the basic graph; as long as the requested change has been met, Pair A may earn the point. The teacher may have to serve as mediator in some cases.

3. The turn then passes to Pair B, who first clear the graphing screen and graph a new basic curve. Pair A now states what change the other pair should make in the basic curve, and play continues. Pair A, however, cannot request the same change that Pair B used during the previous turn; a different change must be used for each new turn in the game. Also, a pair of players may not request the same change of the other pair twice in a row; that is, if on a turn Pair A requests Pair B to "raise the basic curve," then the next time Pair A is to request a change of Pair B, the change cannot be to "raise the curve" again. These directions for *selecting* a curve change will cause students to create and graph a greater variety of quadratic functions during the game.

4. A team might play until time is called, or might play until the first pair earns a total of 10 points.

5. Here is a list of *changes* to be made to the basic quadratic curve that the pairs of students might request of each other:

(**a**) raise the curve

(**b**) lower the curve

(**c**) shift curve to left

(**d**) shift curve to right

(**e**) widen the curve

(**f**) narrow the curve

(**g**) make the curve open downward

Name _____   **Date** _____

WORKSHEET 4–8–3
Curve Transformers

On each turn of the game:

1. The pair of players having the turn clears the view screen and graphs $P(N) = N^2$ as the *basic curve.*

2. The other pair of players states a *change* to be made in the basic curve by the first pair of players. Possible changes to request:

   —raise the curve

   —lower the curve

   —shift curve to left

   —shift curve to right

   —widen the curve

   —narrow the curve

   —make the curve open downward

3. The first pair of players then graphs a new curve over the basic curve and describes the domain and the range of the new curve.

4. If the other pair accepts the new curve as showing the required change, and agrees with the stated domain and range, the first pair of players earns a point.

5. The turn then passes to the other pair of players to become the graphing pair and repeat steps 1 through 4.

OBJECTIVE 9: Given the expression for the general or N-th term of a polynomial (quadratic) sequence and its numerical value for some N, find the value of N.

Activity 1: BUILDING LARGER TERMS

[Developing Action]

Materials: Packet of tiles (from Objective 3, Section 4)
Equation building mats (from Objective 10, Section 3)
Regular pencils
Paper
Worksheet 4–9–1

Management: Partners (50 minutes)

Directions:

1. Give each pair of students an equation building mat and a packet of tiles. The packet of tiles should contain a minimum of 8 quadratic variable tiles (large square tiles with large X on one side for inverse), 12 linear variable tiles (long rectangles with large X on one side for inverse), and 30 unit tiles (small square tiles with X on one side for inverse). See Objective 3 of this section for details on the tile packets. More unit tiles may need to be added to the packets that were used in Objective 3. In this activity students will represent the N-th or general term of a quadratic or second-degree polynomial sequence with tiles and equate that set of tiles to the value of a particular term expressed in unit tiles. While solving quadratic equations with tiles, students will make connections to the figurate number sequences developed in Objective 7 of this section. It is assumed that students have completed the three activities of Objective 7 as preparation for this lesson. Skills developed in Objective 3 of this section (combining like terms) will also be needed in this lesson.

2. Write the following on the board: *The total unit tiles or value for the N-th term of a quadratic sequence will equal $N^2 + 2N$. Ask:* "Since the algebraic expression $N^2 + 2N$ involves the quadratic variable tile, we know that it must represent a product of some kind. Can you arrange 1 quadratic variable tile and 2 linear variable tiles (as indicated by the expression) in a rectangular shape so that we can identify the two factors?" (*yes;* one possible arrangement is to place the 2 long rectangles to the right of the large square tile as shown in the illustration below) "Our tiles now show the product, N rows of (N + 2) unit tiles per row. Using N(N + 2) as a building pattern for the N-th term, can you use the positive unit tiles to build the first term? the second term? What does the N tell you to build? the (N + 2)?" Using N = 1 and N = 2 in the pattern, students should build a *first* term and a *second* term as shown in the illustration below. Have them count the total tiles used to build each term, then record the following number sentences on their own papers: **T(1) = +3 and T(2) = +8 when T(N) = $N^2 + 2N$ = N(N + 2).** Read T(1) as "total unit tiles in the first term, or T of 1," and similarly for T(2).

Possible Product:

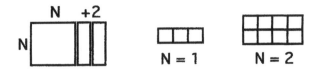

3. *Ask:* "If one of the terms in this sequence uses 24 positive unit tiles in its design, how can we decide which term it is and what the term will look like?" Some students may offer their opinions at this point. Listen to their ideas, then ask them to show the relationship with their tiles on the building mat. The quadratic variable tile and 2 linear variable tiles should be placed on the left side of the mat and arranged to show the product N(N + 2), and 24 positive unit tiles should be placed on the right side of the mat to show +24. ***Ask:*** "Looking at our product in tiles on the left side of the mat, we know that the upper edge of the rectangular shape must be 2 positive units longer than the left edge. Can you arrange the 24 unit tiles on the right side of the mat as a rectangular shape whose upper edge is 2 positive units longer than its left edge?" Students should explore making different arrangements with their unit tiles until they find the 4×6 arrangement. In this case, the upper edge (+6) is 2 units longer than the left edge (+4). Thus, N must have the value of +4 in this particular arrangement. The final tile arrangements on the mat are shown here.

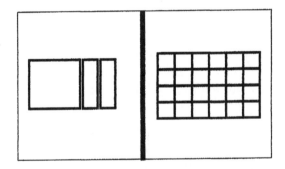

4. Remind students that the variable tiles can represent many different values. Even though the edge length of the large square tile on the left side of the mat **physically** appears to equal the edge length of the rectangular shape on the right side of the mat, this will not always be the case. It is the **relationship between** adjacent edge lengths of the **same** rectangular shape that we really seek, not their actual physical measurements. The tile arrangements now on the mat indicate that the term having a value of **+24** must be the **fourth** term in the sequence. Students should finally record: **T(4) = +24.** Again, read T(4) as "total unit tiles in the fourth term, or T of 4."

5. Now write the following on the board: *The total unit tiles or value for the N-th term of a quadratic sequence will equal $N^2 + N - 2$.* Discuss the idea that this algebraic expression may be considered as 1 of the amount squared combined with 1 of the amount itself, then with +2 removed. An alternative to removing +2, however, is to add on –2; we will use this last approach to find our terms for this example. Ask students to build the *first* term and *second* term of this new sequence with their unit tiles. An example of how each term might be built is shown in the illustration below. After building each term, students should simplify and count the total tiles remaining (which is 0 for the first term) and record the following number sentences or equations on their own papers: **T(1) = 0 and T(2) = +4 when T(N) = N² + N – 2.**

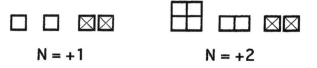

N = +1   N = +2

6. *Ask:* "How can we find the term of this sequence that requires 28 positive unit tiles to build it? Can you build an equation on the building mat to help you decide which term it will be?" For variation, have students place 28 positive unit tiles on the *left* side of the mat, and place 1 quadratic variable tile, 1 linear variable tile, and 2 negative unit tiles on the right side of the mat. The right side will represent the second-degree polynomial, $N^2 + N - 2$, for the total unit tiles in the N-th term. As before, students should try to arrange the tiles on the right side of the mat to form a rectangular shape or product. From this we can identify the factors of the product of tiles; knowing the factors will help us to find the correct arrangement for the 28 positive unit tiles on the left side.

7. A 0-pair of linear variable tiles is needed in order to form a rectangular shape or product. Using the order shown in the illustration below, we have the factors $(N - 1)(N + 2)$. The upper edge factor is 2 more than some amount, while the left edge factor is 1 less than that same amount. This implies that no matter what value is assigned to the linear variable tile, the upper edge length will be 3 more than the left edge length of the rectangular shape. This means that we need to arrange the 28 unit tiles into a similar rectangular shape. Students should experiment with the 28 tiles until they find the 4×7 arrangement, which has an upper edge length of 7 units and a left edge length of 4 units. Remind students that the small square tile has an edge length of 1 unit, but also an area of 1 square unit. Usually we will say "1 unit of length" and "1 unit of area"; the situation will determine which type of "unit" is meant at the time. We use the area when totaling tiles in a *product,* but use the edge length when evaluating *factors.* The two tile stages on the mat are shown below.

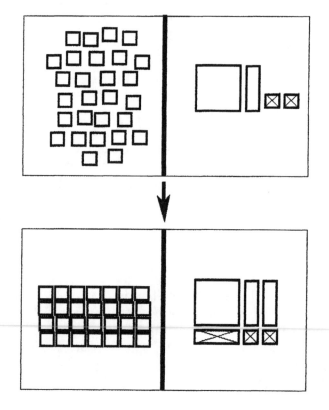

8. The left edge of the unit tiles arrangement equals +4, and the left edge of the variable group equals N − 1. These two lengths must equal each other, since the product-factors relationship is the same for both tile sets shown on the mat. From N − 1 = +4, we have the solution N = +5, which indicates that the **fifth** term should have a total tile value of **+28.** Have students build the fifth term according to the pattern they used for the first and second terms earlier. In other words, they should build 5 rows of 5 positive unit tiles each, followed by another separate row of 5 unit tiles. Finally, 2 positive unit tiles may be removed, or if there are enough unit tiles available, 2 negative unit tiles may be added on instead. Upon simplifying and counting the remaining unit tiles to confirm that the fifth term indeed has a value of +28, students should record on their own papers: **T(5) = +28.**

9. *Extension:* Since this objective deals only with sequences, the value of N is limited to the natural numbers 1, 2, 3, . . . (or positive integers). This would be a good time, however, to have students begin to think in terms of negative values for N, which they will encounter in the next objectives. *Ask:* "In this exercise we know that +4 and +7 are the two factors we need in order to have the product +28, because +7 is 3 more than +4, the required relationship for the two factors. If we did not have to limit the value of N to the positive integers, could you think of two other numbers, whose product is +28, where one number is 3 more than the other number?" Encourage students to think about possible negative numbers once they realize that there are no other positive factors that will work. The new factors will be −7 and −4, since −4 is 3 more than −7 and their product equals +28. Then N − 1 = −7 and N = −6. Discuss the idea that, in general, −6 is another possible solution for $N^2 + N − 2 = +28$; however, when solving any equation for the variable, we must always know the limits of the *situation* that the equation is modeling. Our situation in this activity concerns *sequences*, so N must be a natural number or positive integer. We therefore exclude N = −6 as our solution.

10. Assign other sequences for which students will find specific terms when given their total value in unit tiles. (See Worksheet 4–9–1.) After solving each equation for N by building with the tiles on the mat, students should build the indicated term in unit tiles according to the pattern represented by the original algebraic expression. This will confirm that the term does have the required value. This confirming process will also reinforce students' understanding of second-degree polynomials as *models of situations.* Here are some possible expressions to assign, as well as a term value for which to find N. (Solution for N is shown in brackets with each exercise.)

1. $T(N) = N^2 − 4$;   +21   [5]
2. $T(N) = N^2$;   16   [4]
3. $T(N) = 2N^2$;   +18   [3]
4. $T(N) = N^2 − 1$;   +15   [4]

5. $T(N) = N^2 + 3N$;   +18   [3]
6. $T(N) = 3N^2 + 5N$;   +22   [2]
7. $T(N) = N^2 + 4N + 3$;   24   [3]
8. $T(N) = N^2 − N − 2$;   18   [5]

Name _____ **Date** _____

WORKSHEET 4–9–1
Building Larger Terms

For each N-th term of a sequence, build with tiles on the equation building mat to find the term of the sequence having the given total value (shown in brackets). Also build T(1) and T(2). Record your results below the expression for the N-th term.

Example 1: $T(N) = N^2 + 2N$ [+24]

Example 2: $T(N) = N^2 + N - 2$ [+28]

Exercises:

1. $T(N) = N^2 - 4$ [+21]

2. $T(N) = N^2$ [+16]

3. $T(N) = 2N^2$ [+18]

4. $T(N) = N^2 - 1$ [+15]

5. $T(N) = N^2 + 3N$ [+18]

6. $T(N) = 3N^2 + 5N$ [+22]

7. $T(N) = N^2 + 4N + 3$ [+24]

8. $T(N) = N^2 - N - 2$ [+18]

Activity 2: PICTURING SPECIAL TERMS

[Bridging Action]

Materials: Paper
Regular pencils
Calculators
Worksheet 4–9–2

Management: Partners (30–50 minutes)

Directions:

1. Provide each pair of students with a calculator. The diagramming technique used in this activity will give students another strategy to apply to *situations* involving sequences. In particular, the activity continues to prepare students to solve quadratic equations.

2. Write the following equation on the board: $T(N) = 2N^2 + 4N + 2$. Ask students to calculate $T(1)$ and $T(2)$ and record their work on their own papers as number sentences: $T(1) = 2(1)(1) + 4(1) + 2 = +8$ **and** $T(2) = 2(2)(2) + 4(2) + 2 = +18$. *Ask:* "What set of tiles is suggested by the second-degree polynomial, $2N^2 + 4N + 2$?" *(2 large square tiles, 4 long rectangular tiles, and 2 small square tiles)* "Can you draw a diagram that represents these tiles as a product region?" *(yes; one possible product is (2N + 2)(N + 1))* "Since this product diagram can represent any term in the sequence, can you **equate** it with the term *value* of +50?"

3. Students should draw an equation frame that shows the product region to the left of two vertical bars (the **equals** sign) and a rectangle to the right. The rectangle should be somewhat **similar** to the shape of the product region; that is, if the product region is taller than it is wide when all the shapes are drawn, the rectangle should also be drawn taller than it is wide. The two factors of the polynomial should be labeled on the left edge and upper edge of the product region, and the term value, +50, should be written inside the rectangle. Here is an example of such a diagram.

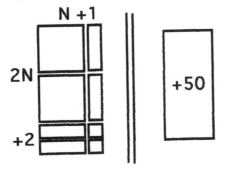

4. Students should now analyze the two factors of the product region to see how they compare sizewise to each other. In this case, $(2N + 2)$ equals twice the size or value of $(N + 1)$, so the left edge of the product region is twice the size of the upper edge. Consequently, we need factors for +50 that have the same relationship: the left factor is twice the value or size of the upper factor. Allow students time to explore the possible factor pairs of 50 to see which pair has this relationship. The factors needed will be +5 and +10. Students should write +10 on the left edge of the rectangle in the diagram and write +5 on the upper edge. These numbers must be in the same order on the rectangle as their corresponding factors on the product region.

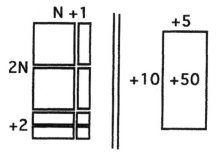

5. Now students may compare either the upper edges or the left edges of the two rectangular shapes in the diagram: **N + 1 = +5, or 2N + 2 = +10.** Solving either linear equation, they will find **N = 4.** Have students record whatever steps they use to solve their chosen equation. Since N = +4 means the **fourth** term in the sequence, students should test for the fourth term by using N = 4 in the original polynomial expression for the N-th term. The result will be the value +50. They should record these substitution steps on their own papers: **T(4) = 2(4)(4) + 4(4) + 2 = +50.** Hence, the fourth term of the sequence does indeed have the value of +50.

6. Again, as we did earlier in Activity 1, probe students for other possible factor pairs. Encourage them to consider negative values. We need two numbers where one is two times the value of the other and their product is +50. Hopefully, students will discover that $-10 = 2(-5)$ and $(-5)(-10) = +50$. This is an example of a number (−10) being "two times another number" (−5), yet −10 is actually **less than** −5 in value, a characteristic of negative numbers that students do not easily accept. So $2N + 2 = -10$ and $N + 1 = -5$, yielding the *general* solution, N = −6. Since our *situation* involves *sequences* where N must be positive, we exclude N = −6 as a solution for our *specific* sequence exercise.

7. Now assign other sequences for students to solve for a particular term. (See Worksheet 4–9–2.) The procedure used in steps 2 through 5 should be followed. T(1) and T(2) should be calculated first, then a diagram drawn to compare the polynomial for the N-th term to the particular term whose *value* has been given. Rectangles will be drawn to represent the products or factored forms being compared. In each exercise, the size relationship between the two factors of the given polynomial will have to be identified and applied to the factors of the given term value. Once the term's position in the sequence has been identified, symbolic steps used in the solving process should be recorded and a test made to confirm that term's value with respect to the general polynomial given for all the terms in the sequence. Later, when checking students' work in class, occasionally ask students to describe the unit tile arrangement for T(1) or T(2) or the new term found with respect to a given polynomial for the N-th term.

8. Here are suggested general polynomials to use for the N-th term, along with the values of the terms being sought, that might be assigned to students. (Solution for N is shown in brackets with each exercise.)

1. $T(N) = N^2 + 7N + 10$;   +88   [6]   5. $T(N) = N^2 + N - 12$;   60   [8]

2. $T(N) = -N^2$;   −81   [9]   6. $T(N) = 4N^2 - 2N$;   +90   [5]

3. $T(N) = N^2 - N$;   42   [7]   7. $T(N) = N^2 - 3N - 18$;   −14   [4]

4. $T(N) = -N^2 - 6N - 9$;   −64   [5]   8. $T(N) = 4N^2 - 9$;   27   [3]

Name _____   **Date** _____

WORKSHEET 4–9–2
Picturing Special Terms

For each N-th term of a sequence, on your own paper draw a diagram and solve equations to find the term of the sequence having the given total value (shown in brackets). Compute T(1) and T(2). Write number sentences on the worksheet to show your results.

Example: $T(N) = 2N^2 + 4N + 2$ [+50]

Exercises:

1. $T(N) = N^2 + 7N + 10$ [+88]

2. $T(N) = -N^2$ [–81]

3. $T(N) = N^2 - N$ [+42]

4. $T(N) = -N^2 - 6N - 9$ [–64]

5. $T(N) = N^2 + N - 12$ [+60]

6. $T(N) = 4N^2 - 2N$ [+90]

7. $T(N) = N^2 - 3N - 18$ [–14]

8. $T(N) = 4N^2 - 9$ [+27]

Activity 3: BACKTRACKING POINTS

[Application/Exploration]

Materials: 5-millimeter grid paper
Red pencils
Regular pencils and paper
Calculators
Graphing calculators (for extension activity only)
Worksheet 4–9–3

Management: Partners (50 minutes)

Directions:

1. Give each pair of students 5 or 6 sheets of 5-millimeter grid paper, a calculator, and a red pencil. Remind students that a **quadratic (polynomial) sequence** is just a special type of **quadratic function** where the first member of each ordered pair is a positive integer or natural number (1,2,3, . . .). That is, the **domain** of the function is the natural numbers. The second member is a value that has been formed according to a specific pattern, which is described with an algebraic expression, a second-degree polynomial. It is the set of **values,** listed according to the order of the first members of the pairs, that students typically see and consider to be the sequence itself. That is, the sequence numbers are just the **range** of the function.

2. Write the equation $T(N) = N^2 - N - 12$ on the board. Ask students to compute $T(1)$ and $T(2)$ on their own papers as follows: $T(1) = (1)(1) - 1 - 12 = -12$ and $T(2) = (2)(2) - 2 - 12 = -10$. Using $(N, T(N))$ as the form for the ordered pairs, students should record the ordered pairs found: $(1,-12)$ and $(2,-10)$, in a 2-column table with headings N and T(N); the pairs should then be plotted on a sheet of the 5-millimeter grid paper. The longer edge should be the (left) vertical axis, labeled as "Term Value T(N)"; each vertical grid segment should equal 5 units for the scale. Since T(N) might be a negative value, use the interval $[-50,+150]$ for the vertical axis. The shorter edge should be the (lower) horizontal axis, labeled as "Term Number N" or "Term Position N"; every 2 horizontal grid segments should equal 1 unit for the scale. Use the interval $[0,13]$ for the horizontal axis. Once the two points are marked on the grid, students should also find points for N = 5, 8, and 10 and mark these new points on the grid. They should then draw a *non-straight* curve through the points in red pencil; no straight path or line segment should be used to connect adjacent points. If students try to draw a *line segment*—for example, between the point for N = 5 and the point for N = 10—have them find the point for N = 7 or N = 8 in order to see that the new point does **not** fall on the line segment; hence, the line segment is **not** the correct path. If necessary, have students plot more points to help them realize how the curve will look. The finished graph will just be a scatterplot of points, not a continuous curve, since the domain for the sequence is the natural numbers and not the real numbers. The red pencil does not represent all points of the function; it only helps students visualize the change in the vertical distance or T(N) when the horizontal distance N changes. The curve drawn in red pencil, however, will represent the right branch of a parabolic path since we are working with a quadratic or second-degree polynomial sequence or function.

3. *Ask:* "If we are looking for the term in this sequence that has the value +8, how might we find the point in our scatterplot that belongs to that term?" This point has already been plotted, but we want students to focus on a particular procedure. The point being sought has the ordered pair (N,+8); the vertical distance, +8, should be located and "boxed" on the vertical axis, then that position "tracked" over to the red curve by drawing in regular pencil a horizontal path that will intersect with the curve. In this first example, since the point has already been plotted, the horizontal path will lead directly to that marked point; this point of intersection should be circled. *Ask:* "What mark on the horizontal axis lies directly below this point on the curve?" Another path or "track" should be drawn vertically from this identified point down to the horizontal axis; the axis mark will be at +5. A box should be drawn around +5. **Note:** Every number found on the horizontal axis by this "backtracking" method will be an *integer,* since this axis represents the term *positions* (counting numbers) in the sequence.

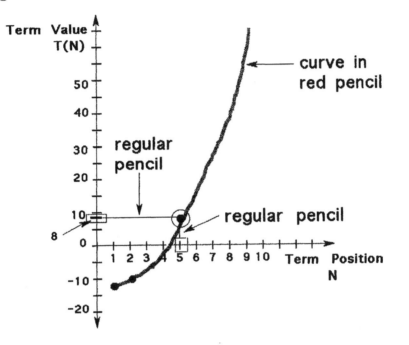

4. The +5 indicates the position of the term whose value is +8. If this were a new point, students would test this solution by substituting +5 in the general expression for a term's value in the sequence: T(5) = (5)(5) − 5 − 12 = +8. So the **fifth** term would indeed have the value **8.** Then students would record their new ordered pair (5,8) in their 2-column table.

5. For more practice with the "tracking" procedure using the *same* sequence, give students the term value of 120 to "track" (or the value for some other N whose point has not been plotted yet). The horizontal and vertical paths will show the corresponding N to equal 12. The N-value +12 should be tested in the expression T(N) to see if T(12) equals 120. If so, then (12,120) will be a solution for the sequence. The **twelfth** term in the sequence will be **+120.**

6. For *new* sequences, assign the general expressions (with given term values) listed below, each expression to be plotted on a *separate* sheet of grid paper. (See Worksheet 4–9–3.) Use the same vertical and horizontal scales as used in the above example; this will allow students to compare all their scatterplots or "curves" when the assignment is completed. For each expression, students should compute T(N) for N = 1, 2, 5, 8, and 10 initially; prepare a table of ordered pairs; plot points and connect them with a red curve; "backtrack" from the given term value to the term position; and last, test the N found.

Ask several students to explain their work when all are finished. Also have them compare their different curves and make observations about their steepness, their horizontal axis intercepts, the upward or downward direction of each curve with regard to the coefficient on the squared term in T(N), etc. [**Note:** As an extension of this lesson, have students use graphing calculators to plot f(N) = T(N) for N as a real number in the interval [−15, +15], scale = +1, and f(N) in the interval [−50, +150], scale = +5; T(N) will be an expression from the sequence assignment. This extension activity will allow students to see how their sequence curves are just a part of a full *parabola,* their being a portion of the total curve with respect to the positive integers on the horizontal axis.] (The solution for N is given in brackets with each exercise below.)

1. $T(N) = -N^2 + 75$;   +59   [4]   3. $T(N) = 5 + 2N^2$;   +103   [7]

2. $T(N) = N^2 + N$;   132   [11]   4. $T(N) = N^2 - 3N - 18$;   −8   [5]

WORKSHEET 4–9–3
Backtracking Points

Complete the table of ordered pairs and make a scatterplot for each general expression provided below. *Backtrack* on the graph to find the value of N for the value of T(N) given in the table. Estimate another value of T(N) from the graph and backtrack to find its possible N value; compute T(N) to test your estimate.

1. $T(N) = -N^2 + 75$

N	T(N)
1	
2	
5	
8	
10	
	+59

2. $T(N) = N^2 + N$

N	T(N)
1	
2	
5	
8	
10	
	132

3. $T(N) = 5 + 2N^2$

N	T(N)
1	
2	
5	
8	
10	
	+103

4. $T(N) = N^2 - 3N - 18$

N	T(N)
1	
2	
5	
8	
10	
	-8

OBJECTIVE 10: Solve quadratic equations of the form: $aX^2 + bX + c = 0$, using the real number factor property: $MN = 0$ implies $M = 0$ or $N = 0$.

Activity 1: ZERO DIMENSIONS

[Developing Action]

Materials: Packet of tiles (from Objective 3, Section 4)
Equation building mats (from Objective 10, Section 3)
Unlined 3 in. by 5 in. index cards
Regular pencils
Paper
Worksheet 4–10–1

Management: Partners (50 minutes)

Directions:

1. Give each pair of students an equation building mat, a packet of tiles, and a 3 in. by 5 in. index card with a large zero written on the card. The packet of tiles should contain a minimum of 8 quadratic variable tiles (large square tiles with large X on one side for inverse), 12 linear variable tiles (long rectangles with large X on one side for inverse), and 30 unit tiles (small square tiles with X on one side for inverse). See Objective 3 of this section for details on the tile packets. More unit tiles may need to be added to the packets that were used in Objective 3. It is assumed that students have completed all three activities in Objective 9 of this section. In that objective, we were interested in finding the value of N that paired or mapped to a particular *nonzero* value of P(N) within a second-degree polynomial sequence. At that time we built on the idea of the area of a rectangular region being equal to the product of the two dimensions of that region. Remind students that sequences are just special functions with the natural numbers as the domain. For this new objective, we will be looking for the N value that produces a *zero* value for the general expression describing a quadratic function. In graphing language, this particular N is where the parabolic curve intersects the horizontal axis. Here in Activity 1, students will return to the rectangular region idea, but this time the area will have only a value of 0. The general expression A(N) will be modeled as the area of a rectangular region with variable and unit tiles; the tile region will be considered **congruent** to another rectangular region with an area of 0 unit tiles. We will then compare the dimensions (edge lengths) of the two regions in order to find a possible value for N. Note that we will be using A(N), rather than P(N), here in order to reflect the context of the activity: area.

2. Write the following on the board: *The area A(N) in unit tiles for a rectangular region will equal $N^2 + 3N$.* **Ask:** "Since the algebraic expression $N^2 + 3N$ involves the quadratic variable tile, we know that it must represent a product of some kind. We also know that the surfaces of the tiles represent areas, and that area can be found from the product of two **perpendicular dimensions.** Can you arrange 1 quadratic variable tile and 3 linear variable tiles (areas indicated by the expression) in a rectangular shape so that we can identify the shape's two dimensions?" (*yes;* one possible arrangement is to place the 3 long rectangles below the large square tile as shown in the following illustration) The tiles now show the product, (N + 3) rows of N unit tiles per row. Since the unit tiles serve as our units of area, this product is another way to describe the *area* of our tile arrangement.

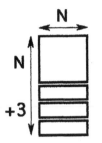

3. Have students place their (N + 3)N tile arrangement on the left side of the equation building mat and then place the index card (containing 0) on the right side of the mat. As before with sequences, we now assume that the two rectangular regions shown on the building mat are **congruent** to each other. This implies that their *corresponding dimensions are equal* and their *areas are equal*. Remind students that the tile region and index card are only *models* of rectangular regions; the "congruent" shapes will **not** necessarily **look** the same size. Discuss the idea that the index card represents a rectangular region with an "area" of 0. In the previous lesson with sequences, we worked with both positive and negative "areas" and looked for two factors whose product equaled a given area value and that also satisfied the characteristics indicated by the factors of the rectangular region made from variable and unit tiles. *Ask:* "If we have a region whose area is 0, what do we know about the two dimensions of the region?" *(at least one of the dimensions must equal 0 if the area is to equal 0)* "Do we know which dimension of our index card region is the 0 dimension?" *(no, since no specific information is given about the dimensions;* either one or both of the two dimensions, the length or the width, might equal 0) Thus, we must assume that each dimension might equal 0. Have students record the following equations on their own papers to show the equal areas and the equal dimensions of the two **congruent** rectangular regions:

(1) *area A(N):* $N^2 + 3N = 0$ **square units**

(2) *dimensions (N + 3) and N:* **N + 3 = 0 units, or N = 0 units**

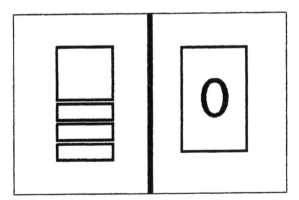

4. Have students solve their two dimension equations for N, using methods for solving linear equations studied in Section 2. The solutions will be N = –3 or N = 0. Students should test the solutions to see if they will produce an area of 0 for the tile region. Clearly, to test N = 0, if zero unit tiles of area replace the large square variable tile (i.e., $N^2 = 0$) and zero unit tiles of area replace each of the 3 long rectangular tiles (i.e., 3 of N becomes 3 of 0), then the total tile area will equal 0 square units, the desired amount. To test N = –3, students should replace the large square tile on the mat with 9 positive units ($N^2 = +9$) of area and each long rectangular tile on the mat with 3 negative units (3 of N becomes 3 of –3) of area. Since there are now 9 positive units and 9 negative units in place of the tile region, the total value of the region's "area" will equal 0 square units. Hence, the solutions N = –3 units or N = 0 units are correct. Students should finally record below the other equations the following statements:

N = –3 units or N = 0 units

Areas A(–3) = 0 and A(0) = 0 when area A(N) = N^2 + 3N

The notation "A(–3)" should be read as "A of –3" or the "area of the region when N = –3," and similarly for "A(0)."

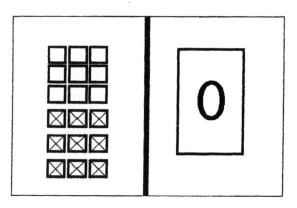

5. Now write the following on the board: *The area A(N) in unit tiles for a rectangular region will equal N^2 – 4.* Have students place a quadratic variable tile (large square tile) and 4 negative units on the *right* side of the building mat (just for variety's sake) to represent N^2 – 4, and place the 0-labeled index card on the left side of the mat. Following the procedures used in steps 2 through 4, students should build a rectangular region with the tiles (as shown below; note that two 0-pairs of linear variable tiles will be needed to complete the tile region) and equate the corresponding dimensions of the left and right regions on the mat. Students should record and solve their equations, then test their solutions by substituting unit tiles for the variable tiles on the mat. They should write the following on their own papers:

(1) area A(N): N^2 – 4 = 0 square units

(2) dimensions (N – 2) and (N + 2): N – 2 = 0 units, or N + 2 = 0 units

N = +2 units, or N = –2 units

Areas A(+2) = 0 and A(–2) = 0 when area A(N) = N^2 – 4

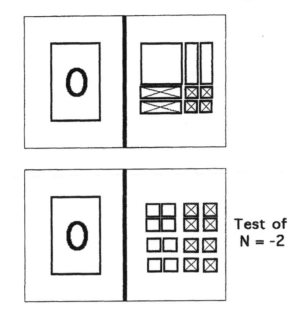

Test of
N = -2

6. Assign other quadratic expressions for students to solve for N when the given expression A(N) equals 0. (See Worksheet 4–10–1.) Each expression should be built as a tile region on one side of the mat and compared to the index card region of 0 area on the other side of the mat. Students should vary the mat side on which they build the tile arrangement. Once the dimensions (edge lengths of the tile region) have been identified, linear equations that equate each dimension to 0 units should be solved for N. Finally, each solution for N should be tested by substituting appropriate unit tiles for each variable tile in the mat arrangement. This will confirm that the area of the tile arrangement has the required value of 0. Students should record their results according to the format used in step 5. Here are some possible expressions to assign. [Solutions for N are provided in brackets with each exercise.]

1. $A(N) = N^2 - 1$ $[+1, -1]$

2. $A(N) = N^2 + 5N + 6$ $[-2, -3]$

3. $A(N) = 2N^2$ $[0, 0]$

4. $A(N) = -N^2 - 2N + 3$ $[-3, +1]$

5. $A(N) = N^2 - 2N$ $[0, +2]$

6. $A(N) = 3N^2 + 6N$ $[0, +2]$

7. $A(N) = N^2 + 4N + 3$ $[-3, -1]$

8. $A(N) = N^2 - N - 2$ $[+2, -1]$

Activity 2: *VISUALIZING WITH AREA*

[Bridging Action]

Materials: Paper
Regular pencils
Calculators
Worksheet 4–10–2

Management: Partners (50 minutes)

Directions:

1. Provide each pair of students with a calculator. The diagramming technique used in this activity is an effective strategy for students to apply to *situations* involving *area*

WORKSHEET 4–10–1
Zero Dimensions

Build a tile region for each given expression, and compare the area of the tile region to an area of 0. Use the edge lengths of the tile region to solve for N. Follow your teacher's instructions to record your results.

Example 1: $A(N) = N^2 + 3N$

Example 2: $A(N) = N^2 - 4$

Solve for N when $A(N) = 0$.

    1. $A(N) = N^2 - 1$

    2. $A(N) = N^2 + 5N + 6$

    3. $A(N) = 2N^2$

    4. $A(N) = -N^2 - 2N + 3$

    5. $A(N) = N^2 - 2N$

    6. $A(N) = 3N^2 + 6N$

    7. $A(N) = N^2 + 4N + 3$

    8. $A(N) = N^2 - N - 2$

measurement. It also may be used to find the horizontal axis intercepts (or X-intercepts) of a parabolic curve or to find the independent values that produce a dependent value of 0 in a quadratic function. Students need to be aware of each of these different ways of interpreting the "solving" of a quadratic equation.

2. Write the following equation on the board: **Area A(b) = 2b^2 + 5b + 3.** Ask students to calculate the areas A(1) and A(2) and record their work on their own papers as number sentences: **A(1) = 2(1)(1) + 5(1) + 3 = +10   and   A(2) = 2(2)(2) + 5(2) + 3 = +21.** *Ask:* "What set of tiles is suggested by the second-degree polynomial, 2b^2 + 5b + 3?" *(2 large square tiles, 5 long rectangular tiles, and 3 small square tiles)* "Can you draw a diagram that represents these tiles as a product or rectangular region?" *(yes;* one possible product is (b + 1)(2b + 3)) "You just found the areas A(1) = +10 and A(2) = +21. Since this product diagram can represent *any* area, can you **equate** it with the area of 0 square units?"

3. Students should draw an equation frame that shows the product region to the left of two vertical bars (the **equals** sign) and a rectangle to the right. The rectangle should be somewhat **similar** to the shape of the product region; that is, if the product region is taller than it is wide when all the shapes are drawn, the rectangle should also be drawn taller than it is wide. The two factors of the polynomial should be labeled on the left edge and upper edge of the product region, and the area measure of 0 should be written inside the rectangle on the right. Here is an example of such a diagram.

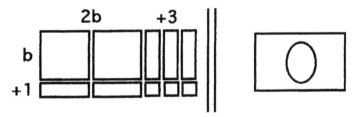

4. Students should now analyze the two dimensions or factors that produce the 0 area on the right side of the diagram. In order to have a product of 0, *at least* one factor must be 0. Students should write 0 on the left edge of the rectangle in the diagram, the word OR at the upper left corner, and another 0 on the upper edge. These numbers should be written on the same sides or edges of the rectangle as their corresponding factors or dimensions of the product region on the left side of the diagram. Students should now record the following equations on their own papers:

(1) *areas:* 2b^2 + 5b + 3 = (b + 1)(2b + 3) = 0

(2) *dimensions:* b + 1 = 0, or 2b + 3 = 0

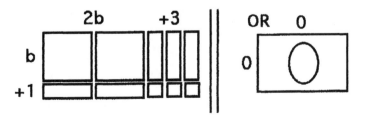

5. Discuss the idea that since we do not know which dimension or edge length of the rectangular region on the right is the 0-factor, we must compare the upper edges of the two rectangular shapes in the diagram, as well as the left edges: **b + 1 = 0, or 2b + 3 = 0.**

Solving each linear equation, students will find **b = –1, or b = ($\frac{1}{2}$)(–3) = –1.5.** Have students record whatever steps they use to solve their chosen linear equations (review Section 2 techniques, if necessary). Students should also test each solution for the variable b in the original polynomial expression A(b) to see if the value will produce an area of 0 square units. They should record their substitution steps on their own papers: **A(–1) = 2(–1)(–1) + 5(–1) + 3 = 0, or A(–1.5) = 2(–1.5)(–1.5) + 5(–1.5) + 3 = 0.** Hence, the solutions for b are correct, because each produces a dimension of 0 units and therefore an area of 0 square units.

6. For students already comfortable with using the *product grid* (see Objective 6) to factor a second-degree polynomial, here are two additional ways to draw a diagram. The first diagram combines the product grid with the equation frame. The second diagram simply adds extra labels to the product grid itself. For any of the three diagrams presented, the main purpose is to provide visual clues that will lead students to the correct relationships and equations needed to solve for the variable.

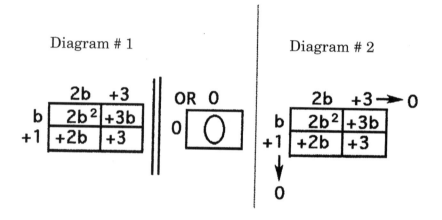

7. Now assign other polynomial expressions for area for students to solve for the linear variable. (See Worksheet 4–10–2.) Use different letters for the variables now. The procedure used in steps 3 through 5 should be followed. For each exercise, a diagram should be drawn to compare the given polynomial region to the rectangular shape having 0 area. Encourage students to alternate the sides of the diagram on which they draw the polynomial region. Each side or edge length of the shapes in the diagram should be labeled with the factor group or dimension it represents. Allow students who are already comfortable with factoring a quadratic expression to use one of the alternative diagrams described in step 6. Symbolic steps used in the solving process should be recorded and a test made to confirm that each solution does indeed produce a product or area of 0 square units. Appropriate equations like those used in steps 3 through 5 should be recorded for each exercise.

8. Here are some general polynomials for area that might be assigned to students. [Solutions are given in brackets with each exercise below.]

1. $A(b) = b^2 + 7b + 10$ [–2, –5]

2. $A(m) = -6m^2$ [0, 0]

3. $A(N) = N^2 - N$ [+1, 0]

4. $A(d) = -d^2 - 6d - 9$ [–3, –3]

5. $A(X) = X^2 - 8X + 16$ [+4, +4]

6. $A(k) = 4k^2 - 2k$ [0, +0.5]

7. $A(w) = w^2 + 3w - 18$ [–6, +3]

8. $A(R) = 4R^2 - 9$ [+1.5, –1.5]

WORKSHEET 4–10–2
Visualizing with Area

For each polynomial expression provided, draw a diagram on your own paper to compare the polynomial region to another rectangular region having 0 area. Follow your teacher's instructions to record your results.

Example: Area $A(b) = 2b^2 + 5b + 3$

Solve for the variable when the area A equals 0.

1. $A(b) = b^2 + 7b + 10$

2. $A(m) = -6m^2$

3. $A(N) = N^2 - N$

4. $A(d) = -d^2 - 6d - 9$

5. $A(X) = X^2 - 8X + 16$

6. $A(k) = 4k^2 - 2k$

7. $A(w) = w^2 + 3w - 18$

8. $A(R) = 4R^2 - 9$

Activity 3: QUADRATIC PATHWAYS

[Application/Exploration]

Materials: Worksheet 4–10–3
  Colored pencils
  Paper
  Regular pencils

Management: Partners (30 minutes)

Directions:

1. Give each pair of students a copy of Worksheet 4–10–3 and a colored pencil (any color). Partners are to work together to find a **path** through the different boxes of each "pathway" puzzle that will lead to correct solutions for the quadratic equation shown in the top box. This path can be drawn in regular pencil. Once students have found the first path, they should try to find an *alternative* path by which to reach the solutions; if one is found, it should be drawn with the colored pencil.

2. Each path will begin at the top box, then pass sequentially through boxes that show appropriate steps needed to find the solutions, which should be recorded in the bottom box. If the step in a particular box is not needed or is incorrect, the path should be drawn along the boundary or edges of the box, rather than through the box's interior. A path can only move to the left or right, or move directly or diagonally downward. It cannot back up on itself or move upward. This prevents students from repeating steps they have already taken, and forces them to think more efficiently about the steps they do take.

3. After all students have found at least one path for each of the two puzzles, have some students describe the different paths they found by telling the number of each box passed through and the order in which the boxes were used. When explaining a path to the class, students should give a reason for each box they select for their path. Possible paths for the sample puzzle shown below are as follows: *path (a)*—top, 3, 5, 9, bottom [uses method of Objective 10]; or *path (b)*—top, 1, 4, 9, bottom [uses method of Objective 9 to find positive factors from which to make linear equations, then uses **inverses** of the positive factors as another set of factors]. Since +9 is a familiar perfect square, some students may choose to skip box 4 in path (b) and go directly from box 1 to box 9; this is permissible. Note that box 8 is not a good choice since it only shows the positive solution and not the negative solution for the given equation.

```
┌─────────────────────────────────────────────┐
│        Solve for N:   N² - 9 = 0             │
├──────────────┬──────────────┬───────────────┤
│  N² = +9     │   N² = -9    │  (N+3)(N-3)   │
│              │              │     = 0       │
│  1           │   2          │  3            │
├──────────────┼──────────────┼───────────────┤
│  N = -√9 or  │  N+3 = 0 or  │  (N-3)(N-3)   │
│  N = +√9     │  N-3 = 0     │     = 0       │
│  4           │   5          │  6            │
├──────────────┼──────────────┼───────────────┤
│  N = -9 or   │   N = +3     │  N = -3 or    │
│  N = +9      │              │  N = +3       │
│  7           │   8          │  9            │
├──────────────┴──────────────┴───────────────┤
│        Solutions:   N = -3,  +3              │
└─────────────────────────────────────────────┘
```

4. Encourage students to use a *product grid* (Objective 6) when factoring a second-degree polynomial. The other types of diagrams discussed in Activity 2 are also available for students to use. Each factor found must then be made to equal 0 in order to solve for the variable.

5. Possible pathways to use for each puzzle on Worksheet 4–10–3:

Puzzle #1: [solutions: +3, −5]
  path *(a)*—top, 1, 5, 7, 8, bottom; or
  path *(b)*—top, 1, 5, 6, 9, 8, bottom

Puzzle #2: [solution: −2]
  path *(a)*—top, 3, 5, 4, 7, 8, bottom; or
  path *(b)*—top, 2, 6, 9, 8, bottom

6. Source for additional "pathway" puzzles:

Thompson, Frances M. (1992). *More Five-Minute Challenges for Secondary School* (Activity Resources Co., Inc., P.O. Box 4875, Hayward, CA 94540)

WORKSHEET 4–10–3
Quadratic Pathways

Find the answer to each problem by drawing a path through appropriate boxes in correct order as needed. The path can only move sideways (left or right), or directly or diagonally downward. It cannot move in an upward direction. To skip a box, draw along its edges. Try to find more than one path that works.

1.

Solve for N: $2N^2+4N-30=0$		
$(2N-6)(N+5)$ $=0$ 1	$(N+3)(2N-5)$ $=0$ 2	$2N^2=$ $30-4N$ 3
$N+3=2N-5$ 4	$2N-6=0$ or $N+5=0$ 5	$2(N-3)=0$ or $N+5=0$ 6
$2N=+6$ or $N=-5$ 7	$N=+3$ or $N=-5$ 8	$N-3=0$ or $N+5=0$ 9

Solutions:

2.

Solve for X: $3X^2+12X+12=0$		
$3X^2=$ $12X+12$ 1	$3(X^2+4X+4)$ $=0$ 2	$(3X+6)(X+2)$ $=0$ 3
$3X=-6$ or $X=-2$ 4	$3X+6=0$ or $X+2=0$ 5	X^2+4X+4 $=0$ 6
$X=1/3(-6)$ or $X=-2$ 7	$X=-2$ 8	$(X+2)^2=0$ 9

Solutions:

OBJECTIVE 11: **Solve quadratic equations of the form:**
$(aX + b)^2 = c$, where X, a, b, and c are real
numbers and $c \geq 0$.

Activity 1: SQUARING OFF!

[Developing Action]

Materials: Packet of tiles and equation building mats from Objective 10
Regular pencils
Paper
Worksheet 4–11–1

Management: Partners (50 minutes)

Directions:

1. Give each pair of students a packet of tiles and an equation building mat. In this objective we will modify the area comparison technique used in Objective 9. Instead of building a *rectangular* tile arrangement to find the two factors of a polynomial product, then building a *similar* arrangement for a given area using unit tiles and comparing the factors of the two arrangements, we will build rectangular arrangements that are shaped more specifically like *squares*. With this new technique, students will look for two **equal** factors in each of the two tile arrangements being compared. Previously students had to look for two factors in the variable tile arrangement, identify the relationship between the two factors (often a **nonequal** relationship), then find factors for the unit tile arrangement that had the same relationship. Factor equality will make the task much easier.

2. Write the following problem on the board: "The area of square A is $(2k - 1)^2$ square yards. The area of square B is 9 square yards. If the area of square A equals the area of square B, what could the value of k be?" Have students build a **square** arrangement of variable and unit tiles on the left side of the equation building mat that will represent the product $(2k - 1)^2$. They should also build a **square** arrangement on the right side of the mat, using 9 positive unit tiles. *Ask:* "Since the tile arrangements shown on the mat are both square regions and are considered to have the same area, what do we know about their dimensions?" *(when two regions are squares and have equal areas, their dimensions must also be equal)* "What do you notice about the quadratic variable tiles in the upper left corner of the tile arrangement on the left side of the mat? What about the unit tiles in the lower right corner?" *(the 4 large variable tiles form a square arrangement themselves;* the single unit tile is also a square shape; if there were more unit tiles, they would still form a square subregion within themselves) Since the two dimensions of each tile region are equal, students only need to work with one dimension to solve for k. The linear equation $2k - 1 = +3$ can easily be solved to yield $k = +2$, a solution for the area equation. Thus, students should write on their own papers the following equations:

(a) *areas:* $(2k - 1)^2 = +9$

(b) *dimensions:* $2k - 1 = +3$, so $k = +2$

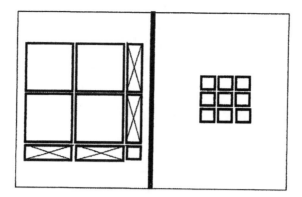

3. Now **ask:** "If we are not restricted to positive numbers to show *measurements,* is there another value we might use in the pair of equal factors for +9?" (*yes; the product* (−3)(−3) *also equals +9*) Have students solve the new linear equation 2k − 1 = −3, then add the following to their previous recording:

(c) *inverse factor:* **2k − 1 = −3, so k = −1**

4. Have students check each solution by replacing the variable tiles on the left side of the mat with the proper amount in unit tiles according to the solution being tested. After a substitution is complete, both sides of the mat should hold the same value in unit tiles. Remind students that if k is the name for the variable tile and k = −1, then the inverse variable tile must be replaced by the opposite value or +1, and k² = (−1)(−1) = +1. Here is the final unit tile substitution for the solution, **k = +2.**

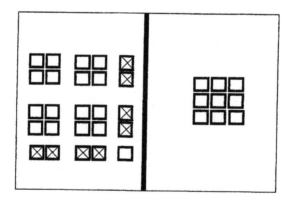

5. Assign other products (areas of square regions) for students to build with tiles on the equation building mat. (See Worksheet 4–11–1.) For each exercise, they should record equations in the format shown in steps 2 and 3 above. Any steps needed to solve the linear equations should also be written on students' papers. Whenever there are enough unit tiles to do so, encourage students to test each solution they find by replacing variable tiles on the mat with the appropriate amount of unit tiles. Here are suggested products to assign. [Solutions are provided in brackets for each exercise.]

(1) $N^2 = +4$ [−2, +2]   (5) $4y^2 = +4$ [+1, −1]

(2) $(X + 1)^2 = +9$ [+2, −4]   (6) $(H + 3)^2 = +16$ [+1, −7]

(3) $b^2 − 4b + 4 = +16$ [+6, −2]   (7) $(m − 1)^2 = +25$ [+6, −4]

(4) $(2A + 1)^2 = +25$ [+2, −3]   (8) $w^2 − 10w + 25 = 0$ [+5, +5]

© 1998 by John Wiley & Sons, Inc

WORKSHEET 4–11–1
Squaring Off!

Build a square region with tiles for each polynomial expression and compare the tile region's area to a square region having the given area. Follow your teacher's instructions to record your results on your own paper.

Example: Area $(2k - 1)^2 = 9$

Solve for the variable where the given area is for a square region.

1. $N^2 = +4$

2. $(X + 1)^2 = +9$

3. $b^2 - 4b + 4 = +16$

4. $(2A + 1)^2 = +25$

5. $4y^2 = +4$

6. $(H + 3)^2 = +16$

7. $(m - 1)^2 = +25$

8. $w^2 - 10w + 25 = 0$

Activity 2: SQUARE PICTURES

[Bridging Action]

Materials: Calculators
Colored pencils (any color)
Paper
Regular pencils
Worksheet 4–11–2

Management: Partners (50 minutes)

Directions:

   1. Give each pair of students a calculator (with square root key) and a colored pencil (any color). In this activity students will first draw squared regions on equation frames to be able to compare dimensions, then they will use a combination of a product grid with a labeled square in order to identify linear equations to solve.

   2. *Product Region Method.* Write the following on the board: "The tile amounts $4N^2 - 12N + 9$ and $+25$ represent the areas of squared regions. If the two areas are equal, what might N equal?" Have students draw a diagram on their own papers to equate the two areas as product regions. A large square with $+25$ written in its interior should be drawn to the left of two vertical, parallel bars and a product region to represent $4N^2 - 12N + 9$ should be drawn to the right of the vertical bars. At least one of the two equal factors should be labeled on each square. A sample diagram is shown here.

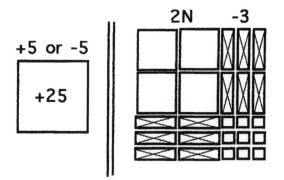

   3. Students should now write equations from their diagram and solve for N, applying linear procedures studied in Section 2:

   (a) *areas:* $4N^2 - 12N + 9 = (2N - 3)(2N - 3) = +25$

   (b) *dimensions:* $2N - 3 = +5$, so $N = +4$

   (c) *inverse factor:* $2N - 3 = -5$, so $N = -1$

   4. Have students compute to test each solution as follows:

   $4(+4)(+4) - 12(+4) + 9 = +25$, and $4(-1)(-1) - 12(-1) + 9 = +25$.

Since each substitution produces $+25$, the values $+4$ and -1 must be correct solutions for N. Some students might prefer to use the *colored pencil* to draw unit tiles directly on top of each variable tile in the diagram. Remind them that if a negative unit is drawn on the linear variable shape to show N = −1, then a positive unit must be drawn on its inverse shape to show −N = +1.

5. ***Product Grid Method.*** Now present another type of diagram to the students. Write the following exercise on the board: **$d^2 - 4d + 4 = +27$.** Have students draw a *product grid* (see Objective 6 for details) in combination with a large square containing +27 in its interior. Since +27 is not a perfect square, students must estimate a decimal value for its square root. If needed, review the method for estimating square roots studied in Objective 11, Section 1. From this new type of diagram, students should write equations like those used in step 3 and solve for d. Substitutions as in step 4 should also be made to test the solutions found. Examples of the equations and diagram are shown below.

(a) ***areas:*** $d^2 - 4d + 4 = +27$

(b) ***dimensions:*** $d - 2 = +\sqrt{27}$, **so d $\approx$ 2 + 5.2 $\approx$ +7.2**

(c) ***inverse factor:*** $d - 2 = -\sqrt{27}$, **so d $\approx$ 2 − 5.2 $\approx$ −3.2**

(+7.2)(+7.2) − 4(+7.2) + 4 = +27.04 $\approx$ +27 and

(−3.2)(−3.2) − 4(−3.2) + 4 = +27.04 $\approx$ +27

6. Assign more exercises for students to practice finding factors and setting up appropriate linear equations to solve. (See Worksheet 4–11–2.) Equations and substitutions, along with diagrams, should be recorded on the students' own papers. Some possible exercises are listed below. Exercises 1 through 4 should be done using the *product region* diagram; exercises 5 through 8 should be done using the *product grid* diagram. Exercise 5 will require estimation of a square root. Exercise 8 will use $(\frac{1}{2}X)(\frac{1}{2}X) = \frac{1}{4}X^2$ on the product grid. Some students may need to continue drawing a detailed product region of tile shapes in order to find the factors; if so, encourage them also to draw the product grid that corresponds to their product region. (Solutions are provided in brackets for each exercise. Note that some solutions are approximate.)

Product Region Method:

(1) $9m^2 = +36$ [+2, −2]   (3) $N^2 - 16N + 64 = 0$ [+8, +8]

(2) $4y^2 + 12y + 9 = +25$ [+1, −4]   (4) $9k^2 + 24k + 16 = 64$ [+$\frac{4}{3}$, −4]

Product Grid Method:

(5) $B^2 + 10B + 25 = +7$ [−2.4, −7.6]   (7) $16c^2 + 16c + 4 = 1$ [−$\frac{1}{4}$, −$\frac{3}{4}$]

(6) $4w^2 = 0$ [0, 0]   (8) $(\frac{1}{4})X^2 - 3X + 9 = +81$ [24, −12]

WORKSHEET 4–11–2
Square Pictures

For each polynomial expression provided, draw a diagram on your own paper to compare the polynomial region to a square region with the given area. Follow your teacher's instructions to record your results. You may need to approximate some solutions.

Example 1: Use a *product region* diagram to solve $4N^2 - 12N + 9 = +25$.

Example 2: Use a *product grid* diagram to solve $d^2 - 4d + 4 = +27$.

Solve each area equation for the variable, using a *product region* diagram.

1. $9m^2 = +36$

2. $4y^2 + 12y + 9 = +25$

3. $N^2 - 16N + 64 = 0$

4. $9k^2 + 24k + 16 = 64$

Solve each area equation for the variable, using a *product grid* diagram.

5. $B^2 + 10B + 25 = +7$

6. $4w^2 = 0$

7. $16c^2 + 16c + 4 = 1$

8. $\frac{1}{4}X^2 - 3X + 9 = +81$

Activity 3: MAKE FOUR!

[Application/Exploration]

Materials: Decks of cards (details given in step 1)
Worksheet 4–11–3 (pattern for card deck)
Calculators
Paper
Regular pencils

Management: Teams of 4 students each (30 minutes)

Directions:

1. Give each team of students a deck of cards and a calculator (with square root key). Each deck will consist of 52 cards: 12 "books" with 4 cards per book, plus 4 distractors. Each book will contain 1 **equation** card, 2 **factor** cards, and 1 **solution** card, and will involve the solving of a quadratic equation, using one of the factoring techniques studied in Objectives 9, 10, and 11. For each **equation** card (two rectangular regions separated by two vertical bars), students must decide what factor pairs are needed for the given *numerical* area, then find two **factor** cards where each shows a region labeled with one of the needed factor pairs. Using the equation and factor information, the solutions of the equation may then be found and the matching **solution** card identified. Labels for a possible deck are provided on Worksheet 4–11–3. Cards may be made from light tagboard cut into 3 in. by 4 in. rectangles, which are then labeled and laminated. Before cards are laminated, the cards in each deck should be uniquely coded on the back with a small symbol or a set of colored or specially arranged dots; this special code will identify cards that belong in the *same deck* in case the cards should become separated for some reason.

2. To begin the game, a team should shuffle its deck of cards well, then one member distribute the cards one at a time to all 4 team members until each person has 7 cards. The remaining 24 cards should be placed face down in a stack in the center of the playing area; this stack will be the **drawing pile** during play.

3. After each player has checked the cards in hand to see if any belong to the same book, any complete book may be placed face up in a stack near the player who "owns" it. Then the players begin to take turns requesting or drawing a card. The player to the right of the "dealer" has the first turn.

4. As an example of play, if it is player A's turn, that player will decide which cards might be needed to form a particular book, then will ask player B (sitting to the right of player A) for only one such *specific* card. If player B has the card, the card must be given to player A; if not, player A must take a new card from the top of the **drawing pile.** If the new card completes a *book,* player A must place that book's four cards face up in a stack on the table. Only one book may be placed on the table during a turn. The other 3 players must agree that the 4 cards put down do correctly form a book. After player A has received or drawn a new card, and possibly put down a book, the turn passes to player B. Player B follows the procedure used by player A and requests a specific card from player C to the right.

WORKSHEET 4-11-3
Card Labels for "Make Four!" Game

$N+2$ [$N+3$] ‖ ? [? / 30]	N [$N+3$] ‖ ? [? / 28]	$N-3$ [$N+4$] ‖ ? [? / 60]
$+5$ [$+6$] -6 [-5]	$+4$ [$+7$] -7 [-4]	$+5$ [$+12$] -12 [-5]
$N= +3$ or $N= -8$	$N= +4$ or $N= -7$	$N= +8$ or $N= -9$
N [$N+1$] ‖ ? [? / 3/4]	$N+1$ [$N+1$] ‖ ? [? / 25]	$N-2$ [$N-2$] ‖ ? [? / 49]
$+1/2$ [$+3/2$] $-3/2$ [$-1/2$]	$+5$ [$+5$] -5 [-5]	$+7$ [$+7$] -7 [-7]
$N= +1/2$ or $N= -3/2$	$N= +4$ or $N= -6$	$N= +9$ or $N= -5$
$N-1$ [$N-1$] ‖ ? [? / 5]	$N+4$ [$N+4$] ‖ ? [? / 36]	$N-3$ [$N+1$] ‖ ? [? / 0]
$+\sqrt{5}$ [$+\sqrt{5}$] $-\sqrt{5}$ [$-\sqrt{5}$]	$+6$ [$+6$] -6 [-6]	? [0] 0 [?]
$N= +3.2$ or $N= -1.2$	$N= +2$ or $N= -10$	$N= +3$ or $N= -1$

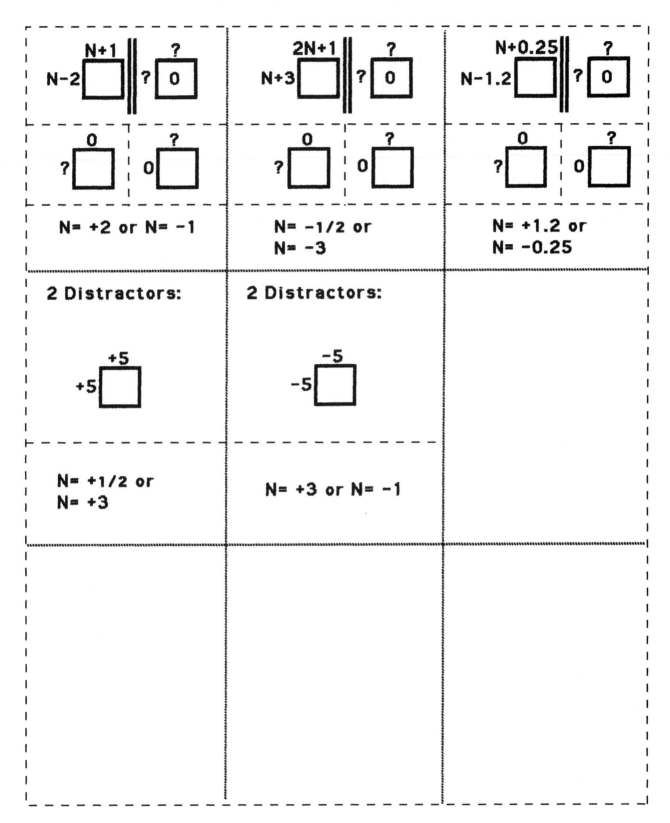

5. Play continues until time is called, or until the drawing pile is empty and the next player to have a turn after that is unable to obtain a new card from a neighbor. The player with the most books at the end will be the winner.

6. Notes about the Card Labels on Worksheet 4–11–3: Expressions or figures for each card in a 52-card deck are listed on Worksheet 4–11–3. This set may be photocopied (and possibly enlarged, if preferred), then each expression or figure cut out and glued on an individual card in order to make a playing deck. The four figures/expressions for each **book** are grouped together in the same column. The first expression will be the **equation** to be solved; the second and third figures shown in the same row will represent the two **factor** pairs needed; and the last expressions will be the **solutions** to the equation. Each **equation** card in the suggested deck will contain *square* rectangles, even though *nonsquare* rectangles may actually be involved. This is to prevent students from matching cards with respect to their *shapes,* rather than their *values.* Also, some **factor** and **solution** cards will involve decimals and fractions, but the amounts will be easy to compute. One book will require students to estimate a decimal value for a numerical square root (see method taught in Objective 11, Section 1). Otherwise, students may just use their calculators to get a value for the square root; however, they must recognize that a square root will be involved.

OBJECTIVE 12: **Develop and apply the technique of "completing the square" to solve equations of the form: $aX^2 + bX + c = 0$, where X, a, b, and c are real numbers and $a \neq 0$; derive the Quadratic Formula from the "completing the square" technique and apply it to solve quadratic equations.**

Activity 1: SQUARING WITH TILES

[Developing Action]

Materials: Packets of tiles, equation building mats, and index cards with "0" from Objective 10
Regular pencils
Paper
Worksheet 4–12–1

Management: Partners (50 minutes)

Directions:

1. Give each pair of students a packet of tiles, an equation building mat, and 3 index cards containing "0." In Objectives 9 through 11, students learned how to solve quadratic equations using a factoring process. The factored product was equated to 0 or to a nonzero value as area. Perhaps the easiest method was the one used in Objective 11, where the polynomial was a perfect square. Then the square root or a root estimate was found for the given numerical area. Objective 12 now addresses the question: How do we solve such an equation if the polynomial is not easy to factor?

2. Write on the board: **$m^2 - 6m + 3 = +5$.** At this point we want students to experience contradictions (or the failure to meet required conditions) when they try to apply the methods previously studied. Have students build the quadratic expression with tiles on the left side of the building mat, then place 5 positive unit tiles on the right side. Ask students to form a rectangular region with each set of tiles. This will require the strategy of *trial-and-error;* students will try a variety of arrangements, but will not be able to form a complete rectangular region with the tiles on the left. Suggest to students that they might try *adding the same amount* of positive unit tiles *to both sides* of the equation. This would maintain the equality of the two sets of tiles and the extra unit tiles would allow students to complete the polynomial region on the left. One such possibility would be to add 5 positive unit tiles to both sides. The product $(m - 4)(m - 2)$ could then be arranged on the left. There should then be 10 positive unit tiles on the right; the 10 unit tiles can be arranged as 1 row of 10 unit tiles, 10 rows of 1 unit tile per row, 5 rows of 2 unit tiles each, or 2 rows of 5 unit tiles each. The factoring method used in Objective 9 requires factor pairs on both sides of the equation to have the same relationship. In $(m - 4)(m - 2)$, the factor $(m - 2)$ is 2 more than the factor $(m - 4)$. Integral factors cannot be found for +10 where one factor is 2 more than the other. We say "integral factors" because we are limited to integers as factors when physically arranging a region of unit tiles. Encourage students to find other products in this manner; for example, by adding 2 positive unit tiles to both sides, students might obtain the product, $(m - 5)$ $(m - 1)$, equal to $+7$. Again, $(m - 1)$ is 4 more than $(m - 5)$, but 7 positive unit tiles cannot be arranged to show integral factors where one factor is 4 more than the other factor. Here are the tile arrangements just discussed.

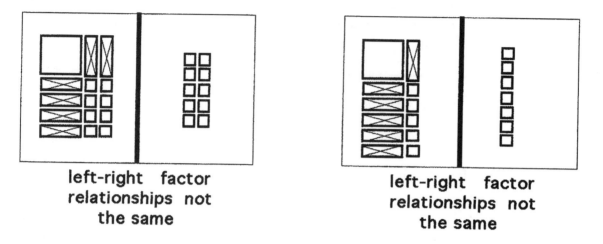

left-right factor relationships not the same   **left-right factor relationships not the same**

3. Now ask students to try the method of Objective 10 where a polynomial equals 0. Continuing with $m^2 - 6m + 3 = +5$ in tiles on the mat, students should now remove the same amount of unit tiles from both sides of the mat until no unit tiles remain on the right. An index card containing a 0 should be placed on the right side to indicate a region of 0 area. (Note that we do not try to adjust any *variable* tiles, since any removal or addition of a variable tile on one side of the mat would just cause other variable tiles to appear on the other side. Our concern is with the unit tiles; we need numerical values for our factors in order to solve for the variable **m** eventually.) If 5 positive unit tiles are removed from the right side, we must introduce 0-pairs of unit tiles on the left in order to remove 5 positive unit tiles in all. This will leave 2 negative unit tiles on the left side of the mat. Again, students will not be able to form a complete rectangular region with the tiles on the left, and no extra unit tiles can be added to the left side of the mat without requiring a similar amount of unit tiles to be added to the *right,* where we really want to have **0.** Thus, the method of factoring a product that equals 0 will not work for our equation either.

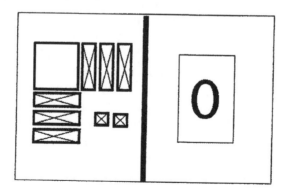

4. The only method remaining to be tested is the perfect square method of Objective 11. Have students build a tile arrangement that represents a polynomial that is a "perfect square" like those studied in Objective 11 and earlier. Two examples might be $(2B +$

3)(2B + 3) or (B − 2)(B − 2). Ask students what they notice about their "perfect square" arrangements. Hopefully they will notice that the upper left and lower right sections both involve *square* arrangements of tiles, with each section having its own type of tile, and that the upper right and lower left sections contain not only the same amount of tiles but also the same type of tile. ***Ask:*** "Now that you know how the tiles look when you build a product that is a perfect square, can you use the tiles for $m^2 − 6m + 3 = +5$ in some way to build such a 'perfect square'? Remember that whatever you do to one side of the mat, you must also do to the other side." Students should place the quadratic variable tile in the upper left position, then arrange 3 inverse linear variable tiles in the upper right and also in the lower left positions of an arrangement on the left side of the mat. Nine positive unit tiles are *needed* in the lower right to complete the "perfect square," but there are only 3 positive unit tiles on the left side. Thus, 6 more positive unit tiles must be added to the left side. To keep the balance of the equation, another 6 positive unit tiles must be added to the right side, making a total of +11 on the right. The mat should now show the equation $m^2 − 6m + 9 = +11$ (see illustration in step 5).

5. Students should now try to make a square arrangement with the 11 positive unit tiles. This will not be physically possible, but an *almost* square arrangement will provide a close estimate of a true square's dimensions. Realizing that each dimension will be the square root of +11, students should either estimate or use their calculators to find a value for $\sqrt{11}$, then use this value in the dimension and inverse equations. The following equations and solution tests may now be recorded on students' papers:

(a) ***areas:*** $m^2 − 6m + 9 = (m − 3)(m − 3) = +11$

(b) ***dimensions:*** $m − 3 = +\sqrt{11}$, so $m \approx 3 + 3.3 \approx +6.3$

(c) ***inverse factor:*** $m − 3 = −\sqrt{11}$, so $m \approx 3 − 3.3 \approx −0.3$

$(+6.3)(+6.3) − 6(+6.3) + 9 = +10.89 \approx +11$ **and**

$(−0.3)(−0.3) − 6(−0.3) + 9 = +10.89 \approx +11$

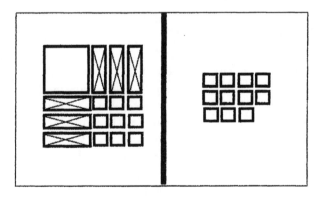

6. Discuss the idea with students that the "perfect square" method used in Objective 11 has now been modified, at least with respect to the unit tiles, so that certain equations involving "non-perfect-square" second-degree polynomials can also be solved. This new method is called "completing the square." Even if the set of unit tiles on one side of the mat will not form a perfect square, students have a method for estimating what the edge length would be if such a square could be formed. (**Note:** For this activity we have explored ways to complete the square without totally removing whatever unit tiles were with the variable tiles initially. *Total removal* will be used in Activity 2.)

7. Now write the following on the board: $3N^2 + 12N + 9 = 0$. Students should show the polynomial with tiles on the left side of the mat and place one index card on the right side to represent the area of **0. *Ask:*** "Can you make a perfect square with your tiles?" (*no;* the 3 quadratic variable tiles will not make a square arrangement as needed within the total square-shaped product region) Discuss the idea that students already have a method for dealing with the unit tiles, but the variable tiles cannot be treated the same way (see discussion in step 3). Thus, we will use a separation technique where the original equation is separated into several equivalent equations. Have students move one large square tile to the upper edge of the mat, another large square tile to the middle section, and the remaining large tile to the lower edge of the mat. They should continue separating their tiles into the three groups until each type of tile is represented equally in each group. Since the left side has been separated into 3 equal groups, the 0 area on the right side must also be separated into 3 equal groups. To show this, students should replace the one index card on the right with 3 rows of one index card each. The tiles should appear on the mat as shown here.

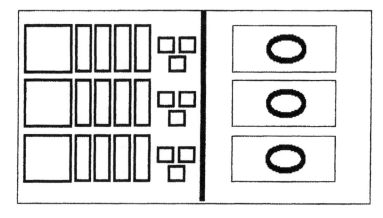

8. Have students remove two of their three groups of tiles and "0" cards, thereby leaving only $N^2 + 4N + 3 = 0$ represented on the mat. They should now "complete the square" being formed by the tiles on the left side. This will require that a new positive unit tile be added to each side of the mat. At this point the "0" card should be removed from the mat. The linear equations obtained from the tile arrangements will be $N + 2 = +1$ and $N + 2 = -1$. ***Ask:*** "If your solutions for this one group of tiles on the equation building mat are $N = -1$ and $N = -3$, will -1 and -3 also be the solutions for the original equation that you built: $3N^2 + 12N + 9 = 0$? Test your values to find out." Students should substitute $N = -1$ and $N = -3$ in the original equation as follows: $3(-1)(-1) + 12(-1) + 9 = 0$ $\checkmark$ and $3(-3)(-3) + 12(-3) + 9 = 0$ $\checkmark$. Therefore, finding solutions to one of several *equivalent* equations also yields the solutions to the *original* equation, that is, the equation that results from combining all the equivalent equations. Actually, the original equation and the three *equivalent* equations are all considered *equivalent to each other*; this is because they all have the *same solutions*. We now have a method for working with equations that have more than one quadratic variable tile.

9. Give students additional equations to solve by "completing the square." (See Worksheet 4–12–1.) Equations and solution tests like those shown in step 5 should be recorded for each equation solved. For exercise 4 below, students should first record the *original* equation, then the new *equivalent* equation that will actually be solved. The tests should

Name _____ **Date** _____

WORKSHEET 4–12–1
Squaring with Tiles

Build *square* regions with tiles to solve the following equations. Some solutions may be approximate. Follow your teacher's instructions to record your results on your own paper.

Example 1: $m^2 - 6m + 3 = +5$

Example 2: $3N^2 + 12N + 9 = 0$

Solve for each variable by building a "complete" square region.

1. $X^2 + 4X + 3 = +15$

2. $4N^2 + 4N - 3 = 5$

3. $d^2 - 8d + 8 = 0$

4. $5a^2 - 10a - 10 = 0$

be made with the *original* equation in this case (see step 8 above). Here are possible equations to assign. (Solutions are provided in brackets with each exercise.)

(1) $X^2 + 4X + 3 = +15$ $[-6, +2]$

(2) $4N^2 + 4N - 3 = 5$ $[-2, +1]$

(3) $d^2 - 8d + 8 = 0$ (use $\sqrt{8} \approx 2.8$) $[+6.8, +1.2]$

(4) $5a^2 - 10a - 10 = 0$ (use $\sqrt{3} \approx 1.7$) $[+2.7, -0.7]$

Activity 2: SQUARING PATTERNS

[Bridging Action]

Materials: Calculators
Worksheet 4–12–2
Colored pencils (at least 3 colors)
Paper
Regular pencils

Management: Partners (50 minutes)

Directions:

1. Give each pair of students only a calculator at first; they will receive Worksheet 4–12–2 and some colored pencils later. For this activity, students will use *product grids* in equation diagrams to solve quadratic equations. Remind students that any second-degree polynomial equation can be transformed so that all variables and nonzero constants are on one side of the equation and only 0 is on the other side. This allows us to begin forming a "perfect square" with the quadratic and linear variables by adjusting the constants as needed. Emphasis in this activity will be on finding a pattern for how the different coefficients of the polynomial in an equation occur in the solution of that equation. Several quadratic equations will be solved with diagrams at first. Then a careful analysis will be made of the steps used to find each solution. After the analysis, Worksheet 4–12–2 will be distributed in order for students to test their pattern found for the coefficients. Our goal is the development of the **Quadratic Formula;** however, some students may not be comfortable with the traditional abstract format. A modified product grid approach may be a more effective method for such students. Hopefully, this activity will provide the careful *connection* they need to see between the **actions** used in "completing the square" and the abstract notation.

2. Write the following equation on the board: **$3N^2 + 12N + 6 = 0$.** This equation is similar to the last example discussed in Activity 1; that is, the 3 quadratic variables will not form a square arrangement in the upper left position as is needed in the main tile arrangement of the product region. *Ask:* "How many equivalent equations should we try to form from this original one?" (*3,* since there are 3 quadratic variables) "Can you describe one of the new equivalent equations you will form?" (*$N^2 + 4N + 2 = 0$*) Students should write both the original equation and an equivalent equation on their own papers.

3. Discuss the idea that we now want to work directly with the *linear variables* in the equivalent equation in order to find the positive units needed to *complete the square,* that is, form a polynomial that is a perfect square. We can do this without considering any positive or negative units already present in the equivalent equation, even though in this case the +2 would just need additional positive units to complete its square arrangement. Remind students that we are looking for a **general** method that will work for **all** second-degree polynomials, regardless of the numbers involved. Students should remove +2 from the left side of the equivalent equation and also from the right side (or add −2 to both sides). An equation diagram should now be drawn, using a *product grid* to show the separation of the linear variables into two equal groups and the factors involved.

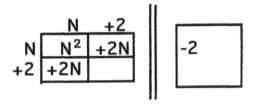

4. Students should observe the integer +2 in each factor on the grid. The product (+2)(+2) will be the new constant needed to complete the product grid. Since +4 must be added on the left side of the equation, +4 must also be added on the right. Factors for the right region should now be labeled on the diagram. Equations should also be recorded as follows:

(a) *areas:* $3N^2 + 12N + 6 = 0$
$$N^2 + 4N + 2 = 0$$

(b) *dimensions:* $N + 2 = +\sqrt{2}$, so $N \approx -2 + 1.4 \approx -0.6$

(c) *inverse factor:* $N + 2 = -\sqrt{2}$, so $N \approx -2 - 1.4 \approx -3.4$

$$3(-0.6)(-0.6) + 12(-0.6) + 6 = -0.12 \approx 0 \text{ and}$$

$$3(-3.4)(-3.4) + 12(-3.4) + 6 = -0.12 \approx 0$$

5. The above procedure may also be applied to an equation having *inverse* quadratic variables. Write the following on the board: **−2d² + 16d − 6 = 0.** *Ask:* "What can we do in this equation if we want just one plain quadratic variable, **d²**, with which to complete the square?" *(use **two** steps: (1) take the opposite of every variable and unit represented on the left, and take the opposite of 0 on the right, which is still 0; and then (2) separate the variables and units into two equivalent equations)* "What will the 'opposites' equation be, and what will one of the two equivalent equations be?" *(2d² − 16d + 6 = 0; d² − 8d + 3 = 0)* Initially it is best for students to find the opposites first, then perform the separation, rather than combine the steps together as though there is just one change to make. Later in our analysis we will combine the two steps as division by –2. Students should now draw a diagram and write equations to show the solution steps:

(a) *areas:* $-2d^2 + 16d - 6 = 0$

$$2d^2 - 16d + 6 = 0$$

$$d^2 - 8d + 3 = 0$$

(b) *dimensions:* $d - 4 = +\sqrt{13}$, so $d \approx +4 + 3.6 \approx +7.6$

(c) *inverse factor:* $d - 4 = -\sqrt{13}$, so $d \approx +4 - 3.6 \approx +0.4$

$-2(+7.6)(+7.6) + 16(+7.6) - 6 = +0.08 \approx 0$ and

$-2(+0.4)(+0.4) + 16(+0.4) - 6 = +0.08 \approx 0$

6. Write two more equations on the board: $5X^2 - 10X - 15 = 0$ and $-w^2 + 4w + 5 = 0$. Partners should work together to draw diagrams and write the necessary equations for solving these two equations. After all have finished, we will begin our analysis and search for a *coefficients pattern.* The solutions for the above two equations will be $X = +3$ or $X = -1$, and $w = +5$ or $w = -1$.

7. Now list all four equations used in this activity on the board, one equation beside the other near the top of the board. Taking one equation at a time, ask students to describe in order each step they used to solve the equation. As teacher, write an equation that reflects each step given by a student. This part will be tedious, so it is important that students not be burdened with recording the detailed notation. We will use the notation from Section 2 for showing division; for example, 2N divided by 2 or separated into **two** equal sets will be recorded as $(\frac{1}{2})(2N)$, rather than as $2N \div 2$ or $\frac{2N}{2}$. Likewise, for the quadratic equation involving the variable w, when the **opposite** of the equation is taken but the variables and constant remain together as **one** set (i.e., are not separated into several equal groups), we will use $w^2 + (\frac{1}{-1})4w$ and $(\frac{1}{-1})(5)$ in the notation in order to follow the same format used with the other three quadratic equations. The descriptions and corresponding notation for solving the equation $-2d^2 + 16d - 6 = 0$ are given on the transparency master as an example of how each of the four equations should be discussed and summarized on the board. Write the description of each step first, followed by the notation that represents that step. *Do not simplify any step at this time;* follow the example for the notation closely in order to show the pattern at the end.

8. After all four equations have been analyzed for the steps needed, give each pair of students two copies of Worksheet 4–12–2 and 3 different colored pencils. The left column of the worksheet will contain the four quadratic equations solved and analyzed in class, each being written in the $aX^2 + bX + c = 0$ format where **plus signs** are used between terms; the right column will contain in corresponding order the *unsimplified* solution equations found for each original quadratic equation. For each quadratic equation in the left column of the worksheet, ask students to draw a circle in color #1 around the coefficient of the quadratic variable, a circle in color #2 around the coefficient of the linear variable, and a circle in color #3 around the constant (also a coefficient). We will consider a **coefficient** to

Description of each step:	*Notation for each step:*
(1) original equation	$-2d^2 + 16d - 6 = 0$
(2) take opposites of all terms and separate into 2 new equivalent equations; use only one new equation	$d^2 + \left(\dfrac{1}{-2}\right)16d + \left(\dfrac{1}{-2}\right)(-6) = 0$
(3) remove constant of variable group from both sides of equation	$d^2 + \left(\dfrac{1}{-2}\right)16d = -\left(\dfrac{1}{-2}\right)(-6)$
(4) separate linear variables into 2 equal groups; **add new squared constant to both sides of equation**	$d^2 + \left(\dfrac{1}{-2}\right)16d + \left[\left(\dfrac{1}{2}\right)\left(\dfrac{1}{-2}\right)(16)\right]^2 =$ $\left[\left(\dfrac{1}{2}\right)\left(\dfrac{1}{-2}\right)(16)\right]^2 - \left(\dfrac{1}{-2}\right)(-6)$
(5) compare factors of two square regions; include inverses	$d + \left(\dfrac{1}{2}\right)\left(\dfrac{1}{-2}\right)(16) = \pm\sqrt{\left[\left(\dfrac{1}{2}\right)\left(\dfrac{1}{-2}\right)(16)\right]^2 - \left(\dfrac{1}{-2}\right)(-6)}$
(6) solve each linear equation for the variable	$d = \left(-\dfrac{1}{2}\right)\left(\dfrac{1}{-2}\right)(16) + \sqrt{\left[\left(\dfrac{1}{2}\right)\left(\dfrac{1}{-2}\right)(16)\right]^2 - \left(\dfrac{1}{-2}\right)(-6)}$ OR $d = \left(-\dfrac{1}{2}\right)\left(\dfrac{1}{-2}\right)(16) - \sqrt{\left[\left(\dfrac{1}{2}\right)\left(\dfrac{1}{-2}\right)(16)\right]^2 - \left(\dfrac{1}{-2}\right)(-6)}$

WORKSHEET 4–12–2
Squaring Patterns

Follow the teacher's instructions to complete this worksheet. You will be looking for a pattern among the coefficients of the different equations.

Quadratic Equation	*Solution Equations*

1. $3N^2 + 12N + 6 = 0$

$$N = -\frac{1}{2}\left(\frac{1}{3}\right)(12) + \sqrt{\left[\left(\frac{1}{2}\right)\left(\frac{1}{3}\right)(12)\right]^2 - \left(\frac{1}{3}\right)(6)}$$

OR

$$N = -\frac{1}{2}\left(\frac{1}{3}\right)(12) - \sqrt{\left[\left(\frac{1}{2}\right)\left(\frac{1}{3}\right)(12)\right]^2 - \left(\frac{1}{3}\right)(6)}$$

2. $(-2)d^2 + 16d + (-6) = 0$

$$d = -\frac{1}{2}\left(\frac{1}{-2}\right)(16) + \sqrt{\left[\frac{1}{2}\left(\frac{1}{-2}\right)(16)\right]^2 - \left(\frac{1}{-2}\right)(-6)}$$

OR

$$d = -\frac{1}{2}\left(\frac{1}{-2}\right)(16) - \sqrt{\left[\frac{1}{2}\left(\frac{1}{-2}\right)(16)\right]^2 - \left(\frac{1}{-2}\right)(-6)}$$

3. $5X^2 + (-10)X + (-15) = 0$

$$X = -\frac{1}{2}\left(\frac{1}{5}\right)(-10) + \sqrt{\left[\frac{1}{2}\left(\frac{1}{5}\right)(-10)\right]^2 - \left(\frac{1}{5}\right)(-15)}$$

OR

$$X = -\frac{1}{2}\left(\frac{1}{5}\right)(-10) - \sqrt{\left[\frac{1}{2}\left(\frac{1}{5}\right)(-10)\right]^2 - \left(\frac{1}{5}\right)(-15)}$$

4. $(-1)w^2 + 4w + 5 = 0$

$$w = -\frac{1}{2}\left(\frac{1}{-1}\right)(4) + \sqrt{\left[\frac{1}{2}\left(\frac{1}{-1}\right)(4)\right]^2 - \left(\frac{1}{-1}\right)(5)}$$

OR

$$w = -\frac{1}{2}\left(\frac{1}{-1}\right)(4) - \sqrt{\left[\frac{1}{2}\left(\frac{1}{-1}\right)(4)\right]^2 - \left(\frac{1}{-1}\right)(5)}$$

be either the number multiplied by a variable that tells how many of that variable are present in the equation or the number that tells how many positive units are present (alias, the "constant"; as an example of the latter, the term –5 in a polynomial indicates that there are –5 of +1 present). After students have circled all the numbers in the quadratic equations, they should try to find those same numbers in the corresponding solution equations in the right column. The same color should be used to draw a circle around any matching numbers; for example, if a circle in color #1 is around –2 in the quadratic equation, then a circle in color #1 should also be around –2 in the corresponding solution equations. Here is an example of one of the sets of equations marked on the worksheet.

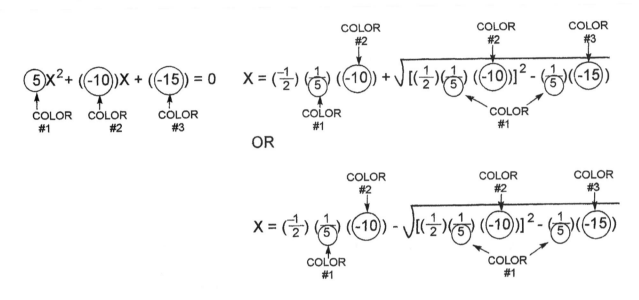

9. After students have completed their markings on the worksheet, ask them to compare the positions of the **coefficients** within the quadratic equations to their positions within the solution equations. Hopefully, students will notice that a quadratic coefficient occurs in the same positions within a solution equation, regardless of which quadratic equation is being used. Similarly, the linear coefficient and constant (or unit coefficient) keep their same positions, regardless of the quadratic equation used. ***Ask:*** "If we are given a new quadratic equation, $-6B^2 + 12B - 7 = 0$, can you predict what the solution equations will be?" Following the pattern of the colored circles, students should be able to predict the following solution equations.

$$B = -\frac{1}{2}\left(\frac{1}{-6}\right)(12) + \sqrt{\left[\frac{1}{2}\left(\frac{1}{-6}\right)(12)\right]^2 - \left(\frac{1}{-6}\right)(-7)}$$

OR

$$B = -\frac{1}{2}\left(\frac{1}{-6}\right)(12) - \sqrt{\left[\frac{1}{2}\left(\frac{1}{-6}\right)(12)\right]^2 - \left(\frac{1}{-6}\right)(-7)}$$

10. More practice will be given with the discovered pattern in Activity 3. In summary, remind students that they can apply the new *coefficient pattern* they have found or they can use the product grid and equation diagram technique to find the solution equations for any quadratic equation, no matter what real numbers might be used as coefficients. As an example, have students guide you in applying both methods to the equation: $2m^2 + (-6)m + 0.8 = 0$. When the linear equations are set up or simplified by either method, using $\sqrt{1.85} \approx 1.4$, the solutions will be $m \approx +2.9$ and $m \approx +0.1$.

(1) **Product Grid Method:**

	m	−1.5
m	m^2	−1.5m
−1.5	−1.5m	+2.25

$+\sqrt{1.85}$ or $-\sqrt{1.85}$

−0.4
+2.25
= +1.85

(2) **Coefficient Pattern Method:**

$$m = -\frac{1}{2}\left(\frac{1}{2}\right)(-6) + \sqrt{\left[\frac{1}{2}\left(\frac{1}{2}\right)(-6)\right]^2 - \left(\frac{1}{2}\right)(0.8)}$$

OR

$$m = -\frac{1}{2}\left(\frac{1}{2}\right)(-6) - \sqrt{\left[\frac{1}{2}\left(\frac{1}{2}\right)(-6)\right]^2 - \left(\frac{1}{2}\right)(0.8)}$$

Activity 3: THE QUADRATIC FORMULA

[Application/Exploration]

Materials: Calculators
Paper
Regular pencils
Worksheet 4–12–3

Management: Partners (30 minutes)

Directions:

1. How you choose to use this last activity will depend on the mathematical maturity of the students. Activities 1 and 2 of this objective and the activities of Objectives 9 through 11 have provided students with an in-depth experience in solving quadratic equations in one variable. At this point, students have sufficient skills—particularly with the product grid and equation diagram technique—to solve such equations. To go further to the **Quadratic Formula** now requires a simplification of the *coefficients pattern* students have discovered. Many students can lose the connection between their pattern and the formula if the algebraic steps used in the simplification are not familiar to them or if the steps become too tedious. Being able to substitute numbers into a formula does not necessarily imply that students understand the processes or the purpose the formula represents. It is possible that for some students the *more expanded* coefficients pattern used in Activity 2 will be easier to remember and apply. Simplification steps that reflect the methods and notation used in earlier sections (e.g., with square roots) will be provided below for presentation to students. It is recommended, however, that students be encouraged to decide for themselves which method they prefer to use: the coefficients pattern, the product grid diagram, or the simplified quadratic formula. Preferred learning styles will determine which method is perceived as "easiest" by individual students. Several exercises will be provided in the last steps of this activity for practice with any of the three methods.

2. *The Quadratic Formula:* Present the simplification steps given below, along with the descriptions, to the class. Only the solution equation using the *positive* square root will be transformed in detail; similar steps may be followed for the *negative* square root. Discuss the processes involved as each change is made. Do not require students to record the steps, but keep them *actively* involved in explaining or justifying each step.

Simplifying Steps:

(1) Use *coefficients pattern* to find one solution to $aX^2 + bX + c = 0$.

(2) Find fraction products.

(3) Apply exponent to fraction:
$$\left(\frac{b}{2a}\right)\left(\frac{b}{2a}\right) = \frac{b^2}{4a^2}$$

(4) Find common denominator for fractions being subtracted:
$$\frac{b^2}{4a^2} - \frac{c(4a)}{a(4a)}$$

(5) Simplify square root with repeated factor method:
$$\sqrt{\left(\frac{1}{4a^2}\right)(b^2 - 4ac)} = \sqrt{\left(\frac{1}{2a}\right)\left(\frac{1}{2a}\right)(b^2 - 4ac)}$$

(6) Combine numerators over same denominator.

Algebraic Notation:

$$X = -\frac{1}{2}\left(\frac{1}{a}\right)b + \sqrt{\left[\frac{1}{2}\left(\frac{1}{a}\right)b\right]^2 - \left(\frac{1}{a}\right)c}$$

$$X = \frac{-b}{2a} + \sqrt{\left[\frac{b}{2a}\right]^2 - \frac{c}{a}}$$

$$X = \frac{-b}{2a} + \sqrt{\frac{b^2}{4a^2} - \frac{c}{a}}$$

$$X = \frac{-b}{2a} + \sqrt{\frac{b^2}{4a^2} - \frac{c(4a)}{4a^2}}$$

$$X = \frac{-b}{2a} + \frac{1}{2a}\sqrt{b^2 - 4ac}$$

$$X = \frac{-b + \sqrt{b^2 - 4ac}}{2a}$$

Steps 1 through 6 can be repeated to find the solution equation using the (additive) *inverse* of the square root.

3. After the simplification or derivation is completed, remind students that this new equation is just a *condensed* form of the coefficients pattern they discovered earlier. As a formula, it must be *memorized* if it is to be useful. Most students will more correctly apply the formula if they write it as two separate equations (+√ and −√ forms) each time. Also encourage them to show **all** substitutions in the formula before they begin to simplify any part of the new expression; this procedure reduces chances of error in computation.

4. Write the four quadratic equations used in Activity 2 on the board. These equations are also shown on Worksheet 4–12–3. Solutions are provided in brackets here.

(1) $3N^2 + 12N + 6 = 0$ [−0.6, −3.4]

(2) $-2d^2 + 16d - 6 = 0$ [+7.6, +0.4]

(3) $5X^2 - 10X - 15 = 0$ [+3, −1]

(4) $-w^2 + 4w + 5 = 0$ [+5, −1]

5. Give each pair of students a calculator. Have students apply the new formula to each of the four equations to find its solutions. Compare the *formula* solutions to those solutions found earlier with a *product grid diagram* in Activity 2. As an example, if solving $5X^2 - 10X - 15 = 0$, students should rewrite the equation as $5X^2 + (-10)X + (-15) = 0$ and label each coefficient in the equation appropriately as **a, b,** or **c** before making the following substitutions:

$$X = \frac{-(-10) + \sqrt{(-10)^2 - 4(5)(-15)}}{2(5)} \text{ or } X = \frac{-(-10) - \sqrt{(-10)^2 - 4(5)(-15)}}{2(5)}$$

$$X = \frac{+10 + \sqrt{100 + 300}}{10} \text{ or } X = \frac{+10 - \sqrt{100 + 300}}{10}$$

$$X = \frac{+10 + 20}{10} = +3 \text{ or } X = \frac{+10 - 20}{10} = -1$$

6. For additional practice with the quadratic formula (or the coefficients pattern or the product grid diagram), assign the following equations for students to solve. (See Worksheet 4–12–3.) Note that some polynomials will need to be rewritten in correct (i.e., descending) order before coefficients can be labeled. (Solutions are provided in brackets for each exercise.)

(1) $-6 + 2B^2 - 8B = 0$ ($\sqrt{7} \approx 2.6$)   [+4.6, −0.6]

(2) $-20m + 2m^2 - 8 = 0$ ($\sqrt{29} \approx 5.4$)   [+10.4, −0.4]

(3) $-g^2 - 4.8g + 7.9 = 0$ ($\sqrt{13.66} \approx 3.7$)   [+1.3, −6.1]

(4) $24K + 24 + 6K^2 = 0$ [−2, −2]

Name _____   **Date** _____

WORKSHEET 4–12–3
The Quadratic Formula

Use the *quadratic formula* to solve the given equations. Rewrite an equation, if necessary, in order to correctly label the coefficients as *a, b,* or *c* for use in the formula. Round any square root value to the nearest tenth.

The Quadratic Formula:

To solve $am^2 + bm + c = 0$ for m, use $m = \dfrac{-b \pm \sqrt{b^2 - 4ac}}{2a}$

Solve for each variable.

1. $3N^2 + 12N + 6 = 0$

2. $-2d^2 + 16d - 6 = 0$

3. $5X^2 - 10X - 15 = 0$

4. $-w^2 + 4w + 5 = 0$

5. $-6 + 2B^2 - 8B = 0$

6. $-20m + 2m^2 - 8 = 0$

7. $-g^2 - 4.8g + 7.9 = 0$

8. $24K + 24 + 6K^2 = 0$

Section 5

SPECIAL APPLICATIONS

OBJECTIVE 1: Transform a linear inequality in two variables, X and Y: aX + bY > c or aX + bY < c, so that one variable is in terms of the other variable; *a, b, c, X* and *Y* are real numbers.

Activity 1: OUT OF BALANCE!

[Developing Action]

Materials: Inequality building mats and paper "equals" markers from Section 3, Objective 12
Sets of tiles (described in step 1)
Worksheet 5–1–1
Regular pencils
Paper

Management: Partners (50 minutes)

Directions:

1. Give each pair of students a set of tiles, an inequality building mat, and a paper "equals" marker. The set of tiles should contain 30 unit tiles and have 8 variable tiles in each of two different sizes (for example, 0.75 in. by 3 in. and 0.75 in. by 3.25 in.). A different color should be used for each variable length. Consider the shorter variable tile as variable A and the longer tile as variable B for notation purposes. Each tile—both unit and variable—should have a large X marked on one side to represent its inverse form. It is assumed that students have successfully completed the three activities for Objective 12 in Section 3 as preparation for this lesson. A review of inequalities in *one* variable might be helpful at this time.

2. Write the inequality 2A − 2B + 3 > −5 on the board. Have students show the inequality with tiles on the inequality building mat. The mat should be rotated to show the word "more" in the lower left corner when partners, sitting beside each other, view the mat. The bold separation bar should appear as a "more than" sign to the students working on the mat; the tiles having the greater *value* (not the greater *amount of tiles*) will be on the left side of the bold bar. Two short variable A tiles, 2 long inverse variable (−B) tiles, and 3 positive unit tiles should be placed on the left side of the mat; 5 negative unit tiles should be placed on the right side.

3. Ask students to solve for the variable A tile in terms of the variable B tile. Remind them that this process requires them to isolate a single variable A tile on one side of the mat, leaving only variable B tiles and unit tiles on the other side of the mat. Remember that, when solving an inequality, we use the add-take away method to isolate a plain variable tile; we do not solve for an inverse variable tile first, then find opposites (that is, we avoid having to change the direction of the inequality sign). In order to isolate the variable A tiles as a group first, students should place 2 variable B tiles and 3 negative unit tiles on each side of the mat. Zero-pairs of tiles should then be formed and removed from the mat, leaving 2 variable A tiles on the left side of the mat and 8 negative unit tiles and 2 variable B tiles on the right side.

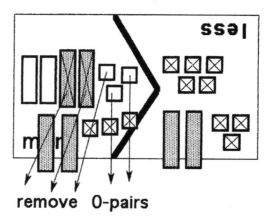

4. Students should now separate the 2 variable A tiles into 2 rows of 1 tile each on the left side of the mat. This requires that the negative unit tiles and variable B tiles on the right side also be separated into 2 rows of 4 negative unit tiles and 1 variable B tile each. One complete row of tiles should be removed from each side of the mat. A single variable A tile then remains on the left side and 4 negative unit tiles and 1 variable B tile remain on the right. Have students record the following sentence on their own papers: **2A − 2B + 3 > −5, so A > −4 + B.**

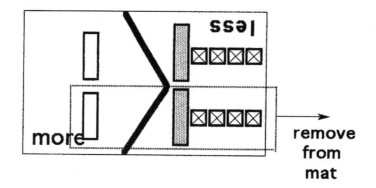

5. *Ask:* "Since there are two different variables involved in our final inequality, what do we know about the possible values of A if B equals +3?" Have students replace the variable B tile with 3 positive unit tiles on the building mat, then remove any 0-pairs formed. Their mat should appear as follows:

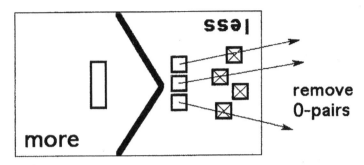

6. *Ask:* "We now know that the solution value of the variable A must be greater than –1 when the variable B equals +3. Can you name a possible value for A that is in the solution interval but is *at least 5 units away* from the *boundary value, –1*?" Students should name several different values for A that are greater than or equal to +4; encourage them to look for nonintegral values, such as +6.5 or +20⅔, as well as integers. Have them record their substitution results on their own papers below the first sentence. If +6 was chosen for the value of A, the new sentences might be as follows: **If B = +3, then A > –1. A can be +6.**

7. Now write a second inequality on the board for students to build on their mats: **B – 3 ≤ –2B + 6A.** Mats should be rotated to show "less" in the lower left corner of the mat from the students' viewpoint. Since the left side may also *equal* the right side this time, the card or paper marker containing an "equals" sign should be placed at the top edge of the mat. One long variable B tile and 3 negative unit tiles should be placed on the left side of the mat and 2 inverse variable B tiles and 6 variable A tiles should be placed on the right side. Ask students to solve for B in terms of A now.

8. In order to isolate one or more plain variable B tiles (and not *inverse* variable B tiles) on one side of the mat, students should place 2 variable B tiles on each side of the mat; 3 positive unit tiles should also be placed on each side. 0-pairs should be formed and removed from the mat, leaving 3 variable B tiles on the left side, and 6 variable A tiles and 3 positive unit tiles on the right side. The mat and tiles for these steps are shown here.

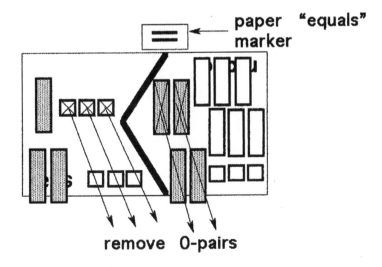

9. Since there are 3 variable B tiles still on the mat, students should separate them into 3 rows of 1 variable B tile each. The variable tiles may be turned horizontally if mat space is limited. The tiles on the right side must also be separated into 3 equal rows,

WORKSHEET 5-1-1
Out of Balance!

Build with tiles to solve each inequality for the variable shown first in the brackets. Substitute the value shown in the brackets for its stated variable in the final inequality on the mat to find a specific solution interval. Identify a number in that solution interval that is *at least 4 units away* from the boundary value of the solution interval. Write sentences to record your results.

1. A + 2B > −1   [A; B = +3]

2. −A ≤ +8 − B   [B; A = −2]

3. (+7) + A > 5B   [A; B = −3]

4. −B + (−3) + 2A ≤ A   [B; A = +7]

5. 5A < +10 − 5B   [A; B = −5]

6. −B − 5 < 3 + A   [A; B = −1]

7. 2B + 3 ≥ −4A + 1   [B; A = 0]

8. −A + 3B < 5A − 12   [B; A = +5]

9. 3A + B < 12 + 7B   [A; B = 0]

10. −4A + B + 6 > −A + 2 + 2B   [B; A = −2]

11. −2A + 3B ≥ −A − 6   [A; B = +4]

12. 4B + 5 ≥ 8A − 3   [B; A = −1]

13. 4 + 2B − 4A ≥ −3A + B + 1   [A; B = +2]

14. −6 − 2B + 4A ≤ A − B   [B; A = +3]

where each row contains 2 variable A tiles and 1 positive unit tile. To finally solve for the variable B tile, students should remove two complete rows of tiles from each side of the mat, thereby leaving a single variable B tile on the left side, and 2 variable A tiles and 1 positive unit tile on the right. Have students now record the following sentence on their own papers: **B − 3 ≤ −2B + 6A, so B < 2A + 1 or B = 2A + 1.**

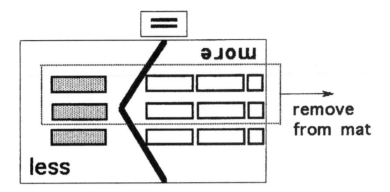

10. *Ask:* "If the variable A has the value −2, what do we know about the specific solution interval for the variable B?" Students should replace each variable A tile on the mat with 2 negative unit tiles, then remove the 0-pairs that form. The solution interval for B will contain all real numbers less than −3 or equal to −3 when A equals −2. ***Ask:*** "When A equals −2, can you name a possible value for B that is in the *solution interval* but is at least 8 units away from the *boundary value, −3*?" Students should name several different numbers for B that are less than or equal to −11. Have students record their substitution results below their first sentence for the exercise. As an example, if −15 was chosen as the value for B, partners might write: **If A = −2, then B < −3 or B = −3. B can equal −15.**

11. Now assign other inequalities for students to solve for one variable in terms of the other. Give each student a copy of Worksheet 5–1–1. Each inequality should be solved for the variable listed first in the brackets. The variable and value listed second in the brackets is the substitution that should be made in the final inequality to find a specific solution interval. Students should state a possible value for the variable found that is *at least 4 units away* from the boundary value of the specific solution interval. Three sentences like the examples in steps 4 and 6 or steps 9 and 10 should be recorded for each exercise on the worksheet. When all students are finished with the worksheet, have several students explain how they solved different inequalities with the tiles. **Note:** If students think they do not have enough variable tiles to solve certain inequalities, remind them that subtracting or *taking* a tile *away from* the mat is equivalent to *adding* the inverse tile *to* the mat.

Answer Key for WORKSHEET 5–1–1

The final inequality in two variables and the specific inequality for each exercise are provided below. Student answers should include these in *word sentences*. The value selected from the specific solution interval will vary with each student.

1. A > −2B − 1
   A > −7

2. B ≤ A + 8
   B ≤ +6

3. A > −7 + 5B
   A > −22

4. (−3) + A ≤ B
   +4 ≤ B

5. $A < 2 - B$
   $A < 7$

6. $-B - 8 < A$
   $-7 < A$

7. $B \geq -2A - 1$
   $B \geq -1$

8. $B < 2A - 4$
   $B < +6$

9. $A < 4 + 2B$
   $A < 4$

10. $-3A + 4 > B$
    $+10 > B$

11. $6 + 3B \geq A$
    $18 \geq A$

12. $B \geq 2A - 2$
    $B \geq -4$

13. $3 + B \geq A$
    $5 \geq A$

14. $-6 + 3A \leq B$
    $+3 \leq B$

Activity 2: PLOTTING HALF-LINES

[Bridging Action]

Materials: Worksheet 5–1–2
Colored pencils (2 different colors)
Regular pencils
Paper

Management: Partners (50 minutes)

Directions:

1. Give each pair of students two copies of Worksheet 5–1–2 and 2 different colored pencils (1 pencil per color). In this activity students will draw diagrams to solve inequalities and also graph their specific solution intervals on grids provided on the worksheet. Each table and its corresponding set of axes will have the independent and the dependent variables already indicated. Various letters will be used as variables since rectangles used for variables in the diagrams can easily be labeled with letters to identify them.

2. Write the following inequality on the board: **3N – W < +6 + 2W.** Have students solve for the variable N in terms of W. Tell students that W will be the *independent* variable. After drawing the initial diagram on their own papers, students should draw another rectangle for the variable W on both sides of the diagram and connect inverses to show 0-pairs. The transformed diagram is shown here.

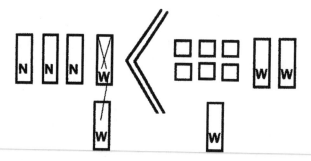

3. There are 3 of the variable N remaining on the left side of the diagram. Since students need to solve for a single N, they should separate the rectangles representing the variable N into 3 equal groups by drawing a path in pencil around each rectangle. The shapes on the right side of the diagram must also be separated into 3 equal groups. This can be done by drawing a path around each group consisting of 1 rectangle (W) and 2 small squares (+2). A horizontal bar should be drawn below the original diagram, then one group from each side of the diagram should be redrawn below the bar to show the final inequality: N < 2 + W. The completed diagrams are shown below.

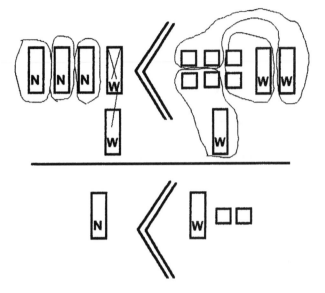

4. Students now need to record in algebraic notation on their own papers the steps they used to solve for N in terms of W. The format used in earlier lessons should be followed. The steps may be written as follows:

$$3N - W \ < \ +6 \ + 2W$$
$$3N + (-W) < (+6) + 2W$$
$$\underline{ + W \qquad\qquad + W}$$
$$3N \qquad\quad < (+6) + 3W$$
$$(\tfrac{1}{3})3N \qquad < (\tfrac{1}{3})(+6) + (\tfrac{1}{3})3W$$
$$N \qquad\qquad < \ (+2) \ + \ W$$

5. The final inequality for N in terms of W is N < +2 + W. ***Ask:*** "If W is our independent variable in this inequality and we want W to equal +3, what could be a value for the variable N?" When W = +3, N must have a real value less than (+2) + (+3), that is, N < +5. In the first table on Worksheet 5–1–2, have students write +3 in the left column under W five times. Have them draw a vertical dashed line in colored pencil (color #1) at W = +3 on the adjacent grid. This line represents potential values for the variable N when W = +3. Students should complete the heading "N" of the right column to show "N < +5." Remind students that +5 is the boundary value for the specific solution interval for N when W equals +3, but in this case, N will not equal +5. Have students write +5 in the first row of the right column of the table, then write "bd value open" beside the +5. An "open" or blank dot should be marked in color #2 on the line drawn at W = +3 on the grid to show that +5 is the boundary value. Now ***ask:*** "Are the values +3.5, +2, +1, and −1.25 possible values for N if N < +5?" *(yes, since each number is less than +5)* Have students record these four values in decreasing order in the next four rows under +5 in the right column of the table, then locate and mark points in color #2 for these values on the dashed line of W = +3. Since all possible solution values for N must be less than +5 on the W = +3 line,

WORKSHEET 5-1-2
Plotting Half-Lines

Draw diagrams to solve each inequality for the variable listed first in the brackets. Record the steps used in algebraic notation. Graph the solution interval with respect to the given value in the brackets. Write a sentence about your results for each inequality.

1. 3N - W < +6 + 2W

W	N

2. $\frac{1}{2}$ B + 3 ≥ M + 1

B	M

WORKSHEET 5-1-2 *(cont.)*
Plotting Half-Lines

3. $\frac{1}{3}$ A + 1 < R - 1 [A; R=2]

A	R

4. -5B +6 ≥ 2X -B [X; B=-2]

X	B

WORKSHEET 5–1–2 *(cont.)*
Plotting Half-Lines

5. -d+(-4) ≤ d+2m [d; m=1]

m	d

6. $\frac{1}{2}$ Y - X > X + 3 [Y; X=0]

X	Y

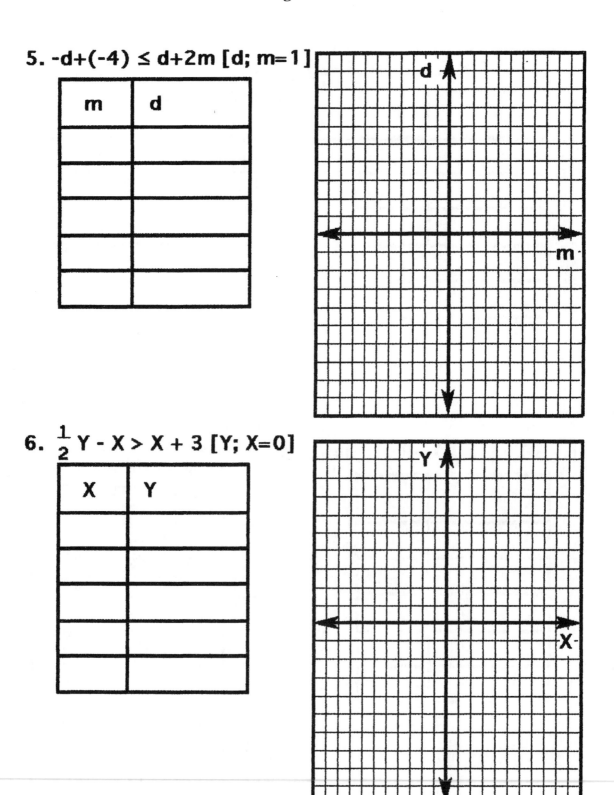

students should complete the graph by drawing a solid arrow in color #2 through the 5 points located on the grid. The final table and graph are shown below.

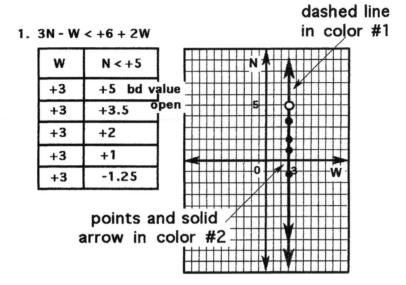

1. 3N - W < +6 + 2W

W	N < +5
+3	+5 bd value
+3	+3.5 open
+3	+2
+3	+1
+3	-1.25

dashed line in color #1

points and solid arrow in color #2

6. Below the completed table of ordered pairs on the worksheet, students should write the following sentence: **If N < W + 2, then N < +5 when W = +3.**

7. Now write another example on the board: $\frac{1}{2}$**B + 3 ≥ M + 1.** Ask students to draw a diagram on their own papers to solve for B in terms of M. We will use M as the *dependent* variable this time. Three negative units should be drawn on both sides of the initial diagram and 0-pairs of units formed. Since only half of the variable B is present at first and a solution requires a whole variable B, a horizontal bar will need to be drawn below the initial diagram to start a new diagram. Two of the half-variable ($\frac{1}{2}$B) should be drawn on the left side to form a whole variable B. This requires that two groups of the variable M and –2 be drawn on the right side of the new diagram. The final inequality will be B ≥ 2M – 4. The completed diagram should appear as shown.

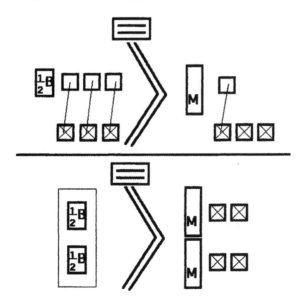

8. Have students now record on their own papers in algebraic notation the steps used to solve for B. The following steps might be recorded:

$$\frac{1}{2}B \quad +3 \ \geq \quad M+1$$
$$\quad \underline{+(-3) \qquad +(-3)}$$
$$\frac{1}{2}B \qquad \geq M+(-2)$$
$$2(\tfrac{1}{2}B) \qquad \geq 2M+2(-2)$$
$$B \qquad \geq 2M-4$$

9. Ask students to graph the solution interval for B when M = –2. Using the second table and grid on Worksheet 5–1–2, students should record the value –2 under M in the right column of the table since M is our dependent variable now. The heading for the left column should be "B ≥ –8." The first entry in the left column should be –8; to the left of –8, students should write "bd value closed" to show that –8 is the boundary value for the solution interval of B and that –8 is also a solution value for B. On the adjacent grid, have students draw a horizontal dashed line in color #1 at M = –2. A "closed" or shaded dot should be marked in color #2 on the dashed line to show the boundary point for B's solution interval when M = –2. Ask students to suggest four more real numbers, including two decimal numbers, that might be solutions for B. For convenience, we will use –5, –2.5, +1, and +4.75 for the four numbers. Since all four are greater than –8, the numbers should be recorded in the left column in increasing order under the first entry, –8. Points for these four numbers should be located and marked in color #2 on the dashed line. Since these four numbers, as well as all real numbers greater than or equal to –8, are solutions for B when M = –2, students should now draw an arrow in color #2 that passes from the boundary point to the right through the other four points. The arrow represents the solution interval for B when M = –2. The completed table and graph are shown here.

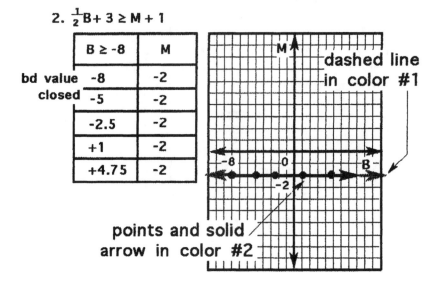

10. Below the completed table on the worksheet, have students record the following sentence: **If B ≥ 2M – 4, then B ≥ –8 when M = –2.**

11. For additional practice, assign six more inequalities that can be represented on Worksheet 5–1–2. Students should solve for one variable in terms of the other and graph the solution interval for the first variable when a value is given for the other variable. For each exercise, diagrams and algebraic notation should be used, and when the table and graph are completed, a sentence like those given in steps 6 and 10 should be written below the table. Here are four inequalities to assign to complete the worksheet:

3. $\frac{1}{3}A + 1 < R - 1$ [A indep; R = +2]   5. $-d + (-4) \leq d + 2m$ [d dep; m = +1]

4. $-5B + 6 \geq 2X - B$ [X indep; B = -2]   6. $\frac{1}{2}Y - X > X + 3$ [Y dep; X = 0]

Answer Key to Exercises 3–8 on WORKSHEET 5-1-2

The final inequalities and the specific solution intervals to be graphed are provided below:

3. $A < 3R - 6$; $A < 0$ when R = +2   **5.** $-2 - m \leq d$; $-3 \leq d$ when m = +1

4. $-2B + 3 \geq X$; $+7 \geq X$ when B = -2   **6.** $Y > 4X + 6$; $Y > +6$ when X = 0

Activity 3: THE GREAT DIVIDE!

[Application/Exploration]

Materials: Worksheet 5–1–3 (pattern for spinner)
  Colored pencils (any 2 bright colors)
  Centimeter grids (on 8.5 in. × 11 in. paper)
  Large paper clips (for spinner needles)
  Paper
  Regular pencils
  Calculators

Management: Teams of 4 students each (30 minutes)

Directions:

1. Give each team a copy of Worksheet 5–1–3 (the spinner), 2 colored pencils (1 pencil per color), a sheet of centimeter grid paper, a large paper clip (the spinner needle), and a calculator. A horizontal and a vertical axis should be drawn on the grid paper with the origin at the center of the grid. Label the horizontal axis with the variable X and the vertical axis with the variable Y. Each centimeter segment on an axis will represent 1 unit of value.

2. Assign a different linear inequality in X and Y to each team. A team will first solve its own inequality for Y in terms of X. Then, taking turns, each team member or player will spin the spinner to generate a value for X and use that value in the simplified inequality to plot in *colored pencil* a specific solution interval for Y on the team's set of axes. If the boundary value computed for Y is a point off the grid paper or if the specific solution interval has already been graphed, the player will spin again to obtain a new number for X.

3. After each player has had one or more turns, the team should work *together* to find the "Great Divide" or boundary that separates all their solution intervals from the rest of the graphing plane. Will the boundary be **curved** or **straight?** Team members must determine the answer to this question. They may need to use other values for X besides those on the spinner in order to graph more solution intervals; encourage this kind of testing. After plotting several solution intervals, they should recognize a linear boundary being formed by the points marking their different boundary values. Even though only two points are needed to locate a line, students must plot *enough* solution intervals to be *convinced* that no matter what value they use for X, the resulting solution interval will lie in the same region of the graphing plane as all their other intervals do. Once they believe the boundary is indeed a line, they should try to identify an equation for this special line. Hopefully they will discover that the **equation** for Y in terms of X that corresponds to their simplified **inequality** (for example, Y = aX + b *corresponds* to Y < aX + b) is the one that defines the mysterious line.

4. As an example of team play, suppose that a team has been assigned the inequality: **X + Y > +2.** The team first solves for Y in terms of X to find **Y > −X + 2.** Player #1 spins to get −5 for X; using this value in the simplified inequality, player #1 graphs in colored pencil the resulting solution interval, **Y > +7 at X = −5,** on the grid. The point for the boundary value +7 will be "open." Player #2 spins to get X = +1.5 and graphs **Y > +0.5 at X = +1.5.** Player #3 then spins to get X = 0 and graphs **Y > +2 at X = 0.** Player #4 spins to get X = +4 and graphs **Y > −2 at X = +4.** At this point the team members begin to look for a pattern in the intervals they have graphed. If necessary, they try other values of X in order to graph more intervals. They conclude that their solution intervals represent half of the graphing plane and are separated from the points in the other half-plane by a line that passes through all of the boundary value points for specific values of X. Using one of the methods studied in Section 3, Objectives 6 through 9, for finding the algebraic equation for a given line, the team decides that the equation **Y = −X + 2** describes the separation line they have found. In this example, the points on the line do not represent solution points of the original inequality because each is also a boundary value point for a given X value, and all the boundary value points were "open." To show this idea, the discovered line should be drawn as a broken or dashed line in colored pencil on the grid. The team's grid after four turns is shown here.

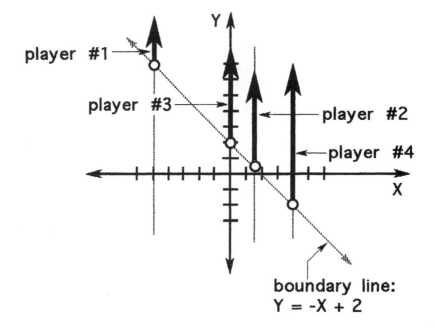

boundary line:
Y = -X + 2

5. After all teams have finished, have them share their "discoveries" with the entire class. Observe that the separation line will be solid if the boundary value points are "closed," but the line will be dashed or broken if the points are "open" and not included in their respective solution intervals.

6. Here are some possible team inequalities to assign. (The final "boundary" equation for each inequality is shown in brackets.)

1. $+1 \leq 2X - Y$
   $[Y = 2X - 1]$

2. $Y - X > +3$
   $[Y = X + 3]$

3. $Y - 2 \geq -X$
   $[Y = -X + 2]$

4. $+6 < -3X - Y$
   $[Y = -3X - 6]$

5. $0 > +0.5X - Y + 4$
   $[Y = +0.5X + 4]$

6. $+0.5X + Y + 2 < 0$
   $[Y = -0.5X - 2]$

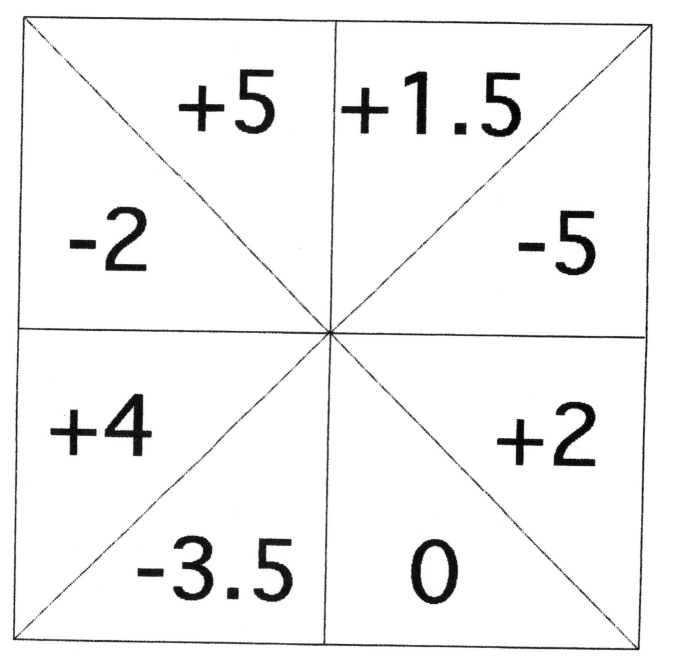

OBJECTIVE 2: **Locate points in disjoint regions formed by one or two given linear boundaries in a plane and compare them to points on the boundaries (two-dimensional space).**

Activity 1: POINT SEARCH

[Developing Action]

Materials: Large grid sheets and small colored markers (described in step 1)
Thin bamboo skewers or straight wire pieces (10–12 inches long)
Paper
Regular pencils

Management: Partners (50 minutes)

Directions:

1. Give each pair of students a large grid sheet, a bag of 6 small colored markers (6 different colors; 1 marker per color), and 2 bamboo skewers or wire pieces. The wire piece should be only thick enough to keep it from bending too easily. The small markers might be commercially available colored centimeter cubes, colored flat buttons (approximately 0.5-inch diameter), or square or hexagonal metal nuts (approximately 0.5-inch diameter; spray-painted in 6 colors, 1 color per nut) from a hardware store. Other materials are possible as well. The grid may be drawn off on heavy bulletin board paper to form approximately a 14 in. × 16 in. grid (unit length of 1 inch), or a grid may be drawn on two sheets of 8.5 in. × 14 in. paper, which can then be taped together at their longer edges to make the larger grid that is needed. Laminating the final grids will make them more durable. Package the 6 small markers in a snack-size, closable, plastic bag to make distribution of materials easier and quicker. (Similar materials were used in Objectives 6 and 8 of Section 3.) In this activity students will observe patterns in sets of points that meet certain conditions.

2. Students should position their grid so that the longer edge is the *horizontal axis* or X-axis. The left vertical edge will be the Y-axis, and the lower left corner of the grid will be the origin. In other words, only the first quadrant of the Cartesian plane will be used in this activity. Ask students to place a colored marker on each of 6 different points on the grid where each point has a vertical distance (ordinate) from the origin that is 2 inches more than the point's horizontal distance (abscissa) from the origin. The sets of points shown will vary, but each set of 6 markers should form a linear arrangement. Have students place the bamboo skewer or wire piece on the grid so that it lies on the points shown by the markers. The markers should then be removed from the grid.

3. Have students place a new marker on the grid at the point for (5, 3). **Ask:** "Do the vertical and horizontal distances for this point have the same relationship as each of the points represented by the skewer or wire?" *(no; for this new point, the horizontal distance is 2 inches more than the vertical distance)* Have students move the marker to the point for (2, 2). **Ask:** "Do the two distances for this point have the same relationship as the distances for each point of the skewer? If not, what relationship do the two distances have?"

(no; the horizontal and vertical distances for this point are equal) "Place markers at other points where the horizontal distance of each point equals its vertical distance. Will any of these points be on the other side of the skewer from (2, 2)? Why or why not?" *(markers might be placed at (3, 3), (4, 4), (6, 6), etc.; each point of the skewer will be 2 inches above its corresponding marker that shares the same horizontal distance;* for example, (3, 5) is covered by the skewer and is 2 inches higher vertically than (3, 3) indicated by a marker; see the illustration below) *Ask:* "Can you describe a set of ordered pairs whose points will be *above* the skewer or wire on the grid?" Answers will vary, but in each set of pairs suggested, the vertical distance in each ordered pair must be *more* than 2 inches greater than the horizontal distance for that pair. For example, one set might contain (1, 4), (2, 5), and (4, 7), where the vertical distance is 3 inches more than the horizontal distance.

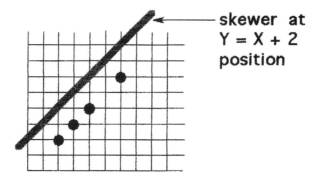

skewer at
Y = X + 2
position

4. Now have students clear their grid of markers and skewer, then place one skewer on the grid so that points (1, 8) and (9, 4) are covered. Have them place the other skewer on the grid to cover the points (1, 2) and (4, 2), adjusting it so that it does not lie on top of the first skewer; however, it is acceptable for the two skewers to be touching each other. Ask students to make observations about each skewer or the line it represents on the grid. Some possible comments might be as follows: (1) the first skewer has a negative slope; its vertical distance-horizontal distance ratio is −1 to +2; (2) the second skewer is parallel to the horizontal axis and has a zero slope; the vertical distance for each point is 2 inches; and (3) if the two skewers are extended, they will intersect each other.

5. *Ask:* "When we had only one skewer on the grid, it acted as a boundary line that separated the grid into two regions, one region on each side of the skewer. Now we have two skewers on the grid. How many regions are now formed by the two skewers?" Discuss the idea that there is a grid region above the first skewer, a region between the two skewers, and a region below the second skewer. If no one mentions a fourth region, ask students to consider what happens if the two skewers are extended to the right, perhaps beyond the visible grid. Hopefully they will realize that to the lower right of the point where the two skewers will intersect each other, another region will be formed. Ask students to find the point where the two skewers will meet if extended. This can be done by carefully sliding the first skewer down to the right, keeping the skewer in its original path, until it crosses the horizontal grid line for Y = +2. Both skewers will cover this point, which is (13, 2). This common point might also be found by applying the slope of $\frac{-1}{+2}$ to the original point (9, 4) of the first skewer. We can subtract 1 inch vertically from +4 as we add 2 inches horizontally to +9 to find another point (11, 3) of the first skewer. Repeating this process, we find the point (13, 2). If the two skewers are moved farther to the right and held so that one overlaps the other, the fourth region will become *visible* to the students. Many students have great difficulty just *imagining* how the two intersecting skewers might look; they need to actually make the skewers cross each other physically. After students recognize the fourth region, have them move the two skewers back to their original positions on the grid.

6. Now have students locate various points on the grid with the colored markers and describe their positions with respect to the two skewers. Here are some possible questions to **ask:**

(1) If X = +4, what integral value might Y have to locate a point *between* the two skewers? (*Y = 3, 4, 5, or 6;* students should show *one* of these points with the color #1 marker)

(2) What must the value of X be for a point to be 1 inch *below* the second (or lower) skewer? (*X can be any value as long as Y = +1;* students should show one such point with the color #2 marker; have a few students state the ordered pairs for their chosen points)

(3) If the X value is *between* +2 and +5, inclusive of endpoints, what Y value will give a point that is above both skewers, no matter which value in the interval is finally chosen for X? (*since the highest point of the top skewer over the given interval for X is at Y = +7.5 when X = +2, the chosen point will need a Y value greater than +7.5;* have students use the color #3 marker to show such a point that satisfies this Y requirement as well as the interval condition for X; have several students name the ordered pair for their chosen point)

(4) What conditions must be on the X-value and Y-value of a point in order for that point to lie in the fourth region formed when the two skewers are extended farther to the right? (*since the skewers will intersect at the point (13, 2), the new point in the fourth region must have X > +13 and Y < +2; however, Y will also have a **lower** limit in order to keep the new point **above** the first skewer in the fourth region;* have students select a point that will be "safe" to use, for example, (15, 1.5) or (16, 1), and, if possible, show it on the grid with the color #4 marker; have different students name the points they choose)

One possible arrangement of markers on the grid for points selected in parts (1) through (3) above is shown here.

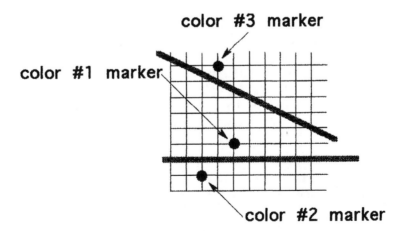

Activity 2: SPACE SNEAKERS

[Bridging Action]

Materials: Worksheet 5–2–1
Colored pencils (at least 4 different colors)
Regular pencils

Management: Partners (30 minutes)

Directions:

1. Give each pair of students 4 copies of Worksheet 5–2–1 and 4 colored pencils (4 different colors; 1 pencil per color). Each grid segment will represent 1 unit of length on an axis.

2. Each student should take an individual copy of Worksheet 5–2–1, secretly select a point somewhere on the grid and draw two diagonal lines so that they intersect each other at the point. Each line should be extended in both directions to the edge of the paper. The two lines will separate the grid into 4 disjoint regions. Each region should be colored with a colored pencil; no two regions should be the same color. The finished worksheet should be hidden from the view of the student's partner. Partners will take turns trying to identify each other's special point. Here is an example of a finished worksheet.

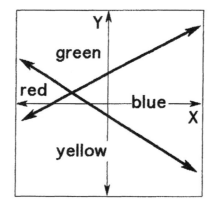

3. As an example of play, suppose that partner A is to try to locate partner B's special point. Partner A will use a clean copy of Worksheet 5–2–1 to keep a record of the different points guessed and what is learned about each point, in particular, the color of the guessed point's region on partner B's finished worksheet. Each time partner A guesses a point [e.g., (–1, 3)], partner B will tell the color of its region (e.g., "red"). If partner A suggests a point that is on one of the two lines, partner B will simply say "line." Partner A will continue to guess points, marking each point on the blank grid of the new worksheet and labeling the point with its color name, until he or she can identify the special point where partner B's two lines intersect. Partner A's score will be the *number of guesses made,* including the final correct guess, in order to find the special point. Following the same procedure used by partner A, but using a new, clean copy of Worksheet 5–2–1, partner B will then try to guess the ordered pair or location of the special point on partner A's finished worksheet. Partner B will try to use fewer guesses than partner A did.

4. After all students have had their turn, have them share some of the strategies they used. Discuss what information they had that finally led them to the correct point. Did

WORKSHEET 5-2-1
Space Sneakers

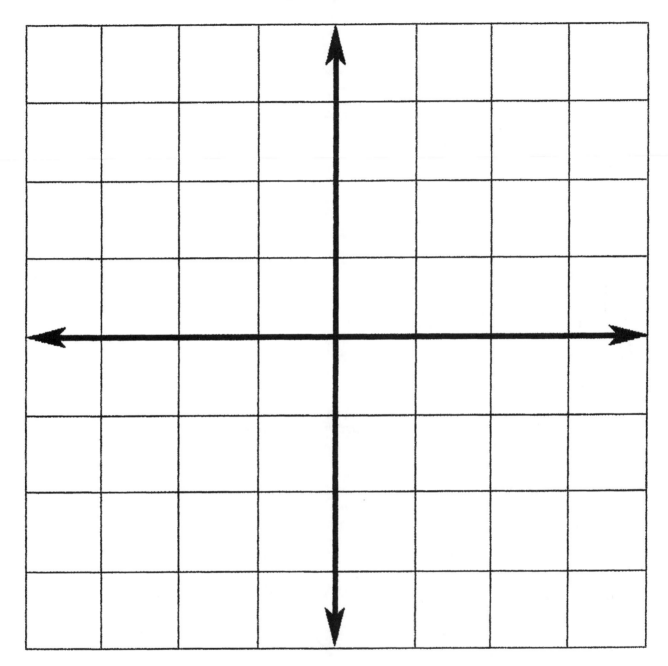

they begin to see "boundaries" forming between different colored regions? How did they use the numbers in the ordered pairs to predict where the two lines might be? In many cases, students will intuitively locate a point and not be consciously aware of their reasons. Discussions about strategies help them to reflect on their own thinking processes and to analyze their steps used in finding a solution.

5. The above game is an adaptation of a game described in the following article: Stephen S. Willoughby, "Activities to Help in Learning about Functions," *Mathematics Teaching in the Middle School,* Vol. 2, No. 4 (February 1997). The article also contains other interesting games designed especially for prealgebra and algebra students.

Activity 3: SPACE MASTERS

[Application/Exploration]

Materials: Graphing calculators
Worksheet 5–2–2
Regular pencils
Paper

Management: Teams of 4 students each (30 minutes)

Directions:

1. Give each team of students a graphing calculator and a copy of Worksheet 5–2–2. In this activity students will take turns locating points in specific regions of the graphing plane. For the graphing calculators, use a viewing screen with $X\varepsilon[-5, 5]$ and $Y\varepsilon[-5, 5]$, scale = 1.

2. Write the following pair of equations on the board: $Y = X + 2$ and $Y = -2X + 3$. Each team should graph the two linear functions on their graphing calculator. In order to match the "region" numbers used on the record sheet on Worksheet 5–2–2, the "regions" (the four disjoint planar regions as well as the two lines) of the graph will be identified as follows:

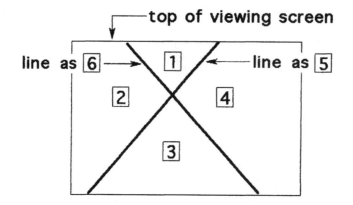

3. The members of each team will take turns identifying points in the six different "regions" of the viewing screen. On a turn, a member or player will select one of the six "regions" listed on the worksheet and name an ordered pair of a point in the selected region. The player will then input the ordered pair into the calculator, using the PLOT key or its equivalent, to see where the selected point will actually be located on the graph. If the "blinking dot" appears in the region stated by the player, the player earns 1 point and records that number in the row of that region in his or her column of the record sheet. If the selected point does NOT appear in the chosen region, the player earns 0 points for that turn.

4. On a turn, a player may state that a point will be chosen so that it lies *on both lines* (regions 5 and 6) of the graph, then select the point and plot it. If the selected point indeed lies on both lines (i.e., the point is the intersection point of the two lines), the player will earn 3 points for each of the two regions or a total of 6 points for the turn. The selected ordered pair, however, must be **tested** to see if it is a true solution of each of the two equations. In this case, it is not enough that the point looks "close" visually. Another player should substitute the X and Y values of the pair in the two equations and compute to see if the equalities hold. **Note:** This opportunity to earn a higher score is designed to encourage students to begin looking for common solutions of two lines in preparation for a later study of systems of linear equations or functions.

5. A player does not have to select the regions according to their numerical order, but must try to locate a point in each of the six regions in order to complete the game. Each player may only find one point per region and may not select a point that has already been plotted on the graph.

6. When all 4 players have completed their columns on Worksheet 5–2–2, the game is over. Each player's final score will be the sum of the points in his or her column.

7. If a team finishes early or if time allows, assign another pair of equations for another game, such as: (1) $X = -3$ and $Y = +2$ (perpendicular lines where one is vertical, the other horizontal); or (2) $Y = 2X + 1$ and $Y = 6X - 4$.

WORKSHEET 5-2-2
Space Masters
Record Sheet

Region	Player 1	Player 2	Player 3	Player 4
1				
2				
3				
4				
5				
6				
Score				

OBJECTIVE 3: Solve systems of linear inequalities in two variables by graphical methods.

Activity 1: COLOR MAGIC

[Developing Action]

Materials: Large inch grids from Activity 1, Objective 2
Transparent, colored plastic sheets (2 colors: red, yellow; see step 1)
Small wooden craft sticks, long flat toothpicks, or small paper strips (see step 1)
Worksheet 5–3–1
Calculators
Paper
Regular pencils

Management: Partners (50 minutes)

Directions:

1. Give each pair of students a large inch grid, 2 copies of Worksheet 5–3–1, a calculator, 4 small wooden craft sticks (approximately 4 in. long and $\frac{3}{8}$ in. wide), and 4 rectangular pieces of transparent plastic (2 red pieces and 2 yellow pieces). Two craft sticks should have one tip colored with a red marker, and two other craft sticks should have one tip colored with a yellow marker. White paper strips (0.5 in. wide by 4 in. long) or long flat toothpicks (not round) may be used instead of craft sticks, and should be colored according to the directions for the craft sticks. Each plastic piece should be 3 inches to 4 inches wide and 10 inches to 12 inches long. The plastic pieces can be made from colored plastic theme covers or other plastic of a similar, medium weight. On one plastic piece of each color, a *solid* black bar should be drawn with a permanent wide-tipped marker along *only one* of the longer edges of the piece. On the other plastic piece of the same color, a *broken* black bar should be drawn along *only one* of the longer edges. In this activity students will be locating regions of a graph where the points satisfy two different inequalities simultaneously. It is assumed that students have completed all the activities of Objective 1 and Objective 2 successfully. We will be using the methods taught in those lessons to identify sets of solution points for inequalities in a system.

2. Students should position their grid so that the longer edge is the *horizontal axis* or X-axis. The left vertical edge will be the Y-axis, and the lower left corner of the grid will be the origin. In other words, only the first quadrant of the Cartesian plane will be used in this activity. Each grid segment will be considered a unit of length or value when locating points on the grid.

3. Write the inequalities of exercise 1 on Worksheet 5–3–1 on the board: **(a) Y ≤ 2X + 1** and **(b) Y > –X + 7.** Ask students to use X = 1 and X = 4 to find two boundary points for inequality (a): **Y ≤ 2X + 1.** For X = 1, Y must be *less than* +3 or *equal to* +3. Have students place a "red" craft stick (or paper strip or toothpick) on and aligned with the vertical grid segment for X = 1 with the red tip touching the horizontal grid segment for Y = 3 and the rest of the craft stick positioned *below* that point. The craft stick represents all

WORKSHEET 5–3–1
Color Magic

For each system of inequalities below, use colored plastic pieces and a large inch grid to find the solution points of the system. In the space below the two given inequalities, make a quick-sketch of the graph of the two boundaries found and circle the point of intersection. Shade the circle if the point represents a solution of the system and shade the region whose points satisfy both inequalities of the system. Write an inequality that describes the domain of the solutions of the system.

1. (a) $Y \leq 2X + 1$

   (b) $Y > -X + 7$

2. (a) $Y \leq 3 + 0.5X$

   (b) $X \leq 4$

3. (a) $Y < (-\frac{7}{3})X + 8$

   (b) $Y > (-\frac{1}{3})X + 2$

4. (a) $X < 6$

   (b) $Y \leq 3$

5. (a) $Y \leq X - 1$

   (b) $Y \leq -X + 7$

6. (a) $Y > 0$

   (b) $X \geq 0$

Y-values satisfying inequality (a) when X = 1. For X = 4, Y must be less than +9 or equal to +9. Students should place the second "red" craft stick on and aligned with the vertical grid segment for X = 4 with the red tip touching the horizontal grid segment for Y = 9 and the rest of the craft stick positioned *below* that point. The craft stick represents all Y-values satisfying inequality (a) when X = 4. **Ask:** "What does the sign in the inequality tell us about the boundary points themselves? Will those points represent solutions of the inequality?" *(the boundary points locate solution points because the sign contains the "equals" sign as well as the "less than" sign)* Thus, the points on the grid marked by the red tips of the two craft sticks must be included in the solution graph. To show this, have students take the red plastic piece with the solid black bar, and place it on top of the two craft sticks so that the edge with the solid black bar touches the boundary points or red ends of the craft sticks. The rest of the two craft sticks must be *under* the red plastic piece. The red plastic piece now represents all points (the points it covers now, as well as other points it would cover if enlarged in all directions except across the solid black bar) whose values satisfy inequality (a). The final placement of the plastic piece and the craft sticks on the grid is shown below.

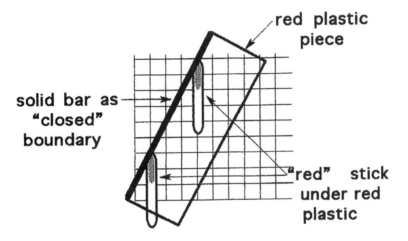

4. Repeat the above process, using inequality (b): **Y > –X + 7.** The "red" craft sticks may now be carefully removed from beneath the red plastic piece, but the red plastic piece should remain in its position on the grid. To avoid confusion, we will use different values for X than were used for inequality (a). For X = 2, Y must be *greater than* +5. Have students place a "yellow" craft stick (or paper strip or toothpick) on and aligned with the vertical grid segment for X = 2 with the yellow tip touching the horizontal grid segment for Y = 5 and the rest of the craft stick positioned *above* that point. If the red plastic piece already happens to be covering the needed grid segment, the "yellow" craft stick may be placed either under or on top of the red plastic piece (the transparent plastic allows the grid segment to be easily seen). The craft stick now represents all Y-values satisfying inequality (b) when X = 2. For X = 6, Y must be greater than +1. Students should place the second "yellow" craft stick on and aligned with the vertical grid segment for X = 6 with the yellow tip touching the horizontal grid segment for Y = 1 and the rest of the craft stick positioned *above* that point. The craft stick represents all Y-values satisfying inequality (b) when X = 6. **Ask:** "What does the sign in the inequality tell us about the boundary points themselves? Will those points represent solutions of the inequality?" *(the boundary points do not represent solution points because the sign does not contain the "equals" sign)* Thus, the points on the grid marked by the yellow tips of the two craft

sticks must not be included in the solution graph. To show this, have students take the yellow plastic piece with the broken black bar, and place it on top of the two "yellow" craft sticks so that the edge with the broken black bar touches the boundary points or yellow ends of the craft sticks. The rest of the two "yellow" craft sticks must be *under* the yellow plastic piece. The yellow plastic piece now represents all points (the points it covers now, as well as other points it would cover if enlarged in all directions except across the broken black bar) whose values satisfy inequality (b). If preferred, once the yellow plastic piece is in place on the grid, the "yellow" craft sticks may carefully be removed from the grid. The final placement—with respect to the red plastic piece—of the yellow plastic piece and the "yellow" craft sticks on the grid is shown here.

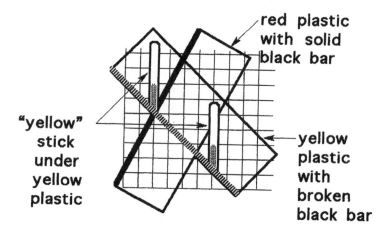

5. In the space below the first exercise on the worksheet, students should make a quick-sketch of the solid bar and the broken bar together on a grid. Grid line segments do not need to be drawn; only unit markings on the axes are needed in order to locate key boundary points and the intersection point of the two boundary lines. Each line on the graph should be labeled with the letter (a or b) of the inequality whose boundary it represents. *Ask:* "Since the plastic pieces show us where the solutions are for *each* inequality, and for the *system* we need solutions that satisfy *both* inequalities *simultaneously*, how can we find those common solutions?" (*find where the two plastic pieces overlap on the grid;* the points covered by *both* plastic pieces satisfy *both* inequalities) The plastic pieces should create an **orange** color (red + yellow = orange) where they overlap. Students should *shade* this identified region on their quick-sketch of the graph of the two boundary lines.

6. *Ask:* "Does (2, 5), the ordered pair for the intersection point of the two boundary lines, satisfy both inequalities?" (*no, it is a solution for only inequality (a)*) Have students draw a plain (unshaded) circle around the intersection point to show that it is not a solution of the system. In later exercises, if the intersection point identifies a solution for *both* inequalities, the circle around the point will be shaded. *Ask:* "By looking at the orange region on your grid, can you describe what the **domain** or values of X will be for the set of solutions or solution pairs?" (*in order for a point to lie in the orange region on the grid, the value for X must be greater than +2;* the intersection point at (2, 5), marked with a plain circle, is not a solution, so X will not equal +2) On the worksheet, have students write the following below their quick-sketch of the graph: **Domain: X > +2.** We will include the **range** later in Activity 2.

7. Students should now work the other exercises on Worksheet 5–3–1, following the procedure used for exercise 1 in steps 3 through 6 above. For each exercise, they should randomly select two values of X on the large grid to use in locating boundary points for each inequality. No X-value should be used for both inequalities in the same system. Monitor their work closely to be sure they are positioning the colored plastic pieces correctly on the large grid. As students work, informally ask various partners if an orange region they have just built has a minimum or a maximum for its values of Y and, if so, what that value might be. Help students to focus on the lengths of vertical segments within the orange region; this will help them better understand, when the algebraic notation is used later, that expressions of the form $Y < aX + b$ or $Y > aX + b$ actually refer to the limits on the vertical lengths or distances.

Answer Key to WORKSHEET 5–3–1

[* marks solution region on graph.]

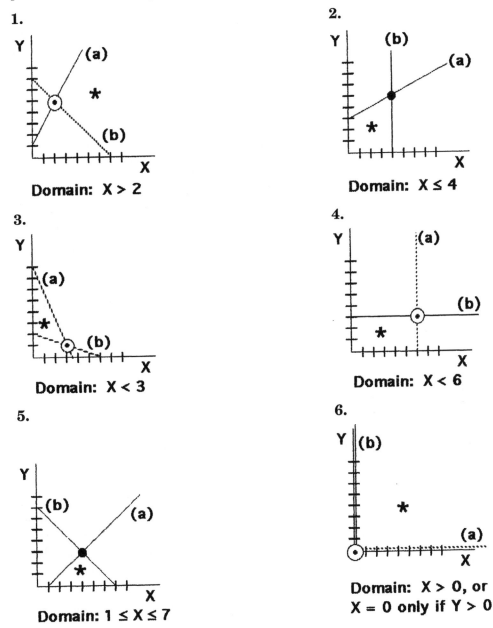

1.

Domain: X > 2

2.

Domain: X ≤ 4

3.

Domain: X < 3

4.

Domain: X < 6

5.

Domain: 1 ≤ X ≤ 7

6.

Domain: X > 0, or
X = 0 only if Y > 0

Activity 2: SHADING SOLUTIONS

[Bridging Action]

Materials: Worksheet 5–3–2
Colored pencils (2 or more bright colors)
Calculators
Paper
Regular pencils

Management: Partners (50 minutes)

Directions:

1. Give each pair of students 2 copies of Worksheet 5–3–2, 2 colored pencils (2 bright colors; 1 pencil per color), and a calculator. In this activity, students will graph each inequality in a system, then find the region on the graph that represents the solutions of the system. They will also state the domain and range of the solution set, which often requires them to first find the ordered pair for the intersection point of the boundary lines of the two inequalities of the system.

2. Write the first set of inequalities from Worksheet 5–3–2 on the board: **(a) Y ≤ X + 2** and **(b) Y < –X + 2.** Following the procedure used in Activity 1, have students use X = –1 (a random choice) to find a boundary point for inequality (a). For this X, Y must be *less than* +1 or *equal to* +1. A point should be marked on the grid for (–1, +1). Similarly, use X = +3 to find Y ≤ +5; a point for (+3, +5) should be plotted on the grid. These two points are boundary points that locate the boundary line for inequality (a). Since the inequality includes an "equals" sign, the boundary points are solution points. Thus, students should draw a solid line through (–1, +1) and (+3, +5) in regular pencil and label it with (a). The "less than" sign indicates that all solution points must be vertically *below* their respective boundary points, or *below* the boundary line. Students should therefore lightly shade with color #1 the region of the grid that lies *below* the solid boundary line. The solid boundary line and colored region appear as follows.

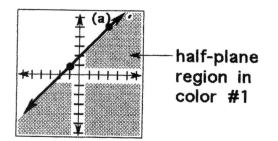

half-plane
region in
color #1

3. Now have students use X = –3 to find a boundary point for inequality (b). The boundary point will be at Y = +5. Students should mark the point for (–3, +5) on the grid; however, since solution points for X = –3 are only those points with Y < +5, this boundary point is not a solution point for inequality (b). Repeating the above process using X = +2, students should find a second boundary point at (+2, 0). With Y < 0, all solutions for X = +2 will lie on the vertical grid line segment below (+2, 0); the boundary point at (+2, 0) will not be a solution. A broken line should be drawn on the grid through the points for

Name _____ **Date** _____

WORKSHEET 5–3–2
Shading Solutions

For each system of inequalities below, graph the boundary lines on the grid provided. Lightly color the solution region of each inequality with a colored pencil; use a different color for each region. The region whose points satisfy both inequalities of the system will be colored with both colors. Circle the point of intersection of the two boundary lines. Shade the circle if the point represents a solution of the system. Write an inequality that describes the **domain** of the solutions of the system and another that describes the **range;** for these two ideas, you may have to find the ordered pair of the intersection point. State the ordered pair of a point that lies in the *interior* of the system's solution region on the graph.

1. (a) $Y \leq X + 2$
   (b) $Y < -X + 2$

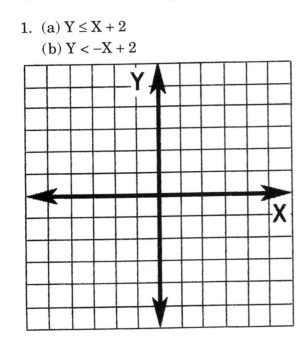

2. (a) $X > -2$
   (b) $Y > -3$

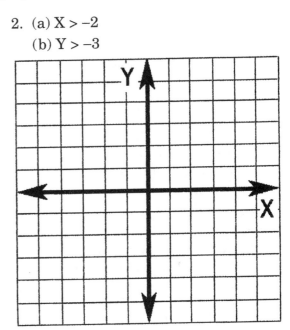

3. (a) $Y \leq -3X + 6$
   (b) $Y \geq 0.75X - 3$

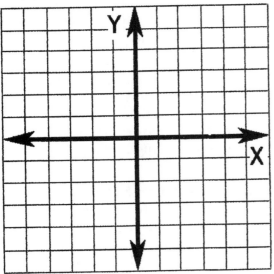

4. (a) $Y \leq 2X - 2$
   (b) $Y > 0.6X - 3.5$

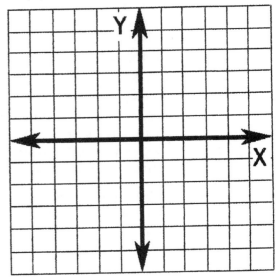

(+2, 0) and (−3, +5) to represent the boundary line for inequality (b), and should be labeled with (b). Since Y-values of solutions for a given X-value must be *less than* the Y-value of the boundary point for that same X, the half-plane *below* the broken boundary line should be lightly shaded with color #2. The graph of the broken boundary line and its colored region are shown in the illustration in step 4.

4. Ask: "Since one boundary line is solid and one line is broken, what does this tell you about their intersection point as a possible solution of *both* inequalities or of the system?" *(the intersection point is a solution point for only inequality (a), as shown by the solid line; therefore, it cannot be a solution point for the system)* Students should draw a circle around the intersection point but not shade the circle. Here is the completed graph, showing the overlapping regions.

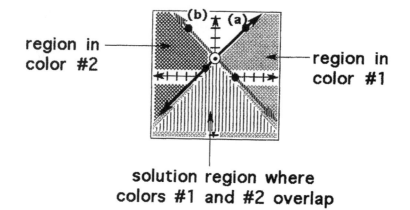

region in color #2

region in color #1

solution region where colors #1 and #2 overlap

5. Ask: "For this solution region for the two inequalities of the system, what do you know about the **domain,** the values of X occurring in the solutions?" *(since the shading of the solution region extends without bounds to the left and to the right as the two lines extend in the plane, X can be any real number)* "What about the **range,** the values of Y in the solutions? Can Y be any real number like X can, or will there be limits on Y?" *(Y cannot be any real number because the two boundary lines control the choices for Y; the upper bound on Y is at the intersection point)* Have students find the ordered pair for the intersection point graphically; it is (0, +2). **Ask:** "Since the upper bound for our Y-values is +2, will +2 be in our **range** for the system?" *(no; the intersection point is not in the solution region, so its Y-value will not be in the range of the system)* Students should now write below the graph on the worksheet the following statements: **Domain: X is any real number** and **Range: Y < +2.**

6. Finally, have students randomly select and mark a point that lies in the **interior** of the solution region of the graph and label the point with its ordered pair. A possible choice might be the point at (−2, −3). Choices will vary, but they should all be located in the two-color region of the graph. Encourage variety in the ordered pairs selected. Points might lie on the solid boundary line, but not the broken line; points might also lie on one of the axes within the solution region.

7. Students should now repeat the procedure followed in steps 2 through 6 to complete the other exercises on Worksheet 5–3–2. Monitor their work carefully to be sure they are locating their lines correctly. Emphasize the method used in this activity and also in Activity 1 where *an X-value is selected first,* then used to find a boundary point for the Y-values that correspond to that X. It is the boundary point, along with the inequality sign, that indicates where the Y-values will be located for solution points (vertically above or below the boundary point for the given X). These vertical sets of points, each determined by a specific X-value, then combine together to form the solution region. (**Note:** Another method often used to help students find the solution region for an inequality has students simply test a single point on either side of the line representing the *related equation* to see if its X and Y values satisfy the given inequality. If the two values make a true statement when substituted in the inequality, students merely shade the half-plane that contains the selected point; if not, they shade the other half-plane on the other side of the line. Many students using this method fail to see the role being played by the boundary line of the inequality and how the boundary points identify the Y-values for the solution set. The method presented in this activity and in Activity 1 hopefully will make the boundary line of an inequality more meaningful.)

8. After students have completed the worksheet, have various students share their ordered pairs selected from the different solution regions. Also, discuss the descriptions they have written for the domain and the range of each system of inequalities; this is important preparation for future studies in functions.

Answer Key for WORKSHEET 5–3–2

The graph and the domain and range statements are provided below for each exercise. In lieu of shading, the different solution regions have been indicated by one or more letters written within each disjoint region; if the letter *a* is present, that region should be shaded for inequality (a); if the letter *b* is present, the region should be shaded for inequality (b); if both letters are present, the region should be shaded in two colors as the solution region for the system. Ordered pairs from the *interior* of the solution region are not indicated here since student choices will vary.

1.

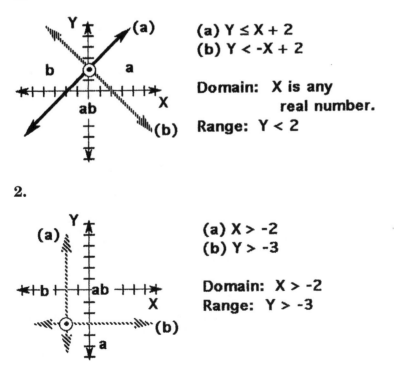

(a) $Y \leq X + 2$
(b) $Y < -X + 2$

Domain: X is any
           real number.
Range: $Y < 2$

2.

(a) $X > -2$
(b) $Y > -3$

Domain: $X > -2$
Range: $Y > -3$

3.

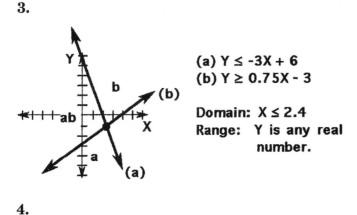

(a) Y ≤ -3X + 6
(b) Y ≥ 0.75X - 3

Domain: X ≤ 2.4
Range: Y is any real
        number.

4.

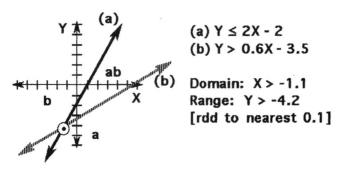

(a) Y ≤ 2X - 2
(b) Y > 0.6X - 3.5

Domain: X > -1.1
Range: Y > -4.2
[rdd to nearest 0.1]

Activity 3: SYSTEM SHAKE-DOWN

[Application/Exploration]

Materials: Decks of cards (see step 1)
Worksheet 5–3–3 (pattern for card deck)
Calculators
Paper
Regular pencils

Management: Teams of 4 students each (30 minutes)

Directions:

1. Give each team of 4 students a deck of cards and a calculator. Each deck of cards will contain two sets of cards, Set A and Set B (see Worksheet 5–3–3). Set A should be a different color from Set B. Cards belonging to the same deck should be coded on the back in some way (a number, set of dots, etc.) so they can be identified as one full deck, if necessary. Cards may be laminated for better endurance. Set A will consist of 8 cards; each card will contain a system of 2 linear inequalities. Some of the system cards will have an inequality in **standard form** (for example, aX + bY < c or aX + bY > c) and may need to be transformed to show Y in terms of X for easier graphing. Set B will have 12 cards. Each of 8 cards will contain a graph that matches to a system listed on a card in Set A; the other 4 cards will be distractors and have graphs that do not match to cards in Set A.

2. A team will randomly distribute Set A, giving 2 cards to each player. All 12 cards in Set B will be placed face up in the center of the table. Since the cards contain graphs, they should all be positioned so that their corresponding axes are oriented the same way. When taking a turn, a player may need to turn or pick up a card to be able to read its graph more easily; the card should be returned to its original position at the end of the turn.

3. The four players on a team will take turns matching a system card in hand to a graph card on the table. Each time a match is made, the player must give reasons for the match to the other players. If the other players agree with the selected graph, the matched graph card is removed from the table and laid aside with its system card. If they do not agree, all four team members will then work together to find the correct graph card. Once the correct match is made, the two cards may be laid aside. After several minutes, if the team cannot find a graph card for the system card being discussed, the system card should be placed face down on the table near the set of graph cards. The turn then passes to the next player. If time remains after all other system cards have been matched to graph cards, the team may ask for help from the teacher, or may ask for a class discussion of that particular system card.

4. As a sample of a turn, a player needs to find the graph card for the system card that contains the following: **(a) 2X − Y < 4** and **(b) Y < 3 − X.** The player has several ways to approach the problem. Here are three possible methods the player might use.

> ***Method 1:*** Following the approach most recently used in Activity 1 and Activity 2, the player selects 2 X-values and substitutes each into, say, inequality (a) in order to locate the *boundary point* for each given X. In this case, it is easier to transform inequality (a) from *standard form* to a form for Y in terms of X: **Y > 2X − 4.** So if X = +1, we have Y > −2; this indicates that we want all points vertically *above* the boundary point (+1, −2) as solution points for inequality (a). Repeating for X = −2, we have Y > −8; so other solution points must be above the boundary point (−2, −8). The player might need to draw a quick sketch of a graph on his or her own paper in order to record or plot any information found. With these first two points, the player knows where the boundary line and solution points are for inequality (a). The process can be repeated for inequality (b). The player should then be able to identify the correct graph card for a match.

> ***Method 2:*** Students discovered in an earlier lesson with inequalities that the boundary line of the solution points for an inequality can be described by an equation whose terms correspond to the terms of the inequality. For example, for the inequality Y > 2X − 4, the equation for the boundary line would be Y = 2X −4. Using this equation in its slope-intercept form, a player can plot the *Y-intercept* of the boundary line, then use the *slope* value on the X term to find a second point; the two points determine the position of the boundary line. Substituting the X-value of either point found in the inequality, the player can compute the Y-value for a *boundary point* and determine where other solution points must lie with respect to the boundary point. The second inequality can be graphed in a similar way, then the system graph identified.

> ***Method 3:*** This method is similar to method 2, except that instead of using the slope to find the second point for the boundary line, the *X-intercept* is used as that point.

These three methods should be reviewed briefly with students before they begin this activity. They need to be *aware* of different strategies available to them, and should be encouraged to *try* the various ways during the game or activity.

5. Worksheet 5–3–3 may serve as an *answer key,* if needed, since each system is already paired with its own graph on the worksheet.

WORKSHEET 5-3-3
Card Deck for "System Shake-Down"

(Each system matches the graph below it. A shaded square marks the solution region.)

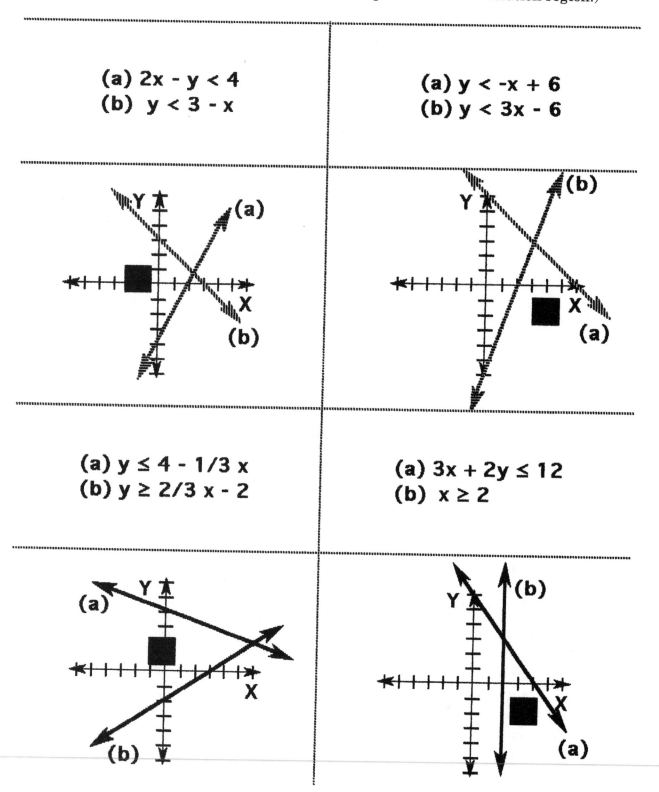

(a) 2x - y < 4
(b) y < 3 - x

(a) y < -x + 6
(b) y < 3x - 6

(a) y ≤ 4 - 1/3 x
(b) y ≥ 2/3 x - 2

(a) 3x + 2y ≤ 12
(b) x ≥ 2

(Each system matches the graph below it. A shaded square marks the solution region.)

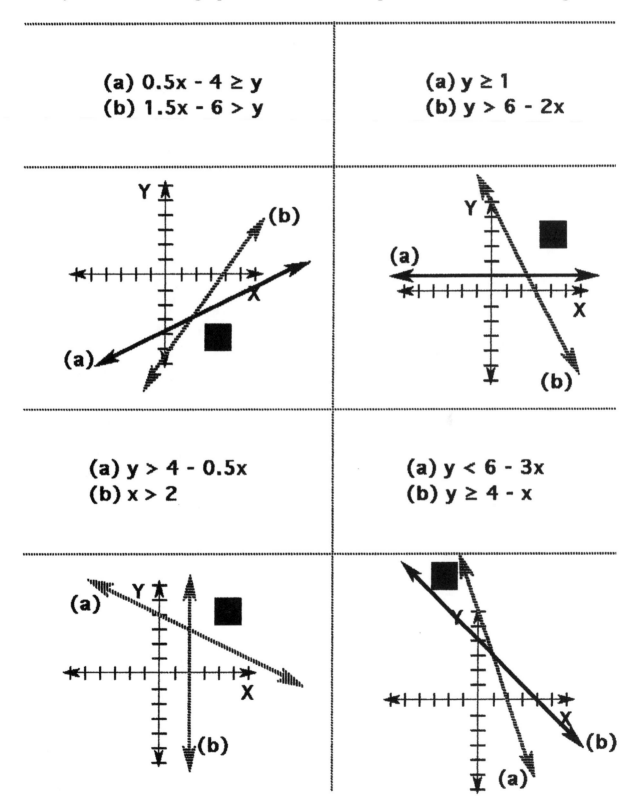

(a) 0.5x - 4 ≥ y
(b) 1.5x - 6 > y

(a) y ≥ 1
(b) y > 6 - 2x

(a) y > 4 - 0.5x
(b) x > 2

(a) y < 6 - 3x
(b) y ≥ 4 - x

(4 distractor graphs for "System Shake-Down")

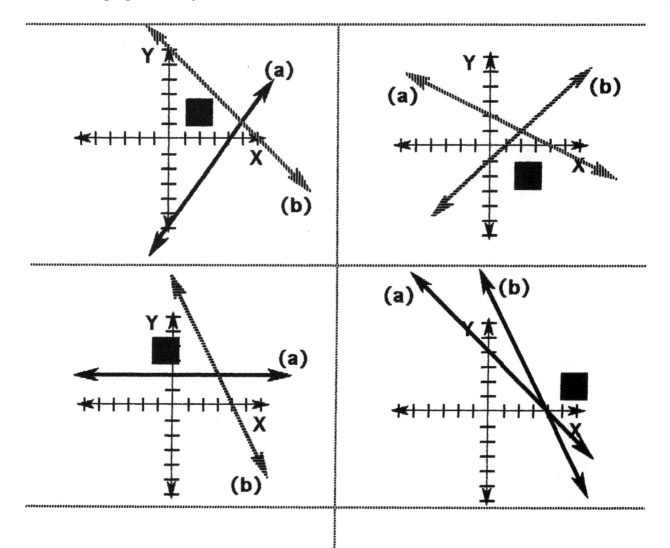

OBJECTIVE 4: Solve systems of linear functions in two variables by graphical methods.

Activity 1: SPARRING SQUARES

[Developing Action]

Materials: Worksheet 5–4–1
Worksheet 5–4–2
Packets of 30 positive unit tiles each
Paper
Regular pencils

Management: Partners (50 minutes)

Directions:

1. Give each pair of students one copy each of Worksheet 5–4–1 (the building mat) and Worksheet 5–4–2, and a packet of 30 positive unit tiles. In this activity students will be given conditions for quantities of unit tiles placed in squares A, B, and C on the worksheet. Partners will work together to place different amounts of unit tiles in each square, checking back and forth (sparring!) between each pair of squares to assure that given conditions for the squares' quantities are met. Three variables (A, B, and C) will actually be used in this introduction to linear systems. Students will be looking for values for A, B, and C that satisfy all three equations simultaneously in a given set or system. This triplet of values will be the **solution** of the given **system.**

2. As a sample, consider the first set of equations on Worksheet 5–4–2: **2A = B, B – 3 = C,** and **C – 1 = A.** Viewing the first equation, students must put *some* (a random amount at first) unit tiles in square A, then double that amount for square B. For example, suppose 3 unit tiles are placed in square A. Then 2×3 or 6 unit tiles must be placed in square B. Since square C holds 3 less than square B holds, 6 – 3 or 3 unit tiles must be placed in square C. According to the third equation, C – 1 = A, square A should hold 1 less tile than square C does; however, square A presently holds 3 unit tiles, not the 2 tiles that the last equation required. Thus, the initial assumption that square A should hold 3 unit tiles is incorrect. Students must now change the amount in square A to something else, perhaps 2 unit tiles or 4 unit tiles, and start over with the checking process. After several trials, students will finally discover that 4 unit tiles in A, 8 unit tiles in B, and 5 unit tiles in C will satisfy all three equations of the system. These amounts should be recorded in the blanks provided on Worksheet 5–4–2. In the remaining space to the right of the answer blanks, students should record number sentences that show their answers substituted in the original equations: **2(4) = 8; (8) – 3 = 5;** and **(5) – 1 = 4.**

3. Encourage students to try different amounts of tiles in each square. Many students are not comfortable with this "trial-and-error" strategy; they need to know that it is a very important strategy in problem solving. Also, the process of beginning with an *assumption,* logically proceeding until a *contradiction* is reached, then changing to a *new assumption* in order to reach a logically correct *conclusion* is likely to be new to most students. Discuss this method with the class; it will be an important *proof* technique to

WORKSHEET 5-4-1
Sparring Squares
Building Mat

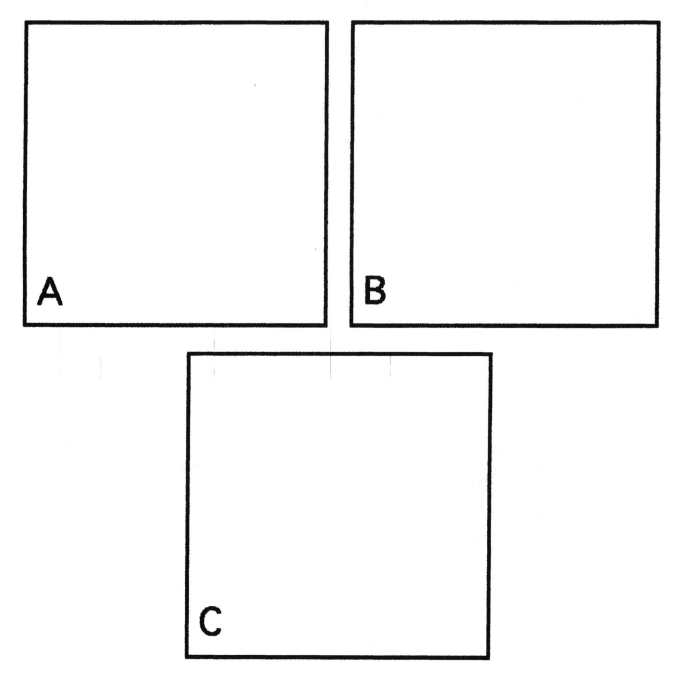

WORKSHEET 5–4–2
Sparring Squares

For each set of equations or conditions given below, place positive unit tiles in squares A, B, and C in amounts that will satisfy the stated conditions. You may need to adjust the amount of tiles in each square several times until all three equations (the "conditions") are satisfied by the final values found in the three squares. Record the value in unit tiles found for each square beside the stated conditions. The value in tiles for a square is represented by the letter A, B, or C written inside the square.

1. $2A = B$

   $B - 3 = C$

   $C - 1 = A$

   A = _____

   B = _____

   C = _____

2. $B = A + 4$

   $C = 2A - 3$

   $B = C$

   A = _____

   B = _____

   C = _____

3. $A = \frac{1}{3}B$

   $A + 1 = C$

   $C = B - 5$

   A = _____

   B = _____

   C = _____

those who continue into geometry and more advanced mathematics courses. Students need to be aware of the thinking processes they are using; awareness leads to mathematical maturity.

Answer Key to WORKSHEET 5–4–2

(1) A = 4, B = 8, C = 5;   (2) A = 7, B = 11, C = 11;   (3) A = 3; B = 9; C = 4

Activity 2: VERTICAL SEARCH

[Bridging Action]

Materials: Worksheet 5–4–3
              Paper
              Regular pencils

Management: Partners (50 minutes)

Directions:

1. Give each pair of students a copy of Worksheet 5–4–3, which contains several graphs of intersecting lines. Students will be asked to find the horizontal or X value on a given graph that maps or belongs to a pair of vertically aligned Y-values, one Y-value on each line, where the two Y-values are related in a certain way. For example, one may be three times as great as the other. For convenience, we will use the notation: Y(1) on Line 1, and Y(2) on Line 2 for a given X.

2. Students must use *trial-and-error* to find differences between vertically aligned points along the two lines. It might be helpful if the edge of a sheet of paper is placed on the graph so that the paper's edge is parallel to the Y-axis and crosses over both lines. Then the place where each line meets the paper's edge can be marked on the paper. The distance between the two marks can then be compared to the Y-axis measures and an estimate of the distance found. This process continues until points are found on the two lines where the vertical distance between the two points is the amount being sought. Then the ordered pairs of the points can be identified. Students should measure distances to the nearest tenth of a unit on the graph.

3. *Challenge:* After all students have completed their worksheets, challenge them with the following *discussion questions:*

What conditions might exist for related Y-values if their two lines—

(**a**) are diagonal (not vertical or horizontal), yet parallel to each other? *[the difference between Y(1) and Y(2) remains the same for all X]*

(**b**) coincide? *[only one line appears on the graph, so Y(1) = Y(2) for all X]*

(**c**) are perpendicular to each other with one line horizontal and the other line vertical? *[only one X-value will have Y-values on both lines and that is the X-value for the point of intersection of the two lines; all other X-values have a Y-value only on the horizontal line; also, the X-value of the intersection point belongs to **infinitely many** Y-values on the vertical line; the vertical line does not identify a **function,** but the horizontal line does]*

For each graph below, three different relationships are given for pairs of vertically aligned Y values, each pair being shown as Y(1) on Line 1 and Y(2) on Line 2. For each relationship, find the X-value that locates the points of the two required Y-values, and record the ordered pairs of the two related points in the space provided. Draw a vertical line segment on the graph through each pair of points to the X-axis.

1. (a) $Y(1) = Y(2)$

   (X,Y): _____

   (b) $Y(1) = Y(2) + 5$

   (X,Y): _____

   (c) $Y(2) = 2Y(1)$

   (X,Y): _____

2. (a) $Y(2) = Y(1) + 4$

   (X,Y): _____

   (b) $Y(1) = Y(2)$

   (X,Y): _____

   (c) $Y(2) - \frac{4}{3} = Y(1)$

   (X,Y): _____

3. (a) $Y(1) = Y(2)$

   (X,Y): _____

   (b) $Y(1) = 6Y(2)$

   (X,Y): _____

   (c) $Y(1) = Y(2) + 3$

   (X,Y): _____

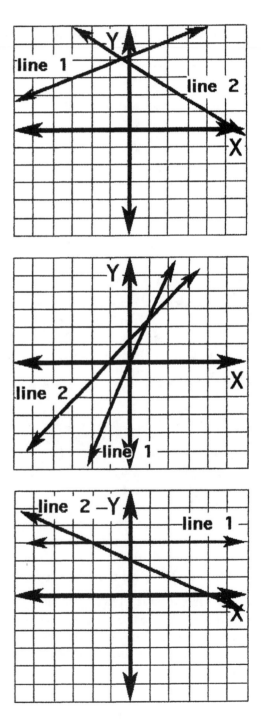

4. ***For background information only:*** The systems used to generate the three graphs for this activity are provided here for the teacher, but are not intended for student use at this time.

(1) $3X - 7Y = -30$ and $5X + 7Y = 27$

(2) $5X - 2Y = 0$ and $3.5X - 3Y = -4$

(3) $Y = 3$ and $0.5X + Y = 2$

Answer Key to WORKSHEET 5–4–3

1. (a) $(-0.4, 4.4)$ [to nearest tenth]
(b) $(4, 6)$ and $(4, 1)$
(c) $(-3, 3)$ and $(-3, 6)$

2. (a) $(-2, -5)$ and $(-2, -1)$
(b) $(1, 2.5)$
(c) $(0, 0)$ and $(0, 1.3)$ [to nearest tenth]

3. (a) $(-2, 3)$
(b) $(3, 3)$ and $(3, 0.5)$ [to nearest tenth]
(c) $(4, 3)$ and $(4, 0)$

Activity 3: MAKING COMPARISONS

[Application/Exploration]

Materials: Worksheet 5–4–4
Graphing calculators
Paper
Regular pencils

Management: Teams of 4 students each (50 minutes)

Directions:

1. Give each team of students 4 copies of Worksheet 5–4–4 and 2 graphing calculators. The worksheet contains 2 application problems with functions to be graphed and analyzed. Each team should discuss and answer the questions given with each problem, then summarize their results on their own papers. For this activity, it will be helpful for TRACING purposes if the graphing calculators have the capability of moving the cursor back and forth between lines graphed on the same screen. This makes it easier to compare Y-values on two different lines for the same X-value. Otherwise, students may need to regraph a particular function when they are ready to TRACE for a certain X or Y value on the graph of that function.

2. An initial viewing screen for Problem 1 might be $X\varepsilon[0, 600]$, scale = \$50, and $Y\varepsilon[0, 100]$, scale = \$10. Students will need to ZOOM IN or change the viewing screen in order to determine the point of intersection of the two lines more accurately. Decimal readings for X and Y on the graphing screen will vary from calculator to calculator. Students will need to round the values to the nearest dollar or nearest \$5.

3. An initial viewing screen for Problem 2 might be $X\varepsilon[0, 6]$, scale = 0.5 hr, and $Y\varepsilon[0, 100]$, scale = 10 miles. Again, students will need to change these parameters as needed.

WORKSHEET 5–4–4
Making Comparisons

For each problem, graph the two given functions on your graphing calculator. Determine what size of viewing screen is needed to represent the data in the problem; adjust the screen size when necessary. TRACE along the lines of the graph to find the values of X and Y needed to answer each question. Record your answers on your own paper. Make a quick sketch of each pair of lines in order to show their general relationship to each other; label each line to show whom or what it represents. Be ready to explain your answers to the entire class.

1. Picayune Bank offers two credit card plans: Gold and Platinum. The Gold card has an APR (annual percent rate) of 10.9% plus an annual fee of $40; the Platinum card has an APR of 14.9% with an annual fee of $25. One way to compare the two offers is to consider the interest rates as **simple** interest, which is computed once a year (APR's are usually *compounded* on a daily basis; methods vary). The rates can then be applied to different amounts of total charges for the entire year to find the expected total interest paid on a year's charges. Here are possible functions you can graph to compare the two offers: (1) *Gold*—$Y = 0.109X + 40$; and (2) *Platinum*—$Y = 0.149X + 25$, where X is the total dollars spent in charges for a year and Y is the total paid in simple interest and annual fees for a year. For convenience, use X as $100, $200, $300, etc. Is there ever a time when one card offer is equally as good as the other? When is the Gold card better with respect to the interest and fees? When is the Platinum card better? Explain your answers.

2. For a 100-mile bike race Louisa averages a speed of 17 mph and Mae averages 20 mph. Using the relationship: distance (Y) in miles = average speed × hours (X) travelled, two functions can be graphed to compare the two bikers' performances during the race: (1) *Louisa*—$Y = 17X$; and (2) *Mae*—$Y = 20X$. For convenience, use X as 1 hr, 2 hrs, 3 hrs, etc. How many hours after the start of the race has one biker ridden about 6 miles farther than the other? At what time is the distance traveled about the same for both bikers? When is Mae about 14 miles ahead of Louisa? Is there a time during the race that the difference in distance between Mae and Louisa is three times as great as their difference is after the first two hours of riding? Explain your answers.

Decimal readings for X on the graphing screen should be rounded to the nearest 0.1 hr and readings for Y should be rounded to the nearest mile.

4. When all teams have finished, have several students share their team's results with the entire class. Interpretation and rounding of numerical answers may vary.

Answer Key to WORKSHEET 5–4–4

Numerical answers and possible interpretations are provided below for each problem on the worksheet.

Problem 1: At X = $375 (to nearest $5) in total charges for the year, both Y(Gold) and Y(Platinum) are about $81 (to nearest dollar) for simple interest and annual fee. Thus, if yearly charges total less than $375, the Platinum card offer is better with respect to amount of interest and fees. If yearly charges are more than $375, the Gold card offer is better. Note that the ordered pair ($375, $81) for the *intersection point* of the two lines is often called the "solution" of the *system* of two equations or functions graphed; however, the comparison statements made about the two card offers are the actual "real-world solutions" to this problem.

Problem 2: If miles are rounded to the nearest mile and hours are rounded to the nearest 0.1 hour, then 2.0 hrs after the start of the race, Mae is about 6 miles ahead of Louisa; points read from the graphing screen might be (2.01, 34.18) for Louisa and (2.01, 40.21) for Mae. At the 4.5 hr mark, Mae is about 14 miles ahead of Louisa; Mae has completed about 91 miles of the 100-mile race and Louisa has completed about 77 miles. The only time when the two bikers have traveled the *same* distance (i.e., they are 0 miles apart) is at the *beginning* of the race; they have ridden 0 miles in 0 hrs. According to the graphs of the two lines, in order for the difference in distance between the two bikers to be three times their difference at 2 hrs, each biker must ride for about 6 hrs. This is impossible, however, since Mae would travel 120 miles in 6 hrs and the race is only 100 miles long; that is, Mae finishes the race in 5 hrs. Note that in this problem, the traditional "solution" to the system of equations or functions is the ordered pair: (0 hrs, 0 miles).

OBJECTIVE 5: Solve systems of linear functions in two variables by combining like sides of equations.

Activity 1: JOINING SIDES

[Developing Action]

Materials: System building mats and sets of tiles (described in step 1)
Worksheet 5–5–1
Regular pencils
Paper

Management: Partners (50 minutes)

Directions:

1. Give each pair of students two copies of Worksheet 5–5–1, a set of tiles, and a system building mat. The set of tiles used in Objective 1, Activity 1, of this section may be used here. The set of tiles should contain 30 unit tiles and have 8 variable tiles in each of two different sizes (for example, 0.75 in. by 3 in. and 0.75 in. by 3.25 in.). A different color should be used for each variable length. Consider the shorter variable tile as variable A and the longer tile as variable B for notation purposes. Each tile, both unit and variable, should have a large X marked on one side to represent its inverse form. It is assumed that students have successfully completed the three activities for Objective 5 in Section 3 as preparation for this lesson and that they have mastered the solving of linear equations in one variable. The *system* building mat may be constructed by taping two *equality* building mats together at their longer edges, then drawing two large arrows across the taped edges. Each equality building mat consists of an 8.5 in. × 14 in. sheet of paper or lightweight tagboard. A bold, black bar should be drawn from the midpoint of one longer edge to the midpoint of the other longer edge of the paper. The color of the mats should contrast with the colors of the tiles. After the two mats are taped together and the arrows drawn, the finished system mat may be laminated. We will refer to the connected equality mats individually as the "top mat" and the "bottom mat" in this activity. The completed *system* mat should appear as shown below.

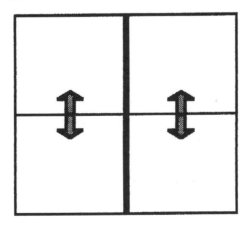

WORKSHEET 5-5-1
Joining Sides

For each *system* of equations given below, solve for variables A and B by building with tiles on a system building mat. Record the values of A and B in the space below the two equations they satisfy. Write a number sentence that shows the values of A and B substituted in one of the system's two original equations.

1. $A - 3 = -B$

    $A + 3B = +1$

2. $B + 2A = -B - 2$

    $-3 + B - A = -B + 1$

3. $A = 3B + 2$

    $A = 4B + 5$

4. $-B + 3A = +4$

    $2B - A = +2$

5. $-1 = A - B$

    $A = -B - 9$

6. $A - 3B = +5$

    $2A - 2B = +10$

2. To introduce students to the new *system* mat, write the following equations on the board: **A = +2** and **B = −1.** Have students use variable and unit tiles to show A = +2 on the top mat and B = −1 on the bottom mat of the system building mat. The shorter variable tile is for variable A and the longer variable tile is for variable B. Remind students that if a group of tiles is placed on each side of an *equality* mat and the arrangement is accepted for some known reason, this indicates that the two groups of tiles are equal in value to each other. ***Ask:*** "If we place a variable B tile on each side of the top equality mat, what do we know about the balance of the two new tile groups on the top mat?" *(left and right tile groups are still equal in value since the same value represented by B has been added to both sides)* "Instead of placing the second variable B tile on the right side of the top mat, can we place something else there that we know equals the value of B?" *(yes, because the value of the new amount of tiles added on the right side of the top mat still balances with the value of the first variable B tile added on the left side)* To show this, have students move the variable B tile from the left side of the bottom mat across the double arrow to the left side of the top mat. Similarly, they should move the negative unit tile from the right side of the bottom mat across the double arrow to the right side of the top mat. The original tile arrangement and the changes are shown here.

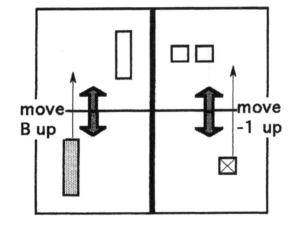

3. After simplifying the tiles by forming and removing 0-pairs, students should have 1 variable A tile and 1 variable B tile on the top left section of the system mat and have 1 positive unit tile on the top right section of the mat. ***Ask:*** "How can we test these two new groups of tiles to see if they are indeed equal in value?" *(substitute the given amount of unit tiles for each variable tile as stated in the original two equations, and compare the left and right totals in unit tiles)* Students should now replace the variable A tile with 2 positive unit tiles and the variable B tile with 1 negative unit tile. Two positive unit tiles and 1 negative unit tile will be on the left side of the top mat, and 1 positive unit tile will be on the right side of the top mat. Since each group of tiles has a value of +1, the *equality* of the top mat is maintained. This tells us that it is *logically correct* for us to combine the top left and bottom left tiles on the system mat and to combine the top right and bottom right tiles on the system mat; the new left group of tiles will still be equal in value to the new right group of tiles. That is, the new combined equation, **A + B = 2 + (−1),** is a true statement.

4. Now write the following equations on the board: **A = +2** and **−1 = B.** Have students show these equations with tiles on the system mat. The new tile arrangements should look like the tiles shown originally in step 2, except that the variable B tile is now on the right side of the bottom mat and the negative unit tile is on the left of the bottom mat. **Ask:** "Does it matter that we have changed sides with the variable B and −1? Will the equality of the tile groups still hold if we move the two left groups together and move the two right groups together?" *(the moves will represent the new combined equation: **A + (−1) = 2 + B**)* Have students move the appropriate groups together onto the top mat, then repeat the substitution process to get 2 positive unit tiles and 1 negative unit on both the left and the right sides of the top mat. Since each side has a value of +1, the equality is maintained. Therefore, the combined equation, A + (−1) = 2 + B, is a true statement just as A + B = 2 + (−1) is a true statement.

5. We now know that different equations can be combined according to the steps we have used here, and that, when doing this, the left and right sides of an equation can be exchanged before they are combined with another equation. This realization leads to a new *strategy* for students.

6. Write the following two equations on the board: **A − 3 = −B** and **A + 3B = +1** (see Worksheet 5–5–1). Students should build the first equation with tiles on the top mat, and build the second equation on the bottom mat. Have them follow the combining process used in steps 2 and 3. The system mat with initial changes is shown below.

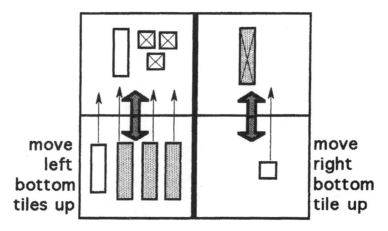

7. The tiles finally appearing on the top mat represent the combined equation: **2A + 3B − 3 = −B + 1.** Note that even though we tried to maintain an order of position when we moved tiles in steps 2 through 4 (that is, each group of bottom tiles was moved to the *right* of the corresponding, original group of tiles on the top mat), it is not necessary because of the commutative property of addition. We kept an order only to help students differentiate between the two sets of equations that were discussed at the beginning of the activity. Ask students to solve the new combined equation for the variable A tile in terms of the variable B tile (see Objective 5 of Section 3). This can be done by adding 3 inverse variable B tiles and 3 positive unit tiles to both sides of the top mat and forming 0-pairs of tiles. The result will be 2 variable A tiles on the left side of the top mat and 4 inverse variable B tiles and 4 positive unit tiles on the right side. The tiles on each side should be separated into 2 equal rows: on the left, 2 rows of one variable A tile each; and on the right, 2 rows of 2 inverse variable B tiles and 2 positive unit tiles each. Only one row is kept on the mat, yielding the equation: **A = –2B + 2.** The separation step prior to the removal of one complete row of tiles from the mat is shown below.

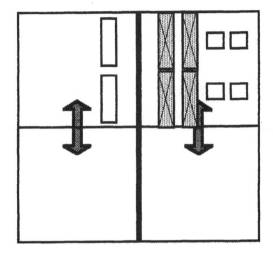

8. Discuss the idea with students that when we have two linear equations that represent what is happening in a given situation, often we are interested in the particular pair of values for the two variables that satisfy both equations simultaneously. In particular, in Activity 3 of Objective 4 earlier, this special pair of values identified the intersection point of the two lines that represented the two equations graphically; the intersection point belonged to both lines *simultaneously.* **Ask:** "We know that whatever values of A and B will satisfy this combined equation will also satisfy the first two equations before you combined them. Can you tell me what the value of A needs to be for this new equation to be true?" *(no; to find the value of A, we need the value of B in the equation; similarly, to find the value of B, we need to know the value of A in the equation)* **Ask:** "If we randomly assign a value, such as +1, to B in the combined equation, we get 0 for the value of A. Do the values A = 0 and B = +1 satisfy each of the first two equations?" *(no)* "If B is –2 in the combined equation, A must be +6. Will A = +6 and B = –2 satisfy the first two equations?" *(no)* Therefore, even though we can find values for A and B that will make the combined equation true, these same values will not necessarily make each of the two original equations in A and B true (see step 6).

9. Now have students rebuild the equations **A – 3 = –B** and **A + 3B = +1** on the system mat. **Ask:** "If A = +2 and B = +1 are substituted in the first equation, **A – 3 = –B,** will they be a solution for the equation?" *(yes; when substituted in the equation, a true statement occurs)* "What about the **opposite** of the first equation, that is, **–A + 3 = B?** Will A = +2 and B = +1 be a solution for that equation as well?" *(yes)* Have students take the opposite of each tile on the top mat to show the new equation: **–A + 3 = B.** Since this equation is satisfied or solved by the same values of A and B that solve its opposite, the original first equation, we can combine this new equation with the original second equation, **A + 3B = +1,** and still look for common solutions to both equations. The system mat should appear as shown here.

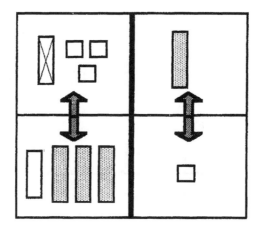

10. Students should now combine the two equations shown on the system mat. Remind them that they need to find values for the variable A and the variable B. When the tiles on the bottom mat are moved to the appropriate sides of the top mat, the variable A tiles will form a 0-pair, which should be removed from the mat. Only variable B tiles and unit tiles remain on the mat. As students continue to work, 3 negative unit tiles and 1 inverse variable B tile might be added to both sides of the top mat. After more 0-pairs are formed and removed, 2 variable B tiles remain on the left side of the top mat and 2 negative unit tiles remain on the right side. Two rows of 1 variable B tile each are made on the left side, and 2 rows of 1 negative unit tile each are made on the right side. Retaining only one complete row on the top mat, the final tiles show the equation: **B = –1.**

11. *Ask:* "What happened this time when you combined equations that did *not* happen when you combined the original two equations?" *(all the variable A tiles were removed from the mat)* "Why were the variable A tiles removed from the mat?" *(they all had formed 0-pairs with their inverses)* "What did this particular *loss in tiles* allow you to do?" *(only variable B tiles and unit tiles remained, so a value could easily be found for B)* Discuss the idea with students that this discovered process of *removing all of one kind of variable tile,* including its inverse form, *by forming 0-pairs* is a major **strategy** in solving a system or set of equations for each type of variable involved.

12. Since the values for A and B together must satisfy all the equations used thus far in this exercise, students may substitute **B = –1** in either one of the original two equations, **A – 3 = –B or A + 3B = +1,** or in the opposites equation, **–A + 3 = B,** to find the value for the variable A. At this stage, students should be able to do the substitution in a written format: **A – 3 = +1** or **A + 3(–1) = +1** or **–A + 3 = –1,** respectively; in either of the three substitutions, **A = +4.** (**Note:** If some students are still not comfortable with using only number sentences to make substitutions, allow them to rebuild one of the original equations, **A – 3 = –B or A + 3B = +1,** with tiles on the mat. They should then replace each variable tile B on the mat with a negative unit tile and solve for A with the remaining tiles. In the space below the exercise on the worksheet, have them record a sentence that reflects the substitution they make with tiles, for example, **A + 3(–1) = +1, so A = +4.**)

13. As a final confirmation that they have indeed found a pair of solution values that are common to all equations in the exercise, have students substitute A = +4 and B = –1 in whichever two equations they did *not* use to find the value of A. This again may be done in written form: **(+4) – 3 = +1** or **(+4) + 3(–1) = +1** or **(–4) + 3 = –1.** Students must realize that the values for A and B that they have found will satisfy the original equations, as well as any equivalent forms. The equations A = +4 and B = −1, along with one of the substitution number sentences, should be recorded on Worksheet 5–5–1 below the first system of equations.

14. For practice with the discovered strategy for deleting one of the variables in a system of linear equations, write the second system of equations from the worksheet on the board: **B + 2A = −B − 2** and **−3 + B − A = −B + 1.** Have students build the first equation on the top mat and the second equation on the bottom mat. Tell them to apply the new strategy to the equations in order to *delete all of the variable B tiles,* including inverses. Allow students time to think about the situation. Remind them that they eventually will be combining two left sides together and two right sides together, but before they do that, they are free to transform the two original equations into other equivalent equations, including opposites and multiples of the two equations. There are several ways to do this. Do not emphasize grouping the tiles in a certain way, for example, placing all *variable* tiles on the same side of the mat. Such ideas will be covered in Activity 2. Have different students share their ideas for this exercise. One possible way is to take the opposite of all the equation tiles on the bottom mat, **3 − B + A = B − 1,** then combine these new tiles with the equation tiles shown on the top mat. One 0-pair of variable B tiles will form on each side of the mat and can be removed from the mat, leaving only variable A tiles and unit tiles on the mat. Students should continue working with the tiles to solve for the value of A and eventually for the value of B. The results and a substitution number sentence should finally be recorded on the worksheet under exercise 2. (**Note:** Another way to solve this system might be to *double* the equation tiles on the bottom mat, then combine the new tiles with the tiles on the top mat. This procedure deletes the variable tile A, so that the value of the variable tile B is found first.)

15. Assign the other systems of equations on Worksheet 5–5–1 for students to solve for A and B by building with tiles on the system building mat. Remind them that the **strategy** is to remove all of one variable type from the mat by forming 0-pairs with that variable tile. Encourage students to look for transformations of a system's equations that will make it easier to apply the strategy. Remind them that a multiple of an equation is equivalent to the equation itself, so their solutions will be the same. For example, if we **triple** all the tiles showing A − 2B = +3 on the mat, then we will have 3A − 6B = +9 in tiles on the mat; both equations are satisfied by A = +7 with B = +2, A = −1 with B = −2, etc. For each system, the values found for A and B should be recorded on the worksheet below the given equations. A number sentence should also be written on the worksheet that shows the values for A and B substituted in one of the system's original equations in order to form a true statement.

16. After students have completed the exercises on the worksheet, have them share the different ways they transformed their equations in order to form 0-pairs when the new equations were combined.

Answer Key for WORKSHEET 5–5–1

Only the solutions for the systems are provided below; substitution number sentences will vary.

(1) A = +4, B = −1   (2) A = −2, B = +1

(3) A = −7, B = −3   (4) A = +2, B = +2

(5) A = −5, B = −4   (6) A = +5, B = 0

Activity 2: SIZING UP THE SIDES

[Bridging Action]

Materials: Worksheet 5–5–2
Paper
Regular pencils

Management: Partners (50 minutes)

Directions:

1. Give each pair of students two copies of Worksheet 5–5–2. In this activity we will focus on which transformations of system equations to use, so that when the new equations are combined, one of the variables in the system will be eliminated easily. We will also include fractional coefficients and solutions in the exercises. It is assumed that students have mastered Objective 5 of Section 3 and can make simple changes in linear equations mentally.

2. Write the following system of equations on the board: $B + 2N = -2B - 2$ and $-3 + B - N = -2B + 1$. We solved this system with tiles in Activity 1, so now we want to draw a diagram that shows the steps we used with the tiles. Using shapes to represent the tiles, students should draw a diagram of the system as shown below.

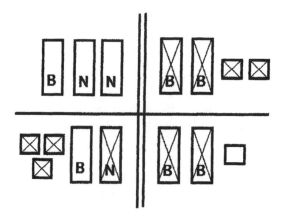

3. The first equation is reflected in the top half of the diagram and the second equation is reflected in the bottom half of the diagram. *Ask:* "If we still want to form 0-pairs of one variable type so that we can remove the 0-pairs and, hence, remove one type of variable from the working frame, do we need to make any changes in the variables and units shown on the left side of each equation, or shown on the right side of each equation, before we combine the equations? If so, what are the changes?" Students might suggest that the bottom equation be transformed to its opposite form so that 0-pairs of the variable B can be made on each side when the different sides are combined. In order to show the opposites, yet not clutter the diagram too much, have students mark out the shapes in the bottom equation. They should then draw at the top of the diagram the inverse of each shape that was marked out in the bottom equation. 0-pairs can be connected without having to connect across another shape in the

WORKSHEET 5–5–2
Sizing Up the Sides

For each system of equations below, on your own paper draw a diagram to solve for each variable, and record your steps symbolically. Below the equations on the worksheet, write the value found for each variable, then rewrite each original equation with its variables replaced by their values, showing a true statement.

1. $B + 2N = -2B - 2$

   $-3 + B - N = -2B + 1$

2. $A + B = -3B$

   $\frac{1}{2} A + 2B = -2 + A$

3. $g + m = -1$

   $5 - g = -m - 2$

4. $3d = (+3) - 2x$

   $-x + d = -2d$

5. $(-\frac{1}{3})W + 4 = P + 3$

   $-2P + 3 = W$

6. $3k + 5 = (\frac{1}{2})b + k$

   $b - 2k = +8$

diagram. The marking out, the new opposites equation, and the 0-pairs are shown in the following illustration.

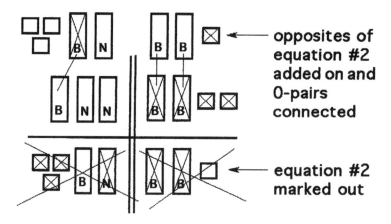

opposites of
equation #2
added on and
0-pairs
connected

equation #2
marked out

4. A horizontal bar should be drawn below the original part of the diagram, then the remaining shapes of the combined equation redrawn below the bar. The variable B and its inverse have been removed; only the variable N and units are present in the new equation. Students should now finish the diagram to solve for N. This is done by adding 3 negative units to both sides of the equation and forming 0-pairs. The three variables on the left side should be separated into 3 equal groups; similarly, the six negative units on the right side should be separated, putting −2 in each group. Only one group should be redrawn from each side to show the solution, **N = −2.** The final diagram is shown below.

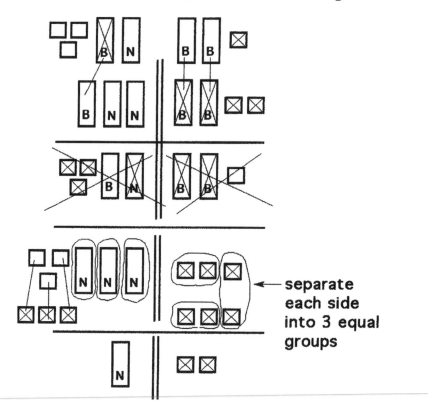

separate
each side
into 3 equal
groups

5. Students should now record in symbols on their own papers beside their completed diagram the transformations they made in the equations and the different steps used to solve for the first variable. The recording for the first exercise might be as follows:

$$
\begin{aligned}
\text{B} + 2\text{N} &= -2\text{B} - 2 \quad \text{(original equations)}\\
-3 + \text{B} - \text{N} &= -2\text{B} + 1\\
\hline
\text{B} + 2\text{N} &= -2\text{B} - 2\\
+3 - \text{B} + \text{N} &= 2\text{B} - 1 \quad \text{(opposites)}\\
\hline
+3 + 3\text{N} &= -3 \quad \text{(combined equation)}\\
-3 & \quad -3 \quad \text{(begin final steps to solve for N)}\\
\hline
3\text{N} &= -6\\
(\tfrac{1}{3})3\text{N} &= (\tfrac{1}{3})(-6)\\
\text{N} &= -2
\end{aligned}
$$

6. Substituting $\text{N} = -2$, students should rewrite one of the original equations or the opposites equation to solve for B. As an example, from the first equation, **B + 2N = –2B – 2,** we have **B + 2(–2) = –2B – 2.** Solving this equation symbolically (or pictorially, if necessary for some students), we have the final steps: $3\text{B} = +2$; $(\tfrac{1}{3})(3\text{B}) = (\tfrac{1}{3})(+2)$; and $\text{B} = +\tfrac{2}{3}$. On Worksheet 5–5–2 below the first exercise, students should record the equations: **N = –2** and **B = +$\tfrac{2}{3}$.**

7. Students need to be continually reminded that they are finding pairs of solution values that must satisfy each equation in the system. Have them substitute the values found for their respective variables in each original equation and record the resulting number sentences on the worksheet below the corresponding solution pair: $(+\tfrac{2}{3}) + 2(-2) = -2(+\tfrac{2}{3})$ **– 2** and **–3 + (+$\tfrac{2}{3}$) – (–2) = –2(+$\tfrac{2}{3}$) + 1.** Students should complete the computations to confirm that the number sentences are true statements.

8. Now that students have been introduced to the system diagramming technique, it is time to look more closely at the equation transformations used to make the new combined equation. In Activity 1, students were allowed to discover which transformations would produce 0-pairs when sides were combined. The systems of equations used for exercises had the variable, which was more likely to be eliminated first, positioned on the same side in both equations. Therefore, the transformation needed could be determined by considering only one term in each equation, or the two terms in the same variable that would be combined when the corresponding sides were joined together. We will now consider situations where the variable appears on both sides of the equation. Write the equations of the second worksheet exercise on the board: **A + B = –3B** and **$\tfrac{1}{2}$A + 2B = –2 + A.** Draw a diagram on the board for this system, drawing shapes for the first equation in the top half of the system frame and shapes for the second equation in the bottom half of the frame. *Ask:* "If we double the shapes in the top equation and take opposites of all the new terms, will all the variable B shapes connect to make 0-pairs when this new top equation combines with the bottom equation?" *(all will on the left side, but 6B will still remain on the right)* "If we double the shapes in the bottom equation and take opposites of all the new terms, will all the variable A shapes connect to make 0-pairs when this new bottom equation combines with the original top equation?" *(all will on the left side, but –2A will remain on the right)* Discuss the idea that, if a particular variable is to be removed through the *0-pair strategy,* all of that variable type within the same equation need to be grouped together as one term. Also, the terms in the two equations that involve the same variable should be on the same side within their respective equations.

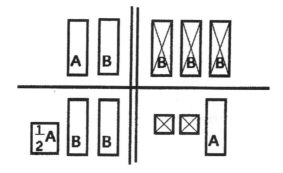

9. Now have students redraw the original equations of exercise 2 on the worksheet so that for each new equivalent equation, all like variables are grouped together on the same side of the equation. At this stage, tell students that they may choose which side to use for each variable. Both variables, A and B, may be grouped on the same side, or on different sides, in the two equations. For discussion, consider the second situation: transform each equation so that the variable B is on the left side and the variable A is on the right side. It is assumed that students can now do simple transformations either mentally or symbolically on paper. Write the new equations on the board and draw a system diagram for them: $4B = -A$ and $2B = -2 + \frac{1}{2}A$. Ask students what needs to be done in order to eliminate the variable A through the 0-pairs strategy. Hopefully they will realize that the bottom equation needs to be doubled to get a whole variable A. Students should repeat each shape of the bottom equation as a new group below the initial diagram. The inverse of a whole variable A can now be connected to the two half-variables of A. See the diagram steps in the illustration below.

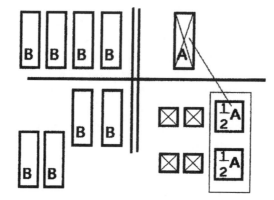

10. Have students simplify their work by drawing a horizontal bar below the first diagram, then redrawing any remaining shapes as a new equation, $8B = -4$, below the horizontal bar. The 8B must be separated into 8 groups in order to solve for B; similarly, -4 must be separated, putting $-\frac{1}{2}$ in each group. The final diagram is as follows.

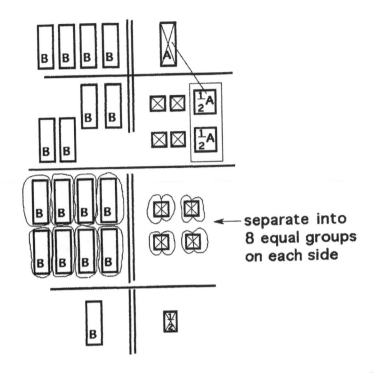

← separate into
8 equal groups
on each side

11. Students should now record in symbols on their own papers beside their completed diagram the transformations they made in the equations and the different steps used to solve for the first variable. The recording for the second exercise might be as follows.

$$A + B = -3B \qquad \text{(original equations)}$$
$$\tfrac{1}{2}A + 2B = -2 + A$$

$$\overline{4B = -A} \qquad \text{(regrouped variables on}$$
$$2B = -2 + \tfrac{1}{2}A \qquad \text{opposite sides in equations)}$$

$$\overline{4B = -A}$$
$$4B = -4 + A \qquad \text{(doubles)}$$

$$\overline{8B = -4} \qquad \text{(combined equation)}$$
$$(\tfrac{1}{8})(8B) = (\tfrac{1}{8})(-4) \qquad \text{(begin final steps to solve for B)}$$
$$B = -\tfrac{4}{8} \text{ or } -\tfrac{1}{2}$$

12. Using $B = -\tfrac{1}{2}$ in any one of the equations containing both A and B, students should now solve for A with number sentences. Substituting for B in $2B = \tfrac{1}{2}A - 2$, we have $2(-\tfrac{1}{2}) = \tfrac{1}{2}A - 2$, or $-1 = \tfrac{1}{2}A - 2$. We have $+1 = \tfrac{1}{2}A$ and finally $2(+1) = 2(\tfrac{1}{2}A)$ or $+2 = A.$ The solution pair, **$A = +2$ and $B = -\tfrac{1}{2}$,** should be recorded on the worksheet below exercise 2. The substitution number sentences for the two original equations of the system should also be recorded on the worksheet: $(+2) + (-\tfrac{1}{2}) = -3(-\tfrac{1}{2})$ and $(\tfrac{1}{2})(+2) + 2(-\tfrac{1}{2}) = -2 + (+2)$. The computation should be done to show that the number sentences are true statements.

13. Discuss the idea that writing the groups for variable A and variable B on the same side of the equation and the units or constants on the other side is often called the **standard form** of an equation. In other words, the first equation, $A + B = -3B$, in the last system would be in standard form when written as **$A + 4B = 0.$** A system of linear equations is often solved, using the equations in standard form.

14. Assign the other exercises on Worksheet 5–5–2 for more practice. Encourage students to group the variables within each equation and also to try solving some of the systems, using their equations in *standard form*. For each exercise, students should draw a system diagram on their own papers to represent the two original equations (but with the variables now grouped in some way), then modify the diagram to use opposites or multiple amounts of one of the equations and solve for one of the variables. Steps used to solve for the first variable should be recorded beside the diagram, as in steps 5 and 11. The value of the second variable may be found by substituting the value of the first variable found into any one of the equations being used. On the worksheet, students should record the solution pair and also write a substitution number sentence for each of the original equations of the system, as shown in step 12.

15. After students have completed the exercises on the worksheet, have some of them share the different types of equations they used in their diagrams. Ask for observations concerning when the use of one type of equation might be more efficient stepwise in the combining process than the use of another type (for example, putting one variable on one side of the equation and the second variable on the other side vs. putting both variables on the same side of the equation as in "standard form"). Standard form can be advantageous in that, after one variable is eliminated, the remaining variable will still be on one side of the combined equation and the constant on the other. The solution comes in just one more step. When the two variables are on opposite sides of the equation, however, a similar situation will occur if students choose to eliminate the variable that is on the same side as the constant. This leaves a variable on one side of the new equation and the constant on the other, as we found earlier with the standard form. Our purpose here is to make students think about their choices when they wish to solve a system of linear equations. Which approach is easier often depends on the coefficients in the equations.

Answer Key to WORKSHEET 5–5–2

The solution pair for each system is provided below:

(1) $N = -2$, $B = +\frac{2}{3}$

(2) $B = -\frac{1}{2}$, $A = +2$

(3) $m = -4$, $g = +3$

(4) $d = +\frac{1}{3}$, $x = +1$

(5) $W = +3$, $P = 0$

(6) $b = +6$, $k = -1$

Activity 3: LADYBUG LEAP

[Application/Exploration]

Materials: Worksheet 5–5–3
Calculators
Rulers
Paper
Regular pencils

Management: Teams of 4 students each (50 minutes)

Directions:

1. Give each team of 4 students 4 copies of Worksheet 5–5–3, a ruler, and a calculator. Team members will work together to complete their worksheets. This activity combines several approaches to solving a system of linear equations: marking positions on a

Ladybug Leap

Two ladybugs, TwoSpot and Dottie, are discovered walking up the door of a storage closet in a classroom. Each walks near the other and makes a path perpendicular to the floor. When first seen by students, TwoSpot is 2 feet up from the floor and Dottie is 1 foot up. The closet door is 6 feet high. TwoSpot is moving 0.75 feet per minute and Dottie is moving 1 foot per minute.

1. On the "distance ruler" below, show where TwoSpot and Dottie are at each minute.

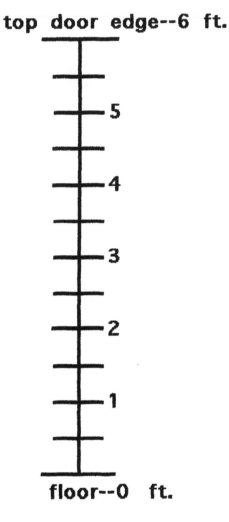

top door edge--6 ft.

5

4

3

2

1

floor--0 ft.

2. Complete the table for each ladybug. Show the steps used. For example: $0.75(3) + 2 = 4.25$ ft. at 3 min.

Minutes (t)	Dottie's distance (d) in feet from floor	Two Spot's distance (d) in feet from floor
0		
1		
2		
3		
4		
5		
6		

3. Graph the ordered pairs from the table on the grid below. Label each ladybug's line. Label the intersection point of the two lines with an estimate of its ordered pair.

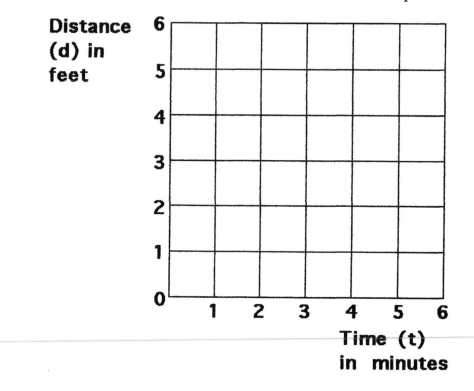

WORKSHEET 5-5-3 *(cont.)*
Ladybug Leap

4. Answer the following questions, using the data from items 1–3.

a. When does Dottie reach the top edge? ____________________

b. When and where does Dottie pass TwoSpot? ____________________

Using the rate-time relationship shown by the computation steps in the numerical table in item 2,

c. write an equation for Dottie's distance d in terms of time t:

____

d. write an equation for TwoSpot's distance d in terms of time t:

____

e. Use the equation in (d) to find when TwoSpot reaches the top edge.

f. Solve the system of the two equations above, using the "combination of like sides" method studied in this lesson. Write a sentence to tell what the obtained solution pair represents in the situation involving Dottie and TwoSpot.

"ruler," recording distances in a numerical table, finding patterns that generate distance equations, graphing equations to estimate a common solution, and combining like sides of equations to find a common solution.

2. After all teams have finished the worksheet, have several students share their methods with the entire class. Discuss differences, if any, in answers found by estimating from a graph or a numerical table and answers found by symbolic methods (combining like sides of equations). Discuss which answers might be more or less accurate and why.

Answer Key to WORKSHEET 5–5–3

(1) For Dottie, use D_0, D_1, etc., to label points at 1, 2, 3, 4, 5, and 6; for TwoSpots, use T_0, T_1, etc., to label points at 2, 2.75, 3.5, 4.25, 5, and 5.75.

(2) Samples of table entries:

time	Dottie's distance	TwoSpot's distance
0	1 ft.	2 ft.
2	(1)(2) + 1 = 3 ft.	(0.75)(2) + 2 = 3.5 ft.

(3) On the grid, Dottie's line will pass through (0, 1) and (2, 3); TwoSpot's line will pass through (0, 2) and (2, 3.5). Possible estimate for intersection point is (4, 5); a graphing calculator might show (4.04, 5.03), if used.

(4) a. 5 minutes

b. 4 minutes at 5 feet above floor

c. Dottie: $d = 1t + 1$

d. TwoSpot: $d = 0.75t + 2$

e. 6 ft. = 0.75t + 2, so t = 5.3 minutes

f. System: $d = 1t + 1$ (sample solving steps shown below)
$$\underline{d = 0.75t + 2}$$
$$d = 1t + 1$$
$$\underline{-d = -0.75t - 2} \quad \text{(opposites)}$$
$$0 = 0.25t - 1 \quad \text{(final steps to solve for t)}$$
$$\underline{+1 \qquad\qquad +1}$$
$$1 = 0.25t$$
$$(\tfrac{1}{0.25})(1) = (\tfrac{1}{0.25})(0.25t)$$
$$4 = t$$
$$d = 1(4) + 1 = 5 \quad \text{(substitution to solve for d)}$$

The system solution, (t, d) = (4, 5), shows that Dottie and TwoSpot are both 5 feet above the floor after 4 minutes of walking.

OBJECTIVE 6: **Solve systems of linear functions in two variables by substitution methods.**

Activity 1: SHARING VALUES

[Developing Action]

Materials: System building mats and sets of tiles from Objective 5
Worksheet 5–6–1
Regular pencils
Paper

Management: Partners (50 minutes)

Directions:

1. Give each pair of students two copies of Worksheet 5–6–1, a set of tiles, and a system building mat. The set of tiles used in Objective 5, Activity 1, of this section may be used here. The set of tiles should contain 30 unit tiles and have 8 variable tiles in each of two different sizes (for example, 0.75 in. by 3 in. and 0.75 in. by 3.25 in.). A different color should be used for each variable length. Consider the shorter variable tile as variable A and the longer tile as variable B for notation purposes. Each tile, both unit and variable, should have a large X marked on one side to represent its inverse form. It is assumed that students have successfully completed the three activities for Objective 5 in Section 3 as preparation for this lesson and that they have mastered the solving of linear equations in one variable. This lesson will focus on solving one equation in a system for one variable in terms of the other variable, then substituting the new expression for its equivalent variable in the other equation.

2. On the board write the first system of linear equations from Worksheet 5–6–1: **(a) A – B = –8** and **(b) B = 2 – A.** Have students show the two equations in tiles on the system building mat. The top equation mat should have one short tile for variable A and one long inverse tile for variable B on the left side and 8 negative unit tiles on the right side. The bottom equation mat should have one long variable tile for B on the left side and 2 positive unit tiles and one short inverse variable tile for A on the right side. Discuss the idea that if two groups of tiles are considered equal in value, either one of the groups can **replace** the other on an equation mat. Also, since equations in a system have the same solutions, this replacement can occur in any equation within the same system. So, since we have B = 2 – A from equation (b), the group of tiles for 2 – A can replace B in equation (a) of the system. **Ask:** "We want to exchange a variable B tile in equation (a) on the top mat for the group of tiles representing 2 – A from the bottom mat, but an *inverse* variable B tile is actually on the top mat. What must we do in order to replace this inverse variable tile?" (*need to use opposite of each tile in the group being moved, so need 2 negative unit tiles and one variable A tile to replace the inverse variable B tile on the top mat;* remember that the *opposite of an inverse* variable tile is the plain variable tile itself) Have students remove the inverse variable B tile from the left side of the top mat and replace

WORKSHEET 5-6-1
Sharing Values

For each system below, build the two equations with tiles on a system building mat and solve for each variable. Record the value found for each variable below the system of equations on the worksheet.

1. (a) $A - B = -8$

   (b) $B = 2 - A$

2. (a) $A - 3B = 7$

   (b) $2A + 2B = 6$

3. (a) $3A + 2B = 12$

   (b) $B = 3$

4. (a) $A + B = -3$

   (b) $2B - 3A = 4$

5. (a) $A - B = 7$

   (b) $B = 2A - 12$

6. (a) $A + B = 6$

   (b) $A - B = 4$

7. (a) $A + 2B = 4$

   (b) $A = B + 1$

8. (a) $3B - 2A = 5$

   (b) $2A - B = 1$

it with 2 negative unit tiles and one variable A tile. The tiles on the bottom mat should then be removed from the mat.

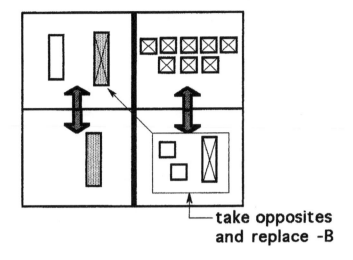

take opposites
and replace -B

3. The left side of the top mat now contains one variable A tile, 2 negative unit tiles, and another variable A tile, and the right side contains 8 negative unit tiles. Students should be quite comfortable by now with the steps needed to solve for the variable A tile when only one type of variable is involved. Two positive unit tiles should be placed on each side of the top mat, then 0-pairs removed (some students may prefer to *remove* 2 negative unit tiles from both sides instead). The two variable A tiles on the left must be separated into 2 rows of 1 variable A tile each, and the 6 negative unit tiles on the right must also be separated into 2 equal rows with 3 negative unit tiles per row. Keeping only one complete row on each side of the top mat and removing the other row of tiles, we find that **A = −3.**

4. To solve for the variable B, have students use equation (b) to write and solve a substitution number sentence below exercise 1 on the worksheet: **B = 2 − (−3) = +5.** The solution **A = −3** should also be recorded there. Have students confirm that their values for A and B are a solution pair for both equations. This should be done by rebuilding the original two equations on the system mat. For A − B = −8 on the top mat, on the left side 3 negative unit tiles should replace the variable A tile and the opposite of 5 positive unit tiles, or 5 negative unit tiles, should replace the inverse variable B tile. The total value on the left side then equals the value −8 shown on the right side of the mat. For B = 2 − A on the bottom mat, 5 positive unit tiles should replace the variable B tile on the left side, and 2 positive unit tiles and the opposite of 3 negative unit tiles, or 3 positive unit tiles, should be on the right side. The equality holds: +5 = 2 + (+3).

5. To focus on a specific *strategy,* write the system from exercise 8 on Worksheet 5–6–1 on the board: **(a) 3B − 2A = 5** and **(b) 2A − B = 1.** Have students build the two new equations on the system mat. Generally, the substitution method will be applied when at least one equation of the system contains a variable in singular form (the variable's coefficient is +1 or −1). This type of equation is easy to solve for the individual variable. For example, in equation (b), 2A − B = 1, we could transform the equation to find 2A − 1 = B, where 2A − 1 becomes the expression to substitute for B in equation (a). Another strategy needs to be considered, however, for systems when the *same* or *opposite* amounts of a particular variable tile appear in both equations. For example, in exercise 8, 2A appears in both equations. As one approach to this exercise, have students isolate the 2 inverse variable A tiles in equation (a) by adding 2 variable A tiles and 5 negative unit tiles to both sides of the top mat. After 0-pairs are removed, 2 variable A tiles will remain on the right side and 3 variable B tiles and 5 negative unit tiles will be on the left side of the mat. Since tiles for 2A also appear on the bottom mat, there is no need to solve for the single variable A tile on the top mat. Have students replace the 2 variable A tiles on the left side of the bottom mat with 3 variable B tiles and 5 negative unit tiles. The bottom mat now contains this new group of tiles and an inverse variable B tile on the left side and 1 positive unit tile on the right side. Students should remove any tiles remaining on the top mat at this time.

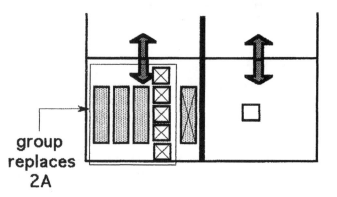

group replaces 2A

6. Students should continue to solve for B by adding 5 positive unit tiles to both sides, then separating the tiles on each side into 2 equal rows. After one complete row of tiles is removed to leave only one row on the bottom mat, the variable B is shown to equal +3. To solve for the variable A, students can use equation (b) to write a substitution number sentence: **2A − (+3) = 1.** This equation should be recorded below exercise 8 on the worksheet. Solving the equation, we find **A = +2.** The system solution pair **A = +2** and **B = +3** should also be recorded below the exercise. Again, students should confirm their solution pair by rebuilding the original equations of the system on the system mat, then substituting appropriate amounts of unit tiles for the variable tiles.

7. Students should solve the other systems on Worksheet 5–6–1, using the procedures discussed in steps 2 through 6. After solving for a first variable, they should write a substitution number sentence on the worksheet that yields the value of the second variable. The values for the solution pair should also be recorded on the worksheet.

Answer Key for WORKSHEET 5–6–1

Substitution number sentences used to solve for the second variable will vary, depending on which variable was isolated and replaced first. Thus, only solution pairs for each system are provided below.

(1) A = −3, B = +5   (2) A = +4, B = −1

(3) A = 2, B = 3   (4) A = −2, B = −1

(5) A = +5, B = −2   (6) A = 5, B = 1

(7) A = +2, B = +1   (8) A = 2, B = 3

Activity 2: DIAGRAM SWITCH

[Bridging Action]

Materials: Worksheet 5–6–2
Calculators *(optional)*
Paper
Regular pencils

Management: Partners (50 minutes)

Directions:

1. Give each pair of students 2 copies of Worksheet 5–6–2 and a calculator. In this activity we will focus on which substitutions to use, so that one of the variables in the system will be eliminated easily. Patterns among the coefficients in a system will be examined. We will also include fractional coefficients and solutions in the exercises. It is assumed that students have mastered Objective 5 of Section 3 and can make simple changes in linear equations mentally.

2. Write the following system of equations on the board: **(a) B − 2N = 2** and **(b) B + 2N = 6.** We want to draw a diagram that shows the steps we used in Activity 1 with the tiles. Using shapes to represent the tiles, students should draw on their own papers a diagram of the system as shown in the illustration in step 3.

3. *Ask:* "What kinds of substitution are possible with this system?" *(can substitute for a single variable B or for 2N)* For discussion purposes, we will work with 2N. Have students draw an inverse variable B on both sides of the bottom frame and form 0-pairs. This shows 2N = 6 − B on the bottom frame.

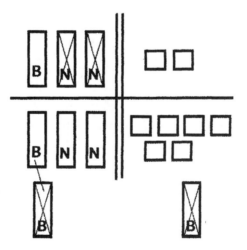

4. Since equation (a) shown in the top frame contains the inverse of 2N, we need the opposite of each shape in the right side of the bottom frame as a replacement for 2N in equation (a) on the top frame. Have students draw a horizontal bar below the initial system frame, then redraw equation (a), showing the substitution for 2N. They should then draw 6 positive units on each side of the new equation frame and form 0-pairs.

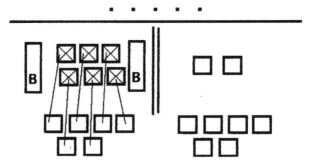

5. Since 2 of the variable B appear on the left side of the equation frame, students need to separate them into 2 equal groups of one variable B each. They must also separate the 8 positive units on the right side into 2 equal groups of 4 positive units each. One group from each side should be redrawn on a new frame to show **B = +4.**

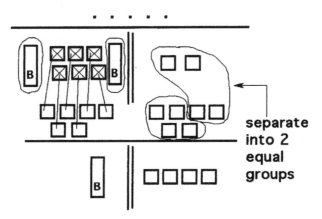

separate
into 2
equal
groups

6. Students should now record in symbols on their own papers beside their completed diagram the transformations they made in the equations and the different steps used to solve for the variable B. A substitution number sentence to find N should then be written to find N, for example, using equation (b). The recording for the first exercise might be as follows:

$$B + (-2N) = +2 \qquad \text{(from } B - 2N = +2\text{)}$$
$$\underline{B + 2N = +6}$$
$$B + 2N = +6$$
$$\underline{+(-B) +(-B)} \quad \text{(omit if done mentally)}$$
$$2N = +6 - B$$
$$-2N = -6 + B$$
$$B + (-6 + B) = +2$$
$$\underline{+6 +6} \quad \text{(omit if done mentally)}$$
$$2B = +8$$
$$(\tfrac{1}{2})(2B) = (\tfrac{1}{2})(+8)$$
$$B = +4$$

7. Substituting B = +4, students should rewrite one of the original equations to solve for N. As an example, from the second equation, **B + 2N = +6,** we have **(+4) + 2N = +6.** Solving this equation symbolically (or pictorially, if necessary for some students), we have the final steps: 2N = +2; $(\tfrac{1}{2})(2N) = (\tfrac{1}{2})(+2)$; and N = +1. On Worksheet 5–6–2 below the first exercise, students should record the equations: **B = +4** and **N = +1.** A *unique (only one) solution* has finally been determined for the system of exercise 1.

WORKSHEET 5-6-2
Diagram Switch

For each system of equations below, on your own paper draw a diagram to solve for each variable, and record your steps symbolically. Below the equations on the worksheet, write the value found for each variable, then rewrite each original equation with its variables replaced by their values, showing a true statement. If a solution is impossible, mark your diagram to show where the difficulty occurs.

1. (a) $B - 2N = +2$
   (b) $B + 2N = +6$

2. (a) $x + 2y = -2$
   (b) $3x + 2y = -8$

3. (a) $X + 5W = 8$
   (b) $W = X + 1$

4. (a) $2A - B = 4$
   (b) $B - 2A = 7$

5. (a) $2x + y = +3$
   (b) $-4x - 2y = -6$

6. (a) $4r - 2d = +1$
   (b) $2r - d = 3$

7. (a) $(\frac{1}{2})m + k = -1$
   (b) $2k + 3m = 2$

8. (a) $3A - 6G = 9$
   (b) $A - 2G = 3$

8. Students need to be continually reminded that they are finding pairs of solution values that must satisfy each equation in the system. Have them substitute the values found for their respective variables in each original equation and record the resulting number sentences on the worksheet below the corresponding solution pair: $(+4) - 2(+1) = +2$ and $(+4) + 2(+1) = +6$. Students should complete the computations to confirm that the number sentences are true statements.

9. Now have students use substitution to find solutions to the other systems on Worksheet 5–6–2. For each system, they should use the solving and recording procedures followed in steps 2 through 8. They may choose which substitution to make first. Tell students they may find that, for some systems, they will not be able to find values for the two variables involved. If so, they should mark the section of their diagram where they realize that they cannot solve for the variables. These particular systems will be discussed after the worksheet has been completed.

10. After students have completed the exercises on the worksheet, have some of them share the different types of substitutions they used in their diagrams, that is, whether for a single variable or for a common multiple of a variable. Our purpose is to make students think about their choices when they wish to solve a system of linear equations. Which approach is easier often depends on the coefficients in the equations.

11. Discuss the idea that, if a system has a solution, it will be a *unique* solution; that is, only one value for each variable will be found. Exercises 4 and 6, however, ended up with one amount of units on one side of the equation frame and a different amount of units on the other side (e.g., $6 \neq 1$). This is an example of a **contradiction.** All variables had been removed; therefore, no solutions could be found. On the board, make a quick-sketch of the graph of the two equations in each of these two exercises to show that each graph will be two parallel lines. Parallel lines do not intersect and therefore cannot have a common point; therefore, there is *no common solution* pair of values for the system. Have students record "no solution possible" below exercise 4 and exercise 6 on the worksheet. Exercises 5 and 8 each ended up with the same amount of units on both sides of the equation frame. The result was a true statement (e.g., $9 = 9$), but the variables had all been removed and specific solutions could not be found. For each exercise, make a quick-sketch on the board of the graph of the two equations; the graph will be a single line. This indicates that all points of one line are the same for the other line. Hence, all solution pairs of one equation are the same for the other equation. Such a system has *infinitely many* solutions. Have students record "many solutions" below exercise 5 and exercise 8 on the worksheet.

12. Each exercise on Worksheet 5–6–2 should now have a specific solution pair recorded for the system, or should have "no solution possible" or "many solutions" written below the system. *Ask:* "Looking at the coefficients on the variables and the constants used in the two equations of each system, do you see any relationships among the numbers? Is there a different kind of relationship that exists in exercises 4, 5, 6, and 8 than exists in the other four exercises? Is there a difference between exercises 4 and 6 and the other two exercises, 5 and 8?" Hopefully students will see that in exercises 5 and 8, one equation in the system is a multiple of the other; for example, we have $aX + bY = c$ with $naX + nbY = nc$. In exercises 4 and 6, one equation is a multiple of the other only with respect to the variable terms; the two constants are not related in the same way. As an example, in exercise 6, we have $2r - d = 3$ and $(2)2r - (2)d \neq (2)3$. Depending on the focus or the ability level of the class, you might wish to mention special labels used for these different types of systems. Systems with "many solutions" (a single line) are **dependent** systems. Systems with "no solutions" (parallel lines) are **inconsistent** systems. Thus, systems with a unique solution (intersecting lines) are both **independent and consistent** systems.

Answer Key to WORKSHEET 5–6–2

The solution pair for each system is provided below.

(1) B = +4, N = +1

(2) x = –3, y = +$\frac{1}{2}$

(3) X = $\frac{1}{2}$, W = 1$\frac{1}{2}$

(4) no solution (parallel lines)

(5) many solutions (one line)

(6) no solution (parallel lines)

(7) m = +2, k = –2

(8) many solutions (one line)

Activity 3: A REAL WHEEL DEAL

[Application/Exploration]

Materials: Worksheet 5–6–3
Graphing calculators
Paper
Regular pencils

Management: Teams of 4 students each (50 minutes)

Directions:

1. Give each team of 4 students 4 copies of Worksheet 5–6–3 and a graphing calculator. Each team will work together to complete Worksheet 5–6–3, which involves three problem-solving strategies: making a numerical table, finding patterns, and writing equations. Students will develop and solve a system of equations during this activity. If they choose to graph their equations to find a common solution, they must determine an appropriate view-screen size for the graphing calculator.

2. Students should complete 8 or 9 rows of the table, using different amounts of vans and bicycles. Encourage them to use an organized approach when selecting the different amounts for the table.

3. The first row of the table shows how the numbers should be recorded in order to show the steps involved. Other rows should be completed similarly. For the last row, students should write expressions that reflect the steps used in each column. For two factors in a product, the first factor (multiplier) should represent the number of vehicles used, and the second factor (multiplicand) should be the number of wheels per vehicle.

4. If we choose the variable v to equal the number of vans and the variable b to equal the number of bicycles, then the last row will show the following column entries from left to right: v, v(4), b, b(2), v + b, and v(4) + b(2). The system of equations based on Saturday's data would then be the following equations: v + b = 53 vehicles total, and v(4) + b(2) = 136 wheels total. When the system is solved for a unique solution, the results should be **v = 15 vans** and **b = 38 bicycles.**

5. After all teams have finished the worksheet, have different students share their team approaches to solving the problem.

WORKSHEET 5-6-3
A Real Wheel Deal

A special city-wide competition was held at Logan High School on Saturday. The algebra teacher helped provide security in the school parking lot all day, and noticed several fascinating things about all the 15-person vans and bicycles parked there. Some of the data are given below, along with a question for you and your team to answer.

Parking lot data: There were 53 vans and bicycles in the parking lot on Saturday. Altogether, these vehicles had 136 wheels.

Question to answer: How many vans and how many bicycles were parked in the school lot on Saturday?

Procedure:

1. Complete several rows of the table with randomly selected amounts of vans and of bicycles. In each row, record all the factors and the terms to be added before you simplify them. This will help you find a pattern among the numbers. Sample data and recording shown in row 1: 8 vans have $8(4) = 32$ wheels; 12 bicycles have $12(2) = 24$ wheels; 8 vans and 12 bicycles together yield $8 + 12 = 20$ vehicles with 56 wheels.

2. On the last row, write a variable in the "vans" column and a different variable in the "bicycles" column. Write an algebraic expression in each of the other columns in terms of either or both of your chosen variables.

3. Using the expressions from part (2) and the data from Saturday, write an equation that relates the amounts of different types of vehicles in some way, and write an equation that relates the amounts of different types of wheels in some way.

4. The two equations from part (3) must be satisfied by the same amounts of vans and bicycles, so the equations form a system. Solve the system by using one of the following methods: combining like sides, graphing, or substitution. If the graphing method is used, remember that there are no fractional vans or bicycles, only whole ones!

Number of Vans	Number of Van Wheels	Number of Bicycles	Number of Bicycle Wheels	Total Number of Vehicles	Total Number of Wheels
8	8(4)=32	12	12(2)=24	8+12=20	8(4)+12(2)=56

OBJECTIVE 7: **Develop the Pythagorean Theorem for right triangles; apply the theorem to real-world situations involving the right triangle.**

Activity 1: SQUARE MOVERS

[Developing Action]

Materials: Large inch grids from Objective 2
Packets of 100 inch paper squares (1 in. × 1 in.)
Thin bamboo skewers or straight wire pieces (10–12 inches long)
Worksheet 5–7–1
Regular pencils

Management: Partners (50 minutes)

Directions:

1. Give each pair of students a large inch grid, 2 packets of 100 inch paper squares, 2 copies of Worksheet 5–7–1, and a bamboo skewer or wire piece. In this activity students will work only with right triangles to discover the Pythagorean Theorem; in Activity 2, they will investigate other triangles in order to determine which conditions of the theorem are really necessary. It is assumed that students have not yet studied the Pythagorean Theorem. This activity is designed to be their first experience with the relationships stated in the theorem and is intended to be a discovery lesson. Allow students to find patterns for themselves.

2. Have students position the large grid so that the longer edge appears like a horizontal axis and the shorter edge appears like a vertical axis on the left. Have them place **3** paper squares along the shorter edge of the large inch grid, starting from the lower left corner of the grid. Then have them place **4** paper squares along the longer edge of the grid, starting from the same corner as the 3 paper squares. Ask students to use more paper squares to build a larger square region that has the 3 paper squares along one side. The new 3 in. by 3 in. square region will extend from the edge of the large grid onto the desktop. Ask students to build another square region that also extends from the grid, using the 4 paper squares along one edge. The grid and newly built square regions should appear as follows.

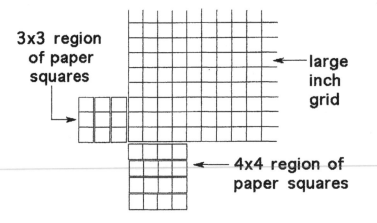

3x3 region of paper squares

large inch grid

4x4 region of paper squares

3. Now have students place the bamboo skewer (or wire piece) on the large grid so that it touches the upper right corner of the 3 × 3 region and the upper right corner of the 4 × 4 region. The segment of each grid edge where the paper squares touch the grid and the segment of the skewer between the two points where the skewer touches the paper squares form a triangle. Since one angle of the triangle is formed by the adjacent or corner edges of the large grid and these corner edges measure 90 degrees, the triangle is a **right triangle.** Here is the arrangement of the skewer on the grid.

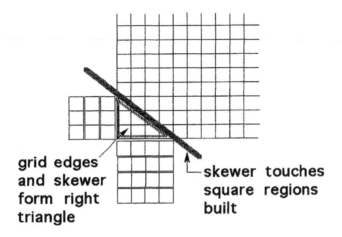

grid edges and skewer form right triangle

skewer touches square regions built

4. Ask: "If you use *only* the paper squares from the two square regions you have already made, will you have enough paper squares to build a new square region with its edge along the skewer, or longer side of the triangle? How many paper squares will fit along this longer side?" Allow students to explore before they answer the question. The paper squares should only touch the skewer segment that lies on the grid, not the skewer sections that extend off the grid. Also, in their new region, some or all of the paper squares will lie on top of the grid instead of extending off the grid as the previous regions did. Students should be able to build a 5 in. by 5 in. region whose edge coincides with the hypotenuse (skewer segment) of the right triangle. Have students record their results on the first line of the table on Worksheet 5–7–1. Remind them that the "area" heading in the table refers to the total amount of paper squares used to make each square region. Each paper square has 1 square inch of "area." The right-most column of the table simply asks whether the combined paper squares from the first two square regions were enough to make the third square region; students should record either "yes" or "no" in this last column. The column entries from left to right for row 1 should read as follows: **right, 3 in., 4 in., 5 in., 9 sq. in., 16 sq. in., 25 sq. in., yes.** The final arrangement of the paper squares on the grid should be as follows.

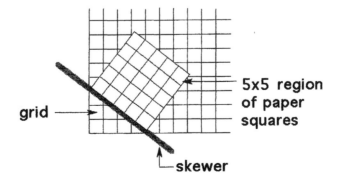

grid

5x5 region of paper squares

skewer

WORKSHEET 5-7-1
Square Movers

Complete the table by building with paper squares in Activity 1 or by drawing on special grids in Activity 2.

Type of Triangle	Edge Lengths			Areas			Area 1+Area 2 = Area 3 ? Yes/No
	Short Side 1	Short Side 2	Long Side 3	Short Side 1	Short Side 2	Long Side 3	
1.							
2.							
3.							
4.							
5.							
6.							
7.							
8.							
9.							
10.							

Describe in your own words the special relationship (called the Pythagorean Theorem) that you have found.

5. Assign two other pairs of sizes of square regions for students to build along the two adjacent edges of the large grid. Following the procedure used in steps 2 through 4, they should try to build a third square region along the skewer side of the right triangle that has formed on the grid, using all the paper squares from the two square regions built along the grid edges. Each pair of numbers given below as amounts of paper squares to place along the two edges to start the square regions will indeed lead to a third square region. Students will not know the length of the *long* side of a triangle they have formed on the grid until they have placed paper squares along the skewer segment or hypotenuse of the triangle. A right triangle will be formed in each example and only side lengths of right triangles that produce integral lengths for the hypotenuse will be used in this exploration. Here are two possible pairs of numbers to use as the lengths of the two short sides of the right triangle (all other Pythagorean triples involve larger quantities of paper squares where building becomes too tedious): **6 and 8; 5 and 12.**

Answer Key to WORKSHEET 5–7–1

Students should record their results for each exercise on Worksheet 5–7–1. The column entries for the two exercises given in step 5 should be as follows (remember that the first example using **3, 4, and 5** has already been recorded as row 1 in the table):

Row 2: right, 6 in., 8 in., 10 in., 36 sq. in., 64 sq. in., 100 sq. in., yes

Row 3: right, 5 in., 12 in., 13 in., 25 sq. in., 144 sq. in., 169 sq. in., yes

Activity 2: WHICH SUM WORKS?

[Bridging Action]

Materials: Worksheet 5–7–1 (table from Activity 1)
Worksheet 5–7–2
Colored pencils (any bright color except yellow)
Small index cards
Calculators *(optional)*
Regular pencils

Management: Partners (50 minutes)

Directions:

1. Give each pair of students 2 copies of Worksheet 5–7–2, an index card, a calculator *(optional),* and two colored pencils (1 pencil/student; any bright color except yellow; two colors do not have to be the same). They should already have Worksheet 5–7–1 from Activity 1. The index card will be used to test for right angles in some of the triangles on Worksheet 5–7–2. In this activity, instead of trying to *transform* two regions into a larger third region, students will draw a square region for each side of a triangle, then *compare* the combined total areas of the two smaller regions to the area of the larger third region. Right, acute, and obtuse triangles will be used. This investigation is a continuation of the one begun in Activity 1.

2. As an example of how to use Worksheet 5–7–2, have students look at the first exercise on the worksheet. It is numbered as exercise 4 there in order to coincide with the

For each triangle, use the side lengths (in units) to mark off square regions on the attached grids. Shade the interior of each square region in colored pencil, and find the total square units in each region. Use an index card to test for right angles. Complete the table on Worksheet 5–7–1.

4.

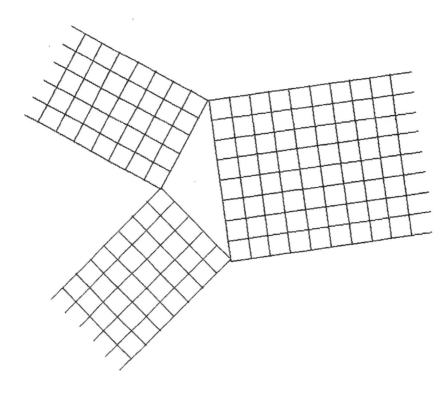

5.

6.

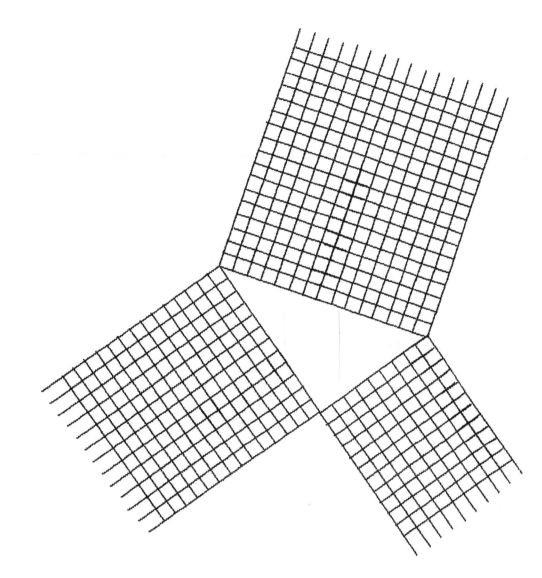

7.

8.

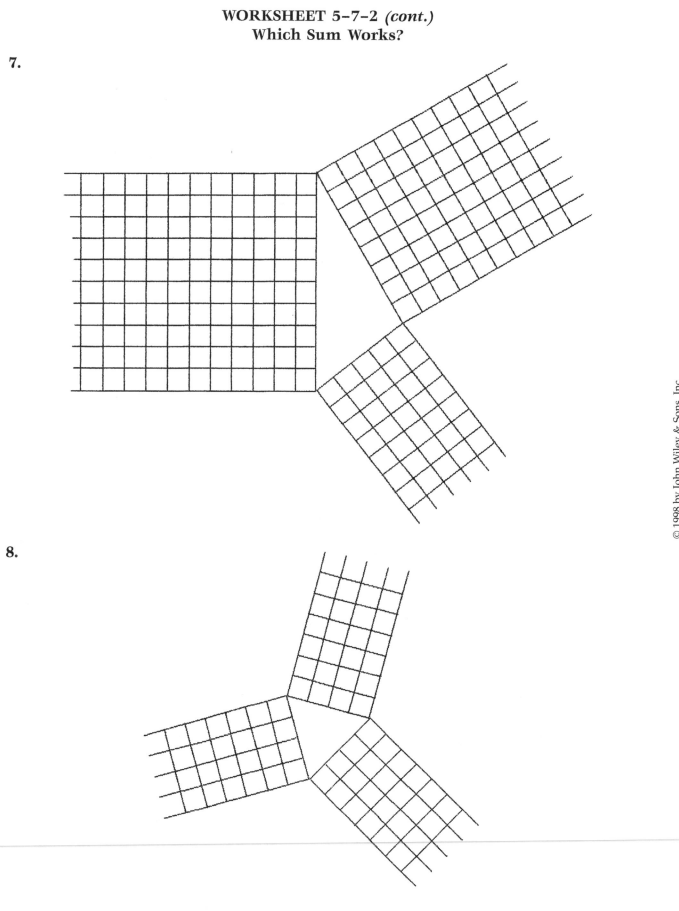

9.

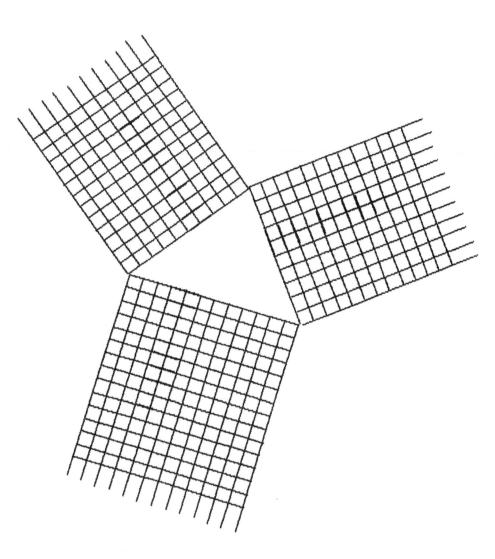

10.

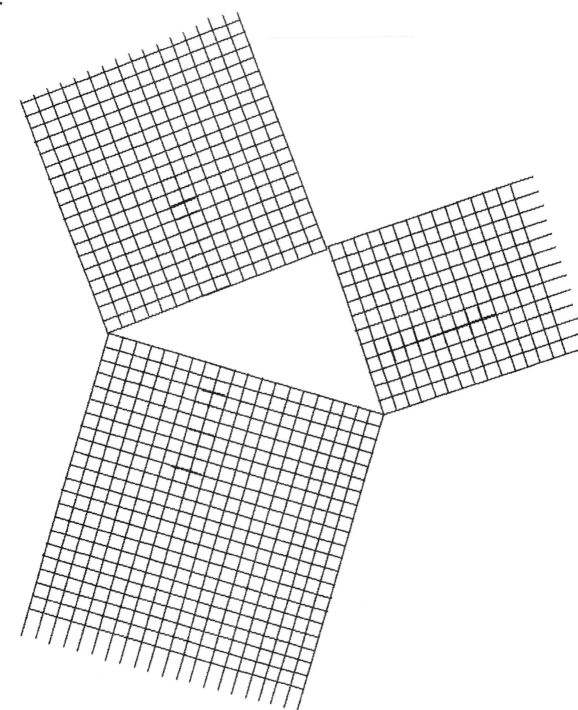

numbering on Worksheet 5–7–1, which already includes the three exercises from Activity 1. The index card should be used to test for a right angle in the triangle (the adjacent edges of each corner represent a 90-degree angle). One angle of the triangle, when tested with the index card, will be greater than 90 degrees, so the triangle is an **obtuse** triangle. A grid extends from each side of the triangle. Students should identify the length of each side of the triangle, then mark off the attached grid to make a square region. For example, if the side measures 5 units of length according to the attached grid, a 5 × 5 region should be marked off and its interior shaded with a colored pencil. If the side is 8 units long, an 8 × 8 square region should be drawn and shaded. Students should then count or compute the total square units shaded in each region's interior, and fill in the fourth row of the table on Worksheet 5–7–1. The column entries for this exercise should read from left to right as follows: **obtuse, 5 units, 5 units, 8 units, 25 sq. un., 25 sq. un., 64 sq. un., no.** The shaded regions of the triangle are shown below.

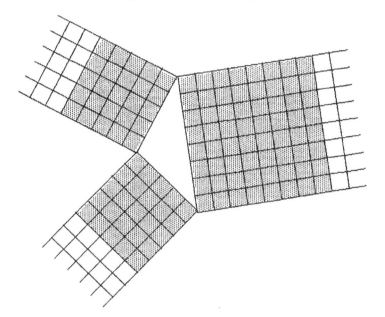

3. Students should continue the procedure and complete the other exercises on Worksheet 5–7–2. A row in the table of Worksheet 5–7–1 should be completed for each exercise. All completed rows of the table for exercises 1–10 are shown here:

Row 1: right, 3 in., 4 in., 5 in., 9 sq. in., 16 sq. in., 25 sq. in., yes

Row 2: right, 6 in., 8 in., 10 in., 36 sq. in., 64 sq. in., 100 sq. in., yes

Row 3: right, 5 in., 12 in., 13 in., 25 sq. in., 144 sq. in., 169 sq. in., yes

Row 4: obtuse, 5 units, 5 units, 8 units, 25 sq. un., 25 sq. un., 64 sq. un., no

Row 5: acute, 6 un., 6 un., 6 un., 36 sq. un., 36 sq. un., 36 sq. un., no

Row 6: right, 9 un., 12 un., 15 un., 81 sq. un., 144 sq. un., 225 sq. un., yes

Row 7: obtuse, 5 un., 8 un., 10 un., 25 sq. un., 64 sq. un., 100 sq. un., no

Row 8: acute, 4 un., 4 un., 4 un., 16 sq. un., 16 sq. un., 16 sq. un., no

Row 9: acute, 10 un., 10 un., 12 un., 100 sq. un., 100 sq. un., 144 sq. un., no

Row 10: right, 12 un., 16 un., 20 un., 144 sq. un., 256 sq. un., 400 sq. un., yes

4. After students have completed both worksheets, ***ask:*** "Looking at your table results on Worksheet 5–7–1, what kinds of triangles had 'yes' in the last column?" *(only right triangles)* "What special relationship do you now know about the sides of a right triangle?" *(the sum of the areas of the square regions belonging to the two short sides equals the area of the square region belonging to the long side)* It is important for students to use *words* to describe this relationship at first. If they seem comfortable with their written version of the theorem, tell them that the relationship is often presented in textbooks in the following form: $a^2 + b^2 = c^2$, **where a and b are the measures of the two short sides and c is the measure of the long side of a right triangle.** In Activity 3, we will consider applications of this "newly discovered" Pythagorean Theorem.

Activity 3: A TRIANGULAR PERSPECTIVE

[Application/Exploration]

Materials: Worksheet 5–7–3
Calculators
Paper
Regular pencils

Management: Teams of 4 students each (50 minutes)

Directions:

1. Give each team of 4 students 4 copies of Worksheet 5–7–3 and a calculator. In this activity, students will experience a variety of applications that require the Pythagorean Theorem.

2. To prepare students for the worksheet, draw a right triangle on the board. Label the two short sides as 3 ft. and 5 ft. and the hypotenuse as N. ***Ask:*** "How do the two side measures, 3 and 5, relate to the long side's measure N?" *(the long side's measure squared, N × N, equals (3 × 3) + (5 × 5), or 34)* "Then how do we find the measure of the long side itself?" *(since N × N = 34, estimate the square root of 34 to the nearest tenth; N = $\sqrt{34}$ ≈ 5.8 ft.)*

3. Now draw another right triangle on the board. Label the hypotenuse as 100 yd., one short side as 40 yd., and the other short side as N yd. ***Ask:*** "What equation shows the relationship between the three sides now?" *(100 × 100 = (40 × 40) + (N × N))* "What does N × N equal?" *(10,000 − 1,600, or 8,400)* "How do we find the value of N?" *(N = $\sqrt{8,400}$, or N ≈ 91.7 yd. to the nearest tenth of a yard)*

4. Stress the importance of drawing diagrams and labeling them with given or inferred values or expressions. Diagrams make it easier for students to write equations that represent the relationships shown in the diagrams. In helping students set up their equations that involve the Pythagorean Theorem, avoid writing more than one term under a square root sign. Find the sum first, then find the square root of the simplified value. All work shown in the answer key for Worksheet 5–7–3 follows this procedure. Only problem 4 requires more knowledge of square root properties. In that problem, students must find the square root of the expression 2(d × d). Applying the pattern used for square roots in the first section of the text, we have for the area, d × d, the edge length d written as $\sqrt{d \times d}$. Extending this idea, we have for the area 2 × d × d, or (d$\sqrt{2}$)(d$\sqrt{2}$), the edge length of d$\sqrt{2}$. This can then be estimated as d(1.4) or 1.4d. We do not want to

WORKSHEET 5–7–3
A Triangular Perspective

Work with your team to solve the problems on this worksheet. For each problem, draw and label a diagram for the situation on your own paper. Use the diagram and the Pythagorean Theorem to find your answer. Be ready to show your diagram or explain your steps to the entire class.

1. A sailboat has two long poles—a mast and a boom—to which the mainsail is attached. The boom is connected to the vertical mast at a 90-degree angle. The mainsail is shaped like a right triangle. If the mainsail's edge that attaches to the mast is 100 ft. long and its edge that attaches to the boom is 60 ft. long, estimate to the nearest tenth of a foot the length of the longest edge of the mainsail.

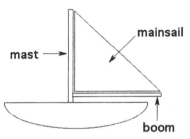

2. Plot the following points on an X-Y plane: A(0, –1), B(–1, –1), C(0, 0.5), D(0.5, –0.5), and E(0.5, 0.5). Find how far in units each point is from the origin. Estimate square roots to the nearest tenth of a unit.

3. In a factory two steam pipes are mounted so that one is directly above the other, but the two pipes are not parallel to each other (see illustration below). The top pipe has one end higher than the other and is 6 feet long. Estimate to the nearest tenth of a foot the length of the lower pipe.

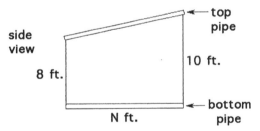

4. A cube has an edge length of d. Point C is at the center of the top face of the cube. Express the length of the path from vertex A to vertex B to the center point C in terms of d. Use the idea that the square root of (N × N) is N. Estimate any numerical square roots needed to the nearest tenth.

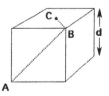

5. A kitchen had a square skylight with an area of 4 square feet that was built into its ceiling. After the kitchen was remodeled, a new skylight had the same height and width of the original one, but the new area equaled half the area of the original skylight. The new skylight was also square. How is this change in area possible?

confuse students at this time by requiring too much simplification of radicals involving algebraic expressions.

Answer Key for WORKSHEET 5-7-3

Some labeled drawings and steps, as well as final answers, are provided below.

(1) $N \times N = 10,000 + 3,600 = 13,600$; $N = \sqrt{13,600} \approx 116.6$ ft.

(2) dist A = 1 unit; dist B = $\sqrt{2} \approx 1.4$ units; dist C = 0.5 unit;

dist D × dist D = 0.25 + 0.25 = 0.50, so dist D = $\sqrt{0.50} \approx 0.7$ unit;

dist E × dist E = 0.25 + 0.25 = 0.50, so dist E = $\sqrt{0.50} \approx 0.7$ unit;

notice that C is closer to the origin than D or E.

(3) $36 = N \times N + 4$; $N \times N = 32$; $N = \sqrt{32} \approx 5.7$ ft.

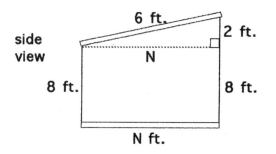

(4) $(d \times d) + (d \times d) = 2(d \times d)$; m(seg AB) = $d\sqrt{2} \approx d(1.4)$;

m(seg BC) = $\frac{1}{2}$ of m(seg AB);

path length = (1.4d) + 0.5(1.4d) = 1.5(1.4d) = 2.1d in terms of d

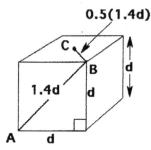

(5) a puzzle-type problem; the height and width of the new skylight actually measure diagonals of another square that fits inside the space of the old skylight; $N \times N = (1 \times 1) + (1 \times 1) = 2$; $N = \sqrt{2} \approx 1.4$ ft.; the new area is (1.4)(1.4) = 1.96 ≈ 2 sq. ft.

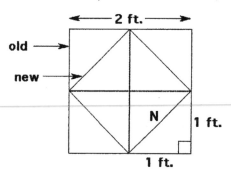

OBJECTIVE 8: Investigate exponential functions of the form $Y = b^X$, where b is a positive constant, and b, X, and Y are real numbers.

Activity 1: GROWTH PATTERNS

[Developing Action]

Materials: Lightweight, unlined paper (8.5 in. × 11 in.)
Worksheet 5–8–1
Calculators *(optional)*
Paper luncheon napkins (6 in. × 6 in. after folded twice; thin paper)
Scissors
Regular pencils

Management: Partners (50 minutes)

Directions:

1. Give each pair of students 2 copies of Worksheet 5–8–1, 2 sheets of unlined paper, 2 paper napkins, 1 pair of scissors, and a calculator. Use the luncheon napkins that have been prefolded twice and that measure about 12.5 inches by 12.5 inches when unfolded; they should be made of lightweight paper or tissue for easy folding. In this lesson students will do two different paper-folding activities in order to collect data and look for patterns. Each set of data will represent an exponential function with a base value greater than one.

2. *Paper Folding, Part I. Ask:* "If you have a sheet of paper that has not been folded and cut apart yet, how many pieces of paper do you have?" *(1 piece of paper)* For the first data table on Worksheet 5–8–1, for the top row that shows 0 cuts in the left column, tell students to record the number 1 in the column for "Pieces of Paper." Ask partners to fold 1 sheet of unlined paper in half along the long edge of the paper, then cut along the fold, making 2 pieces of paper. Students should record the number 2 in the right column on the row for 1 cut. Continuing, they should stack the 2 new pieces of paper together and fold along the longer edge of the stack of paper. Cutting each piece along the new fold, students will make 4 separate pieces of paper. Counting from the beginning, two cuts have now been made, so on the row for 2 cuts, the number 4 should be recorded in the right column.

3. Have students continue the process of stacking the pieces of paper, then folding and cutting them to make a new set of separate pieces. They should record the number of new pieces formed after each cut. Have students fold and cut up to 10 times, if possible; only 5 or 6 folds may be possible because of the thickness of the paper stacks. If folding becomes impossible, encourage students to look for patterns among the numbers in the right column and apply those patterns to complete the table. The final table should contain the following ordered pairs: (0, 1), (1, 2), (2, 4), (3, 8), (4, 16), (5, 32), (6, 64), (7, 128), (8, 256), (9, 512), and (10, 1024).

4. After students have completed the table, except for the row N, *ask:* "How are the numbers in the right column changing each time?" *(doubling)* "Do you see a relationship between the number of cuts and the number of pieces of paper made each time?" *(the right number is a product of factors of 2; if the table number is written as a power of 2, the*

WORKSHEET 5-8-1
Growth Patterns

Follow the directions given by your teacher for completing the two tables below.

Part I: Data Table

Number of Cuts	Pieces of Paper
0	
1	
2	
3	
4	
5	
6	
7	
8	
9	
10	
N	

Part II: Data Table

Number of Cuts	Holes in Napkin
0	
1	
2	
3	
4	
5	
6	
7	
8	
9	
10	
N	

exponent will equal the number in the left column; for example, 8 is $2 \times 2 \times 2$ or 2 to the third power, where 3 is also the number of cuts in the left column) "So if we have made N cuts in the paper, what expression can we write in the right column to represent the number of pieces of paper made?" *(for N cuts, we will have N factors of 2 or 2 to the Nth power for the number of pieces of paper made;* 2^N should be recorded in the last row of the right column) "Do you think the ordered pairs shown on the table represent a **linear function?**" *(no; for a linear function, the numbers in the right column would increase at a constant rate)* "Do you think the ordered pairs represent a **quadratic function?**" *(no; for a quadratic function, the numbers in the right column would increase by a different and greater amount each time, but would not increase as rapidly as these numbers do here)* "What is the **domain** of the new function you have found? What is the **range?**" Have students record a description of the domain and of the range below the first table on Worksheet 5–8–1 as follows: **Domain: all whole numbers,** and **Range: integers of the form 2^N for any integer $N \geq 0$.**

5. *Paper Folding, Part II.* Have partners take 1 paper napkin in its folded form and unfold it. ***Ask:*** "Before you cut your napkin with the scissors, how many holes does it have?" *(0 cuts, so 0 holes)* Have students record the number 0 in the right column of the first row of the second data table. Have them refold the napkin into its original form and find the corner that is the midpoint of the first fold of the napkin, the point where the first fold bends over on itself. We will call such a corner the **fold corner.** Students should cut off a *small* portion of this corner, then unfold the napkin to count the number of holes made in the entire napkin. There should be 1 hole in the paper. Thus, in the right column of the row for 1 cut, students should record the number 1 for the number of holes.

6. Have students refold the napkin into its original folded form, then fold the napkin in half along its second fold. The new corner formed by the point where the second fold bends upon itself is another **fold corner.** Students should cut off a small portion of this corner, then unfold the napkin again to count the total holes now in the whole paper. There should be 3 holes. The number 3 should be recorded in the right column of the row for 2 cuts.

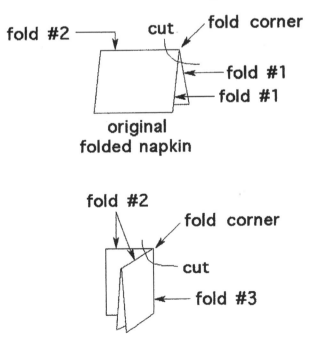

7. Students should continue the folding and unfolding process described above, recording the number of cuts and related number of holes made on the table. Using the thin paper napkin, students should be able to make at least 6 cuts at fold corners before the paper becomes too thick to cut. For cuts 5 and 6, a larger portion of the corner may need to be cut off in order for the cut to be made through every layer of paper. Ask students to look for patterns in the sequence of numbers in the right column, then try to apply those patterns to finish the table. The final table should contain the following pairs of numbers: (0, 0), (1, 1), (2, 3), (3, 7), (4, 15), (5, 31), (6, 63), (7, 127), (8, 255), (9, 511), and (10, 1023).

8. *Ask:* "How do the numbers in the right column of this table compare to the numbers in the right column of the first table on the worksheet?" *(for the same row on each table, the right column number in the second table is 1 less than the corresponding right column number in the first table)* "Then for N cuts in the napkin, what expression describes the number of holes we can expect?" *(for N cuts, the number of holes will equal 2 to the Nth power decreased by 1; $2^N - 1$ should be recorded in the last row of the right column)* Repeat the questions used in Part I: "Do you think the ordered pairs shown on the table represent a **linear function?**" *(no; for a linear function, the numbers in the right column would increase at a constant rate)* "Do you think the ordered pairs represent a **quadratic function?**" *(no; for a quadratic function, the numbers in the right column would increase by a different and greater amount each time, but would not increase as rapidly as these numbers do here; also, the quadratic values would eventually begin to decrease)* "What is the **domain** of this second function you have found? What is the **range?**" Have students record a description of the domain and of the range below the second table on Worksheet 5–8–1 as follows: **Domain: all whole numbers,** and **Range: integers of the form $2^N - 1$ for any integer $N \geq 0$.**

9. Note: Both of the functions found in Activity 1 are examples of exponential functions that are **growth functions,** since the *base* number used, **2,** is greater than one. That is, the rate of change or "growth" from one cutting to the next equals 2. The measuring of the growth of a colony of bacteria over a short period of time would be a possible example of a growth function. Also, money invested at a rate of interest that is *compounded* over time represents a growth function.

Activity 2: STEPPING DOWN!

[Bridging Action]

Materials: 5-millimeter grid paper
Colored pencils (any bright color)
Regular pencils

Management: Partners (50 minutes)

Directions:

1. Give each pair of students a sheet of 5-mm grid paper and a colored pencil (any bright color). The exponential function {(N, $(\frac{1}{2})^N$) where N is a whole number} will be developed in this activity. The development of powers here will be similar to the development of exponents in Activity 1 of Objective 1, Section 4, except that $\frac{1}{2}$ will be the *base* now instead of the integer 2.

2. Have students turn the grid paper so that the longer side will be on the left and form the vertical axis. The lower left corner of the grid will serve as the origin of the horizontal and vertical axes. Have students count off 48 grid segments and mark that length on the axis as "1"; if the grid does not go to 48 spaces vertically, a few more spaces can be drawn free-hand at the top of the grid to extend it. Using the new marking for "1" as the whole, students should then mark $\frac{1}{2}$, $\frac{1}{4}$, $\frac{1}{8}$, $\frac{1}{16}$, $\frac{1}{32}$, and $\frac{1}{64}$ on the vertical axis. Students should also make equally spaced markings on the horizontal axis and label them as 0, 1, 2, 3, 4, 5, and 6, starting with 0 at the vertical axis.

3. Now guide students through making a bar graph where each bar is half the height of the preceding bar to its left. Starting with the first column to the right of the vertical axis, have students draw and color a bar that has "1" as its height. The top of the bar should be labeled with "1." The 0-mark on the horizontal axis will mark the lower left corner of this first bar. The next bar to the right should begin in the grid column just to the right of the 1-mark on the horizontal axis and should be half the length of the first bar; it will have a height of "$\frac{1}{2}$." Label the top of this second bar as "$\frac{1}{2}$." Similarly, the third bar should be drawn to the right of the 2-mark on the horizontal axis and should be half of $\frac{1}{2}$, or $\frac{1}{4}$, in height. Label the top of this bar as "$\frac{1}{2} \times \frac{1}{2}$." Continue this drawing process until all seven bars have been drawn and colored on the grid paper. Then have the students go back to each bar to write a new label in exponential form for each product of factors of $\frac{1}{2}$. Discuss the idea that the general expression for each bar length will be $(\frac{1}{2})^N$ for each whole number N. The horizontal axis should now be labeled with N and the vertical axis should be labeled with $(\frac{1}{2})^N$. The final graph is shown below.

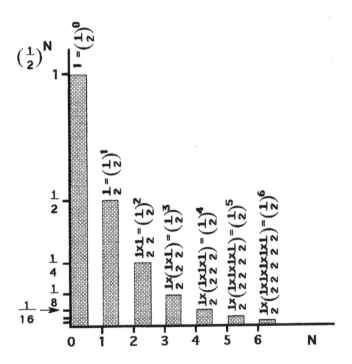

4. *Ask:* "In what way are the bar lengths changing as you view them from left to right?" (*bar lengths are decreasing, but the difference in length between adjacent bars is not constant; the difference or change in length is getting smaller as N increases*) "Do you think this *sequence* of bar lengths represents a **linear** or a **quadratic** function then?" (*no; a linear change must be constant, and a quadratic graph of the lengths of the bars*

would not drop or descend this quickly at first, then level off; instead, it would rise back up again)

5. Have students record on the final graph what the domain and range will be for their new function if they continued to draw more bars. These two sets should reflect the conditions imposed by the construction. The following should be written: **Domain: the whole numbers,** and **Range: positive rational numbers ≤ 1 that have the form $(\frac{1}{2})^N$ for the integer N ≥ 0.**

6. **Note:** The function studied in Activity 2 is an example of an exponential function that is a **decay function,** since the *base* number used, $\frac{1}{2}$, is positive but less than one. That is, the rate of change or "growth" from one bar length to the next equals $\frac{1}{2}$. Examples of decay are found in the study of the half-life expectancy of radioactive materials.

Activity 3: EXPONENTIAL FUNCTIONS

[Application/Exploration]

Materials: Worksheet 5–8–2
Graphing calculators
Colored pencils (at least 4 colors)
Regular pencils

Management: Teams of 4 students each (50 minutes)

Directions:

1. Give each team of 4 students one copy of Worksheet 5–8–2, a graphing calculator, and 4 colored pencils (4 different colors; 1 pencil per color). In this activity students will graph several different functions and compare their graphs. View screens on the graphing calculators should be set initially for Xε[0, 5], scale = 1, and for Yε[0, 50], scale = 5. Students may need to change the view screen as they investigate the behavior of each function's curve more closely.

2. Ask students to graph the following functions on their graphing calculators: $Y = X^2$ (a power function), $Y = 2^X$ (an exponential growth function with base, 2), $Y = (\frac{1}{2})^X$ (an exponential decay function with base, $\frac{1}{2}$), and $Y = e^X$ (an exponential function with special base, e, which is a numerical value that will be studied in future mathematics courses). They should make a quick-sketch of each curve on the grid on Worksheet 5–8–2. Each curve should be drawn with a different color of pencil and should be labeled with the function it represents.

3. Below the grid on Worksheet 5–8–2, team members should write their observations about the following ideas: (a) how the four curves differ in their rates of change or growth as X increases in value from 0; (b) the upper or lower limits on the values of Y for each function for X ≥ 0; and (c) the horizontal or vertical axis intercepts for each curve.

4. After all teams have finished writing their observations, have a member from each team share the team's findings with the entire class.

WORKSHEET 5-8-2
Exponential Functions

Use your graphing calculator to graph the following functions: $Y = X^2$, $Y = 2^X$, $Y = (\frac{1}{2})^X$, and $Y = e^X$. Make a quick-sketch of each function's graph on the grid provided on the worksheet. TRACE or ZOOM as needed. Sketch each graph in a different color and label the graph with its function name. In the blank space below the grid, write any observations your team makes when comparing the four graphs with respect to each curve's: (a) rate of change or growth, (b) upper and lower limits on Y, and (c) axis intercepts. Use the back of this worksheet if more writing space is needed.

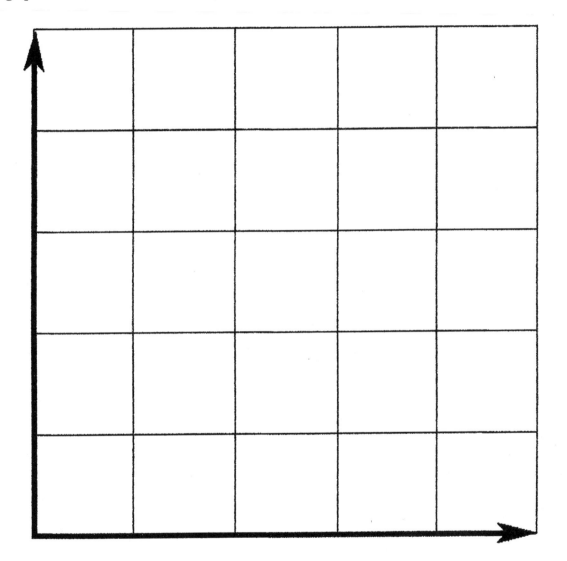

5. Here are some possible observations students might make for each idea mentioned in step 3.

(a) The curves for $Y = X^2$ and $Y = 2^X$ increase at somewhat similar rates until $X = 4$; for $X > 4$, $Y = 2^X$ grows more rapidly. The curve for $Y = e^X$ begins to increase faster than $Y = X^2$ and $Y = 2^X$ just before $X = 1$. $Y = (\frac{1}{2})^X$ decreases or decays and is falling below the other three curves before $X = 1$.

(b) Only $Y = (\frac{1}{2})^X$ has an upper limit of $+1$ on its Y-values; the other three functions have no upper limit as X increases. $Y = 2^X$ and $Y = e^X$ have a lower limit of $Y = 1$, which occurs at $X = 0$, but $Y = (\frac{1}{2})^X$ has a lower limit of $Y = 0$, which the curve never reaches. $Y = X^2$ has a lower limit of $Y = 0$ at $X = 0$.

(c) Only $Y = X^2$ has both axis intercepts, and both occur at $(0, 0)$. The other three functions do not have X-intercepts, but all three intercept the Y-axis at $Y = 1$.

OBJECTIVE 9: Investigate inverse variation, using the form: $Y = \frac{k}{X}$, where k is a positive integer and X and Y are real numbers with $X \neq 0$.

Activity 1: DIMINISHING FRACTIONS

[Developing Action]

Materials: Unlined paper (8.5 in. × 11 in.)
5-millimeter grid paper (contrasting color to unlined paper)
Calculators
Scissors
Rulers
Transparent tape
Worksheet 5–9–1
Colored markers (any color; medium-width)
Regular pencils

Management: Partners (50 minutes)

Directions:

1. Give each pair of students 2 copies of Worksheet 5–9–1, 1 sheet of unlined paper (any color or white), a calculator, 1 sheet of 5-mm grid paper (contrasting color to unlined paper), scissors, transparent tape, a ruler (cm/in.), and a colored marker (any color). In this activity, students will build a vertical bar graph to represent the function $Y = \frac{1}{X}$, where X is a positive integer. Worksheet 5–9–1 will be needed for Activity 2 as well.

2. Have students prepare a **baseline** for their graph by drawing a line segment with the colored marker along one longer side of the unlined paper. The segment should be drawn parallel to and one inch from the edge of the paper. Rotating the paper so that the colored segment is at the lower edge as viewed by the students, they should mark off equal intervals along the segment from 0 at the left end to 10 at the right end; the marks for 0 and 10, however, should not be right at the edge of the paper, but about a half-inch from the edge (see the illustration of a finished graph in step 5). An **X** should be written near the 10-mark at the right end of the baseline.

3. Students should then cut from the 5-mm grid paper a strip of grid spaces or square units that is 36 grid spaces long and 1 grid space wide. This first strip will represent the "unit" or vertical value "1" on the graph. The strip should be taped onto the unlined paper so that it extends upward from and perpendicular to the baseline at the mark for "1." Have students record the equation $\frac{1}{1} = \mathbf{1.00}$ in the first row of the right column of the worksheet table.

4. For the second strip to mount at the 2-mark on the baseline, have students cut a grid strip that is half the length of the "1" or "unit" strip. The strip should be 18 grid spaces long and 1 grid space wide. After the strip is taped on the unlined paper, students should record the equation $\frac{1}{2} = \mathbf{0.50}$ on the second row of the worksheet table.

5. Students should continue this process of cutting and taping strips until 10 strips have been mounted in order on the unlined paper. They will need to make strips that are $\frac{1}{3}$ of the first strip's length, $\frac{1}{4}$ of the first strip's length, $\frac{1}{5}$ of that length, etc. The number of grid spaces needed for the length of a strip may have to be estimated by students; for example, to make a strip that is $\frac{1}{7}$ of the first strip's length, a strip that is about 5.1 grid spaces long and 1 grid space wide will be needed. Have students write the common fraction name of each strip's length just above the top edge of the strip on the unlined paper. The fraction and decimal equivalents that each strip represents should be recorded on the table in the appropriate row of the right column. Rounding decimals to the nearest *hundredth,* the right column entries in order should be the following: $\frac{1}{1} = \textbf{1.00}$, $\frac{1}{2} = \textbf{0.50}$, $\frac{1}{3} = \textbf{0.33}$, $\frac{1}{4} = \textbf{0.25}$, $\frac{1}{5} = \textbf{0.20}$, $\frac{1}{6} = \textbf{0.17}$, $\frac{1}{7} = \textbf{0.14}$, $\frac{1}{8} = \textbf{0.13}$, $\frac{1}{9} = \textbf{0.11}$, **and** $\frac{1}{10} = \textbf{0.10}$. The completed graph is shown below.

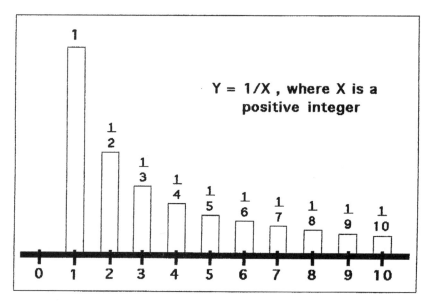

6. When all students have completed their graphs and tables, *ask:* "What do you notice about the lengths of the paper strips as the value of X increases? Does the length seem to change or decrease by the same amount each time?" *(the lengths do not decrease at a constant rate of change; the lengths change rapidly at first, then more slowly)* "Assuming that we are able to *physically cut* a strip of paper for any length, no matter how short it has to be, will we ever need a strip that is 0 grid spaces long?" *(no; no matter how great the X-value becomes, the fraction $\frac{1}{x}$ will always determine a non-zero length of some kind for a paper strip; the strip length eventually becomes a "microscopic paper sliver," but it still exists)* Ask students to compare how the paper strip lengths are physically and visually decreasing to how the *decimal* numbers in the right column of the worksheet table are changing (it is easier for students to recognize changes in numbers when they are written in decimal form rather than when written in fractional or ratio form). Have them record their observations on Worksheet 5–9–1. Possible comments they might make are as follows: (a) As the top ends of the paper strips from left to right appear to be dropping quickly at first, then later leveling off a little but still lowering toward the baseline, the decimal numbers in the table also appear to decrease in value quickly at first, then decrease only by one or two hundredths near the bottom of the table; (b) Just as the paper strip length continues to exist, though quite small, the numbers in the table continue to be positive, yet low in value.

Diminishing Fractions

Follow your teacher's instructions for building a special "paper strip" graph and record the values you find on the table below. Write your observations about the graph and the table in the space provided.

X	Y= 1/X
1	
2	
3	
4	
5	
6	
7	
8	
9	
10	

Record your observations here:

7. Now have students record in the upper right corner of their paper strip graph the equation that describes their special function $Y = \frac{1}{x}$, **where X is a positive integer.** Students should retain Worksheet 5–9–1 for use in Activity 2.

Activity 2: A SEARCH FOR INFINITY

[Bridging Action]

Materials: 5-millimeter grid paper
Calculators
Worksheet 5–9–1 from Activity 1
Regular pencils

Management: Partners (50 minutes)

Directions:

1. Give each pair of students 2 sheets of 5-mm grid paper and a calculator. They should already have Worksheet 5–9–1 from Activity 1. In this activity, students will continue to investigate the graph of the function $Y = \frac{1}{x}$, where X is a real number greater than 0. The concept of **infinity** will be discussed.

2. Students should draw X and Y axes on each of the two sheets of grid paper to show the *first quadrant only.* Label one grid sheet as "Graph A" and the other as "Graph B." For *Graph A,* the horizontal or X axis should go from 0 to about 30, using each grid segment as 1 unit of length; that is, each grid mark will represent a positive integer. On the vertical or Y axis (drawn on the left edge of the grid), each grid segment will equal a length of 0.05 unit; thus, the Y axis will go from 0 to about 1.0. For *Graph B,* the X axis should be marked from 0 to about 3.0, using each grid segment as 0.1 unit of length. The Y axis should go from 0 to about 10, with each grid segment marked as 0.5 unit of length. Graph A will be used to investigate what happens to the vertical distance Y as X increases. Graph B will be used to investigate changes in Y as X approaches 0 in value.

3. Have students plot points for the ordered pairs already recorded in the table on Worksheet 5–9–1 on each of the two grids (for graphs A and B), using the decimal values recorded for Y. Beginning with Graph A, students should plot additional points on that graph, using $Y = \frac{1}{x}$ and $X = 11, 12, \ldots, 30$. Y-values should be rounded to the nearest *hundredth* each time and written on Graph A near their corresponding points. Since the value of X no longer has to be limited to the integers, but can be any positive real number, have students draw a curve to connect all the dots plotted on Graph A. Discuss the appearance of the curve as it moves from left to right. *Ask:* "As the value of X increases on the graph, what happens to the value of Y?" *(the value of Y decreases as X increases)* "Do you think the curve will ever cross the X-axis?" *(no, because $\frac{1}{x}$ will always be positive as long as X is positive; the Y value will never be 0 or negative)* "We say that if the value of X continues to increase positively without any limit or bound, **X is approaching infinity.** Thus, when X approaches infinity, what does Y seem to do?" *(the value of Y decreases closer and closer to 0, but never equals 0; we say that **Y approaches 0**)* Have students record their observations, such as the above, in the upper right corner of Graph A's grid paper. Their statements should mention what X and Y are each *approaching* as we move along the curve to the right. Since Y decreases as X increases (or Y increases as

X decreases), we can say that as **Y varies inversely as X varies.** That is, the function $Y = \frac{1}{X}$ for X > 0 is an example of **inverse variation.** The function may also be written as XY = +1. If appropriate, introduce the following notation: **as X → ∞, Y → 0.**

4. Now have students plot additional points on Graph B. A new point needs to be plotted for each grid mark between 0 and 1.0 on the X-axis. Y-values should be rounded to the nearest *tenth,* and each Y-value should be recorded on the grid near its corresponding point. These new points will represent the following ordered pairs: (0.1,10), (0.2, 5), (0.3, 3.3), (0.4, 2.5), (0.5, 2), (0.6, 1.7), (0.7, 1.4), (0.8, 1.3), and (0.9, 1.1). These extra ordered pairs might be recorded *below* the table on Worksheet 5–9–1, but they will not necessarily be in order with those pairs recorded in the table during Activity 1. In this activity, we focus on the values written on the graphs *directly* rather than on the sequence of numbers in the table. Ask students to predict what will happen to the curve in Graph B for X-values between 0 and 0.1 (the curve will continue to rise as we move along the curve to the left toward the Y-axis). Ask them to compute the Y-value for X = 0.05 (Y will equal 20) and for X = 0.01 (Y will equal 100). These new Y-values cannot be plotted on Graph B, but they will give students a stronger awareness of Y's behavior as X gets closer to 0. *Ask:* "As X continues to decrease positively and approach 0, what do you predict for the upper limit or bound on Y?" *(there will be no such limit on Y as long as X equals some nonzero value; there is no end to how small X can become when it is a decimal fraction between 0 and 1)* Encourage students to use different "extreme" values for X to compute $Y = \frac{1}{X}$ on their calculators. For example, if X = 0.000001, Y will be 1,000,000! Challenge students to see who in the class, using calculators, can find the largest Y-value for the smallest X-value. Finally, state that **as X approaches 0 from the right, Y approaches infinity.** Students should record similar statements in the upper right corner of Graph B's grid paper. If appropriate, introduce the following notation: **as X → 0, Y → ∞.**

Activity 3: INVESTIGATING INVERSE VARIATION

[Application/Exploration]

Materials: Worksheet 5–9–2
Graphing calculators
Colored pencils (at least 4 colors)
Regular pencils

Management: Teams of 4 students each (50 minutes)

Directions:

1. Give each team of 4 students one copy of Worksheet 5–9–2, a graphing calculator, and 4 colored pencils (4 different colors; 1 pencil per color). In this activity students will graph several different functions and compare their graphs. View screens on the graphing calculators should be set initially for Xε[0, 5], scale = 1, and for Yε[0, 50], scale = 5. Students may need to change the view screen as they investigate the behavior of each function's curve more closely.

2. Ask students to graph the following functions on their graphing calculators: $Y = \frac{1}{X}$, $Y = (\frac{1}{X})^2$, $Y = \frac{10}{X}$, and $Y = (\frac{1}{2})^X$. They should make a quick-sketch of each curve on the grid on Worksheet 5–9–2. Each curve should be drawn with a different color of pencil and should be labeled with the function it represents.

3. Below the grid on Worksheet 5–9–2, team members should write their observations about the following ideas: (a) how the four curves differ in their rates of change as X increases in value from 0; (b) the upper or lower limits on the values of Y for each function for $X \geq 0$; and (c) the horizontal or vertical axis intercepts for each curve.

4. After all teams have finished writing their observations, have a member from each team share the team's findings with the entire class.

5. Many observations are possible as students change the view screen on their graphing calculators to investigate the functions over different intervals for X. Here are some observations students might make for each idea mentioned in step 3 above:

(a) All four curves have Y decreasing as X increases. The three curves for $Y = (\frac{1}{x})^2$, $Y = \frac{1}{x}$, and $Y = (\frac{1}{2})^X$ descend at somewhat similar rates for $X \geq 2$; the curve for $Y = \frac{10}{X}$ is higher than the other three curves and descends more slowly over the initial interval, $0 < X \leq 5$, and continues to have a greater Y-value than the other curves for the same X-value. For very large values of X, the four curves appear to coincide; that is, the differences between corresponding Y-values of the four functions become very small, or less than 0.01, for $X > 1,000$. In other words, the functions behave the same beyond some particular value of X.

(b) Only $Y = (\frac{1}{2})^X$ has an upper limit of $+1$ on its Y-values; the other three functions have no upper limit as X approaches 0. The lack of an upper limit for Y as X approaches 0 is a characteristic of functions that are **inverse variations.** Y **varies inversely as X** in $Y = \frac{1}{x}$ and in $Y = \frac{10}{X}$, and varies **inversely as X²** in $Y = (\frac{1}{x})^2$ or $\frac{1}{(X^2)}$. $Y = (\frac{1}{2})^X$ is not an inverse variation; it is an exponential decay function. All four curves have a lower limit of $Y = 0$ for $X > 0$, but none of them ever has $Y = 0$ for $X > 0$.

(c) Only $Y = (\frac{1}{2})^X$ has a Y-intercept, which occurs at (0, 1). The other three functions do not have X- or Y-intercepts; that is, they do not have a Y-value at $X = 0$ (or they do not **exist** at $X = 0$).

6. If time permits, students might want to investigate the four functions for $X < 0$.

WORKSHEET 5-9-2
Investigating Inverse Variation

Use your graphing calculator to graph the following functions: $Y = (\frac{1}{X})^2$, $Y = \frac{1}{X}$, $Y = (\frac{1}{2})^X$, and $Y = \frac{10}{X}$. Make a quick-sketch of each function's graph on the grid provided on the worksheet. TRACE or ZOOM as needed. Sketch each graph in a different color and label the graph with its function name. In the blank space below the grid, write any observations your team makes when comparing the four graphs with respect to each curve's: (a) rate of change, (b) upper and lower limits on Y, and (c) axis intercepts. Use the back of this worksheet if more writing space is needed.

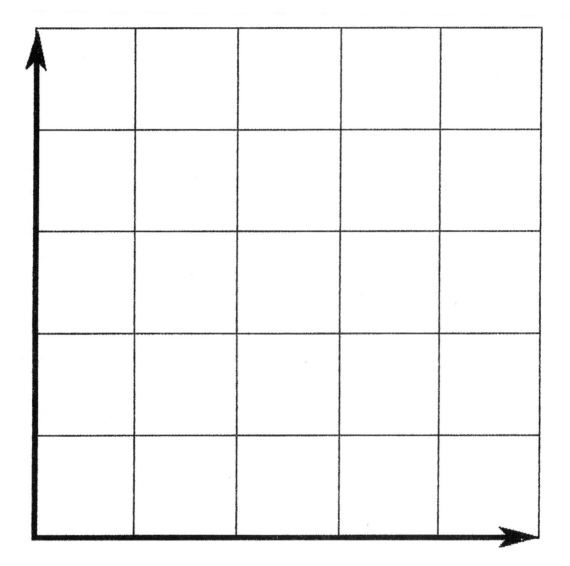

Appendix

TILE PATTERNS

For your convenience, here is an assortment of tile patterns that can be easily photocopied as many times as needed for student use in completing the games and activities located throughout this resource.

(print in color #1)

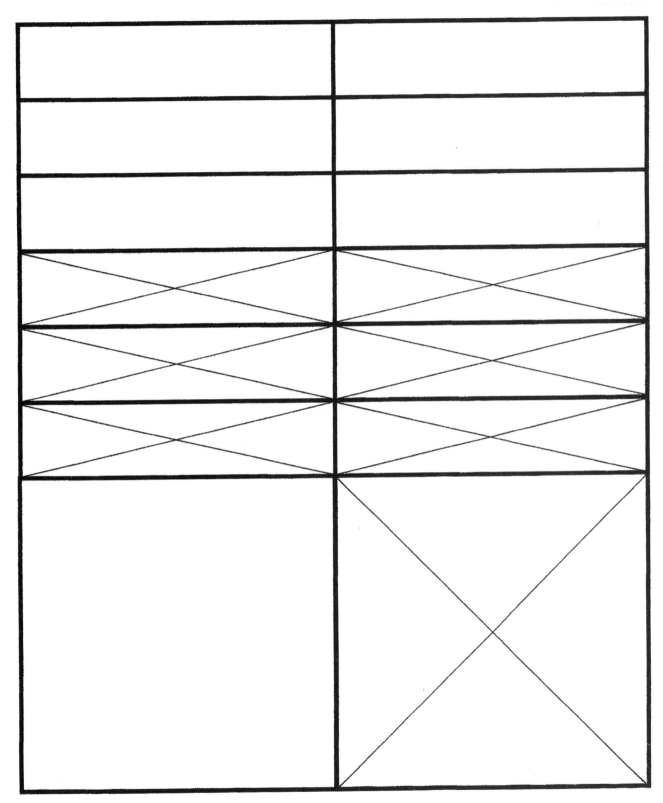

(print in color #3)

(print in color #4)

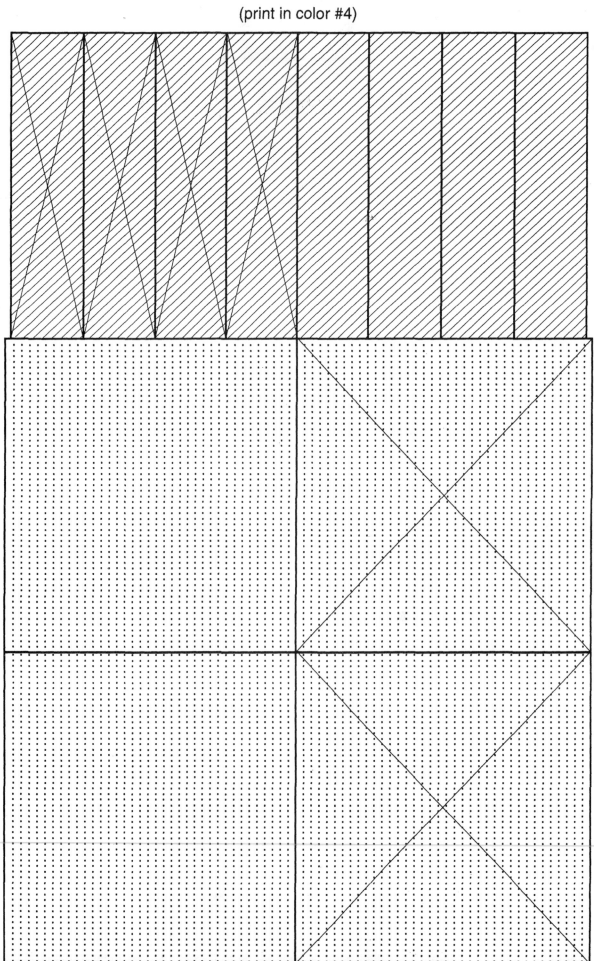